k is to be returned on or before th

*International Review of
Industrial
and Organizational
Psychology
2006   Volume 21*

International Review of Industrial and Organizational Psychology 2006 Volume 21

Edited by

Gerard P. Hodgkinson
The University of Leeds, UK

and

J. Kevin Ford
Michigan State University, USA

John Wiley & Sons, Ltd

Other Wiley Editorial Offices

John Wiley & Sons Inc., 111 River Street, Hoboken, NJ 07030, USA

Jossey-Bass, 989 Market Street, San Francisco, CA 94103-1741, USA

Wiley-VCH Verlag GmbH, Boschstr. 12, D-69469 Weinheim, Germany

John Wiley & Sons Australia Ltd, 42 McDougall Street, Milton, Queensland 4064, Australia

John Wiley & Sons (Asia) Pte Ltd, 2 Clementi Loop #02-01, Jin Xing Distripark, Singapore 129809

John Wiley & Sons Canada Ltd, 22 Worcester Road, Etobicoke, Ontario, Canada M9W 1L1

Wiley also publishes its books in a variety of electronic formats. Some content that appears
in print may not be available in electronic books.

Library of Congress Cataloging-in-Publication Data

International review of industrial and organizational psychology.
    —1986—Chichester; New York; Wiley, c1986–
    v.: ill.; 24cm.
    Annual.
    ISSN 0886-1528 $^1/_4$ International review of industrial and organizational psychology
    1. Psychology, Industrial—Periodicals.   2. Personnel management—Periodicals.
    [DNLM: 1. Organization and Administration—periodicals.   2. Psychology,
Industrial—periodicals. W1IN832UJ]
HF5548.7.I57   158.7005—dc 19 86-643874   AACR 2 MARC-S
Library of Congress [8709]

British Library Cataloguing in Publication Data

A catalogue record for this book is available from the British Library

ISBN-10 0-470-01606-X (hbk)
ISBN-13 978-0-470-01606-0 (ppc)

Typeset in 10/12pt Plantin by TechBooks, New Delhi, India
Printed and bound in Great Britain by TJ International Ltd, Padstow, Cornwall, UK
This book is printed on acid-free paper responsibly manufactured from sustainable forestry
in which at least two trees are planted for each one used for paper production.

CONTENTS

ABOUT THE EDITORS

Gerard P. Hodgkinson *Leeds University Business School, The University of Leeds, Leeds LS2 9JT, UK*

J. Kevin Ford *Department of Psychology, 129 Psychology Research Building, Michigan State University, E. Lansing, MI 48824, USA*

Gerard P. Hodgkinson is Professor of Organizational Behaviour and Strategic Management at the University of Leeds, UK. He earned his BA, MSc, and PhD degrees at Wolverhampton Polytechnic and the Universities of Hull and Sheffield, respectively. He has published over 40 articles and chapters and two books on topics of relevance to the field of industrial and organizational psychology and in 2001 he was elected a Fellow of both the British Psychological Society and the British Academy of Management, in recognition of his pioneering contribution to the psychology of strategic management as an emergent field of study. This and related work on managerial and organizational cognition is currently being taken forward (2004–2006) through the award of a Fellowship of the Advanced Institute of Management Research (AIM), the UK's research initiative on management, funded by the Economic and Social Research Council (ESRC) and the Engineering and Physical Sciences Research Council (EPSRC). He is the Editor-in-Chief of the *British Journal of Management* and an Editorial Board Member of the *Academy of Management Review*, the *Journal of Occupational and Organizational Psychology*, and *Organization Science*. A practising chartered occupational psychologist, he has conducted numerous consultancy assignments for leading private and public sector organizations. Further information about Gerard and his work can be found at the following addresses: (1) *http://www.leeds.ac.uk/lubs/*; (2) *http://www.aimresearch.org*.

Kevin Ford is a Professor of Psychology at Michigan State University. His major research interests involve improving training effectiveness through efforts to advance our understanding of training needs assessment, design, evaluation, and transfer. Dr Ford also concentrates on understanding change dynamics in organizational development efforts and building continuous learning and improvement orientations within organizations. He has published over 50 articles and chapters and four books relevant to Industrial and Organizational Psychology. Currently, he serves on the editorial boards of the *Journal of Applied Psychology* and *Human Performance*. He is an active consultant with private industry and the public sector on training, leadership, and organizational change issues. Kevin is a Fellow of the American Psychological Association and the Society of Industrial and Organizational Psychology. He received his BS in Psychology from the University of Maryland and his MA and PhD in Psychology from the Ohio State University. Further information about Kevin and his research and consulting activities can be found at: *http://www.io.psy.msu.edu/jkf.*

CONTRIBUTORS

John Annett   Department of Psychology, University of Warwick, Coventry CV4 7AL, UK

Kamaljit Birdi   Institute of Work Psychology, University of Sheffield, Mushroom Lane, Sheffield S10 2TN, UK

Michael J. Burke   Freeman School of Business, Tulane University, New Orleans, LA 70118, USA

Catherine Cassell   Manchester Business School, University of Manchester, Booth Street West, Manchester M15 6PB, UK

Renée E. DeRouin   Department of Psychology and Institute for Simulation and Training, University of Central Florida, PO Box 161390, Orlando, FL 32816-1390, USA

Scott C. Douglas   School of Business Administration, University of Montana, Missoula, MT 59812, USA

Paul Harvey   College of Business, The Florida State University, Tallahassee, FL 32306, USA

David Holman   Institute of Work Psychology, University of Sheffield, Mushroom Lane, Sheffield S10 2TN, UK

Cameron Klein   Department of Psychology and Institute for Simulation and Training, University of Central Florida, PO Box 161390, Orlando, FL 32816-1390, USA

Gary P. Latham   Rotman School of Management, University of Toronto, 105 St George St, Toronto, ON M5S 3E6, Canada

Karen S. Lyness   Department of Psychology, Baruch College, City University of New York, One Bernard Baruch Way, New York, NY 10010, USA

Sara Mann   Rotman School of Management, University of Toronto, 107 St George St, Toronto, ON M5S 3E6, Canada

Mark J. Martinko   College of Business, The Florida State University, Tallahassee, FL 32306, USA

Eduardo Salas *Department of Psychology and Institute for Simulation and Training, University of Central Florida, PO Box 161390, Orlando, FL 32816-1390, USA*

Paul R. Sparrow *Manchester Business School, University of Manchester, Booth Street West, Manchester M15 6PB, UK*

Neville Stanton *School of Engineering and Design, Brunel University, Uxbridge UB8 3PH, UK*

Gillian Symon *Department of Organizational Psychology, Birkbeck College, University of London, Malet Street, London WC1E 7HX, UK*

Jolie M.B. Terrazas *Department of Psychology, Baruch College, City University of New York, One Bernard Baruch Way, New York, NY 10010, USA*

EDITORIAL FOREWORD

This is the twenty-first volume of the *International Review of Industrial and Organizational Psychology*. As with past volumes in the series, we have commissioned a wide-ranging collection of chapters from some of the world's leading researchers, reflecting the rich diversity of advances occurring both within the mainstream and at the leading-edge of the field. Several of the topics covered in the present volume, although well established as areas of theory, research, and application, are new to the series, including workplace interpersonal skills, applications of learning theory to the development of effective health and safety training, attribution theory, and task analysis. Another topic featured for the first time, and worthy of special mention, is qualitative research. In a highly critical survey, Catherine Cassell and Gillian Symon raise a series of issues with which many of our readers are likely to be distinctly uncomfortable, challenging researchers, reviewers, and editors alike to rethink a number of practices now commonplace in the analysis and reporting of quantitative data, but which may be wholly inappropriate in the context of qualitative work. Other chapters (e.g., the chapters on 'Women in Management' by Karen Lyness and Jolie Terrazas, 'Advances in the Science of Performance Appraisal' by Gary Latham and Sara Mann, and 'International Management' by Paul Sparrow) revisit topics covered in previous volumes, offering detailed overviews of the scientific literature amassed over the interim.

Now entering its twenty-second year, the *International Review of Industrial and Organizational Psychology* has become the primary reference work of choice for individuals seeking authoritative, up-to-the-minute coverage of developments around the globe.

GPH
JKF
June 2005

Chapter 1

A WALK ON THE SAFE SIDE: THE IMPLICATIONS OF LEARNING THEORY FOR DEVELOPING EFFECTIVE SAFETY AND HEALTH TRAINING

Michael J. Burke
Freeman School of Business, Tulane University, USA
and
David Holman and Kamaljit Birdi
Institute of Work Psychology, University of Sheffield, UK

Knowledge and motivation represent two broad categories of determinants of safe work behavior in organizations. A considerable amount of research and practice in disciplines as diverse as psychology, occupational medicine, and engineering focus on how safety and health training affects the development of worker characteristics in these domains and the transfer of knowledge to the job (e.g., see Colligan & Cohen, 2004; Johnston, Cattledge, & Collins, 1994). Findings from this large and diverse body of research generally show that safety and health training is sometimes positively associated with knowledge acquisition, safe work behavior, and the reduction of accidents, illnesses, and injuries (Colligan & Cohen, 2004). However, a cursory examination of this literature indicates that not only do the learning theories and theoretical approaches that underlie safety training efforts differ, but also that potentially relevant learning theories and research findings are not necessarily incorporated into the design and conduct of worker safety and health training.

To date, no unified discussion of the implications of learning theory and research for safety and health training research and practice has been presented in a disciplinary literature. This gap in the literature is particularly noteworthy given that the amount of requisite knowledge and skills can be considerable in many types of safety work, and learning research indicates that infrequently performed tasks or complex skills can quickly deteriorate without

International Review of Industrial and Organizational Psychology, 2006, Volume 21
Edited by G.P. Hodgkinson and J.K. Ford. © 2006 John Wiley & Sons, Ltd.

practice (Adams, 1987; Arthur, Bennett, Stanush, & McNelly, 1998). This point can relate to knowledge and skill development or maintenance in work related to many critical skills occupations (e.g., emergency response, firefighting) and work involving infrequent critical incidents (e.g., mining explosions, hazardous waste emissions, and transportation equipment failure). An integrative discussion of the role and relevance of learning theory and research with current safety training research and practice would be helpful for suggesting how best to achieve different types and levels of knowledge acquisition through training and optimize the transfer of training to the job. In particular, an integrative discussion of the learning literature and safety training research would shed light on why and how different methods of safety training, as well as methods of training program evaluation, affect proximal training outcomes (e.g., knowledge, skills, and attitudes) and more distal outcomes (e.g., on-the-job performance and performance outcomes such as accidents, illnesses, and injuries). In addition, an integrative discussion would offer suggestions for improving safety and health training research and practice, especially in relation to work in critical skills occupations affecting the public in an age of terrorism (e.g., emergency response, protective services, transportation security) and occupations involving significant worker injuries (e.g., nursing, construction, mining).

A problem faced in the rapprochement of historically different paradigms and bodies of literature as they might relate to safety knowledge acquisition is where to provisionally begin in terms of a theoretical foundation. For our purposes, we begin with a discussion of the nature of general safety performance, the actions or behaviors that employees exhibit in almost all types of work to promote their own health and safety and that of their coworkers, clients, the public, and the environment. Given that safety knowledge is posited as a direct antecedent of safety performance (Neal & Griffin, 2004), specifying the construct domain of general safety performance will permit a discussion of the nature and content of requisite safety knowledge affected by training. Consistent with Ackerman's (1996) arguments for the importance of systematically inquiring about the content of intellect in particular domains, identifying the content of safety knowledge is not only important for understanding what workers know, but is also critical for studying whether and how that knowledge changes with respect to training applications of particular learning theories. Surprisingly, many training evaluation studies are mute on the specific content of learning and specific attributes associated with this content (e.g., novelty and complexity; Sonnentag, Niessen, & Ohly, 2004). Although the focus of this chapter is on knowledge acquisition in safety training contexts, we will discuss, where appropriate, motivational issues in relation to knowledge and skill acquisition and its transfer to the job.

Subsequent to our discussion of the nature of general safety performance and safety knowledge, we begin our presentation of learning theories with a brief description of a long-standing theoretical approach or paradigm for knowledge and skill acquisition in the applied psychology literature, which is the stage or phase approach to learning (see Anderson, 1985, 1987; Bryan & Harter, 1899; Fitts, 1962). The discussion of stage approaches is followed by a description of the role and relevance of (a) reinforcement and feedback intervention theories (Geller, 2001; Kluger & DeNisi, 1996; Skinner, 1974), (b) social learning theory (Bandura, 1977), goal-setting theory (Locke & Latham, 1990), and action regulation theory (Hacker, 2003), and (c) experiential-learning theory (Kolb, 1984; Weil & McGill, 1989) and theories of distance learning (Garrison, 2000; Moore, 1993). We have chosen to focus on particular learning theories and selected studies on learning or behavior modification which, in our opinion, are most directly relevant to improving our understanding of knowledge and skill acquisition in safety training contexts and offer the greatest possibility of enhancing safety training research and practice. Our discussion of these clusters of theories is not intended to imply that the various learning theories and approaches are mutually exclusive.

Following each set of learning theories, we discuss the implications of the respective theories for safety training. Thereafter, we indicate how the various learning theories are being applied to safety training methods and discuss the relative effectiveness of these applications. Our chapter concludes with a focus on selected individual difference, situational, and training process variables, which are concerned with the limits of our current state of knowledge and practice in relation to safety and health training, and offer the most promise for expanding these limits. Finally, while our discussion of learning theories and their implications for safety training often has direct relevance for learning with respect to leader safety behavior and individuals functioning within teams or work groups, our focus is on individual learning per se.

THE NATURE OF GENERAL SAFETY PERFORMANCE AND SAFETY KNOWLEDGE

General Performance

In terms of task-relevant behavior, workers are required to display core, basic safety behaviors to some degree across jobs in most industries, including manufacturing, health care, mining, chemical processing, nuclear power plant operations, and protective services. For the most part, a single-factor model relating to safety compliance has dominated conceptual and empirical research on the nature of safety task performance in these industries and types of work (Cheyne, Cox, Oliver, & Tomas, 1998; Chhokar, 1990; Griffin & Neal, 2000; Hofmann & Stetzer, 1996; Lingard & Rowlinson, 1997; McDonald, Corrigan, Daly, & Cromie, 2000; Neal & Griffin, 2004; Rudmo, 2000). Safety compliance refers to the extent to which employees adhere to required safety procedures and carry out work in a correct and safe manner. Notably, Marchand, Simard, Carpentier-Roy, and Ouellet (1998) found a weak fit for a confirmatory factor model involving safety compliance, with follow-up analyses indicating that safety compliance is not a consistent dimension.

In a few cases, researchers have argued that multiple performance factors underlie worker safety-related task behavior, including leader safety behavior (see Hofmann & Morgeson, 2004; Simard & Marchand, 1997). Furthermore, in a more general sense, Burke, Sarpy, Tesluk, and Smith-Crowe (2002) confirmed, across 23 jobs, a grounded theoretical model of general safety performance, with four factors labeled (1) using personal protective equipment, (2) engaging in work practices to reduce risk, (3) communicating health and safety information, and (4) exercising employee rights and responsibilities. Notably, these factors were confirmed for individuals working in dyads, work groups, and teams. These four factors are consistent with knowledge content areas and lesson plans (in terms of how safety training is segmented into modules) for a number of major labor unions and organizations (e.g., International Brotherhood of Teamsters, 1993). These findings offer progress toward a taxonomy of general safety performance in so far as safety task performance is concerned, and provide potentially useful categories for describing the content of requisite safety knowledge in a broad set of jobs and types of work. We note that our discussion is not intended to preclude the consideration of more specific safety performance constructs and knowledge areas, including more specific team processes (see Marks, Mathieu, & Zaccaro, 2001), but is intended to identify theoretically meaningful performance and knowledge constructs that help to drive our discussion of the relative effectiveness of safety training interventions.

Drawing on work in the area of contextual performance (Borman & Motowidlo, 1993), a second type of behavior, discretionary or extra-role behavior—referred to as safety participation or safety initiative—has also been studied (e.g., Griffin & Neal, 2000; Marchand et al., 1998; Neal, Griffin, & Hart, 2000). Notably, Marchand et al. found that a two-factor model of safety performance (with factors relating to safety compliance and safety initiative) did not provide a good fit to the data. This result is not surprising, given that the research literature on contextual performance suggests that more specific dimensions underlie discretionary work behaviors (Motowidlo, Borman, & Schmitt, 1997).

Safety Knowledge and Skills

For any task-related safety performance construct, the content of safety knowledge can be characterized in terms of the factual material the trainee needs to acquire (i.e., often referred to as declarative knowledge or verbal information: Gagne & Medsker, 1996; Kraiger, Ford, & Salas, 1993). Trainees in almost all occupational domains will need to acquire declarative knowledge of fundamental information related to using personal protective equipment, engaging in work practices to reduce risk, communicating health and safety information, and exercising employee rights and responsibilities. The literature is replete with examples of safety training directed toward the development of workers' understanding of fundamental information in each of these broad content domains in industries as diverse as agriculture (Barnett et al., 1984), health care (Foster, 1996), mining (Fiedler, 1987), and transportation (Saari & Nisanen, 1989).

While more advanced knowledge concerning how to undertake cognitive or physical tasks (i.e., often referred to as procedural knowledge and skill and can include mental models: Kraiger et al., 1993) can be described for each general knowledge area, another useful distinction is the type and level of procedural knowledge or skill. For the purpose of our discussion, we will use the term 'skill' interchangeably with the concept of 'procedural knowledge.' Moving beyond the acquisition of fundamental or declarative knowledge, the development of safety and health knowledge in each of the four content domains can be considered with respect to at least two levels of advanced skill: recognition and awareness skills, and analytical and decision-making skills (Baker & Wallerstein, 1998). For the most part, recognition and awareness skills pertain to observing and inspecting the workplace for potential hazards, and properly reporting these hazards. Analytical and decision-making skills focus on controlling hazards and engaging in social action to proactively prevent work-related accidents, illnesses, and injuries. As such, in safety work, the latter skills often have cognitive/intellectual (applying concepts and generating solutions) and motor components (executing physical action with a degree of precision)—occasionally referred to as cognitive-psychomotor skills (Arthur, Bennett, Edens, & Bell, 2003). As we will point out below, particular learning theories and methods of safety and health training are often closely tied to the type and level of knowledge being acquired.

LEARNING THEORIES AND THEIR IMPLICATIONS FOR SAFETY AND HEALTH TRAINING

All theoretical frameworks that address adult knowledge development describe a process for how learning unfolds with respect to the systematic ordering of concepts that are germane to the respective framework. In addition, the theories can be further differentiated in terms of the extent to which notions of action or behavior, reflection (thinking), feedback (and dialogue), and motivational constructs are incorporated into the framework. We note that individual reflection can be of an abstract or more concrete nature, with more concrete reflection often posited to be associated with actions considered or taken. We also distinguish feedback from dialogue, where the latter refers to discussions with others, including virtual others, and often with respect to actions considered or taken. Feedback refers to information learners receive from either external sources (e.g., trainers, peers, and supervisors) or intrinsically (e.g., kinesthetic, tactile, visual, and olfactory) concerning their progress in the acquisition of knowledge or demonstration of behavior.

For each learning theory, we discuss key concepts and their ordering within the theory as well as how the various theories incorporate notions of action, reflection, feedback, dialogue, and motivation. These discussions highlight commonalities and differences among the theories, and set the stage for a discussion of how safety training is based on each theory. Table 1.1 provides a summary of the key features of each approach and the implications of each learning theory for knowledge development and its transfer, which are detailed below.

Stage-learning Theories

Historically, many learning theorists (e.g., Bryan & Harter, 1899; Fitts, 1962) have described knowledge acquisition in terms of stages that delineate different aspects of the learning process. For instance, Anderson (1985) and Kanfer and Ackerman (1989) segment learning into three phases: acquisition of declarative knowledge, followed by knowledge compilation, and, subsequently, the proceduralization of knowledge. Declarative knowledge refers to one's mastery of factual material (i.e., knowledge of facts and things), whereas procedural knowledge concerns the routines for undertaking cognitive or physical tasks (i.e., knowledge about how to perform a task).

In the declarative knowledge phase, the learner is viewed as a non-autonomous consumer of information delivered by one or more experts. An important aspect of the declarative knowledge phase is that knowledge acquisition requires substantial attentional resources. For instance, a hazardous waste worker learning how to use air respirators needs to devote considerable cognitive and motor resources to acquire facts and routines related to components of the task (e.g., selecting the appropriate air respirator, properly fitting the respirator, cleaning the respirator). As a result, when an individual is confronted with information-processing requirements that are tangential to the task or learning goal related to using an air respirator (e.g., communicating health and safety information), he or she is often unable to devote attention to such a secondary task (e.g., see Nissen & Bullemer, 1987). Consequently, declarative knowledge acquisition is slow and error prone.

Once the learner has developed an adequate cognitive representation of the task, he or she progresses to the knowledge compilation phase. During the knowledge compilation phase, with practice, the learner is posited to integrate the sequences of cognitive and motor processes necessary for engaging in the task. The attentional demands are reduced and the learner moves acquired knowledge from short-term to long-term memory. The notion of moving knowledge acquired through action and practice into long-term memory or knowledge structures is analogous to the development of an 'operative imaging system' (the sum of internal long-term representations of stimulus–response–consequence relations) through acting as described within action-regulation theory (see Frese & Zapf, 1994; Hacker, 2003).

Table 1.1   Prominent features of learning theories

Learning theory emphases and features	Stage theories	Reinforcement	Feedback intervention	Social learning	Action regulation	Experiential learning	Distance learning
Knowledge development							
Development of declarative knowledge is considered	•				•	•	•
Content of knowledge is important					•		
Multiple methods (e.g., lecture, case studies) are employed	•				•	•	
Aids for retention of observed skills (e.g., notes, guides) are provided				•			
Action/Behavior							
Development of procedural knowledge and skill is emphasized	•			•	•	•	
Physical practice is encouraged	•			•	•	•	
Error training is used to aid transfer					•		
Motivation							
Development of learning valence beliefs is encouraged				•			•
Rewards/punishment are used to reinforce behaviors		•		•			
Goal setting is used as an aid to transfer			•	•	•		
Self-management strategies (e.g., relapse prevention) are taught				•		•	
Feedback							
Specific actions are targeted		•		•			
Informational feedback is provided	•	•	•	•	•		
Feedback is considered better as task grows subjectively familiar or objectively simple			•				
Feedback is recommended on task rather than person			•				
Dialogue and reflection							
Reflection considered important for knowledge development					•	•	•
Action-focused reflection is viewed as critical to knowledge development					•	•	
Dialogue is considered important					•	•	•
Role of teacher in facilitating reflection and dialogue is considered						•	•
Learning strategies are considered—deep learning is encouraged						•	•
Mental practice is used					•		
Small group, collaborative learning is considered						•	
Contextualization							
Importance is placed on learning skills in context					•	•	
Individuals build upon their experiences	•				•	•	
Experiential methods (e.g., problem-based learning, project work, role plays, simulations) are promoted						•	
Learning in non-redundant contexts is encouraged for transfer					•	•	

In the final phase, procedural knowledge and skills are acquired when the learner can perform the task with little attentional resources—that is, the task is said to be automated or proceduralized, such that once a signal or stimulus is presented, the task is performed with little conscious activity. In many respects, advanced proceduralized knowledge is analogous to notions of implicit knowledge (Broadbent, Fitzgerald, & Broadbent, 1986; Gardener, Chmiel, & Wall, 1996), that is, knowledge that is developed through action and cannot necessarily be verbalized. For tasks that are infrequently carried out (such as responding to an emergency), extra learning opportunities subsequent to the proceduralization of knowledge have been found to have positive effects on procedural knowledge retention (Driskell, Willis, & Copper, 1992; Wagner, 1997). Also, as would be expected from stage theories of learning, meta-analytic research has shown stronger associations between post-training levels of procedural knowledge and performance than between post-training levels of declarative knowledge and performance (see Alliger, Tannenbaum, Bennett, Traver, & Shotland, 1997; Colquitt, LePine, & Noe, 2000).

Implications of stage-learning theories for safety training

For training objectives related to the acquisition of procedural knowledge, stage-learning theories imply that safety training for individuals and work groups begin with the standardized presentation of factual material, possibly via a lecture-based format by a recognized expert, followed by opportunities for substantial practice. This point is in line with Atherley and Robertson's (1998) observation that a stage approach to learning calls for the use of multiple training methods or instructional techniques for the development of different levels of safety knowledge. These points are also consistent with Halpern and Hakel's (2003) arguments that substantial practice during training under varied conditions will promote long-term retention and transfer of knowledge. In addition, stage-learning theorists emphasize expert feedback, often of a unidirectional nature throughout the learning process. Notably, the theoretical role of dialogue (within and between trainers and trainees) in the development of knowledge structures is typically not considered in stage-learning theories. Furthermore, stage-learning theorists allude to reflection or thinking via the notion of knowledge compilation, but the process for how knowledge compilation occurs or can be stimulated is rather vaguely described. Finally, with the notable exception of Kanfer and Ackerman's (1989) work, stage-learning theorists have not emphasized the role of motivational variables.

Reinforcement and Feedback Theories

Behaviorists, such as Skinner (1974), propose that learning results from the association between behaviors (actions) and rewards (consequences). The basic premise is that actions are controlled by the immediate consequences; that is, individual or team behavior can be increased, suppressed, or decreased depending on what happens immediately after its occurrence. A key focus of behavior modification is on positive reinforcement, following a desired behavior with a reward (praise, recognition, cash reward, etc.) so as to increase its probability of occurrence. As a learning mechanism, positive reinforcement is useful in pointing out when the desired action is demonstrated, and has been shown to be effective in increasing individual and team task performance across a wide range of working populations and work settings (see reviews by Hackman & Wageman, 2005; Stajkovic & Luthans, 1997, 2001).

Feedback intervention theory (Kluger & DeNisi, 1996, 1998) has been proposed as a related framework for understanding why and how worker behavior changes as a result of external consequences. The three basic arguments of feedback intervention theory are (a) behavior is regulated by comparisons of feedback with goals or standards (and the identification of gaps between the two), (b) attentional resources are limited, and only those feedback-goal gaps that receive attention affect self-regulation, and (c) feedback interventions change the locus of attention (self versus task) and thus behavior. For example, feedback interventions that direct attention to the self on complex tasks are seen as depleting the resources needed for adequate performance. In contrast, feedback interventions that direct attention to the self on simple tasks may increase performance. Notably, Kluger and DeNisi's (1998) meta-analytic findings indicate that the effects of feedback interventions grow more positive either as the task becomes more subjectively familiar (e.g., skills for engaging in the task are proceduralized) or objectively simple.

Implications of behavior-based safety and feedback intervention theory for modifying safety performance

For modifying safety-related behavior, behavior-based safety implies that interventions must always target specific actions. For the most part, targeting specific behaviors implies that workers know how to engage in the action (i.e., the skill is proceduralized) or that the action is relatively simple. Feedback intervention theory also suggests that simple actions or complex actions (which are proceduralized) are most likely to be positively affected by feedback interventions. In addition, feedback intervention theory suggests that targeting simple actions or actions related to proceduralized skills should be accompanied by goal setting in order to further motivate behavioral change (Kluger & DeNisi, 1998).

Clearly, the emphasis in reinforcement theory is on *acting workers into thinking differently* rather than targeting internal individual differences (such as declarative knowledge or attitudinal variables) in order to *think people into acting differently* (Geller, 2001). Although not denying the existence of internal states, reinforcement theory implies that trainers or others (e.g., supervisors) should look for external factors (positive as opposed to negative consequences) to improve worker safety performance. This position leads to a lack of emphasis placed on reflection about actions taken. Rather, emphasis is placed on identifying signals that activate behavior and expert unidirectional feedback to modify worker actions. Likewise, feedback intervention theory stresses unidirectional, external feedback related to task behavior (as opposed to the self as the locus of attention).

Social-learning and Action-regulation Theories

Social-learning theory (Bandura, 1977) within the Anglo-American tradition and action-regulation theory (Hacker, 2003) within German psychology developed as alternatives to behaviorist approaches. Below, we discuss the two approaches and then provide an integrated discussion of the implications of these social-cognitive theories for safety and health training.

Social-learning theorists believe that behavior is a result of continual, dynamic, and reciprocal interaction between the person and the environment. Similar to behaviorists, they consider that response consequences, such as rewards or punishments, will influence the likelihood of a behavior occurring in a given situation. However, the key difference with behaviorists is the proposed active role of cognition in mediating between stimulus and response, and the view that learning not only takes place through direct experience (enactive learning) but can also occur vicariously through watching others (observational learning). In terms of workplace learning, the most influential of this school of theorists is Albert Bandura (Bandura, 1977, 2001; Bandura & Locke, 2003; Wood & Bandura, 1989). The three most relevant contributions of this theory are, with regards to the operation of observational learning, the focus on active *self-management* of the individual, and the acknowledged importance of factors such as *motivation* and *self-efficacy* in influencing learning and behavior.

Bandura's theoretical position on observational learning considers four interrelated processes. The first necessary condition for modeling to occur is that the learner needs to attend to the model (*attentional* processes). An individual's level of attention can be affected by many factors including the characteristics of the behavior, the model characteristics, and their own distractedness or tiredness. Greater modeling occurs where the behavior is demonstrated in a clear and specific manner by an identified and trusted model (Goldstein & Ford, 2002). Second, observed activities are transformed into symbolic mental representations (as images or semantic code), which guide subsequent behavior (*retention* processes). Factors that aid long-term memory (e.g., repetition of modeled behavior) or help with the recovery of information (e.g., contextual cues) will influence the degree of modeling (Weeks & Anderson, 2000). The third phase involves the translation of what has been observed and coded into covert behavior (*production* processes). Individuals compare their conceptions of what should be produced with what they are actually producing. Abilities improve with direct practice and even usage of mental rehearsal (e.g., Davis & Yi, 2004; Driskell, Copper, & Moran, 1994; Salas & Cannon-Bowers, 2001). Feedback is also an important component here in helping individuals to identify the discrepancy between target and actual behaviors and allowing the gap to be closed (Smith-Jentsch, Salas, & Baker, 1996). The fourth aspect concerns the role of *motivational* processes. Individuals may learn how to do certain behaviors but they also need to be motivated or confident enough to display the behavior (Tannenbaum & Yukl, 1992). Social-learning theory considers that motivation can be influenced by the individual being directly reinforced through tangible rewards and punishments, by observing the reinforcement of others, or engaging in self-reinforcement (e.g., through self-praise or self-reproach).

One popular organizational application of social-learning theory has been the development of behavior-modeling training, which utilizes the processes described above to operationalize an observational-learning methodology. In practice, behavior-modeling training has three main steps, which apply to individual trainees or trainees as a work group or team. First, a model (e.g., an expert) demonstrates the behavior and skills the trainee has to learn. Second, the trainee is encouraged to rehearse and practice the model's behavior. Third, feedback or reinforcement from the trainer, and possibly other trainees, is provided as the trainee's behavior approximates closer to the behavior of the model. This approach has been widely used and shown to effect with respect to a wide range of training topics including computer software use (e.g., Bolt, Killough, & Koh, 2001; Chou, 2001; Gist, Schwoerer, & Rosen, 1989; Simon, Grover, Teng, & Whitcomb, 1996; Simon & Werner, 1996), negotiation skills (Nadler, Thomson, & van Boven, 2003), job search skills (Eden & Aviram, 1993), and innovative problem solving (Gist, 1989). Notably, behavior-modeling training has been found to be more effective than traditional lecture-based methods in improving immediate knowledge, skill outcomes, and, to a lesser extent, work performance outcomes (Burke et al., in press; Callahan, Kiker, & Cross, 2003; Goldstein & Ford, 2002). Finally, in a meta-analysis of 117 behavior-modeling studies, Taylor, Russ-Eft, and Chan (in press) found that transfer was greatest when mixed models (positive and negative models, see Baldwin, 1992), as opposed to only positive models, were presented, when practice included trainee-generated scenarios, when trainees' superiors were also trained, and when rewards/sanctions were instituted in the trainees' work environment.

Another key aspect of Bandura's agentic approach is that individuals undertake extensive self-reflection on their experience and the adequacy of their thoughts and actions. With respect to this point, he highlights the importance of self-efficacy, defined as people's judgments of their ability to perform specific activities to a designated standard (Bandura, 1986). It is thought to be significant that the greater the sense of self-efficacy, the greater will be the effort, persistence, and resilience of the individual in performing a behavior (Gist & Mitchell, 1992).

Self-efficacy has been shown to relate to training effectiveness measures, such as knowledge acquisition and work performance itself (see Colquitt et al., 2000; Ford, Quinones, Sego, & Sorra, 1992; Gist & Mitchell, 1992; Mathieu, Martineau, & Tannenbaum, 1993; McNatt & Judge, 2004). In addition, a number of studies have demonstrated relationships between post-training levels of self-efficacy and transfer (Ford, Smith, Weissbein, Gully, & Salas, 1998; Frayne & Latham, 1987; Morin & Latham, 2000; Warr, Allan, & Birdi, 1999). Furthermore, Colquitt et al.'s (2000) training meta-analysis showed that post-training self-efficacy had a significant relationship with transfer over and above levels of declarative knowledge, skill acquisition, and reactions to the training.

Bandura's highlighting of self-management by individuals and the role of motivation and self-efficacy in influencing learning outcomes has contributed to two other types of interventions designed to improve these aspects and, in particular, to improve the transfer of training: relapse prevention/behavioral self-management and goal-setting approaches. Relapse prevention was introduced into the training context by Marx (1982), who proposed a theoretical process to describe how some individuals may fail to transfer their skills to the workplace. He suggested that early in the post-training period, if individuals failed to apply their skills in a challenging situation, they would suffer a decline in self-efficacy and a subsequent reduced likelihood of using their learned skills (i.e., an increased probability of relapse). The relapse prevention approach involves teaching participants a set of self-control strategies including behavioral coping skills (anxiety reduction, stress management, assertion training) and cognitive strategies for reinterpreting negative and irrational outcomes to help trainees to become successful in their transfer (e.g., see Marx & Ivey, 1988).

Reviews of research in clinical and penal contexts (Dowden, Antonowicz, & Andrews, 2003; Mueser et al., 2002) have shown that the teaching of relapse prevention strategies has had a measure of success. Several authors have recommended the use of relapse prevention or self-management strategies for training (e.g., Noe, 1986) and some empirical research has been done on the method in work settings—that is, studies by Burke and Baldwin (1999), Frayne and Latham (1987), Frayne and Geringer (2000), Godat and Brigham (1999), and Hickman and Geller (2003) have shown that self-management training can lead to greater changes in workplace behavior compared to those not provided with self-management strategies.

Another approach for improving motivation is through the setting of goals that are specific, challenging, and accepted by the individual (Locke & Latham, 1990). Goals can be operationalized through behavioral checklists, action plans, or learning contracts. Most training studies on the topic have shown that goal setting can help to improve the transfer of training (e.g., Cheng & Ho, 2001; Shoenfelt, 1996); yet, inconsistent results have been reported (e.g., Morin & Latham, 2000; Murtada & Haccoun, 1996). In addition, several

studies have attempted to directly compare the relative effectiveness of relapse prevention or self-management methods with goal-setting techniques.
Although results have been mixed, they do suggest that goal setting promotes effort and persistence toward a particular target outcome and that self-
management approaches may be particularly helpful in aiding skill mastery and
transfer of skills to new and difficult situations (Gist & Stevens, 1998).

Action-regulation theory

Action-regulation theory is another cognitive, information-processing theory
concerned with goals and the processes that intervene between environmental
input and actions of workers (Frese & Zapf, 1994; Hacker, 2003). Action-
regulation theory focuses on various stages or phases of action regulation, which
begin with action preparation (goal development and orienting oneself to the
characteristics of the situation under which a goal must be accomplished),
implementing the goal (which includes feedback on goal progress), and evaluation of the final outcome. The most important aspect of action regulation
is that actions are controlled by goals—anticipations of the results that one
or more individuals in the case of teams intend to achieve (Hacker, 2003).
From a motivational perspective, the goals can be viewed as intentions. Furthermore, the goals are posited to be stored in memory until the action is
completed.

An important characteristic of this theory is the development of the
'operative-imaging system.' The operative-imaging system is the sum of the internal, long-term representations of condition–action–consequence relations.
Importantly, these associations in the operative-imaging system, and thus
knowledge, are regarded as content specific (Hacker, 2003). Also, action theorists regard substantial parts of knowledge (which would include portions
of procedural knowledge in any content area) as being implicit, unarticu-
lated pieces of knowledge that cannot be elicited by questioning alone. The
operative-imaging system is the cognitive base incorporating all knowledge
gained, analogous to notions of long-term memory, which enables a person to
act. Operative-imaging systems also bear some relation to mental models in
that the information they store is not viewed as a true copy of reality. Yet, the
concept of a mental model is more an internal model of an external system,
whereas an operative-imaging system is built up or learned through acting.

Along with acting, experiencing errors is believed to be helpful in the construction of realistic operative-imaging systems and learning (Frese & Zapf,
1994), and can be successfully incorporated into training efforts (Heimbeck,
Frese, Sonnentag, & Keith, 2003; Ivancic & Hesketh, 2000). Experiencing errors and acting in non-redundant, dynamic environments is expected to prevent
premature routinization of action. In addition, Bransford, Brown, and Cocking
(2000) caution that knowledge that is overly contextualized can reduce the
transfer of knowledge. These points are relevant not only for individuals, but

also for teams that may need to deal with crisis events, where updating and deviating from planned action may be necessary (Doerner, 1996). Furthermore, while feedback is regarded as important, dialogue with a real or virtual partner concerning actions is regarded as critical to learning and the development of the operative-imaging system. The reason for this effect is that dialogue is expected to initiate and stimulate reflection concerning actions taken. In effect, action theorists argue that workers learn and *think in and by action*.

The implications of social-learning and action-regulation theories for safety training

For training objectives relating to the development of procedural knowledge, observational modeling should improve safety training beyond just lecturing. With observational-learning approaches, the model or models must be credible, trusted, and demonstrate the desired behavior in a clear and precise manner. As with stage theories of learning, both social-learning theory and action-regulation theory argue that trainees must be given the opportunity to practice the behavior a number of times, with appropriate levels of feedback. For routine tasks, repetitive practice and feedback not only help to consolidate the requisite knowledge and skill, but also help in the development of task self-efficacy, which is known to influence learning and work behavior. However, as pointed out by action theory and social-learning theory, trainees would potentially benefit from the incorporation of error training or positive and negative role models into the training effort and possibly acting in non-redundant and dynamic (where relevant) contexts to enhance learning (e.g., with respect to different training props and changing scenarios as is done in hands-on emergency responder training; see Smith-Crowe, Burke, & Landis, 2003). The latter features are not only expected to aid in the development of a cognitive operating system, but may also facilitate anticipatory thinking and the development of strategies for handling non-routine and dynamic emergency events or critical incidents. This conclusion is consistent with the assertions of Wall, Cordery, and Clegg (2002) and Kozlowski et al. (2001) that knowledge application facilitates knowledge development, and that both foster more proactive and adaptive orientations. Also, see Ford and Schmidt (2000) for a related discussion of how training might be conducted to enhance the generalization of knowledge acquired through training to deal with non-routine events involving teams.

Attending to the motivational and self-efficacy needs of trainees is also important within both social-learning and action-regulation theories (Frese & Zapf, 1994; Machin & Fogarty, 2003). The use of goal setting should aid the transfer of training (especially for routine safety behavior) and this can be done through usage of behavioral checklists, action plans, or learning contracts. In addition, self-efficacy can be developed through four types of experience, each of which relates to many potential aspects of safety training activities: mastery (e.g., direct attempts to try out skills in a class setting or real or virtual simulations); vicarious learning (e.g., learning by watching others such as facilitators or workers demonstrating procedural skills); verbal persuasion (e.g., being instructed and encouraged by course facilitators, peers, and supervisors); and positive emotional arousal (e.g., increasing feelings of comfort during training related to dealing with actual hazards). Furthermore, the teaching of self-regulatory strategies, which help trainees to monitor their own behaviour and anticipate and cope with difficult situations, should also prove beneficial in improving the transfer of training. This effect is partly (along with well-developed cognitive strategies) a result of helping trainees to maintain their self-efficacy in challenging contexts.

Beliefs about the potential value of training have also been indicated as influencing training success (Tannenbaum, Mathieu, Salas, & Cannon-Bowers, 1991) and participation in learning activities in the first place (Tharenou, 2001). In fact, Colquitt et al.'s (2000) meta-analytic results indicated that there was a strong relationship between valence beliefs and the motivation to learn. Therefore, it may be reasonable to assume that safety training programs that emphasize the value of performing the behaviors (e.g., showing or allowing trainees to experience the negative consequences of not performing the correct safety procedures) should improve the motivation of trainees to learn the content and transfer it to the job. In effect, directly or indirectly experiencing the negative consequence of unsafe behavior or error training may have not only cognitive, but also motivational benefits for safety trainees. More research is needed to address these issues in safety and health training contexts.

Experiential-learning and Distance Education Theories

Theories of experiential learning posit that the learning process ideally involves the following key activities: (a) integrating new knowledge and experiences into existing experience, i.e., the personal knowledge derived from direct participation in the world; (b) constructing more complex and differentiated understandings of self (e.g., one's skills, abilities) and the world; (c) applying experience and new understandings to real-life or life-like situations and problems; and (d) reflecting on experience (Weil & McGill, 1989). These activities are often viewed as a cycle and Kolb's (1984) definition of the learning cycle has been particularly influential in organizational research and practice. Kolb argues that there are four relatively independent stages in a learning cycle, namely, concrete experience, reflective observation, abstract conceptualization, and active experimentation. Notably, learning involves reflecting on experience. From the insight gained, new concepts, theories, or plans can be constructed, which in turn are subsequently tested out in action, leading to further concrete experience. Others place less emphasis on the learning process as a cycle of distinct stages, arguing that the different aspects of learning can be combined or occur in different orders (Marsick & Watkins, 1997; Mezirow, 1990).

Like action-regulation theorists, Schön (1983), for example, suggests that an important aspect of learning is reflection-in-action.

Historically, experiential-learning theorists have emphasized the internal cognitive aspects of learning. More recently, sociocultural and dialogical approaches to experiential learning have begun to highlight the social and contextually situated nature of the learning process (Cunliffe, 2002; Dixon, 1994; Fenwick, 2000; Holman, 2000a; Holman, Pavlica, & Thorpe, 1997; Schein, 1993). Learning is social, not only in the obvious sense that individuals learn from others, but also because social interaction mediates the learning process (Lave & Wenger, 1991; Vygotsky, 1987). For example, a teacher's questioning can enable students to reflect on their experience, as can the discussion generated by receiving feedback from others, and group discussion can help to clarify understanding and develop new perspectives (Webb, Troper, & Fall, 1995). As a result, not only are the process and outcomes of learning improved in any one instance, but these external patterns of dialogue and interaction may also be internalized and lead to an improvement in the individual's learning skills and capabilities, e.g., more critical reflection, and better ability to construct meaning. As such, cognitive acts of learning and learning skills can be seen to originate within social interaction.

Learning is also viewed as contextually situated, as knowing how to act properly within a context requires the learner to develop an understanding of the rules, shared meanings, values, relationships, types of language, and technologies that exist within that context (Lave & Wenger, 1991). An implication is that knowledge is embedded within a context, and that the transfer of knowledge from one context to another may be problematic (Wilson, 1992; see also Anderson, Reder, & Simon, 1996, for a critique of this position). Recognizing that learning occurs within a context, Halpern and Hakel (2003) discuss how increasing variability or novelty of stimuli during learning may not only make the learning process more effortful, but also make the memory 'trace' more durable and resistant to forgetting. We will return to a discussion of the more specific implications of contextual aspects of learning, especially in relation to the development of observational and awareness skills needed for identifying and dealing with workplace hazards.

The learning process in experiential-learning theory is normally seen as having specific and general aims (Holman, 2000b). Specific aims include the development of knowledge *and* skill. Indeed, a hallmark of learning in experiential-learning theory is not simply the development of theoretical or experiential knowledge but the development of a person's ability to take effective, skilled action. Emphasis is also placed on learning skills, e.g., critical thinking, planning, self-directedness. As noted, these skills are thought to be developed through engagement in the experiential-learning process itself and are recognized as crucial to meeting the general aims of experiential learning, namely, individual responsibility for learning and personal autonomy (Brookfield, 1987; Mezirow, 1990).

Experiential training and development methods are relatively diverse and include problem-based learning, project work, action learning, group work, work placement, role playing, outdoor training, simulation, and learning contracts (Henry, 1989). Each method might be used to support a particular aspect of the experiential-learning process. Methods might also be combined enabling the learner to have the opportunity to engage in all aspects of the learning cycle. For example, a teacher might employ problem-based learning to encourage students to reflect on the theoretical knowledge obtained in a lecture and as a means of applying knowledge to a life-like situation (Evensen & Hmelo, 2000). Or a trainer might use an action-learning program in which employees apply their theoretical and experiential knowledge to a practical problem at work and then use group work to encourage reflection and the construction of understanding (Revans, 1971). We should note that advocates of experiential learning do not entirely dismiss methods such as lectures. Rather, lectures are viewed as one technique that can be used if conducted in an engaging manner (deWinstanley & Bjork, 2002; Galliano, 1999).

It is evident that proponents of experiential learning posit that experiential training and development methods facilitate the learning process, which in turn leads to the development of knowledge, skill, and personal autonomy. Moreover, they argue that experiential methods are more effective than more passive, academic methods such as lecture. Evidence for the veracity of experiential-learning theory and its superiority over academic methods in adults can be surmised from studies on three topics: the effects of experiential methods on the learning process; the effects of experiential learning on outcomes; and the effects of training and development methods on outcomes.

With regard to the first of these, research findings are generally supportive of the idea that experiential methods can be used to facilitate learning within individuals (Burgoyne & Hodgson, 1983; Herz & Merz, 1998; Kolb, 1984; Schön, 1983) and between individuals (Frederiksen, 1999; Glenn, Koschmann, & Conlee, 1999; Kneser & Ploetzner, 2001; Raelin, 2001). In addition, particular methods have been shown to facilitate different aspects of the experiential-learning process. For example, problem-based learning, action learning, and simulations are likely to facilitate the application of knowledge to life-like or real-life contexts and problems (Blackler & Kennedy, 2004; Evensen & Hmelo, 2000; Gow & Kember, 1993; Keys & Wolfe, 1990). Research on student learning has also demonstrated that when lectures are more experientially based (e.g., by utilizing students' existing experience and theoretical knowledge and relating new knowledge to these understandings), students are more adept at facilitating the integration of ideas and the construction of meaning (Entwistle, 1987, 1995; Prosser, 1987). However, it needs to be noted that evidence for the effects of experiential methods on the learning process is mainly derived from qualitative case studies (the research on student learning is one exception but was not conducted from the perspective of experiential-learning theory). There is a need for further research on the types of cognitive and social-learning activities that occur while participating in experiential-training and development methods (Noe, 1986).

Evidence for the effects of experiential learning can be garnered from research that has focused directly on experiential learning, as well as from other more indirect sources. Direct examinations of the experiential-learning process in educational and organizational settings have illuminated how its different aspects—particularly reflection and application—facilitate the development of knowledge and skill (Boud, Cohen, & Walker, 1994; Pedler, 1983). Other direct examinations of the experiential-learning process can be found in the work of Kolb (Kolb & Kolb, 2000). For example, Mainemelis, Boyatzis, and Kolb (2002) examined whether one of four learning styles, a preference for engaging in one of the four stages of the learning cycle, would be associated with skills hypothesized as being developed through training. They reported that, as expected, an abstract conceptualization style was positively correlated with analytical skills such as logical inference, building conceptual models, and experimenting with new ideas. In addition, a concrete experience style was positively associated with interpersonal skills, such as relationship skills and empathy. The other two learning styles—reflective observation and active experimentation—showed no positive association with the expected skill areas.

Indirect evidence for the effects of experiential learning can be obtained from research on learning strategies, some of which are conceptually similar to aspects of the experiential-learning process (Leung & Kember, 2003). Thus, certain cognitive-learning strategies are comparable to reflection and integration, while certain behavioral strategies are comparable to practical application. With regard to cognitive strategies, research in undergraduate populations has consistently demonstrated an association between a deep approach to learning (a mixture of integration and reflection) and more sophisticated understandings of subject matter (Balla, Biggs, Gibson, & Chang, 1990; Biggs & Collis, 1982; Marton & Saljo, 1976), improved long-term recall (Marton & Wenestam, 1979), and higher grades (Biggs, 1989; Entwistle, 2002).

In occupational samples, the findings with regard to cognitive strategies are less consistent. On the one hand, Ford et al. (1998) found that a meta-cognitive strategy akin to reflection (i.e., one that permitted trainees' control over the learning process) was positively associated with knowledge gain and performance, and Sonnentag and Kliene (2000) reported that insurance agents who engaged in deliberate practice received higher supervisor ratings. Deliberate practice activities—which included running mental simulations, asking for feedback, and planning for difficult situations—can be compared to the types of activity involved in reflection and abstract conceptualization. Warr and Bunce (1995) also reported a positive association between an analytical learning strategy (a measure that included integration activities) and tutor-based measures of cognitive and skill-based outcomes. On the other hand, Warr and Downing (2000) found no relationship between a measure of integration (called active reflection) and knowledge change in trainee mechanics. Duff (2003) found that the deep approach predicted academic performance of MBA students in continuous assessments, but not exam grades. With regard to behavioral-learning strategies, research in occupational samples has demonstrated that the use of strategies akin to practical application in training programs is positively related to knowledge gain, performance (Ford et al., 1998), self-reported competence (Warr et al., 1999), and tutor-based measures of cognitive and skill-based outcomes (Warr & Allen, 1998).

Other indirect evidence of the usefulness of experiential-learning theory comes from traditional reviews and meta-analytic studies in industrial and organizational (I/O) psychology where a general conclusion is that more engaging methods of training (e.g., behavior modeling, lectures combined with role playing and discussion) have a greater effect on outcomes than less engaging methods, particularly, lectures (e.g., see Burke & Day, 1986; Colligan & Cohen, 2004). These conclusions are consistent with those reached in the educational literature by Vernon and Blake (1993) that problem-based learning is superior to lecture-based methods, and by Springer, Stanne, and Donovan (1999) that small group learning is superior to individualistic and non-collaborative methods.

Distance education theories

Distance education refers to learning contexts where the instructor may not be present in the learning situation or where the learning group may be scattered and connected to differing degrees (Chen & Willits, 1998). These situations might include correspondence study, videoconference learning environments, use of interactive databases, and Internet-based learning environments. Moore's (1973, 1993) distance-learning theory identifies the degree of course structure, learner autonomy, and dialogue between teachers and learners as the key components of distance learning. Essentially, Moore argues that these components affect the amount of transactional distance between teachers and learners, defined as the relative psychological (as opposed to geographical) separation between understandings and perceptions of participants in learning situations. Notably, Moore contends that it is possible to manipulate the communications medium (e.g., computer, video, or teleconference) to increase dialogue between teachers and learners, thus reducing transactional distance and allowing for more effective learning. Furthermore, tests of Moore's theory (e.g., Chen & Willits, 1998) indicate that the dimensions of structure, learner autonomy, and dialogue are multidimensional, and that in-class discussion (one of the dimensions of dialogue) in a videoconferencing learning environment has direct effects on perceived learning outcomes. Chen's (2001) research with respect to the World Wide Web learning environment also indicates that the construct domain for transactional distance is multidimensional, and will need to be taken into account and overcome for learning to occur.

Like Moore, D.R. Garrison's (1989, 2000) theory of distance learning stresses the critical role of two-way communication between the teacher (or other subject-matter experts) and the learner. Importantly, D.R. Garrison (1989) asserted that at the heart of education is the process of critical reflection and perspective formation, which is a result of dialogue between the teacher and the learner. Consistent with arguments of action-regulation and experiential-learning theorists, D.R. Garrison is one of a number of educational researchers who acknowledge the role of dialogue or shared inquiry as important for permitting learners to transcend the limitations of their own experience and generate better solutions to problems (e.g., see Harrington & J.W. Garrison, 1992; King, 1990; Schacter, 2000).

Implications of experiential-learning and distance education theories for safety and health training

Experiential-learning theories would imply that in order for safety and health training to be meaningful and effective it should be grounded in the experience of the trainee. That is, trainees need to be actively engaged in the learning process and not relatively passive receivers of knowledge. Both experiential and theoretical knowledge need to be considered in the learning process, and that the opportunities to apply both types of knowledge and reflect on them are essential for the effective development of safety knowledge and skill. These points are also advocated within the adult learning literature (Knowles, 1983, 1996). Furthermore, in both experiential-learning and distance education theories, dialogue is regarded as important for enhancing reflection and learning. The latter point is particularly important relative to the emphasis being placed on more passive, computer-based, and distance-training methods within the public health workforce (e.g., see Eckerman et al., 2002; NIEHS, 1999) and the need to consider technological advancements in educating this workforce (Gebbie & Huang, 2000).

Experiential-learning theory suggests that learning is embedded within a context and, thus, transfer of knowledge from one context to another may be problematic. This point, and empirical research supportive of this proposition (McCarley, Kramer, Wickens, Vidoni, & Boot, 2004), would imply that health and safety trainers should ensure that contextual features of the training be varied. For example, McCarley et al. (2004) advocate for varying target materials during training of airport security workers in order to enhance the generalization of recognition and awareness skills. More research is needed in regard to the generalization of hazard recognition and awareness skills developed within training contexts. Chmiel and Wall's (1994) related work on how more advanced procedural knowledge of an implicit nature in fault prevention is acquired through active involvement in fault management, would imply that problem-solving and decision-making skills be developed in order to generalize. Where training is part of the skill development, the latter situation would call for trainees to acquire knowledge via experiential-training methods with respect to multiple problem scenarios to develop anticipatory responses to problem situations. Experiential-learning theory further implies that multiple training methods would lead to optimal learning, as different methods could be used to support particular aspects of the learning process.

Finally, consideration also needs to be given to learning strategies and trainees' capabilities to learn from experiential methods. For example, trainers might ensure that trainees possess basic literacy skills, a familiarity with jargon, and an understanding of how to work with other trainees prior to training (Warr, 2001). Pre-training activities directed toward ensuring these capabilities would be, for example, beneficial in 40-hour HAZWOPER (Hazardous Waste Operations and Emergency Response) training where trainees acquire considerable jargon-laden declarative and procedural knowledge and skills in interaction with other trainees over multiple types of training exercises and methods.

APPLICATIONS OF LEARNING THEORIES TO SAFETY AND HEALTH TRAINING

In practice, a fair amount of safety and health training is based on multiple training methods, and these interventions are not always directly linked to a particular theory of learning. In this section, our discussion of applications of learning theories focuses on selected safety and health training efforts that are more closely aligned with a particular theory and the training methods employed in these efforts. This section concludes with a brief discussion of the relative effectiveness of safety and health training methods for knowledge acquisition, performance improvement, and the reduction of accidents, illnesses, and injuries.

Safety and health training programs that are consistent with a stage approach often initiate the learning process with a passive (lecture, video, or pamphlet) presentation of fundamental information relating to personal protective equipment (e.g., Azizi et al., 2000), the work practices that reduce risk (e.g., Albers et al., 1997), health and safety communication (e.g., Brnich, Derick, Mallett, & Vaught, 2002), or employee rights and responsibilities (e.g., Saarela, Saari, & Alltonen, 1989). Substantial practice often follows in an attempt to proceduralize knowledge, with the use of multiple training methods or instructional techniques for the development of more advanced recognition, problem-solving, and decision-making skills (Albers et al., 1997; Atherley & Robertson, 1998). Examples abound including how stage-learning theory is applied in the Australian Eco-Skills training modules (Cohen-Rosenthal, 1998), the New England Consortium's safety and health training programs for hazardous waste workers and emergency responders (see Lushkin, Somers, Wooding, & Levenstein, 1992), and with respect to more specific safety training systems (e.g., Kanfer & Ackerman, 1989). These applications include safety training consistent with the tenets of stage-learning theory at the business unit level of analysis (e.g., 94 restaurants, Cotterchio, Gunn, Coffill, Tormey, & Barry, 1998; 216 farms, Landsittel, Murphy, Kiernan, Hard, & Kassab, 2001). While there are notable exceptions, applications of stage learning in safety and health training contexts tend to emphasize expert feedback (e.g., Kanfer & Ackerman, 1989; Sniezek, Wilkins, Wadlington, & Baumann, 2002). Expert feedback has varied from no feedback for most trainees (Arcury, Quandt, Austin, Preisser, & Cabrera, 1999) to continuous feedback throughout the learning process for all trainees (Sniezek et al., 2002). Also, as pointed out by Sniezek et al. (2002), expert feedback can involve two-way communication. This bidirectional feedback is of the form where the expert can choose to deliver advice or feedback, or the learner can request such assistance. The use of interactive feedback and multiple training methods has generally produced meaningful changes in trainee declarative knowledge, procedural knowledge, and transfer of training to the job.

Some research on stage-learning theories has examined the role of motivational factors in procedural knowledge and skill development in safety and health training (Kanfer & Ackerman, 1989). This research suggests that goal setting has its greatest effect in the later stages of complex skill acquisition, and is likely to have a greater impact on low- versus high-ability trainees. To date, little research has followed in regard to addressing the effects of proximal motivational processes on procedural knowledge development in safety and health training contexts.

The literature is also replete with studies applying principles of reinforcement theory, under the label of behavior-based safety, to modify individual behaviors related to using personal protective equipment (e.g., Komaki, Heinzmann, & Lawson, 1980), engaging in work practices to reduce risk (e.g., Lingard & Rowlinson, 1997), and communicating health and safety information (e.g., Fox & Sulzer-Azaroff, 1987). In addition, reinforcement theory has been applied to the modification of safe work behavior at the department (four poultry processing departments: Komaki, Collins, & Penn, 1982) and work group levels of analysis (five shipyard crews: Smith, Anger, & Uslan, 1978). These interventions usually begin with a lecture or orientation meeting that alerts workers or work groups to the target behaviors or actions (e.g., see Mattila & Hyodynmaa, 1988; Zohar, Cohen, & Azar, 1980), followed by different forms of feedback and in some cases goal setting (Sulzer-Azaroff, Loafman, & Merante, 1990). In general, reviews of the literature on behavior-based safety indicate that these types of feedback interventions have been effective in modifying more routine, task behaviors across different types of work at the individual and work group levels of analysis (Geller, 2001; Sulzer-Arnoff & Austin, 2000). As noted above, these interventions are not necessarily applicable in modifying or developing more complex skills necessary for handling non-routine events.

Several notable safety interventions, consistent with principles of feedback intervention theory, have been directed at modifying work practices to reduce risk at the individual (e.g., Arnetz & Arnetz, 2000; Van Poppel, Koes, Van der

Ploeg, Smid, & Bouter, 1998) and business unit (e.g., Lazovich et al., 2002) levels of analysis. For instance, Arnetz and Arnetz's (2000) study focused on feedback and group discussions related to handling violent incidents, and demonstrated the effective use of feedback for enhancing more advanced, problem-solving and decision-making skills in this area. Van Poppel et al. (1998) coupled a lecture (instructional session on lifting techniques) with in-dividualized on-the-job feedback on working methods to produce a decrease in sick leave related to low back pain. Likewise, in a study evaluating the effective-ness of a lecture-based safety training program for manufacturing employees, Reber, Wallin, and Chhokar (1984) found that knowledge of results (perfor-mance feedback) subsequent to training and the setting of specific goals was a beneficial condition for the achievement of maximum performance.

A large number of safety and health training interventions are consistent with principles of social-learning, action-regulation, and experiential-learning theories (e.g., Calabro, Weltge, Parnell, Kouzekanani, & Ramirez, 1998; Cole, Berger, Vaught, Haley, & Lacefield, 1988; Curwick, Reeb-Whitaker, & Connon, 2003; Lueveswanij, Nittayananta, & Robison, 2000). These inter-ventions often employ more hands-on, experiential training methods such as role plays, demonstrations with practice, and simulations involving individu-als, dyads, and teams. Along with the use of multiple training methods in the delivery of training, many of these training programs emphasize individualized feedback and dialogue in small groups (e.g., Brown & Nguyen-Scott, 1992; Lushkin et al., 1992).

Across different types of safety work, experiential-training methods have been found to be effective with respect to trainees' knowledge acquisition and performance improvement (e.g., Colligan & Cohen, 2004), in particular with respect to procedural knowledge development. These findings are consistent with training evaluation research in other domains. While Arthur et al.'s (2003) meta-analysis of training methods did not directly address the effectiveness of experiential-training methods, Burke and Day's (1986) meta-analysis of man-agerial training methods and Taylor et al.'s (in press) meta-analysis of behavior-modeling training were supportive of the effectiveness of different types of experiential-training methods.

Turning to research on the relative effectiveness of safety and health training methods, several narrative reviews have concluded that most safety and health training interventions have produced improvements in safety knowledge and the adoption of safe work behaviors, as well as reductions in accidents and injuries (Burke & Sarpy, 2003; Colligan & Cohen, 2004). An unanswered question from these qualitative reviews is: 'What is the relative effectiveness of different methods of safety and health training?'

Recently, Burke et al. (in press) addressed this question in terms of meta-analytically examining the relative effectiveness of training methods categorized according to learner participation in the learning process: least engaging (e.g., lecture, pamphlets, films/videos), moderately engaging (e.g., programmed instruction, feedback interventions), and most engaging (e.g., behavioral modeling training, hands-on training). The knowledge and performance variables in their study focused on using personal protective equipment and engaging in work practices to reduce risk. The knowledge assessments in their meta-analysis included both tests of declarative knowledge and assessments of procedural knowledge and skill. Their meta-analytic results based on 95 quasi-experimental studies ($n = 20,991$) were consistent with propositions that as the method of safety and health training becomes more engaging, the effect of training is greater for knowledge acquisition, safety performance improvements, and the reduction of negative outcomes. Importantly, their findings indicated that the most engaging methods of safety training were, on average, approximately two times more effective than the moderately engaging methods and three times more effective than the least engaging methods with respect to knowledge acquisition. The maintenance of declarative knowledge was also greater over comparable time periods as training became more engaging and experientially based. Clearly, more research is needed on the maintenance (decay) in safety and health knowledge subsequent to safety training interventions, especially in regard to the maintenance of procedural knowledge and skill.

General Practice Recommendations

The greater effectiveness of more engaging, participatory, dialogue-based experiential training methods across dependent variable categories lends empirical support to principles of social-learning, experiential-learning, and action-regulation theories. Furthermore, learning theory and empirical research suggests that lecture as well as more passive computer-based and distance-training methods should incorporate some form of active participation from the learner (e.g., dialogue with a virtual or real person concerning facts acquired and actions taken) in order to engender reflection and enhance knowledge acquisition and its maintenance. When the focus of safety and health training is on procedural as opposed to only declarative knowledge development, the suggestion would be to encourage action-focused reflection. Importantly, these suggestions concerning active learner participation apply to the development of both declarative knowledge and procedural knowledge and skill in the four primary content areas: (1) using personal protective equipment, (2) engaging in work practices to reduce risk, (3) communicating health and safety information, and (4) exercising employee rights and responsibilities.

More specifically, learning theories and empirical research on training support the following practice recommendations for enhancing the acquisition and maintenance of procedural knowledge and skill:

- Ensure the development of training valence beliefs and declarative knowledge as bases for procedural knowledge development.
- Facilitate observational learning using credible role models and aids for recall.

- Use multiple training methods with emphasis on experiential and learner-centered methods for both declarative and procedural knowledge development.
- Encourage practice, including mental practice.
- Provide informational feedback to trainees, with focus on the task rather than on the person.
- Encourage dialogue and action-focused reflection.
- Motivate trainees to utilize acquired knowledge via the teaching of self-regulation strategies, and use of reinforcers (for proceduralized knowledge or simple tasks).
- Attend to individual, training-related, and situational factors that might affect the transfer of training.

Our practice recommendations for safety and health training derived from this integration of above literatures should not be viewed as advocating a 'one-for-all practice recipe.' Certainly, we should guard against such theoretical excesses. Yet, at the same time, we should encourage research and research-based practice that are grounded in theory. This point is not new relative to safety and health interventions (e.g., see Sauter et al., 2002). In the present case, we encourage theory-based training methodology/design research and research related to the maintenance of training to further evaluate the efficacy of our practice recommendations. In this regard, below we discuss several additional avenues for research to advance our understanding of the effectiveness of safety and health training and its practice.

EXTENDING WHAT WE KNOW

We begin this section noting how the four general safety performance dimensions may, in part, guide future safety and health training research. We then discuss how safety and health training has been evaluated and suggest future research for improving our understanding of changes in knowledge and performance resulting from safety and health training. Tied to this discussion is a brief review and commentary on how the literature on assessments would lead to further modifications in training program evaluations for enhancing declarative and procedural knowledge acquisition. This section concludes with a discussion of needed research relative to key situational variables and individual differences that offer the most promise for advancing our understanding of the transfer of safety and health training to the job.

The four general safety performance dimensions can be distinguished in terms of the extent to which they are conceptualized as being more physical, skill based (i.e., using personal protective equipment), more cognitive-motor skill based (i.e., engaging in work practices to reduce risk), and cognitive and interpersonal in nature (i.e., communicating health and safety information, exercising employee rights and responsibilities—see Arthur et al., 2003; Kraiger et al., 1993). Distinguishing the dimensions in this regard would suggest that knowledge and motivational variables differentially relate to performance on the dimensions, with motivational factors having a potentially stronger impact on the more affective-based interpersonal dimensions related to communicating safety information and exercising one's rights. Future research examining the possible differential role of knowledge versus motivational determinants of general safety performance dimensions is needed as such findings have important implications for focusing safety training research and practice both in terms of content and methodology.

In regard to the latter point, we encourage research to examine whether greater practice variability with respect to incorporating novel stimuli/situations (or training that incorporates error training) has a differential impact on safety knowledge and skills and subsequent performance on the four safety performance dimensions. Our expectation would be that increased practice variability would be most beneficial for the development and transfer of the cognitive-motor skills that underlie the performance dimension of engaging in work practices to reduce risk, but also would be important for the development and transfer of safety communication skills for individuals and teams that must handle non-routine events. Furthermore, research along these lines should attend to possible difference in training effects associated with immediate post-training performance versus long-term transfer, as one would expect variability in training conditions to have its greatest impact on long-term transfer (Hesketh, 1997; Holladay & Quinones, 2003).

Also, given that the cognitive and physical requirements for engaging in work on the four general safety performance dimensions differs, we also encourage research to examine the extent to which spaced versus massed practice (training sessions), along with differences in time between training sessions, impacts the acquisition of requisite skills across the dimensions (Donovan & Radosevich, 1999). In particular, further research on the effects of spaced versus massed practice on the acquisition of skills for more routine, criterion (standard)-referenced safety performance, such as using personal protective equipment according to specifications, would be helpful. Research demonstrates that spacing individual trials (e.g., three trials, time off, followed by three additional trials) versus massed practice (e.g., six consecutive trials) may be more effective in the achievement of criterion (standard)-referenced performance (see Hagman & Rose, 1983).

Another future research issue concerns the manner in which safety training is conducted. Training can be carried out relative to different knowledge and skills that underlie the safety performance dimensions. Presently, safety training in many critical skills occupations, such as hazardous waste work and emergency response work, is segmented into homogeneous, non-alternating training modules for the four general safety knowledge and skill areas. It would be helpful if future research focused on how alternating training modules with respect to safety knowledge and skill areas (e.g., communications training, then problem-solving training, followed by communications training, and another round of problem-solving training) improves retention and transfer relative to the present manner in which safety training is conducted. This research suggestion is in line with Goettl, Yadrick, Connolly-Gomez, Regian, and Shebilske's (1996) work that supports alternating training modules to enhance knowledge retention.

In regard to the continued learning process, research might also be directed toward how several factors, in particular dialogue and action-focused reflection, and means for encouraging these processes in the post-training environment, support learning (knowledge and skill maintenance and enhancement), and the application of knowledge and skills. While goal-setting and feedback interventions have been employed in the post-training contexts to encourage retention and application of knowledge and skills, little, if any, research attention has been given to the role of dialogue and action-focused reflection in the maintenance of knowledge and skills. Field studies including field experiments examining the impact of these concepts (e.g., via modifications in how regular safety meetings are conducted) on procedural knowledge, safety performance, and safety outcomes would be informative.

In terms of assessing the effectiveness of safety and health training, the knowledge measures in the safety and health training program evaluation literature have typically been short written tests. Future research might attend to the development of well-designed, standardized measures of safety knowledge that tap both declarative and procedural knowledge with respective to one or more of the four general safety knowledge areas. For example, items such as the situational knowledge items and assessments developed by the Midwest Consortium for Hazardous Waste Worker Training (see United Brotherhood of Carpenters, 1992) might be given greater consideration.

Likewise, improvements could be made in assessment of safety performance related to evaluating more complex actions (proceduralized skills) over time from either supervisory or worker perspectives (e.g., see Burke, Bradley, & Bowers, 2003). Presently, safety performance measures are often limited to trained observer ratings of the frequency with which workers engage in more or less routine, discrete actions. This research should also consider examining the effectiveness of training relative to health and safety communication and exercising employee rights and responsibilities for declarative knowledge, procedural knowledge and skill, and performance. To date, the vast majority of safety training evaluation studies has focused on two of the four primary content domains: using personal protective equipment and engaging in work practices to reduce risk.

Future research might also be directed at increasing our understanding of discretionary safe work behaviors and concomitant training issues. That is, confirmatory factor analytic research on the dimensionality of safety initiative/participation would assist in clarifying the behavioral criterion space for evaluating the efficacy of safety training interventions, especially those interventions designed to impact worker attitudes and motivation. Work motivation constructs related to attitudes and self-efficacy are posited to be direct antecedents of discretionary safety behaviors (Neal & Griffin, 2004; Turner & Parker, 2004).

Another under-researched aspect of safety and health training is how the evaluation of trainees' learning outcomes impacts the learning processes and scores on these outcome measures. Evaluation practices on undergraduate courses have been shown to influence student behavior (Becker, Geer, & Hughes, 1968), a phenomena that is exacerbated when students are cue conscious (Miller & Bartlett, 1974). For example, evaluation procedures such as multiple-choice tests have been shown to encourage rote memorization and surface approaches to learning (Elton & Laurilard, 1979; Ramsden, 1983, 1984). As a consequence, such assessment procedures may affect the quality of knowledge learned; and while this may not be problematic for certain subjects, it may be so for more complex knowledge and skills. This point has important implications for mandated safety and health training, including annual refresher courses, which, for the most part, use true–false and multiple-choice test formats for the assessment of both declarative and procedural knowledge (e.g., see Sinclair et al., 2003, for a multiple-choice test of procedural knowledge). In addition, future research examining the usefulness of more dynamic evaluation procedures that are embedded within training programs (e.g., stopping training at particular points to encourage dialogue and action-focused reflection) on learning outcomes and transfer would be informative.

In terms of transfer of knowledge, Ford et al. (1998) and Rouillier and Goldstein (1993) found that learning at the end of training predicted performance after training, but other studies have not found similar support for more distal criteria such as injuries (Sinclair et al., 2003; Tracey, Tannenbaum, & Kavanagh, 1995). For example, Sinclair et al. (2003) evaluated a safety training program in three food service organizations and found that although the training improved trainees' procedural knowledge, no significant relationship existed between knowledge and subsequent injuries. Given these findings, and noting that training effects for distal outcomes such as safety performance and injuries are likely to be more affected by intervening, time-related variables than training effects for more proximal measures such as knowledge, a need exists for future research to examine the moderating influence of situational variables on training effectiveness. In addition, the fact that safety and health training has a greater impact on knowledge acquisition and lesser impacts on performance and safety outcomes would be predicted from theories of job performance (e.g., Campbell, 1990), where performance is posited to mediate the relationship between knowledge and outcomes such as injuries. To date, a test of this general expectation has not been presented in the safety and health literature.

One class of situational characteristics, safety climate variables (i.e., characteristics of work environments such as management support—see Flin, Mearns, O'Connor, & Bryden, 2000; Seo, Torabi, Blair, & Ellis, 2004), offer particular promise for understanding the role of situational variables in the transfer of safety and health training. At the individual level of analysis, workers' safety climate perceptions have been found to be related to safety knowledge and the extent to which workers engage in safe work behaviors (e.g., Cooper & Phillips, 2004; Griffin & Neal, 2000; Hofmann & Stetzer, 1996; Zohar, 2000). At the organizational level of analysis, Smith-Crowe et al. (2003) and Baer and Frese (2003) have found that safety climate has moderated the effectiveness of safety training as well as process innovations related to management practices. Notably, Smith-Crowe et al.'s (2003) results suggest that researchers as well as training program evaluators should attend to management commitment toward safety, the appropriateness of safety and health training, and overt attempts to discourage the transfer of training as key potential moderators of the effectiveness of safety and health training interventions. Future research at the individual, team, and organization levels on the extent to which these variables moderate training transfer, especially in regard to the exhibition of safe work behaviors, would be informative. This research might also attend to how the strength of these climate variables (or the degree to which a safety climate has emerged) influences the transfer of safety training (e.g., see Gonzalez-Roma, Peiro, & Tordera, 2002).

Researchers and practitioners might also broaden their conceptualizations and measurement of safety climate to include employee perceptions of how the work environment impacts other key stakeholders. This direction might be informative as Ford and Fisher (1994) have discussed the importance and need for multiple stakeholder groups such as management, clients, safety regulators, and the public to be working cooperatively in safety contexts. Tied to this discussion, Burke, Borucki, and Kaufman (2002) have recently discussed how models of climate, including safety climate, might be expanded to incorporate employee perceptions of how work environment characteristics impact multiple stakeholder groups.

The type of workplace hazards (e.g., physical, ergonomic, chemical, and biological) and worker perceptions of risks associated with these hazards are also theoretically important situation-related variables in safety and health training research. This point is noteworthy for several reasons. First, social-learning theory would suggest that reducing negative emotional arousal during training (through helping trainees to deal with feelings of discomfort that might be produced when dealing with actual hazards) might enhance worker self-efficacy and transfer of training to the job. Related literature on psychological climate (James & James, 1989) would suggest that workers will attend to and be motivated to learn about how to deal with work environment characteristics that are most threatening to personal well-being. Third, empirical research with coal-mining personnel indicates that workers who can be characterized as having direct experience, and hence potential exposure to risks, report higher levels of perceived risk (i.e., they are not necessarily susceptible to habituation and resultant underestimation of risks—Weyman & Clarke, 2003). This point is important as Morrow and Crum's (1998) research, in a study of railroad employees, shows that worker perceptions of risk associated with workplace hazards are predictive of worker attitudes and behaviors. Together, these literatures are supportive of the proposition that researchers and practitioners could more explicitly examine how to make risks associated with various types of workplace hazards more salient in order to enhance the development of worker self-efficacy and transfer of training to the job.

Making risks associated with hazards more salient would be particularly relevant to training related to hazards (e.g., ergonomic and safety/injury) that might not be viewed by some workers as immediate or impending threats to personal well-being. Advances in simulated video and virtual reality training would be a fruitful method of studying possible effects associated with enhancing the salience of risks associated with ergonomic and safety/injury hazards. Although Whitby, Stead, and Najman's (1991) study concerns training associated with biological hazards, it does provide an example for how trainers can make the acquisition of an illness (Hepatitis B) resulting from an inappropriate work action salient via simulation within a videotape and subsequent discussion with trainees.

The above discussion implies that workplace hazards in and of themselves might engender heightened attentional processes along a continuum (e.g., from more personally threatening chemical/biological hazards to less threatening ergonomic/injury hazards) and lead to greater motivation to apply acquired procedural knowledge. As a result, one would expect the effectiveness of safety and health training interventions and methods to be moderated by workplace hazards (in particular, the transfer of training). Future research is needed in this regard.

Research incorporating situational variables could also attend to the role of national/culture variables (see Hofstede, 2001; Triandis, 2004) in determining the nature and effectiveness of safety and health training. Our reason for offering this research suggestion is that health and safety training is often closely linked to national legislation, and national culture variables have been found to be related not only to the nature and use of human resource management practices (Ryan, McFarland, Baron, & Page, 1999), but also to affect worker attitudes and motivational processes (e.g., see Huang & Van de Vliert, 2004). Thus, national culture variables such as uncertainty avoidance (the extent to which a culture values predictability and control) might be expected to affect the nature of health and safety training as well as the transfer of the training to the job.

In addition to work environment characteristics that might affect the transfer of training, increased attention has been devoted to identifying other determinants of transfer including individual cognitive (e.g., general mental ability) and affective (e.g., job satisfaction, openness to change) variables, and also training-related characteristics (task fidelity, stimulus variability—Axtell, Maitlis, & Yearta, 1997; Gregoire, Propp, & Poertner, 1998; Kontoghiorghes,

2004; Machin & Fogarty, 2003; Ruona, Leimbach, Holton, & Bates, 2002). In terms of dispositional traits, research has indicated that general mental ability shows stronger relationships than personality factors with training effectiveness (Colquitt et al., 2000). Nevertheless, Schmidt and Hunter (1998) showed that conscientiousness (one of the Big Five personality dimensions—see McCrae & Costa, 1989) accounts for variance in training performance beyond that accounted for by general mental ability. It has been proposed that conscientiousness influences learning outcomes by affecting proximal factors such as goal orientation (Zweig & Webster, 2004), motivation (Colquitt & Simmering, 1998), and self-efficacy (Martocchio & Judge, 1997; Perlow & Kopp, 2004). While safety and health training practitioners can do little to alter these dispositions, they can take trainees' ability and personality characteristics into account when tailoring particular aspects of training (e.g., allowing more practice time for trainees who are less able; using goal cues, reminders, and follow-up assessments for those low in conscientiousness), and focus on creating learning states irrespective of trainees' stable traits (see Ford & Oswald, 2003). Also, training researchers can include trait-related variables in tests of causal models of the transfer process (see Kozlowski et al., 2001). In regard to modeling the transfer process, future research directed toward examining the joint effects of individual, training-related, and work environment characteristics on the transfer of training would be advantageous to advancing our understanding of the effectiveness of safety and health training interventions (e.g., see Pidd, 2004; Stewart, Carson, & Cardy, 1996).

In conclusion, our integration of the literatures on learning theories was written to encourage the transfer of principles from these theories to the development of new ideas and ways for addressing safety and health training research and practice questions. Our integration emphasized that much progress has been made, and further advances are possible with respect to research and practice that attends more to the level of trainee participation in the learning process, and the critical roles of practice, dialogue, action-focused reflection, and self-regulation in the development of procedural knowledge and skills and the transfer of this knowledge to the job. In arguing for greater consideration of prominent theoretical learning contributions, we hope this work advances the link between learning theory and safety and health training research and practice. The time for learning theory and its principles to move off of the sidelines of safety and health training is long overdue.

REFERENCES

Ackerman, P. (1996). A theory of adult intellectual development: Process, personality, interests, and knowledge. *Intelligence*, 22, 227–257.

Adams, J.A. (1987). Historical review and appraisal of research on the learning, retention, and transfer of human motor skills. *Psychological Bulletin*, 101, 41–74.

Albers, J.T., Li, Y., Lemasters, G., Sprague, S., Stinson, R., & Bhattacharya, A. (1997). An ergonomic education and evaluation program for apprentice carpenters. *American Journal of Industrial Medicine*, **32**, 641–646.

Alliger, G., Tannenbaum, S., Bennett, W., Traver, H., & Shotland, A. (1997). A meta-analysis of the relations among training criteria. *Personnel Psychology*, **50**, 341–358.

Anderson, J.R. (1985). *Cognitive psychology and its implications* (2nd edn). New York: Freeman.

Anderson, J.R. (1987). Skill acquisition: Compilation of weak-method problem solutions. *Psychological Review*, **94**, 192–210.

Anderson, J.R., Reder, L.M., & Simon, H.A. (1996). Situated learning and education. *Educational Researcher*, **25**, 5–11.

Arcury, T.A., Quandt, S.A., Austin, C.K., Preisser, J., & Cabrera, L.F. (1999). Implementation of EPA's Worker Protection Standard training for agricultural laborers: An evaluation using North Carolina data. *Public Health Reports*, **114**, 459–468.

Arnetz, J.E. & Arnetz, B.B. (2000). Implementation and evaluation of a practical intervention programme for dealing with violence towards health care workers. *Journal of Advanced Nursing*, **31**, 668–680.

Atherley, G. & Robertson, D. (1998). Principles of training. In J.M. Stellman (Ed.), *Encyclopedia of occupational health and safety* (pp. 18.5–18.7). Geneva: International Labour Office.

Arthur, W., Bennett, W., Edens, P.S. & Bell, S.T. (2003). Effectiveness of training in organizations: A meta-analysis of design and evaluation features. *Journal of Applied Psychology*, **88**, 234–245.

Arthur, W., Bennett, W., Stanush, P., & McNelly, T. (1998). Factors that influence skill decay and retention: A quantitative review and analysis. *Human Performance*, **11**, 57–101.

Axtell, C., Maitlis, S., & Yearta, S. (1997). Predicting immediate and longer-term transfer of training. *Personnel Review*, **26**, 201–213.

Azizi, E., Flint, P., Sadetzki, S., Solomon, A., Lerman, Y., Harari, G. et al. (2000). A graded work site intervention program to improve sun protection and skin cancer awareness in outdoor workers in Israel. *Cancer Causes and Control*, **11**, 513–521.

Baer, M. & Frese, M. (2003). Innovation is not enough: Climate for initiative and psychological safety, process innovations, and firm performance. *Journal of Organizational Behavior*, **24**, 45–68.

Baker, R. & Wallerstein, N. (1998). Worker education and training. In J.M. Stellman (Ed.), *Encyclopedia of occupational health and safety* (pp. 18.7–18.12). Geneva: International Labour Office.

Baldwin, T. (1992). Effects of alternative modeling strategies on outcomes of interpersonal skills training. *Personnel Psychology*, **77**, 147–154.

Baldwin, T. & Ford, J. (1988). Transfer of training: A review and directions for future research. *Personnel Psychology*, **41**, 63–105.

Balla, S., Biggs, J., Gibson, M., & Chang, A,. (1990). The application of basic science concepts to clinical problem solving. *Medical Education*, **24**, 137–144.

Bandura, A. (1977). *Social learning theory*. Englewood Cliffs, NJ: Prentice-Hall.

Bandura, A. (1986). *Social foundation of thought and action*. Englewood Cliffs, NJ: Prentice-Hall.

Bandura, A. (2001). Social cognitive theory: An agentic perspective. *Annual Review of Psychology*, **52**, 1–26.

Bandura, A. & Locke, E. (2003). Negative self-efficacy and goal effects revisited. *Journal of Applied Psychology*, **88**, 87–99.

Barnett, P.G., Midtling, J.E., Velasco, A.R., Romero, P., O'Malley, M., Clements, C. et al. (1984). Educational intervention to prevent pesticide-induced illness of field workers. *Journal of Family Practice*, **19**, 123–125.

Barnett, R. (1990). *The idea of higher education*. Milton Keynes: SRHE/OU Press.

Barrick, M. & Mount, M. (1991). The Big Five personality dimensions and job performance: A meta-analysis. *Personnel Psychology*, **44**, 1–26.

Becker, S.H., Geer, B., & Hughes, E.C. (1968). *Making the grade: The academic side of college life*. New York: John Wiley & Sons.

Biggs, J. (1989). Approaches to the enhancement of tertiary teaching. *Higher Education Research and Development*, **8**, 7–25.

Biggs, J. & Collis, K. (1982). *Evaluating the quality of learning*. New York: Academic Press.

Blackler, F. & Kennedy, A. (2004). The design and evaluation of a leadership programme for experienced chief executives from the public sector. *Management Learning*, **35**, 181–203.

Bolt, M.A., Killough, L.N., & Koh, H.C. (2001). Testing the interaction effects of task complexity in computer training using the social cognitive model. *Decision Sciences*, **32**, 1–20.

Borman, W.C. & Motowidlo, S.J. (1993). Expanding the criterion domain to include elements of contextual performance. In N. Schmitt & W.C. Borman (Eds), *Personnel selection in organizations* (pp. 71–98). San Francisco: Jossey-Bass.

Boud, D., Cohen, R., & Walker, D. (1994). *Using experience for learning*. Milton Keynes: SRHE/OU Press.

Bransford, J.D., Brown, A.L., & Cocking, R.R. (2000). *How people learn: Brain, mind, experience, and school*. Washington, DC: National Academy Press.

Brnich, M.J., Derick, R.L., Mallett, L., & Vaught, C.(2002). Innovative alternatives to traditional classroom health and safety training. In R.H. Peters (Ed.), *Strategies for improving miners' training* (pp. 19–24). Cincinnati, OH: Department of Health and Human Services (National Institute for Occupational Safety and Health) Publication No. 2002-156.

Broadbent, D.E., Fitzgerald, P., & Broadbent, M.H.P. (1986). Implicit and explicit knowledge in the control of complex systems. *British Journal of Psychology*, **77**, 33–50.

Brookfield, S. (1987). *Developing critical thinkers*. San Francisco: Jossey-Bass.

Brown, M.P. & Nguyen-Scott, N. (1992). Evaluating a training-for-action job health and safety program. *American Journal of Industrial Medicine*, **22**, 739–749.

Bryan, W.L. & Harter, N. (1899). Studies on the telegraphic language: The acquisition of a hierarchy of habits. *Psychological Review*, **6**, 345–375.

Burgoyne, J. & Hodgson, V. (1983). Natural learning and managerial action: A phenomenological study in the field setting. *Journal of Management Studies*, **20**, 387–399.

Burke, L. & Baldwin, T. (1999). Workforce training transfer: A study of the effect of relapse prevention training and transfer climate. *Human Resource Management*, **38**, 227–242.

Burke, M.J., Borucki, C.C., & Kaufman, J.D. (2002). Contemporary perspectives on the study of psychological climate: A commentary. *European Journal of Work and Organizational Psychology*, **11**, 325–340.

Burke, M.J., Bradley, J., & Bowers, H.N. (2003). Health and safety training programs. In J.E. Edwards, J. Scott, & N.S. Raju (Eds), *The human resources program-evaluation handbook* (pp. 429–446). Thousand Oaks, CA: Sage.

Burke, M.J. & Day, R. (1986). A cumulative study of the effectiveness of managerial training. *Journal of Applied Psychology*, **71**, 232–245.

Burke, M.J. & Sarpy, S.A. (2003). Improving worker safety and health through interventions. In D.E. Hofmann & L. Tetrick (Eds), *Health and safety: A multilevel perspective* (pp. 56–90). San Francisco: Jossey-Bass.

Burke, M.J., Sarpy, S.A., Smith-Crowe, K., Chan-Serafin, S., Islam, G., & Salvador, R. (in press). The relative effectiveness of worker safety and health training methods. *American Journal of Public Health.*

Burke, M.J., Sarpy, S.A., Tesluk, P.A., & Smith-Crowe, K. (2002). General safety performance: A test of a grounded theoretical model. *Personnel Psychology,* **55,** 429–457.

Calabro, K., Weltge, A., Parnell, S., Kouzekanani, K., & Ramirez, E. (1998). Intervention for medical students: Effective infection control. *American Journal of Infection Control,* **26,** 431–436.

Callahan, J., Kiker, S., & Cross, T. (2003). Does method matter? A meta-analysis of the effects of training method on older learner training performance. *Journal of Management,* **29,** 663–680.

Campbell, J.P. (1990). Modeling the performance prediction problem in industrial and organizational psychology. In M.D. Dunnette & L.M. Hough (Eds), *Handbook of industrial and organizational psychology* (pp. 687–732). Palo Alto, CA: Consulting Psychologists Press.

Candy, P. (1991). *Self-direction for lifelong learning.* San Francisco: Jossey-Bass.

Chen, Y. (2001). Dimensions of transactional distance in the world wide web learning environment: A factor analysis. *British Journal of Educational Technology,* **32,** 459–470.

Chen, Y. & Willits, F.K. (1998). A path analysis of the concepts in Moore's Theory of transactional distance in a videoconferencing learning environment. *Journal of Distance Education,* **13,** 51–65.

Cheng, E.W.L. & Ho, D.C.K. (2001). A review of transfer of training studies in the past decade. *Personnel Review,* **30,** 102–118.

Cheyne, A., Cox, S., Oliver, A., & Tomas, J.M. (1998). Modeling safety climate in the prediction of levels of safety activity. *Work & Stress,* **12,** 255–271.

Chhokar, J.S. (1990). Behavioral safety management. *Vikalpa,* **15,** 15–22.

Chmiel, N. & Wall, T. (1994). Fault prevention, job design, and the adaptive control of advanced manufacturing technology. *Applied Psychology: An International Review,* **43,** 455–473.

Chou, H.W. (2001). Effects of training method and computer anxiety on learning performance and self-efficacy. *Computers in Human Behavior,* **17,** 51–69.

Cohen-Rosenthal, E. (1998). Worker education and environmental improvement. In J.M. Stellman (Ed.), *Encyclopedia of occupational health and safety* (pp. 18.15–18.18). Geneva: International Labour Office.

Cole, H.P., Berger, P.K., Vaught, C., Haley, J.V., & Lacefield, W.E. (1988). *Research and evaluation methods for measuring nonroutine mine health and safety skills: Volume 1.* Pittsburg, PA: US Bureau of Mines.

Colligan, M.J. & Cohen, A. (2004). The role of training in promoting workplace safety and health. In J. Barling & M.R. Frone (Eds), *The psychology of workplace safety* (pp. 223–248). Washington, DC: American Psychological Association.

Colquitt, J., Lepine, J., & Noe, R. (2000). Toward an integrative theory of training motivation: A meta-analytic path analysis of 20 years of research. *Journal of Applied Psychology,* **85,** 678–707.

Colquitt, J. & Simmering, M. (1998). Conscientiousness, goal-orientation and motivation to learn during the learning process: A longitudinal study. *Journal of Applied Psychology,* **83,** 654–665.

Cooper, M.D. & Phillips, R.A. (2004). Exploratory analysis of the safety climate and safety behavior relationship. *Journal of Safety Research,* **35,** 497–512.

Cotterchio, M., Gunn, J., Coffill, T., Tormey, P., & Barry, M.A. (1998). Effect of a manager training program on sanitary conditions in restaurants. *Public Health Reports*, **113**, 353–359.

Cunliffe, A.L. (2002). Reflexive dialogical practice in management learning. *Management Learning*, **33**, 35–61.

Curwick, C.C., Reeb-Whitaker, C., & Connon, C.L. (2003). Reaching managers at an industry association conference: Evaluation of ergonomics training. *AAOHN Journal*, **51**, 464–469.

Davis, F.D. & Yi, M.Y. (2004). Improving computer skill training: Behavior modeling, symbolic mental rehearsal, and the role of knowledge structures. *Journal of Applied Psychology*, **89**, 509–523.

Day, E.A., Arthur, W., & Gettman, D. (2001). Knowledge structures and the acquisition of complex skill. *Journal of Applied Psychology*, **86**, 1022–1033.

Detrick, P., Chibnall, J.T., & Luebbert, M.C. (2004). The Revised NEO Personality Inventory as predictor of police academy performance. *Criminal Justice and Behavior*, **31**, 676–694.

Dewey, J. (1938). *Experience and education*. New York: Macmillan.

deWinstanley, P.A. & Bjork, R.A. (2002). Successful lecturing: Presenting information in ways that engage effective processing. In D. Halpern & M. Hakel (Eds), *Applying the science of learning to university teaching and beyond*. San Francisco: Jossey-Bass.

Dixon, N. (1994). *The organizational learning cycle: How we can learn collectively*. London: McGraw-Hill.

Doerner, D. (1996). *The logic of failure: Recognizing and avoiding error in complex systems*. New York: Basic Books.

Donovan, J.J. & Radosevich, D.J. (1999). A meta-analytic review of the distribution of practice effect: Now you see it, now you don't. *Journal of Applied Psychology*, **84**, 795–805.

Dowden, C., Antonowicz, D., & Andrews, D.A. (2003). The effectiveness of relapse prevention with offenders: A meta-analysis. *International Journal of Offender Therapy and Comparative Criminology*, **47**, 516–528.

Driskell, J., Copper, C., & Moran, A. (1994). Does mental practice enhance performance? *Journal of Applied Psychology*, **79**, 481–492.

Driskell, J.E., Willis, R.P., & Copper, C. (1992). Effect of overlearning on retention. *Journal of Applied Psychology*, **77**, 615–622.

Duff, A. (2003). Quality of Learning on an MBA Programme: The impact of approaches to learning on academic performance. *Educational Psychologist*, **23**, 123–139.

Eckerman, D.A., Lundeen, C.A., Steele, A., Rercho, H.L., Ammerman, T.A., & Anger, K. (2002). Interactive training versus reading to teach respiratory protection. *Journal of Occupational Health Psychology*, **7**, 313–323.

Eden, D. & Aviram, A. (1993). Self-efficacy training to speed reemployment: Helping people to help themselves. *Journal of Applied Psychology*, **78**, 352–360.

Elton, L. & Laurilard, D. (1979). Trends in research on student learning. *Studies in Higher Education*, **4**, 87–102.

Entwistle, N. (1987). A model of the teaching-learning process. In J. Richardson, M. Eysenck, & D. Piper (Eds), *Student Learning: Research in education and cognitive psychology*. Milton Keynes: SRHE/OU Press.

Entwistle, N.J. (1995). Influences of instructional settings on learning and cognitive-development—introduction. *Educational Psychologist*, **30**, 1–3.

Entwistle, N.J. (2002). Understanding academic performance at university: A research retrospective. In C. Desforges & R. Fox (Eds), *Teaching and learning: The essential readings. Essential readings in development psychology* (pp. 108–123). Malden, MA: Blackwell.

Evenson, D.H. & Hmelo, C.E. (Eds) (2000). *Problem-based learning: A research perspective on learning interactions*. Mahwah, NJ: Lawrence Erlbaum.

Fenwick, T.J. (2000). Expanding conceptions of experiential learning: A review of the five contemporary perspectives on cognition. *Adult Education Quarterly*, **50**, 243–272.

Fiedler, F.E. (1987). *Structure management training in underground mining—five years later* (Information Circular 9145). Pittsburgh, PA: US Bureau of Mines.

Fitts, P.M. (1962). *Factors in complex training*. In R. Glaser (Ed.), *Training research and education*. Pittsburg, PA: University of Pittsburg.

Flin, R., Mearns, K., O'Connor, P., & Bryden, R. (2000). Measuring safety climate: Identifying the common features. *Safety Science*, **34**, 177–192.

Ford, J.K. & Fisher, S. (1994). The transfer of safety training in work organizations: A systems perspective to continuous learning. *Occupational Medicine*, **9**, 241–259.

Ford, J.K. & Oswald, F.L. (2003). Understanding the dynamic learner: Linking personality traits, learning situations, and individual behavior. In M. Barrick & A.M. Ryan (Eds), *Personality and work* (pp. 229–261). San Francisco: Jossey-Bass.

Ford, J.K., Quinones, M., Sego, D., & Sorra, J. (1992). Factors affecting the opportunity to perform trained tasks on the job. *Personnel Psychology*, **45**, 511–527.

Ford, J.K. & Schmidt, A. (2000). Training in emergency preparedness: Strategies for enhancing real world performance. *Journal of Hazardous Materials*, **75**, 195–215.

Ford, J. K., Smith, E.M., Weissbein, D.A., Gully, S.M., & Salas, E. (1998). Relationships of goal orientation, metacognitive activity, and practice strategies with learning outcomes and transfer. *Journal of Applied Psychology*, **83**, 218–233.

Foster, L. (1996). Manual handling training and changes in work practices. *Occupational Health*, **11**, 402–406.

Fox, C.J. & Sulzer-Azaroff, B. (1987). Increasing completion of accident reports. *Journal of Safety Research*, **18**, 65–71.

Frayne, C.A. & Geringer, J.M. (2000). Self-management training for improving job performance: A field experiment involving salespeople. *Journal of Applied Psychology*, **85**, 361–372.

Frayne, C. & Latham, G. (1987). Application of social learning theory to employee self-management of attendance. *Journal of Applied Psychology*, **72**, 387–392.

Frederiksen, C.H. (1999). Learning to reason through discourse in problem-based learning groups. *Discourse Processes*, **27**, 135–160.

Frese, M. & Zapf, D. (1994). Action as the core of work psychology: A German approach. In M.D. Dunnette, L.M. Hough, & H.C. Triandis (Eds), *Handbook of industrial and organizational psychology*, Vol. 4 (2nd edn). Palo Alto, CA: Consulting Psychologists Press.

Gagne, R.M. & Medsker, K.L. (1996). *The conditions of learning*. Fort Worth, TX: Harcourt-Brace.

Galliano, G. (1999). Enhancing student learning through exemplary examples. In B. Perlman, L. McCann, & S. McFadden (Eds), *Lessons learned: Practical advice for the teaching of psychology*. Washington, DC: American Psychological Society.

Gardner, P.H., Chmiel, N., & Wall, T.D. (1996). Implicit knowledge and fault diagnosis in the control of advanced manufacturing technology. *Behaviour and Information Technology*, **15**, 205–212.

Garrison, D.R. (1989). *Understanding distance education: A framework for the future*. London: Routledge.

Garrison, D.R. (2000). Theoretical challenges for distance education in the 21st century: A shift from structural to transactional issues. *International Review of Research in Open and Distance Learning*, **1**, 1–17.

Gebbie, K.M. & Huang, I. (2000). Preparing currently employed public health nurses for changes in the health system. *American Journal of Public Health*, **90**, 716–721.

Geller, E.S. (2001). Behavior-based safety in industry: Realizing the large-scale potential of psychology to promote human welfare. *Applied and Preventive Psychology*, **10**, 87–105.

Gist, M.E., (1989). The influence of training method on self-efficacy and idea generation among managers. *Personnel Psychology*, **42**, 787–805.

Gist, M.E., Bavetta, A., & Stevens, C. (1990). Transfer training method: Its influence on skill generalization, skill repetition and performance level. *Personnel Psychology*, **43**, 501–523.

Gist, M.E., & Mitchell, T. (1992). Self-efficacy: A theoretical analysis of its determinants and malleability. *Academy of Management Review*, **17**, 183–211.

Gist, M.E., Schwoerer, C., & Rosen, B. (1989). Effects of alternative training methods on self-efficacy and performance in computer software training. *Journal of Applied Psychology*, **74**, 884–891.

Gist, M.E., & Stevens, C. (1998). Effects of practice conditions and supplemental training method on cognitive learning and interpersonal skill generalisation. *Organizational Behavior and Human Decision Processes*, **75**, 142–169.

Glenn, P.J., Koschmann, T., & Conlee, M. (1999). Theory presentation and assessment in a problem-based learning group. *Discourse Processes*, **27**, 119–133.

Godat, L.M. & Brigham, T. A. (1999). The effect of a self-management training program on employees of a mid-sized organization. *Journal of Organizational Behavior Management*, **19**, 65–83.

Goettl, B.P., Yadrick, R.M., Connolly-Gomez, C., Regian, W., & Shebilske, W.L. (1996). Alternating tasks modules in isochronal distributed training of complex tasks. *Human Factors*, **38**, 330–346.

Goldstein, I. & Ford, J. (2002). *Training in organizations* (4th edn). Belmont, CA: Wadsworth.

Gonzalez-Roma, V., Peiro, J.M., & Tordera, N. (2002). An examination of the antecedents and moderator influences of climate strength. *Journal of Applied Psychology*, **87**, 465–473.

Gow, L. & Kember, D. (1993). Conceptions of teaching and their relationship to learning. *British Journal of Educational Psychology*, **63**, 20–33.

Gregoire, T.K., Propp, J., & Poertner, J. (1998). The supervisor's role in the transfer of training. *Administration in Social Work*, **22**, 1–18.

Griffin, M.A. & Neal, A. (2000). Perceptions of safety at work: A framework for linking safety climate to safety performance. *Journal of Occupational Health Psychology*, **5**, 347–358.

Hacker, W. (2003). Action regulation theory: A practical tool for the design of modern work processes? *European Journal of Work and Organizational Psychology*, **12**, 105–130.

Hackman, J.R. & Wageman, R. (2005). A theory of team coaching. *Academy of Management Review*, **30**, 269–287.

Hagman, J. & Rose, A. (1983). Retention of military tasks: A review. *Human Factors*, **25**, 199–213.

Halpern, D.F. & Hakel, M.D. (2003). Applying the science of learning to the university and beyond: Teaching for long-term retention and transfer. *Change*, **35** (4), 36–41.

Handy, C. (1987). *The making of managers*. London: NEDO.

Harrington, H.L. & Garrison, J.W. (1992). Cases as shared inquiry: A dialogical model of teacher preparation. *American Educational Research Journal*, **29**, 715–735.

Hartmann, E., Sunde, T., Kristensen, W., & Martinussen, M. (2003). Psychological measures as predictors of military training performance. *Journal of Personality Assessment*, **80**, 87–98.

Heimbeck, D., Frese, M., Sonnentag, S., & Keith, N. (2003). Integrating errors into the training process: The function of error management instructions and the role of goal orientation. *Personnel Psychology*, **56**, 333–361.

Henry, J. (1989). Meaning and experience in experiential learning. In S. Weil & I. McGill (Eds), *Making sense of experiential learning: Diversity in theory and practice.* (pp. 25–37). Milton Keynes: SRHE/OU Press.

Herz, B. & Merz, W. (1998). Experiential learning and the effectiveness of economic simulation games. *Simulation and Gaming,* **29,** 238–250.

Hesketh, B. (1997). Dilemmas in training for transfer and retention. *Applied Psychology: An International Review,* **43,** 317–386.

Hickman, J.S. & Geller, E.S. (2003). A safety self-management intervention for mining operations. *Journal of Safety Research,* **34,** 299–308.

Hofmann, D.A. & Morgeson, F.P. (2004). The role of leadership in safety. In J. Barling & M.R. Frone (Eds), *The psychology of workplace safety* (pp. 159–180). Washington, DC: American Psychological Association.

Hofmann, D.A. & Stetzer, A. (1996). A cross-level investigation of factors influencing unsafe behaviors and accidents. *Personnel Psychology,* **49,** 307–339.

Hofstede, G. (2001). *Cultures consequences* (2nd edn). Thousand Oaks, CA: Sage.

Holladay, C. & Quinones, M. (2003). Practice variability and transfer of training: The role of self-efficacy generality. *Journal of Applied Psychology,* **88,** 1094–1103.

Holman, D. (2000a). A dialogical approach to skill and skilled activity. *Human Relations,* **53,** 957–980.

Holman, D. (2000b). Contemporary models of management education in the UK. *Management Learning,* **31,** 197–218.

Holman, D., Pavlica, K., & Thorpe, R. (1997). Rethinking Kolb's theory of experiential learning: The contribution of social constructionism and activity theory. *Management Learning,* **28,** 135–149.

Hough, L., Eaton, N., Dunnette, M., Kamp, J., & McCloy, R. (1990). Criterion-related validities of personality constructs and the effect of response distortion on those validities [Monograph]. *Journal of Applied Psychology,* **75,** 581–595.

Huang, Xu & Van de Vliert, E. (2004). Job level and national culture as joint roots of job satisfaction. *Applied Psychology: An International Review,* **53,** 329–348.

International Brotherhood of Teamsters (1993). *International Brotherhood of Teamsters hazardous waste worker training program: Student manual.* Washington, DC: International Brotherhood of Teamsters.

Ivancic, K. & Hesketh, B. (2000). Learning from errors in a driving simulation: Effects of driving skill and self-confidence. *Ergonomics,* **43,** 1966–1984.

James, L.A. & James, L.R. (1989). Integrating work perceptions: Explorations into the measurement of meaning. *Journal of Applied Psychology,* **69,** 85–98.

Johnston, J.J., Cattledge, G.T.H., & Collins, J.W. (1994). The efficacy of training for occupational injury control. *Occupational Medicine,* **9,** 147–158.

Kanfer, R. & Ackerman, P.L. (1989). Motivation and cognitive abilities: An integrative/aptitude-treatment interaction approach to skill acquisition. *Journal of Applied Psychology,* **74,** 657–690.

Keys, B. & Wolfe, J. (1990). The role of management games and simulations in education and research. *Journal of Management,* **16,** 307–336.

King, A. (1990). Enhancing peer interaction and learning in the classroom through reciprocal questioning. *American Educational Research Journal,* **27,** 664–687.

Kluger, A.N. & DeNisi, A. (1996). The effects of feedback interventions on performance: Historical review, a meta-analysis and a preliminary feedback intervention theory. *Psychological Bulletin,* **119,** 254–284.

Kluger, A.N. & DeNisi, A. (1998). Feedback interventions: Toward an understanding of a double-edged sword. *Current Directions in Psychological Science,* **7,** 67–72.

Kneser, C. & Ploetzner, R. (2001). Collaboration on the basis of complementary domain knowledge: Observed dialogue structures and their relation to learning success. *Learning and Instruction*, **11**, 53–83.

Knowles, M. (1983). Andragogy: An emerging technology for adult learning. In M. Tight (Ed.), *Adult learning and education* (pp. 53–70). London: Croom Hall.

Knowles, M.S. (1996). Adult learning. In R.L. Craig (Ed.), *The ASTD training and development handbook* (pp. 253–265). New York: McGraw-Hill.

Kolb, A. & Kolb, D.A. (2000). *Bibliography of research on experiential learning theory and the learning style inventory*. Cleveland, OH: Department of Organizational Behavior, Weatherhead School of Management, Case Western Reserve University.

Kolb, D.A. (1984). *Experiential learning: Experience as the source of learning and development*. Englewood Cliffs, NJ: Prentice-Hall.

Komaki, J.L., Collins, R.L., & Penn, P. (1982). The role of performance antecedents and consequences in work motivation. *Journal of Applied Psychology*, **67**, 334–340.

Komaki, J., Heinzmann, A.T., & Lawson, L. (1980). Effect of training and a component analysis of a behavioral safety program. *Journal Applied Psychology*, **65**, 261–270.

Kontoghiorghes, C. (2004). Reconceptualising the learning transfer conceptual framework: Empirical validation of a new systemic model. *International Journal of Training and Development*, **8**, 210–221.

Kozlowski, S.W.J., Toney, R.J., Mullins, M.E., Weissbein, D.A., Brown, K.G., & Bell, B.S. (2001). Developing adaptability: A theory for the design of integrated-embedded training systems. In E. Salas (Ed.), *Advances in human performance and cognitive engineering research* (Vol. 1, pp. 59–123). Amsterdam: JAI/Elsevier Science.

Kraiger, K., Ford, J.K., & Salas, E. (1993). Application of cognitive, skill-based, and affective theories of learning outcomes to new methods of training evaluation [Monograph]. *Journal of Applied Psychology*, **78**, 311–328.

Landsittel, D.P., Murphy, D.J., Kiernan, N.E., Hard, D.L., & Kassab, C. (2001). Evaluation of the effectiveness of educational interventions in the Pennsylvania central region farm safety pilot program. *American Journal of Industrial Medicine*, **40**, 145–152.

Latham, G. & Saari, L. (1979). The application of social learning theory to training supervisors through behavioral modeling. *Journal of Applied Psychology*, **64**, 239–246.

Lave, J. & Wenger, E. (1991). *Situated learning: Legitimate peripheral participation*. New York: Cambridge University Press.

Lazovich, D., Parker, D.L., Brosseau, L.M., Miton, T., Dugan, S.K., Pan, W. et al. (2002). Effectiveness of a worksite intervention to reduce an occupational exposure: The Minnesota wood dust study. *American Journal of Public Health*, **92**, 1498–1505.

Leung, D.Y.P. & Kember, D. (2003). The relationship between approaches to learning and reflection upon practice. *Educational Psychologist*, **23**, 61–71.

Lingard, H. & Rowlinson, S. (1997). Behavior-based safety management in Hong Kong's construction industry. *Journal of Safety Research*, **28**, 243–256.

Locke, E.A. & Latham, G.P. (1990). *A theory of goal setting and task performance*. Englewood Cliffs, NJ: Prentice-Hall.

Lueveswanij, S., Nittayananta, W., & Robison, V.A. (2000). Changing knowledge, attitudes, and practices of Thai oral health personnel with regard to AIDS: An evaluation of an educational intervention. *Community Dental Health*, **17**, 165–171.

Lushkin, J., Somers, C., Wooding, J., & Levenstein, C. (1992). Teaching health and safety: Problems and possibilities for learner-centered training. *American Journal of Industrial Medicine*, **22**, 665–676.

Machin, M.A. & Fogarty, G.J. (2003). Perceptions of training-related factors and personal variables as predictors of transfer implementation intentions. *Journal of Business and Psychology*, **18**, 51–71.

Mainemelis C., Boyatzis, R.E., & Kolb, D.A. (2002). Learning styles and adaptive flexibility—Testing experiential learning theory. *Management Learning*, **33**, 5–33.

Marchand, A., Simard, M., Carpentier-Roy, M.C., & Ouellet, F. (1998). From a unidimensional to a bi-dimensional concept and measurement of workers' safety behavior. *Scandinavian Journal of Work, Environment, and Health*, **24**, 293–299.

Marks, M.A., Mathieu, J.E., & Zaccaro, S.J. (2001). A temporally based framework and taxonomy of team processes. *Academy of Management Review*, **26**, 356–376.

Marsick, V. & Watkins, K. (1997). Lessons from informal and incidental learning. In J. Burgoyne & M. Reynolds (Eds), *Management learning*. Oxford: Blackwell.

Martocchio, J. & Judge, T. (1997). Relationship between conscientiousness and learning in employee training: Mediating influences of self-deception and self-efficacy. *Journal of Applied Psychology*, **82**, 764–773.

Marton, F. & Saljo, R. (1976). On qualitative differences in learning (1) Outcome and process. *British Journal of Educational Psychology*, **46**, 4–11.

Marton, F. & Wenestam, C. (1979). Qualitative differences in understanding and retention of the main points in some texts based on principle–example structure. In M. Gruneburg et al. (Eds), *Practical aspects of memory*. London: Falmer Press.

Marx, R. (1982). Relapse prevention for managerial training: A model for maintenance of behaviour change. *Academy of Management Review*, **7**, 433–441.

Marx, R. & Ivey, A. (1988). Communication skills programs that last: Face to face and relapse prevention. *International Journal for the Advancement of Counselling*, **11**, 135–151.

Mathieu, J., Martineau, J., & Tannenbaum, S. (1993). Individual and situational influences on the development of self-efficacy: Implications for training effectiveness. *Personnel Psychology*, **46**, 125–147.

Mattila, M. & Hyodynmaa, M. (1988). Promoting job safety in building: An experiment on the behavior analysis approach. *Journal of Occupational Accidents*, **9**, 255–267.

Mayer, S. & Russell, J. (1987). Behaviour modeling training in organizations: Concerns and conclusions. *Journal of Management*, **13**, 21–40.

McCarley, J.S., Kramer, A.F., Wickens, C.D., Vidoni, E.D., & Boot, W.R. (2004). Visual skills in airport-security screening. *Psychological Science*, **15**, 302–306.

McDonald, N., Corrigan, S., Daly, C., & Cromie, S. (2000). Safety management systems and safety culture in aircraft maintenance organizations. *Safety Science*, **34**, 151–176.

McNatt, D.B. & Judge, T.A. (2004). Boundary conditions of the Galatea effect: A field experiment and constructive replication. *Academy of Management Journal*, **47**, 550–565.

McRae, R. & Costa, P. (1989). More reasons to adopt the five-factor model. *American Psychologist*, **44**, 451–452.

Meyer, H. & Raich, M. (1983). An objective evaluation of a behavior modeling training program. *Personnel Psychology*, **36**, 755–761.

Mezirow, J. (Ed.) (1990). *Fostering critical thinking in adulthood: A guide to transformative and emancipatory learning*. San Francisco: Jossey-Bass.

Miller, C. & Bartlett, M. (1974). *Up to the mark: A study of the examination game*. London: SRHE.

Moore, M.G. (1973). Toward a theory of independent learning and teaching. *Journal of Higher Education*, **44**, 661–679.

Moore, M.G. (1993). Transactional distance theory. In D. Keegan (Ed.), *Theoretical principles of distance education*. New York: Routledge.

Morin, L. & Latham, G.P. (2000). The effect of mental practice and goal setting as a transfer of training intervention on supervisors' self-efficacy and communication skills: An exploratory study. *Applied Psychology: An International Review*, **49**, 566–578.

Morrow, P.C. & Crum, M.R. (1998). The effects of perceived and objective safety risk on employee outcomes. *Journal of Vocational Behavior*, **53**, 300–313.

Motowidlo, S.J., Borman, W.C., & Schmitt, M.J. (1997). A theory of individual differences in task and contextual performance. *Human Performance*, **10**, 71–83.

Mueser, K.T., Corrigan, P.W., Hilton, D.W., Tanzman, B., Schaub, A., Gingerich, S. et al. (2002). Illness management and recovery: A review of the research. *Psychiatric Services*, **53**, 1272–1284.

Murtada, N. & Haccoun, R.R. (1996). Self-monitoring and goal setting as determinants of the transfer of applied training. *Canadian Journal of Behavioural Science*, **28**, 92–101.

Nadler, J., Thompson, L., & van Boven, L. (2003). Learning negotiation skills: Four models of knowledge creation and transfer. *Management Science*, **49**, 529–540.

Neal, A. & Griffin, M.A. (2004). Safety climate and safety at work. In J. Barling & M.R. Frone (Eds), *The psychology of workplace safety* (pp. 15–34). Washington, DC: American Psychological Association.

Neal, A., Griffin, M.A., & Hart, P.M. (2000). The impact of organizational climate on safety climate and individual behavior. *Safety Science*, **34**, 99–109.

NIEHS (1999). *HAZWOPER training: Utilizing advanced training technologies* (NIEHS Technical Workhop: Computer and Internet-Based Learning Methods for Safety and Health Training). Bethesda, MD: National Institute of Environmental Health Sciences and National Clearinghouse for Worker Safety and Health Training.

Nissen, M.J. & Bullemer, P. (1987). Attentional requirements of learning: Evidence from performance measures. *Cognitive Psychology*, **19**, 1–32.

Noe, R. (1986). Trainees' attributes and attitudes: Neglected influences on training effectiveness. *Academy of Management Review*, **11**, 736–749.

Pedler, M. (1983). *Action learning in practice*. Aldershot: Gower.

Perlow, R. & Kopp, L.S. (2004). Conscientiousness and ability as predictors of accounting learning. *Human Performance*, **17**, 359–373.

Pidd, K. (2004). The impact of workplace support and identity on training transfer: A case study of drug and alcohol safety training in Australia. *International Journal of Training and Development*, **8**, 274–288.

Prosser, M. (1987). The effects of cognitive structure and learning strategy on student achievement. In J. Richardson, M. Eysenck, & D. Piper (Eds), *Student learning: Research in education and cognitive psychology*. Guildford, England: SRHE/OU Press.

Raelin, J.A. (2001). Public reflection as a basis for learning. *Management Learning*, **32**, 11–30.

Ramsden, P. (1983). Institutional variations in British students' approaches to learning and experiences of teaching. *Higher Education*, **12**, 275–286.

Ramsden, P. (1984). The context of learning. In F. Marton, D. Hounsell, & N. Entwistle (Eds), *The experience of learning*. Edinburgh: SAP.

Reber, R.A., Wallin, J.A., & Chhokar, J.S. (1984). Reducing industrial accidents: A behavioral experiment. *Industrial Relations*, **23**, 119–125.

Revans, R. (1971). *Developing effective managers*. New York: Appleton Century Holt.

Rouillier, J. & Goldstein, I. (1993). The relationship between organizational transfer climate and positive transfer of training. *Human Resource Development Quarterly*, **4**, 377–390.

Rudmo, T. (2000). Safety climate, attitudes, and risk perception in Norsk Hydro. *Safety Science*, **34**, 47–59.

Ruona, W., Leimbach, M., Holton III, E., & Bates, R. (2002). The relationship between learner utility reactions and predicted learning transfer among trainees. *International Journal of Training and Development*, **6**, 218–228.

Ryan, A.M., McFarland, L., Baron, H., & Page, R. (1999). An international look at selection practices: Nation and culture as explanations for variability in practice. *Personnel Psychology*, **52**, 359–391.

Saarela, K.L., Saari, J., & Alltonen, M. (1989). The effects of an informational safety campaign in the shipbuilding industry. *Journal of Occupational Accidents*, **10**, 255–266.

Saari, J. & Nisanen, M. (1989). The effect of positive feedback on industrial housekeeping and accidents: A long-term study at a shipyard. *International Journal of Industrial Ergonomics*, **4**, 201–211.

Sadri, G. & Robertson, I. (1993). Self-efficacy and work-related behaviour: A review and meta-analysis. *Applied Psychology: An International Review*, **42**, 139–152.

Salas, E. & Cannon-Bowers, J. (2001). The science of training: A decade of progress. *Annual Review of Psychology*, **52**, 471–499.

Sauter, S.L., Brightwell, W.S., Colligan, M.J., Hurrell, J.J., Katz, T.M., LeGrande, D.E. et al. (2002). *The changing organization of work and the safety and health of working people: Knowledge gaps and research directions* (DHSS (NIOSH) Publication No. 2002–116). Cincinnati, OH: National Institute for Occupational Safety and Health.

Schacter, J. (2000). Does individual tutoring produce optimal learning? *American Educational Research Journal*, **37**, 801–829.

Schein, E.H. (1993). On dialogue, culture and organizational learning. *Organizational Dynamics*, **22**, 40–51.

Schmidt, F. & Hunter, J. (1998). The validity and utility of selection methods in personnel psychology: Practical and theoretical implications of 85 years of research findings. *Psychological Bulletin*, **124**, 262–274.

Schön, D. (1983). *The reflective practitioner: How professionals think in action*. London: Maurice Temple Smith.

Seo, D., Torabi, M.R., Blair, E.H., & Ellis, N.T. (2004). A cross-validation of safety climate scale using confirmatory factor analytic approach. *Journal of Safety Research*, **35**, 427–445.

Shoenfelt, E.L. (1996). Goal setting and feedback as a posttraining strategy to increase the transfer of training. *Perceptual and Motor Skills*, **83**, 176–178.

Simard, M. & Marchand, A. (1997). Workgroups' propensity to comply with safety rules: The influence and effectiveness in occupational safety. *Safety Science*, **17**, 169–185.

Simon, S.J., Grover, V., Teng, J.T.C., & Whitcomb, K. (1996). The relationship of information system training methods and cognitive ability to end-user satisfaction, comprehension, and skill transfer: A longitudinal field study. *Information Systems Research*, **7**, 466–490.

Simon, S.J. & Werner, J.M. (1996). Computer training through behavior modeling, self-paced, and instructional approaches: A field experiment. *Journal of Applied Psychology*, **81**, 648–659.

Sinclair, R.C., Smith, R., Colligan, M., Prince, M., Nguyen, T., & Stayner, L. (2003). Evaluation of a safety training program in three food service companies. *Journal of Safety Research*, **34**, 547–558.

Skinner, B.F. (1974). *About behaviorism*. New York: Alfred A. Knopf.

Smith, M.J., Anger, W.K., & Uslan, S.S. (1978). Behavior modification applied to occupational safety. *Journal of Safety Research*, **10**, 87–88.

Smith-Crowe, K., Burke, M.J., & Landis, R.S. (2003). Organizational climate as a moderator of safety knowledge–safety performance relationships. *Journal of Organizational Behavior*, **24**, 861–876.

Smith-Jentsch, K., Salas, E., & Baker, D. (1996). Training team performance-related assertiveness. *Personnel Psychology*, **49**, 909–935.

Sniezek, J., Wilkins, D.C., Wadlington, P.L., & Baumann, M.R. (2002). Training for crisis decision-making: Psychological issues and computer-based solutions. *Journal of Management Information Systems*, **18**, 147–168.

Sonnentag, S. & Kliene, B.M. (2000). Deliberate practice at work: A study with insurance agents. *Journal of Organisational and Occupational Psychology*, **73**, 87–102.

Sonnentag, S., Niessen, C., & Ohly, S. (2004). Learning at work: Training and development. In C. Cooper & I. Robertson (Eds), *International review of industrial and organizational psychology* (pp. 249–289). Chichester: John Wiley & Sons.

Springer, L., Stanne, M.R., & Donovan, S.S. (1999). Effects of small-group learning on undergraduates in science, mathematics, engineering, and technology: A meta-analysis. *Review of Educational Research*, **69**, 21–51.

Stajkovic, A. & Luthans, F. (1997). A meta-analysis of the effects of organizational behavior modification on task performance, 1975–1995. *Academy of Management Journal*, **40**, 1122–1149.

Stajkovic, A.D. & Luthans, F. (2001). Differential effects of incentive motivators on work performance. *Academy of Management Journal*, **44**, 580–590.

Stewart, G., Carson, K., & Cardy, R. (1996). The joint effects of conscientiousness and self-leadership training on employee self-directed behavior in a service setting. *Personnel Psychology*, **49**, 143–164.

Sulzer-Arnoff, B. & Austin, J. (2000). Does BBS work? Behavior-based safety and injury reduction: A survey of the evidence. *Professional Safety*, **45**, 19–24.

Sulzer-Azaroff, B., Loafman, B., & Merante, R.J. (1990). Improving occupational safety in a large industrial plant: A systematic replication. *Journal of Organizational Behavior Management*, **11**, 99–120.

Tannenbaum, S., Beard, R., & Salas, E. (1992). Team building and its influence on team effectiveness: An examination of conceptual and theoretical developments. In K. Kelley (Ed.), *Issues, theory and research in industrial/organisational psychology*. Amsterdam: Elsevier Science Publishers BV.

Tannenbaum, S., Mathieu, J., Salas, E., & Cannon-Bowers, J. (1991). Meeting trainees' expectations: The influence of training fulfillment on the development of commitment, self-efficacy and motivation. *Journal of Applied Psychology*, **76**, 759–769.

Tannenbaum, S. & Yukl, G. (1992). Training and development in work organisations. *Annual Review of Psychology*, **43**, 399–441.

Taylor, P.A., Russ-Eft, D.F., & Chan, D.W.L. (in press). A meta-analytic review of behavior modeling training. *Journal of Applied Psychology*.

Tharenou, P. (2001). The relationship of training motivation to participation in training and development. *Journal of Occupational and Organizational Psychology*, **74**, 599–621.

Tracey, J., Tannenbaum, S., & Kavanagh, M. (1995). Applying trained skills to the job: The importance of the work environment. *Journal of Applied Psychology*, **80**, 239–252.

Triandis, H.C. (2004). The many dimensions of culture. *Academy of Management Executive*, **18**, 88–93.

Turner, N. & Parker, S.K. (2004). The effect of teamwork on safety processes and outcomes. In J. Barling & M.R. Frone (Eds), *The psychology of workplace safety* (pp. 35–62). Washington, DC: American Psychological Association.

Tziner, A., Haccoun, R., & Kadish, A. (1991). Personal and situational characteristics influencing the effectiveness of transfer of training improvement strategies. *Journal of Occupational Psychology*, **64**, 167–177.

United Brotherhood of Carpenters Health & Safety Fund of North America (1992). *Hazardous waste participants manual*. Cincinnati, OH: Midwest Consortium for Hazardous Waste Worker Training.

Van Poppel, M.N., Koes, B.W., Van der Ploeg, T., Smid, T., & Bouter, L.M. (1998). Lumbar supports and education for the prevention of low back pain in industry: A randomized controlled trial. *Journal of the American Medical Association*, **279**, 1789–1794.

Vernon, D.T. & Blake, R.L. (1993). Does problem-based learning work? A meta-analysis of evaluative research. *Academic Medicine*, **68**, 550–563.

Vygotsky, L. (1987). *Thought and language* (trans. A. Kozulin). Cambridge, MA: Harvard University Press.

Wagner, R.K. (1997). Intelligence, training, and employment. *American Psychologist*, **52**, 1059–1069.

Wall, T.D., Cordery, J.L., & Clegg, C.W. (2002). Empowerment, performance, and operational uncertainty: A theoretical integration. *Applied Psychology: An International Review*, **51**, 146–169.

Warr, P. (2001). Age and work behaviour: Physical attributes, cognitive abilities, knowledge personality traits and motives. In C.L. Cooper & I.T. Robertson (Eds), *International Review of Industrial and Organizational Psychology*, **16**, 1–36.

Warr, P. & Allen, C. (1998). Learning strategies and occupational training. In C.L. Cooper & I.T. Robertson (Eds), *International review of industrial and organizational psychology* (Vol. 13, pp. 83–121). Chichester: John Wiley & Sons.

Warr, P., Allen, C., & Birdi, K. (1999). Predicting three levels of training outcome. *Journal of Organisational and Occupational Psychology*, **72**, 351–375.

Warr, P. & Bunce, D. (1995). Trainee characteristics and the outcomes of open learning. *Personnel Psychology*, **48**, 347–375.

Warr, P. & Downing, J. (2000). Learning strategies, learning anxiety and knowledge acquisition. *British Journal of Psychology*, **91**, 311–333.

Webb, N.M., Troper, J.D., & Fall, R. (1995). Constructive activity and learning in collaborative small groups. *Journal of Educational Psychology*, **87**, 406–423.

Weeks, D.L. & Anderson, L.P. (2000). The interaction of observational learning with overt practice: Effects on motor skill learning. *Acta Psychologica*, **104**, 259–271.

Weil, S. & McGill, I. (1989). *Making sense of experiential learning*. Buckingham, UK: SRHE/OU Press.

Weitlauf, J., Smith, R., & Cervone, D. (2000). Generalization effects of coping-skills training: Influence of self-defense training on women's efficacy beliefs, assertiveness and aggression. *Journal of Applied Psychology*, **85**, 625–633.

Weyman, A.K. & Clarke, D.D. (2003). Investigating the influence of organizational role on perceptions of risk in deep coal mines. *Journal of Applied Psychology*, **88**, 404–412.

Whitby, M., Stead, P., & Najman, J.M. (1991). Needlestick injury: Impact of a re-capping device and an associated education program. *Infection Control and Hospital Epidemiology*, **12**, 220–225.

Wilson, A. (1992). The promise of situated cognition. In S. Merriam (Ed.), *An update on adult learning theory* (pp. 71–80). San Francisco: Jossey-Bass.

Wood, R. & Bandura, A. (1989). Impact of conceptions of ability on self-regulatory mechanisms and complex decision-making. *Journal of Personality and Social Psychology*, **56**, 407–415.

Zohar, D. (2000). A group-level model of safety climate: Testing the effect of group climate on microaccidents in manufacturing jobs. *Journal of Applied Psychology*, **85**, 587–596.

Zohar, D., Cohen, A., & Azar, N. (1980). Promoting increased use of ear protectors in noise through information feedback. *Human Factors*, **22**, 69–79.

Zweig, D. & Webster, J. (2004). What are we measuring? An examination of the relationships between the big-five personality traits, goal orientation, and performance intentions. *Personality and Individual Differences*, **36**, 1693–1708.

Chapter 2

TASK ANALYSIS

John Annett
Department of Psychology, University of Warwick, UK
and
Neville Stanton
School of Engineering and Design, Brunel University, UK

This chapter will provide a general historical and theoretical introduction to task analysis followed by accounts of the principal methods currently in use for both individual and team tasks. Further sections review the various uses of task analysis (e.g., in the design of equipment, estimating human reliability and workload, the analysis of team tasks, and the design of training). A final section will be concerned with questions of the reliability, validity, and usability of these methods.

The terms 'task' and 'job' are almost synonymous, 'task' being derived from the Old English term for a feudal duty or imposition, while 'job' first emerged in the sixteenth century to denote a piece of work done for payment, itself an interesting reflection on changes in economic and social organization. In modern usage 'job' may mean both an item of paid work, such as an annual car service, or more generally a position or appointment within an organization. The use of the word 'task', on the other hand, implies some activity resulting in a specified outcome or goal and is typically used to refer to discrete elements, the constituents of a job. In practice, task analysis comprises a set of techniques providing a detailed description and understanding of goal-directed work activities, while job analysis refers to a range of techniques for estimating the skills and abilities required of the occupant of a given employment or position and the evaluation of the associated mental and physical costs, sometimes directly related to determining the rate of pay. While the two fields often meet, both in their general objectives of making work more productive and acceptable to the worker, and in the empirical appraisal of work, the methods they use are different, the job analyst typically using rating scales to measure various dimensions of work and the abilities and effort required to inform policy on recruitment, selection, and remuneration. The task analyst, in contrast, typically uses expert

International Review of Industrial and Organizational Psychology, 2006, Volume 21
Edited by G.P. Hodgkinson and J.K. Ford. © 2006 John Wiley & Sons, Ltd.

opinion coupled with direct observation to produce a functional analysis of the processes involved in performing the task. Job analysis was reviewed in this series by Spector, Brannick, and Coovert (1989) but task analysis has not previously received attention.

Task analysis is not merely descriptive but is 'a process whose results provide data about human functions which, in turn, are used to determine the characteristics of job aids, training programmes and the assessment of performance of the system and its components' (Miller, 1962). To put it in a slightly different way, *task analysis refers to any method of inquiry into the actual or probable functionality of an individual or team in achieving some specified goal or goals with a given set of tools or equipment, within a given environmental context.* To describe something requires only a common vocabulary with which to denote the observations made, but an understanding implies that these observations fit into some theoretical framework that will enable the successful manipulation of the objects and processes involved. In short, task analysis is best understood as a means of asking questions directed towards the identification and solution of performance problems of the entire system, including operators, equipment, and environment. Given the almost infinite variety of performance goals, of individuals and teams, of tools and equipment, and of operational contexts it is not surprising that very many different methods have been developed (Annett & Stanton, 2000; Booher & Hewitt, 1990; Diaper & Stanton, 2004; Hollnagel, 2003; Kirwan & Ainsworth, 1992; Schraagen, Chipman, & Shalin, 2000; Stanton, Hedge, Brookhuis, Salas, & Hendrick, 2005; Wilson & Corlett, 2005).

HISTORICAL AND THEORETICAL BACKGROUND

Scientific Management

Such a broad definition of task analysis as that of Miller (1962) could embrace virtually the whole field of 'human factors' since the focus is on the interface of the worker and the machine, including the wider system and its environment. It is not, therefore, surprising that the earliest endeavours of the 'scientific management' movement (Gilbreth, 1911; Taylor, 1911) to use empirical methods to design equipment and methods of work to optimize human performance are the *fons et origo* of task analysis. We shall not deal in detail with these work study methods but concentrate instead on developments that began to emerge in the mid-twentieth century prompted by the demands of rapidly developing industrial and military technology. Two historical trends are particularly noteworthy: first, the development of mass production of complex items such as motor vehicles and radios by semi-skilled workers; and, second, the development of sophisticated communication and control systems for managing chemical processes, power generation and distribution, rail and air traffic control, and, not least, military command and control systems.

The first of these two trends resulted in the progressive loss of ownership of the skills of production by individual work people. For millennia skilled tradesmen had kept tight control of the secrets of their trade but mass production, by breaking down specialist skills into a series of simple elements each of which could be mastered by semi-skilled operators with minimal training, gave industrialists much greater control over the methods used with a consequent reduction in costs. Mass production required the methods of time and motion study to simplify complex tasks but the result was often highly repetitive work of the kind satirized in Charlie Chaplin's film 'Modern Times'. The prevalence of routine repetitive work with little or no intellectual content tended to support the notion that task analysis meant simply specifying the *actions* required of the operator, a view consistent with behaviourism which came to dominate psychology during the first half of the twentieth century. By the early 1950s the shortcomings of behaviourism as a theoretical foundation for psychological science were beginning to be apparent and with the development of information theory advances were made in the understanding of human skills on both sides of the Atlantic (Annett & Kay, 1956, 1957; Fitts, 1954; Hick, 1952). In Birmingham, UK, a training consultant, W. Douglas Seymour (Seymour, 1954, 1968), developed a method called 'skills analysis training' which recognized the importance of perceptual and decision-making components of even relatively simple manual skills (Annett, Golby, & Kay, 1958; Fitts, 1954). At the same time R.B. Miller (1953a, 1953b) had developed a method for man–machine task analysis for the US Air Force.

Systems Psychology

The trend towards the automation of industrial processes progressively reduced the physical demands of work while, in many cases, increasing its intellectual content, requiring operators to monitor many sources of coded information and 'troubleshoot' actual, or potential, system failures. This trend was especially marked in advanced military systems which, with the introduction of sophisticated sensors and servos, were rapidly becoming complexes of human and machine with functions shared between the two. Military psychologists began to think of *systems* and their properties and the implications for the design of equipment and the training of operators. The aim was to determine the psychological factors essential for criterion performance in such a way as to aid the design of training equipment. Miller's method (Miller, 1953a, 1953b) was both rational and empirical. It was rational in the sense that the analysis must determine what *functions* were required in order to achieve the desired system output, and empirical in that it should be possible to determine whether the human physical and psychological capabilities could meet these functional demands.

By the 1950s the role of psychological methods in the design of complex systems was well established. In May 1952, a specialist panel of the Human

Resources Research and Development Board of the US Department of Defense recommended that the three branches of the armed services jointly develop a *Human Engineering Guide to Equipment Design* which was eventually published under that title (Morgan, Cook, Chapanis, & Lund, 1963). Chapanis (1959) also described a number of techniques including activity sampling, process analysis, including flow charting and link analysis, and the critical incident technique that were being used to investigate problems in the design and operation of equipment. Both publications took a systems view which began with consideration of the system goals and the functionality of its components, both human and machine, and of their interactions.

METHODS OF ANALYSIS

Stanton and Annett (2000) pointed out that the variety of uses for task analysis is perhaps too great for any one method to be adequate. The most common uses include determining knowledge requirements, understanding how devices are used, defining training needs, predicting human error, describing multi-agent systems, and designing computer interfaces, and each requires a different approach and often different types of data. Despite the wide variation in the uses of task analysis, the fundamental strategy common to most analytical methods is to search for and remedy the sources of unsatisfactory performance, whether failures of individual attention and perception, inadequate knowledge and understanding, or failures of team coordination. Some of these sources may lie in the design of the equipment, some in capabilities of the operator, and some in the standard operating procedures, but in many cases identification of the source helps to provide the 'cure'. Given this basic diagnostic strategy the analysis proceeds by identifying the goals of the system and systematically decomposing these into sub-goals and sub-sub-goals until the sources of the problem have been identified. A key feature of the strategy is not just to collect information about what *should* happen but to look for data relevant to system failures. The method, pioneered by Fitts and Jones (1947) and elaborated by Flanagan (1954) as the *critical incident technique*, has become one of the most valuable tools of task analysis.

Hierarchical Decomposition

The systems philosophy favours a 'top-down' approach and this was adopted by Miller (1953b) in his method of 'man–machine task analysis' and by Folley (1964) in recommendations for the design of naval training equipment. Rather than adopting an arbitrary level of description, say 'activities' or 'micro-movements', these two authors recommended that the analysis begins with the system goals, which are then further broken down into sub-goals. Folley, for example, proposed a 'system block analysis' in which major system operations are specified, followed by the identification of their component tasks and relationships among them and thence to detailed task activities and their psychological characteristics, such as the demands made on sensory discrimination, decision making, and other features that had long been studied by experimental psychologists.

The method of hierarchical decomposition of tasks had become established and was widely adopted in military procurement and training procedures during the 1960s (Drury, Paramore, Van Cott, Grey, & Corlett, 1987; Miller, 1962). The systems approach thus formed a basis for the method of decomposition subsequently known as Hierarchical Task Analysis (HTA) developed in the UK (Annett & Duncan, 1967; Annett, Duncan, Stammers, & Gray, 1971; Shepherd, 2001). HTA, which was initially used in the analysis of process control tasks in the petrochemical industry (Duncan, 1972), was widely adopted in process industries, including power generation and distribution and by the military (see reviews by Ainsworth & Marshall, 1998; Kirwan & Ainsworth, 1992; Stanton, in press).

Cognitive Task Analysis

Although HTA went largely unnoticed in the USA (Kieras & Meyer, 2000), the functional analysis of complex man–machine systems led to increased attention to the cognitive aspects of tasks. Whereas manual control tasks such as flying, steering, and even managing chemical plant had been prominent up to mid-century, advanced automation began to make these manual skills largely redundant and decision making became the most significant function of the human operator. During the 1970s 'cognitive' psychology had largely overtaken and replaced the American behaviourist orthodoxy of the previous decades. The term 'cognitive task analysis' began to appear in studies of complex tasks involving intellectual skills and the use of expert knowledge (Annett, 2000; Gallagher, 1979; Rothkopf, 1986; Scandura, 1982). British and European psychologists, who had never been totally sold on behaviourism, had long believed that skilled actions and the underlying mental processes should be considered as an integrated whole and that it made little sense to analyse tasks without taking both into account. Indeed, HTA constituted an explicit attempt to account for the performance of intellectually demanding skills such as controlling large-scale petrochemical installations (Annett & Duncan, 1967; Duncan, 1972).

Research into long- and short-term memory, procedural and declarative knowledge, decision making and problem solving, and in 'artificial intelligence' provided theoretical bases for Cognitive Task Analysis (CTA). In particular the idea from computer science that human 'expertise' could be captured and incorporated into a computer-based 'expert system' also began to emerge in the 1980s. Both the psychologist analysing a complex task and the software engineer building an expert system needed reliable methods of 'knowledge elicitation' and useful cross-fertilization took place between the two disciplines (see Hoffman, 1992). From the 1970s onwards the widespread use of computers as components of complex systems also contributed to the range of ideas and techniques in the analysis of tasks involving human–computer interaction. The Goals, Operators, Methods, and Selection rules (GOMS) system (Card, Moran, & Newell, 1983) was aimed specifically at analysing such tasks and the need for sophisticated analytical tools for representing the flow of materials and information between system components led to computer-based methods such as Systems Analysis of Integrated Networks of Tasks (SAINT) (Laughery, 1984).[1]

CTA techniques are used to describe, represent, and evaluate the unobservable cognitive aspects of task performance. According to Schraagen et al. (2000), CTA represents an extension of traditional task analysis techniques and is used to describe the knowledge, thought processes, and goal structures underlying observable task performance. Militello and Hutton (1998) describe CTA techniques as those that focus on describing and representing the cognitive elements that underlie goal generation, decision making, and judgements. Redding (1989) indicated that the following components are essential to CTA: assessing individual abilities, assessing changes in the knowledge base, identifying task components, identifying differences between novices and experts, identifying the conceptual and procedural knowledge of similar components, and specifying the conditions that best facilitate progression from one knowledge state to another (see also Seamster, Redding, & Kaempf, 2000). Various CTA techniques have been subject to widespread use over the past two decades, with applications in a number of domains, such as firefighting (Militello & Hutton, 1998), aviation, white-water rafting, and emergency services (O'Hare, Wiggins, Williams, & Wong, 1998), command and control (Chin, Sanderson, & Watson 1999), military operations (Klein, 2000), and naval maintenance (Schaafstal & Schraagen, 2000). CTA techniques and outputs are used for a variety of purposes including the informing of the design of procedures and processes, the design of new technology and systems, the allocation of functions, the development of training procedures and interventions, and the evaluation of individual and team performance within complex systems.

Data Collection

At least 10 different data collection methods are described in the standard sources (Drury et al., 1987; Kirwan & Ainsworth, 1992; Stanton, et al. 2005). These include structured interviews and focus groups comprising subject-matter experts, direct observation (including walkthroughs and participant observation, audio and video recording), and documentary sources (including standard operating procedures, training manuals, fault-finding guides, and

---

[1] A computerized version is known as Micro-SAINT.

even accident records). Researchers from Folley (1964) to Annett (2005) have stressed that before data collection can begin it is necessary to establish the nature of the system goals, i.e., the desired output or result of task performance. This is not always easy when dealing with complex multi-person systems, since individuals can have goals that do not always map neatly onto the stated 'mission' of senior management. The balance of output with risk and operating costs is not always explicit and may be subject to individual interpretation. The analyst must, therefore, devote some effort to obtaining agreement between the various stakeholders as to the criteria of acceptable performance. Another vital preliminary to data collection is the identification of the people, objects, locations, conditions, and processes to which reference must be made. This can often be achieved by obtaining explanations from one or more subject-matter experts, reference to supporting documentation, and/or by straightforward observation. The latter may not be possible where a prospective task analysis is to be carried out into a system that is in the planning stage and not yet operational. As Lim and Long (1994) point out, a future system often has precedents in earlier versions that can be used as an initial point of reference.

The general strategy of goal decomposition is best accomplished by interviews with subject-matter experts before attempting to collect detailed information on the performance of individual operators. Again, both Folley (1964) and Annett (2005) have stressed the desirability of cross-checking this initial gross analysis with as many available sources as possible. One very useful interview technique is to ask what would be the consequences of failure to attain a given goal or sub-goal. In many complex tasks a critical failure might not be observed in months of direct observation. The evidence is often anecdotal but can sometimes be supported by data on material wastage, equipment failure and downtime, and accidents. This is essentially the critical incident method of Fitts and Jones (1947) and Flanagan (1954). Detailed observation of operator performance, which was the classical 'work study' method, is only justified when the devil really is in the detail. This is the justification for the $p \times c$ 'stop rule' proposed by Annett and Duncan (1967) that further decomposition is unnecessary when the product of the probability of failure with its cost is deemed acceptable. Sometimes it is useful to record details of performance in order to determine, for example, the cues actually used (O'Hare et al., 1998) or the occasions on which certain types of interaction occur (Annett, Cunningham, & Mathias-Jones, 2000) but the value of collecting such data is to identify potential sources of performance failure rather than simply a description of actual performance in normal circumstances.

As a general rule data should be collected, not simply 'because it is there' but because it serves the purpose of the analysis, such as identifying the sources of error or knowledge that the operator must have to perform successfully. CTA approaches use a combination of traditional knowledge elicitation methods such as observation, semi-structured and structured interviews, and questionnaires in order to retrospectively elicit data regarding the mental processes used by system operators during task performance. For example, the Cognitively Orientated Task Analysis (COTA) framework is a collection of procedures, including verbal protocol analysis and interviews, that are used to describe the expertise involved during task performance (DuBois & Shalin, 2000). The Critical Decision Method (CDM—Klein, Calderwood, & MacGregor, 1989) uses direct observation and semi-structured interviews in order to analyse the cognitive processes underlying decision making in complex environments. The Applied Cognitive Task Analysis (ACTA) approach (Militello & Hutton, 1998) uses probe questions designed to elicit information regarding the cognitive processes employed during task performance, such as 'What are the major elements you have to know and keep track of?' Data collected by these methods can be invaluable in the design of information sources and decision support systems and training.

Presentation of Results

The manner in which task analysis information is recorded and presented is varied. Perhaps the most common method is a representation of the task hierarchy in either diagrammatic or tabular form (Annett et al., 1971; Shepherd, 2001) but other formats may better represent important facets of the task. Link diagrams (Chapanis, 1959) and state-space diagrams (Stanton & Baber, 2005) can usefully represent important interactions between people and between people and machines, while critical path analysis (Baber, 2005) is a useful way of representing processes. The variety of documentation and presentation methods is considerable, as indicated by the number of compendia published in recent years (Booher, 1990; Diaper & Stanton, 2004; Hollnagel, 2003; O'Brien & Charlton, 1996; Stanton et al., 2005). However presented, the final product of a task analysis should provide some answers to the questions initially posed. These answers may be hypotheses, such as a suggested design change, and should be advanced only with the degree of confidence merited by the existing state of knowledge about, for instance, instrument design or the effectiveness of the training method. Published reports of analyses rarely report empirical tests of hypothetical solutions—a question to which we shall return in the final section.

Computer-based Task Analysis

Finally, mention should be made of a number of computer-based task analysis methods which support both data collection and presentation of results. Micro-SAINT (Laughery, 1984) represents data flow. ATLAS (Hamilton, 2000) offers a variety of formats including both the hierarchical decomposition of goals and an event timeline for individual or multi-role tasks, and data may be recorded and presented on the perceptual, cognitive, and psychomotor attributes required to perform task elements. A version of HTA is available in Mackintosh Apple™ format (Bass, Aspinal, Walter, & Stanton, 1995), and a Windows™-based software package for conducting HTA called Task Architect has recently been published (Stuart, 2004). A freeware HTA program is also available from the Communications and Systems Engineering Group at Cranfield University, UK. It must be emphasised that none of the authors of these packages claims to reduce task analysis to a mere clerical exercise but rather their purpose is to aid the expert analyst. An emerging role for computerized task analysis is in task modelling. GOMS (Card et al., 1983; Kieras, 2004) was developed as a means of modelling HCI tasks and Williams (2000) describes a Cognitive Analysis Tool (CAT) which extends the basic idea to the modelling of declarative task knowledge consistent with the COGNET[2] architecture (Zachary, Ryder, & Hincinbotham, 2000). Kieras and Meyer (2000) point to the potential value of predictive computer modelling in the design of complex tasks, including multi-agent systems. Analysis and modelling are closely related technologies that have much to offer.

TASK ANALYSIS IN SYSTEM DESIGN AND PERFORMANCE ASSESSMENT

Wilson (1995) divides ergonomics methods into five basic types: (1) for collecting data about people (e.g., their physical, physiological, and psychological capacities); (2) methods used in system development (e.g., collection of data on current and proposed system design); (3) methods to evaluate human–machine system performance (e.g., collection of data on quantitative and qualitative measures); (4) methods of assessing the task demands and effects on people (e.g., collection of data on short-term and longer-term effects on the well-being of the person performing the tasks being analysed); and (5) methods used in the development of an ergonomics management programme, such as strategies for supporting, managing, and evaluating sustainable ergonomics interventions. Task analysis methods may fall into several of these categories. Some of the approaches occupy more than one category because of their generic nature. For a full range of methods see Stanton et al. (2005) or Wilson and Corlett (2005). The point of task analysis is not just the description of the tasks or goals: as Wilson has indicated, it is the purpose to which those descriptions are put.

Stages in System Development

Task analysis can be carried out at different stages of the design lifecycle, Concept, Assessment, Demonstration, Manufacture, In-service, and Disposal (CADMID), and the choice of method is dependent upon the stage at which it is used. The concept stage, which represents the beginning of any project,

---

[2] COGnition as a NETwork of tasks.

should address the principal human issues and make a preliminary assessment of the associated risks and requirements. This process is normally referred to as Early Human Factors Analysis (EHFA). During the assessment stage, more detailed work is conducted in order to evaluate and, where possible, quantify the Human Factors/Engineering (HF/E) requirements and risks. Information regarding the user tasks, working conditions, and expected performance is normally required during this stage and issues such as manpower reduction, workload, and performance shortfalls are also assessed. During the demonstration stage, specifications are refined to ensure that robust HF/E content and clear human performance targets are specified. During the manufacture stage, the analysis ensures integration with training development, tactics development, and general support strategy. End user trials are also conducted in order to build confidence in equipment operability, which leads to acceptance and subsequent handover. While in-service, task evaluation helps to identify any human-related performance shortfalls or failures of human–equipment integration. Finally the aim of the disposal stage is to dispose of the equipment safely, efficiently, and effectively.

In *A Guide to Task Analysis*, Kirwan and Ainsworth (1992) provide 10 case studies illustrating most of these stages, except decommissioning. These range from assessing the effects of staffing levels in a nuclear power plant (Fewins, Mitchell, & Williams, 1992, pp. 241–251; Pennington, Joy, & Kirwan, 1992, pp. 289–299) through safety assessment on an offshore oil platform (Pennington, 1992, pp. 253–265) and in a nuclear power plant (Pendelbury & Ainsworth, 1992, pp. 311–326; Rycraft, Brown, & Leckey, 1992, pp. 355–362), potential human error in a nuclear power plant (Reed, 1992, pp. 267–288), workload assessment (McLeod & Sherwood-Jones, 1992, pp. 301–310), maintenance training in a chemical processing plant (Shepherd, 1992, pp. 327–339), inspection and faultfinding (Williams, 1992, pp. 341–353), and finally a programme of analysis for a nuclear chemical reprocessing plant is described (Kirwan, 1992, pp. 363–388). In a survey of the use of task analysis in the defence industry, Ainsworth and Marshall (1998) found allocation of function together with workload assessment and interface design to be the most common purposes and this pattern was reflected in 60 analyses in the nuclear industry. It is of note that the majority of analyses were carried out at the in-service stage, perhaps reflecting caution in their acceptance as adequate predictors of performance.

In the large-scale design and development of a new nuclear reactor, Staples (1993) describes how task analysis was used as the basis for virtually all of the human factors and ergonomics studies. The task analysis was produced through reviews of contemporary operating procedures, discussions with subject-matter experts, and interviews with operating personnel from another reactor. The resultant task analysis was used to examine potential errors and their consequences, the interface design verification, identification of training procedures, development and verification of operating procedures, workload assessment, and communication analysis. Staples argued that task analysis is of major benefit in system design as it makes possible a detailed and systematic assessment of the interactions between human operators and their technical systems. Conducting the task analysis helps the analyst to become familiar with the processes and procedures to enable the crucial aspects of the work to be critically assessed. Staples also notes that reference to the task analysis for the analysis of all aspects of the system can highlight inconsistencies between training, procedures, and system design and draws the general conclusion that the broad application of task analysis can make it a very cost-effective approach to system design.

Lim and Long (1994) describe a Method of Usability Engineering (MUSE) which aims to anticipate human factor problems at an early stage of system development, having in mind especially the design of computer-based systems. MUSE is essentially a top-down approach for developing and refining a task model, usually beginning with the analysis of an existing or 'extant' task in a hierarchical format. This is used as the basis for a more generalized task model which specifies functions rather than detailed specification of the actual user interface. A model of the needs of the system user is then developed which, in conjunction with the generalized task model, opens up consideration of the interaction of user and task. A comparable approach to design is the Sub-Goal Template (SGT) method (Ormerod, 2000; Ormerod & Shepherd, 2003; Richardson, Ormerod, & Shepherd, 1998). SGT is based on HTA and aims to specify the information requirements of the task. The idea of a sub-goal template is that the 'stop rule' in HTA is taken as the lowest level at which the information requirements of the task may be independent of any actual implementation, such as specific display or communication systems. What is important is information processing; the manner in which it is presented is something for later consideration, when all the information requirements are known.

Human Error Identification (HEI)

Human reliability is a major concern of system designers and a number of methods for human error prediction have been developed, including: the Systematic Human Error Reduction and Prediction Approach (SHERPA—Embrey, 1986); Cognitive Reliability and Analysis Method (CREAM—Hollnagel, 1998); Hazard and Operability (HAZOP—Kletz, 1991); Technique for Human Error Rate Prediction (THERP—Swain & Guttman, 1983); Technique for Retrospective and Predictive Analysis of Cognitive Errors (TRACE—Shorrock & Kirwan, 2002); and Human Error Recovery Assessment (HERA—Kirwan, 1998a, 1998b). Task analysis techniques are used to describe normative behaviour and the error identification methodologies such as those enumerated above are used to help to identify what could go wrong. The taxonomic approaches of Norman (1988) and Reason (1990) have enabled the development and formal definition of several categories of human error (such as capture errors, description errors, data-driven errors, associated activation errors, and loss of activation errors). However, the work of Reason (1990) and also Wickens (1992) goes beyond mere classification by proposing a theory of the psychological mechanisms that combine to cause errors (such as failure of memory, poor perception, errors of decision making, and problems of motor execution). Reason (1990), in particular, has argued that we need to consider the activities of the individual if we are to be able to identify what may go wrong. Rather than viewing errors as unpredictable events, this approach regards them to be wholly predictable occurrences based upon an analysis of an individual's activities.

Most HEI techniques work in much the same manner (Kirwan, 1994). First, the activity needs to be broken down into a sequence of sub-stages by, for example, using hierarchical task analysis. Second, possible and plausible errors are identified for each of the sub-stages in turn. Third, the HEI technique may indicate the possible psychological error mechanisms underlying these identified errors, and, finally, the HEI technique may be able to specify a recovery or error reduction pathway. In essence these methods work by associating up to 10 error modes with each action. In the hands of a novice, it is typical for there to be an over-inclusive strategy for selecting error modes. The novice user would rather be safe than sorry and tends to predict many more errors than actually occur. This might be problematic as 'crying wolf' too many times might ruin the credibility of the approach. Task Analysis For Error Identification (TAFEI—Baber & Stanton, 1994), in contrast, is a convergent error prediction technique: it works by identifying the possible transitions between the different states of a device and uses the normative description of behaviour (provided by the HTA) to identify potentially erroneous actions. Even in the hands of novices the technique seems to prevent individuals generating too many false alarms, certainly no more than they do using heuristics. In fact, by constraining the user of TAFEI to the problem space surrounding the transitions between device states, it should exclude extraneous error prediction.

THE ANALYSIS OF TEAM TASKS

As with all methods of analysis, the form and content in team level applications must depend on the purpose and anticipated use of the data. In an early example, Chapanis (1959) plotted the frequency of communication links between members of a naval command team in order to facilitate redesign of the physical layout of a warship's combat information centre. This link analysis procedure employed the classic principle of economy of effort on which motion study was based to simplify the physical layout and thus improve intra-team communication. In recent years highly publicized failures of complex technological systems have drawn attention to a variety of structural and training problems of teams.

The 1988 incident in which a US Navy ship, the USS *Vincennes*, accidentally shot down an Iranian civil airliner over the Persian Gulf led an extensive research programme on 'Tactical Decision Making Under Stress' (TADMUS) to investigate factors affecting the performance of naval command teams. The programme resulted in a number of significant publications on teams and team working summarized by Cannon-Bowers and Salas (1998). Since the design of military teams is largely dictated by the command structure and the nature of the equipment, a strong focus has been on team training and performance assessment.

One major effort was to analyse and model the cognitive aspects of the task of the ship's Anti-Air Warfare Controller (AAWC—Zachary et al., 1998, 2000). This used the software language COGNET, inspired by the distinctive Carnegie-Mellon approach to the analysis of cognition (Newell, 1980), to model the knowledge used by the AAWC in performing a series of tasks involved in correctly identifying and responding to air threats. Data were collected by recording the actual performance of experts in a combat information centre simulator and having other experts provide commentaries on the information and rules underlying the decisions made by the operators and building them into a GOMS type task model. Data collection was arduous and the analysis was not focused on any particular problem, although both system design and training were thought of as possible uses. Although the aim was to examine teamwork, in this example at least COGNET, like most classical methods of task analysis, modelled only the work of an individual operator, the AAWC, and the analysis concerned only the tasks of that individual and not of the team as such. Distinguishing 'task work' from 'team work' is a central problem for the analysis of team tasks.

Team Process and Team Product

It has long been known that when two or more individuals work together to a common goal, their joint product is rarely the exact sum of their individual contributions. Both 'social facilitation' (an increase in total product: Zajonc, 1965) and 'social loafing' (a reduction in total product: Latané, Williams, & Harkins, 1979) have been observed in group working. When individuals form part of a team with some degree of role specialization, further complications arise with reference to how the work is shared in terms of individual effort and the coordination of team effort; team 'process' can affect team 'product' in a variety of ways. The analysis of team tasks, therefore, involves factors additional to those affecting individual performance which concern the structure and functioning of the team as an entity.

Teams are complex entities with many facets that may merit analysis for any of several different purposes, each of which may call for different methods. However, team tasks are no different from individual tasks in the sense that they are defined by their goals. A team task is only complete when the specified goal, including any relevant sub-goals, has been attained, but in some cases team goals can be hard to specify. It may, for example, be difficult to specify precisely the goals of a creative team and perhaps some problem-solving teams, but where tasks are constrained by the nature of the problem and the resources (equipment and personnel) available, an approach via goal identification is feasible. This would normally be the case in multi-person tasks such as air traffic control and military command teams. Such teams are normally well structured and features such as information flow between team members and the authority hierarchy may be worthy of attention. This can be the case where communication is via some electronic medium such as a voice or video link or by access to a common (computerized) database and where special problems in team working have been encountered (McGrath & Hollingshead, 1994). Essens, Post, and Rasker (2000) describe the modelling of some of the key functional features of a naval command centre. This involved modelling the organizational structure, the flow of information through the system, the knowledge required, the physical and human agents, and goals and events. As they remark, 'modelling is no sinecure of a system . . .' (p. 388), and the task of collecting and analysing data was considerable. The practical approach was to begin by interviewing as many experts as were available, taking each aspect of the system in turn and representing the results on flowcharts. The development of these flowcharts, like the diagrams used in HTA, force both the expert and the analyst to demonstrate and agree a common understanding of some aspect of the system which had not been formally documented in either the engineering or the organizational design. The information derived from the analysis was then available for incorporation into training materials and as a basis for design developments.

Structure and Process

Steiner (1972) has developed a theory of how task and team structure interact to affect team processes, which in turn affect outcomes or team products. For example, in a 'divisible' task each member has a distinct role and, unless the organization contains some functional redundancy, failure can result when a single individual fails to fulfil his or her assigned role. In contrast 'unitary' team tasks are those in which each individual has the same role. Some unitary tasks, such as tug-of-war, depend on a combination of individual efforts and are termed 'additive', whereas a 'disjunctive' unitary task requires only one member of the team to be successful—for example, a quiz team needs only one really bright member. Again, some unitary tasks are 'conjunctive', requiring every member to attain a specified goal—for example, getting every member across a crocodile-infested river.

Each of these structures has different implications for overall team success and may draw attention to some specific feature of the task that will make a particular team process critical to success and hence in need of analysis.

Among the most important features are the human and physical resources required. In unitary tasks these would ideally be distributed according to whether the task is additive, disjunctive, or conjunctive. In divisible tasks resources of skill and knowledge, access to information and communication channels, and, sometimes critically, backup in the event of overload require special attention. Further, one should not neglect the fact that in many tasks the possible scenarios that present themselves to the team may introduce a significant degree of variability in the demands made on both individuals and the group, and it is therefore essential to specify not only the normal task routine but also ways in which the team may be faced with unusual and demanding situations.

Process Taxonomies

Two broadly contrasting strategies have attracted the attention of researchers, one of which focuses on identifying the characteristics of successful teams, such as the degree of team cohesion. The other attempts a functional analysis of the processes, for example, communication between team members, which lead to one or more successful team products. The former is represented by the work of Fleishman and Zaccaro (1992), who developed a taxonomy of team performance functions comprising seven categories, including team orientation, resource distribution, timing, response coordination, motivation, systems monitoring, and procedure maintenance. The latter attempts to analyse the team task in terms of the flow of information between team members and the ways in which the behaviour of each may affect that of the others; that is, the two primary processes of communication and collaboration. In the taxonomic approach, team function is typically treated as a general characteristic capable of measurement, usually by an expert, but subjective, rating, while, in the analytic approach, team processes are defined in more concrete terms, such as which individual or sub-group is required to make a particular contribution to the team product(s) and how this is brought into play in a given scenario.

A subjective approach is commonly adopted by team trainers, as illustrated by the account of training for nuclear power plant operation by Caddy and Wachtel (1992). They suggest that a job or task database be examined for task action verbs, such as 'inform', 'direct', 'decide', which imply 'generic' team skills of communication and collaboration. Since control room operations are often complex and, to a degree, unpredictable, a table top review is carried out by subject-matter experts who identify scenarios that may involve potentially critical interactions. A taxonomy such as that by Fleishman and Zaccaro (1992) could, of course, be applied but the analysis would have to be based on a combination of subject-matter expertise and consistent use of technical (psychological) terms which may be only loosely defined.

Klein (2000) identified five main types of cognitive process believed, on the basis of extensive research, to be important in effective team functioning, namely, control of attention, shared situation awareness, shared mental models, application of strategies to plan, make decisions and solve problems and metacognition (i.e., being aware of one's own cognitive processes). These five types of process should be captured by a team task analysis which represents the overall decision requirements. A study of a US Marine Corps command post (Klein et al., 1996) collected data on 200 decision-making incidents in order to identify critical team decisions and the reasons why they sometimes failed. Failure to build and maintain team situation awareness was found to be a prime cause of failure and much of this could be attributed to the way in which information was combined and displayed and to individual communication errors. Planning failures were likewise often due to poor communications, including lack of awareness by the commander that the state of communications would not support a rapid change of plan, however desirable in principle. Klein rightly points out that the use of critical incidents in identifying sources failure of team cognitive processes does not depend on a highly detailed account of the formal team structure, standard procedures and individual duties. However, much of this information is normally available and the analyst would be well advised to master the basic facts of team design, structure, and procedures before attempting to interview busy subject-matter experts in the manner described. It is therefore somewhat disingenuous to claim that what Klein refers to as a 'behavioural' task analysis is unnecessarily detailed.

Decomposing Team Tasks

It is, of course, the case that detailed recording of the activities of even a small team making difficult decisions can present almost insurmountable problems for the analyst, but that is precisely where the top-down hierarchical decomposition recommended by Annett and Duncan (1967) can be so useful in identifying team goals. Just as the task of an individual operator can be represented as a hierarchy of goals and sub-goals structured by a set of plans, team tasks can also be represented as a hierarchy of team goals and sub-goals. As the analysis becomes more detailed, some sub-goals are likely to be the responsibility of sub-teams and, at an even more detailed level, individual operators may be responsible for the attainment of sub-sub-goals. Annett and Cunningham (2000) showed how the task of a naval command team, normally comprising over 20 individuals, could be decomposed in this way. A further study (Annett et al., 2000) analysed the tasks of a three-man anti-submarine warfare (ASW) team comprising the principal warfare officer (PWO), action picture supervisor (AcPS), and active sonar director (ASD). As noted earlier, the principle enunciated by Annett and Duncan (1967) was that task decomposition should proceed to the level at which the product of the cost of failure to the system and the probability of failure was deemed acceptable. Applied as a rule of thumb, without the necessity of detailed numerical estimation, the stop rule allows the analyst to identify sources of performance failure and thus to propose solutions, whether the design of the equipment and operating procedures or the training of operators. The same general principle can be applied to the analysis of team tasks. If one proceeds down the hierarchy to the lowest level at which failure is probable and costly, one can ask: 'What must the team do to succeed?' To answer this question we need to turn to a theory of team process and the relation to team product.

As indicated by Klein (2000) and others, such as Paris, Salas, and Cannon-Bowers (2000), there is a degree of consensus as to the characteristics of good teamwork. Annett (1997) proposed that team product (degree of success and failure to attain team goals) can be related to three interrelated types of process designated as *behavioural, cognitive,* and *affective.* These are arranged in a hierarchy of influence such that affective processes, such as team loyalty, will affect cognitive processes, including adoption of a common team model, which in turn will affect team behaviours such as acts of communication. Only the latter are directly observable while cognitive and affective processes must be inferred from introspective accounts of what team members perceived or believe. CTA lays particular stress on collecting this type of data—see, for example, Militello and Hutton (1998). Affective processes can be assessed by the use of attitude scales, such as measures of group cohesion, which are popularly employed by team coaches (Martens & Petersen, 1971). An attempt was made by Annett and Cunningham (2000) to estimate the influence of attitudinal factors on the success of 16 naval command teams involving 270 naval personnel using a 30-item questionnaire. Eight factors accounted for 66% of the variance, the most important being identified as familiarity with and liking for other team members (18.6%), familiarity with the action information system used in the exercise (12.4%), and intra-team communication and situation awareness (10.1%). However, it was only the second factor, familiarity with the system, that was predictive of team performance as assessed by experienced instructors, and so the research focus returned to the cognitive and behavioural processes.

Teamwork in its various aspects is typically assessed by experienced observers but a task analysis can identify sub-tasks where teamwork is critical. Objectivity can be enhanced by specifying events in a pre-planned scenario which should trigger particular kinds of team activity. To this end the TARGET (Targeted Acceptable Responses to Generated Events or Tasks) method (Dwyer, Fowles, Oser, & Lane, 1997) was applied to an anti-submarine warfare exercise. The 25-minute exercise conducted in a realistic simulator involved the three-man ASW team in responding to 14 'trigger' events. The appropriate team responses had been identified by the standard method of hierarchical decomposition. For example, when a new sonar contact is presented the team must establish whether it is likely to be a submarine by first checking the charts for known wrecks, rock pinnacles, etc. The teamwork involved in this example is described, in plain language, as follows: 'ASD passes information to PWO who then calls for chart check at a given range and bearing. The position is plotted by the officer of the watch and the ASD directs the sonar operator to investigate the location and the AcPS enters the data to the system. After receiving information from these sources the PWO, in consultation with AcPS and ASD, declares contact classification (e.g., possible submarine).'

The next question was how to deal with this information in relation to the broad categories of team process identified in the theoretical model. The behaviour of the team was recorded during the exercise and their responses to the 14 critical events were allocated to up to 5 categories: send information, receive information, discuss, collaborate, synchronize actions. Responses were then scored 0 for non-appearance of the appropriate response, 1 for a partially correct response, and 2 for fully correct. The scores were then summed over the 14 trigger events and expressed as a percentage of the maximum possible score. The experimental team of relatively inexperienced trainees scored 31.3% at sending information correctly, but only 25% for receiving and using it correctly, and a miserable 16.7% for discussing the course of action with colleagues. In sum, hierarchical task analysis can provide an economic way to identify significant team processes while TARGET provides a more objective method of teamwork assessment, thus enabling instructors to focus on the specific strengths and weaknesses of team behaviour.

TASK ANALYSIS FOR TRAINING

As mentioned in the introduction, modern techniques of task analysis have been strongly influenced by the development of information processing and cognitive psychology and the requirement to define new training needs associated with the introduction of advanced technical systems. Task analysis for training has two fundamental aims, first to define the task and, second, more subtly, to clarify the nature of the underlying skills and how they might be acquired. The first, a statement of the duties, activities, goals, and performance levels of the fully trained operator together with 'how to . . .' instructions, is a normal and necessary requirement, typically providing documentary support for a range of purposes. The second, in contrast, must attempt to identify the physical and psychological demands of the task, the knowledge and skills needed for successful performance, and to specify an optimal training regime. For the first, the analysis must provide a guarantee that nothing of significance is omitted from the support documentation and the training syllabus, but the second should provide a basis for a training strategy and must therefore address issues of performance and learning.

Many 'semi-skilled' tasks in industry and the military have traditionally been procedural, involving a series of relatively easily learned actions, but more highly skilled tasks may involve difficult discriminations, the interpretation of complex data, the use of effective diagnostic strategies, making difficult decisions, and developing new strategies to meet novel situations employing the gamut of intelligent cognitive processes. Miller's (1953b) method recognized perceptual discrimination and decision making as significant task components and drew attention to the importance of feedback information, both as indicating task and sub-task completion and as a crucial factor in skill acquisition. Miller (1953a) also provided a good deal of practical advice on training methods, including the use of training devices and simulators. He emphasized the role of verbal explanation in the early stages of training but recognized the importance of the transition, through carefully controlled practice, to a non-verbal stage where skill becomes automatic.[3] The control of error through guidance and the provision of feedback also featured strongly with an especially important distinction between 'action feedback' and 'learning feedback', the former providing only a temporary prop to performance, the latter providing error correction and lasting performance improvement. The training process involved transfer from guided practice, often using simplified simulations, to the operational equipment unsupported by instructor intervention. Despite this useful advice, Miller gave no direct indication of how to take the step from analysis to training prescription.

Seymour (1954) recommended task analysis as a means of identifying relatively difficult task elements, such as perceptual discriminations, which might benefit from training and practice in isolation before being integrated with the whole task. For example, he describes (p. 66) a pressure-sensitive device that provides external feedback in order to teach difficult kinaesthetic discriminations[4] and other devices for practising essential hand–eye coordination. This was an important step towards ensuring direct links between the analysis and the training prescription, but he made no detailed recommendations concerning the method of analysis beyond using standard work study methods enhanced by reference to perceptual processes associated with specific actions. This was regarded as sufficient to identify training needs for perceptual-motor skills. Annett et al. (1971) extended this basic idea by identifying two kinds of perceptual component in their basis unit of analysis: the 'operation'. Each operation comprises an 'input', normally the information that signals a requirement for action, and 'feedback', information that signals the successful completion of that action. The trainee has to become familiar with both of these components in order to acquire the skills required for successful goal attainment for each operation or set of operations, and so it is important that these are identified in the analysis.

Training Objectives and Task Taxonomies

An influential contribution to the definition of skills was made by Bloom, Engelhart, Furst, Hill, and Krathwohl (1956) who developed a taxonomy of

---

[3] The 'stage' theory was subsequently promoted by Fitts (Fitts & Posner, 1967) and corresponds to later theories of 'controlled' versus 'automatic' processing (Schneider & Shiffrin, 1977) and the distinction between 'declarative' and 'procedural' knowledge (Anderson, 1980).

[4] There is some doubt as to whether such a device could be effective (see Annett, 1959).

educational objectives with three broad categories or domains: cognitive, affective, and psychomotor. These ideas were developed by others, notably Gagné (1965), who proposed that it was possible to prescribe ideal learning conditions for each category of knowledge or skill identified in a task analysis. The categories were ordered from simple S–R associations through behaviour chains or sequences to concepts and strategies, the latter becoming increasingly important in tasks in which the operator is required to control and troubleshoot complex systems. The taxonomic approach to the analysis of skills has its intellectual roots in psychometric theory (Fleishman & Quaintance, 1984), as distinct from systems theory, and taxonomies vary with the theoretical orientation and the context of the analyst. As in psychometrics, there is general agreement concerning the broad distinctions, such as between skill and knowledge or between procedure following and problem solving, but the variety and number of categories is at best a matter of preference and depends on the subjective judgement of the analyst. Patrick (1991, 1992), reviewing task taxonomies, concluded that methods based on estimates of the ability requirements of tasks were not particularly helpful to training designers.

Duncan (1972) provided a thorough, and somewhat sceptical, review of learning taxonomies but showed how the hierarchical decomposition of an industrial process control task identified different kinds of operation, including manual tracking, the discrimination of different states of the plant, following complex procedures, and using effective diagnostic strategies. The analysis was helpful in a variety of ways. For example, since operations at the lowest level of analysis are essential to the successful execution of superordinate operations it will, in general, be useful to learn these first. The gross structure of the analysis can indicate those operations that are grouped together, start-up and shut-down procedures, and diagnostic strategies, for example, and thus guide the assembly of component sub-tasks into behavioural and cognitively coherent wholes. Knowledge of the plant layout and the identity of control valves and instruments are often best learned prior to practising specific procedures in which these items feature. Probably the most important part of the analysis is in identifying operations that are difficult to perform and where failure is costly since these are likely to be more difficult to learn and the benefit of good training is most valuable.

Shepherd (1989, 2001) provides some useful guidance on how Hierarchical Task Analysis can be used to generate training prescriptions. First, the general rule is that decomposition proceeds to identify specific problems, including failure to identify a significant cue, not knowing how to respond, and so on: the analysis should stop only when a plausible training solution has been found—for example, training in cue identification, rehearsing a response sequence, and so forth. Second, the analysis can highlight underlying concepts and strategies that can be the subject of initial orientation training before being put into practice in specific training scenarios. Third, the task structure revealed by the analysis can guide a part/whole training strategy by identifying those operations that typically hang together and showing how they may be built up from their component sub-operations. Finally, the option of redesigning the task by changing the equipment, procedures, or manning should be available, if no training solution can be offered, or if a proposed solution turns out to be ineffective.

Defining Task Knowledge

The pioneers of modern task analysis methods recognized that, despite the commonly made distinction between 'knowing how' and 'knowing that', skill and expertise are inextricably interrelated (Annett, 1996; Duncan, 1972). Nevertheless, the technological revolution of the late twentieth century has led to an even greater emphasis on the analysis of knowledge requirements of complex tasks and the development of 'cognitive' task analysis (see the earlier section of this review on CTA) sometimes contrasted with 'traditional' or 'behavioural' methods. A number of recent studies described in an earlier section have demonstrated how CTA can be used to develop training materials. These have included detailed descriptions of knowledge elicitation techniques to extract the knowledge base (largely of hydrodynamics) which underpins the skill of manoeuvring two ships in close proximity during refuelling at sea (Williams & Pierce, 1999), for aircrew training (Seamster, Redding & Kaempf, 2000), troubleshooting electronic equipment (Schaafstal & Schraagen, 2000), managing firefighting teams (Militello & Hutton, 1998), and general aviation and white-water rafting (O'Hare et al., 1998). Although varying in methodological detail, CTA procedures generally involve interviews with experts to extract declarative task statements and build knowledge structures showing the relationships between principles and concepts on the one hand and more specific items of knowledge on the other, especially those items relating to the recognition of significant patterns in the task environment and critical choices between course of action. It is worthy of note that the principle of hierarchical decomposition underlies all these variations on the basic theme of using task analysis to identify sources of success and failure.

Training Simulators

The implementation of training is typically based on a model, either explicit or implicit, of the training system. Models of instructional system design typically place task analysis as a fundamental requirement to precede decisions about what is taught and how it is to be taught (see Patrick, 1992). One consideration recognized as important by Miller (1953a) is whether or not to use simulation as a vehicle for practice. To meet this need, Annett (1991) devised a procedural guide to be used in the British Army to span the apparent gap between task analysis and the provision of appropriate training equipment. Specialized equipment for training military tasks was often considered as an afterthought to the procurement process and the guide was designed to be used at what was then identified as the 'project definition' stage preceding full development of the actual equipment. At that stage the nature of the various operator tasks would be specified, at least in outline, and it would be possible to use HTA as a coarse-grained analysis of the tasks supported by the proposed equipment to indicate the types of training equipment that would be required. The guide, called TEAS (Training Equipment Advisory System), was implemented in a Mackintosh HyperCard™ program. It asks a series of questions concerning the nature of the tasks and sub-tasks identified in the analysis and takes the user through a relatively simple algorithm. The algorithm guides choices between using the actual equipment and using simulation or embedded training. In the case of simulation, the guide uses the analysis to choose between full mission and part task trainer and between high- and low-fidelity simulation. TEAS was intended as a simple aid to be used in the early stages of equipment procurement, but more elaborate systems were developed for military use in the USA, such as HARDMAN (HARDware and MANpower—Kaplan & Holman, 1989) or OSBATS (Optimization of Stimulus-BAsed Training Systems—Sticha et al., 1988), computer-based expert systems for specifying manning and training requirements for equipment already at an advanced stage of development.[5]

A similar approach was taken by the Royal Australian Air Force. Wallace and Northam (1998) describe a method for selecting flight simulation facilities based on an analysis for the tasks required by different crew members of a maritime patrol aircraft. Task hierarchies are described at whatever seems an appropriate level of granularity in order to identify the key sensory and perceptual cues (visual, vestibular, kinaesthetic, etc.) required for each task. The parameters that instructors need to control in training, such as difficulty level and student assessment and progress records, are related to the identified tasks and candidate training simulators assessed for the best available match to these two factors.

Variations on this general approach are now widely used where investment in training equipment is necessarily high. TTRAM (Task and Training Requirements Analysis Methodology—Swezey, Owens, Burgondy, & Salas, 1998) was designed to aid the identification of networked simulation requirements for teamwork-intensive tasks, especially those that are in need of protection from possible skill decay due to their infrequency. Task components are given a skill decay index rated by experts on difficulty, degree of prior learning, and frequency of performance. Training needs are then matched to appropriate training media by reference to a skill taxonomy of 16 different classes, ranging from simple detection through pattern recognition, procedure following, mission analysis (planning), and adapting to situational demands. Training media vary in terms of technical provision, including the degrees of difficulty of the supported tasks, fidelity of their representation, and the facilities (such as scoring, feedback, and debriefing) that are provided. The range of training media include use of the actual equipment, classroom demonstrations, whole and

---

[5] See Booher and Hewitt (1990) for a review of the tools available to the MANPRINT program.

part-task simulators, and network-supported simulation exercises. TTRAM draws eclectically on a wide range of basic and applied work in both team task analysis and training and is consequently a flexible rather than a precisely defined procedure.

Shepherd and Hinde (1989) suggest that formal methods for analysing training needs are often regarded by experts as a last resort since many contextual factors affect the choice of content, level, and training aids in any given situation. Experts in training design typically work by analogy, recognizing the type of task, the type of content, and the organizational context to draw on their previous experience of tasks with similar features to determine an appropriate training prescription. In sympathy with this alternative approach, Shepherd and Hinde (1989) constructed a model specifying the information required to determine which task and context prototype matched the new exemplar. A training need is established by reference to symptoms of unsatisfactory performance such as high reject rate, machine downtime, etc., and the training consultant conducts a dialogue with the user to reach a diagnosis and training solution. Both a computer implementation and a paper version were piloted with limited success but the Shepherd and Hinde's study usefully illustrates some of the difficulties in moving from task analysis via training needs analysis to training prescription in a systematic manner.

Methods of analysis and the design of training have been supported by a variety of theoretical approaches and empirical research findings. Training design is like international cooking, characterized by common general themes but varying with locally preferred ingredients. The studies reported in the literature use systematic, but not standard, methods of analysis and appeal to generally accepted psychological principles of learning without being tightly bound to specific theories. The advantages of basing training design on task analysis rather than custom or intuition include: assurance of a comprehensive specification of performance goals; the identification of critical skills and those aspects of the task presenting learning problems; a route to planning part-task training; the provision of an appropriate level of simulation; and the provision of student feedback and goal-related performance data.

VALIDITY, RELIABILITY, AND USABILITY

Task analysis methods are among the most commonly used tools available to the human factors specialist. Stanton and Young (1998, 1999) and Stanton and Stevenage (1998) have drawn attention to the relative paucity of evaluative studies producing data comparable to the measures of validity and reliability normally taken as essential for standardized psychometric tools. This view is confirmed in recent compendia of human factors and ergonomics methods (Booher & Hewitt, 1990; Diaper & Stanton, 2004; Hollnagel, 2003; O'Brien & Charlton, 1996; Wilson & Corlett, 1995, 2005). Only Stanton et al. (2005)

make a serious attempt to cite data on validity and reliability of the methods described but results of anything resembling a standardization study are rare and the few that are quoted are typically based on very small samples of both tasks and analyses. Similar conclusions were reported by Ainsworth and Marshall (1998) who reviewed nearly 100 task analyses, finding that the reported results varied considerably in quality due to two main factors: the inadequate specification of the purpose of the analysis and the varying levels of expertise of the analysts.

Annett (2002) suggested that the analogy between standardized psychometric tests and methods of analytical enquiry is not perfect. A distinction can be made between those methods designed, like psychometric tests, to measure a specified parameter and those aimed primarily at understanding the functional properties of a complex human–machine system. The purpose of the former is to measure characteristics of a given task such as workload, usability, comfort fatigue, and other variables. The latter include task analysis methods used as a design aid to specify equipment and manning requirements and establish training needs in future systems and for diagnosing sources of performance failure in existing systems. If we consider the various possible meanings of validity in these two cases, the evaluative and the analytic, differences can be clearly seen.

The Problem of Validity

The construct validity of a psychometric test depends on an estimate of 'how well the test results capture the hypothetical quality or trait it was designed to measure' (Reber, 1985). Thus a measure of the workload of a task must be underpinned by a well-articulated theory of workload and the results should correlate with other established tests of workload. In contrast, the construct validity of a task analysis must surely depend on how well it represents the task itself. Perhaps the most convincing demonstration of this kind of validity would be a computer model of the task, which behaves in the same way as the 'real' task. Although progress is being made in the construction of task models that can be run on a computer-simulating system (Kieras, 2004; Kieras & Meyer, 2000; Marken, 2003; Williams, 2000; Zachary et al., 2000) this is not yet a fully developed technology. A more practical view of the validity of a task analysis is whether it provides answers to the questions that prompted the analysis— for example, whether it identifies sources of performance failure or identifies training needs.

Militello and Hutton (1998) assessed the validity of a cognitive task analysis method (Applied Cognitive Task Analysis: ACTA) by checking the output against three criteria:

1. Do the results address cognitive issues?
2. Do the results deal with experience-based (as opposed to formal classroom-based) knowledge?
3. Is the instructional content accurate and necessary?

Two different tasks were used and the analysts and a dozen students received training in two versions of the method. Two experts applied the three criteria to the outputs and found acceptably—in some cases very—high agreement with the criteria. In other words the method did what it claimed to do in addressing the questions posed.

It is clear from the Ainsworth and Marshall (1998) survey that many task analyses, especially those carried out in the defence industries, are done as a matter of routine rather than for any specific purpose other than acting as a users' procedural guide. In this case accuracy and ease of use are the only meaningful way of evaluating the method. However, when the analysis is used as a diagnostic tool, and even as a source of hypotheses about how task needs and design shortcomings can be met, then the analogy with the *predictive validity* of a psychometric test appears to be reasonably close, but even here the analogy is not perfect. When task analysis is used in this way it would be normal for the task or equipment design to be modified to prevent the anticipated performance failure or for the analyst to recommend a particular training scheme. It would be virtually unprofessional to leave matters as they stand and wait for evidence of performance failure or the need for adequate training; indeed, the situation would be rather like evaluating a medical diagnosis by waiting to see how many untreated patients recovered spontaneously or died. Unlike a psychometric test aiming to measure a persistent trait, a task analysis is part of a process of deliberate change. Only when there is already a history of performance failure or of unsatisfactory training can the results obtained from a task analysis be shown to have some benefit, but such results tend to be anecdotal rather than statistical simply because most reported analyses constitute a single case study.

Reliability

Analytic methods typically have an empirical content derived either from direct observation, performance records or questionnaires or by interviewing experts. Each of these is open to error and bias since, unlike a standardized psychometric test, the questions are rarely pre-specified; nor are the responses subject to systematic scoring conventions. Nevertheless one would expect two analysts to produce highly similar results and recommendations when applying the same method to the same task. Baber and Stanton (1996) and Stanton and Baber (2002) report reliability coefficients ranging from 0.4 to 0.9 for two methods of error prediction based on hierarchical task analysis. In each case there was only one task and in both cases the number of analysts was small, 2 and 8 respectively. Reliability was higher with better-trained analysts, a result confirmed in a study by Patrick, Gregov, and Halliday (2000) and consistent with Ainsworth and Marshall's (1998) view that better-trained analysts produce higher quality analyses.

Militello and Hutton (1998) addressed the question of the reliability of ACTA in terms of consistency of the information specifying cognitive demands generated by different analysts. Consistency was generally high but given that the outputs are open-ended statements, judgements of the evaluators were nec-essarily subjective. This illustrates another difference between task analysis and psychometric methods. In the latter the questions posed to the individual being tested are highly standardized and responses scored in strict conformity with predetermined criteria, while in the former the actual questions are uncon-strained and the replies are necessarily subject to interpretation by the individ-ual analyst. With respect to both validity and reliability, the most that can be said is that analysts must be thorough in questioning and cross-questioning all available sources in order to obtain the best possible account of the task. Reli-ability depends principally on the care taken in data collection (Annett, 2005).

Usability

All proponents of particular task analysis methods aim for usability and often go to considerable lengths to explain how to use the method. At the same time it is clear that task analysis is a highly sophisticated procedure, demanding clar-ity of purpose, well-developed interpersonal skills, patience, and hard work. Extensive knowledge of human abilities and their limitations is undoubtedly helpful, but prior knowledge of the specific task is not always an advantage—the politely posed naïve question can often be useful. Many of the methods require training and supervised practice. Stanton and Young (1998) reported that a small sample of professional ergonomists estimated that of 11 different meth-ods including checklists, link analysis, and repertory grid, HTA required by far the most training and practice time to achieve proficiency. Some of the most so-phisticated computer-supported methods require specialist training in the use of specific software packages, some of which are available for purchase (Stuart, 2004) and others, such as ATLAS (Hamilton, 2000), are available only through the agency of the originator. Although some users, typically those in the defence industries, would like to treat task analysis as a more-or-less standard clerical procedure, there is no doubt that it more closely resembles the sophisticated set of diagnostic strategies used by medical and human factors consultants.

SUMMARY

Questions regarding the validity, reliability, and usability of task analysis meth-ods find no straightforward answers in the literature. Validity and reliability are open to different interpretations depending on the purpose of the analysis and the quality of the data collection process and, in practice, few published studies have been able to collect a sufficient sample of both tasks and analysts to justify conventional measures comparable to those expected of standardized psycho-metric procedures. The published methods tend to be statements of strategy rather than rigid procedures. A method such as HTA can, for example, be illustrated in a textbook by the task of operating a toaster (Shepherd, 2001) but can also be applied to the tasks of a military command and control team (Annett et al., 2000). The former takes a few minutes to understand while the latter may depend on weeks or even months of concentrated work to determine how well the team is functioning, what may lead to a dangerous malfunction, and how best to organize equipment, procedures, and training. Task analysis is still very much a craft rather than an industry.

CONCLUDING COMMENTS

Over the past century the nature of work has undergone considerable change, and methods of analysis have undergone extensive development. Work, and the tasks that must be performed in modern industry, are the product of a complex interplay between economic goals, human skills and learning abilities, and the opportunities offered by new technology. Task analysis methods attempt to unravel this complexity by analysing system interactions, often focusing on the cognitive dimension and structural complexity to produce a multifaceted representation of the system's performance potential. In the future, task analysis methods may be integrated with fully functional software support to produce compatible models of the human–technology interaction, including the distributed cognitive activity within the system. A foretaste of these developments can be seen in recent studies of computerized task models, briefly reviewed here, and in new approaches to the analysis of multi-person systems. Fully functional task models will support system and instructional design by providing valid diagnoses and functional specifications. The analysis of the functionality of multi-person systems may add a new dimension to the understanding of organizational problems of the socio-technical systems of the future.

ACKNOWLEDGEMENT

Professor Stanton's contribution to this work was undertaken as part of his role in the Human Factors Integration Defence Technology Centre, part funded by the Human Sciences Domain of the UK Ministry of Defence Scientific Research Programme.

REFERENCES

Ainsworth, L. & Marshall, E. (1998). Issues of quality and practicability in task analysis: Preliminary results from two surveys. *Ergonomics*, **41**, 1607–1617. [Reprinted in J. Annett & N. Stanton (Eds) (2000) *Task analysis* (pp. 79–89). London: Taylor & Francis.]
Anderson, J.R. (1980). *Cognitive psychology and its implications*. New York: Freeman.

Annett, J. (1959). Learning a pressure under conditions of immediate and delayed knowledge of results. *Quarterly Journal of Experimental Psychology*, **11**, 3–15.

Annett. J. (1991). *Guidelines on training requirements*. Interim report to the Army Personnel Research Establishment, D/ER1/9/4/2187/031/APRE.

Annett, J. (1996). On knowing how to do things: A theory of motor imagery. *Cognitive Brain Research*, **3**, 65–69.

Annett, J. (1997). Analysing team skills. In R. Flin, E. Salas, M. Strub, & L. Martin (Eds), *Decision making under stress: Emerging themes and applications* (pp. 315–325). Aldershot: Ashgate Publishing.

Annett, J. (2000). Theoretical and pragmatic influences on task analysis methods. In J.-M. Schraagen, S.F. Chipman, & V.L. Shalin (Eds), *Cognitive task analysis* (pp. 25–37). Mahwah, NJ: Lawrence Erlbaum.

Annett, J. (2002). A note on the validity and reliability of ergonomics methods. *Theoretical Issues in Ergonomics Science*, **3** , 229–232.

Annett, J. (2005). Hierarchical Task Analysis (HTA). In N.A. Stanton, A. Hedge, K. Brookhuis, E. Salas, & H. Hendrick (Eds), *Handbook of human factors and ergonomics methods*. Boca Raton: CRC Press.

Annett, J. & Cunningham, D. (2000). Analysing command team skills. In J.-M. Schraagen, S.F. Chipman, & V.L. Shalin (Eds), *Cognitive task analysis* (pp. 401–445). Mahwah, NJ: Lawrence Erlbaum.

Annett, J., Cunningham, D., & Mathias-Jones, P. (2000). A method for measuring team skills. *Ergonomics*, **43**, 1076–1094.

Annett, J. & Duncan, K.D. (1967). Task analysis and training design. *Occupational Psychology*, **41**, 211–221.

Annett, J., Duncan, K.D., Stammers, R.B., & Gray, M. (1971). *Task analysis*. Training Information Paper, Number 6. London: Her Majesty's Stationery Office.

Annett, J., Golby, C., & Kay, H. (1958). Measurement of elements in an assembly task: The information output of the human motor system. *Quarterly Journal of Experimental Psychology*, **10**, 1–11.

Annett, J. & Kay, H. (1956). Skilled performance. *Occupational Psychology*, **30**, 112–117.

Annett, J. & Kay, H. (1957). Knowledge of results and skilled performance. *Occupational Psychology*, **31**, 69–79.

Annett, J. & Stanton, N.A. (2000). *Task analysis*. London: Taylor & Francis.

Baber, C. (2005). Critical path analysis for multi-modal activity. In N. Stanton, A. Hedge, K. Brookhuis, E. Salas, & H. Hendrick (Eds), *Handbook of human factors and ergonomics methods* (pp. 41-1 to 41-8). Boca Raton: CRC Press.

Baber, C. & Stanton, N.A. (1994). Task analysis for error identification: A methodology for designing error-tolerant consumer products. *Ergonomics*, **37**, 1923–1941.

Baber, C. & Stanton, N.A. (1996). Observation as a technique for usability evaluations. In P. Jordan, B. Thomas, B. Weerdmaster, & I. McLelland (Eds), *Usability in industry* (pp. 85–94). London: Taylor & Francis.

Bass, A., Aspinal, J., Walter, G., & Stanton, N.A. (1995). A software toolkit for hierarchical task analysis. *Applied Ergonomics*, **26**, 147–151.

Bloom, B.S., Engelhart, M.D., Furst, E.J., Hill, W.H., & Krathwohl, D.R. (1956). *Taxonomy of educational objectives*. New York: Longmans Green.

Booher, H.R. (Ed.) (1990). *MANPRINT*. New York: Van Nostrand.

Booher, H.R. & Hewitt, G.M. (1990). MANPRINT tools and techniques. In H.R. Booher (Ed.), *MANPRINT* (pp. 343–390). New York: Van Nostrand.

Caddy, C.D. & Wachtel, J.A. (1992). Team skills training in nuclear power stations. In R.W. Swezey & E. Salas (Eds), *Teams: Their training and performance* (pp. 379–396). Norwood, NJ: Ablex.

Cannon-Bowers, J.A. & Salas, E. (Eds) (1998). *Making decisions under stress: Implications for individual and team training*. Washington, DC: American Psychological Association.

Card, S.K., Moran, T.P., & Newell, A. (1983). *The psychology of human–computer interaction*. Hillsdale, NJ: Lawrence Erlbaum.

Chapanis, A. (1959). *Research techniques in human engineering*. Baltimore: Johns Hopkins Press.

Chin, M., Sanderson, P., & Watson, M. (1999). Cognitive work analysis of the command and control work domain. *Proceedings of the 1999 Command and Control Research and Technology Symposium* (CCRTS), June 29–July 1, Newport, RI, USA, Vol. 1, pp. 233–248.

Diaper, D. & Stanton, N.A. (2004). *The handbook of task analysis for human–computer interaction*. Mahwah, NJ: Lawrence Erlbaum.

Drury, C., Paramore, B., Van Cott, H.P., Grey, S.M., & Corlett, E.N. (1987). Task analysis. In G. Salvendy (Ed.), *Handbook of human factors* (pp. 370–401). New York: John Wiley & Sons.

DuBois, D. & Shalin, V.L. (2000). Describing job expertise using cognitively-oriented task analysis. In J.-M. Schraagen, S.F. Chipman, & V.L. Shalin (Eds), *Cognitive task analysis* (pp. 41–56). Mahwah, NJ: Lawrence Erlbaum.

Duncan, K.D. (1972). Strategies for analysis of the task. In J.R. Hartley (Ed.), *Programmed instruction: An educational technology* (pp. 19–81). London: Butterworth.

Dwyer, D.J., Fowles, J.E., Oser, R.L., & Lane, N.E. (1997). Team performance measurement in distributed environments: The TARGETs methodology. In M.J. Brannick, E. Salas, & C. Prince (Eds), *Team performance assessment and measurement* (pp. 137–153). Mahwah, NJ: Lawrence Erlbaum.

Embrey, D.E. (1986). *SHERPA: A systematic human error reduction and prediction approach*. Paper presented at the International Meeting on Advances in Nuclear Power Systems, Knoxville, Tennessee

Essens, P., Post, W.M., & Rasker, P.C. (2000). Modeling a command center. In J.-M. Schraagen, S.F. Chipman, & V.L. Shalin (Eds), *Cognitive task analysis* (pp. 385–399). Mahwah, NJ: Lawrence Erlbaum.

Fewins, A., Mitchell, K., & Williams, J.C. (1992). Balancing automation and human action through task analysis. In B. Kirwan & E. Marshall (Eds), *A guide to task analysis* (pp. 241–251). London: Taylor & Francis.

Fitts, P.M. (1954). The information capacity of the human motor system in controlling the amplitude of movement. *Journal of Experimental Psychology*, 47, 381–391.

Fitts, P.M. & Jones, R.E. (1947). *Analysis of factors contributing to 460 'pilot error' experiences in operating aircraft controls*. Report TSEAA-694-12 Aero-medical Laboratory, USAF, Wright-Patterson AFB, Dayton, Ohio. [Reprinted in H.W. Sinaiko (Ed.), *Selected papers on human factors in the design and use of control systems* (pp. 332–358). New York: Dover Publications.]

Fitts, P.M. & Posner, M.I. (1967). *Human performance*. Belmont, CA: Brooks/Cole.

Flanagan, J.C. (1954). The critical incident technique. *Psychological Bulletin*, 51, 327–358.

Fleishman, E.A. & Quaintance, M.K. (1984). *Taxonomies of human performance*. New York: Academic Press.

Fleishman, E.A. & Zaccaro, S.J. (1992). Toward a taxonomy of team performance functions. In R.W. Swezey & E. Salas (Eds), *Teams: Their training and performance* (pp. 31–56). Norwood, NJ: Ablex.

Folley, J.D. (1964). *Guidelines for task analysis*. US Naval Training Device Center Technical Report NAVTRADEVCEN 1218-2.

Gagné, R.M. (1965). *The conditions of learning*. New York: Holt, Reinhart & Winston.

Gallagher, J.P. (1979). Cognitive/information-processing psychology and instruction. Reviewing recent theory and practice. *Instructional Science*, **8**, 393–414.

Gilbreth, F.B. (1911). *Motion study*. Princeton, NJ: Van Nostrand.

Hamilton, W.I. (2000). Cognitive task analysis using ATLAS. In J.-M. Schraagen, S.F. Chipman, & V.L. Shalin (Eds), *Cognitive task analysis* (pp. 215–236). Mahwah, NJ: Lawrence Erlbaum.

Hick, W.E. (1952). On the rate of gain of information. *Quarterly Journal of Experimental Psychology*, **4**, 11–26.

Hoffman, R. (1992). *The psychology of expertise*. New York: Springer-Verlag.

Hollnagel, E. (1998). *Cognitive reliability and error analysis method (CREAM)*. Oxford: Elsevier Science.

Hollnagel, E. (2003). *Handbook of cognitive task design*. Mahwah, NJ: Lawrence Erlbaum.

Kaplan, J.D. & Holman, C. (1989). *HARDMAN III Decision Support System*. Army Research Institute, Alexandria, Va.

Kieras, D. (2004). GOMS models for task analysis. In D. Diaper & N. Stanton (Eds), *Handbook of task analysis for human–computer interaction* (pp. 83–116). Mahwah, NJ: Lawrence Erlbaum.

Kieras, D. & Meyer, D. (2000). The role of cognitive task analysis in the application of predictive models of human performance. In J.-M. Schraagen, S.F. Chipman, & V.L. Shalin (Eds), *Cognitive task analysis* (pp. 237–260). Mahwah, NJ: Lawrence Erlbaum.

Kirwan, B. (1992). A task analysis programme for a large nuclear chemical plant. In B. Kirwan & L.K. Ainsworth (Eds), *A guide to task analysis* (pp. 363–388). London: Taylor & Francis.

Kirwan, B. (1994). *A guide to practical human reliability assessment*. London: Taylor & Francis.

Kirwan, B. (1998a). Human error identification techniques for risk assessment of high-risk systems—Part 1: Review and evaluation of techniques. *Applied Ergonomics*, **29**, 157–177.

Kirwan, B. (1998b). Human error identification techniques for risk assessment of high-risk systems—Part 2: Towards a framework approach. *Applied Ergonomics*, **29**, 299–318.

Kirwan, B. & Ainsworth, L.K. (1992). *A guide to task analysis*. London: Taylor & Francis.

Klein, G. (2000). Cognitive task analysis of teams. In J.-M. Schraagen, S.F. Chipman, & V.L. Shalin (Eds), *Cognitive task analysis* (pp. 417–429). Mahwah, NJ: Lawrence Erlbaum.

Klein, G.A., Calderwood, R., & MacGregor, D. (1989). Critical decision method for eliciting knowledge. *IEEE Transactions on Systems, Man and Cybernetics*, **19**, 462–472.

Klein, G., Schmitt, J., McClosky, M., Heaton, J., Klinger, D., & Wolf, S. (1996). *A decision-centred study of the regimental command post*. Fairborn, OH: Klein Associates.

Kletz, T. (1991). *An engineer's view of human error* (2nd edn). Rugby, UK: Institution of Chemical Engineers.

Latané, B., Williams, K., & Harkins, S. (1979). Many hands make light work: Causes and consequences of social loafing. *Journal of Personality and Social Psychology*, **37**, 822–833.

Laughery, K.R. (1984). Computer modeling of human performance on microcomputers. *Proceedings of the Annual Meeting of the Human Factors Society*, pp. 884–888.

Lim K.Y. & Long, J. (1994). *The MUSE method for usability engineering*. Cambridge: Cambridge University Press.

Marken, R. (2003). Error in skilled performance: A control model of prescribing. *Ergonomics*, **46**, 1200–1214.

Martens, R. & Petersen, J.A. (1971). Group cohesiveness as a determinant of success and member satisfaction in team performance. *International Review of Sport Sociology*, **6**, 49–61.

McGrath, J.E. & Hollingshead, A.B. (1994). *Groups interacting with technology*. Thousand Oaks, CA: Sage.

McLeod, R.W. & Sherwood-Jones, B.M. (1992). Simulation to predict operator workload in a command system. In B. Kirwan & L.K. Ainsworth (Eds), *A guide to task analysis* (pp. 301–310). London: Taylor & Francis.

Militello, L. & Hutton, R.J.B. (1998). Applied Cognitive Task Analysis (ACTA): A practitioner's toolkit for understanding cognitive task demands. *Ergonomics*, **41**, 1618–1641.

Miller, R.B. (1953a). *Handbook of training and training equipment design*. Wright Air Development Center Technical Report 53-136.

Miller, R.B. (1953b). *A method for man–machine task analysis*. Wright Air Development Center Technical Report 53-137.

Miller, R.B. (1962). Task description and analysis. In R.M. Gagné (Ed.), *Psychological principles in system development* (pp. 187–228). New York: Holt, Reinhart & Winston.

Morgan, C.T., Cook, J.S., Chapanis, A., & Lund, M.W. (1963). *Human engineering guide to equipment design*. New York: McGraw-Hill.

Newell, A. (1980). *Unified theories of cognition*. Cambridge, Mass.: Harvard University Press.

Norman, D.A. (1988). *The psychology of everyday things*. New York: Basic Books.

O'Brien, T.G. & Charlton, S.G. (1996). *Handbook of human factors testing and evaluation*. Mahwah, NJ: Lawrence Erlbaum.

O'Hare, D., Wiggins, M., Williams, A., & Wong, W. (1998). Cognitive task analyses for decision centred design and training. *Ergonomics*, **41**, 1698–1718. [Reprinted in J. Annett & N. Stanton (Eds) (2000), *Task analysis* (pp. 170–190). London: Taylor & Francis.]

Ormerod, T.C. (2000). Using task analysis as a primary design method: The SGT approach. In J.-M. Schraagen, S.F. Chipman, & V.L. Shalin (Eds), *Cognitive task analysis* (pp. 181–200). Mahwah, NJ: Lawrence Erlbaum.

Ormerod, T.C. & Shepherd, A. (2003). Using task analysis for information requirements specification: The sub-goal template (SGT) method. In D. Diaper & N. Stanton (Eds), *The handbook of task analysis for human–computer interaction* (pp. 347–366). Mahwah, NJ: Lawrence Erlbaum.

Paris, C.R., Salas, E., & Cannon-Bowers, J.A. (2000). Teamwork in multi-person systems: A review and analysis. *Ergonomics*, **41**, 1052–1075.

Patrick, J. (1991). Types of analysis for training. In J.E. Morrison (Ed.), *Training for performance: Principles of applied human learning* (pp. 127–166). Chichester: John Wiley & Sons.

Patrick, J. (1992). *Training: Research and practice*. London: Academic Press.

Patrick, J., Gregov, A., & Halliday, P. (2000). Analysing and training task analysis. *Instructional Science*, **28**, 51–79.

Pendelbury, G. & Ainsworth, L.K. (1992). Task analysis of operator safety actions. In B. Kirwan & L.K. Ainsworth (Eds), *A guide to task analysis* (pp. 311–326). London: Taylor & Francis.

Pennington, J. (1992). A preliminary communications systems assessment. In B. Kirwan & L.K. Ainsworth (Eds), *A guide to task analysis* (pp. 253–265). London: Taylor & Francis.

Pennington, J., Joy, M., & Kirwan, B. (1992). A staffing assessment for a local control room. In B. Kirwan & L.K. Ainsworth (Eds), *A guide to task analysis* (pp. 289–299). London: Taylor & Francis.

Reason, J. (1990). *Human error.* Cambridge: Cambridge University Press.

Reber, A.S. (1985). *The Penguin dictionary of psychology.* Harmondsworth: Penguin.

Redding, R.E. (1989). Perspectives on cognitive task-analysis: The state of the state of the art. *Proceedings of the Human Factors Society*, **33**, 1353–1357. Santa Monica, CA: Human Factors Society.

Reed, J. (1992). A plant local panel review. In B. Kirwan & L.K. Ainsworth (Eds), *A guide to task analysis* (pp. 267–288). London: Taylor & Francis.

Richardson, J., Ormerod, T.C., & Shepherd, A. (1998). The role of task analysis in capturing requirements for interface design. *Interacting with Computers*, **9**, 367–384.

Rothkopf, E.Z. (1986). Cognitive science applications to human resource problems. *Advances in Reading/Language Research*, **4**, 283–289.

Rycraft, H., Brown, F., & Leckey, N. (1992). Operational safety review of a solid waste storage plant. In B. Kirwan & L.K. Ainsworth (Eds), *A guide to task analysis* (pp. 355–362). London: Taylor & Francis.

Scandura, J.M. (1982). Structural (cognitive task) analysis: A method for analysing content. 1. Background and empirical research. *Journal of Structural Learning*, **7**, 101–114.

Schaafstal, A. & Schraagen, J.-M. (2000). Training of troubleshooting: A structured, task analytical approach. In J.-M. Schraagen, S.F. Chipman, & V.L. Shalin (Eds), *Cognitive task analysis* (pp. 57–71). Hillsdale, NJ: Lawrence Erlbaum.

Schneider, W. & Shiffrin, R.M. (1977). Controlled and automatic information processing: 1. Detection, search and attention. *Psychological Review*, **84**, 1–66.

Schraagen, J.-M., Chipman, S.F., & Shalin, V.L. (Eds) (2000). *Cognitive task analysis.* Mahwah, NJ:. Lawrence Erlbaum.

Seamster, T.L., Redding, R.E., & Kaempf, G.L. (2000). A skill-based cognitive task analysis framework. In J.-M. Schraagen, S.F. Chipman, & V.L. Shalin (Eds), *Cognitive task analysis* (pp. 135–146). Hillsdale, NJ: Lawrence Erlbaum.

Seymour, W.D. (1954). *Industrial training for manual operations.* London: Pitman.

Seymour, W.D. (1968). *Skills analysis training.* London: Pitman.

Shepherd, A. (1989). Analysis and training in information technology tasks. In D. Diaper (Ed.), *Task analysis for human–computer interaction* (pp. 15–55). Chichester: Ellis Horwood.

Shepherd, A. (1992). Maintenance training. In B. Kirwan & L.K. Ainsworth (Eds), *A guide to task analysis* (pp. 327–339). London: Taylor & Francis.

Shepherd, A. (2001). *Hierarchical task analysis.* London: Taylor & Francis.

Shepherd, A. & Hinde, C.J. (1989). Mimicking the training expert: A basis for automating training needs analysis. In L. Bainbridge & S.A.R. Quintanilla (Eds), *Developing skills with information technology* (pp. 153–175). Chichester: John Wiley & Sons.

Shorrock, S.T. & Kirwan, B. (2002). Development and application of a human error identification tool for air traffic control. *Applied Ergonomics*, **33**, 319–336.

Spector, P.E., Brannick, M.T., & Coovert, M.D. (1989). Job analysis. In C.L. Cooper & I.T. Robertson (Eds), *International review of industrial and organizational psychology* (pp. 281–328). Chichester: John Wiley & Sons.

Stanton, N.A. (in press). Hierarchical task analysis: Developments, applications and extensions. *Applied Ergonomics.*

Stanton, N.A. & Annett, J. (2000). Future directions for task analysis. In J. Annett & N.A. Stanton (Eds), *Task analysis* (pp. 229–234). London: Taylor & Francis.

Stanton, N.A. & Baber, C. (2002). Error by design: Methods to predict device usability. *Design Studies*, **23**, 363–384.

Stanton, N.A. & Baber, C. (2005). Task analysis for error identification. In N.A. Stanton, A. Hedge, K. Brookhuis, E.Salas, & H. Hendrick (Eds), *Handbook of human factors methods* (pp. 38-1 to 38-9). Boca Raton: CRC Press.

Stanton, N.A., Hedge, A., Brookhuis, K., Salas, E., & Hendrick, H. (Eds) (2005). *Handbook of human factors methods*. Boca Raton: CRC Press.

Stanton, N.A. & Stevenage, S.V. (1998). Learning to predict human error: Issues of acceptability, reliability and validity. *Ergonomics*, **41**, 1737–1756.

Stanton, N.A. & Young, M.S. (1998). Is utility in the mind of the beholder? A review of ergonomics methods. *Applied Ergonomics*, **29**, 41–54.

Stanton, N.A. & Young, M.S. (1999). *A guide to methodology in ergonomics*. London: Taylor & Francis.

Staples, L.J. (1993). The task analysis process for a new reactor. *Proceedings of the Human Factors and Ergonomics Society 37th Annual Meeting—Designing for Diversity*. Seattle, Washington, October 11–15, 1993 (pp. 1024–1028). Santa Monica, CA: The Human Factors and Ergonomics Society.

Steiner, I.D. (1972). *Group process and productivity*. New York: Academic Press.

Sticha, P.J., Blacksten, H.R., Buede, D.M., Singer, M.J., Gilligan, E.L., Mumaw, R.J. et al. (1988). *Optimisation of simulation-based training systems: Model description, implementation and evaluation*. HumRRO FR-PRD-88-26.

Stuart, J. (2004). Taking the work out of task analysis. *The Ergonomist*, September 2004, p. 3.

Swain, A.D. & Guttman, H.E. (1983). *Handbook on human reliability analysis with emphasis on nuclear power plant applications*. Sandia National Laboratories, NM: NUREG/CR 1278, US-NRC.

Swezey, R.W., Owens, J.M., Burgondy, M.L., & Salas, E. (1998). Task and training requirements analysis methodology (TTRAM): An analytic methodology for identifying potential training uses of simulator networks in team-intensive task environments. *Ergonomics*, **41**, 1678–1697. [Reprinted in J. Annett & N. Stanton (Eds) (2000). *Task analysis* (pp. 150–169). London: Taylor & Francis.]

Taylor, F.W. (1911). *Principles of scientific management*. New York: Harper & Row.

Wallace, P. & Northam, G. (1998). A training task analysis. *Military Simulation and Training*, Pt 4, pp. 11–19.

Wickens, C.D. (1992). *Engineering psychology and human performance*. New York: Harper Collins.

Williams, J.C. (1992). A method for quantifying ultrasonic inspection of effectiveness. In B. Kirwan & L.K. Ainsworth (Eds), *A guide to task analysis* (pp. 341–353). London: Taylor & Francis.

Williams, K.E. (2000). An automated aid for modeling human–computer interaction. In J.-M. Schraagen, S.F. Chipman, & V.L. Shalin (Eds), *Cognitive task analysis* (pp. 165–180). Mahwah, NJ: Lawrence Erlbaum.

Williams, K.E. & Pierce, K.A. (1999). Designing human/virtual technology interaction for training effectiveness: A cognitive task modelling approach. In E. Salas (Ed.), *Human–technology interaction in complex systems*, Vol. 9, pp. 31–86.

Wilson, J.R. (1995). A framework and context for ergonomics methodology. In J.R. Wilson & E.N. Corlett (Eds), *Evaluation of human work* (2nd edn, pp. 1–39). London: Taylor & Francis.

Wilson, J.R. (2005). Methods in the understanding of human factors. In J.R. Wilson & N. Corlett (Eds), *Evaluation of human work* (3rd edn, pp. 1–31). London: Taylor & Francis.

Wilson, J.R. & Corlett, E.N. (1995). *Evaluation of human work* (2nd edn). London: Taylor & Francis.

Wilson, J.R. & Corlett, E.N. (2005). *Evaluation of human work* (3rd edn). London: Taylor & Francis.
Zachary, W.W., Ryder, J.M., & Hincinbotham, J.H. (1998). Cognitive task analysis and modeling of decision making in complex environments. In J.A. Cannon-Bowers & E. Salas (Eds), *Making decisions under stress: Implications for individual and team training* (pp. 315–344). Washington, DC: American Psychological Association.
Zachary, W.W., Ryder, J.M., & Hincinbotham, J.H. (2000). Building cognitive task analyses and models of a decision-making team in a complex real-time environment. In J.-M. Schraagen, S.F. Chipman & V.L. Shalin (Eds), *Cognitive task analysis* (pp. 365–385). Mahwah, NJ: Lawrence Erlbaum.
Zajonc, R.B. (1965). Social facilitation. *Science*, **149**, 269–274.

Chapter 3

UNCOVERING WORKPLACE INTERPERSONAL SKILLS: A REVIEW, FRAMEWORK, AND RESEARCH AGENDA

Cameron Klein, Renée E. DeRouin, and Eduardo Salas
Department of Psychology and Institute for Simulation and Training, University of Central Florida

Many of the most memorable and important moments of our working lives involve social interactions. Through these interactions, we gain knowledge of ourselves, other individuals, our organizations, and the world. The success of these interactions depends largely on the proper use of our interpersonal skills (IPS). In fact, these skills are widely considered to be essential components of workplace success. Consider a 1979 survey in which members of the American Society for Training and Development (ASTD) were asked to report what they believed to be the most important skills or knowledge requirements for success as a professional (Clement, Walker, & Pinto, 1979). Over 35% indicated human relations skills, with the next largest group of respondents (25.4%) citing the importance of communication skills (Clement et al., 1979). A more recent survey by ASTD supported these results; over one-third of the respondents in this survey reported that communication or interpersonal relationship skills were the most important qualities in a good boss (ASTD, 2000).

Training and development professionals are not the only ones who need good IPS—interns and job seekers do too! For instance, a recent survey of 100 Society for Industrial and Organizational Psychology practitioners suggested that teamwork and IPS are the most important skill areas for interns to have (Munson, Phillips, Clark, & Mueller-Hanson, 2004). US Marines also need to learn people skills and are receiving training to improve their social skills before going to Iraq for peace-keeping duties (Phillips, 2004). In fact, IPS are essential in virtually every field of endeavor—they are important in health care (McConnell, 2004), accounting (Messmer, 2001), entrepreneurship and sales

International Review of Industrial and Organizational Psychology, 2006, Volume 21
Edited by G.P. Hodgkinson and J.K. Ford. © 2006 John Wiley & Sons, Ltd.

(Baron & Markman, 2000; Garavan, 1997; Sojka & Deeter-Schmelz, 2002), management (Kilduff & Day, 1994; Wayne, Liden, Graf, & Ferris, 1997), and the military (DiGiambattista, 2003; Phillips, 2004; Russell, Crafts, & Brooks, 1995). Social skills also have documented relationships to important outcomes, including task performance, job dedication, interpersonal facilitation, and overall performance (Ferris, Witt, & Hochwarter, 2001). Taken together, this vast and pervasive support demonstrates the value of good IPS in the workplace. Possessing a high level of IPS is an important workplace competency, and one that is critical for work success (Secretary's Commission on Achieving Necessary Skills, 1991).

The purpose of this chapter is to review the extant literature on IPS. First, we describe the current workplace environmental conditions that foster the need for strong IPS and offer a definition of IPS in organizational settings. Next, we introduce an organizing framework for understanding what contributes to good IPS performance, along with a preliminary taxonomy that together serve to outline the remainder of the chapter. We then highlight individual components of the framework, including antecedent conditions for interpersonal interactions (e.g., previous experience, individual differences), situational characteristics of interaction episodes (e.g., environmental settings, individual goals, motivation), and the perceptual/cognitive filtering processes inherent in IPS performance. Following our discussion of these factors, we direct our attention to some of the most common IPS portrayed in the literature. We conclude with a brief discussion of the techniques used to develop IPS and offer several important future research directions.

IPS IN THE WORKPLACE

Current Workplace Conditions that Necessitate Good IPS

In today's service-oriented and information-focused marketplace, IPS are critical. Simply put, people, now more than ever, spend a significant amount of their working day relating to and interacting with others. Employees are expected to possess the personality traits and people skills that will enable them to work well in teams (McIntyre & Salas, 1995), provide superior customer service (Schneider & Bowen, 1995), and engage in behaviors that help coworkers to accomplish organizational goals (Borman & Motowidlo, 1993). Because people enter the work context with different personalities and experiences, a premium has been placed on individuals who are able to navigate the interpersonal milieu that characterizes this dynamic work environment.

It is widely recognized that, as the service industry evolves, there will be an increasingly greater need for individuals who are able to maximize people-to-people interactions for the good of the organization. In fact, there is evidence to suggest that both decisions to continue purchasing goods and services (Oliva & Lancioni, 1996) and customer satisfaction (Humphreys, 1996) are

impacted by the IPS of service providers. Further, the continued advancement of team-based management and self-directed work teams as alternatives
to traditional, hierarchical structures requires that individuals be able to communicate and collaborate effectively with other employees (Ferris, Perrewé,
Anthony, & Gilmore, 2000; Messmer, 1999).

Definition of IPS

While most people believe they know what good and poor social skills are, it is
much harder to define them adequately. Many reviews, articles, and books addressing interpersonal and social skills have been published (e.g., Bishop, 1997;
Boyatzis, 1982; Carpenter & Wisecarver, 2004; Clark et al., 1985; de Janasz,
Dowd, & Schneider, 2002; DuBrin, 1997; Hayes, 1994, 2002; Hogan & Lock,
1995; Lewis, 1973; O'Conner, 2003; Porras & Anderson, 1981; Robbins &
Hunsaker, 1996).

In general, IPS may be described as the skills employed when persons interact with one another. The IPS label is really an umbrella term that refers
to a wide variety of concepts and associated terms, such as social skills, social
competence, people skills, face-to-face skills, human skills, and soft skills. In
fact, these terms are often used interchangeably. Although the labels applied to
these skills vary, it is clear that many of the basic concepts overlap around issues
of effective communication, interacting and managing relationships with others, and correctly interpreting social situations. Consolidating these ideas, we
define IPS as: *goal-directed behaviors, including communication and relationship-
building competencies, employed in interpersonal interaction episodes characterized
by complex perceptual and cognitive processes, dynamic verbal and nonverbal interaction exchanges, diverse roles, motivations, and expectancies.* These behaviors can
be employed in both face-to-face and computer-mediated interactions and are
important for individuals at all organizational levels. Additionally, it is important to note that IPS are situation specific; that is, they may be appropriate in
one situation and inappropriate in another. It is both the ability to enact these
behaviors and the success at interpreting and understanding the behaviors of
others that forms the basis of IPS.

Having reviewed the workplace conditions that necessitate IPS and provided
a definition of IPS, we are now ready to present both a framework of IPS performance and a comprehensive taxonomy of the specific skills. These additions
represent an important contribution to the diverse and often fragmented literature on the topic of IPS.

A FRAMEWORK OF IPS PERFORMANCE

The constructs (i.e., antecedents, situational characteristics, specific IPS, and
outcomes) described in this chapter are depicted graphically in Figure 3.1 in
the form of an organizing framework. This framework is meant to guide future

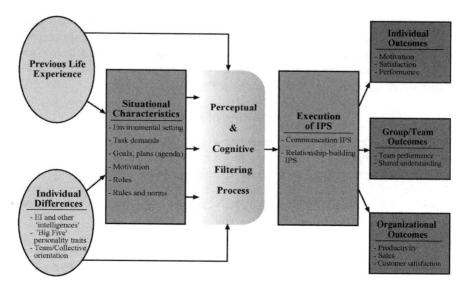

Figure 3.1   Framework of interpersonal skills (IPS) performance

research on IPS as well as some human resource (HR) applications such as training. It is not offered as a testable model; it is a practical heuristic that, we hope, in time will turn into a precise, robust, and testable model of what contributes to IPS. While predominantly theoretical (its basis in cognitive theory), a number of recent findings from fields as diverse as personality, customer service, teamwork, and management provide it with practical appeal. In short, this framework depicts how antecedent variables (including previous life experience and individual differences), together with facets of interpersonal interactions, contribute to the perceptual and cognitive activity that takes place in any interaction. From these interaction episodes and their associated perceptual and cognitive activity, individuals portray, to a greater or lesser degree of success, specific IPS. As discussed periodically throughout this chapter, these skills have documented relationships with several important individual, group/team, and organizational outcomes.

A NEW TAXONOMY OF IPS

Although the surveys and reviews we noted above indicate the significance of good IPS in the workplace, current models of job performance (e.g., Borman & Motowidlo, 1993; Campbell, McCloy, Oppler, & Sager, 1993) fail to provide a comprehensive (and deeper) picture of the interpersonal requirements of jobs. As part of our larger framework, we will review and discuss 12 specific IPS and classify them under two overarching themes (i.e., interpersonal communication skills, relationship-building skills).

Any time one is trying to classify objects, one must be cognizant of the purpose for doing so. According to Fleishman and Quaintance (1984), the primary purpose of scientific classification is to describe the structure and relationships among similar objects in terms that afford general statements about classes of objects. Additional objectives include the definition of essential object properties, generation of hypotheses, and provision of a terminology that facilitates organization, understanding, and communication (Fleishman & Quaintance, 1984). It is generally the last purpose for which we have labored—to provide a terminology and organizing framework that facilitates organization, understanding, and discussion of important workplace IPS. The skills included in this review were chosen for two reasons. First, the wide applicability to interpersonal interactions that occur on the job makes their logical organization under the rubric of workplace interpersonal skills a useful endeavor. Second, although most IPS frameworks include skills listed in this review, the majority of them are not as comprehensive.

A comprehensive taxonomy of workplace IPS can serve a number of purposes, including job analysis and description, performance appraisal, skills assessment, skill training, personnel selection, personnel placement, group and team staffing, and supervisory appraisal and development (Hogan & Lock, 1995). Further, we agree with Hogan and Lock (1995), who maintain that we need a common language for describing the array of workplace IPS. To develop their taxonomy of social skills, Hogan and Lock employed a critical incident methodology and obtained 600 incidents of exceptional IPS in the workplace from working adults across a range of industries. From these 600 incidents, seven dimensions of interpersonal performance emerged. The two most frequently identified themes were 'sensitivity to others' and 'responsibility and accountability.' A subsequent analysis of these themes indicated that the interpersonal dimensions were not independent of each other; in fact, in most of these incidents more than one interpersonal dimension was operating (Hogan & Lock, 1995).

A second attempt at creating a taxonomy of IPS was carried out by Carpenter and Wisecarver (2004). These authors conducted an extensive literature review of the interpersonal performance behaviors required for Special Forces Soldiers and completed two studies which helped to validate their proposed taxonomy. In the first study, empirical evidence for the taxonomy was obtained using a content analysis of over 1000 critical incidents previously collected from US Army Special Forces Soldiers. Over 30% of the obtained critical incidents of job performance contained examples of interpersonal performance, indicating that interpersonal performance is an important aspect of work for Special Forces Soldiers. The proposed taxonomy was supported in the second study by a confirmatory factor analysis. Moreover, the findings suggested that interpersonal performance is multidimensional in nature.

These taxonomies represent a firm foundation, and many of the components therein should be included in any review of IPS. However, we feel that the classification scheme offered in the present chapter is more comprehensive and descriptive of the wide range of interpersonal behavior that takes place in organizations. Further, we suggest that the framework and taxonomy presented here will enable researchers to begin to use a common terminology to discuss and investigate IPS. Widespread use of such an organizing framework will facilitate the accumulation of meaningful empirical findings and direct research to understudied areas.

We present our taxonomy in Table 3.1, which provides a comprehensive accounting of the IPS that are reviewed in this paper, along with subcategories of these skills and sources for finding more information on each. In short, an examination of 12 critical IPS is organized into two major sections: (1) interpersonal communication skills, and (2) relationship-building skills.

In order to determine which of these particular skills to include in our review, we performed an extensive content sampling of the available literature, including articles, book chapters, websites, and other sources for taxonomies, lists, and frameworks of IPS. At the time this literature review was conducted, we found 58 distinct and original sources presenting IPS frameworks or lists. Each of these sources typically listed multiple IPS, so the total number of skills discussed in these frameworks numbered well over 400. In order to simplify and organize this information, we counted the cumulative number of times each skill (and sub- or related skill) was mentioned. Using the most commonly applied labels for each, we were able to identify 12 skills that, together, represent a comprehensive index of IPS found in the workplace. Each of the 12 IPS was found at least 10 times in the literature, within the available IPS frameworks. As more books, articles, chapters, and practitioner resources are published, inevitably these skills will surface again.

In our review, communication skills were far and away the most frequently mentioned. Variations of these skills were mentioned 78 times within the 58 sources—clearly indicating that a number of sources listed more than one communication skill in their framework. Communication skills were followed in frequency by conflict resolution and negotiation, which were mentioned at least 37 times in discussions of IPS frameworks. In short, we believe the framework presented here is sufficient to describe the myriad of IPS in the workplace. Further, as the total number of skills presented in these frameworks numbered well over 400, we suggest that their integration and reduction down to 12 common skills is a useful and much-needed endeavor.

The ability to know when and how to employ particular IPS is influenced by many factors, two of which are discussed in the next section and are considered to be main ingredients or antecedent conditions of IPS, and include previous life experience and individual differences. The concept of previous life experience is conceptualized here as the totality of one's interactions with others over the course of a lifetime. The discussion of individual differences centers on theories of multiple intelligence (including emotional intelligence), personality traits, and team/collective orientation. This discussion is germane

Table 3.1 Interpersonal skills (IPS) taxonomy

Interpersonal skills	Description	Related skill(s)	Source(s)
Communication skills			
Active listening	Paying close attention to what is being said, asking the other party to explain exactly what he or she means, and requesting that ambiguous ideas or statements are repeated	Listening with empathy and sympathy; listening for understanding	de Janasz et al. (2002); DuBrin (1997); Hayes (1994); Guilar (2001); O'Conner (2003); Robbins & Hunsaker (1996); Rogers & Farson (1976)
Oral communication	Sending verbal messages constructively	Enunciating; expressing yourself clearly; communicating emotion; interpersonal communication	Bigelow (1995); de Janasz et al. (2002); DeVito (1999); DuBrin (1997); Hogan & Lock (1995); Rapisarda (2002); Stevens & Campion (1999); Sullivan (1993)
Written communication	Writing clearly and appropriately	Clarity; communicating intended meaning	de Janasz et al. (2002); DuBrin (1997); Sullivan (1993)
Assertive communication	Directly expressing one's feelings, preferences, needs, and opinions in a way that is neither threatening nor punishing to another person	Proposing ideas; social assertiveness; defense of rights; directive; asserting your needs	de Janasz et al. (2002); DuBrin (1997); Guilar (2001); Lorr, Youniss, & Stefic (1991); O'Conner (2003); Silberman (2001); Smith-Jentsch, Salas, & Baker (1996); Sullivan (1993)
Nonverbal communication	Reinforcing or replacing spoken communication through the use of body language, gestures, voice, or artifacts	Expression of feelings; perception/recognition of feelings; facial regard	DeVito (1999); DuBrin (1997); Gifford, Ng, & Wilkinson (1985); Hayes (1994); O'Conner (2003); Stevens & Campion (1999); Yancey, Clarkson, Baxa, & Clarkson (2003)

(Continued)

Table 3.1 (*Continued*)

Interpersonal skills	Description	Related skill(s)	Source(s)
Relationship-building skills			
Cooperation and coordination	Understanding and working with others in groups or teams; includes offering help to those who need it and pacing activities to fit the needs of the team	Adaptability; shared situational awareness; performance monitoring and feedback; interpersonal relations; communication; decision making; cohesion; group problem solving; being a team player	Cannon-Bowers, Tannenbaum, Salas, & Volpe (1995); de Janasz et al. (2002); DuBrin (1997); Fleishman (1953); Hayes (1994); O'Conner (2003); Robbins & Hunsaker (1996); Salas, Sims, & Burke (in press); Salas, Sims, & Klein (2004); Silberman (2001)
Trust	An individual's faith or belief in the integrity or reliability of another person or thing; willingness of a party to be vulnerable to the actions of another party based on the expectation that certain actions important to the trustor will be performed	Self-awareness; self-disclosure; swift trust	de Janasz et al. (2002); Hogan & Lock (1995); Mayer, Davis, & Schoorman (1995)
Intercultural sensitivity	Appreciating individual differences among people	Acceptance; openness to new ideas; sensitivity to others; cross-cultural relations	Bhawuk & Triandis (1996); de Janasz et al. (2002); DuBrin (1997); Hogan & Lock (1995); Triandis (1989, 1995)
Service orientation	A set of basic individual predispositions and an inclination to provide service, to be courteous and helpful in dealing with customers, clients, and associates	Exceeding customer's expectations; customer satisfaction skills; ability to maintain positive client relationship; selling; building rapport; representing the organization to customers and the public	Borman & Brush (1993); Cran (1994); Garavan (1997); Jiang, Klein, Van Slyke, & Cheney (2003); Parasuraman, Zeithaml, & Berry (1985)

Self-presentation	Process by which individuals attempt to influence the reactions and images people have of them and their ideas; managing these impressions encompasses a wide range of behaviors designed to create a positive influence on work associates	Self-expression; face-saving and impression management; managing perceptions; self-promotion	Baron & Markman (2000); Baumeister (1982, 1989); de Janasz et al. (2002); DuBrin (1997); Goffman (1955, 1959)
Social influence	Guiding people toward the adoption of specific behaviors, beliefs, or attitudes; influencing the distribution of advantages and disadvantages within an organization through one's actions	Business etiquette; reasoning; friendliness; coalition building; bargaining; appeals to higher authority; imposing sanctions; networking; persuasion, positive political skills	Baron & Markman (2000); Bigelow (1995); de Janasz et al. (2002); DuBrin (1997); Farrell & Petersen (1982); Giacalone & Rosenfield (1989); Girodo (1998); Hayes (1994); Jiang et al. (2003); Robbins & Hunsaker (1996); Silberman (2001); Rapisarda (2002)
Conflict resolution and negotiation	Advocating one's position with an open mind, not taking personally other members' disagreements, putting oneself in the other's shoes, following rational argument and avoiding premature evaluation, and trying to synthesize the best ideas from all viewpoints and perspectives	Conflict-handling style; conflict management; conflict prevention; compromising; problem solving; integrative bargaining; principled negotiation; cultural negotiation; mediation	Adair, Okumura, & Brett (2001); Bigelow (1995); Bordone (2000); Borman & Brush (1993); de Janasz et al. (2002); DuBrin (1997); Fisher, Ury, & Patton (1991); Gist & Stevens (1998); Guilar (2001); Hayes (1994); O'Conner (2003); Pruitt (1981); Rapisarda (2002); Robbins & Hunsaker (1996); Silberman (2001); Stevens & Campion (1999); Tinsley (2001); Wilson, Cai, Campbell, Donohue, & Drake (1995); Yancey et al. (2003)

to the story for two reasons: (1) these individual difference variables are often discussed in the same context as IPS, and (2) they are regularly mistaken for IPS, especially in the popular literature.

ANTECEDENTS OF IPS

Previous Life Experience

Humans are social creatures from birth, early in life seeking to communicate with others through eye contact, touch, smiles, and eventually by verbal systems. As children advance through clearly defined stages of psychosocial development (cf. Erikson, 1963), they develop the foundations of what will comprise their workplace IPS. From their initial social interactions with parents, siblings, and friends, they learn what constitutes acceptable behavior. The more contact with others, the better, it seems, when it comes to developing IPS. In fact, one recent nationally representative study of more than 20,000 kindergarteners indicated that children with siblings consistently exhibited better social and IPS (as rated by teachers who assessed the quality of students' interactions with others and the ability to control anger) than children without siblings (Miller, 2004).

As children grow older, this learning continues, much of it depending purely upon opportunity (Fontana, 1990). No doubt, by the time they have reached adulthood, they have participated in a countless number and variety of interpersonal interactions. These experiences include both family/peer relationships and work experience, the latter of which requires the frequent development of new relationships, new expectations, and new demands. Exposure to more complex social situations at work (e.g., managing subordinates, clients, vendors) enhances the development of effective interpersonal relationship-building strategies. In the end, the totality of each individual's life experience prepares him or her (to a greater or lesser extent) for future interaction episodes.

Individual Differences

A number of individual difference variables have been proposed to impact the proper use of IPS. These individual difference variables include elaborations on the ideas of social intelligence, emotional intelligence (EI), personality traits (e.g., the 'Big Five'), and team/collective orientation. The importance of these individual differences results from the fact that they can strongly influence the nature of interpersonal relations in work settings (cf. Baron, 1996).

Theories of 'multiple intelligence'

From a theoretical standpoint, the concept of IPS is not new. Many trace the concept of both EI and IPS to E.L. Thorndike's (1920) discussion of *social intelligence*. Actually, Thorndike (1920) discussed three modes of intelligence

—abstract, mechanical, and social. This reference, from the popular but unscientific *Harper's Magazine*, is often considered to be the first discussion of the importance of social skills, and led to 'spotty interest in the development of measures of social intelligence but little serious research on the construct per se' (Landy, 2005, p. 413). However, this connection may be weaker than many supposed, as Thorndike's son, R.L., the eminent psychometrician, later concluded that social intelligence can be largely explained by two already existing constructs—abstract intelligence and interest in people (Thorndike & Stein, 1937). E.L. Thorndike did, nevertheless, use the term 'social intelligence' to inform the lay public that g, or general cognitive ability, is multifaceted. He was not necessarily calling for a new 'type' of intelligence but rather cautioning against using narrowly construed measures of intelligence (Landy, 2005). Accordingly, it should not come as a surprise that traditional and contemporary measures of intelligence fall short in assessing interpersonal competencies, or social skills. Specifically, social abilities relating to social adaptation and problem solving are widely acknowledged as important domains not addressed in traditional intelligence tests (Snyderman & Rothman, 1987).

Although we still lack an integrated framework for identifying multiple intelligence (Riggio & Pirozzolo, 2002), the influence of Thorndike continues. There are at least two well-known frameworks for identifying multiple intelligences— Sternberg's Triarchic Theory of Intelligence (Sternberg, 1985) and Gardner's Multiple Intelligences Theory (Gardner, 1983, 1999). In fact, the more recent impetus for examining IPS largely ensued from Gardner's (1983) book, *Frames of Mind: The Theory of Multiple Intelligences*. In this book, Gardner described *personal intelligence* as the ability to manage our inner feelings and our ability to work well with others. Building from this, Marlowe (1986) described *social intelligence* as 'the ability to understand the feelings, thoughts, and behaviors of persons, including oneself, in interpersonal situations and to act appropriately upon that understanding' (p. 52). Social intelligence provides people with the readiness necessary for the events of social life and includes both declarative knowledge (concepts and memories of events) and procedural expertise (rules that operate on concepts and memories) for working on social tasks (Cantor & Kihlstrom, 1987).

Other terms relating to social intelligence that appear in the literature include 'interpersonal acumen' (Aditya & House, 2002) and 'social competence' (Schneider, Ackerman, & Kanfer, 1996). Aditya and House (2002) described interpersonal acumen as the ability to read the underlying intentions and motivations in others' behavior. This construct addresses a fundamental aspect of social intelligence—the ability to decipher underlying motives in other people's behavior. Social competence, likewise, is defined as socially effective behavior that allows people to achieve social goals (Schneider et al., 1996; Schneider, Roberts, & Heggestad, 2002).

It is clear that early studies and theories on social intelligence have paved the way for future discussions of social skills and other forms of social effectiveness

(Ferris, Perrewé, & Douglas, 2002). For example, authors such as Witt and Ferris (2003) now view social skill as the ability to effectively read, understand, and control social interactions. Similarly, Riggio (1986) described social skill in terms of learned social abilities and strategies for interpersonal interaction.

Social skill typically concerns translating interpersonal aspirations into actions; having this skill allows one to achieve his or her interpersonal goals just as strength and hand–eye coordination allow one to hit a golf ball far and straight. In this sense, social skill has been described as a moderator variable that translates peoples' intentions into observer evaluations. In line with social intelligence and competence, social skill allows individuals to successfully translate goals and intentions into effective social behaviors that will be perceived by observers.

Emotional intelligence (EI)

The construct of EI has received an enormous amount of attention (and generated controversy) in both the popular press and academic journals. EI refers to the competency to identify and express emotions, understand emotions, assimilate emotions into thought, and regulate both positive and negative emotions in oneself and others (Matthews, Zeidner, & Roberts, 2002). It is an ability to recognize the meanings of emotions and their relationships and to reason and solve problems on that basis. Evolving from multiple intelligences theories espoused by Gardner (1983, 1999) and Williams and Sternberg (1988), EI acknowledges that not all problem-solving situations are cognitive; in fact, perceiving, interpreting, and reacting to one's own emotions and those of others are critical capabilities in terms of socialization skills.

Salovey and Mayer's initial article on the construct (1990) was the first to clearly delineate the theory and offer a systematic program of research. Popular efforts to promote the construct accelerated with the publication of Goleman's (1995) book. In general, Goleman asserts that socially skilled people tend to have a wide circle of acquaintances and the talent for finding common ground with people of diverse backgrounds; in other words, they have a knack for building rapport. Despite the fact that this book brought increased focus on the topic of EI, it did not provide for a systematic scientific program of research.

The topic of EI is rather controversial, as evidenced by the general skepticism of academics (e.g., Landy, 2005; Locke, 2005) and the relative acceptance from practitioners. One of the main fault lines lies in whether one views EI as trait based (e.g., Goleman, 1995) or as an ability model composed of mental abilities, skills, or capacities (e.g., Mayer, Salovey, & Caruso, 2000). Trait-based approaches view EI as involving innate attitudes, preferences, and values— essentially a reconceptualization of personality traits. This view has been met with considerable skepticism, and specific arguments against EI caution: (1) the definition of the concept is constantly changing; (2) most definitions are so all-inclusive as to make the concept unintelligible; (3) there is no such thing as an actual EI, although intelligence can be applied to emotions as well as other life domains; (4) research on EI has failed to demonstrate incremental validity over traditional models of personality and social behavior; and (5) much of the current research on EI has neglected well-documented research in the areas of emotion and intelligence (Landy, 2005; Locke, 2005; Matthews et al., 2002).

While these criticisms have merit for trait-based views of EI, ability-based conceptualizations are largely immune from these critiques. Ability approaches to EI conceptualize it as the ability to solve emotional problems—a view that stresses the concept of an intelligence that processes and benefits from emotions. Thus, EI is composed of mental abilities. It is developed in childhood and can be strengthened over time through experience and training (Ashkanasy & Daus, 2002). An emotionally competent person is actively able to identify, understand, process, and influence his or her own emotions and those of others to guide feeling, thinking, and action (Mayer & Salovey, 1997). Thus, it is argued that industrial and organizational psychologists should conceptualize EI as ability based and assess the construct with behaviorally based measures, rather than with self-reports of attitudes, preferences, or values (Ashkanasy & Daus, 2005; Daus & Ashkanasy, 2003). This view recognizes that individuals have different capacities and levels of EI but focuses on behaviorally based measurement systems of EI that have ultimately proven to be more psychometrically sound.

Regardless of one's theoretical stance on the construct, evidence suggests that EI is at least somewhat predictive of important workplace outcomes. For example, EI has been demonstrated to be positively related to customer service (Feyerherm & Rice, 2002). Furthermore, the US Air Force has effectively used EI measures to select recruiters. In their experience, the most successful recruiters scored significantly higher in the EI competencies of assertiveness, empathy, happiness, and emotional self-awareness (Cherniss, 2003). Other dependent variables that would be expected to be positively related to EI include leader emergence, satisfaction, and organizational citizenship or contextual behavior (Landy, 2005).

Although the ability-based conceptualization of EI is a good starting point for understanding IPS, it is not comprehensive enough to describe the myriad of skills employed in workplace interactions. That is, while EI competencies, such as assertiveness and empathy, are certainly interpersonal in nature, the construct in its totality does not fully characterize the domain of IPS. Recall our definition of IPS as 'goal-directed behaviors, including communication and relationship-building competencies, employed in interpersonal interaction episodes characterized by complex perceptual and cognitive processes, dynamic verbal and nonverbal interaction exchanges, diverse roles, motivations, and expectancies.' IPS are undoubtedly behaviorally based and result from many influences, including more than simple perception, understanding, and regulation of emotion. Therefore, EI will be considered as just one (albeit important) antecedent of IPS. Specifically, it will be treated as an individual difference variable that, together with other factors, can influence the enactment of desired IPS.

Personality traits

Research on managerial incompetence at the Center for Creative Leadership and Personnel Decisions, Inc., has come to similar conclusions; many managers who are bright, hard-working, ambitious, and technically competent fail (or are in danger of failing), because they are perceived as arrogant, vindictive, untrustworthy, selfish, emotional, compulsive, overcontrolling, insensitive, abrasive, aloof, too ambitious, or unable to delegate or make decisions (Kaplan, Drath, & Kofodimos, 1991; Lombardo & McCauley, 1988; McCall & Lombardo, 1983; Peterson & Hicks, 1993). In general, these potential career derailers describe established personality characteristics.

It should be emphasized that personality and social skills are quite distinct. That is, personality is relatively stable and enduring whereas social skills are relatively trainable (Hogan & Shelton, 1998; Leary, 1995). More importantly, one can have acceptable social skills and still possess a deeply flawed personality. The distinction between social skills and personality then lies in the fact that social skills allow personality dispositions to demonstrate their positive effects, moderating the relationship between personality and job performance (Leary, 1995). Thus, personality traits comprise another antecedent of social skills.

Although distinct conceptually, modest correlations do exist between measures of social skills and personality. These correlations suggest that personality and social skills are moderately related. Further, knowledge of personality traits may be important for understanding manifested IPS. Researchers are in the initial stages of examining this suggestion empirically.

Ferris and colleagues (2001), for example, found social skills, defined as 'interpersonal perceptiveness and the capacity to adjust one's behavior to different situational demands and to effectively influence and control the responses of others' (p. 1076), to be related to agreeableness ($r = 0.22$, $p < 0.01$), conscientiousness ($r = 0.21$, $p < 0.05$), emotional stability ($r = 0.27$, $p < 0.01$), extraversion ($r = 0.44$, $p < 0.01$), and openness to experience ($r = 0.18$, $p < 0.05$). Taken together, the five-factor traits accounted for about 20% of the variance in social skills. Of these traits, the importance of agreeableness to social skills seems to be particularly well documented. Supporting this assertion, Neuman and Wright (1999), in a study that involved 316 human resource personnel (79 teams) from a large, wholesale department store organization, found agreeableness to be an antecedent condition of social skills. IPS were defined by these authors as the ability to resolve conflict and communicate openly, and results showed, at both the individual ($r = 0.35$, $p < 0.01$) and group level ($r = 0.39$, $p < 0.01$), that measures of agreeableness predicted the IPS of conflict resolution and open communication. They caution, however, that with different types of teams and tasks requiring different amounts of interaction, these findings may not generalize. For example, for tasks requiring extensive social interaction, extraversion should be predictive of performance (Piedmont & Weinstein, 1993).

Costa and McCrae (1989) define 'agreeableness' as a quality of interpersonal interaction characterized by six personality facets: (1) the tendency to attribute benevolent intentions to others (trust); (2) the tendency to be frank and straightforward with people (straightforwardness); (3) the tendency to be altruistic, selfless, and concerned about others (altruistic); (4) the willingness to cooperate in conflict situations (compliance); (5) the ability to demonstrate social humility and a lack of arrogance (modesty); and (6) the ability to express sympathy and empathy (tender-mindedness). Particularly important in team settings, agreeable individuals facilitate the process of conflict resolution. Thus, it is argued that agreeableness may enhance team performance through improved group cohesion and cooperation (Greene, 1989; Neuman & Wright, 1999). A key component of cohesiveness is interpersonal attraction among group members (e.g., Berkowitz, 1954; Festinger, Schachter, & Back, 1950). Agreeable team members are sympathetic toward others and eager to help. These traits should increase interpersonal attraction in the team and result in enhanced team task cohesion (Stogdill, 1972). Finally, in addition to the other 'Big Five' traits (e.g., conscientiousness, openness to experience), the traits of altruism, trust, team/collective orientation, and tender-mindedness have demonstrated potential to enhance the IPS required to relate to others.

The constructs of social intelligence, EI, and the 'Big Five' personality constructs are interrelated in complex ways. In particular, social intelligence embraces a variety of competencies dealing with effective interpersonal relations such as sociability, social boldness, friendliness, cooperativeness, thoughtfulness, and self-monitoring. In addition, it includes the extraversion, agreeableness, and openness to experience dimensions of the 'Big Five' model of personality (Barrick & Mount, 1991). Because social skills represent interpersonal perceptiveness and behavioral flexibility, they reflects a different set of abilities relative to g. IPS are also distinct from personality in that: (1) they can be trained, and (2) personality serves as an antecedent to manifested social skills.

Team/collective orientation

Although the terms 'team orientation' and 'collective orientation' are often used interchangeably, they are not synonymous. Collective orientation is a general predilection to accomplish group goals rather than individual goals and to cooperate with others (e.g., Hofstede, 1984; Wagner, 1995; Wagner & Moch, 1986). As a more general construct than team orientation, collective orientation is based on Hofstede's cultural dimension of individualism/collectivism (i.e., the degree to which individuals are expected to look after themselves versus the group; Hofstede, 1984, 2001) and is context free (i.e., it does not have to be work related or always take place within teams or small groups; Wagner & Moch, 1986).

In contrast, team orientation is not steeped in culture and is described as a preference for working with others. It refers to the tendency to enhance individual performance through the coordination, evaluation, and utilization of task inputs from other group or team members (Driskell & Salas, 1992). Research investigating team orientation has found that it facilitates team performance on decision-making tasks (e.g., Driskell & Salas, 1992) and results in increased cooperation and coordination between team members (Eby & Dobbins, 1997). Research also suggests that team orientation may be a malleable attitude (Eby & Dobbins, 1997).

Due to its focus on group interaction and accomplishing team goals, it is clear that team/collective orientation is an important antecedent to IPS. Individuals with a collective orientation will likely display better IPS in social interactions as they are generally more willing to work with others, to cooperate in groups, and to accomplish group rather than individual goals. In addition, they are also likely to improve work processes due to their willingness to accept feedback and assistance from others in the pursuit of group goals (Salas et al. in press).

Another critical aspect of IPS performance falls into the area of situational characteristics, or facets of the interaction episodes themselves. These include the environmental setting, task demands, individuals' goals and motivations, roles, and social rules and norms.

FACETS OF INTERPERSONAL INTERACTION EPISODES

What are the ingredients of interaction? First and foremost, there must be agendas and there must be parts to play. That is, social and occupational life consists of episodes (Motowidlo, Borman, & Schmit, 1997) or interaction sequences, each of which involves a purpose and associated roles. Argyle's model of social interaction is a frequently cited model of social skills (Argyle, 1975, 1994; Argyle & Kendon, 1967). This model grew out of research into social interaction at Oxford in the 1960s and posits that in any social encounter, individuals have plans or goals that they attempt to realize through the continuous correction of their social performance in light of others' reactions (Hayes, 2002). In this model, social performance is presented as a set of motor responses. Additionally, it assumes that people are purposeful and interact with others in order to secure desired outcomes. As with motor skills, such as those involved in snowboarding, typing, or swinging a golf club, some people are more skilled than others. Specifically, they are more effective in attaining the required goals. A discussion of important characteristics of interpersonal interactions is provided in the following sections.

Environmental Setting

Environmental and situational settings have important influences on interpersonal interactions. That is, if we want to explain and understand social behavior, we must clearly comprehend how different situations influence it (Argyle, Furnham, & Graham, 1981). A situation could be described as the sum of the features of the behavioral system for the duration of a social encounter (Argyle et al., 1981). This description takes into account the fact that individuals contribute to the situations in which they are a part. Previous life experiences and individual differences impact the skillful use of IPS. At the same time, a number of studies by Milgram, Zimbardo, and others have demonstrated the extraordinary extent to which behavior is affected by situations—that is, behavior is at least as much determined by situation and personality–situation interactions as it is by general traits of personality or individual variations due to experience.

In order to properly evaluate IPS in context, it is important to assess the nature of the relationship. Is it hierarchical? Is the setting team-based? Is it an important relationship with a key customer? Each of these settings may require a different combination and level of IPS—that is, the situation prescribes and allows certain patterns of behavior in any social interaction (Trower, 1979). Similarly, the nature of the task at hand can influence the need for particular forms of interpersonal interaction. In any given work group situation, task interdependence results from the requirements and constraints inherent in the group's task (Goodman, 1986). Task interdependence refers to the degree to which group members must rely on one another to perform their tasks effectively given the design of their jobs (Georgopoulos, 1986; Kiggundu, 1981, 1983). Research suggests the level of task interdependence affects the level of cooperation within a group (Shaw, 1973), the group's performance in general (Shea & Guzzo, 1987), and the nature of interpersonal interactions among members of work groups (Gersick, 1988, 1989; Kelley & McGrath, 1985). Thus, the situation and the demands of the task are also important to consider when analyzing IPS.

Moreover, we may view environmental settings as social systems, with interdependent parts or features. If one feature is altered, other features must also change. Argyle and colleagues (1981) document a number of features of social situations, including environmental settings, boundaries, props, and modifiers. They note that the nature of the situation, including the cultural and organizational environment, will undoubtedly influence the nature of the interaction episode. Boundaries (described as enclosures within which social interaction takes place) and props (e.g., chairs, tables) serve a particular social function and often dictate the formality of an interaction. Additionally, modifiers, or physical aspects of the environment (e.g., color, light, noise, heat), affect the emotional tone of the interpersonal behavior being enacted (Argyle et al., 1981). Accordingly, aspects of the environmental setting will undoubtedly influence the timing, pace, and formality of interpersonal interaction episodes.

Goals and Motivation

Most social behavior is goal-directed. People have goals in the form of needs, drives, and wants that they bring to situations, which, in turn, provide the means for satisfying certain wants and stimulating others (Argyle et al., 1981). These goals are constrained and are related to other factors, such as situational rules, roles, and sequential structures, and, as a result, have to be considered in relation to these other features (Argyle et al., 1981).

Hogan and Shelton (1998) suggest that people are motivated in a deep and often unconscious way to get along, get ahead, and render their lives interpretable. In the context of interpersonal interactions, people who want to get along will cooperate, comply, work well in teams, display a friendly attitude, and try not to stand out from the group. People who want to get ahead will volunteer, take initiative, seek responsibility, delight in standing out from the group, and try to ensure that their supervisors notice their performance (see Hogan, Rybicki, Motowidlo, & Borman, 1998). Thus, there are logical reasons to suggest that individual goals and motivations influence interaction episodes.

Roles

Hogan and Warrenfeltz (2003) suggest that the domain of IPS is the traditional subject matter of role theory (cf. Sarbin, 1954). Roles may be defined as the expectations regarding the responsibilities and requirements of a particular job or social interaction (Landy & Conte, 2004). Consequently, the roles people enact and the relationships they engage in greatly impact the interpersonal interaction process. Each situation can be drastically different in terms of formality, the number of people interacting, and the role expectations of each individual. That is, every possible social situation comes with its own roles for interacting with others. Further, in any given situation we all have a large repertoire of possible roles and behavioral styles to bring to bear (Schein, 1999). When analyzing interpersonal behavior, one must consider the relationship and roles of 'actors' in the interaction.

Argyle and colleagues (1981) describe how specified roles are enacted in the social situation and provide the individual with a fairly clear model for interaction. These roles can be seen as encompassing the duties, obligations, or rights of the social position of the actors. Moreover, the roles are dynamic and are prone to change, depending on the particular situation.

Social Rules and Norms

Social situations are often uniquely bounded by their own rule systems (Trower, 1979). Social rules are described as behaviors that members of a group generally believe should or should not occur within a particular situation or across a range of situations (Argyle & Henderson, 1985). They are generated in social situations in order to regulate behavior so that individuals' goals can be attained. They can be thought of as expectations about appropriate behavior in specific situations that, in turn, influence people's perceptions and judgments about the appropriateness of enacted behavior in those same contexts. For example, general or universal social rules include being polite, avoiding embarrassment or conflict, being friendly, and having good manners (Argyle et al., 1981; Argyle & Henderson, 1985). These rules govern all face-to-face relationships and make life predictable and safe (Schein, 1999).

The social contexts of our interactions (including the relationship and roles of the 'actors') influence our dealings with others. Many social interactions, especially those that occur between strangers, are ritualized, formal, and largely predefined (Goffman, 1955, 1959; Grice, 1975). For example, there is often little variation in how we greet a stranger in an empty hallway or sidewalk. A slight head nod or a quick 'hello,' or 'good morning/afternoon' will usually suffice. Put another way, '. . . any time we enter a situation in which we are interacting and communicating with others, we immediately and unconsciously play by the rules that we perceive to govern that particular situation' (Schein, 1999, p. 106).

Equal in importance to the characteristics inherent in any social context is the perceptual and cognitive filtering process that governs the execution of IPS. In the following section we briefly review and discuss these perceptual and cognitive processes. Particular importance is placed on the need to accurately interpret others' motivations and constraints.

PERCEPTUAL AND COGNITIVE PROCESSES OF SOCIAL BEHAVIOR

Expertise in IPS performance requires competence in several key areas—accurate perception, effective nonverbal communication, appropriate self-presentation, and mastery of skilled sequences (Hayes, 2002). As Trower (1979) notes, 'In order to produce skilled behavior the individual needs (1) information on the state of affairs in the immediate situation and (2) information concerning outcomes of possible strategies, gained from either trial-and-error experience or observation of modeled displays' (pp. 4–5). Armed with this information, the 'actor' in any interpersonal interaction may proceed to enact positive IPS.

Perception must be relevant and accurate if performance is to be skilled (Trower, 1979). The ability to perceive nonverbal cues and the capacity to recognize, understand, and manage emotions are critical components of any model of IPS. Perception, recognition, and eventual understanding of the nonverbal behaviors and emotions of others provides actors with critical information, allowing them to adapt their behaviors in order to more effectively reach their goal(s). Thus, a cognitive feedback process is operating between the perception and performance of skilled social behavior. This cognitive stage allows a mechanism for problem solving in the interpersonal interaction episode (Trower, 1979).

The role of perceptual and cognitive processes in the enactment of IPS is not trivial. These processes allow for social problem solving and for individuals to continuously adapt their behavior based on the feedback they are receiving. Not all social situations are prescribed; in fact, relationships that occur between friends, coworkers, clients, and managers/subordinates often leave much room for both interpretational errors and behavioral variability. Schein (1999) describes the intrapsychic processes involved in interpersonal interactions and summarizes them in his ORJI model (i.e., observation, emotional reaction, judgment, and intervention). He reasons that in any relationship we may fall prey to four 'traps' or biases: (1) misperception, (2) inappropriate emotional response, (3) rational analysis based on incorrect data, and (4) intervention based on misinformation. These biases can be avoided but not without some level of self-insight, inquiry, and time to analyze and reflect (Schein, 1999).

Simply stated, when we misinterpret others' responses, we have not developed a reasonable understanding of the social situation. It is important then to avoid perceptual and interpretive errors, which are commonplace, but nonetheless tend to negatively impact the quality of our social interactions. This is where the ideas of social and emotional intelligence are directly linked. The ability to understand the feelings, thoughts, and behaviors of persons, including oneself, in interpersonal situations and to act appropriately upon that understanding (i.e., social intelligence; Marlowe, 1986) is crucial. Similarly, the competency to identify, express, understand, and assimilate emotions into thought, as well as the regulation of both positive and negative emotions in oneself and others (i.e., emotional intelligence; Matthews et al., 2002), are important to successful IPS performance. Together with aspects of the situation, and previous life experience, these individual differences feed into the perceptual and cognitive filtering processes that result in the effective use of IPS.

In the next section, we turn our discussion of workplace IPS toward a brief review of 12 specific workplace IPS. These IPS have been reported in the literature as related to successful job performance and other important outcomes, including sales, productivity, and customer satisfaction.

REVIEW OF SPECIFIC IPS

This review spans the research on workplace IPS. As aptly stated many years ago, 'If we do not restrain ourselves and put some limits on the construct of social skill, it will expand to include all human behavior' (Curran, 1979, p. 323). With that thought in mind, in the sections that follow we discuss two overarching categories of IPS: (1) communication skills, and (2) relationship-building skills.

Communication Skills

Many organizations have supported the need for communication skills improvement, as effective communication continues to be a major deficiency of new-hires and current employees (Cassady & Wasson, 1994). For example, the Chief Executive Officers of the 'Big Eight' Accounting Firms (1989), the American Society for Training and Development (Carnevale, Gainer, Meltzer, & Holland, 1998), and the Carnegie Foundation for the Advancement of Teaching (1986) have all called for increased emphasis on communication skills in business education.

As an example of effective communication, consider the case of one of the most influential world leaders of our time—former US President Ronald Reagan. 'President Reagan had a remarkable ability to communicate and relate to people on their level and to inform and persuade, often through a personally friendly approach and positive, optimistic message' (Coburn, 2000, p. 8). Reagan's admirers note that his exceptional communication skills were developed over his lifetime of stage and leadership roles, including his experiences as a sportscaster, leading actor, tenure as President of The Screen Actors Guild, national conservative spokesman, and successful Governor of California (Coburn, 2000).

However, communication does not merely mean oral communication skills. In general, communication can be oral, written, or nonverbal. In this chapter, five specific communication skills considered to be crucial to effective interpersonal interactions are presented. These include active listening, oral communication, written communication, assertive communication, and nonverbal communication. Taken together, these skills allow individuals to effectively exchange information with others.

Active listening

Listening is considered to be one of the most important workplace IPS (Nurick, 1993; Robbins & Hunsaker, 1996), especially for managers (Crocker, 1978). Active listening is important, because it ensures that the communication is well understood and delivered. Effective listening includes paying close attention to what is being said, asking other parties to explain exactly what they mean, and requesting that ambiguous ideas or statements be repeated (Fisher et al., 1991). Rogers and Farson (1976) outline four components to active listening: intensity, empathy, acceptance, and willingness to take responsibility for completeness. Active listening is important for minimizing the interrelated risks of misperception, inappropriate emotional reactions, and biased judgments (Schein, 1999). In most interpersonal interactions, including problem solving, collaborating, negotiating, and counseling, the successful employment of active listening techniques is imperative.

Oral communication

Effective listening is a necessary but insufficient component of good communication as it is also important that speakers be able to send verbal messages successfully. Aspects of language and speech communication, such as vocabulary, grammar, codes, and voice tone, are partially situation-specific. Some situations are more restricted and may constrain individuals in their use of language. While not everyone is blessed with exceptional oratory skills, it is important to sidestep potential pitfalls in oral communication. For example, interruptions and inattentiveness may convey disrespect (Goffman, 1955). Additionally, one effective strategy when using oral communication is to use 'I' rather than 'You' statements (O'Conner, 2003). 'You' messages have a tendency to generate defensiveness in the other party and are typically met with a similar response.

Written communication

Another important skill is the ability to effectively send written messages. Unfortunately, many new-hires are seen as lacking the basic communication skills necessary to successfully handle the writing responsibilities of their new positions (Sharplin, Sharplin, & Birdsong, 1986; Vaughn, 1985). Written communication skills include not only clarity of writing but also the appropriateness of the message sent. It is important for the sender to realize when the content, tone, or format of his or her messages is likely to be misinterpreted by others. This can be a particular problem in the current workplace environment where the use of email is ubiquitous. Because of the lack of nonverbal cues in electronic communication, misunderstanding of the sender's intentions is commonplace.

Assertive communication

It is imperative that our ideas get conveyed accurately and completely, and assertive communication ensures that this is accomplished. The basic premise underlying the traditional assertiveness paradigm has been that the expression of one's rights in a problematic interpersonal situation will produce positive outcomes (Wolpe, 1973). Dimensions of assertiveness have been outlined by Lorr and More (1980) and include directiveness, interdependence, defense of interests, and social assertiveness. Smith-Jentsch and colleagues (1996) examined these dimensions using university participants in a flight simulation decision-making task and found that the directiveness and independence dimensions are relatively independent from defense of interests and social assertiveness.

Recently, a consistent pattern of findings has demonstrated that the assertive expression of personal rights might produce negative as well as positive evaluations of the asserter. Thus, the skill component of this communication competency presents itself in the ability to find a balance of assertive behavior—not too passive or too aggressive—that maximally facilitates positive outcomes in an interpersonal interaction episode. Situations generally termed 'assertive contexts' (e.g., request refusal, expressing a difference of opinion) are best defined as a group of partially independent, situation-specific response classes (Rakos, 1991; Rich & Schroeder, 1976).

Like other IPS, assertive communication skills can be trained. Smith-Jentsch and colleagues (1996) found that assertiveness training that follows a behavior role modeling format produced more effective team performance-related assertive behavior than training that relied on information, demonstration, and motivation arguments. This finding supports the contention that team performance-related assertiveness is more than just a context-specific attitude; it is a construct with a significant skill component (Smith-Jentsch et al., 1996).

Nonverbal communication

Nonverbal communication includes such diverse behaviors as facial expressions; bodily orientations, movements, and postures; vocal cues (other than words); aspects of physical appearance; interpersonal spacing; and touching (DePaulo, 1992). These signals have been studied extensively, with the general finding that socially inadequate people make less use of nonverbal signals or use them in the wrong way (Trower, 1980).

The study of nonverbal behavior has a distinguished place in the history of science (DePaulo, 1992). Beginning with Charles Darwin, some of the most eminent scientific scholars, including Wundt, Boring, Titchener, Gordon, and Floyd Allport, and even Hull, have written about nonverbal expressive behavior (Goldstein, 1983). DePaulo (1992) outlines a number of reasons why nonverbal behaviors should be of interest to scholars studying the dynamics of social situations. Specifically, nonverbal behaviors are: (1) irrepressible, (2) linked to emotion, (3) less accessible to actors than to observers, (4) off the record, (5) communications with unique meanings, and (6) quick to occur. Essentially, one may consider nonverbal communication to be the glue holding most interaction episodes together, especially those that are conducted face-to-face. For instance, spoken communication is often reinforced through nonverbal signals that offer clues about the other person's internal situation beyond the words he or she is uttering (O'Conner, 2003). Further, in social interactions, people often exert more control over their nonverbal expressive behavior than they do over their verbal communications. This attempted control is not always conscious, and it is not always successful. One may find it difficult, for instance, to feign excitement or truthfulness under the wary eye of an individual trained and experienced in detecting nonverbal signals.

Empirical evidence supports the value of nonverbal communication skills. For example, Gifford and colleagues (1985) investigated the role of nonverbal behavior in the employment interview process. Specifically, 34 job interviews were conducted and videotaped, with 18 judges rating applicants on motivation, social skill, and 'hireability.' Results indicated that social skill was more accurately inferred by the judges as a group than was motivation to work. Of particular relevance to the current chapter, applicants' social skills were apparently transmitted to the judges via three nonverbal cues (Gifford et al., 1985).

To conclude, no IPS is possible without some form of communication to transfer the thoughts, feelings, intentions, and behaviors of individuals interacting socially. Thus, communication skills are vital components of all IPS. These skills allow individuals to effectively communicate with others in the course of their work and nonwork lives. They relate to the overt and subtle ways in which people communicate with each other and thus, are, clearly interpersonal in their nature.

Relationship-building Skills

There are a number of relationship-building skills that can be appropriately placed under the banner of IPS including: cooperation and coordination; trust; intercultural sensitivity; service orientation; self-presentation; social influence; and conflict resolution and negotiation. These skills are important for all employees seeking to develop and foster relationships with others.

Cooperation and coordination

With an ever-expanding global economy and the continued surge of team-based work arrangements, the importance of having good teamwork skills has never been greater (Cohen & Bailey, 1997). Barlex (1994) outlines five categories of effective teamwork skills, including both communication and cooperation. Having already discussed communication skills at length, a brief discussion of cooperation is in order.

Cooperation has been described as a team skill competency that includes offering help to those team members who need it, pacing activities to fit the needs of the team, and behaving in a way such that actions are not misinterpreted by others (Salas et al., 2004). Research generally supports the idea that cooperation promotes team performance (Campion, Medsker, & Higgs, 1993; Campion, Papper, & Medsker, 1996; Deutsch, 1949; Leavitt, 1951). Problems of cooperation involve getting individuals to become interested in group goals and to trust the people with whom they work. In addition, while the ability to cooperate with others during interpersonal interactions is an important workplace IPS, it is not one that is limited to team-based work. For example, we all must cooperate with others on a daily basis—we cooperate when we plan social activities, shop for groceries, or even when we need to negotiate a reasonable rate with the baby-sitter.

Also important is the idea of coordination, which includes coordinating the response, sequencing, and pacing of team member activities (Fleishman & Zaccaro, 1992). Coordination requires members of social groups to align their behavior for the good of the group. Like cooperation, coordination need not require a team-based setting to be useful; we all coordinate every time we take our automobiles on the freeway, by (hopefully) obeying traffic laws and norms of the road. Earlier, we discussed how the attitudinal variable of team/collective orientation can increase both cooperation and coordination between team members (Eby & Dobbins, 1997). This increased cooperation and coordination leads to important individual, team/group, and organizational outcomes.

Essentially, teamwork can be characterized by behaviors, cognitions, and attitudes such as cooperation, communication, and coordination (explicit or implicit) among interdependent team members (see Salas et al., in press). However, other researchers have considered interpersonal relations itself to be an important teamwork skill dimension (e.g., Cannon-Bowers et al., 1995; Jordan, Jensen, & Terebinski, 1963; Tannenbaum, Beard, & Salas, 1992). These researches define interpersonal relations as the ability to optimize the quality of team members' interactions through resolution of dissent, utilization of cooperative behaviors, or use of motivational reinforcing statements (Cannon-Bowers et al., 1995). That is, it is defined as the ability to resolve conflict, cooperate, and motivate others through communication.

Trust

As we increasingly move from individual- to team-based work, employees have less structure and fewer authority figures on which to rely. This situation increases the need to work collaboratively and enhances the importance of trust in work groups. Trust is a multifaceted concept that is described as 'the willingness of a party to be vulnerable to the actions of another party based on the expectation that the other party will perform a particular action important to the trustor, irrespective of the ability to monitor or control that other party' (Mayer et al., 1995, p. 52). Trust is built through a combination of shared experience over time and the sharing of information about aspects of oneself that are relevant to one's relationships. It is especially important in organizations where relationships with customers, colleagues, and business associates must be developed (de Janasz et al., 2002).

Although trust is beneficial to collaboration (Sheppard, 1995), it also involves some level of risk. For example, if a manager places his or her trust in a subordinate to complete a project by a stated deadline, that trust is broken when the project is not completed on time; customers or clients may be lost, and the manager may no longer be able to count on that employee in the future.

Without trust, employees become overly protective of themselves and their immediate work environment, choosing to withhold information and avoid taking risks (Costigan, Ilter, & Brown, 1998). Further, the ability to trust is both person- and situation-dependent. We do not automatically trust every individual in every situation (de Janasz et al., 2002); however, the appropriate use of self-disclosure can build trust through interpersonal liking. In a team setting, lack of sufficient trust will lead team members to expend time and energy protecting, checking, and inspecting each other as opposed to collaborating to provide value-added ideas (Cooper & Sawaf, 1996).

Intercultural sensitivity

Since the 1970s, cultural diversity in the workplace has surged due to an influx of women and ethnic minorities into work organizations (Arai, Wanca-Thibault, & Shockley-Zalabak, 2001). Predictions for the next decade indicate that such groups will fill approximately 75% of the over 20 million new jobs created in the USA (Arai et al., 2001). As a result of these changing workplace demographics, it is important for employees at all organizational levels to understand differences among cultural values and how these differences can potentially affect others' behavior (de Janasz et al., 2002; Russell et al., 1995). Having this type of multicultural awareness should allow employees to make appropriate attributions about diverse colleagues (Landy & Conte, 2004).

Dimensions of differences in cultural values include: (1) individualism/collectivism; (2) power distance; (3) uncertainty avoidance; (4) masculinity/femininity; (5) long-term/short-term orientation; (6) formality/informality; (7) urgent-time/casual-time orientation; and (8) high-context/low-context culture (Hofstede, 1984, 1993; Kennedy & Everest, 1991). One of the most prevalent of these topics in the literature on cross-cultural relations is the distinction between individualism and collectivism. Most studies support the idea that countries such as the USA and the UK are more individualistic, whereas Asian countries (e.g., Japan) are typically more collectivistic. Work by Triandis (1995) suggests that the cultural syndromes of individualism and collectivism have four defining attributes: (1) independent versus interdependent definitions of the self; (2) goals independent from those of the in-groups versus goals compatible with those of the in-groups; (3) emphasis on attitudes versus norms; and (4) emphasis on rationality versus relatedness. These different attributes cause collectivists to view relationships as communal in nature and individualists to view relationships as exchange-oriented (Bhawuk, 1997). Thus, it is important that individuals understand, and are sensitive to, other members of their work organizations who may differ on cultural dimensions.

Dunbar (1996) describes intercultural sensitivity as the ability to interpret events in the same way as those from other cultures. It consists of: (1) comfort with other cultures; (2) positive evaluation of other cultures; (3) understanding cultural differences; (4) empathy for people in other cultures;

(5) open-mindedness; (6) sharing cultural differences with others; (7) seeking feedback about how one is received in other cultures; and (8) adaptability. Similarly, Offermann and Phan (2002) describe 'culturally intelligent' people as those that are able to function successfully in a variety of cultures. Training programs that target intercultural sensitivity include cross-cultural and diversity training. For example, Barker (2004) examined the effects of cross-cultural instruction on the interpersonal job skills of students. This intervention was designed to enhance students' understanding of the effects of diverse cultures with respect to school and career success. In this quasi-experimental study, post-test mean scores on a measure of interpersonal relations were significantly higher for students receiving the intervention. However, because the experimental and control group samples were chosen for convenience, and not randomly selected, the results should be interpreted with caution. In general, as business relationships continue to span international boundaries, intercultural sensitivity skills are likely to become increasingly important in organizations (DuBrin, 1997; Landy & Conte, 2004).

Service orientation

Service sector jobs have grown at a rapid pace in the last 50 years as the continued expansion of the service sector has become an organizational reality. This expansion requires that employees have the necessary customer service skills (which often include communication and negotiation skills) to interact effectively with clients (Gist, Stevens, & Bavetta, 1991). Further, individuals should be able to vary their social behavior for different clients and different situations. This social adaptability is critical for establishing business relationships with strangers (i.e., cold calling) and working with people from diverse cultures (Baron & Markman, 2000).

The concept of social adaptability is similar to the construct of emotional labor, which refers to 'the effort, planning, and control needed to express organizationally desired emotion during interpersonal transactions' (Morris & Feldman, 1996, p. 987). For example, a customer service employee at Disney may be required by his or her manager to continuously smile and be agreeable with customers, even when he or she is not in a good mood. Emotional labor is highest in jobs that involve a high amount of interaction with customers and clients and often result in negative effects on employees in terms of high stress, burnout, and lower satisfaction (Daus & Ashkanasy, 2005; Grandey, 2002). The extent to which effective interpersonal skills may ameliorate these negative individual outcomes has yet to be explored.

In the hospitality literature, service quality is essentially perceived as the customers' subjective interpretation of their experience. In more concrete terms, Parasuraman and colleagues (1985) identify both structural and interpersonal determinants of service quality. Heavily loaded interpersonal dimensions include responsiveness, courtesy, and communication (Parasuraman et al., 1985). A related term, customer service orientation, is defined as a 'set of basic individual predispositions and an inclination to provide service, to be courteous and helpful in dealing with customers and associates' (Cran, 1994, p. 36).

Garavan (1997) examined behaviors that hinder or facilitate transactions between people in a service environment. This study found that social skills training had a positive impact on the delivery of quality service to hotel customers (as indexed by greeting, speed of service, personal recognition, and appreciation). Similarly, the marketing literature indicates that an employee's IPS positively impact customer satisfaction (Humphreys, 1996). There is also support for the premise that strong social competence would be related to the likelihood of obtaining outside entrepreneurial funding (Baron & Markman, 2000).

Self-presentation

Individuals manage impressions through self-presentational behavior (i.e., behavior motivated by individuals' desires to establish, maintain, and refine their images in the minds of others; Baumeister, 1982; Goffman, 1959). The effective use of self-presentation is clearly a vital ingredient to a successful career (Baumeister, 1989) and a pervasive feature of organizational life. Further, because organizations can be considered as networks of interdependency, a person's success or failure in an organizational career is at least partially dependent upon others (Baumeister, 1989). Therefore, individuals are motivated to do the things necessary to get others to think well of them.

A related concept is 'impression management,' which has been described as a way in which individuals attempt to influence the reactions and images people have of them and their ideas (de Janasz et al., 2002). Managing these impressions encompasses a wide range of behaviors designed to create a positive influence on work associates (DuBrin, 1997). Some examples include: being punctual, dressing appropriately, flattering legitimately, having a good sense of humor, being friendly and approachable, and making friends (de Janasz et al., 2002). The effective use of self-presentation and impression management behaviors is another important IPS.

Social influence

Efforts to influence one or more others—to change others' attitudes or behaviors—are a very common aspect of interpersonal relations. Tactics used for this purpose include both persuasion and politicking. Persuasion has been defined as the conscious manipulation of face-to-face communication to induce others to take action (Robbins & Hunsaker, 1996). It is a form of influence and refers to the process of guiding people toward the adoption of some behavior, belief, or attitude preferred by the persuader (de Janasz et al., 2002).

Three general strategies of persuasion have been identified: persuasion through credibility, persuasion through logical reasoning, and persuasion through emotional appeal (Verderber & Verderber, 1986). Robbins and Hunsaker (1996) discuss how persuasion through credibility requires that the persuader be liked by others, and be able to instill confidence in them. However, this credibility has to be earned. With respect to reasoning, these authors suggest a manager or supervisor is more likely to persuade others when he or she can cite logical reasons for subordinates to behave in a certain way. Finally, persuasion through emotional appeal to a person's fears, loves, joys, frustrations, and other emotions can improve the effectiveness of persuasion based on logical reasoning alone.

Another form of social influence, organizational politicking, involves the collective set of actions taken to influence, or to attempt to influence, the distribution of advantages and disadvantages within an organization (Farrell & Petersen, 1982). In other words, it is the use of power and information to move resources toward preferred objectives (Farrell & Petersen, 1982). As the complexities of the global marketplace and other changes in the nature of work continue to proliferate, the importance of politicking will steadily increase. Organizational managers and leaders who develop effective political skills understand the ways in which their business is constantly evolving and seek to remain well informed to enable them to adapt to changing circumstances.

Political tactics and strategies clearly are reflective of the opportunistic social world within which we all interact. That is not to say that organizational and individual values should be compromised, but rather that we should recognize that individuals often engage in behavior designed merely to further their own self-interests. However, when these interests are pursued to the detriment of others, interpersonal interactions are sure to suffer. Individuals should consider whether the action they are considering might cause an imbalance in their or someone else's area of the organization (de Janasz et al., 2002). If so, they may want to reconsider their actions.

Conflict resolution and negotiation

It is estimated that managers spend approximately 20% of their time dealing with conflict (Baron, 1989). Thus, it is important that conflicts do not fester—managing them is critical for sustaining organizational efficiency and effectiveness (McCann & Galbraith, 1981). Conflict is any situation in which there are incompatible goals, cognitions, or emotions within or between individuals that lead to opposition, antagonistic interaction, or mutually exclusive goals, values, or events (de Janasz et al., 2002; DuBrin, 1997). One underlying cause of job conflict concerns organizational factors, such as competition over scarce resources and ambiguity over responsibility (Rahim, 1990). Because the resource pool in organizations is usually finite, the various units within an organization must often compete against one another. That is, individuals in organizations often have directly opposing interests. When people compete for what they consider to be their fair share of resources—such as money, time, senior management attention, technology, supplies, equipment, and human talent—conflict inevitably results (de Janasz et al., 2002). Another leading cause of incompatibility is related to interpersonal factors, i.e., factors related to individuals, their social relationships, and the way in which they think about and perceive others' intentions (Baron, 1990). Like other sources of conflict, differences in personal style may result in conflict and unproductive work behaviors if not properly managed. No matter the source of the conflict, the manner in which it is managed determines whether the outcome is positive or negative.

A recent meta-analysis of relationship conflict and team effectiveness showed that, across 10 studies, there is small negative association between relationship conflict and team effectiveness ($r = -0.08$, $p < 0.05$; De Dreu & Van Vianen, 2001). Nine other studies, when combined, showed a strong negative association between relationship conflict and measures of satisfaction ($r = -0.48$, $p < 0.001$; De Dreu & Van Vianen, 2001). While the association between relationship conflict and team effectiveness was modest, taken together these results suggest that relationship conflict is negatively related to both team effectiveness and satisfaction. Future research should examine the role of IPS in ameliorating the negative effects of conflict.

Three classes of conflict responses include collaborating, contending, and avoiding. A recent field study with a heterogeneous sample of teams performing a complex, nonroutine task indicated that collaborating and contending responses to conflict negatively related to team functioning (i.e., voice, compliance, and helping behavior) and overall team effectiveness (De Dreu & Van Vianen, 2001). Interestingly, avoiding responses to conflict were associated with high team functioning and effectiveness. It is perhaps the case that collaborating and contending responses to conflict distract team members from their tasks (De Dreu & Van Vianen, 2001).

Resolving conflict is a skill that does not come naturally, but it can be learned (de Janasz et al., 2002). Some individual suggestions for effectively resolving conflict include: (a) advocating one's position with an open mind; (b) not taking personally other members' disagreements and rejection of their ideas; (c) putting oneself in the other person's shoes; (d) following rational argument and avoiding premature evaluation; and (e) trying to synthesize the best ideas from all viewpoints and perspectives (Johnson & Johnson, 2000; Smith, 2001).

Another way of dealing with conflict is through negotiation. Negotiation is a basic means of getting what one wants from others. It is back-and-forth communication designed to reach an agreement despite the fact that the two parties may not share the same interests (Fisher et al., 1991). Any method of negotiation can be judged by three criteria: (1) it should produce a wise agreement, if agreement is possible; (2) it should be efficient; and (3) it should improve, or at least not damage, the relationship between the parties (Fisher et al., 1991). The desire to maintain a positive relationship throughout the negotiation process is particularly important and individuals with strong IPS are able to accomplish this. Clearly, conflict resolution and negotiation are important IPS for organizational employees to master.

Having reviewed antecedents of IPS, the facets of IPS interactions, and two classes of interpersonal behaviors, we next present a brief discussion of IPS training and development. Following that, we conclude with a discussion of future research needs and some final thoughts.

DEVELOPING INTERPERSONAL SKILLS

Given the growing number of jobs in the service industry and the ever-increasing use of teams in organizations, expenditures on IPS training have swelled (Gist & Stevens, 1998; Landy & Conte, 2004). Annual surveys by *Training* magazine have consistently demonstrated that, across all industries, half the training budget is spent on improving the IPS of essential organizational members (US Banker, 2000). In general, this training is targeted toward employees whose images and behaviors have the most impact on the company, specifically senior executives, managers, and customer service personnel (Poe, 2001).

As Goldstein and Ford (2002) point out, '. . . teaching interpersonal skills creates the same kind of challenges as teaching employees how to work with products coming off the assembly line' (p. 15). Further, interpersonal task stimuli are often subtle, ambiguous, and emotionally stressful (Gist & Stevens, 1998). Interpersonal tasks are dynamically complex; that is, they are complicated due to high levels of uncertainty and change in the task–performance environment (Wood, 1986). This characteristic of interpersonal tasks can make them difficult areas in which to provide training (Stevens & Gist, 1997).

In general, the accumulated evidence on IPS training suggests that such training should focus on specific, optimal social skills, and not on increased general sensitivity or insight. For example, at AT&T training methods are focused on a few critical areas, such as sales negotiation, and substantial investments are made in these areas (Henderson & Crawford, 2002). Further, IPS training may be directed at developing cognitive, behavioral, or affective components of these skills (Bailey & Butcher, 1983; Harrison, 1992). Focusing on only one component to the exclusion of the others may not lead to a successful intervention. Finally, similar to the development of other competencies, a combination of information, demonstration, practice, and feedback is needed to develop IPS.

Bradley, White, and Mennecke (2003) reviewed the effects of various interpersonal interventions on indicators of team performance. In this review, IPS were conceptualized as 'social process skills,' 'teamwork,' and 'soft interpersonal skills.' Results of interpersonal interventions were placed in one of four quadrants representing the temporal characteristics of both teams and tasks (i.e., ongoing team, short task; ongoing team, long task; short-term team, short task; short-term team, long task). They found that for short-term teams working on contrived tasks of brief duration, interpersonal interventions did not seem to affect team performance as much as task interventions. On the other hand, for both ongoing teams and for short-term teams working on real tasks of longer duration, the effects of interpersonal interventions on team performance were more positive. The authors explained these results by suggesting that the expectation of benefit mediated the effectiveness of interpersonal interventions on team performance—that is, the expectation of benefit from the IPS intervention was higher in the ongoing teams and in the short-term teams performing long tasks. They concluded that temporal components of tasks and teams are key to understanding the effects of IPS on team performance.

Formal Strategies

Based on our review of the literature, it appears that, in general, different training methods are more or less useful for the development of IPS. Further complicating the issue is the fact that the choice of training method is often dictated by organizational (e.g., time and money) and individual (e.g., willingness to participate in training) constraints. Role playing is one method of training that has been used extensively to develop interpersonal and human relations skills, including sales techniques (Berry, 1998; Connerley, 1997; Holsbrink-Engels, 1997; Muchinsky, 2003). One particular role-playing technique, *behavioral modeling*, is often used to train IPS. This technique applies principles of *social learning theory* (Bandura, 1977) to the development of IPS in managers and supervisors. Behavioral modeling typically consists of observing actual job incumbents, or videos of job incumbents, that demonstrate positive modeling behaviors, rehearsing the behavior using a role-play technique, receiving feedback on the rehearsal, and, finally, trying out the behavior on the job.

Baldwin (1992) studied effects of alternate behavioral modeling strategies on IPS training that focused on assertive communication. He found that showing trainees a video of a person using both correct and incorrect behaviors was more effective for enhancing trainee generalization than showing only a video of positive modeling behaviors. Similarly, May and Kahnweiler (2000) used behavioral modeling to improve active listening skills using role-play practice exercises. They found that practice sessions that broke down tasks into manageable parts led to high retention rates and high scores on a simulated IPS case study. However, this study is potentially limited due to the use of a small sample of supervisors and managers from a single manufacturing plant. Moreover, while improvements in retention and behavioral demonstration were found, there was no documented effect on transfer of improvements in listening skills.

Goldstein and Sorcher (1974) reported the results of an extensive behavioral modeling program at General Electric that focused on improving the IPS of first-line supervisors. This program was aimed at improving common supervisor–employee interactions, such as giving recognition and discussing potential disciplinary action. Results from this study showed that production measures from employees of the trained supervisors consistently surpassed those from the employees of the untrained supervisors. Similarly, Burnaska (1976) presented evidence of improved IPS as a result of role-play exercises. He compared 62 randomly selected and trained mid-level managers with 62 randomly selected managers who served as the control group. Three role-play situations were presented and evaluated: (1) performance problem discussion; (2) work assignment discussion; and (3) giving recognition to an average employee. Results obtained from behavioral measures showed significantly improved IPS for the trained managers.

Rapid improvements and increasingly sophisticated computer-based technologies are creating ample opportunities to use computers as training tools for developing IPS. And, there is evidence that computer-based role playing enhances IPS (cf. Holsbrink-Engels, 1997). As an example, the Federal Bureau of Investigation (FBI) has developed a unique simulator to help agents to develop interview skills by providing meaningful experience in detecting deception during interviews (Olsen, Sellers, & Phillips, 2004). In this simulation, law enforcement agents use verbal and nonverbal clues to detect deception in human behavior. In general, training simulation technology has progressed to the point where it can successfully be used to help to develop a variety of IPS. For example, the technology could be expanded to teach a large range of interpersonal abilities, including investigative and peer-pressure resistance skills as part of a drug prevention program (Olsen et al., 2004).

Moreover, advances in simulation-based training have enabled both military and industry teams to train in 'virtual' environments that reduce both training costs and consequences of error during practice. For example, both low- and high-fidelity flight simulators have been used extensively to improve the communication skills of military and commercial aviation crews (e.g., Salas, Burke, Bowers, & Wilson, 2001). As computer technology continues to advance, we expect it will be increasingly used for the development of IPS.

Informal Strategies

Beyond role playing (including behavioral role modeling) and advancements in computer technology, more basic developmental strategies apply. For example, motivating and goal setting, coaching and mentoring, and providing feedback are all ways in which individuals can improve their IPS. Locke, Shaw, Saari, and Latham (1981) postulate that goals affect task performance by 'directing energy and attention, mobilizing energy expenditure or effort over time (persistence), and motivating the individual to develop relevant strategies for goal attainment' (p. 145). The following conditions of goal setting have been found to improve performance: (1) creating specific goals rather than a vague set of intentions; (2) matching goals to individual ability levels; (3) providing continuous feedback concerning the degree to which a goal is being achieved; and (4) ensuring that the individual accepts the assigned goal (Locke et al., 1981). Effective organizational managers and leaders use goal setting to motivate and inspire their employees to improve both task and interpersonal performance.

Similarly, coaching and mentoring are two techniques recently adapted and formalized by organizations as ways to motivate and develop employees toward superior performance. Coaching can be defined as a method of helping workers to grow and improve their job performance by providing suggestions and encouragement (DuBrin, 2005). A coach analyzes an employee's performance, provides insight for performance improvement, and offers the leadership, motivation, and supportive climate necessary to help the employee to achieve that improvement (Robbins & Hunsaker, 1996). In contrast to coaching, mentoring generally involves an individual with advanced experience and knowledge (usually a friend or adviser) who is committed to working long term and one-on-one with a less experienced protégé (DuBrin, 1997). Mentoring can result in increased morale, productivity, and enhanced interpersonal working relationships (de Janasz et al., 2002).

Receiving constructive feedback is also important to the development of IPS. Feedback can be defined as any communication that provides a person with information about his or her behavior and its effect on others (Mill, 1976), and, when given properly, feedback can lead to improved employee performance (Locke & Latham, 1990). Hunt and Baruch (2003) examined the influence of subordinate feedback on the development of IPS for 252 executives following a five-day training workshop. They found a modest impact of IPS training on executives' IPS and suggested that refinement, rather than radical change, is possible. However, it is important to note that their population included top level managers and chief executives, who, presumably, already possess a high level of IPS. The provision of IPS feedback to lower level employees may result in even greater gains.

In summary, prior research has supported the effectiveness of behavioral modeling over other approaches to training IPS (Gist, Schwoerer, & Rosen 1989). Further, behavioral modeling has been proven effective in all industries and at all educational levels (Pescuric & Byham, 1996). At the same time, however, more research is needed to determine when and where other training strategies will be effective for improving specific IPS. In particular, more research is needed on the viability of relatively low-cost information- and demonstration-based IPS training methods. The majority of the literature reviewed for this chapter employed more time-consuming practice-based methods.

A RESEARCH AGENDA

'Good theory illuminates and clarifies, often by organizing, and thus simplifying, a set of previously unorganized and scattered observations' (Klein & Zedeck, 2004, p. 932). Further, 'good theory is theory that can be used to address problems in organizations' (Klein & Zedeck, 2004, p. 933). And finally, as noted by Kurt Lewin (1951), while there is nothing so challenging as a practical problem, there is also nothing so practical as a good theory. While the purpose of this chapter is to review and organize the diverse literature on the construct of IPS, we also hope it helps to identify and stimulate research designed to solve organizational problems. Specifically, from this review and its associated framework, a number of future research ideas are evident.

First and foremost, research should be done to expand, test, and refine the organizing framework presented here. For example, as depicted in our framework and discussed elsewhere, it will be useful to further examine the role of IPS as a moderator of the relationship between personality and performance (e.g., Riggio, 1986; Schneider et al., 1996)—that is, while personality is relatively fixed, efforts to improve IPS may lead to improved performance for individuals with lower measured levels of social and emotional intelligence. Additionally, while a modest number of studies have examined outcomes of good IPS, few have indexed antecedents. Another likely antecedent, general mental ability (GMA), was largely absent from the current review. However, at least one study has demonstrated an interaction between GMA and social skill in the prediction of job performance (e.g., Ferris et al., 2001). In short, further refinement of the nomological network of IPS—to empirically assess its antecedents and consequences—is needed to advance the literature in this area.

Second, it is clear that we need better measures to assess and evaluate IPS. No existing measures of IPS (e.g., Connerley, 1997; Ferris et al., 2001; Lorr et al., 1991; Riggio, 1986) clearly capture all 12 skills presented in this chapter. For measures that attempt to capture some of them, there is a disconcerting over-reliance on self-report methodologies. We believe that researchers should begin to focus more on behavioral markers of IPS, as these behavioral indicators can be designed to assess work-specific or profession-specific IPS.

In addition, the increased use of a situational judgment approach to develop measures of IPS is welcome in this area. Situational judgment tests (SJTs) are essentially low-fidelity work samples and may be particularly useful for selecting service personnel (e.g., Weekley & Jones, 1997). They are relatively inexpensive to develop and have been shown to add incremental validity to the prediction of job performance above and beyond job knowledge, cognitive ability, job experience, and conscientiousness (Clevenger, Pereira, Wiechmann, Schmitt, & Harvey, 2001). Specifically, the use of SJTs that assess IPS is likely to add incremental validity to predictions of job performance, particularly for jobs characterized by a high level of interpersonal interaction.

Third, research is needed to ascertain the effect of IPS on the bottom line or on return-on-investment (ROI) in organizations. Specifically, how can HR directors and corporate trainers relate training in IPS to the organization's bottom-line? Moreover, what is the financial impact of selecting individuals who are high on IPS? Most of the current research on IPS and outcomes has stopped short of determining the impact on organizational financials, settling instead to examine trainee reactions and self-reports of behavioral change. Before training and selection programs based on IPS are commonly implemented, it is important to determine their impact on the organization. Along these lines, we suggest that a meta-analysis (or series of meta-analyses) examining the overall influence of IPS on important individual, group/team, and business outcomes would represent a substantial contribution to the literature.

Fourth, it will be interesting to further investigate the impact of distance and distribution on the performance of IPS. While not explicitly depicted in our framework, the variable of distribution would be considered a characteristic of the situation that should undoubtedly influence the nature and presentation of IPS. With more work groups and teams than ever accomplishing work at a distance, this appears to be a particularly critical research avenue (see Salas, Stagl, & Burke, 2004).

Fifth, it will be important to ensure that the current framework and taxonomy can generalize to other cultural settings. For example, it is suggested that most of the IPS training programs delivered in the workplace have been designed for a white middle-class rather than a diverse population (Barker, 2004). Thus, it is important to ask how well these constructs and interventions generalize to other cultures. Similarly, with the rise of multinational organizations, how do cultural differences impact the use of IPS? Is there an increased premium on good IPS in organizations that span cultures and nations? Is it harder to develop a shared understanding among group or team members when their cultures, backgrounds, and experiences are different?

Finally, much is still to be learned concerning the most effective ways of training specific IPS. While not depicted in the model, training is expected to directly influence both the accuracy of social perception and cognitive problem solving as well as the execution of specific IPS. Yet, we still have little understanding about the best way to develop IPS, as there has been little advance in content or method of IPS training since the 1970s (Hunt & Baruch, 2003). Currently, studies suggest that behavioral modeling is the most effective method for training some IPS (cf. Burke & Day, 1986; Decker, 1980; Latham & Saari, 1979), but research is needed, however, on how trainee characteristics and pedagogical factors influence both immediate training performance and the maintenance (i.e., retention) of IPS beyond the initial training session (Baldwin & Ford, 1988). Interestingly, it is possible that integrating psychological and pharmacological interventions may positively influence the enactment of IPS. Among others, Bellack and colleagues (2004) have investigated this avenue and examined whether clozapine and risperidone could improve the social competence and problem-solving skills of patients with schizophrenia. While they did not find a statistically significant effect of medication on either social competence or problem solving, the low power of their study and the unique nature of the participant population warrant further investigation. More research is clearly needed in this area, which might be ripe for cross-functional research collaboration.

CONCLUDING REMARKS

Mead (1934) is reputed to have said that the secret to human exchange is to give to the other person behavior that is more valuable to him than costly to you, and to get from the other person behavior that is more valuable to you than costly to him (Hayes, 2002). If only social interactions were that easy, but regardless of difficulty or ease, there is little argument that IPS are critical to workplace functioning.

Challenges and opportunities abound in the current organizational milieu. Growth-oriented organizations are customer focused, motivated by change, creative, and adaptive. Today, much more so than in the past, people-focused leadership and management is now essential, and this requires excellent IPS, including the ability to communicate effectively at all levels of the organization.

One conclusion from this research that bears repeating is that expertise in skilled social performance requires competent performance in several different areas—accurate perception, effective nonverbal communication, appropriate self-presentation, and mastery of skilled sequences of behavior (Argyle, 1981). Two further points regarding IPS are notable: (1) they are likely to make a more discernible difference in fluid situations where roles and interactions are free to vary, and (2) there are probably different uses for the same skills—that is, they can be used for either prosocial or selfish purposes (Hogan & Lock, 1995). Psychotherapists and selection interviewers, for example, as well as all supervisors, must have strong social performance skills. Even in jobs that don't appear to involve interpersonal interaction (e.g., landscaping), social episodes still emerge and individuals are required to communicate and cooperate with others.

In this chapter we have discussed antecedents of IPS, facets of interpersonal interaction episodes, perceptual and cognitive phenomena related to IPS, and training strategies for developing IPS. In addition, we provided both a framework and comprehensive taxonomy of 12 critical IPS, organized into two general sections. At the same time, we have uncovered even more questions, answers to which still need to be addressed in future research. For the present and the foreseeable future, we believe that the importance of and interest in IPS and their influence on organizational functioning are likely to continue.

REFERENCES

Adair, W.L., Okumura, T., & Brett, J.M. (2001). Negotiation behavior when cultures collide: The United States and Japan. *Journal of Applied Psychology*, 86, 371–385.

Aditya, R.N. & House, R.J. (2002). Interpersonal acumen and leadership across cultures: Pointers from the GLOBE study. In R.E. Riggio, S.E. Murphy, & F.J. Pirozzolo (Eds), *Multiple intelligences and leadership* (pp. 215–240). Mahwah, NJ: Lawrence Erlbaum.

American Society for Training and Development (ASTD) (2000, February). More than one-third of people surveyed identified communication skills or interpersonal relationship skills as the most important quality in a good boss. *Training and Development Journal*, 16.

Arai, M., Wanca-Thibault, & Shockley-Zalabak, P. (2001). Communication theory and training approaches for multiculturally diverse organizations: Have academics and practitioners missed the connection? *Public Personnel Management*, 30 (4), 445–455.

Argyle, M. (1975). *Bodily communication*. London: Methuen.

Argyle, M. (1981). Methods of social skill training. In M. Argyle (Ed.), *Social skills and work* (pp. 195–220). London: Methuen.

Argyle, M. (1994). *The psychology of interpersonal behavior*. London: Penguin.

Argyle, M., Furnham, A., & Graham, J.A. (1981). *Social situations*. Cambridge, MA: Cambridge University Press.

Argyle, M. & Henderson, M. (1985). *The anatomy of relationships*. London: Heinemann.

Argyle, M. & Kendon, A. (1967). The experimental analysis of social performance. *Advances in Experimental Social Psychology*, 3, 55–98.

Ashkanasy, N.M. & Daus, C.S. (2002). Emotion in the workplace: The new challenge for managers. *Academy of Management Executive*, 16 (1), 76–86.

Ashkanasy, N.M. & Daus, C.S. (2005). Rumors of the death of emotional intelligence in organizational behavior are vastly exaggerated. *Journal of Organizational Behavior*, 26, 441–452.

Bailey, C.T. & Butcher, D.J. (1983). Interpersonal skills training. I: The nature of skill acquisition and its implications for training design and management. *Management Education and Development (Workshop)*, 14 (1), 48–54.

Baldwin, T.T. (1992). Effects of alternative modeling strategies on outcomes of interpersonal-skills training. *Journal of Applied Psychology*, 77, 147–154.

Baldwin, T.T. & Ford, J.K. (1988). Transfer of training: A review and direction for research. *Personnel Psychology*, 41, 63–105.

Bandura, A. (1977). *Social learning theory*. Englewood Cliffs, NJ: Prentice-Hall.

Barker, S.A. (2004). Improving interpersonal skills by applying cross-cultural training. *Journal of European Industrial Training*, 28 (2–4), 215–235.

Barlex, D. (1994). Organizing project work. In F. Banks (Ed.), *Teaching technology* (pp. 124–143). London: Routledge.

Baron, R.A. (1989). Personality and organizational conflict: The Type A behavior pattern and self-monitoring. *Organizational Behavior and Human Decision Processes*, 44, 281–297.

Baron, R.A. (1990). Environmentally induced positive affect: Its impact on self-efficacy, task performance, negotiation, and conflict. *Journal of Applied Social Psychology*, 20, 368–384.

Baron, R.A. & Markman, G.D. (2000). Beyond social capital: How social skills can enhance entrepreneurs' success. *Academy of Management Executive*, 14 (1), 106–116.

Barrick, M.R. & Mount, M.K. (1991). The big five personality dimensions and job performance: A meta-analysis. *Personnel Psychology*, 44, 1–26.

Baumeister, R.F. (1982). A self-presentational view of social phenomena. *Psychological Bulletin*, 91, 3–26.

Baumeister, R.F. (1989). Motives and costs of self-presentation in organizations. In R.J. Giacalone & P. Rosenfeld (Eds), *Impression management in the organization* (pp. 57–72). Hillsdale, NJ: Lawrence Erlbaum.

Bellack, A.S., Schooler, N.R., Marder, S.R., Kane, J.M., Brown, C.H., & Yang, Y. (2004). Do clozapine and risperidone affect social competence and problem solving. *American Journal of Psychiatry*, 161 (2), 364–367.

Berkowitz, L. (1954). Group standards, cohesiveness, and productivity. *Human Relations*, 7, 509–519.

Berry, L.M. (1998). *Psychology at work: An introduction to industrial and organizational psychology*. Boston, MA: McGraw-Hill.

Bhawuk, D.P.S. (1997). Leadership through relationship management: Using the theory of individualism and collectivism. In K. Cushner & R.W. Brislin (Eds), *Improving intercultural interactions: Modules for cross-cultural training programs* (pp. 40–56). Thousand Oaks, CA: Sage.

Bhawuk, D.P.S. & Triandis, H.C. (1996). Diversity in the work place: Emerging corporate strategies. In G.R. Ferris & M.R. Buckley (Eds), *Human resource management: Perspectives, context, functions, and outcomes* (pp. 84–96). Englewood Cliffs, NJ: Prentice-Hall.

Bigelow, J.D. (1995). Interpersonal skills. In N. Nicholson, R.S. Schuler, & A.H. Van de Ven (Eds), *The Blackwell encyclopedic dictionary of organizational behavior* (pp. 256–260). Malden, MA: Blackwell.

Bishop, S. (1997). *The complete guide to people skills.* Brookfield, VT: Gower.

Bordone, R.C. (2000, October). Teaching interpersonal skills for negotiation and for life. *Negotiation Journal*, **16**(4), 377–385.

Borman, W.C. & Brush, D.H. (1993). More progress towards a taxonomy of managerial performance requirements. *Human Performance*, **6** (1), 1–21.

Borman, W.C. & Motowidlo, S.J. (1993). Task performance and contextual performance: The meaning for personnel selection research. *Human Performance*, **10**, 99–109.

Boyatzis, R.E. (1982). *The competent manager: A model for effective performance.* New York: John Wiley & Sons.

Bradley, J., White, B.J., & Mennecke, B.F. (2003). Teams and tasks: A temporal framework for the effects of interpersonal interventions on team performance. *Small Group Research*, **34** (3), 353–387.

Burke, M.J. & Day, R.R. (1986). A cumulative study of the effectiveness of managerial training. *Journal of Applied Psychology*, **71**, 232–245.

Burnaska, R.F. (1976). The effects of behavior modeling training upon managers' behaviors and employees' perceptions. *Personnel Psychology*, **29**, 329–335.

Campbell, J.P., McCloy, R.A., Oppler, S.H., & Sager, C.E. (1993). A theory of performance. In N. Schmitt, W.C. Borman, & Associates (Eds), *Personnel selection in organizations* (pp. 35–70). San Francisco: Jossey-Bass.

Campion, M.A., Medsker, G.J., & Higgs, A.C. (1993). Relations between work group characteristics and effectiveness: Implications for designing effective work groups. *Personnel Psychology*, **46**, 823–850.

Campion, M.A., Papper, E.M., & Medsker, G.J. (1996). Relations between work team characteristics and effectiveness: A replication and extension. *Personnel Psychology*, **49**, 429–452.

Cannon-Bowers, J.A., Tannenbaum, S.I., Salas, E., & Volpe, C.E. (1995). Defining team competencies and establishing team training requirements. In R. Guzzo, E. Salas, & Associates (Eds), *Team effectiveness and decision making in organizations* (pp. 333–380). San Francisco: Jossey-Bass.

Cantor, N. & Kihlstrom, J.F. (1987). *Personality and social intelligence.* Englewood Cliffs, NJ: Prentice-Hall.

Carnegie Foundation for Advancement of Teaching (1986). *College: The undergraduate experience in America.* Princeton, NJ: Carnegie Foundation for the Advancement of Teaching.

Carnevale, D.J., Gainer, L.J., Meltzer, A.S., & Holland, S.L. (1998, October). Workplace basics: The skills employers want. *Training and Development Journal*, 22–30.

Carpenter, T.D. & Wisecarver, M.M. (2004). *Identifying and validating a model of interpersonal performance dimensions* (Technical Report 1144). Alexandria, VA: US Army Research Institute for the Behavioral and Social Sciences.

Cassady, M. & Wasson, L. (1994). Written communication skills of international business persons. *Bulletin of the Association for Business Communication*, **57**, 36–40.

CEOs of Big Eight Accounting Firms (1989). *Perspectives on education: Capabilities for success in the accounting profession.* New York: Anderson & Co., Arthur Young, Coopers and Lybrand, Deloitte Haskins and Sells, Ernst and Whinney, Peat Marwick Main & Co., Price Waterhouse, and Touche Rosse.

Cherniss, C. (2003). The business case for emotional intelligence. *The Consortium for Research on Emotional Intelligence in Organizations.* Retrieved April 15, 2004, from http://www.eiconsortium.org/research/business_case_for_et.htm.

Clark, H.B., Wood, R., Kuchnel, T., Flanagan, S., Mosk, M., & Northrup, J.T. (1985). Preliminary validation and training of supervisory interactional skills. *Journal of Organizational Behavior Management,* 7 (1–2), 95–115.

Clement, R.W., Walker, J.W., & Pinto, P.R. (1979). Changing demands on the training professional. *Training and Development Journal,* 29, 3–7.

Clevenger, J., Pereira, G.M., Wiechmann, D., Schmitt, N., & Harvey, V.S. (2001). Incremental validity of situational judgment tests. *Journal of Applied Psychology,* 86, 410–417.

Coburn, W.E. (2000). *The Reagan way: Using leadership skills for strategic success.* USAWC Strategy Research Project (No. 20000320 086). Carlisle Barracks, PA: US Army War College.

Cohen, S.G. & Bailey, D.E. (1997). What makes teams work? Group effectiveness research from the shop floor to the executive suite. *Journal of Management,* 23, 239–290.

Connerley, M.L. (1997). The influence of training on perception of recruiters' interpersonal skills and effectiveness. *Journal of Occupational and Organizational Psychology,* 70, 259–272.

Cooper, R. & Sawaf, A. (1996). *Executive EQ: Emotional intelligence in leadership and organizations.* New York: Perigee Books.

Costa, P.T., Jr & McCrae, R.R. (1989). *The NEO Personality Inventory manual.* Odessa, FL: Psychological Assessment Resources.

Costigan, R.D., Ilter, S.S., & Brown, J.J. (1998). A multidimensional study of trust in organizations. *Journal of Management Issues,* 10 (3), 303–318.

Cran, D.J. (1994). Towards validation of the service orientation construct. *The Service Industries Journal,* 14, 34–44.

Crocker, J. (1978). Developing management skills. In D.A. Whetten & K.S. Cameron (Eds), *Developing management skills* (p. 218). Glenview, IL: Scott-Foresman.

Curran, J.P. (1979). Social skills: Methodological issues and future directions. In A.S. Bellack & M. Hersen (Eds), *Research and practice in social skills* (pp. 319–354). New York: Plenum Press.

Daus, C.S. & Ashkanasy, N.M. (2003). Will the real emotional intelligence please stand up? On deconstructing the emotional intelligence 'debate.' *The Industrial–Organizational Psychologist,* 41 (2), 69–72.

Daus, C.S. & Ashkanasy, N.M. (2005). The case for the ability-based model of emotional intelligence in organizational behavior. *Journal of Organizational Behavior,* 26, 453–466.

Decker, P.J. (1980). Effects of symbolic coding and rehearsal in behavior-modeling training. *Journal of Applied Psychology,* 65, 627–634.

De Dreu, C.K.W. & Van Vianen, A.E.M. (2001). Managing relationship conflict and effectiveness of organizational teams. *Journal of Organizational Behavior,* 22, 309–328.

de Janasz, S.C., Dowd, K.O., & Schneider, B.Z. (2002). *Interpersonal skills in organizations.* New York: McGraw-Hill.

DePaulo, B.M. (1992). Nonverbal behavior and self-presentation. *Psychological Bulletin,* 111 (2), 203–243.

Deutsch, M. (1949). An experimental study of the effects of cooperation and competition upon group process. *Human Relations*, 2, 199–231.

DeVito, J.A. (1999). *Messages: Building interpersonal communication skills*. New York: Longman.

DiGiambattista, J.P. (2003). *Accepting the challenge: Examining infantry and military police employment of competencies on the twenty-first century battlefield* (Master's thesis). Fort Leavenworth, KS: US Army Command and General Staff College.

Driskell, J.E. & Salas, E. (1992). Collective behavior and team performance. *Human Factors*, 34, 277–288.

DuBrin, A.J. (1997). *Human relations: Interpersonal, job-oriented skills*. Upper Saddle River, NJ: Prentice-Hall.

DuBrin, A.J. (2005). *Coaching and mentoring skills*. Upper Saddle River, NJ: Pearson Prentice-Hall.

Dunbar, E. (1996). Sociocultural and contextual challenges of organizational life in Eastern Europe. In D. Landis & R.S. Bhagat (Eds), *Handbook of intercultural training* (pp. 349–365). Thousand Oaks, CA: Sage.

Eby, L.T. & Dobbins, G.H. (1997). Collectivistic orientation in teams: An individual and group-level analysis. *Journal of Organizational Behavior*, 18, 275–295.

Erikson, E.H. (1963). *Childhood and society*. New York: Norton.

Farrell, D. & Petersen, J.C. (1982, July). Patterns of political behavior in organizations. *Academy of Management Review*, 7, 403–412.

Ferris, G.R., Perrewé, P.L., Anthony, W.P., & Gilmore, D.C. (2000). Political skill at work. *Organizational Dynamics*, 28 (4), 25–37.

Ferris, G.R., Perrewé, P.L., & Douglas, C. (2002). Social effectiveness in organizations: Construct validity and research directions. *Journal of Leadership and Organizational Studies*, 9, 49–63.

Ferris, G.R., Witt, L.A., & Hochwarter, W.A. (2001). Interaction of social skill and general mental ability on job performance and salary. *Journal of Applied Psychology*, 86 (6), 1075–1082.

Festinger, L., Schachter, S., & Back, K. (1950). *Social pressures in informal groups*. New York: Harper & Row.

Feyerherm, A.E. & Rice, C.L. (2002). Emotional intelligence and team performance: The good, the bad and the ugly. *International Journal of Organizational Analysis*, 10 (4), 343–362.

Fisher, R., Ury, W., & Patton, B. (1991). *Getting to yes: Negotiating agreement without giving in*. New York: Penguin.

Fleishman, E.A. (1953). Leadership climate, human relations training, and supervisory behavior. *Personnel Psychology*, 6, 205–222.

Fleishman, E.A. & Quaintance, M. (1984). *Taxonomies of human performance: The description of human tasks*. New York: Academic Press.

Fleishman, E.A. & Zaccaro, S.J. (1992). Toward a taxonomy of team performance functions. In R.W. Swezey & E. Salas (Eds), *Teams: Their training and performance* (pp. 31–56). Norwood, NJ: Ablex.

Fontana, D. (1990). *Social skills at work*. London: The British Psychological Society and Routledge.

Garavan, T.N. (1997). Interpersonal skills training for quality service interactions. *Industrial and Commercial Training*, 29 (3), 70–79.

Gardner, H. (1983). *Frames of mind: The theory of multiple intelligences*. New York: Basic Books.

Gardner, H. (1999). *Intelligence reframed: Multiple intelligences for the 21st century*. New York: Basic Books.

Georgopoulos, B.S. (1986). *Organizational structure, problem solving, and effectiveness.* San Francisco: Jossey-Bass.

Gersick, C.J.G. (1988). Time and transition in work teams: Toward a new model of group development. *Academy of Management Journal*, **31**, 9–41.

Gersick, C.J.G. (1989). Marking time: Predictable transitions in task groups. *Academy of Management Journal*, **32**, 274–309.

Giacalone, R.A. & Rosenfeld, P. (Eds) (1989). *Impression management in the organization.* Hillsdale, NJ: Lawrence Erlbaum.

Gifford, R., Ng, C.F., & Wilkinson, M. (1985). Nonverbal cues in the employment interview: Links between applicant qualities and interviewer judgments. *Journal of Applied Psychology*, **70** (4), 729–736.

Girodo, M. (1998). Machiavellian, bureaucratic, and transformational leadership styles in police managers: Preliminary findings of interpersonal ethics. *Perceptual and Motor Skills*, **86**, 419–427.

Gist, M.E., Schwoerer, C., & Rosen, B. (1989). Effects of alternate training methods on self-efficacy and performance in computer software training. *Journal of Applied Psychology*, **74**, 884–891.

Gist, M.E. & Stevens, C.K. (1998). Effects of practice conditions and supplemental training method on cognitive learning and interpersonal skill generalization. *Organizational Behavior and Human Decision Processes*, **75**, 142–169.

Gist, M.E., Stevens, C.K., & Bavetta, A.G. (1991). Effects of self-efficacy and post-training intervention on the acquisition and maintenance of complex interpersonal skills. *Personnel Psychology*, **44**, 837 861.

Goffman, E. (1955). On face work: An analysis of ritual elements in social interaction. *Psychiatry*, **18**, 213–231.

Goffman, E. (1959). *The presentation of self in everyday life.* New York: Doubleday.

Goldstein, A.G. (1983). Behavioral scientists' fascination with faces. *Journal of Nonverbal Behavior*, **7**, 223–255.

Goldstein, A.P. & Sorcher, M. (1974). *Changing supervisory behavior.* New York: Pergamon.

Goldstein, I.L. & Ford, J.K. (2002). *Training in organizations: Needs, assessment, development, and evaluation.* Belmont, CA: Wadsworth.

Goleman, D. (1995). *Emotional intelligence.* New York: Bantam.

Goodman, P.S. (1986). Impact of task and technology on group performance. In P.S. Goodman (Ed.), *Designing effective work groups* (pp. 120–167). San Francisco: Jossey-Bass.

Grandey, A. (2002). Emotion regulation in the workplace: A new way to conceptualize emotional labor. *Journal of Occupational Health Psychology*, **5**, 95–110.

Greene, C. (1989). Cohesion and productivity in work groups. *Small Group Behavior*, **20**, 70–86.

Grice, H.P. (1975). Logic and conversation. In P. Cole & J.L. Morgan (Eds), *Syntax and semantics: Speech acts* (pp. 41–58). New York: Academic Press.

Guilar, J.D. (2001). *The interpersonal communication skills workshop: Listening, assertiveness, conflict resolution, collaboration: A trainer's guide.* New York: AMACOM.

Harrison, R. (1992). *Employee development.* London: Institute of Personnel Management.

Hayes, J. (1994). *Interpersonal skills: Goal-directed behaviour at work.* New York: Routledge.

Hayes, J. (2002). *Interpersonal skills at work.* New York: Routledge.

Henderson, J. & Crawford, G. (2002, April). Ten ways to wire sales training. *T+D Magazine*, 48–50.

Hofstede, G. (1984). *Culture's consequences: International differences in work related values.* Newbury Park, CA: Sage.

Hofstede, G. (1993, Spring). A conversation with Geert Hofstede. *Organizational Dynamics,* 53–61.

Hofstede, G. (2001). *Culture's consequences: Comparing values, behaviors, institutions, and organizations across nations.* Thousand Oaks, CA: Sage.

Hogan, J. & Lock, J. (1995, May). *A taxonomy of interpersonal skills for business interactions.* Paper presented at the 10th Annual Conference of the Society for Industrial and Organizational Psychology, Orlando, FL.

Hogan, R., Rybicki, S.L., Motowidlo, S.J., & Borman, W.C. (1998). Relations between contextual performance, personality, and occupational advancement. *Human Performance,* 11, 189–207.

Hogan, R. & Shelton, D. (1998). A socioanalytic perspective on job performance. *Human Performance,* 11 (2/3), 129–144.

Hogan, R. & Warrenfeltz, R. (2003). Educating the modern manager. *Academy of Management Learning and Education,* 2 (1), 74–84.

Holsbrink-Engels, G.A. (1997). Computer-based role-playing for interpersonal skills training. *Simulation and Gaming,* 28, 164–180.

Humphreys, M.A. (1996). Exploring the relative effects of salesperson interpersonal process attributes and technical product attributes on customer satisfaction. *Journal of Personal Selling and Sales Management,* 16, 47–57.

Hunt, J.W. & Baruch, Y. (2003). Developing top managers: The impact of interpersonal skills training. *Journal of Management Development,* 22 (8), 729–752.

Jiang, J.J., Klein, G., Van Slyke, C., & Cheney, P. (2003). A note on interpersonal and communication skills for IS professionals: Evidence of positive influence. *Decision Sciences,* 34 (4), 799–812.

Johnson, D.W. & Johnson, F.P. (2000). *Joining together: Group therapy and group skills.* Boston: Allyn & Bacon.

Jordan, N., Jensen, B., & Terebinski, S. (1963). The development of cooperation among three-man crews in a simulated man–machine information processing system. *Journal of Social Psychology,* 59, 175–184.

Kaplan, R.E., Drath, W.H., & Kofodimos, J.R. (1991). *Beyond ambition: How driven managers can lead better and live better.* San Francisco: Jossey-Bass.

Kelley, J.R. & McGrath, J.E. (1985). Effects of time limits and task types on task performance and interaction of four-person groups. *Journal of Personality and Social Psychology,* 49, 395–406.

Kennedy, J. & Everest, A. (1991, September). Put diversity in context. *Personnel Journal,* 50–54.

Kiggundu, M.N. (1981). Task interdependence and the theory of job design. *Academy of Management Review,* 6, 499–508.

Kiggundu, M.N. (1983). Task interdependence and job design: Test of a theory. *Organizational Behavior and Human Performance,* 31, 145–172.

Kilduff, M. & Day, D.V. (1994). Do chameleons get ahead? The effects of self-monitoring on managerial careers. *Academy of Management Journal,* 37, 1047–1060.

Klein, K.J. & Zedeck, S. (2004). Introduction to the special section on theoretical models and conceptual analysis. *Journal of Applied Psychology,* 89 (6), 931–933.

Landy, F.J. (2005). Some historical and scientific issues related to research on emotional intelligence. *Journal of Organizational Behavior,* 26, 411–424.

Landy, F.J. & Conte, J.A. (2004). *Work in the 21st century: An introduction to industrial and organizational psychology.* Boston: McGraw-Hill.

Latham, G.P. & Saari, L.M. (1979). The application of social learning theory to training supervisors through behavioral modeling. *Journal of Applied Psychology*, **64**, 239–246.

Leary, M.R. (1995). *Self-presentation: Impression and interpersonal behavior*. Boulder, CO: Westview.

Leavitt, H.J. (1951). Some effects of certain communication patterns on group performance. *Journal of Abnormal and Social Psychology*, **46**, 38–50.

Lewin, K. (1951). *Field theory in social psychology*. New York: Harper & Raw.

Lewis, B.D. (1973, September). The supervisor in 1975. *Personnel Journal*, 815–818.

Locke, E.A. (2005). Why emotional intelligence is an invalid concept. *Journal of Organizational Behavior*, **26**, 425–431.

Locke, E.A. & Latham, G.P. (1990). *A theory of goal setting and task performance*. Englewood Cliffs, NJ: Prentice-Hall.

Locke, E.A., Shaw, K.N., Saari, L.M., & Latham, G.P. (1981). Goal setting and task performance. *Psychological Bulletin*, **90**, 125–152.

Lombardo, M.M. & McCauley, C.D. (1988). *The dynamics of management derailment* (Technical Report No. 34). Greensboro, NC: Center for Creative Leadership.

Lorr, M. & More, W. (1980). Four dimensions of assertiveness. *Multivariate Behavioral Research*, **15**, 127–138.

Lorr, M., Youniss, R.P., & Stefic, E.C. (1991). An inventory of social skills. *Journal of Personality Assessment*, **57** (3), 506–520.

Marlowe, H.A., Jr (1986). Social intelligence: Evidence for multidimensionality and construct independence. *Journal of Educational Psychology*, **78**, 52–58.

Matthews, G., Zeidner, M., & Roberts, R.D. (2002). *Emotional intelligence: Science and myth*. Cambridge, MA: MIT Press.

May, G.L. & Kahnweiler, W.M. (2000). The effect of mastery practice design on learning and transfer in behavior modeling training. *Personnel Psychology*, **53**, 353–373.

Mayer, R.C., Davis, J.H., & Schoorman, F.D. (1995). An integrative model of organizational trust. *Academy of Management Review*, **20**, 709–734.

Mayer, J.D. & Salovey, P. (1997). What is emotional intelligence? In P. Salovey & D.D. Sluyter (Eds), *Emotional development and emotional intelligence: Implications for educators* (pp. 3–31). New York: Basic Books.

Mayer, J.D., Salovey, P., & Caruso, D.R. (2000). Competing models of emotional intelligence. In R.J. Sternberg (Ed.), *Handbook of human intelligence* (pp. 396–420). New York: Cambridge University Press.

McCall, M.W., Jr & Lombardo, M.M. (1983). *Off the track: Why and how successful executives get derailed* (Technical Report No. 21). Greensboro, NC: Center for Creative Leadership.

McCann, J.E. & Galbraith, J.R. (1981). Interpersonal relations. In P.C. Nystrom & W.H. Starbuck (Eds), *Handbook of organizational design* (pp. 60–84). Oxford: Oxford University Press.

McConnell, C.R. (2004). Interpersonal skills: What they are, how to improve them, and how to apply them. *The Health Care Manager*, **23** (2), 177–187.

McIntyre, R.M. & Salas, E. (1995). Measuring and managing for team performance: Emerging principles from complex environments. In R.A. Guzzo & E. Salas (Eds), *Team effectiveness and decision making in organizations* (pp. 9–45). San Francisco: Jossey-Bass.

Mead, G.H. (1934). *Mind, self, and society*. Chicago: University of Chicago Press.

Messmer, M. (1999, August). Skills for a new millennium. *Strategic Finance Magazine*, 10.

Messmer, M. (2001). Interpersonal skills: The new essential in accounting. *The National Public Accountant*, **46** (1), 28–29.

Mill, C.R. (1976). Feedback: The act of giving and receiving help. In L. Porter & C.R. Mill (Eds), *The reading book for human relations training* (pp. 18–19). Bethel, ME: National Institute for Applied Behavioral Science.

Miller, K.A. (2004). Siblings help boost social skills: Study suggests 'only child' is missing out. *WebMD Medical News*, Tuesday, July 27, 2004. Article retrieved from http://my.webmd.com/content/Article/91/101119.htm, April 21, 2005.

Morris, J.A. & Feldman, D.C. (1996). The dimensions, antecedents, and consequences of emotional labor. *Academy of Management Review*, 21 (4), 986–1010.

Motowidlo, S.J., Borman, W.C., & Schmit, M.J. (1997). A theory of individual differences in task and contextual performance. *Human Performance*, 10, 71–83.

Muchinsky, P.M. (2003). *Psychology applied to work*. Belmont, CA: Thomson-Wadsworth.

Munson, L.J., Phillips, G., Clark, C.C., & Mueller-Hanson, R. (2004). Everything you need to know about I-O internships: Results from the 2003 SIOP internship survey. *The Industrial-Organizational Psychologist*, 42 (1), 117–126.

Neuman, G.A. & Wright, J. (1999). Team effectiveness: Beyond skills and cognitive ability. *Journal of Applied Psychology*, 84 (3), 376–389.

Nurick, A.J. (1993). Facilitating effective work teams. *SAM Advanced Management Journal*, 58 (1), 22–26.

O'Conner, T. (2003). *Interpersonal skills module* (Generic Skills Integration Project—GENSIP). Dublin: University of Dublin, Trinity College.

Offermann, L.R. & Phan, L.U. (2002). Culturally intelligent leadership for a diverse world. In R.E. Riggio, S.E. Murphy, & F.J. Pirozzolo (Eds), *Multiple intelligences and leadership* (pp. 187–214). Mahwah, NJ: Lawrence Erlbaum.

Oliva, R.A. & Lancioni, R. (1996). Identifying key traits of good industrial service reps. *Marketing Management*, 4, 44–51.

Olsen, D.E., Sellers, W.A., & Phillips, R.G., Jr (2004). The simulation of a human subject for interpersonal skills training. *Proceedings of the Interservice/Industry Training, Simulation and Education Conference* (IITSEC), Orlando, FL.

Parasuraman, A., Zeithaml, V.A., & Berry, L.L. (1985). A conceptual model of service quality and its implications for future research. *Journal of Marketing*, 49, 41–50.

Pescuric, A. & Byham, W.C. (1996, July). When unveiled 20 years ago, behavior modeling was predicted to do wonder for training. It has. And, now, an enhanced version is keeping up with our changing times. *Training and Development*, 25–30.

Peterson, D.B. & Hicks, M.D. (1993, May). *How to get people to change*. Workshop presented at the Eighth Annual Conference of the Society for Industrial and Organizational Psychology, San Francisco.

Phillips, M.M. (2004). Simper nice: Before heading to Iraq, Marines learn people skills. *Wall Street Journal* (Eastern edition). Retrieved December 6, 2004, from ProQuest database.

Piedmont, R.L. & Weinstein, H.P. (1993). Predicting supervisor ratings of job performance using the NEO Personality Inventory. *Journal of Psychology*, 128, 255–265.

Poe, A.C. (2001). Mind their manners. *HR Magazine*, 46.

Porras, J. & Anderson, B. (1981). Improving managerial effectiveness through modeling-based training. *Organizational Dynamics*, 9(4), 60–77.

Pruitt, D.G. (1981). *Negotiation behavior*. New York: Academic Press.

Rahim, M.A. (1990). *Theory and research in conflict management*. New York: Praeger.

Rakos, R.F. (1991). *Assertive behavior: Theory, research, and training*. London: Routledge.

Rapisarda, B.A. (2002). The impact of emotional intelligence on work team cohesiveness and performance. *The International Journal of Organizational Analysis*, 10 (4), 363–379.

Rich, A.R. & Schroeder, H.E. (1976). Research issues in assertiveness training. *Psychological Bulletin*, **83**, 1081–1096.

Riggio, R.E. (1986). Assessment of basic social skills. *Journal of Personality and Social Psychology*, **51**, 649–660.

Riggio, R.E. & Pirozzolo, F.J. (2002). Multiple intelligences and leadership: Implications for leadership research and training. In R.E. Riggio, S.E. Murphy, & F.J. Pirozzolo (Eds), *Multiple intelligences and leadership* (pp. 241–250). Mahwah, NJ: Lawrence Erlbaum.

Robbins, S.P. & Hunsaker, P.L. (1996). *Training in inter-personal skills: TIPS for managing people at work*. Upper Saddle River, NJ: Prentice-Hall.

Rogers, C.R. & Farson, R.E. (1976). *Active listening*. Chicago: Industrial Relations Center of the University of Chicago.

Russell, T.L., Crafts, J.L., & Brooks, J.E. (1995). *Intercultural communication requirements for Special Forces teams* (Research Report 1683). Alexandria, VA: US Army Research Institute for the Behavioral and Social Sciences.

Salas, E., Burke, C.S., Bowers, C.A., & Wilson, K.A. (2001). Team training in the skies: Does crew resource management (CRM) training work? *Human Factors*, **43** (4), 641–674.

Salas, E., Sims, D.E., & Burke, C.S. (in press). Is there a big five in teamwork? To appear in *Small Group Research*.

Salas, E., Sims, D.E., & Klein, C. (2004). Cooperation at work. *Encyclopedia of Applied Psychology*, **1**, 497–505.

Salas, E., Stagl, K.C., & Burke, C.S. (2004). 25 years of team effectiveness in organizations: Research themes and emerging needs. In C.L. Cooper & I.T. Robertson (Eds), *International review of industrial and organizational psychology* (pp. 47–91). Chichester, UK: John Wiley & Sons.

Salovey, P. & Mayer, J.D. (1990). Emotional intelligence. *Imagination, Cognition, and Personality*, **9**, 185–211.

Sarbin, T.R. (1954). Role theory. In G. Lindzey (Ed.), *Handbook of social psychology*, Vol. 1, pp. 122–187.

Schein, E.H. (1999). *Process consultation revisited: Building the helping relationship*. Reading, MA: Addison-Wesley.

Schneider, B. & Bowen, D.E. (1995). *Winning the service game*. Boston: Harvard Business Press.

Schneider, R.J., Ackerman, P.L., & Kanfer, R. (1996). To 'act wisely in human relations': Exploring the dimensions of social competence. *Personality and Individual Differences*, **21**, 469–481.

Schneider, R.J., Roberts, R.D., & Heggestad, E.D. (2002, April). Exploring the structure and construct validity of a self-report social competence inventory. In L.M. Hough (Chair), *Compound traits: The next frontier in I/O personality research*. Symposium conducted at the 17th Annual Conference of the Society for Industrial and Organizational Psychology, Toronto, Ontario, Canada.

Secretary's Commission on Achieving Necessary Skills (1991). *What work requires of schools: SCANS report for American 2000*. US Department of Labor. Washington, DC: US Government Printing Office.

Sharplin, A.D., Sharplin, W.S., & Birdsong, T.P. (1986). Knowing the market: Are writing teachers out of touch? *Journal of Education for Business*, **11**, 80–84.

Shaw, M.E. (1973). Scaling group tasks: A method for dimensional analysis (MS. No. 294). *JSAS Catalog of Selected Documents in Psychology*, **3**, 8.

Shea, G.P. & Guzzo, R.A. (1987). Groups as human resources. In G.R. Ferris & K.M. Rowland (Eds), *Research in personnel and human resources management* (pp. 323–356). Greenwich, CT: JAI Press.

Sheppard, B.H. (1995). Negotiating in long-term mutually interdependent relationships among relative equals. In R.J. Bies, R.J. Lewicki, & B.H. Sheppard (Eds), *Research on negotiation in organizations* (pp. 3–44). Greenwich, CT: JAI Press.

Silberman, M. (2001). Developing interpersonal intelligence in the workplace. *Industrial and Commercial Training*, 7 (5), 266–269.

Smith, B. (2001). *Working with others, improving own learning and performance problem-solving*. Harlow: Longman.

Smith-Jentsch, K.A., Salas, E., & Baker, D.P. (1996). Training team performance-related assertiveness. *Personnel Psychology*, 49, 909–936.

Snyderman, M. & Rothman, S. (1987). Survey of expert opinion on intelligence and aptitude testing. *American Psychologist*, 42, 137–144.

Sojka, J.Z. & Deeter-Schmelz, D.R. (2002). Enhancing the emotional intelligence of salespeople. *Mid-American Journal of Business*, 17 (1), 43–50.

Sternberg, R.J. (1985). *Beyond IQ: A triarchic theory of human intelligence*. New York: Cambridge University Press.

Stevens, C.K. & Gist, M.E. (1997). Effects of self-efficacy and goal-orientation on negotiation skill maintenance: What are the mechanisms? *Personnel Psychology*, 50, 955–978.

Stevens, M.J. & Campion, M.A. (1999). Staffing work teams: Development and validation of a selection test for teamwork settings. *Journal of Management*, 25 (2), 207–228.

Stogdill, R.M. (1972). *Group process and productivity*. New York: Academic Press.

Sullivan, P.A. (1993). Communication skills training for interactive sports. *The Sport Psychologist*, 7, 79–91.

Tannenbaum, S.I., Beard, R.L., & Salas, E. (1992). Team building and its influence on team effectiveness: An examination of conceptual and empirical developments. In K. Kelley (Ed.), *Issues, theory, and research in industrial/organizational psychology* (pp. 117–153). New York: Elsevier Science.

Thorndike, E.L. (1920). Intelligence and its use. *Harper's Magazine*, 140, 227–235.

Thorndike, R.L. & Stein, S. (1937). An evaluation of the attempts to measure social intelligence. *Psychological Bulletin*, 34, 275–285.

Tinsley, C.H. (2001). How negotiators get to yes: Predicting the constellation of strategies used across cultures to negotiate conflict. *Journal of Applied Psychology*, 86 (4), 583–593.

Triandis, H.C. (1989). Cross-cultural studies of individualism and collectivism. In J. Berman (Ed.), *Nebraska symposium on motivation* (pp. 43–133). Lincoln, NB: University of Nebraska Press.

Triandis, H.C. (1995). *Individualism and collectivism*. Boulder, CO: Westview.

Trower, P. (1979). Fundamentals of interpersonal behavior: A social-psychological perspective. In A.S. Bellack & M. Hersen (Eds), *Research and practice in social skills* (pp. 3–40). New York: Plenum Press.

Trower, P. (1980). Situational analysis of the components and processes of behavior in socially skilled and unskilled patients. *Journal of Consulting and Clinical Psychology*, 48, 327–339.

US Banker (2000). Hard lessons in soft skills. *US Banker*, 110, 44.

Varney, G.H. (1989). *Building productive teams: An action guide and resource book*. San Francisco: Jossey-Bass.

Vaughn, J. (1985). The basis of English: Foundations for success in technical communications. *Technical Writing Teacher*, 12, 19–22.

Verderber, K.S. & Verderber, R.F. (1986). *Inter-act: Using interpersonal communication skills*. Belmont, CA: Wadsworth.

Wagner, J.A. (1995). Studies of individualism–collectivism: Effects on cooperation in groups. *Academy of Management Journal*, 38, 152–172.

Wagner, J.A. & Moch, M.K. (1986). Individualism–collectivism: Concept and measure. *Group and Organization Studies*, **11**, 280–303.

Wayne, S.J., Liden, R.C., Graf, I.K., & Ferris, G.R. (1997). The role of upward influence tactics in human resource decisions. *Personnel Psychology*, **50**, 979–1006.

Weekley, J.A. & Jones, C. (1997). Video-based situational testing. *Personnel Psychology*, **50**, 25–49.

Williams, W. & Sternberg, R. (1988). Group intelligence: Why some groups are better than others. *Intelligence*, **12** (4), 351–377.

Wilson, A.R., Cai, D.A., Campbell, D.M., Donohue, W.A., & Drake, L.E. (1995). Cultural and communication processes in international business negotiations. In A.M. Nicotera (Ed.), *Conflict and organizations: Communicative processes* (pp. 201–237). Albany, NY: SUNY Press.

Witt, L.A. & Ferris, G.R. (2003). Social skill as a moderator of the conscientiousness–performance relationship: Convergent results across four studies. *Journal of Applied Psychology*, **88** (5), 809–820.

Wolpe, J. (1973). *The practice of behavior therapy*. New York: Pergamon.

Wood, R.E. (1986). Task complexity: Definition of the construct. *Organizational Behavior and Human Decision Processes*, **37**, 60–82.

Yancey, G.B., Clarkson, C.P., Baxa, J.D., & Clarkson, R.N. (2003). Examples of good and bad interpersonal skills at work. *Eye on Psi Chi*, **7** (3), 40–41.

Chapter 4

ATTRIBUTION THEORY IN INDUSTRIAL AND ORGANIZATIONAL PSYCHOLOGY: A REVIEW

Mark J. Martinko
Department of Management, The Florida State University, USA
Scott C. Douglas
Department of Management, University of Montana, USA
and
Paul Harvey
Department of Management, The Florida State University, USA

The purpose of this chapter is to review the empirical and conceptual literature that has applied attribution theory to the domain of Industrial and Organizational Psychology (IOP) over the last 30 years and provide guidance on how this area will continue to evolve. At the outset, it is important to note that several other reviews of the status of attribution theory in the organizational sciences are also available (Martinko, 1995, 2004), but these have focused more on the contributions of attribution theory to the managerial literature as opposed to IOP. In presenting this review, particular emphasis will be given to the areas that have had the greatest impact on both theory and practice in IOP and/or seem to have the greatest potential to impact the long-term development of the field. We will begin with a general overview of the emergence of attributional perspectives in the IOP literature followed by a discussion of the various definitions and conceptualizations of attributional processes. We will then address the issue of measurement and review the various procedures and instruments that have been proposed as well as the respective applications, advantages, and disadvantages of these procedures. The majority of the chapter will focus on major themes in the attribution literature, including the role of attributional styles and biases, individual differences, counterproductive behavior, leader–member relations, impression management in selection and interviewing processes, emotions, and group and organizational level

International Review of Industrial and Organizational Psychology, 2006, Volume 21
Edited by G.P. Hodgkinson and J.K. Ford. © 2006 John Wiley & Sons, Ltd.

attributions for performance. The final major section of the chapter will identify emerging themes and discuss the potential of attribution theory with respect to both theory and applications in the IOP literature.

THE EMERGENCE OF ATTRIBUTION THEORY

As with many of the major theories in IOP, the roots of attribution theory in IOP can be traced back to the disciplines of psychology and social psychology. Fritz Heider (1958) is most often identified as the first person to propose a coherent theory of attributions, observing that people can be characterized as naive psychologists trying to ascertain the causes of outcomes for both themselves and others. Heider viewed this preoccupation with causation as a necessity for evolution and survival, suggesting that one's causal interpretation of the world was a primary motivating force for adaptive behavior.

After Heider, the two most influential contributors were Weiner and Kelley. Kelley (1973) focused on the front end of the attribution process, describing how people use information (i.e., consensus, consistency, and distinctiveness) to make causal inferences. On the other hand, Weiner et al. (1971) focused on the consequences of attributional explanations (e.g., ability and effort) and their dimensions (e.g., internal/external and stable/unstable) for expectancies, emotions, and behavior. In addition, Jones (1976) and his colleagues (Jones & Davis, 1965; Jones & Nisbett, 1971) as well as many others (e.g., Abramson, Seligman, & Teasdale, 1978; Deiner & Dweck, 1978) have made significant contributions to the development of attribution theory.

The emergence of attribution theory in the IOP literature occurred in the middle and late 1970s but was gradual and piecemeal. While some articles appeared in the social psychology journals (e.g., Feldman & Hilterman, 1975, 1977) that were relevant to IOP, very little was published in the mainstream IOP literature. Examples of the articles that did appear include Chacko, Stone, and Brief's (1979) article on goal setting, Kovenklioglu and Greenhaus's (1975) paper relating attributions to expectancies and task performance, Staw's (1975) paper regarding attributions for corporate performance, and the Yates and Kulick (1977) paper that discussed the relationship between attributions of control and effort.

The first major stream of attribution research in the IOP area began with Green and Mitchell's (1979) theory of leadership, which emphasized how attributional processes shape leader–member relations. This paper was followed by a flurry of leadership research in the early 1980s (e.g., Knowlton & Ilgen, 1980; Knowlton & Mitchell, 1980; McFillen & New, 1979; Mitchell & Kalb, 1981, 1982; Mitchell & Wood, 1980), which appeared to taper off quickly after a paper by Mitchell (1982) expressed disappointment regarding the explanatory power of attributions. More about this stream of research will be said later in the chapter.

During the next 25 years, attribution theory contributed to a wide variety of IOP topics including performance appraisal (e.g., Feldman, 1981; Goerke, Moller, Schulz-Hardt, Napiersky, & Frey, 2004), interview and selection processes (e.g., Silvester, 1997; Silvester, Anderson-Gough, Anderson, & Mohamed, 2002), leader–member relations (Ashkanasy, 1989, 1995), counterproductive behaviors, such as aggression (Aquino, Douglas, & Martinko, 2004; Douglas & Martinko, 2001), learned helplessness and burnout (e.g., Campbell & Martinko, 1998; Martinko & Gardner, 1982), emotions (Dasborough & Ashkanasy, 2002; Weiner, 1985a), organizational level attributions for performance (e.g., Michalisin, Karau, & Tangpong, 2003), and a variety of papers relating attributions to individual differences including core self-evaluations (Judge & Kammemeyer-Mueller, 2004), gender (e.g., Crittenden & Bae, 1994; Dobbins, Pence, Orban, & Sgro, 1983; Langford & Mackinnon, 2000), culture (e.g., Diener & Diener, 1995; Morris & Peng, 1994), age (e.g., Ferris, Yates, Gilmore, & Rowland, 1985; Mezulis, Abramson, Hyde, & Hankin, 2004), self-efficacy (Silver, Mitchell, & Gist, 1995), locus of control (e.g., Kinicki & Vecchio, 1994; Perlow & Latham, 1993; Storms & Spector, 1987), and trait anger (Douglas & Martinko, 2001). Major international conferences on the contributions of attribution theory to the organizational sciences were held in 1994 and 2004 (see Martinko, 1995, 2004). The importance of attribution theory to organizational theory was underscored by Shaffritz and Ott (2000) who named the book resulting from the 1994 conference (Martinko, 1995) as one of the two most significant contributions to organizational theory in 1995. While many of the topics addressed in the conferences built upon issues that had previously appeared in the IOP literature, such as leadership and motivation, many of the topics addressed were new or relatively new applications of attribution theory to organizational contexts. These topics included core self-evaluations, organizational politics, organizational aggression, emotions, justice, burnout, work family conflict, role conflict, the process by which groups make attributions, and negotiations (for further details see Martinko, 1995, 2004).

When we look at the volume of contributions over the last 30 years, we are impressed by the wide range of applications to virtually every major area of IOP. On the other hand, we are somewhat puzzled by the apparent failure of attribution theory to emerge as a major theory of motivation within the context of IOP. Thus, most texts in IOP (e.g., Lawson & Shen, 1998), human resource management (e.g., Dessler, 2005), and organizational behavior (e.g., Robbins, 2003; Wagner & Hollenbeck, 2005) devote relatively little space to the explanation and application of attribution theory as a separate topic. Instead, the contributions of attribution theory are interspersed among the various applications. More will be said about this issue after we have reviewed the major developments that have occurred across the basic content areas.

Before beginning our review of the content areas, it is appropriate to describe the criteria we have adopted for including works in this review. A search of the major research indexes, which included ABI/Inform, APA PsychArticles, Elsevier Science Direct, Expanded Academic ASAP, and JSTOR, yielded more than 900 articles concerned with attribution processes. We used three criteria to help us to achieve our goals and make the review manageable. First, we included only those articles concerned with major issues and topics in the IOP area. Second, we tried to balance the amount of conceptual and empirical work. More specifically, we observed that there were many more conceptual as opposed to empirical contributions and that many of the former simply described applications of attribution theory to other domains without suggesting any major adaptions or changes in attribution theory. Therefore, we elected to focus on the empirical works but, recognizing that conceptual works often provide guidance for empirical work, we also included those of the more recent conceptual works that appear to be most promising for forecasting the longer term direction of the field. Finally, we also focused on articles from journals that are well respected by the IOP community, namely, the *Journal of Applied Psychology*, *Personnel Psychology*, *Journal of Occupational Health Psychology*, *Organizational Behavior and Human Decision Processes*, *Academy of Management Review*, *Academy of Management Journal*, *Journal of Personality and Social Psychology*, *Psychological Bulletin*, *Journal of Occupational and Organizational Psychology*, *Personality and Social Psychology Bulletin*, *European Journal of Personality*, *Journal of Organizational Behavior*, *Journal of Vocational Behavior*, and the *International Journal of Selection and Assessment*.

DEFINITION AND CONSTRUCT

An attribution is a causal explanation (Martinko, 2004). As Kelley and Michela (1980) have noted, there are a number of variations of attribution theory but the majority focus on either the information processing required to make an attribution (Kelley, 1973) or the consequences of attributions (Weiner, 1986). More specifically, Kelley's model (1973) focused on how people use consensus, consistency, and distinctiveness information to determine whether the cause of an outcome is due to the person, an entity, or the situation. As suggested by Martinko (1995), this model of the attribution process is most often used to describe how people make attributions for the outcomes of others (i.e., social attributions) and is typified by the Green and Mitchell (1979) leadership model.

A second major thrust of attribution theory has been within the context of intrapersonal achievement-oriented behavior (Weiner, 1985a, 1986). Within this context, attribution theories typically seek to describe the consequences of causal explanations (e.g., ability and effort) and causal dimensions (e.g., internal/external and stable/unstable) with respect to individuals' expectancies, emotions, and behaviors. Thus, for example, counterproductive aggressive behavior and the accompanying anger are viewed as a consequence of external and stable attributions (i.e., blaming the organization) for negative outcomes (e.g., being fired).

In addition to the two most traditional variations of attribution theory described above, Brewin and Antaki (1987) have noted that attributions can also serve other purposes such as moral evaluation, self-presentation, and labeling or description. Likewise, Lord and Smith (1983) suggest that attributions can be used not only to identify the cause of an outcome, but can also be used to refer to personal qualities such as leadership and can be used to identify responsibility for an event.

As Martinko (2004) has noted, the many different forms that attribution theory has taken can sometimes be confusing and, at times, it also appears as if the term 'attribution' is synonymous with 'perception.' However, this problem is more apparent than real since the term almost always refers to perceptions of causation. Within the context of our review, we will focus on the two major forms of attribution theory identified above: the process by which people form attributions and the consequences of attributions in terms of expectancies, emotions, and behavior.

MEASURING ATTRIBUTIONS

Before beginning our review of the various topic areas, it is important to discuss the processes and issues related to the measurement of attributions and also to point out that other more comprehensive reviews and discussions of these methods are available (e.g., Kent & Martinko, 1995; Russell, 1991). As indicated above, there are many different types of attributions and domains to which attribution theory has been applied. Each of these different purposes and applications requires somewhat different measurement procedures.

Measurement Procedures

When measuring intrapersonal attributions for achievement, researchers typically measure attributional explanations, the dimensions of the explanations, or both. Explanations are the immediate cause of an outcome such as ability, effort, task difficulty, or luck. Typically, explanations are assessed by asking respondents to identify the extent to which an explanation is appropriate on a Likert-type scale. Dimensions are viewed as a means of assessing the underlying cognitive structure of explanations. Thus an explanation such as ability can be viewed along the dimensions of locus of causality (i.e., internal or external) and stability (stable or unstable) on a Likert-type scale.

Whether or not one measures explanations or dimensions is somewhat of a dilemma (Kent & Martinko, 1995). Since explanations are the subjects' most immediate and cognitively salient expression of their views of causation, it would seem that explanations would be the most appropriate measure. However, as Weiner (1986) and others (e.g., Russell, 1991) have noted, explanations do not always predict emotion, expectancies, or behaviors because the underlying structure and intent of the explanation is not always known. More specifically, it has been asserted that the underlying cognitive dimensions of the explanations are the key to predicting expectancies, emotions, and outcomes. To illustrate this issue, we will use the example of a salesperson failing to make an important sale and attributing the failure to a lack of ability (explanation). Whether or not this explanation will affect expectancies, emotions, and behaviors depends on the dimensions that underlie the subject's concept of ability. If the subject views ability as internal, she will experience negative affect. If she also views ability as stable, she will expect to fail in the future in similar situations and, as a consequence of her views of ability as internal and stable, she will be unlikely to exert effort in the future. On the other hand, if ability is viewed as internal and unstable, the subject may still feel badly, but if she views ability as unstable and changeable, she is less likely to expect failure and more likely to expend effort in the future. Thus, a good argument can be made for measuring the dimensions of explanations rather than the explanations themselves. However, it can also be argued that the explanation is the subject's most natural response, and that asking about the underlying dimensions may confuse people and result in cognitive processes that are not normal, resulting in findings that are an artifact of the method rather than typical cognitive processes. Our recommendation is that, when in doubt, measure both the explanations and the dimensions. A recent study suggested that there is almost no difference in the results of the two methods and that subjects most often identify the dimensions of explanations that are predicted by theory (e.g., Martinko & Moss, 2004).

There is also some disagreement about the explanations that should be measured, and researchers have been criticized for limiting attributional explanations to ability, effort, task difficulty, and luck or chance (e.g., Falbo & Beck, 1979). Weiner (1983, 1985a) notes that these are the four causes that are most often given in the motivation–achievement domain, but other domains can also produce different causal ascriptions (Reno, 1979). This potential highlights the need for conducting pilot studies to identify the most salient causes when we move beyond the achievement context into other areas, such as judging responsibility, assigning blame, and ethics. As researchers begin to explore different applications, the number of potential causal explanations increases exponentially and, as Benson (1989) has observed, building a parsimonious attributional framework appears unlikely unless we measure the underlying causal dimensions. Thus focusing measurement on dimensions rather than explanations may be a more efficacious strategy for theory building since it is more likely to allow comparisons across studies and is more amenable to meta-analyses.

Scales

A number of scales have been developed to measure attributions. Some of these scales, such as Russell's Causal Dimension Scale (Russell, 1982), have been designed to measure individuals' reactions to specific events. However, many of the standardized scales are designed to measure attribution style, which is the notion that people have cross-situational consistencies (i.e., biases) in the way they make attributions (Cutrona, Russell, & Jones, 1985; Peterson et al., 1982). Thus, for example, some people may have an optimistic style, and tend to attribute success to their own internal and stable characteristics (i.e., ability) and failure to external and unstable causes such as luck. On the other hand, people who are pessimistic tend to attribute failure to their own internal and stable characteristics (e.g., ability) and success to external and unstable causes such as luck. In general, research has demonstrated that these styles are related to people's attributional tendencies (Martinko, 2004). The scales that are most frequently used to measure attributions and attribution styles are discussed below.

The Causal Dimension Scale

This scale (Russell, 1982) is a direct-rating instrument that asks subjects to provide open-ended responses for achievement outcomes and then requires them to rate their attributions along the locus of causality, stability, and controllability dimensions. Although this scale has been widely accepted (e.g., Russell, McAuley, & Tarico, 1987; Vallerand, 1987) and has demonstrated reliability (e.g., Abraham, 1985; Henry & Campbell, 1995), several criticisms have been made concerning the factorial structure of the causal dimensions, particularly controllability (Vallerand & Richer, 1988). McAuley, Duncan, and Russell (1992) addressed this concern in developing the CDSII. In so doing, they expanded the controllability dimension to include both personal and external control dimensions. The results of four studies (McAuley et al., 1992) demonstrated average internal consistencies between 0.67 and 0.82 for the four dimensions and confirmatory factor analysis indicated support for the hypothesized four-factor structure (McAuley et al., 1992). Nevertheless, the original scale still appears to be used more frequently than the revised scale.

The Multidimensional–Multiattributional Causality Scale

This 48-item scale (Lefcourt, von Baeyer, Ware, & Cox, 1979) employs a derived-score approach and is used to measure attribution style (e.g., Powers, Douglas, & Choroszy, 1983; Reasinger & Brownlow, 1996). Although more thorough reviews of this scale have been conducted by Lefcourt (1991) and Hamilton and Akhter (2002), we provide a brief summary of the main findings pertaining to the scale. The scale includes items that assess subjects' reactions to failure and success in both the achievement and affiliation domains. Within each of these domains, there are three items relating to ability, effort, context, and luck. Cronbach alphas for this scale have ranged from 0.50 to 0.88, while test–retest scores range between 0.50 and 0.70 (Lefcourt, 1991). In their review of the scale, Hamilton and Akhter (2002) concluded that there was partial support for the scale's factorial validity.

The Attributional Style Questionnaire (ASQ)

The ASQ (Peterson et al., 1982) is another measure of attribution style. With this instrument, individuals are asked to speculate about the causes for 12 hypothetical success and failure situations and then indicate on a seven-point Likert-type scale the extent to which each cause is: due to the characteristics of the person (internal) or of the situation (external); likely to persist over time (stable) or is only temporary (unstable); and, likely to influence other areas of the person's life (global) or is specific to similar situations (specific) (Shaver & Brennan, 1991). The reliabilities for each of the dimensions are generally low (Barnett & Gottlib, 1988). However, the reliabilities for the composite scores for the six positive and six negative items tend to exceed 0.70 (Shaver & Brennan, 1991). In light of this, Petersen et al. (1982) recommended that those who use the scale report the reliabilities for the composite scores and not discriminate between achievement and affiliation items unless there are specific and relevant reasons to do so. A more recent version of this instrument (Peterson & Villanova, 1988) has higher reliabilities but the original version appears to be used more extensively and, despite the problems noted above, the original version of the ASQ is probably the most extensively used scale to measure attribution style.

Organizational Attributional Style Questionnaire (OASQ)

The OASQ (Kent & Martinko, 1995) is similar to the ASQ but focuses specifically on organizational situations rather than the general scenarios presented in the ASQ. The rationale for this scale was a reaction, in part, to criticisms that the earlier attribution style questionnaires resulted in low reliabilities because of the wide range and disparity in the situations that were described (e.g., Cutrona et al., 1984; Russell, 1982). Kent and Martinko (1995) argued that narrowing the scope of achievement-oriented events would result in greater reliability. In the original study the reliabilities for the dimensions of stability (0.80), internality (0.69), externality (0.68), controllability (0.70), globality (0.76), and intentionality (0.80) were within the range suggested by Nunnally (1978). However, following the results of a principal components analysis with an oblique rotation, they suggested that the scale be limited to three dimensions: stability, controllability, and intentionality (Kent &

Martinko, 1995). This scale, or a modified version, has been used in several subsequent studies. In a study of empowerment and learned-helplessness, the Cronbach alphas were 0.77 and higher (Campbell & Martinko, 1998). Douglas and Martinko (2001) used a modified version of the OASQ, which included the locus of causality dimension to study the association between a hostile attribution style and workplace aggression. They reported a Cronbach alpha of 0.89 for the composite score. Aquino et al. (2004) also used the modified version employed by Douglas and Martinko (2001) to study the relationship between hostile attribution style, perceived victimization, and overt expressions of anger and reported a composite score of $\alpha = 0.88$. The relatively higher reliabilities for the OASQ as compared to the ASQ suggest that this instrument may be a more appropriate measure of attribution style in organizational contexts.

Social Attributional Style Questionnaire (SASQ)

The SASQ (Thomson & Martinko, 2004) is similar to the OASQ (Kent & Martinko, 1995) with the exception that it inquires about one's social attributions, rather than self-attributions, in the workplace. In constructing this scale the authors conducted confirmatory factor analyses on data obtained in two separate studies. The results yielded two interpretable factors: stability and intentionality with Cronbach alphas of 0.81 and 0.86, respectively. This scale appears promising in that it confirmed that observers have consistent styles (i.e., attributional biases) in the way that they evaluate the behavior of others, which has important implications for IOP, particularly with respect to appraisals and judgments of the causes of member and organizational performance. However, because it is so new, information on the validity of the scale is limited.

The ROASQ

The Revised Occupational Attributional Style Questionnaire (ROASQ) by Furnham, Brewin, and O'Kelly (1994) is similar to both the ASQ (Petersen et al., 1982) and the OASQ (Kent & Martinko, 1995). Unfortunately, the scales developed by Furnham et al. (1994) and Kent and Martinko (1995) can easily be confused, since they are both referred to in the literature as the OASQ. To limit this confusion, we will refer to the Furnham et al. (1994) scale as the ROASQ. The ROASQ is an extended version of the original scale developed by Furnham, Sadka, and Brewin (1992). Like the Kent and Martinko (1995) scale, the ROASQ incorporates 16 hypothetical scenarios—including the 10 original items from Furnham et al. (1992)—describing eight positive and negative events. Like the OASQII (Martinko & Moss, 2004), the ROASQ asks the subjects to write down the single most likely cause for the outcomes and then score them along a series of seven-point scales reflecting different attributional dimensions. The ROASQ differs from the scales developed by Martinko and his colleagues in terms of the dimensions of interest. Specifically, the ROASQ measures the internality, stability, globality, externality, and personal controllability dimensions. The average reliability for all dimensions was 0.67. Both internality and personal control had reliabilities of less than 0.60 (Furnham et al., 1994). Concerning evidence of validity, there is some indication of construct validity as varying patterns of attribution style were predictably correlated with organizational measures such as organizational commitment, job involvement, and job satisfaction (Furnham et al., 1994).

It is difficult to compare the relative efficacy of the OASQ by Martinko and his colleagues and that of Fuhrnam et al. since the amount of empirical data and validation is limited for both measures. It is worth noting, however, that although both scales were developed independently and the stems they used are different, the scales are very similar. The positive findings for both scales, along with their reasonably high reliabilities, suggest that they are better alternatives than the original ASQ for measuring attributional styles in organizational contexts.

Coding Systems

In addition to standardized scales, researchers have also developed coding systems for the analysis of spoken attributions, which are described in the work of Campbell and Martinko (1998), Henry and Campbell (1995), Silvester (1997), Silvester, Anderson, and Patterson (1999), and Weiner (1983, 1985a). Readers should consult these articles for descriptions of the relevant coding procedures. In addition to the systems that were developed for specific studies, at least two systems have been developed to serve as generic templates for coding attributions and are described below.

The Leeds Attributional Coding System (LACS)

Developed by Stratton, Munton, Hanks, Heard, and Davidson (1988), this system provides a method for extracting and coding spoken attributions. Although Munton, Silvester, Stratton, and Hanks (1999) provide a detailed review and description for the LACS, we will touch upon a few of its highlights here. The system provides binary ratings (0, 1) on five causal dimensions: internal–external, stable–unstable, controllable–uncontrollable, global–specific, and personal–universal. However, Silvester et al. (1999) note that only the first four of these dimensions are relevant to organizational settings and that it is possible to add a third rating of 'uncertain' in those cases where the coders cannot ascertain the spoken attribution. Additionally, the locus of causality and controllability dimensions can be coded separately, depending on whether one is speaking about self- or social attributions. Like all verbal coding schemes, the validity of the LACS is largely contingent upon the training of the coders. With regard to reliabilities, the results of several studies indicate that coders can reliably identify and extract spoken attributions from general discourse (Wendel, Miklowitz, Richards, & George, 2000). Acceptable inter-rater reliabilities have been achieved by Silvester et al. (1999), Silvester et al. (2002), and Wendel et al. (2000).

Content Analysis of Verbal Explanations (CAVE)

Another fairly widely used technique for analyzing causal attributions in written text and speech is CAVE (Peterson, Bettes, & Seligman, 1985). This procedure requires the analyst to examine written or spoken text, either manually or with specially designed software, in order to identify key words that denote causality. For example, the term 'responsibility' often implies an attribution of control and/or intent (e.g., Gundlach, Douglas, & Martinko, 2003). The statements containing these terms are then analyzed and coded along the relevant attributional dimensions. In this way contextual analysis can be used as an alternative or as a supplement to more direct methods for the measurement of attributional tendencies, such as the OASQ. Like the LACS, the CAVE technique may be more advantageous than laboratory-based methods and structured questionnaires, in that it captures individuals' causal perceptions in natural settings, thereby reducing the possibility of data contamination arising from the artificial nature of the data collection process, as encountered in experimental settings.

Other procedures

Apparently there are no well-known scales for assessing Kelley's (1967, 1972) sources of information. Nevertheless, several studies have been able to evaluate the notion that people use consensus, distinctiveness, and consistency information to form attributional explanations. For instance, of the subordinates with whom they had to deal, Ashkanasy (1995) asked subjects to recall one who had performed well and one who had performed poorly. Afterward, the subjects were asked to rate each subordinate's past performance on the same task (consistency), performance on other types of tasks (distinctiveness), and the performance of the subordinate's colleagues on the same task (consensus) along a seven-point Likert-type scale. Other studies that assess the hypothesized influence of the three sources of information on attributional explanations have used short scenarios (e.g., Ashkanasy, 1989; Mitchell & Wood, 1980) and role plays (e.g., Ashkanasy & Gallois, 1994; Green & Liden, 1980; Mitchell & Kalb, 1981) in which they manipulated consistency, consensus, and distinctiveness information. Additionally, some researchers have used verbal protocol analysis (e.g., Martin & Klimosky, 1990) to test Kelley's (1972) co-variation hypothesis. Thus, although there appear to be no standardized rating instruments for assessing Kelley's dimensions, they have nonetheless been measured or manipulated with the techniques described above.

Conclusions: Measurement

Over 15 years ago, Benson (1989) argued that the absence of an overarching framework for attributional measurement, and the lack of integration across the wide variety of measurement techniques, had limited research. Kent and Martinko echoed similar concerns in 1995, stating that the wide variety of methods makes it difficult to gain a more comprehensive understanding of the role of attributions in organizations. However, there may also be some resolution of these issues with the movement toward measuring dimensions of attributions that can be compared across studies through techniques such as meta-analysis. In addition, the growing body of evidence that spoken attributions can be validly and reliably assessed is promising for researchers who want to study attributional processes in organizational field settings.

ATTRIBUTIONAL BIASES

Research on attributions has identified several common attributional biases that appear to distort causal perceptions. These biases are important because they have the potential to disrupt strategic planning efforts (Bernardin, 1989), reduce the reliability and effectiveness of selection interviews (Herriot, 1981), and promote conflict between leaders and subordinates (Martinko & Gardner, 1987). In addition, because of our knowledge of these biases, they can enhance our ability to predict attributions, expectancies, emotions, and behavior. In this section we will define and describe four of the most prevalent attributional biases that have been identified: the actor–observer bias, the self-serving bias, the false consensus bias, and the hedonic relevance bias.

Actor–observer Bias

The actor–observer bias refers to the 'pervasive tendency of actors to attribute their actions to situational requirements, whereas observers tend to attribute the same actions to stable personal dispositions' (Jones & Nisbett, 1972, p. 2). Bernardin (1989) explained that this tendency often causes employees (i.e., the actors) to make attributions that differ from those made by supervisors (i.e., the observers). For instance, if an employee succeeds or fails at a task, a supervisor might be inclined to attribute the outcome to a cause such as ability. Conversely, the employee is more likely to attribute the outcome to situational factors such as leadership, resource levels, or coworkers' efforts. Martinko and Gardner (1987) reasoned that subordinates make situational attributions more frequently than leaders because they are more aware of the external circumstances affecting their performance.

Empirical research

Numerous empirical studies have demonstrated the existence of the actor–observer bias (e.g., Bernardin, 1989; Bernardin & Beatty, 1984; Epley, Savitsky, & Gilovich, 2002; Feldman, 1981; Mitchell & Wood, 1980; Miyamoto & Kitayama, 2002; Pruitt & Insko, 1980; Ross, 1977; Sillars, 1981; Van Boven, Kamada, & Gilovich, 1999). For instance, Bernardin and Beatty (1984) and Ross (1977) both showed the existence of the bias in laboratory settings. Bernardin (1989) built upon these laboratory findings by demonstrating a reliable difference in the attributions made by supervisors and subordinates in a workplace setting. He found that mid-level managers tended to attribute subordinate failures to dispositional characteristics of the employees. When evaluating their own failures, however, the same mid-level managers were more likely to attribute outcomes to external factors. Ironically, the most common external attribution made by these subjects was the poor performance of their own supervisors.

The severity of attributional bias between supervisors and subordinates appears to increase as the former become further removed from the activity the subordinates are performing. Several studies (i.e., Fedor & Rowland, 1989; Mitchell & Kalb, 1982) show that supervisors are more susceptible to dispositionally biased attributions when they have less first-hand familiarity with the situational factors affecting subordinate performance. Mitchell and Kalb (1982) demonstrated that supervisors are less biased toward dispositional attributions if they have experience with the task they are observing. Similarly, Fedor and Rowland (1989) found that supervisors exhibited stronger dispositional biases the longer they held supervisory positions and did not perform the work they supervise.

Although the actor–observer bias appears to be a fairly common human tendency, research indicates that its prevalence may vary by culture. Martinko and Douglas (1999) argued that this variation might be explained by the extent to which different cultures emphasize dispositional or situational explanations of outcomes. In support of this argument, Van Boven et al. (1999) found that Japanese subjects were less biased toward attributing actor behaviors to dispositional factors than were subjects from more individualistic cultures. Similarly, Miyamoto and Kitayama (2002) found that American observers showed stronger dispositional biases for actor behavior than did Japanese subjects.

Research suggests that the actor–observer bias can complicate the process of administering rewards, promotions, and punishments. These problems appear to arise as a result of attributional conflict between supervisors and subordinates (e.g., Baron, 1985; Martinko, 2002; Martinko & Douglas, 1999). Martinko (2002) explained that the different attributions that actors and observers form can lead to disagreements concerning the assignment of responsibility, especially when the outcomes are negative. As a result, supervisors may punish employees for negative outcomes when employees feel that situational factors are responsible (Martinko & Douglas, 1999). Such punishments are likely to have negative affects on employee perceptions of fairness and satisfaction.

Training prescriptions might also be flawed as a result of actor–observer biases. Several authors (i.e., Gist & Mitchell, 1992; Green & Mitchell, 1979; Ilgen & Knowlton, 1980; Mitchell & Wood, 1980) noted that the type of training assigned to subordinates is typically a function of supervisors' diagnoses of the causes of poor performance. Managers that focus on dispositional causes of poor subordinate performance might therefore administer ineffective training techniques when the poor performance is actually caused by situational factors.

Self-serving Bias

The self-serving bias refers to the tendency of individuals to take credit for successful outcomes while blaming other people or situational factors for negative outcomes (Zuckerman, 1979). A common example of this bias is an employee who takes credit for an important sale but blames the failure to make a sale on a lack of organizational support. In both cases the employee is making a potentially inaccurate attribution that places him or her in a positive light, hence the name 'self-serving' bias.

There are at least three reasons why individuals might exhibit a self-serving bias (Clapham & Schwenk, 1991; Martinko & Gardner, 1987). First, people may communicate self-serving attributions under the belief that doing so will make them look good (Bradley, 1978; Salancik & Meindl, 1984; Staw, McKechnie, & Puffer, 1983). A second reason is that self-serving attributions may serve as an ego-defense mechanism (Huff & Schwenk, 1990; Zuckerman, 1979). Finally, the motivation for the self-serving bias can be seen as a strategy for maximizing rewards and minimizing punishments for failures.

Empirical research

Numerous studies have confirmed the existence of the self-serving bias. Dobbins and Russell (1986) found that the leaders of groups that were told they had performed at a low level blamed the internal characteristics of their subordinates for the poor performance, whereas the subordinates attributed the poor performance to internal factors of their leaders. Thus, both subordinates and leaders made self-serving attributions by blaming each other for the poor performance. Additional research documents the self-serving bias in shareholder letters signed by corporate executives (Bettman & Weitz, 1983;

Clapham & Schwenk, 1991; Salancik & Meindl, 1984; Staw et al., 1983), demonstrating that executives often take credit for successful organizational outcomes while attributing negative outcomes to external factors.

It has also been suggested that the self-serving bias affects people at the group level as well as at the individual level. Several studies have shown that people often make self-serving attributions for the outcomes of the groups to which they belong (Al-Zahnrani & Kaplowitz, 1993; Islam & Hewstone, 1993; Taylor & Jaggi, 1974). Thus, it appears that employees who identify strongly with their organization, or workgroup within their organization, are relatively more self-serving when evaluating the behaviors of their group as opposed to other groups.

As with the actor–observer bias, there is some evidence that self-serving attributions are more prevalent in some cultures. Specifically, the self-serving bias appears to be most prevalent in individualistic cultures such as the USA (Martinko & Douglas, 1999; Mezulis et al., 2004; Van Boven et al., 1999). It does not appear, however, that self-serving biases are solely a Western, individualistic phenomenon. A meta-analysis by Mezulis et al. (2004) concluded that the self-serving bias is common in most human subjects, but is exacerbated in individualistic societies.

False Consensus Bias

Martinko (2002) explains that the false consensus bias 'is the result of observers believing that their own behaviors and choices are typical and appropriate and then using them as a standard to judge the behavior and performance of others' (p. 75). The term 'false consensus' therefore refers to the belief that one's behaviors are appropriate and consistent with behavioral norms (Krueger & Clement, 1994; Krueger & Zeiger, 1993; Ross, 1977). Thus, this bias denotes a tendency to believe that one's behaviors are high on Kelley's (1967) consensus dimension of attributions.

This bias particularly affects the attributions that individuals make concerning the behaviors they observe in others. When individuals believe that their own behaviors are 'average,' they also tend to believe that behaviors that do not conform to their standards are somehow deviant from the social norm. When observing others, individuals exhibiting the false consensus bias may therefore attribute nonconforming behaviors to stable dispositional factors of those being observed (Martinko & Gardner, 1987). This is consistent with research on the consensus dimension discussed above, which shows that observed behaviors perceived to be low on consensus are commonly attributed to dispositional rather than situational factors. On the other hand, behaviors that are consistent with the observers' own behavioral preferences are more likely to be attributed to situational factors.

Empirical research

Relatively little empirical research has investigated the prevalence of the false consensus bias (Martinko, 2002). However, Krueger and Zeiger (1993) found that subjects demonstrated the false consensus bias more frequently when interacting with individuals of the same gender. This finding indicates that individuals are more likely to overgeneralize themselves to others of the same gender, but are less likely to do so when interacting with members of the opposite gender. Thus, obvious differences between individuals (such as gender differences) may attenuate false consensus biases.

The false consensus bias has negative implications for a manager's ability to accurately evaluate employees and job candidates. The net effect of the bias is likely to be that managers use their own behaviors as a basis for judging employees (Feldman, 1981). As such, it is likely that managers will favor employees that mimic their own behavior when evaluating employees and making reward and promotion decisions. Similarly, when conducting selection interviews, interviewers might be biased toward candidates whose behaviors are similar to those of the interviewer. More will be said about this bias in the section on personnel selection and assessment below.

Hedonic Relevance Bias

Hedonic relevance refers to the perceived personal benefit associated with an outcome or behavior (Martinko, 2002). Jones and Davis (1965) argued that the hedonic relevance of outcomes and behaviors influences the attributions of observers such that they are biased toward making dispositional attributions when there are strong affective consequences.

Empirical research

Although there has not been a great deal of empirical research concerning the hedonic relevance bias, a study by Dossett and Greenberg (1981) demonstrated the effect of hedonic relevance in performance evaluations. The authors argued that the hedonic relevance of subordinate goal-achievement to a supervisor would likely increase based on the extent to which the supervisor participated in the setting of the goal. The basis for this argument, according to the authors, is that the success or failure of a subordinate in achieving a goal reflects strongly on a supervisor. In support of this notion, Dossett and Greenberg (1981) found that supervisors that were involved in the goal-setting process made more favorable attributions concerning their subordinates' successful performances (e.g., high ability and effort) and more unfavorable attributions for subordinate failures (e.g., low ability and effort).

Implications

As stated in the introduction to this section, biases are critical to understanding interpersonal behaviors and evaluative situations such as selection and assessment activities. Biases are important in understanding these processes because they help to forecast attributions, expectancies, affect, and behaviors. Understanding that biases such as those discussed above can lead people to attribute the same behaviors and outcomes to different causes enables leaders to both anticipate and manage conflict (Baron, 1985; Feldman, 1981). The research discussed above suggests that unless this conflict is recognized and managed, it can impair a leader's ability to effectively evaluate employees, administer training and rewards, and make selection decisions. More about the effects of attributional errors and biases will be discussed in later sections, particularly with respect to selection and assessment and leader–member relations.

INDIVIDUAL DIFFERENCES AND ATTRIBUTIONS

During the last 30 years research has identified a number of significant relationships between individual difference variables and attributions. Although it is often difficult to ascertain the exact nature of these relationships, they are important because the individual difference variables can be used as a proxy for identifying attribution styles. These relationships are described below.

Gender

Findings from this research indicate that males and females demonstrate differences in their attribution styles. These differences appear to exist when male and female subjects evaluate their own performance or the performance of others (e.g., Feather, 1969; Feldman-Summers & Kiesler, 1974; McElroy & Morrow, 1983; Molm, 1985).

Gender and self-evaluations

Feather (1969) and McElroy and Morrow (1983) found that female employees tend to attribute their performance to external factors whereas males often make more self-serving attributions—taking credit for successful outcomes and blaming external factors for negative outcomes. McElroy and Morrow (1983) explained that these differences have important implications for employees' performance. As noted in our discussion on empowerment elsewhere in this chapter, the tendency to attribute positive outcomes to internal factors while attributing negative outcomes to external factors can promote high levels of motivation and performance. It therefore appears that men may be somewhat predisposed toward empowering attributions, even if these attributions are not always accurate.

Males also tend to express more empowering attributions because of their heightened tendency to demonstrate self-serving (Cash, Gillen, & Burns, 1977; Dobbins et al., 1983) or hostile (Douglas & Martinko, 2001; Martinko & Moss, 2004; Neuman & Baron, 1998) attributional biases. As noted elsewhere in this chapter, subjects exhibiting these types of biases blame external factors for negative outcomes. Additionally, the self-serving bias promotes the attribution of positive outcomes to internal characteristics. The finding that men are more likely than women to demonstrate these tendencies might explain results indicating that men tend to take more credit than women do for successes, while accepting less blame for failures.

A study by Molm (1985) also indicated that men and women base their self-evaluations on different causal factors. She found that male subjects often cited their level of power and their use of that power as a primary cause of positive or negative self-evaluations. Females, on the other hand, were more likely to attribute their evaluations to stable personality and behavioral characteristics. This finding implies that males and females differ in their opinions concerning the factors that lead to high levels of performance.

Gender and evaluations of others

Feldman-Summers and Kiesler (1974) found that when males and females performed at the same high level, observers often attributed the performance of females to effort while attributing the performance of males to ability. They also noted that this tendency was stronger for male raters than for female raters, suggesting that men may be more biased in rating female performance than females. The authors reasoned that observers, especially males, expected the males to succeed while expecting females to fail. Thus, when females performed at the same level as males, the subjects in this study may have assumed that the females exerted more effort than the males in order to compensate for lower ability.

McElroy and Morrow (1983) came to a similar conclusion, taking into account the nature of the tasks the subjects observed. They argued that the effects found by Feldman-Summers and Kiesler (1974) are most likely to occur when female actors are observed working in traditionally male-dominated jobs (e.g., firefighters and construction workers). They reasoned that many observers would be socialized to believe that men are better suited to such jobs and would therefore attribute successful performance by men to their inherent abilities. Females, on the other hand, might be seen as less fit for such occupations, causing raters to assume that women must rely on factors such as high levels of effort, luck, or assistance from others to succeed.

Gender might also impact individuals' evaluations of other employees due to its potential to induce attributional biases. As noted above, at least two studies have indicated that males tend to show higher levels of self-serving bias than females. This type of bias might cause male managers to take credit for successes at work while blaming subordinates for failures. Conversely, it is possible that females are more objective in their evaluations.

On the other hand, research by Powell and Butterfield (1980) suggested that gender only has significant effects on evaluations when information about the performer and the performance environment is limited. More specifically, their research showed that the gender of actors did not significantly influence observers' attributions when the observers were aware of information, other than gender, that was relevant to the actors' performance. They reasoned that gender-related biases and stereotypes have significant effects on attributions only when performance-related information is limited. As a result, they concluded that bias and discrimination are most likely to occur in ambiguous situations where information is limited. In a review of the discrimination literature, Martinko and Gardner (1983) arrived at a similar conclusion, asserting that job discrimination and bias were attenuated in information-rich environments such that gender stereotypes and biases only played a significant role when little information was available. We believe that a similar situation exists with respect to attributional biases. More specifically, when objective information is available regarding the causes of performance, attributional biases are less likely to occur than in situations with little information and high ambiguity.

Attributions and Culture

One can argue whether or not culture should be considered an individual difference variable. We will avoid this argument by simply observing that culture is often used as a categorical and control variable and treated as an individual difference. A considerable body of work has evolved demonstrating that attributions and attribution styles are related to culture.

Differences in attributions across cultures

One of the most consistent findings in cross-cultural attribution research is that cultures tend to differ in their members' displays of internal and external attribution styles. Research has demonstrated that Chilean (Betancourt & Weiner, 1982), Indian (Inkeles, 1983), Chinese (Morris & Peng, 1994), and Korean (Cha & Nam, 1985; Jae-Ho & Ki-Dok, 1985) subjects all tend to make attributions that are more external than subjects from the United States.

In explaining these findings, several researchers have argued that members of individualistic societies tend to have dispositional attribution styles, whereas members of collective cultures tend to have more situationally oriented styles (Diener & Diener, 1995; Martinko & Douglas, 1999; Morris & Peng, 1994). Martinko and Douglas (1999) argued that members of individualistic cultures would be more likely to attribute behaviors and outcomes to internal, low-consensus factors because they are socialized to believe that individuals are responsible for their own successes and failures. As Landrine and Klonoff (1992) noted, in such cultures the ultimate explanation for most outcomes is generally the self. Members of collective cultures, on the other hand, are socialized to 'downplay individual independence and distinction' (Martinko & Douglas, 1999, p. 273), focusing instead on the role of society and other factors when explaining the causes of outcomes and behaviors. As a note of caution, it should be stated that cultural factors besides individualism appear to influence attribution styles. Crittenden and Bae (1994) explained that individuals in different Asian countries (all of which represent relatively collectivistic cultures) varied in their tendencies to make either self-serving or self-effacing attributions. They reported that additional situational factors such as setting (i.e., work or school) could influence the types of attributions deemed appropriate and that these social rules differed between the Asian countries.

The economic and geographical position of a country might also influence the attributions made by its citizens. Payne and Furnham (1990) provided an example of this effect by studying the attributions made by employed and unemployed citizens of Barbados. Among the six most common attributions made by subjects, four were situational in nature (failure of trade unions, government policy, global and regional changes, and industrial management). Only two of the most common attributions were dispositional (lack of ability and effort). The authors suggested that because of Barbados' position as a relatively small and undeveloped country heavily influenced by external forces, its citizens are more sensitive to external factors when making attributions for outcomes such as job loss.

Although the majority of cross-cultural attribution research has focused on locus of causality, culture can also influence other attributional dimensions. For instance, Betancourt and Weiner (1982) found that Chilean subjects generally perceived causes to be less stable and less controllable than did American subjects.

Dimensions across cultures

Members of different cultures may also differ in how they conceptualize the dimensions of attributions. As discussed earlier in the chapter, attributions are often conceptualized in terms of effort, ability, task difficulty, and luck (Weiner et al., 1971). Little (1987) has noted that this taxonomy is rooted in Western culture and may carry different meanings in different cultures. For example, Little found that children in Sri Lanka were more likely to attribute scholastic performance to luck than were British children. However, she also discovered that individuals from Sri Lanka often equate luck with good fortune whereas Britons are more likely to equate luck with chance. Whereas chance denotes a random occurrence, good fortune simply refers to a positive occurrence. When conceptualized in this way, the fact that scholastic performance is rarely random is likely to explain the different attributions made by the two cultures.

Additional research indicates that members of some cultures may make attributions that are not considered by many Western researchers. As an example, Morris and Peng (1994) explained that karma, the belief that outcomes are influenced by good and bad deeds performed in a previous life, is an important causal factor for members of Hindu cultures. Karma, however, is rarely, if ever, considered by Western researchers. Thus, it is possible that there are factors influencing the attributions of some cultures' members that current attribution research has yet to identify.

Biases between cultures

A final note about the influence of culture on attributions relates to a phenomenon known as 'egocentric assumptions' (Kelley, 1973) or intergroup bias (Islam & Hewstone, 1993). This phenomenon describes the tendency of members of a culture to make self-serving attributions for the behaviors and outcomes of other members of that culture (in-group members) while making derogatory attributions for the actions and outcomes of members of other cultures (out-group members). These attributional tendencies appear to be a common phenomenon and can promote negative stereotypes between cultures.

Intergroup attributional bias was discussed by Taylor and Jaggi (1974), who found that subjects from Hindu and Muslim cultures often made internal attributions when in-group members performed socially desirable acts, but generally made external attributions when members of the other culture performed the same socially desirable acts. Conversely, subjects from each culture made external attributions when in-group members performed undesirable acts and generally made internal attributions when members of the other culture did the same. A more recent study by Islam and Hewstone (1993) produced similar results with individuals attributing internal, stable, global, and controllable causes for desirable behaviors by in-group members while making the opposite attributions for desirable behaviors by out-group members.

This research on cross-cultural attributional bias has important implications for managers. Clearly, culture-driven attribution styles can promote negative stereotypes and are a potential source of conflict between members of different cultures. Martinko and Douglas (1999) have suggested that such culturally biased attribution styles might help to explain the high frequency of failure among expatriate managers. It would seem that leaders as well as other organizational members could benefit greatly from training interventions designed to help members to recognize and attenuate the negative effects of culturally related attributional biases.

Age

Age is another factor that has been found to be related to self- and social attributions.

Age and self-attributions

Several studies document a relationship between age and self-attributions. Erikson (1963) argued that as people age it becomes less likely that they will initiate the attribution process in response to any given stimulus. Frieze (1984) suggested that this occurs because people experience more outcomes over the course of their lives, and each individual success or failure becomes less meaningful. Because it is generally believed that outcomes must be perceived as relevant in order to initiate the causal search process (Weiner, 1985a), the frequency with which attributions are formed may decrease with age.

When older individuals engage in self-attributions, there is evidence that they demonstrate self-serving biases more frequently than do younger adults (Mezulis et al., 2004). This finding might help to explain the study by Ferris et al. (1985), which indicated that older employees tend to rate their performance higher than do their supervisors. Additionally, Maehr and Kleiber (1980), Rodriguez (1997), and Greer, Halgin, and Harvey (2004) suggested that older and younger people might conceptualize successes and failures differently. Again, this is probably a result of the larger range and quantity of outcomes experienced by older individuals over the course of their lives. For instance, a failure in the workplace such as being passed over for a promotion might appear to be a major setback for a young employee but less severe to a more experienced person who has become acclimatized to the ups and downs of organizational life. Conversely, a negative outcome such as an injury might seem especially severe to older individuals whose bodies are less resilient than those of younger people. Thus, different stimuli may be more or less likely to initiate the attribution process for older versus younger individuals.

Age and observer attributions

The stereotypes often applied to the elderly have stimulated research concerning social attributions about the performance of elderly individuals (Frieze, 1984). Ferris et al. (1985) found that observers frequently attributed successful outcomes by older employees to causes other than ability. Similarly, Banzinger and Drevenstedt (1982) found that observers attributed the failures of older individuals to a lack of ability more frequently than they did for younger individuals.

There are also some interesting contrasts between the social attributions of older versus younger observers. Chen and Blanchard-Fields (1997) found that older subjects tended to initially attribute performance to mostly situational factors, but made more dispositional attributions when given time to think about the performance they witnessed. Younger adults, in contrast, displayed the opposite tendency. This finding suggests that both younger and older managers might make erroneous initial attributions regarding employee performance. As with culture, this body of work has significant practical implications. Biases related to age can result in a number of unintended consequences that can be harmful to organizations including: inappropriate rewards and punishments; faulty attempts at corrective actions such as training and job assignments; and possible charges of discrimination. As in the case of other types of attributional errors, the probability of these kinds of negative consequences can be attenuated through training and the design of recruitment, selection, and performance appraisal systems that have checks and balances for these types of errors.

Core Self-evaluations

A number of individual difference variables that relate to core self-evaluations (Judge, Locke, & Durham, 1997) are also related to attributions. Specifically, Judge and his colleagues have argued that self-efficacy, self-esteem, locus of control, and neuroticism are all highly related constructs that influence individuals' overall assessments of 'themselves, the world, and others' (Bono & Judge, 2003, p. S6). These self-evaluations (i.e., attributions) are thought to have significant implications for job satisfaction and performance (e.g., Bono & Judge, 2003; Erez & Judge, 2001; Judge, Erez, & Bono, 1998). Below, we will discuss the importance of these constructs in the context of attribution theory.

Self-efficacy

Self-efficacy refers to 'beliefs in one's capabilities to mobilize the motivations, cognitive resources, and courses of action needed to meet given situational demands' (Wood & Bandura, 1989, p. 408). Self-efficacy is relevant from a human resource management perspective because there appears to be a strong correlation between self-efficacy and high levels of performance and success (e.g., Campbell & Hackett, 1986; Gist & Mitchell, 1992; Hill, Smith, & Mann, 1987; Singer, 1989; Taylor, Locke, Lee, & Gist, 1984; Wood & Locke, 1987).

Empirical research by Thomas and Mathieu (1994) and by Silver et al. (1995) indicates that attributions and levels of self-efficacy are closely related. Specifically, the Silver et al. study concluded that people with high self-efficacy make more internal and stable attributions for positive outcomes and less internal and stable attributions for negative outcomes than do those with low self-efficacy. This conclusion seems logical, given that self-efficacy is related to confidence in one's level of ability, an internal and stable factor.

Silver et al. (1995) also concluded that a reciprocal relationship between self-efficacy and attributions might exist such that self-efficacy not only promotes self-serving attributions, but also that self-serving attributions for past outcomes increase self-efficacy. The logic behind this relationship is that the attribution of successful outcomes to internal and stable factors increases individuals' expectations for future success. This expectation, in turn, is a fundamental component of Wood and Bandura's (1989) concept of self-efficacy.

Self-esteem

Self-esteem is defined as the extent to which individuals believe they are 'capable, significant, successful, and worthy' (Coopersmith, 1967, pp. 4–5) and has been linked to behavior and performance. One consistent finding among a number of studies is that there appears to be an attributional component to self-esteem. More specifically, Romney (1994) found that tendencies toward attributing negative outcomes to internal, stable, and global causes were associated with low self-esteem and depression. Similarly, Stake (1990) found that females with high self-esteem attributed positive events to more stable causes than did females with low self-esteem. Additionally, she found that women with low self-esteem made more pessimistic attributions than did women with high self-esteem or men with any level of self-esteem, suggesting that there may be an interaction between gender and self-esteem on the attributions that individuals make. Another study, by Piers (1977), found that subjects with high self-esteem took more credit for success and less credit for failures than did subjects with low self-esteem. Consistent with these findings, Girodo, Dotzenroth, and Stein (1981) and Burke, Hunt, and Bickford (1985) found that subjects with high self-esteem were more internal in their attributions for successful outcomes and external in their attributions for negative outcomes than were subjects with low self-esteem.

Locus of control

Locus of control refers to perceptions concerning the relationship between behaviors and outcomes (Rotter, 1966). Those with an external locus of control tend to believe that outcomes are not under their control. Instead, their tendency is to believe that their fate is determined by factors outside their control, such as other people or luck. People with an internal locus of control are said to perceive a strong link between their efforts and their outcomes. Put differently, these individuals are inclined to believe that they control their own fate (Anderson & Schneier, 1978).

A fairly clear parallel appears to exist between the concepts of locus of control and locus of causality. As noted by Martinko and Douglas (1999), an internal locus of control seems to also imply an internal locus of causality. However, although there are numerous studies that demonstrate that locus of control is related to behavior and performance (Anderson, Hellriegel, & Slocum, 1977; Goodstadt & Hjelle, 1973; Kinicki & Vecchio, 1994; Mitchell, Smyser, & Weed, 1975; Perlow & Latham, 1993; Storms & Spector, 1987), we are not aware of any studies that directly investigate the relationship between locus of control and locus of causality. There is a study that indicates that subjects in a culture characterized by an external locus of control (e.g., Japan) often show external tendencies in their attributions. Specifically, Markus and Kitayama (1991) reported that Japanese students referred to situational characteristics twice as frequently as did American students when describing themselves. Thus it would seem that further investigation into the relationship between locus of control and the types of attributions people make would be worthwhile, since both constructs appear to be related to each other and to performance in a variety of contexts.

Neuroticism and negative affectivity

Thoms, Moore, and Scott (1996) define neuroticism as 'a person's degree of emotional stability, anxiety, self-confidence, pessimism, and self-consciousness' (p. 352). Various researchers have found that neuroticism is related to undesirable traits (Larson & LaFasto, 1989; Petterson, 1991; Thoms et al., 1996). Although we are not aware of any research explicitly linking neuroticism and attributions, Perrewé and Spector (2002) have noted that neuroticism and negative affectivity (NA) are highly similar constructs and NA appears to be related to attribution style. More specifically, Martinko, Gundlach, and Douglas (2002) argue that NA is likely to affect the frequency with which people perceive negative outcomes and exhibit pessimistic attributions. They assert that high NA individuals tend to focus on negative aspects of their environment and themselves, often blaming stable factors (either internal or external) for negative events, which can promote counterproductive behaviors. Although the Douglas and Martinko (2001) study did not specifically test the relationship between NA and attribution styles, their data revealed a significant positive ($p < 0.05$) relationship between NA and hostile attribution styles. Thus, it would seem that the relationship between NA and attribution style merits investigation.

Impulsivity

Impulsivity refers to individuals' tendencies toward sporadic and unpredictable behavior. Martinko, Douglas, Harvey, and Joseph (2005) and Martinko and Zellars (1998) argued that overly impulsive individuals are likely to make hostile attributions for negative outcomes. They also predicted that impulsive individuals are more likely than ordinary people to react to such attributions in violent ways. Thus impulsive individuals appear to be a potential liability due to their capacity for unpredictable, and possibly dangerous, behaviors.

Trait Anger

Like impulsivity, trait anger among employees may create a dangerous working atmosphere within an organization. This construct refers to the frequency and severity with which individuals feel anger. A study by Gibson and Barsade (1999) indicated that those with high levels of trait anger have a heightened tendency to feel disrespected by others, and this finding implies that the anger felt by employees high on trait anger is likely to be directed at other employees. Building upon this notion, Douglas and Martinko (2001) found that individuals high on trait anger tend to attribute negative outcomes to external and stable factors and demonstrate a higher proclivity toward aggressiveness than subjects lower on trait anger.

As with a number of the individual difference variables discussed in this section, trait anger is a factor that organizations should take into account when screening, placing, and training individuals. More will be said about human resource management processes later in this chapter.

COUNTERPRODUCTIVE BEHAVIOR

In recent years, increasing attention has been devoted to explaining various forms of counterproductive workplace behavior, including other-directed aggressive behaviors, such as violence, vandalism, and harassment, as well as self-directed dysfunctional behaviors, such as absenteeism, alcoholism, and drug abuse. As this area has developed, researchers have proposed that many of the same individual difference variables that we described above are also related to counterproductive behavior, including age, gender, ethnicity, self-monitoring, self-efficacy, self-esteem (Dalton & Wimbush, 1998; Harris & Greising, 1998; Neuman & Baron, 1998), neuroticism, negative affect, the Big-Five personality characteristics (Folger & Skarlicki, 1998), and trait-anger and control beliefs (Douglas & Martinko, 2001; Fox & Spector, 1999). In addition, researchers have also argued that situational factors, including adverse working conditions, rigid policies and controls (Dalton & Wimbush, 1998; Folger & Skarlicki, 1998; Martinko & Gardner, 1982), leadership style (Folger & Skarlicki, 1998; Fox & Spector, 1998; Martinko & Zellars, 1998), and unjust reward systems (Martinko & Gardner, 1982; O'Leary-Kelly, Griffin, & Glew, 1996) are related to counterproductive work behaviors. Throughout the development of this area, although researchers often emphasized either individual difference factors or situational variables, they also discussed or at least recognized the importance of causal analyses (i.e., attributional processes) at some level, as an explanation as to why these individual and situational factors may or may not result in counterproductive behavior at work.

In this section we will describe and discuss the research relating to how attributional frameworks help to explain both other-directed counterproductive behaviors, such as violence, stealing, and sabotage, and self-directed counterproductive behaviors characterized by learned helplessness behaviors, such as alcoholism, drug abuse, and absenteeism.

Other-directed Counterproductive Behavior

Martinko and Zellars (1998) put forth an attributional framework which integrates both individual and situational variables to explain why some but not other organizational members engage in workplace aggression or violence. Their main thesis is that attributions about the causes of workplace events are primary factors motivating the expectancies and emotions related to aggressive workplace behaviors. Their model can be described as a five-step process: Negative Event → Perception of Disequilibria → Attributional Analysis → Emotional State → Acts of Aggression or Violence. Although they proposed a number of hypotheses, a central tenet of their theory is that individuals who tend to attribute negative outcomes to external, stable, intentional, and controllable causes, while perceiving few mitigating circumstances, are more likely than others to engage in counterproductive aggressive work behaviors.

The results of recent studies appear to support the Martinko and Zellars (1998) model. Douglas and Martinko (2001) and Aquino et al. (2004) found that workers who exhibit a hostile attribution style (a cross-situational tendency to make attributions to external, stable, controllable, and intentional causes when faced with a negative outcome) are more likely to overtly express their anger and engage in acts of aggression than are workers who do not exhibit this attribution style. In a study contrasting the attributional tendencies of MBA students and criminals incarcerated for violent crimes, Martinko and Moss (2004) found that the people who were incarcerated exhibited an enhanced self-serving bias.

In addition to the above studies, which directly supported the Martinko and Zellars (1998) model, it should be noted that the work on individual differences described above also supports an attributional interpretation. More specifically, as described above, individual difference variables are often related to both attributional style and counterproductive behaviors. Thus, by inference, the individual differences that are related to counterproductive behaviors suggest that attribution styles are also related to counterproductive behaviors. While a complete description of all of these relationships is beyond the scope of this chapter, these relationships are discussed in more detail in Martinko and Zellars (1998), Martinko et al. (2002), and Martinko, Douglas, Ford, & Gundlach (2004).

Self-directed Counterproductive Behaviors and Learned Helplessness

Although Martinko and Zellars (1998) proposed an integrative model of workplace aggression and violence, they did not specifically address self-destructive workplace behaviors, such as depression, drug, and alcohol abuse. However, a later paper by Martinko et al. (2002) asserted that the same process underpinning the Martinko and Zellars (1998) model could be applied to this context. It should also be noted that the attributional model of learned helplessness suggested by Martinko and Gardner (1982) applied the same basic attributional framework to address the issue of self-directed counterproductive behavior: however, at the time, it was termed 'organizationally induced helplessness.' Regardless of terminology, both of these models represent essentially the same attributional paradigm, asserting that self-directed counterproductive behavior is at least partially a function of stable and internal attributions for poor performance. The internality dimension results in negative affect and the stability dimension results in expectations of future failure. As a result of the negative affect and expectations of future failure, the person gives up and 'learns helplessness.'

There has been considerable support for the learned helplessness model in the psychological literature (Abramson et al., 1978) and, while there has been less research in the IOP area, it has also been supportive. A multi-method study conducted by Campbell and Martinko (1998) found that both empowerment and learned helplessness were related to attributional styles. These findings were consistent with Abramson et al.'s (1978) distinction between personal and universal helplessness and Martinko, Henry, and Zmud's (1996) distinction between Dispositionally Related Helplessness (DRH) and Organizationally Induced Helplessness (OIH). Whereas universal helplessness and DRH appear to have trait origins, personal helplessness and OIH appear to have contextual origins (Campbell & Martinko, 1998), suggesting that by altering environmental conditions, human resource managers can affect both attributions and the occurrence of dysfunctional self-directed behaviors.

Work exhaustion or burnout has been explored with an attributional lens as well. Most recently, Moore (2000) argued that some individuals will not exhibit many of the job attitudes and behaviors often associated with burnout since these outcomes are likely to depend upon their attributions as to why they are exhausted. More specifically, she proposes that varying patterns of attributions that fall along the locus of causality, stability, and controllability dimensions are associated with work-based self-esteem, affective organizational commitment, organizational cynicism, depersonalization, voluntary turnover, and efforts to change both the organization and oneself. Evidence supporting this model has been demonstrated: Hablesleban and Buckley (2004) found that several of the consequences associated with burnout are related to the attributions for the cause of burnout.

LEADER–MEMBER INTERACTIONS

The first comprehensive description of the role of attributions in the leader–member interaction process was presented by Green and Mitchell (1979). In Green and Mitchell's model, the member's performance on an achievement related task serves as a trigger event, which is observed by the leader who then uses Kelley's informational cues (i.e., consensus, consistency, and distinctiveness information) to develop an attributional explanation (i.e., ability, effort, task difficulty, or luck) for the performance, which in turn influences how the leader behaves toward the member. Given this temporal sequence of events, Green and Mitchell (1979) describe their model as a three-step process: subordinate behavior → leader attributions → leader behavior. Before we turn our attention to the results of these studies, we note that although Green and Mitchell's (1979) model illustrates that a leader's behavior can have an impact on the member's future performance, they gave little attention to how the member's attributions for the leader's behavior can also affect the nature of the leader–member relationship.

Martinko and Gardner (1987) proposed an interactive model of leader–member relations that incorporates member attributions. Their model represents an extension of Green and Mitchell's (1979) work and can be roughly described as a five-step process: subordinate behavior → leader attributions → leader behavior → subordinate attributions → subordinate behavior. We frame the remainder of our discussion within the context of these five steps.

The majority of the early work on attribution and leadership was conducted by Mitchell and his colleagues and was concerned with the first three steps of the model, focusing on how leaders' attributions for members' performance affected disciplinary actions. In many of these studies they manipulated consensus, consistency, and distinctiveness information to induce attributions and then observed how these attributions affected disciplinary actions. Thus, Mitchell and Wood (1980) manipulated information and found that internal as opposed to external attributions were more likely to result in disciplinary actions. Ilgen and Knowlton (1980) looked at how attributional explanations affected leaders' evaluations of poor member performance and found that attributions of effort resulted in the most severe evaluations, whereas attributions of ability resulted in evaluations that were more positive than was warranted.

Additional studies in the early 1980s (Green & Liden; 1980; Ilgen, Mitchell, & Fredrickson, 1981; Mitchell & Wood, 1980; Wood & Mitchell, 1981), as well as more recent studies (e.g., Anderson, 1992; Ashkanasy & Gallois, 1994), employed similar designs and, in general, confirmed the notion that attributions and the dimensions of information described by Kelley were related to leadership behaviors. However, throughout this series of studies, a variety of other variables were also found to account for as much or more of the variance in leaders' behaviors as the attributions of leaders. Thus, for example, they found that the consequence of members' negative performances and the leaders' experiences influenced the severity of the discipline in the Mitchell and Kalb (1981) and (1982) studies, respectively. Similarly, Ilgen and Knowlton (1980) found that, in addition to attributions, whether or not ratees would have access to their ratings, accounted for a significant proportion of the variance in leaders' evaluations of members' performances. Mitchell (1982) expressed frustration with the attribution paradigm, warning that other factors (e.g., the social context and polices) played as much or more of a role than attributions in explaining the behaviors of leaders. Shortly after this paper there was a marked decline in the attribution research by Mitchell and his colleagues, as well others in the field in general.

Although we are uncertain as to whether or not the Mitchell paper caused the decline in research, we believe that some researchers may have overreacted to Mitchell's warnings. More specifically, while we agree with Mitchell's observations, it is important to note that in virtually all of the above studies, attributions accounted for a significant portion of the variance and therefore must be considered as part of any theory that attempts to explain leader reactions to member behavior. The observation that other factors besides attributions affect behavior has been acknowledged throughout the development of attribution theory and is emphasized in Weiner's recent work (e.g., Weiner, 1995) as well as our own work (Martinko et al., 2004). Thus, for example, in the case of aggressive behavior, although a victim may hold a perpetrator responsible (i.e., attribute a negative outcome to the internal stable and intentional actions of a perpetrator), the victim may still not retaliate because of societal sanctions. Similarly, a leader may not direct disciplinary action against a member even though the leader attributes the failure to the internal, controllable, and intentional actions of the member because of company polices, union contracts, or a difficult job market. In the studies by Mitchell and his colleagues, many of the leaders were nursing supervisors who may have felt the constraints of a shallow labor pool. Thus the observation that actions do not always follow attributions is not unique and it is somewhat naive to expect any single variable to account for the majority of the variation in any type of human behavior.

Much of the work that followed in the late 1980s through today has addressed the last three steps of the model concerning followers' reactions to leader behavior. An example is the work of Dasborough and Ashkanasy (2002), which argued that leadership is an emotional process in which leaders display particular emotions and attempt to induce those emotions in their members. In so doing, they proposed that the mood (state affect) of both leaders and members influences members' attributions for leader behavior such that positive mood states manifest positive perceptions of leader behavior (e.g., transformational), whereas negative mood states result in negative perceptions of leader behavior (e.g., pseudo-transformational). A study by Sechrist, Swim, and Mark (2003) provides support for Dasborough and Ashkanasy's (2002) arguments, in that they found that women who are in a negative mood state are more likely to report discrimination than women who are in a positive mood state. However, when women believed that their mood state (positive or negative) was due to external causes, mood had no effect on reports of discrimination. Thus it appears that the attributions that members develop for their negative mood influences the extent to which these states manifest negative perceptions of their leaders.

In a more recent contribution, Davis and Gardner (2004) propose a model showing how member attributions shape member perceptions of organizational cynicism and politics. Their propositions suggest that members who attribute their poor performance to external causes will perceive higher levels of organizational politics and cynicism when leaders react punitively to the poor performance. Perhaps most interestingly, Davis and Gardner also touch upon how the distance in leader–member relationships can affect a member's level of cognitive processing, which in turn influences the extent to which cognitive biases can shape his or her attributions for a leader's behavior. In short, they argue that members who are in distant leader–member relationships are more likely to rely on automatic rather than controlled cognitive processes to shape their attributions and thus these attributions are more likely to be influenced by cognitive biases than the attributions of members in close leader–member relationships. Their work supports the work of Lord and his colleagues (Lord, 1985, 1995; Lord & Maher, 1990, 1991, 1993; Lord & Smith, 1983) which contends that people do not always engage in systematic or rational cognitive processes, but also adds to that work by specifying the conditions under which overt processing is likely rather than unlikely.

Several papers employ a systems-based perspective when looking at leader–member relations by considering all five steps in the model rather than focusing exclusively on the last two. Martinko and Gardner (1987) proposed one of the earliest attribution models to focus on the dyadic nature of the leader–member relationship. In developing their model, they recognized that several attributional biases and individual differences are likely to affect both leader and member attributions for member performance and, in turn, influence their behaviors toward one another. They also proposed that the level of congruence between leader and member attributions for member performance is negatively associated with the level of conflict in leader–member relationships. Recently, Martinko et al. (2003) tested one of the implications of Martinko and Gardner's (1987) model. Specifically, Martinko and Gardner proposed that under conditions of poor member performance, the leaders' and members' self-serving and actor–observer biases interact such that they predispose leaders to attribute members' poor performance to the latters' internal characteristics. In contrast, the interaction of these same biases would predispose members to attribute their poor performance to external causes. Thus, over time and repeated instances of poor member performance, leader–member relations would become more contentious to the extent that leaders and members exhibited these biases. Martinko et al. (2003) tested for and found evidence indicating that there was a negative relationship between the leaders' pessimistic attribution style for the members' negative outcomes and the members' perception of the quality of their leader–member relationship. Moreover, this negative relationship was stronger to the extent that members' attribution styles were more optimistic for their negative outcomes.

Bitter and Gardner (1995) proposed a model similar to that of Martinko and Gardner (1987) in that its focus is also on the dyadic, leader–member exchange and incorporates attributional biases and individual differences.

However, their model focuses on how the leader's and the member's impression management behaviors effect each other's perceptions, attributions, and behaviors as well as the perceptions, attributions, and behaviors of other leaders and members.

In conclusion, it appears that work in this area is trending toward another level of analysis. The earlier work was mostly leader-centric, focusing on leader attributions and reactions to member performance. More recent work has been more dynamic and has focused on the reciprocal influences inherent in the leader–member social interaction process. This progression is likely to present several new challenges as we move to test these contemporary models. Higher levels of conceptual analysis (e.g., dyad, group, organizational) will often require higher levels of statistical analysis and more complex research designs, which may be difficult to execute in field settings. Thus, we expect to see a new wave of lab-based studies that will be necessary to test these dyadic and dynamic exchange processes, which, as suggested by Gilbert's (1995) snowball process, are critical to understanding the leader–member social interaction process: 'What I think affects how I behave, which affects what you think, which affects how you behave, which affects what I think' (p. 126). Thus, like rolling a snowball, a small attributional error in the beginning can produce large consequences over time (Gilbert, 1995). In conclusion, although Mitchell (1982) is right in noting that attributions may only account for a small amount of variance in some situations, it is also important to recognize that those small differences can compound their effects over time.

IMPRESSION MANAGEMENT AND HUMAN RESOURCE MANAGEMENT

Manipulating behavior in an attempt to generate favorable responses from others (i.e., impression management: Goffman, 1959) is common whenever organizational members interact (Decker, 1990). Although attributions are most often thought of as mediators between outcomes and behaviors, they can also serve as cues that are intended to manipulate the perceptions of others. A recent paper by Martinko et al. (2004) makes the case that, very frequently, the goal of impression management in organizational contexts is to influence the audience to make a specific type of attribution. This type of impression management process is most apparent in selection interviews and performance appraisal processes.

Interviews and Selection Decisions

Although job interviews are the most common form of employee selection device, they are frequently poor predictors of future performance (Robbins, 2003). Herriot (1981, 1989) argued that the poor reliability and validity of interviews is partially caused by the attributional errors made by interviewers. Research indicates that these errors are likely to stem from a number of sources (e.g., Degroot & Motowidlo, 1999; Dipboye, Stramler, & Fontenelle, 1984; Ramsay, Gallois, & Cannon, 1997) and can jeopardize an organization's ability to attract and hire qualified employees (Ployhart & Ryan, 1997).

Recent studies indicate that both interviewers and job candidates believe that specific patterns of attributions lead to more or less favorable impressions. Silvester et al. (2002) found that both interviewers and prospective applicants believed that candidates convey a more positive image when the interviewee attributes past events to internal and controllable factors. The results confirmed those of an earlier study by Silvester (1997), which found that applicants who attributed negative events to internal and controllable causes were rated more highly by interviewers than those who attributed negative outcomes to other causes.

The results from a study on attraction shed some light on how the applicants' attributions for their success in interviews affects their interest in the job opening. Based on Kelley's (1967) covariation model, Kimble and Moriarty (1997) argued and found support for the hypothesis that positive interview outcomes (i.e., being called back for another interview or being offered a job) are most personally meaningful and likely to generate the most positive responses from targets when they perceive that the outcome covaried with their behavior since this infers that they are responsible for the positive results. Thus, maximum attraction occurs when the interviewer is more positive toward the interviewee (i.e., low consensus) than toward any other interviewee (Kimble & Moriarty, 1979), leading the interviewees to make internal attributions for their success in the interview.

Role expectations are also thought to influence the attributions that interviewers make concerning candidates. Herriot (1981) explained that certain behaviors are generally expected of interviewees, such as allowing the interviewer to control the flow of the conversation and answering questions in a fluent and concise manner. He argued that deviations from these norms are likely to reduce interviewers' satisfaction with the interviews. He further argued that the interviewer is likely to attribute the poor interview to the candidate's deviance (i.e., an internal attribution based on consensus information), reducing the likelihood that the candidate will be hired.

Additional research indicates that perceptions of similarity (i.e., false consensus bias) between interviewers and candidates might also influence interviewers' attributions. Based on studies by Byrne (1969), Keenan (1976), and Rand and Wexley (1975), Herriot (1981) argued that interviewers will make more optimistic attributions for candidates they see as similar to themselves. Thus, the false consensus bias may hinder organizational attempts to increase diversity as managers make overly optimistic attributions for members with whom they identify (see also Herriot, 1989).

Performance Appraisal and Assessments

In the section on leader–member relations earlier in this chapter, we discussed the research on the effects of leader attributions for poor member performance from the perspective of how it affects member reactions. In this section we will focus on evaluations from the perspective of how attributional errors affect formal appraisals and the accuracy of the ratings of the performance of both leaders and members.

Feldman and Hilterman (Feldman, 1981; Feldman & Hilterman, 1975, 1977) were among the first to point out the importance of attributions in appraisal processes. Feldman (1981) demonstrated the importance of the actor–observer, false consensus, and hedonic relevance biases. Later research by Goerke et al. (2004) indicated that self-serving biases can cause managers to attribute too much blame to subordinates when negative outcomes occur, resulting in overly negative performance evaluations.

In addition to these biases, researchers have identified a number of other factors that might also influence the attributions made by evaluators. These factors include the nature of the relationship between managers and the employees they evaluate and the managers' experience with the task. Mitchell and Kalb (1982) argued that the amount of experience that managers have at the jobs they are evaluating influences their attributions concerning subordinate performance. Specifically, they found that observers made more situational attributions for poor subordinate performance if they had experience with the task being performed. Conversely, they found that observers who had no experience with the task tended to attribute poor performance to the internal characteristics of the actors. On the other hand, Fedor and Rowland (1989) showed that the amount of time managers and subordinates work together could influence the attributions that managers make concerning subordinate performance. They found that managers made more optimistic attributions for employees with whom they shared a longer relationship. Additionally, some studies have indicated that managers make more optimistic attributions for employees they like on a personal level (Johnson, Erez, Kiker, & Motowidlo, 2002; Reagan, Strauss, & Fazio, 1974), although support for this relationship is mixed (Fedor & Rowland, 1989).

Another factor that appears to influence the attributions of evaluators is specific attempts to manage impressions. Giacalone and Riordan (1986) found that people give higher ratings to managers who attribute their success to internal factors and disclose obstacles that had to be overcome as opposed to crediting their subordinates. However, Silvester et al. (2002) argue that members are likely to develop negative attributions regarding their leader's behavior when it is seen as inconsistent, distinct, and nonconsensual, such as when a leader seems to take credit for only successful outcomes. Along this line of reasoning, Decker (1990) demonstrated that, under conditions where credit taking is likely to be seen as particularly self-serving, people react most favorably when managers share credit with their subordinates and disclose obstacles that had to be overcome to achieve success. When leaders and members experience negative outcomes they often give excuses or justifications that can impact on the attributions that others form. More specifically, in a study of nursing supervisors, Wood and Mitchell (1981) demonstrated that external accounts for poor performance lessened the amount of responsibility assigned by supervisors, and that both external accounts and apologies reduced the amount of punishment by supervisors. Similar relationships are suggested by Weiner, Figueroa-Munoz, and Kakihara (1991), Martinko and Zellars (1998), and Gundlach et al. (2003), who describe how excuses and apologies can be used to shift attributions along the locus of causality, stability, and controllability dimensions. In so doing, actors can communicate that they are not responsible for the negative outcome and that the outcome is unlikely to recur, thereby reducing the probability of punishment.

Research has also indicated that managers often attribute the performance of individuals and teams to different causes. This phenomenon, known as the team halo effect, refers to the tendency of evaluators to hold individuals within teams responsible for negative outcomes while attributing positive outcomes to the team as a unit (Naquin & Tynan, 2003). Naquin and Tynan explained that this bias is commonly observed in sports fans, when an individual player is blamed for a loss. Such an attribution is unfair because it ignores the many significant positive and negative contributions of the entire team over the course of a sporting event. Similarly, managers who focus on team members, as opposed to the entire team, when negative outcomes occur might unfairly penalize certain individuals.

Within teams, or larger collectives such as departments, it appears that some individuals are more likely to be singled out than others as the cause of a failure. Feldman (1981) noted that individuals who deviate from collective norms (i.e., exhibit low consensus behaviors) stand out in the mind of observers and are often seen as being a more important causal factor than others. Thus, the only Asian member of a team, or the only female member of a group, is more likely to be blamed for negative outcomes than the more 'typical' members. Additionally, employees that behave in ways that deviate from established norms appear more likely to be blamed for poor performance (Herriot, 1981; Kelley, 1971; Ramsay et al., 1997).

The fact that so many factors appear to influence performance-related attributions is concerning, given the importance of evaluations in determining training needs, reward allocations, and placement and termination decisions. Research indicates that managers' attributions for poor performance often influence the types of training or punishment they deem appropriate (Gist & Mitchell, 1992; Green & Mitchell, 1979; Ilgen & Knowlton, 1980; Mitchell & Wood, 1980). For example, Mitchell and Wood's (1980) study showed that managers were more likely to administer punitive measures intended to modify employee behavior when dispositional attributions for poor performance were made. Additionally, Ilgen and Knowlton's (1980) study concluded that failures attributed to a lack of subordinate ability often cause managers to use skill-based training techniques. Conversely, poor performance attributed to lack of subordinate effort was associated with decisions to use motivational techniques.

Attributions regarding the motivation of employees also appear to be relevant to the distribution of organizational rewards and punishment. Green and Mitchell (1979) first made this prediction, arguing that managers will allocate more rewards to employees whose behaviors are thought to be driven by altruistic motives. More recently, a study by Johnson et al. (2002) supported the notion that managers reward helpful employee behaviors more frequently if they attribute those behaviors to altruistic motives.

Supervisor attributions concerning employee performance also have important implications for employee satisfaction and motivation. As described above, numerous studies indicate that employees are more likely to experience learned helplessness if they are led to believe that their failures are caused by internal and stable factors (Campbell & Martinko, 1998; Martinko & Gardner, 1982). Conversely, Campbell and Martinko (1998) demonstrated a link between employee empowerment and internal and stable attributions for successful outcomes. It is clear that the attributions made by managers, and communicated through evaluations, can influence these motivational states by influencing employees' attributions for their own performance.

In conclusion, there are many convincing conceptual arguments and there is overwhelming empirical evidence to demonstrate that attributions are an important component of the evaluation process and that errors and other perceptual distortions can jeopardize the accuracy and effectiveness of evaluations, which inevitably affect decisions regarding selection, training, placement, and reward systems in organizations.

ATTRIBUTIONS AND EMOTIONS

It has been argued that the relationship between attributions and behaviors is not direct, but that attributions influence behaviors via their effect on emotions (Weiner, 1985a, 1987). In this section we describe the research on the nature of the relationships between attributions, emotions, and behaviors in organizational contexts.

Attributions, Emotions, and Behaviors

Weiner's (1985a) cognition–emotion model predicts that attributions influence the emotions that people feel, and that these emotions then drive behavioral responses to outcomes. A simplified model of this process is as follows:

Outcome → Initial Affect → Causal Search and Attribution → Refined Emotional Reaction → Behavioral Response. The model indicates that, as with all attributional processes, the attribution–emotion–behavior process begins when a person experiences a personally relevant outcome followed by an initial affective response (i.e., happy, sad, frustrated).

Weiner (1985a) explained that the purpose of the attribution process in this model is to determine the cause of the outcome that generated the initial affective response. Based on the attribution a person makes, a more refined emotional response is developed. For instance, Weiner argued that failures that are attributed to stable causes will produce feelings of helplessness because the stability of the cause promotes the expectation of future failures. Other possible attribution-driven emotional responses include shame (internal and uncontrollable attribution for a negative outcome), guilt (internal and controllable attribution for a negative outcome), anger (external and controllable attribution for a negative outcome), pride (internal attribution for a positive outcome), gratitude (external and intentional attribution for a positive outcome), and surprise (external and unstable attribution for success or failure).

Each of these emotional responses is then argued to promote different behaviors. For instance, Douglas and Martinko (2001) argued and demonstrated that feelings of anger directed toward external causes promote aggressive behaviors, as discussed earlier in this chapter. Feelings of helplessness have been linked to withdrawal behaviors, decreased motivation, and heightened passivity whereas feelings of hopefulness have been associated with heightened levels of effort and motivation (Campbell & Martinko, 1998; Douglas & Martinko, 2001). Additionally, feelings of guilt resulting from internal and unstable attributions (e.g., lack of effort) for negative outcomes are argued to promote increased effort toward positive outcomes in the future.

Controlling the Emotions of Others

Because emotions are linked to behaviors, and because attributions appear to influence emotions, practicing managers have an incentive to try to control the attributions that subordinates make, to the extent that such control is reasonable and ethical. Several recent works have described how leaders influence emotions and the consequences of attempts at emotional control. From a managerial perspective, a supervisor might deliberately lie about the causes of poor performance in order to avoid hurting a subordinate's feelings. Conversely, the supervisor might falsely attribute positive outcomes to internal traits of the subordinate, such as effort or ability, instead of an external cause, such as luck, in order to increase the subordinate's esteem (Weiner, 1987). However, recent research suggests that there is a downside to inaccurate feedback. A study by Newcombe and Ashkanasy (2002) showed that leaders who displayed a positive facial expression while giving positive feedback were rated higher than those who appeared angry or upset while giving positive feedback. This study indicates that leaders will be effective in manipulating subordinates' emotions through communicated attributions only to the extent that they give emotional cues that are consistent with what they are saying.

Similarly, Dasborough and Ashkanasy (2002) argued that leaders high on emotional intelligence would be effective in aligning their causal statements (i.e., attributions) with the emotional cues they present to subordinates. However, they also suggested that subordinates with high levels of emotional intelligence are capable of perceiving incongruence between emotional cues and the attributions a leader communicates. Thus, a leader's ability to manage subordinates' emotions and behaviors through communicated attributions appears to be a function of the perceived truth of the attributions. While leaders with high levels of emotional intelligence appear to be more convincing in this regard, emotional intelligence also seems to make subordinates more aware of false attributions.

At least one study indicates that attributional training can be used to promote positive emotional and, therefore, behavioral responses to outcomes. Hall, Hladkyi, Perry, and Ruthig (2004) found that training designed to promote unstable and uncontrollable attributions for failures was associated with increased levels of positive emotions (pride and hope) and decreased levels of negative emotions (guilt and shame). These emotions, in turn, were associated with increased levels of performance. This finding replicates earlier research linking attributional training and performance (e.g., Schunk, 1998) and indicates that positive emotions play an important mediating role in this relationship.

Research also suggests that positive and negative emotional states can influence the accuracy of employees' attributions. Based on past emotion research (e.g., Bodenhausen, 1993; Fiedler, 1988), Forgas (1998) reasoned that individuals in a positive mood state are likely to base their causal assessments on readily available dispositional factors as opposed to less salient situational factors. Conversely, he argued that those in a negative mood state are generally more methodical and systematic in forming attributions, and will therefore consider both situational and dispositional factors. A study by Forgas (1998) showed that individuals experiencing a positive mood state after succeeding at a task were likely to commit the fundamental attribution error (i.e., the tendency to overlook situational explanations for outcomes in favor of dispositional explanations) when evaluating the performance of others. Those experiencing a negative mood state after failing at a task demonstrated less of a dispositional tendency. Forgas's (1998) findings suggest that negative emotional states might decrease the influence of the actor–observer bias because observers in a negative mood might be more diligent in seeking out situational explanations for others' performances. Thus supervisors who experience negative emotions and empathize when subordinates fail at a task might form more accurate attributions for failures than those who are not emotionally affected by their subordinates' failures.

The potential influence of emotions on attributions was also investigated in a study by de Castro, Slot, Bosch, Koops, and Veerman (2003) who concluded that negative emotional states increased subjects' tendencies toward hostile attributions. This conclusion and Forgas's (1998) findings both suggest that the initial affective response to outcomes noted in the description of Weiner's (1985a) model above can affect the accuracy of attributions. Thus it would seem that organizational members who are responsible for evaluating performance could benefit from attributional training designed to promote accurate attributions in adverse circumstances.

GROUP AND ORGANIZATIONAL LEVEL ATTRIBUTIONS

A number of studies conducted since the late 1970s have demonstrated relationships between organizational performance and the attributions leaders make for that performance. These studies typically measure executives' attributions in shareholder reports or speeches, using contextual analysis techniques such as CAVE, as described above. A consistent finding among these studies is that leaders typically make self-serving attributions. When their organizations are successful they tend to attribute the success to internal factors but tend to attribute poor organizational performance to external and uncontrollable factors (Bettman & Weitz, 1983; Bowman, 1976, 1978, 1984; Clapham & Schwenk, 1991; Michalisin et al., 2003; Salancik & Meindl, 1984). We now review and discuss the implications of these findings.

A series of studies by Bowman (1976, 1978, 1984) used a contextual analysis of annual reports to examine the attributions that leaders make for poor organizational performance. He concluded that leaders typically attributed poor performance to external and uncontrollable factors, such as bad weather or government legislation. In terms of positive outcomes, Salancik and Meindl (1984) found that CEOs typically attributed favorable performance to internal factors, such as management policy and decisions. Similarly, Bettman and Weitz (1983) found that CEOs tended to attribute high levels of performance and other desirable outcomes to internal, stable, and controllable factors. Their analysis also indicated that poor performance and other negative organizational outcomes were commonly attributed to external, unstable, and uncontrollable causes.

Salancik and Meindl's (1984) study also indicated that the stability of an organization's performance can affect leader attributions. They found that CEOs of organizations with erratic performance levels often made internal attributions for both the good and bad levels of performance in their letters to shareholders. CEOs of organizations with more consistent performance, either good or bad, generally demonstrated the more self-serving attribution styles noted in the previous paragraph. The authors reasoned that the internally biased attributions of CEOs of unstable organizations might be an impression management device intended to convince investors that the CEO is in control, despite the organization's unstable performance.

Bowman (1976) and Clapham and Schwenk (1991) also noted that the biasing influence of organizational performance on attributions might hinder a manager's ability to accurately predict future performance. If leaders convince themselves that high levels of performance are related to internal, stable, and controllable factors, for example, they might overlook important external, unstable, and uncontrollable influences. These factors might then affect performance in a negative and unexpected way in the future. Such an unexpected downturn might leave managers with a workforce that is too large and improperly trained to handle a more challenging economic and competitive environment.

There has also been a recent trend in the literature exploring the nature and consequences of attributions regarding team performance and the attributions team members make about each other. In studying leader attributions in a team context, Michalisin et al. (2003) found that self-serving attributions for performance frequently led team leaders to attribute positive outcomes to their team members as well as to themselves. Negative performance was generally associated with external attributions. This evidence suggests that leaders of teams within organizations make the same self-serving attributions as organizational leaders. It also suggests that team leaders are biased in the assessment of their team members' efforts and abilities.

Attribution theory has also been used recently to explain helping behaviors at the group and organizational levels. LePine and Van Dyne (2001) use attribution theory to address how group members engage in attributional processes when one of their members performs poorly. Based on their analysis, they proposed that group members experience an affective reaction and form expectations about the member's ability to perform in the future, which influences how they respond to the poorly performing member. The results of a study conducted by Jackson and LePine (2003) support the LePine and Van Dyne (2001) model. Specifically, they found that when group members attributed the poor performance of a group member to low task-related ability that was seen as uncontrollable, they felt sympathy toward the low-performing member, were less likely to reject the member, and were more likely to work around the low-performing member and provide training. On the other hand, when group members attributed low performance to a lack of effort that was seen as highly controllable, they did not feel sympathy toward the low-performing member, were more likely to reject the member, and were less likely to work around or provide training for the member.

Jackson and LePine (2003) also examined and found limited support for the direct effects of the observers' personality characteristics (e.g., the Big Five traits of extraversion, openness, agreeableness, emotional stability, and conscientiousness) on their behavioral response to a group member who had performed poorly. However, they did not examine how these and other characteristics might shape observers' attributional explanations in the first place. This could be a fruitful exploration at the group level, given McDonald's (1995) discussion on attributional biases in newly formed n-person groups. He argues that to the extent that members of newly formed groups have a previously established and positive basis of identity with other group members, they will make situational rather than dispositional attributions for the other members' negative performance, which in turn influences their willingness to cooperate with them in the future. Perhaps personality characteristics are related to the propensity to establish identity with others and thus influence the type of attributions people make when interacting in group settings.

Allred (1995) uses attribution theory to discuss intra- and interorganizational relations. Similar to McDonald (1995), LePine and Van Dyne (2001), and Jackson and LePine (2003), he explores the role of attributions in determining whether organizational parties cooperate or compete with each other. Allred's emphasis, however, is clearly on how emotions mediate the relationship between attributions and decisions to cooperate or compete at the intra- and interorganizational levels. He argues that group membership (in-group vs out-group) biases the attributions (controllable vs uncontrollable) the members make for negative performance outcomes, which in turn stimulate feelings of gratitude or anger that directly influence levels of cooperation or competition seen at both intra- and interorganizational levels.

Silvester et al. (1999) recently conducted an empirical investigation of the role attributions can play at the intraorganizational level. In this study, they performed an attributional analysis of key stakeholder groups in a multinational corporation who were involved in a culture change program. They found evidence indicating considerable intergroup differences in how managers, trainers, and trainees perceived the change process. Hence, the results suggest that attributions can operate at a group level when group members share an underlying causal schema for interpreting important work-related events.

EMERGING ISSUES

In addition to the areas described above that have been the focus of attention for attribution theory in IOP, there are several other areas that have begun to emerge in the last few years that deserve attention.

Optimism and Positive Psychology

The focus of this emerging area is on those aspects of the human condition that encourage productive and functional as opposed to dysfunctional behavior (Luthans, 2002a, 2002b; Luthans & Avolio, 2003; Seligman, 1999; Seligman & Csikszentmihalyi, 2000; Sheldon & King, 2001). Basic questions addressed by this area are concerned with why some people are able to persist, adapt, remain hopeful, and display resilience and functional behavior under adverse conditions, whereas others become learned helpless and dysfunctional. Although a complete exposition of this area is beyond the scope of this chapter, Seligman's (1990) work on learned optimism is a cornerstone concept in this developing area, which can be viewed as the reciprocal of his earlier work on learned helplessness. More specifically, Seligman (1998) defines optimism as a mental process that combines positive expectations and an attribution style that favors internal, stable, and global attributions for positive outcomes and external, unstable, and specific attributions for negative outcomes. Optimistic individuals are argued to be more motivated because they expect to succeed and view failures as temporary setbacks (Luthans & Avolio, 2003). Luthans and Avolio have also argued that an optimistic attribution style is associated with higher levels of job satisfaction and morale.

Another core concept in positive psychology is resilience (Masten, 2001, p. 228). Huey and Weisz (1997) demonstrated that individuals with low levels of resilience tend to make overly internal or external attributions for negative outcomes. Thus many non-resilient individuals have a tendency to consistently blame external factors for negative outcomes (Huey & Weisz, 1997) and experience frustration and aggressive tendencies as a result (Martinko et al., 2002; Weiner, 1985b). Others overly blame themselves for negative outcomes, resulting in learned helplessness and/or depression (Huey & Weisz, 1997; Martinko & Gardner, 1982).

In our view of this emerging area, it is—as its proponents have suggested—a reaction to the focus on dysfunctional behavior in psychology that borrows heavily on attribution theory for a major part of its foundation. Thus the emergence of this area can be viewed as a sound application of attribution theory principles. We are optimistic that, as this area develops more fully, it will shift the focus of attributional research to a wider arena and, as empirical work and applications develop, it will undoubtedly enrich our knowledge of and applications of attribution theory in the workplace.

Conflict Resolution

Betancourt (2004) recently reviewed studies that test an attribution–emotion model of conflict and violence (Betancourt & Blair, 1992). He concluded that the attribution processes involved in conflict situations are likely to promote feelings of empathy and anger, which are associated with the conflict resolution behaviors of compromising and dominating, respectively. Joseph and Douglas (2004) make similar arguments but also propose a model illustrating how attributions and attribution styles are related to a wider range of conflict resolution behaviors, such as dominating, integrating, obliging, avoiding, and compromising (cf. Rahim & Bonoma, 1979). They argue that people engage in an attributional analysis to determine their own and the other party's role in causing a conflict. More specifically, they argue that individuals make both self- and social attributions as to why the conflict occurred and that these attributions fall along the locus of causality and stability dimensions. They propose that to the extent that people see conflict as due to their own internal characteristics, they are inclined to pursue an avoiding or obliging approach as opposed to a dominating or integrating approach to resolving the conflict. On the other hand, to the extent that people attribute the conflict to the other party's internal characteristics, they are likely to pursue an avoiding or dominating approach, as opposed to an integrative or obliging approach. Lastly, Joseph and Douglas (2004) argue that people must perceive that the causes of the conflict are changeable on the part of both parties (i.e., they make unstable self- and social attributions) in order to pursue a compromising approach. Clearly this is an area where empirical work is badly needed.

Ethics, Moral Judgments, Responsibility, and Justice

Several high-profile incidents of organizational wrongdoing have brought renewed interest from IOP scholars who are concerned with moral judgments and justice. Some of these researchers have proposed models to explain why members can vary in their perceptions of whether their organization is engaged in wrongdoing. Others have focused on understanding why some members but not others report organizational wrongdoing. Regardless of their research interest, attribution theory has been used as an underlying framework for explaining these perceptions and behaviors.

One focus of interest in this area is on how attribution theory is used to shape judgments of responsibility for perceived wrongdoing. Based on Jones and Nisbett's (1971) work on the actor–observer bias, Payne and Giacalone (1990) argued that the same action can be seen as more or less moral depending upon whether the person is the actor or the observer. They point out that the parties directly involved in the questionable action (e.g., actor or decision maker) are inclined to attribute their behaviors to external causes and thus less likely to perceive that they are responsible for the consequences of their actions. Accordingly, when their acts are called into question, they tend to disassociate themselves from the wrongdoing. On the other hand, observers are inclined to attribute the wrongdoing to internal causes, such as the actors' lack of morals, and thus see the actors as responsible (Payne & Giacalone, 1990).

According to Payne and Giacalone's arguments, responsibility is dependent on whether the outcome is attributed to dispositional or environmental causes. Weiner (1995) later pointed out that the relationship between attributions and judgments of responsibility is more complex than just reflecting an underlying actor–observer bias. More specifically, he argued that to hold another party responsible for an act, we must believe that the act was caused by the party's internal characteristics, the party had control over the action, and they intended it to occur.

Gundlach et al. (2003) recently proposed an attributional framework for explaining whistle-blowing decisions. Based on Weiner's (1995) work on attributions and judgments of responsibility and the work of Martinko and Zellars (1998) on attributions and workplace aggression, they proposed that organizational members would hold another party responsible for perceived wrongdoing, become angry, and decide to blow the whistle when they attributed their acts to internal, stable, controllable, and intentional causes. Their model also incorporates the impact of the wrongdoers' impression management tactics (e.g., excuses, justifications, and intimidation) on the potential whistle-blower's attributions as well as how the perceived credibility of these attempts influences their effectiveness. The results of a recent test of their model (Gundlach et al., 2003) showed that observers are more likely to see another party as responsible for wrongdoing, become angry, and decide to blow the whistle when they attribute the wrongdoing to controllable and stable causes. Moreover, the effects of both the observers' attributions and judgments of responsibility on their whistle-blowing decisions were fully mediated by the emotion of anger.

The criminology literature raises some interesting implications for the Gundlach et al. (2003) model. Grasmick and McGill (1994) and Cullen, Clark, Cullen, and Mathers (1985) suggest that dispositional attributions are consistent with the classical view of crimes (more punishment, less rehabilitative responses to crime), whereas situational attributions are consistent with the positivist view of crimes (less punishment, more rehabilitative responses to crime). To the extent that these arguments are valid, they imply that observers of organizational wrongdoing who attribute the behavior to internal, stable, controllable, and intentional causes will be more interested in punishing the organization rather than in bringing about positive change. Empirical work in this area is needed to check the validity of this important implication.

The relationship between attributions and judgments of responsibility has also been used to explain prejudice, which can result in a variety of undesirable consequences (e.g., hostility, aggression, and various forms of discrimination). In an interesting twist, Crandall and Eshleman (2003) propose that attributions of control and judgments of responsibility serve as reasons that people use to justify prejudice. From this perspective, when individuals attribute their negative outcomes to other people, they infer that they are bad people that deserve bad treatment. Hence, attributions and subsequent judgments of responsibility are often used to justify bad (i.e., prejudicial) treatment of others (Crandall & Eshleman, 2003). As in the case of the other topics in this section, research in this area is sparse but needed because the implications are so important.

Finally, some comment on the relationships between attributions, judgments of justice, and impression management is warranted. In a conceptual article, Martinko et al. (2004) describe how information and attributions lead to perceptions of justice. More specifically, they link social justice with low consensus and dispositional attributions, high consistency with stable attributions and distributive justice, and low distinctiveness with global attributions and procedural justice. Since we are not aware of empirical data documenting these linkages, this appears to be an area that would benefit from additional conceptual and empirical attention.

Criticisms

Before concluding our review, it should be noted that in addition to criticisms by Mitchell (1982) that were discussed earlier in this chapter, Gilbert (1989), Maher (1995), and Lord (1995) have all questioned the depiction of people as rational information processors and point to research and theory on cognitive load which suggests that, in complex situations such as social interactions, cognitive load requirements mitigate against the type of deliberate information processing described by Kelley's principles of covariation. Although we agree with these criticisms, we do not believe that they require us to 'throw out the baby with the bath water.' Overreacting to these criticisms takes attribution theory to task for claims it has never made. More specifically, Weiner (1985a, 1986) has never contended that people engage in causal search and analysis in everyday routine situations but rather that attributions are prompted by outcomes that are surprising, important, or very negative. Thus, for routine situations, the categorization processes and cognitive shortcuts described by Gilbert (1989), Maher (1995), and Lord (1995) appear to be valid depictions of everyday mundane situations. On the other hand, when critical outcomes do occur, we believe that the 'naive psychologist' perspective that originated with Heider (1958) is probably appropriate. Moreover, it is also plausible that, as Martinko (1995, p. 353) has suggested, both explicit and implicit information processing may occur in parallel. However, regardless of how we describe the mechanics of information processing (i.e., through the type of explicit attributional processes described by Kelley or implicitly thorough schema and cognitive shortcuts), it is critical to note that the empirical demonstrations of attribution biases and the empirical relationships between attributions and individual differences, emotions, and behavior that are described in this chapter are not conceptual depictions of cognitive processes, but are the result of hard data. Thus even if we disagree about the origins and processes that maintain these relationships, they nonetheless exist and need to be explained. At this point, attribution theory appears to be the most comprehensive explanation. Finally, it is worth noting that Weiner never emphasized the cognitive processes associated with making attributions, but has always focused more on the dimensions and consequences of attributional explanations. From this perspective, it does not matter whether or not attributional explanations are arrived at through implicit processes such as those suggested by Lord and his colleagues, or by Kelley's covariation principles. What matters most is that these explanations and the dimensions of these explanations are related to expectancies, emotions, and behaviors. Thus, at this juncture, it can be argued that it is more important to focus on the consequences of attributions rather than the process by which they are derived. Of course, we need to understand both, but the criticisms of the processing mechanisms do not affect the validity of the empirical relationships that have been documented.

CONCLUSIONS

As we look over our review, several impressions emerge. The first is that the empirical work documents that attributions and attributional processes are related to a wide range and scope of IOP topics. In fact, it appears that just about every form of goal-related behavior has an attributional component. This observation fits well with Martinko's (2004, p. 298) observation that attributions, in the broad sense, are people's beliefs about the causes of their rewards (i.e., successes) and punishments (i.e., failures). If we accept the premise that most goal-oriented behavior is influenced by its consequences, as most IOP theorists do, then it follows that beliefs about these consequences, often formed through prior experience, will affect expectancies, emotions, and behavior. Thus, it is not surprising that attributions are related to a wide range of variables that are central to IOP.

Second, while empirical work usually confirms that attributions are related to behavior, expectancies, and affect, they do not always account for the largest proportion of variance in research designs. This should be no more surprising than the finding that many behaviors in organizations are not a function of organizational rewards, because, in addition to organizationally controlled rewards, most behaviors are supported by multiple consequences mediated through social systems. Thus, although behaviors may be a function of consequences, there are multiple consequences and a limited number are controlled by organizations. Following this line of thinking, if there are multiple consequences for behaviors, there are also multiple attributions for these different consequences. As a result, a fundamental problem with the most frequently used experimental procedures for measuring attributions is that they assess the 'major' cause of the outcome, when there are usually multiple causes and there should be multiple attributions. Hence, it is not surprising that a small proportion of the variability in the behavior is related to the attributions regarding one of these outcomes because there are multiple outcomes for most complex behaviors. In addition, as we indicated in our prior discussion of this issue, other factors, such as norms and sanctions, limit the influence of attributions on behavior. Thus, we should not be surprised that attributions account for a limited proportion of the variance in behavior, but should keep in mind that this proportion is significant. Two analogies help to put the 'small' proportion of variance issue into perspective: Gilbert's (1989) snowball analogy and the notion of compound interest. Both of these analogies suggest that although attributions may account for a small amount of variance in some situations, over time, these differences compound and eventually become practically and theoretically significant. In today's economic climate, most investors would be happy with a real return of 7% on an investment. Similarly, we believe that researchers and practitioners can benefit greatly by investing their time and interest in the variance attributable to attributions.

A third observation is that the majority of the research we have reviewed is primarily oriented toward the application and demonstration of attributional processes, as opposed to theory building. More specifically, many of the current works take the standard attribution paradigm and apply it to a new area, sometimes describing empirical work that documents the relations depicted by their models. Moreover, when theory building does occur, as in the case of the work on poor performance, the theory builds around the issue (e.g., poor performance) without a concurrent effort to enhance or make modifications to attribution theory per se. At this juncture, we would like to see theory diverge from asking 'if' attribution helps to explain IOP phenomena and begin a more concerted effort to expand our theories of how attribution processes work and affect IOP processes.

A fourth observation, and one that we think is most surprising, is that despite the activity in this area documented by our literature search, there appears to have been very little effort to implement the knowledge we have about attribution theory in terms of training or other types of organizational interventions. More specifically, we believe that the empirical evidence and the theory surrounding the data clearly demonstrate that attributional biases, such as the actor–observer and self-serving biases, have significant impacts on leader–member relations, performance feedback, formal appraisals, and personnel selection processes. Despite this knowledge, there have been only a few formal efforts to implement attributional training and a limited number of descriptions of how such training interventions could be implemented (e.g., Martinko, 2002; Martinko & Gardner, 1982; Schulman, 1999). The basic theory and instruments for both diagnosing attributional biases and developing training interventions to reduce the destructive impacts of attributional biases is available. Kelley's theory describes the types of information people need to make accurate attributions, and the general attribution paradigm describes how the dimensions of information, attributions, expectancies, emotions, and behavior are related. Based on the knowledge of these relations, we should be able to diagnose potential aggression and other types of counterproductive behaviors, and, based on the observed pattern of information, attributions, expectancies, emotions, and behaviors, we should be able to design interventions and training to nurture productive behaviors. Similarly, with the knowledge we have of how attributional errors affect selection interview and performance appraisal processes, we should be able to design appraisal and selection processes that reduce the effects of attributional errors by doing things such as making sure that we have information on all three of Kelley's dimensions, checking to ensure that displayed emotion is consistent with attributional patterns, and structuring questions to more clearly identify attributions and attribution styles. Thus, we look forward to the time when IOP and human resource management texts treat attributions as an important component of the general paradigm of motivation, include sections on attributional training, and apply principles of attribution theory to human resource management processes such as appraisals and selection interviews.

Finally, as we have noted above, attribution theory has been and is being applied to a wide range of theories. As Weiner (2004) has noted, these extensions of application will also result in new theory building. In particular, it appears that as we attempt to describe interactive dyadic and group attribution processes, there will have to be both theoretical and research design innovations in order to capture the true complexity of these dynamic types of interactions. These new research designs will require equally new statistical procedures, as well as an open-minded perspective on the part of reviewers and editors with regard to these innovations.

In conclusion, a review of the attribution research in the IOP area unequivocally documents that attributions play a significant role in behaviors associated with the topics that are central to IOP, such as individual differences, counterproductive behavior, leader–member interactions, impression management, conflict resolution, training, selection interviewing, and performance appraisal. Our biggest challenge, at this point, is to go beyond documenting the role of attributional processes and begin to understand more about how these processes work by building new theory and engaging in applications that begin to take advantage of the knowledge that we have already accumulated. We hope that this review will play a constructive role in this endeavor.

REFERENCES

Abraham, I.L. (1985). Causal attributions of depression: Reliability of the causal dimension scale in research on clinical inference. *Psychological Reports*, **56**, 415–418.
Abramson, L.Y., Seligman, M.E.P., & Teasdale, J.D. (1978). Learned helplessness in humans: Critique and reformulation. *Journal of Abnormal Psychology*, **87**, 49–74.
Allred, K.G. (1995). Realizing the advantage of organizational interdependencies: The role of attributional mediated emotions. In M.J. Martinko (Ed.), *Attribution theory: An organizational perspective* (pp. 253–271). Delray Beach, FL: St Lucie Press.
Al-Zahrani, S.S. & Kaplowitz, S.A. (1993). Attributional biases in individualistic and collectivistic societies: A comparison of Americans and Saudis. *Social Psychology Quarterly*, **56**, 223–233.
Anderson, C.R., Hellriegel, D., & Slocum, J.W., Jr (1977). Managerial response to environmentally induced stress. *Academy of Management Journal*, **20**, 260–272.
Anderson, C.R. & Schneier, C.E. (1978). Locus of control, leader behavior and leader performance among management students. *Academy of Management Journal*, **4**, 690–698.

Anderson, L.R. (1992). Leader interventions for distressed group members: Overcoming leaders' self-serving attributional biases. *Small Group Research*, **23**, 503–523.

Aquino, K., Douglas, S.C., & Martinko, M.J. (2004). Overt expressions of anger in response to perceived victimization: The moderating effects of attributional style, hierarchical status, and organizational norms. *Journal of Occupational Health Psychology*, **9**, 152–164.

Ashkanasy, N.M. (1989). Causal attributions and supervisors' response to subordinate performance: The Green and Mitchell model revisited. *Journal of Applied Social Psychology*, **19**, 309–330.

Ashkanasy, N.M. (1995). Supervisory attributions and evaluative judgments of subordinate performance: A further test of the Green and Mitchell model. In M.J. Martinko (Ed.), *Attribution theory: An organizational perspective* (pp. 211–228). Delray Beach, FL: St Lucie Press.

Ashkanasy, N.M. & Gallois, C. (1994). Leader attribution and evaluations: Effects of locus of control, supervisory control, and task control. *Organizational Behavior and Human Decision Processes*, **59**, 27–50.

Banzinger, G. & Drevenstedt, J. (1982). Age as a variable in achievement attributions. *Journal of Gerontology*, **37**, 468–474.

Barnett, P.A. & Gottlib, L.H. (1988). Psychosocial functioning and depression: Distinguishing among antecedents, concomitants, and consequences. *Psychological Bulletin*, **104**, 97–126.

Baron, R.A. (1985). Reducing organizational conflict: The role of Attributions. *Journal of Applied Psychology*, **70**, 434–441.

Benson, M.J. (1989). Attributional measurement techniques: Classification and comparison of approaches for measuring causal dimensions. *Journal of Social Psychology*, **129**, 307–323.

Bernardin, H.J. (1989). Increasing the accuracy of performance measurement: A proposed solution to erroneous attributions. *Human Resource Planning*, **12**, 239–250.

Bernardin, H.J. & Beatty, R.W. (1984). *Performance appraisal: Assessing human behavior at work*. Boston, MA: PWS-Kent.

Betancourt, H. (2004). An attribution–empathy approach to conflict and negotiation in multicultural settings. In M.J. Martinko (Ed.), *Attribution theory in the organizational sciences* (pp. 243–256). Greenwich, CT: Information Age Publishing.

Betancourt, H. & Blair, I. (1992). A cognition (attribution)–emotion model of violence in conflict situations. *Personality and Social Psychology Bulletin*, **18**, 343–350.

Betancourt, H. & Weiner, B. (1982). Attributions for achievement-related events, expectancy, and sentiments: A study of success and failure in Chile and the United States. *Journal of Cross-Cultural Psychology*, **13**, 362–374.

Bettman, J. & Weitz, B. (1983). Attributions in the boardroom: Causal reasoning in corporate annual reports. *Administrative Science Quarterly*, **28**, 165–183.

Bitter, M.E. & Gardner, W.L. (1995). A mid-range theory of the leader/member attribution process in professional service organizations: The role of the organizational environment and impression management. In M.J. Martinko (Ed.), *Attribution theory: An organizational perspective* (pp. 171–192). Delray Beach, FL: St Lucie Press.

Bodenhausen, G.V. (1993). Emotions, arousal, and stereotypic judgments: A heuristic model of affect and stereotyping. In D.M. Mackie & D.L. Hamilton (Eds), *Affect, cognition, and stereotyping* (pp. 13–37). San Diego, CA: Academic Press.

Bono, J.E. & Judge, T.A. (2003). Core self-evaluations: A review of the trait and its role in job satisfaction and job performance. *European Journal of Personality*, **17**, S5–S18.

Bowman, E. (1976). Strategy and the weather. *Sloan Management Review*, **15**, 35–50.

Bowman, E. (1978). Strategy, annual reports, and alchemy. *California Management Review*, **20**, 64–71.

Bowman, E. (1984). Content analysis of annual reports for corporate strategy and risk. *Interfaces*, 14, 61–71.

Bradley, G.W. (1978). Self-serving biases in the attribution process. A reexamination of the fact or fiction question. *Journal of Personality and Social Psychology*, 45, 199–209.

Brewin, L.R. & Antaki, C. (1987). *Journal of Clinical and Social Psychology*, 5, 79–98.

Burke, J.P., Hunt, J.P., & Bickford, R.L. (1985). Causal internalization of academic performance as a function of self-esteem and performance satisfaction. *Journal of Research in Personality*, 19, 321–329.

Byrne, D. (1969). Attitudes and attraction. In L. Berkowitz (Ed), *Advances in experimental social psychology* (Vol. 4). New York: Academic Press.

Campbell, C.R. & Martinko, M.J. (1998). An integrative attributional perspective of empowerment and learned helplessness: A multi-method field study. *Journal of Management*, 24, 173–200.

Campbell, N.K. & Hackett, G. (1986). The effects of mathematics task performance on math self-efficacy and task interest. *Journal of Vocational Behavior*, 28, 149–162.

Cash, T.F., Gillen, B., & Burns, D.S. (1977). Sexism and 'beautyism' in personnel consultant decision making. *Journal of Applied Psychology*, 62, 301–310.

Cha, J.-H. & Nam, K.D. (1985). A test of Kelley's cube theory of attribution: A cross-cultural replication of McArthur's study. *Korean Social Science Journal*, 12, 151–180.

Chacko, T.I., Stone, T.H., & Brief, A.P. (1979). Participation in goal-setting programs: An attributional analysis. *Academy of Management Review*, 4, 433–437.

Chen, Y. & Blanchard-Fields, F. (1997). Age differences in stages of attributional processing. *Psychology and Aging*, 12, 694–703.

Clapham, S.E. & Schwenk, C.R. (1991). Self-serving attributions, managerial cognition, and company performance. *Strategic Management Review*, 12, 219–229.

Coopersmith, S. (1967). *The antecedents of self-esteem*. San Francisco: Freeman.

Crandall, C.S. & Eshleman, A. (2003). A justification–suppression model of expression and experience of prejudice. *Psychological Bulletin*, 129, 414–446.

Crittenden, K.S. & Bae, H. (1994). Self-effacement and social responsibility: Attribution as impression management in Asian cultures. *American Behavioral Scientist*, 37, 653–671.

Cullen, F., Clark, G.A., Cullen, J.B., & Mathers, R.A. (1985). Attribution, salience, and attitudes toward criminal sanctioning. *Criminal Justice and Behavior*, 12, 305–331.

Cutrona, C., Russell, D., & Jones, R. (1984). Cross-situational consistency in causal attributions: Does attributional style exist? *Journal of Personality and Social Psychology*, 47, 1043–1058.

Dalton, D.R. & Wimbush, J.C. (1998) Absence does not make the heart grow fonder. In R.W. Griffin, A. O'Leary-Kelly, & J.M. Collins (Eds), *Dysfunctional behavior in organizations: Violent and deviant behavior*. Stamford, CT: JAI Press.

Dasborough, M.T. & Ashkanasy, N.M. (2002). Emotion and attribution of intentionality in leader–member relationships. *Leadership Quarterly*, 13, 615–634.

Davis, W.D. & Gardner, W.L. (2004). Perceptions of politics and organizational cynicism: An attributional and leader–member exchange perspective. *The Leadership Quarterly*, 15, 439–465.

de Castro, B.O., Slot, N.W., Bosch, J.D., Koops, W., & Veerman. J.W. (2003). Negative feelings exacerbate hostile attributions of intent in highly aggressive boys. *Journal of Clinical Child and Adolescent Psychology*, 32, 55–56.

Decker, W.H. (1990). Managing impressions of individual and group achievement through self-presentation. *Journal of Social Behavior and Personality*, 5, 287–296.

Degroot, T. & Motowidlo, S.J. (1999). Why visual and vocal interview cues can affect interviewers' judgments and predict job performance. *Journal of Applied Psychology*, 84, 986–993.

Dessler, G. (2005). *Human resource management* (10th edn). Upper Saddle River, NJ: Pearson Prentice-Hall.

Diener, C.T. & Dweck, C.S. (1978). An analysis of learned helplessness: Continuous changes in performance, strategy, and achievement cognitions following failure. *Journal of Personality and Social Psychology*, 36, 451–462.

Diener, E. & Diener, M. (1995). Cross-cultural correlates of life satisfaction and self-esteem. *Journal of Personality and Social Psychology*, 68, 653–663.

Dipboye, R.L., Stramler, C.S., & Fontenelle, G.A. (1984). The effects of the application on recall of information from the interview. *Academy of Management Journal*, 27, 561–575.

Dobbins, G.H., Pence, E.C., Orban, J.A., & Sgro, J.A. (1983). The effects of sex of the leader and sex of the subordinate on the use of organizational control policy. *Organizational Behavior and Human Performance*, 32, 325–343.

Dobbins, G.H. & Russell, J.M. (1986) Self-serving biases in leadership: A laboratory experiment. *Journal of Management*, 12, 475–483.

Dossett, D.L. & Greenberg, C.I. (1981). Goal setting and performance evaluation: An attributional analysis. *Academy of Management Journal*, 24, 767–779.

Douglas, S.C. & Martinko, M.J. (2001). Exploring the role of individual differences in the prediction of workplace aggression. *Journal of Applied Psychology*, 86, 547–559.

Epley, N., Savitsky, K., & Gilovich, T. (2002). Empathy neglect: Reconciling the spotlight effect and the correspondence bias. *Journal of Personality and Social Psychology*, 83, 300–312.

Erez, A. & Judge, T.A. (2001). Relationship of core self-evaluations to goal setting, motivation, and performance. *Journal of Applied Psychology*, 86, 1270–1279.

Erikson, E. (1963). *Childhood and society.* New York: Norton.

Falbo, T. & Beck, R.C. (1979). Naïve psychology and the attributional model of achievement. *Journal of Personality*, 47, 185–195.

Feather, N.T. (1969). Attribution of responsibility and valence of success and failure to initial confidence and task performance. *Journal of Personality and Social Psychology*, 13, 129–144.

Fedor, D.B. & Rowland, K.M. (1989). Supervisor attributions for subordinate performance. *Journal of Management*, 15, 37–48.

Feldman, J.M. (1981). Beyond attribution theory: Cognitive processes in performance appraisal. *Journal of Applied Psychology*, 66, 127–148.

Feldman, J.M. & Hilterman, R.J. (1975). Stereotype attribution revisited: The role of stimulus characteristics, racial attitude, and cognitive differentiation. *Journal of Personality and Social Psychology*, 31, 1177–1188.

Feldman, J.M. & Hilterman, R.J. (1977). Sources of bias in performance evaluation: Two experiments. *International Journal of Intercultural Relations*, 1, 35–57.

Feldman-Summers, S. & Kiesler, S.B. (1974). Those who are number two try harder: The effect of sex on attributions of causality. *Journal of Personality and Social Psychology*, 30, 846–855.

Ferris, G.R., Yates, V.L., Gilmore, D.C., & Rowland, K.M. (1985). The influence of subordinate age on performance ratings and causal attributions. *Personnel Psychology*, 38, 545–557.

Fiedler, K. (1988). Emotional mood, cognitive style, and behavior regulation. In K. Fiedler & J. Forgas (Eds), *Affect, cognition and social behavior* (pp. 100–119). Toronto: Hogrefe.

Folger, R. & Skarlicki, D.P. (1998). A popcorn metaphor for employee aggression. In R.W. Griffin, A. O'Leary-Kelly, & J.M. Collins (Eds), *Dysfunctional behavior in organizations* (pp. 43–81). Stamford, CT: JAI Press.

Forgas, J.P. (1998). On being happy and mistaken: Mood affects on the fundamental attribution error. *Journal of Personality and Social Psychology*, 75, 318–331.

Fox, S. & Spector, P.E. (1999). A model of work frustration-aggression. *Journal of Organizational Behavior*, 20, 915–933.

Frieze, I.H. (1984). Causal attributions for the performances of the elderly: Comments from an attribution theorist. *Basic and Applied Social Psychology*, 5, 127–130.

Furnham, A., Brewin, C.R., & O'Kelly, H. (1994). The occupational attributional style questionnaire and attitudes to work. *Human Relations*, 47 (12), 1509–1522.

Furnham, A., Sadka, V., & Brewin, C. (1992). The development of an organizational attribution style questionnaire. *Journal of Organizational Behavior*, 13, 27–39.

Giacalone, R. & Riordan, C.A. (1986). Effects of self-presentation on perceptions in an organization. *Proceedings of the Academy of Management, Southwest Division* (pp. 91–95).

Gibson, D.E. & Barsade, S.G. (1999). The experience of anger at work: Lessons from the chronically angry. In R.R. Callister (Chair), *Anger in organizations: Its causes and consequences.* Symposium conducted at the annual meeting of the Academy of Management, Chicago.

Gilbert, D. (1989). Thinking lightly about others: Automatic components of the social inference process. In J.S. Uleman & J.A. Bargh (Eds), *Unintended thought.* New York: Guilford Press.

Gilbert, D. (1995). Attribution and interpersonal perception. In A. Tesser (Ed.), *Advanced social psychology* (pp. 99–147). New York: McGraw-Hill.

Girodo, M., Dotzenroth, S.F., & Stein, S.J. (1981). Causal attribution bias in shy males: Implications for self-esteem and self-confidence. *Cognitive Therapy and Research*, 5, 325–338.

Gist, M.E. & Mitchell, T.R. (1992). Self-efficacy: A theoretical analysis: Of its determinants and malleability. *Academy of Management Review*, 17, 183–211.

Goerke, M., Moller, J., Schulz-Hardt, S., Napiersky, U., & Frey, D. (2004). 'It's not my fault—but only I can change it': Counterfactual and prefactual thoughts of managers. *Journal of Applied Psychology*, 89, 279–292.

Goffman, E. (1959). *The presentation of self in everyday life.* Oxford, UK: Doubleday.

Goodstadt, B.E. & Hjelle, L.A. (1973). Power to the powerless: Locus of control and the use of power. *Journal of Personality and Social Psychology*, 27, 190–196.

Grasmick, H.G. & McGill, A.L. (1994). Religion, attribution style, and punitiveness toward juvenile offenders. *Criminology*, 32, 23–46.

Green, S.G. & Liden, R.C. (1980). Contextual and attributional influences on control decisions. *Journal of Applied Psychology*, 65, 453–458.

Green, S.G. & Mitchell, T.R. (1979). Attributional processes of leaders in leader–member interactions. *Organizational Behavior and Human Performance*, 23, 429–458.

Greer, J., Halgin, R., & Harvey, E. (2004). Global versus specific symptom attributions: Predicting the recognition and treatment of psychological distress in primary care. *Journal of Psychosomatic Research*, 57, 521–527.

Gundlach, M.J., Douglas, S.C., & Martinko, M.J. (2003). The decision to blow the whistle: A social information processing framework. *Academy of Management Review*, 28, 107–123.

Hablesleban, J.R. & Buckley, M.R. (2004). Attribution and burnout: Explicating the influence of individual factors in the consequences of workplace exhaustion. In M.J. Martinko (Ed.), *Attribution theory in the organizational sciences: Theoretical and empirical contributions* (pp. 83–110). Greenwich, CT: Information Age Publishing.

Hall, N.C., Hladkyi, S., Perry, R.P., & Ruthig, J.C. (2004). The role of attributional retraining and elaborative learning in college students' academic development. *Journal of Social Psychology*, 114, 591–612.

Hamilton, R.J. & Akhter, S. (2002). Psychometric properties of the multidimensional–multiattributional causality scale. *Educational and Psychological Measurement*, **62**, 802–817.

Harris, M.H. & Greising, L.A. (1998). Alcohol and drug use as dysfunctional workplace behaviors. In R.W. Griffin, A. O'Leary-Kelly, & J.M. Collins (Eds), *Dysfunctional behavior in organizations: Violent and deviant behavior*. Stamford, CT: JAI Press.

Heider, F. (1958). *The psychology of interpersonal relations*. New York: John Wiley & Sons.

Henry, J.W. & Campbell, C. (1995). A comparison of the validity, predictiveness, and consistency of a trait versus situational measure of attributions in attribution theory. In M.J. Martinko (Ed.), *An organizational perspective* (pp. 35–52). Delray Beach, FL: St Lucie Press.

Herriot, P. (1981). Towards an attributional theory of the selection interview. *Journal of Occupational Psychology*, **54**, 165–173.

Herriot, P. (1989). Attribution theory and interview decisions. In R.W. Eder & J.R. Ferris (Eds), *The employment interview: Theory, research and practice* (pp. 97–106). Newbury, CA: Sage.

Hill, T., Smith, N.D., & Mann, M.F. (1987). Role of efficacy expectations in predicting the decision to use advanced technologies. *Journal of Applied Psychology*, **72**, 307–314.

Huey, S.J. & Weisz, J.R. (1997). Ego control, ego resiliency, and the five-factor model as predictors of behavioral and emotional problems in clinic-referred children and adolescents. *Journal of Abnormal Psychology*, **106**, 404–415.

Huff, A. & Schwenk, C. (1990). Bias and sensemaking in good times and bad. In A.S. Huff (Ed.), *Mapping strategic thought* (pp. 85–108). Chichester, UK: John Wiley & Sons.

Ilgen, D.R. & Knowlton, W.A., Jr (1980). Performance attributional effects on feedback from superiors. *Organizational Behavior and Human Performance*, **25**, 441–456.

Ilgen, D.R., Mitchell, T.R., & Fredrickson, J.W. (1981). Poor performance: Supervisors' and subordinates' responses. *Organizational Behavior and Human Performance*, **27**, 386–410.

Inkeles, A. (1983). 'The American character.' *The Center Magazine*, **16**, 25–39.

Islam, M.R. & Hewstone, M. (1993). Intergroup attributions and affective consequences in majority and minority groups. *Journal of Personality and Social Psychology*, **64**, 936–950.

Jackson, C.L. & LePine, J.A. (2003). Peer responses to a team's weakest link: A test and extension of LePine and Van Dyne's Model. *Journal of Applied Psychology*, **88**, 459–475.

Jae-Ho, C. & Ki-Dok, N. (1985). A test of Kelley's cube theory of attribution: A cross-cultural replication of McArthur's study. *Korean Social Science Journal*, **12**, 151–180.

Johnson, A.L., Luthans, F., & Hennessey, H.W. (1984). The role of locus of control in leader influence. *Behavior Personnel Psychology*, **37**, 61–75.

Johnson, D.E., Erez, A., Kiker, D.S., & Motowidlo, S.J. (2002). Liking and attributions of motives as mediators of the relationships between individuals' reputations, helpful behaviors, and raters' reward decisions. *Journal of Applied Psychology*, **87**, 808–815.

Jones, E.E. (1976). How do people perceive the causes of behavior? *American Scientist*, **64**, 300–305.

Jones E.E. & Davis, K.E. (1965). A theory of correspondent inferences: From acts to dispositions. In L. Berkowitz (Ed.), *Advances in experimental social psychology* (Vol. 2, pp. 219–266). New York: Academic Press.

Jones, E.E. & Nisbett, R.E. (1972). The actor and the observer: Divergent perceptions of the causes of behavior. In E.E. Jones, D.E. Kanouse, H.H. Kelley, R.E. Nisbett,

S. Valins, & B. Weiner (Eds), *Attribution: Perceiving the causes of behavior* (pp. 79–94). Morristown, NJ: General Learning Press.

Joseph, C.V. & Douglas, S.C. (2004). Conflict management: An attributional perspective. In M.J. Martinko (Ed.), *Attribution theory in the organizational sciences: Theoretical and empirical contributions* (pp. 225–242). Greenwich, CT: Information Age Publishing.

Judge, T.A., Erez, A., & Bono, J.E. (1998). The power of being positive: The relationship between positive self-concept and performance. *Human Performance*, 11, 167–187.

Judge, T.A. & Kammemeyer-Mueller, J.D. (2004). Core self-evaluations, aspirations, success, and persistence: An attributional model. In M.J. Martinko, (Ed.), *Attribution theory in the organizational sciences: Theoretical and empirical contributions* (pp. 111–132). Greenwich, CT: Information Age Publishing.

Judge, T.A., Locke, E.A., & Durham, C.C. (1997). The dispositional causes of job satisfaction: A core evaluations approach. *Research in Organizational Behavior*, 19, 181–188.

Keenan, A. (1976). Interviewers' evaluations of applicant characteristics: Differences between personnel and non-personnel managers. *Journal of Occupational Psychology*, 49, 223–230.

Kelley, H.H. (1967). Attribution theory in social psychology. In D. Levine (Ed.), *Nebraska symposium on motivation* (Vol. 15). Lincoln, NB: University of Nebraska Press.

Kelley, H.H. (1971). *Attributions in social interaction*. New York: General Learning Press.

Kelley, H.H. (1972). Causal schemata and the attribution process in attribution: Perceiving the causes of behavior. In E. Jones, D. Kanouse, H. Kelley, R. Nisbett, S. Valins, & B. Weiner (Eds), *Attribution: Perceiving the causes of behavior*. Morristown, NJ: General Learning Press.

Kelley, H.H. (1973). The process of causal attributions. *American Psychologist*, 28, 107–128.

Kelley, H. & Michela, J. (1980). Attribution theory and research. *Annual Review of Psychology*, 31, 457–501.

Kent, R. & Martinko, M.J. (1995). The development and evaluation of a scale to measure organizational attribution style. In M. Martinko (Ed.), *Attribution theory: An organizational perspective* (pp. 53–75). Delray Beach, FL: St Lucie Press.

Kimble, C.E. & Moriarty, B.F. (1979). An attributional view of attraction: Evaluative gains versus favorable comparisons. *Psychological Reports*, 45, 199–207.

Kinicki, A.J. & Vecchio, R.P. (1994). Influences on the quality of supervisor–subordinate relation: The role of time-pressure, organizational commitment, and locus of control. *Journal of Organizational Behavior*, 15, 75–82.

Knowlton, W.A. & Ilgen, D.R. (1980). Performance attributional effects on feedback from superiors. *Organizational Behavior and Human Performance*, 25, 441–456.

Knowlton, W.A. & Mitchell, T.R. (1980). Effects of causal attributions on a supervisor's evaluation of subordinate performance. *Journal of Applied Psychology*, 64, 459–466.

Kovenklioglu, G. & Greenhaus, J.H. (1975). Causal attributions, expectations, and task performance. *Journal of Applied Psychology*, 63, 698–705.

Krueger, J. & Clement, R.W. (1994). The truly false consensus effect: An ineradicable and egocentric bias in social perception. *Journal of Personality and Social Psychology*, 67, 596–610.

Krueger, J. & Zeiger, J.S. (1993). Social categorization and the truly false consensus effect. *Journal of Personality and Social Psychology*, 65, 670–680.

Landrine, H. & Klonoff, E.A. (1992). Culture and health-related schemas: A review proposal for interdisciplinary integration. *Health Psychology*, 11, 267–276.

Langford, T. & Mackinnon, N.J. (2000). The affective bases for the gendering of traits: Comparing the United States and Canada. *Social Psychology Quarterly*, **68**, 34–48.

Larson, C.E. & LaFasto, F.M.J. (1989). *Teamwork: What must go right/what can go wrong*. Newberry Park, NJ: Sage.

Lawson, R.B. & Shen, Z. (1998). *Organizational psychology: Foundations and applications*. New York: Oxford University Press.

Lefcourt, H.M. (1991). The multidimensional–multiattributional causality scale. In J.P. Robinson, P.R. Shaver, & L.S. Wrightsman (Eds), *Measures of personality and social psychological attitudes* (Vol. 1, pp. 454–457). San Diego, CA: Academic Press.

Lefcourt, H.M., von Baeyer, C.L., Ware, E.E., & Cox, D.J. (1979). The multidimensional–multiattributional causality scale: The development of a goal-specific locus of control scale. *Canadian Journal of Behavioural Science*, **11**, 286–304.

LePine, J.A. & Van Dyne, L. (2001). Peer responses to low performers: An attributional model of helping in the context of groups. *Academy of Management Review*, **26**, 67–84.

Little, A. (1987). Attributions in a cross-cultural context. *Genetic, Social, and General Psychology Monographs*, **113**, 63–79.

Lord, R.G. (1985). An information processing approach to social perceptions, leadership and behavioral measurement in organizations. In L.L. Cummings & B.M. Staw (Eds), *Research in organizational behavior* (Vol. 7, pp. 87–128). Greenwich, CT: JAI Press.

Lord, R.G. (1995). An alternative perspective on attributional processes. In M. Martinko (Ed.), *Attribution theory: An organizational perspective* (pp. 333–350). Delray Beach, FL: St Lucie Press.

Lord, R.G. & Maher, K.J. (1990). Alternative information-processing models and their implications for theory, research, and practice. *Academy of Management Review*, **15**, 9–28.

Lord, R.G. & Maher, K.J. (1991). Cognitive theory in industrial and organizational psychology. In M.D. Dunnette & L.M. Hough (Eds), *Handbook of industrial and organizational psychology* (2nd edn, Vol. 2). Palo Alto, CA: Consulting Psychologists Press.

Lord, R.G. & Maher, K.J. (1993). *Leadership and information processing: Linking perceptions and performance*. London: Routledge.

Lord, R.G. & Smith, J.E. (1983). Theoretical, informational, information processing, and situational factor affecting attributional theories of organizational behavior. *Academy of Management Review*, **8**, 50–60.

Luthans, F. (2002a). The need for and meaning of positive organizational behavior. *Journal of Organizational Behavior*, **23**, 695–706.

Luthans, F. (2002b). Positive organizational behavior: Developing and managing psychological strengths. *Academy of Management Executive*, **16**, 57–75.

Luthans, F. & Avolio, B.J. (2003). Authentic leadership development. In K.S. Cameron, J.E. Dutton, & R.E. Quinn (Eds), *Positive organizational scholarship* (pp. 241–261). San Francisco: Barrett-Koehler.

Maehr, M.L. & Kleiber, D.A. (1980). The graying of America: Implications for achievement research and theory. In L.J. Fyans (Ed.), *Recent trends in achievement motivation theory and research* (pp. 171–189). New York: Plenum Press.

Maher, K. (1995). The role of cognitive load in supervisor attributions of subordinate behavior. In M.J. Martinko (Ed.), *Attribution theory: An organizational perspective*, (pp. 193–210). Delray Beach, FL: St Lucie Press.

Markus, H.R. & Kitayama, S. (1991). Culture and the self: Implications for cognition, emotion, and motivation. *Psychological Review*, **98**, 224–253.

Martin, S.L. & Klimoski, R.J. (1990). Use of verbal protocols to trace cognitions associated with self and supervisor evaluations of performance. *Organizational Behavior and Human Decision Processes*, **46**, 135–154.

Martinko, M.J. (Ed.) (1995). *Attribution theory: An organizational perspective.* Delray Beach, FL: St Lucie Press.

Martinko, M.J. (2002). *Thinking like a winner: A guide to high performance leadership.* Tallahassee, FL: Gulf Coast Publishing.

Martinko, M.J. (2004). Parting thoughts: Current issues and future directions. In M.J. Martinko (Ed.), *Attribution theory in the organizational sciences: Theoretical and empirical contributions* (pp. 297–305). Greenwich, CT: Information Age Publishing.

Martinko, M.J. & Douglas, S.C. (1999). Culture and expatriate failure: An attributional explication. *The International Journal of Organizational Analysis,* 7, 265–293.

Martinko, M.J., Douglas, S.C., Ford, R., & Gundlach, M.J. (2004). Dues paying: A theoretical explication and conceptual model. *Journal of Management,* 30, 49–69.

Martinko, M.J., Douglas, S.C., Harvey, P., & Joseph, C. (2005). Managing organizational aggression. In R. Kidwell & C. Martin (Eds), *Managing organizational deviance: Readings and cases* (pp. 237–260). Thousand Oaks, CA: Sage.

Martinko, M.J. & Gardner, W.L. (1982). Learned helplessness: An alternative explanation for performance deficits. *Academy of Management Review,* 7, 195–204.

Martinko, M.J. & Gardner, W.L. (1983). A methodological review of sex-related access discrimination problems. *Sex Roles: A Journal of Research,* 9, 825–839.

Martinko, M.J. & Gardner, W.L. (1987). The leader–member attribution process. *Academy of Management Review,* 12, 235–249.

Martinko, M.J., Gundlach, M.J., & Douglas, S.C. (2002). Toward an integrative theory of counterproductive workplace behavior: A causal reasoning perspective. *International Journal of Selection and Assessment,* 10 (1/2), 36–50.

Martinko, M.J., Henry, J., & Zmud, R. (1996). Learned helplessness: A theoretical explication of reactions to information technologies in the workplace. *Behavior and Information Technology,* 15, 313–330.

Martinko, M.J. & Moss, S.E. (2004). An exploratory study of workplace aggression. In M.J. Martinko (Ed.), *Attribution theory in the organizational sciences: Theoretical and empirical contributions* (pp. 133–150). Greenwich, CT: Information Age Publishing.

Martinko, M.J., Moss, S.E., & Douglas, S.C. (2003). *The effects of attribution styles on leader–member relations.* Presented at the Annual Meeting of the Academy of Management 2003, Seattle.

Martinko, M.J. & Zellars, K.L. (1998). Toward a theory of workplace violence: A cognitive appraisal perspective. In R. Griffin, A. O'Leary-Kelly, & J. Collins (Eds), *Dysfunctional behavior in organizations: Violent and deviant behavior* (pp. 1–42). Stanford, CT: JAI Press.

Masten, A.S. (2001). Ordinary magic: Resilience processes in development. *American Psychologist,* 56, 227–238.

McAuley, E., Duncan, T.E., & Russell, D.W. (1992). Measuring causal attributions: The revised causal dimension scale (CDSII). *Personality and Social Psychology Bulletin,* 18, 566–573.

McDonald, D.M. (1995). Fixing blame in *n*-person attributions: A social identity model for attributional processes in newly formed cross-functional groups. In M.J. Martinko (Ed.), *Attribution theory: An organizational perspective* (pp. 273–288). Delray Beach, FL: St Lucie Press.

McElroy, J.C. & Morrow, P.C. (1983). An attribution theory of sex discrimination. *Personnel Review,* 12, 11–13.

McFillen, J.M. & New, J.R. (1979). Situational determinants of supervisor attributions and behavior. *Academy of Management Review,* 4, 793–809.

Mezulis, A.H., Abramson, L.Y., Hyde, J.S., & Hankin, B.L. (2004). Is there a universal positivity bias in attributions? A meta-analytic review of individual, developmental, and cultural differences in the self-serving attributional bias. *Psychological Bulletin*, **130**, 711–747.

Michalisin, M.D., Karau, S.J., & Tangpong, C. (2003). The effects of performance and team cohesion on attribution: A longitudinal simulation. *Journal of Business Research*, **57**, 1108–1115.

Mitchell, T. (1982). Attributions and actions: A note of caution. *Journal of Management*, **8**, 65–74.

Mitchell, T.R. & Kalb, L.S. (1981). Effects of outcome knowledge and outcome valence on supervisors' evaluations. *Journal of Applied Psychology*, **66**, 604–612.

Mitchell, T.R. & Kalb, L.S. (1982). Effects of job experience on supervisor attributions for a subordinate's poor performance. *Journal of Applied Psychology*, **67**, 181–188.

Mitchell, T.R., Smyser, C.M., & Weed, S.E. (1975). Locus of control: Supervision and work satisfaction. *Academy of Management Journal*, **18**, 623–630.

Mitchell, T.R. & Wood, R.E. (1980). Supervisor's responses to subordinate poor performance: A test of an attributional model. *Organizational Behavior and Human Performance*, **25**, 123–138.

Miyamoto, Y. & Kitayama, S. (2002). Cultural variation in correspondence bias: The critical role of attitude diagnosticity of socially constrained behavior. *Journal of Personality of Social Psychology*, **83**, 1239–1248.

Molm, L.D. (1985). Gender and power use: An experimental analysis of behavior and perceptions. *Social Psychology Quarterly*, **48**, 285–300.

Moore, J.E. (2000). Why is this happening? A causal attribution approach to work exhaustion consequences. *Academy of Management Review*, **25**, 335–349.

Morris, M.W. & Peng, K. (1994). Culture and cause: American and Chinese attributions for social and physical events. *Journal of Personality and Social Psychology*, **67**, 949–971.

Munton, A.G., Silvester, J., Stratton, P., & Hanks, H.G.I. (1999). *Attributions in action: Coding qualitative data*. Chichester: John Wiley & Sons.

Naquin, C.E. & Tynan, R.O. (2003). The team halo effect: Why teams are not blamed for their failures. *Journal of Applied Psychology*, **88**, 332–340.

Neuman, J.H. & Baron, R.A. (1998). Workplace violence and workplace aggression: Evidence concerning specific forms, potential causes, and preferred targets. *Journal of Management*, **24**, 391–420.

Newcombe, M.J. & Ashkanasy, N.M. (2002). The role of affect and affective congruence in perceptions of leaders: An experimental study. *Leadership Quarterly*, **13**, 601–614.

Nunnally, J.C. (1978). *Psychometric theory* (2nd edn). New York: McGraw-Hill.

O'Leary-Kelly, A., Griffin, R.W., & Glew, D.J. (1996). Organization-motivated aggression: A research framework. *Academy of Management Review*, **21**, 225–253.

Payne, M. & Furnham, A. (1990). Causal attributions for unemployment in Barbados. *The Journal of Social Psychology*, **130**, 169–181.

Payne, S.L. & Giacalone, R.A. (1990). Social psychological approaches to the perception of ethical dilemmas. *Human Relations*, **43**, 649–665.

Perlow, R. & Latham, L.L. (1993). Relationship of client abuse with locus of control and gender: A longitudinal study in mental retardation facilities. *Journal of Applied Psychology*, **78**, 831–834.

Perrewé, P.L. & Spector, P.E. (2002). Personality research in the organizational sciences. In G.R. Ferris (Ed.), *Research in personnel and human resources management* (Vol. 21, pp. 1–64). Oxford: JAI Press.

Peterson, C., Bettes, B.A., & Seligman, M.E.P. (1985). Depressive symptoms and unprompted causal attributions: Content analysis. *Behavior Research and Therapy*, **23**, 379–382.

Peterson, C., Semmel, A., Von Baeyer, C., Abramson, L., Metalsky, G., & Seligman E. (1982). The attributional style questionnaire. *Cognitive Therapy and Research*, **6**, 287–300.

Peterson, C. & Villanova, P. (1988). An expanded attributional style questionnaire. *Journal of Abnormal Psychology*, **97**, 87–89.

Petterson, N. (1991). Selecting project managers: An integrated list of procedures. *Project Management Journal*, **22**, 21–26.

Piers, E.V. (1977). Children's self-esteem, level of esteem certainty, and responsibility for success and failure. *Journal of Genetic Psychology*, **130**, 295–304.

Ployhart, R.E. & Ryan, A.M. (1997). Toward an explanation of applicant reactions: An examination of organizational justice and attribution frameworks. *Organizational Behavior and Human Decision Processes*, **72**, 308–335.

Powell, G.N. & Butterfield, D.A. (1980). The female leader: Attributional effects of group performance. *Psychological Reports*, **47**, 891–897.

Powers, S., Douglas, P., & Choroszy, M. (1983). The factorial validity of the multidimensional–multiattributional causality scale. *Educational and Psychological Measurement*, **43**, 611–615.

Pruitt, D.J. & Insko, C.A. (1980). Extension of the Kelley attribution model: The role of comparison-object consensus, distinctiveness, and consistency. *Journal of Personality and Social Psychology*, **39**, 39–58.

Rahim, M.A. & Bonoma, T.V. (1979). Managing organizational conflict: A model for diagnosis and intervention. *Psychological Reports*, **44**, 1323–1344.

Ramsay, S., Gallois, C., & Callan, V.J. (1997). Social rules and attributions in the personnel selection interview. *Journal of Occupational and Organizational Psychology*, **70**, 189–203.

Rand, T.M. & Wexley, K.N. (1975). Demonstration of the effect 'similar to me' in simulated employment interviews. *Psychological Reports*, **36**, 535–544.

Reagan, D.T., Strauss, E., & Fazio, R. (1974). Liking and the attribution process. *Journal of Experimental Social Psychology*, **10**, 385–397.

Reasinger, R. & Brownlow, S. (1996). *Putting off until tomorrow what is better done today: Academic procrastination as a function of motivation toward college work*. Salisbury, NC: Catawba College.

Reno, R. (1979). Perceived causality for success in occupations. *Journal of Vocational Behavior*, **14**, 190–208.

Robbins, S.P. (2003). Organizational behavior (10th edn). Upper Saddle River, NJ: Prentice-Hall.

Rodriguez, Y.G. (1997). Learned helplessness or expectancy-value? A psychological model for describing the experiences of different categories of unemployed people. *Journal of Adolescence*, **20**, 321–332.

Romney, D.M. (1994). Cross-validating a causal model relating attributional style, self-esteem, and depression: An heuristic study. *Psychological Reports*, **74**, 203–207.

Ross, L. (1977). The intuitive psychologist and his shortcomings: Distortions in the attribution process. In L. Berkowitz (Ed.), *Advances in experimental social psychology* (Vol. 10, pp. 173–219). New York: Academic Press.

Rotter, J.B. (1966). Generalized expectancies for internal versus external control of reinforcement. *Psychological Monographs: General and Applied*, **1**, 1–28.

Russell, D. (1982). The causal dimension scale: A measure of how individuals perceive causes. *Journal of Personality and Social Psychology*, **42**, 1137–1145.

Russell, D.W. (1991). The measurement of attribution process: Trait and situational approaches. In S.L. Zelen (Ed.), *New models, new extensions of attribution theory*. New York: Springer-Verlag.

Russell, D.W., McAuley, E., & Tarico, V. (1987). Measuring causal attributions for success and failure: A comparison of methodologies for assessing causal dimensions. *Journal of Personality and Social Psychology*, **52**, 1248–1257.

Salancik, G. & Meindl, J. (1984). Corporate attributions as strategic illusions of management control. *Administrative Science Quarterly*, **28**, 238–254.

Schulman, P. (1999). Applying learned optimism to increase sales productivity. *Journal of Personal Selling and Sales Management*, **19**, 31–37.

Schunk, D.H. (1998). Teaching elementary students to self-regulate practice of mathematical skills with modeling. In D.H. Schunk & B.J. Zimmerman (Eds), *Self-regulated learning: From teaching to self-reflective practice* (pp. 137–159). New York: Guilford Press.

Sechrist, G.B., Swim, J.K., & Mark, M.M. (2003). Mood as information in making attributions to discrimination. *Personality and Social Psychology Bulletin*, **29**, 524–531.

Seligman, M.E.P. (1990). *Learned optimism*. New York: Pocket Books.

Seligman, M.E.P. (1999). The president's address. *American Psychologist, 1998 Annual Report*, pp. 559–562.

Seligman, M.E.P. & Csikszentmihalyi, M. (2000). Positive psychology: An introduction. *American Psychologist*, **55**, 5–14.

Shaffritz, J.M. & Ott, J.S. (2000). *Classics of organization theory* (5th edn). New York: Harcourt College Publishers.

Shaver, P.R. & Brennan, K.A. (1991). Attributional style questionnaire. In J.P. Robinson, P.R. Shaver, & L.S. Wrightsman (Eds), *Measures of personality and social psychological attitudes* (Vol. 1, pp. 225–229). San Diego, CA: Academic Press.

Sheldon, K.M. & King, L. (2001). Why positive psychology is necessary. *American Psychologist*, **56**, 216–217.

Sillars, A.L. (1981). Attributions and interpersonal conflict-resolution. In J.H. Harvey, W. Ickes, & R.F. Kidds (Eds), *New directions in attributional research* (Vol. 3, pp. 279–305). Hillsdale, NJ: Lawrence Erlbaum.

Silver, W.S., Mitchell, T.R., & Gist, M.E. (1995). Responses to successful and unsuccessful performance: The moderating effect of self-efficacy on the relationship between performance and attributions. *Organizational Behavior and Human Decision Processes*, **62**, 286–299.

Silvester, J. (1997). Spoken attributions and candidate success in graduate recruitment interviews. *Journal of Occupational and Organizational Psychology*, **70**, 61–73.

Silvester, J., Anderson, N.R., & Patterson, F. (1999). Organizational culture change: An inter-group attributional analysis. *Journal of Occupational and Organizational Psychology*, **72**, 1–23.

Silvester, J., Anderson-Gough, F.M., Anderson, N.R., & Mohamed, A.R. (2002). Locus of control, attributions and impression management in the selection interview. *Journal of Occupational and Organizational Psychology*, **75**, 59–76.

Singer, M.S. (1989). Individual differences in leadership aspirations: An exploratory study from valence, self-efficacy and attribution perspectives. *Journal of Social Behavior and Personality*, **4**, 253–262.

Stake, J.E. (1990). Exploring attributions in natural settings: Gender and self-esteem effects. *Journal of Research in Personality*, **24**, 468–486.

Staw, B.M. (1975). Attribution of the 'cause' of performance: A general alternative interpretation of cross-sectional research on organizations. *Organizational Behavior and Human Performance*, **13**, 414–432.

Staw, B.M., McKechnie, P., & Puffer, S. (1983). The justification of organizational performance. *Administrative Science Quarterly*, **28**, 582–600.

Storms, P.L. & Spector, P.E. (1987). Relationships of organizational frustration with reported behavioral reactions: The moderating effects of locus of control. *Journal of Occupational Psychology*, **60**, 635–637.

Stratton, P., Munton, A.G., Hanks, H.J.I., Heard, D., & Davidson, C. (1988). *Leeds Attributional Coding System Manual*. Leeds, UK: University of Leeds Press.

Taylor, D.M. & Jaggi, V. (1974). Ethnocentrism and causal attribution in a south Indian context. *Journal of Cross Cultural Psychology*, **5**, 162–171.

Taylor, M.S., Locke, E.A., Lee, C., & Gist, M.E. (1984). Type A behavior and faculty research productivity: What are the mechanisms? *Organizational Behavior and Human Decision Processes*, **34**, 402–418.

Tessler, R. & Suschelsky, L. (1978). Effects of eye contact and social status on the perception of a in an employment interview situation. *Journal of Vocational Behavior*, **13**, 338–347.

Thomas, K.M. & Mathieu, J.E. (1994). Role of causal attributions in dynamic self-regulation and goal processes. *Journal of Applied Psychology*, **79**, 812–818.

Thoms, P., Moore, K.S., & Scott, K.S. (1996). The relationship between self-efficacy for participating in self-managed work groups and the Big Five personality dimensions. *Journal of Organizational Behavior*, 349–362.

Thomson, N.F. & Martinko, M.J. (2004). Social attributional style: A conceptual and empirical extension of attributional style. In M.J. Martinko (Ed.), *Attribution theory in the organizational sciences* (pp. 173–201). Greenwich, CT: Information Age Publishing.

Vallerand, R.J. (1987). Antecedents of self-related affects in sport: Preliminary evidence on the intuitive–reflective appraisal model. *Journal of Sport Psychology*, **9**, 161–182.

Vallerand, R.J. & Richer, F. (1988). On the use of the Causal Dimension Scale in a field setting: A test with confirmatory factor analysis in success and failure situations. *Journal of Personality and Social Psychology*, **54**, 704–712.

Van Boven, L., Kamada, A., & Gilovich, T. (1999). The perceiver as perceived: Everyday intuitions about the correspondence bias. *Journal of Personality and Social Psychology*, **77**, 1188–1199.

Wagner, J.A. & Hollenbeck, J.R. (2005). *Organizational behavior: Securing a competitive advantage* (5th edn). Mason, OH: Thomson/South-Western.

Weiner, B. (1983). Some methodological pitfalls in attributional research. *Journal of Educational Psychology*, **75**, 530–543.

Weiner, B. (1985a). An attributional theory of achievement motivation and emotion. *Psychological Review*, **92**, 548–573.

Weiner, B. (1985b). 'Spontaneous' causal thinking. *Psychological Bulletin*, **97**, 74–84.

Weiner, B. (1986). *An attributional theory of motivation and emotion*. New York: Springer-Verlag.

Weiner, B. (1987). The social psychology of emotion: Applications of a naïve psychology. *Journal of Social and Clinical Psychology*, **5**, 405–419.

Weiner, B. (1995). *Judgments of responsibility: A foundation for a theory of social conduct*. New York: Guilford Press.

Weiner, B. (2004). Social motivation and moral emotions: An attributional perspective. In M.J. Martinko (Ed.), *Attribution theory in the organizational sciences: Theoretical and empirical contributions* (pp. 5–24). Greenwich, CT: Information Age Publishing.

Weiner, B., Figueroa-Munoz, A., & Kakihara, C. (1991). The goals of excuses and communication strategies related to causal perceptions. *Personality and Social Psychology Bulletin*, **17**, 4–13.

Weiner, B., Frieze, I., Kukla, A., Reed, L., Rest, S., & Rosenbaum, R.M. (1971). *Perceiving the causes of success and failure*. Morristown, NJ: General Learning Press.

Wendel, J.S., Miklowitz, D.J., Richards, J.A., & George, E.L. (2000). Expressed emotion and attributions in the relatives of bipolar patients: An analysis of problem-solving interactions. *Journal of Abnormal Psychology*, **109**, 792–796.

Wood, R.E. & Bandura, A. (1989). Impact of conceptions of ability on self-regulatory mechanisms and complex decision making. *Journal of Personality and Social Psychology*, **56**, 407–415.

Wood, R.E. & Locke, E.A. (1987). The relation of self-efficacy and grade goals to academic performance. *Educational and Psychological Measurement*, **47**, 1013–1024.

Wood, R.E. & Mitchell, T.R. (1981). Manager behavior in a social context: The impact of impression management on attributions and disciplinary action. *Organizational Behavior and Human Performance*, **28**, 356–378.

Yates, J.F. & Kulick, R.M. (1977). Effort control and judgments.*Organizational Behavior and Human Performance*, **20**, 54–65.

Zuckerman, M. (1979). Attribution of success and failure revisited, or The motivational bias is alive and well in attribution theory. *Journal of Personality*, **47**, 245–287.

Chapter 5

INTERNATIONAL MANAGEMENT: SOME KEY CHALLENGES FOR INDUSTRIAL AND ORGANIZATIONAL PSYCHOLOGY

Paul R. Sparrow

Manchester Business School, University of Manchester, UK

International management as a field has been developing at a dramatic pace, as evidenced by a rapid increase in publications. Increasingly psychology in general and the field of industrial and organizational (I/O) psychology in particular are making their presence felt. Since important aspects of international management were reviewed in this series only five years ago by Smith, Fischer, and Sale (2001a), the present chapter will adopt a rather different focus. The context for international management has changed radically even within this relatively short period of time and therefore the territory covered by this review must by necessity be broad. The territory on which I have chosen to focus is that associated with the globalization process taking place within firms. The review draws primarily upon journal articles published in this period in reputable I/O psychology journals. As will be seen, this includes not just the A list journals frequently used in research assessment processes but also specialized (and more recent) outlets such as the *International Journal of Cross-Cultural Management* where appropriate. Material is also sourced not just from I/O psychology journals, but from journals in cognate areas such as international human resource management. Computerized searches were conducted on databases such as ABI-Inform using keyword analysis. A manual search of the dominant journals in the field was also conducted. Finally, several review chapters from international research volumes have been accessed. The intention is to relay the discourse taking place within the field and to position this in the context of general developments in the international management literature. In this chapter I draw upon papers published since 2000, referring to earlier work where it is necessary to trace the roots of the academic discourse. This five-year timeframe

International Review of Industrial and Organizational Psychology, 2006, *Volume 21*
Edited by G.P. Hodgkinson and J.K. Ford. © 2006 John Wiley & Sons, Ltd.

captures most developments in the field and enables my review to build upon the earlier chapter of Smith et al. (2001a) in this series.

Most of the research discussed in this chapter comes from a cross-cultural or comparative perspective. The review is structured as follows. The opening sections review the debates that have arisen in the last five years from a Comparative Human Resource Management (CHRM) perspective (post Smith et al.'s 2001a chapter in this series) around the issue of national culture and our need to develop better theories that explain its impact on I/O psychology. The starting point for the present chapter, therefore, is a brief reminder of the main inheritance that still guides much work in the comparative field. I then note some new data that have emerged from this perspective. This is followed by a critical review of the research assumptions and subsequent methodological biases associated with three different types of study that have come to dominate the field. The multiple cultures perspective is introduced, and specific criticisms of cross-national research are covered. On the basis of these criticisms, the need to contextualize national culture differences is considered along with the need to understand a number of processes that probably underpin culturally embedded behaviour. This leads into a discussion of cultural convergence or the continuance of cultural differences. The debate about convergence brings with it the need to understand change processes in national cultures and the need to develop multilevel frameworks. A number of continuing theoretical challenges, principally about how best to formulate such theories, are revisited. One of the messages that arises from this discussion is the need to be clear about the nature of underlying human functioning within the level of analysis most familiar to I/O psychologists—that of organization–individual linkages. Having reported on a number of studies at this level of analysis on issues such as job satisfaction, commitment, and the psychological contract, I finally move onto some new directions for research that are emerging from the globalization process taking place within firms. The latter sections consider work of relevance to the new agenda in the International Human Resource Management (IHRM) field. I use current research on the process of globalization within firms to identify a series of pressing concerns. Of these concerns, I draw attention to two particular issues: understanding global knowledge transfer and understanding mutual adjustment processes among a more diverse group of international employees.

THE TERRITORY FOR RESEARCH IN INTERNATIONAL MANAGEMENT

Before identifying some of the key challenges for I/O psychologists in relation to international management, we must understand the territory in which psychological knowledge is currently making (or potentially could make) a significant contribution. Werner (2002) recently carried out an analysis of the research that has been published in the field of international management. He concentrated his analysis on research that has looked at the management of firms in a multinational context by analysing systematically research published in the top US journals, i.e., the discourse that is important within the US (and increasingly non-US) academic promotion system. It should be noted that the list of journals relevant to the US career system excludes many relevant journals for the field of cross-cultural management such as the *International Journal of HRM*, *International Journal of Cross-Cultural Management*, and *Applied Psychology: An International Review*. This review chapter is based on a search of the broader set of journals. Returning to Werner's (2002) analysis, it provides us with a clear picture of the field as traditionally defined (see Figure 5.1). It shows that early international management research could broadly be divided

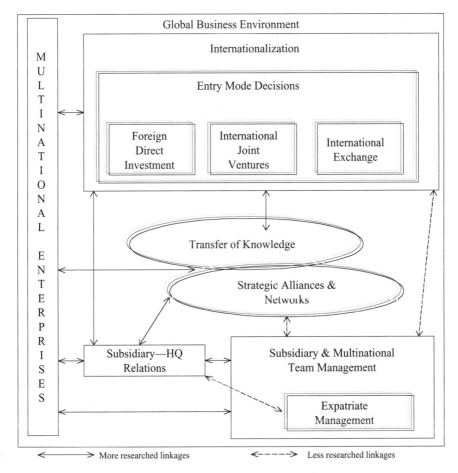

Global Business Environment

Internationalization

Entry Mode Decisions

Foreign Direct Investment

International Joint Ventures

International Exchange

Transfer of Knowledge

Strategic Alliances & Networks

Subsidiary—HQ Relations

Subsidiary & Multinational Team Management

Expatriate Management

MULTINATIONAL ENTERPRISES

——————▷ More researched linkages   ◁ — — — ▷ Less researched linkages

Figure 5.1   Current themes in international management research
Source: Werner, S. (2002). Recent developments in international management research: A review of 20 top management journals. *Journal of Management*, **28** (3), 277–305.

into three categories:

1. Studies that look at the management of firms in a multinational context, i.e., the international aspects of management that do not exist in domestic firms, such as the internationalization process, entry mode decisions, foreign subsidiary management, and expatriate management.
2. Comparisons of management practices across different cultures (cross-cultural studies) and nations (cross-national comparisons).
3. Studies that look at management in specific (single) countries within the domain of international management (in order to overcome the bias of early work that had a North American perspective).

According to Werner (2002), a total of 271 articles were published from 1996 to 2000, representing 5.5% of total journal content, up from 1.8% of content over the previous 20 years. International management, then, is still a small, but increasingly important, focus of academic study. Werner contends that the field as defined by these 271 articles can be broken down into 12 domains:

- *Global business environment*: Threats and opportunities of global economy, global markets, political and regulatory environments, and international risk.
- *Internationalization*: Descriptions and measurement of internationalization as a process, its antecedents and consequences.
- *Entry mode decisions*: Predictors of entry mode choices, equity ownership levels, and consequences of entry mode decisions.
- *Foreign direct investment (FDI)*: Timing, motivation, location, and firm and host country consequences of FDI.
- *International exchange*: International exchange, determinants of exporting, export intermediaries, and consequences of exporting.
- *International joint ventures (IJVs)*: Partner selection, partner relations, and consequences of IJVs.
- *Strategic alliances and networks*: Alliance relationships, networks, and outcomes of strategic alliances.
- *Transfer of knowledge*: Antecedents of knowledge transfer, processes, and consequences of transfer.
- *Multinational enterprises (MNEs)/multinational corporations (MNCs)*: Multinational enterprise strategies and policies, models of MNEs.
- *Subsidiary-HQ relations*: Subsidiary role, strategies and typologies, subsidiary control and performance.
- *Subsidiary and multinational team management*: Subsidiary HRM practices, subsidiary behaviours, multinational negotiations, and multinational team management.
- *Expatriate management*: Expatriate management, issues for expatriates, expatriate and repatriate reactions.

Reflecting the direction of the broader field of international management, early research in the narrower field of IHRM also focused on the role of MNCs.

Finding and nurturing the people able to implement international strategy was seen as critical for such firms and considerable attention was given to the management of expatriates. IHRM was considered to have the same main dimensions as HRM in a national context but to operate on a larger scale, with more complex strategic considerations, more complex coordination and control demands, and some additional HR functions considered necessary to accommodate the need for greater operating unit diversity, more external stakeholder influence, higher levels of risk exposure, and more personal insight into employees' lives and family situation (Dowling, Welch, & Schuler, 1998). Research therefore focused on understanding those HR functions that had to change when firms went international. It began to identify important contingencies that influenced the HR function as it became more internationalized, such as the country in which the MNC operated, the size and life cycle stage of the firm, and the type of employee (parent company national, home country national, and third country national). IHRM, then, focuses on how different organizations manage their people across national borders.

In the CHRM field (generally but not exclusively of more interest to European I/O psychologists, but a different field in its own right) researchers have traditionally incorporated a country comparison perspective, asking the following questions: How is HRM structured in individual countries? What strategies are discussed? What is actually put into practice? What are the main differences and similarities between countries? To what extent are HR policies influenced by national factors such as culture, government policy, and educational systems? The bulk of work in the CHRM field has then concentrated on the culture-bound versus the culture-specific thesis; consideration of which HRM practices are more or less culture sensitive; and an empirical examination of patterns of convergence or divergence in HRM practices across national borders. Returning to Werner's (2002) outline of international management research, the CHRM field has covered his second and third categories, i.e., comparisons of management practices across different cultures and nations and studies that look at management in specific (single) countries. It concentrates (still) on how people are managed differently in different countries by analysing practices within firms of different national origin in the same country or by comparing practices between different nations or regions. In relation to the work of I/O psychologists, most of the research on cross-cultural psychology and the impact of culture on work behaviours are located within this tradition.

CULTURAL VALUE ORIENTATIONS: THE INHERITANCE

So what, then, was the inheritance for people beginning research in this area around 2000 and where did the main expertise lie? If we look within the field of psychology, we find that cross-cultural psychologists, cultural psychologists, indigenous psychologists, and psychological anthropologists were all contributing to our understanding of how and why behaviour appears in specific cultural contexts (Smith, Harb, Lonner, & Van de Vijver, 2001b). To this list of expertise we can, of course, add the anthropologists, sociologists, and international management researchers. Yet, despite a host of models, frameworks, and theoretical propositions to explain the connection between culture and ethnicity and human thought and behaviour: '... one can also say with certainty that it has yet to be determined exactly how and when culture and ethnicity affect [it]' (Smith et al., 2001b, p. 9). The international management field has, however, done much to bring the topic of national culture to the attention of researchers, through the work successively of Hofstede (1980), Trompenaars (1993), Schwartz (1994), and Inglehart, Basanez, and Moreno (1998). Indeed, today's international management researchers have 'inherited' a number of constructs from these initial studies that still dominate the field today. The majority of these constructs provide some representation of values, which Schwartz (1992) defined as desirable, trans-situational, but motivational goals that vary in importance but serve as guiding principles in people's lives. Some of the finer points of difference are alluded to later, but from Hofstede (1994) came the value dimensions of power distance, uncertainty avoidance, individualism, and masculinity/femininity. From Schwartz's (1994, 1999) analysis of value preferences of 60,000 individuals in 63 countries, 45 values were found to have similar meaning across countries but these were reduced by multidimensional scaling to seven values, organized along three major dimensions of conservatism (embeddedness) versus autonomy (intellectual and affective), hierarchy versus egalitarianism, and mastery versus harmony. Trompenaars and Hampden-Turner (1998) surveyed the values of over 11,000 organizational employees in 46 countries, which were reduced by Smith, Peterson, and Wang (1996) to an egalitarian commitment versus conservatism dimension and a utilitarian involvement versus loyal involvement dimension.

There have since been two additional pieces of work that have specifically addressed values that fall within the review period:

1. Schwartz and Bardi's (2001) work on values structures.
2. The GLOBE (Global Leadership and Organizational Behaviour Effectiveness) research programme (House et al., 1999).

Schwartz and Bardi (2001) asked an important and reverse question, observing that '... researchers, including ourselves, have focused almost exclusively on differences in value priorities. When we switch our focus to ask about similarities, we discover a striking degree of consensus across individuals and societies' (p. 268). They established a near-universal structure of relations among 10 value types (each with different goals and specific actions leading to its attainment: power; achievement; hedonism; stimulation; self-direction; universalism; benevolence; tradition; conformity; and security). Although individuals and groups may differ substantially in the importance they attribute to these values, the same structure of opposite motivations and compatibilities was considered to exist across samples. In the 2001 study they reported additional evidence on agreement around the world on the relative importance of these different values and argued that analysing a group's value profile in isolation creates a distorted view of culture. Data were analysed for 8043 adults in 13 nations, and then generalized to two other datasets of 14,000 schoolteachers from 56 nations and 19,000 college students from 54 nations. They looked at the average value hierarchy across the 13 nations and assessed how similar each nation's structure was to the overall pattern. Considerable overlap in value hierarchies was found. Schwartz and Bardi (2001, p. 275) noted that:

> ... given the widespread research evidence of value differences between individuals and groups, the observed similarity of the average value hierarchies may seem surprising at first sight. It is important to recognise, therefore, that even when the value hierarchies are ordered similarly, value ratings may differ meaningfully and reliably.

Such differences were indeed found, so the second analysis assessed the level of consensus, asking whether the same hierarchy of values merely represented averages, or agreement on the value priorities across the nations. Across the nations the mean correlation was $r = 0.92$ (ranging from 0.80 to 0.97). Within the teacher samples the mean correlation was $r = 0.90$ and for the student sample $r = 0.91$. The analysis showed high cross-cultural consensus regarding the value hierarchy. When considering the question of why this should be, the researchers noted that their instrument taps three universal human requirements: biological needs, requisites of coordinated social interaction, and demands of group survival. Schwartz and Bardi (2001, p. 280) concluded that:

> ... individual differences in the importance attributed to values reflect individuals' unique needs, temperaments, and social experiences. But the pan-cultural similarities in value importance are likely to reflect the shared bases of values in human nature and the adaptive functions of each type of value in maintaining societies.

They argued that once researchers switch from analysing differences to analysing similarities (in the context of values embedded in cultures) three insights arise: there is a common pan-cultural baseline of value priorities; this hierarchy can tentatively be understood as reflecting adaptive functions; and we can only really understand the distinctiveness of any particular nation once we analyse its value priorities as they differ against this pan-cultural baseline. On a technical footnote, during the period of review an analysis was also carried out to test the measurement equivalence of 10 value types from the Schwartz Value Survey across countries (Spini, 2003). A total of 3787 psychology and law students were sampled in 21 countries using the 57-item Schwartz Value Survey and a range of demographic variables. Multigroup confirmatory factor analysis was used to test for configural and metric equivalence of the scales and nine of the 10 values were found to be suitable for cross-cultural research.

Within the review period work has also been conducted to ask whether there are conditions that elicit universal responses from employees regardless of culture. Perhaps the best-known and largest cross-cultural framework new to the literature during this period concerns the topic of global leadership. Cross-cultural studies have generally indicated a strong connection between national culture and preferred leadership styles. The GLOBE project has reported on its main findings in recent years. It has made a contribution to the debate about the interrelationships between societal culture, organizational culture, and organizational leadership. The topic of global leadership continues to receive attention, not least because:

> . . . as companies rely more and more on global strategies, they require more and more global leaders. This tie between strategy and leadership is essentially a two-way street: the more companies pursue global strategies, the more global leaders they need; and the more global leaders companies have, the more they pursue global strategies.
>
> (Morrison, 2000, p. 119)

The GLOBE project was a multiphase, multimethod project in which investigators spanning the world examined the interrelationships between societal culture, organizational culture, and organizational leadership. It involved 170 social scientists and management scholars (Country Co-Investigators).

The idea was actually conceived in 1991, and the grant proposal was awarded in 1993. The initial outline of the research summarized by House et al. (1999) has been followed by a number of reports (see, for example, Ashkanasy, Trevor-Roberts, & Earnshaw, 2002; House, Javidan, Hanges, & Dorfman, 2002; House et al., 2004). The meta-goal of GLOBE was to develop an empirically based theory to describe, understand, and predict the impact of specific cultural variables on leadership and organizational processes, and the effectiveness of these processes. House et al. (2002) asked four questions about global leadership:

1. Are there leader behaviours, attributes, and organizational practices that are accepted and effective across cultures?
2. Are there leader behaviours, attributes, and organizational practices that are accepted and effective only in some cultures?
3. How do attributes of societal and organizational cultures affect the kinds of leader behaviours and organizational practices that are accepted and effective?
4. Can the universal and culture-specific aspects of leader behaviours, attributes, and organizational practices be explained in terms of an underlying theory that accounts for systematic differences across cultures?

The research used a pool of 753 questionnaire items and identified nine psychometrically sound dimensions of national culture (cf. my later comments on the psychometric properties of Hofstede's scales). The GLOBE project therefore introduced another cross-cultural framework into the literature and positioned societies into clusters that provided a link between cultural background and preferred leadership styles. Many of the nine cultural dimensions were already in the literature, such as uncertainty avoidance and power distance. Hofstede's masculinity dimension was perhaps reflected in the dimensions of gender egalitarianism and assertiveness, and long-termism in future orientation. The organizational level of analysis undoubtedly gave rise to two additional dimensions of *Performance Orientation* (the extent to which an organization or society encouraged and rewarded group members for performance improvement and excellence) and *Humane Orientation* (the degree to which individuals in organizations or societies encouraged and rewarded individuals for being fair, altruistic, friendly, generous, caring, and kind to others). Given the discussion of different forms of collectivism (see the next section but also Bandura, 2002; Triandis, 2001) it is of interest to note that the GLOBE project differentiated between *Societal Collectivism*, which reflected the degree to which organizational and societal institutional practices encouraged and rewarded collective distribution of resources and collective action, and *In-Group Collectivism*, which reflected the degree to which individuals express pride, loyalty, and cohesiveness in their organizations or families.

Each of the nine cultural dimensions was translated into questionnaire items that measured both 'what should be' (i.e., shared modal values of collectives), and 'what is' or 'what are' (i.e., the common behaviours, institutional practices, and prescriptions). As noted by Erez and Gati (2004), the GLOBE study operates at both the mid-level of analysis (through its measurement of aspired values of 'should be') and a more surface and visible level, reflected in behaviours and practices ('as is'). The questionnaires were distributed to middle managers in 62 national cultures. Ten distinct national clusters emerged within the overall sample. A total of 23 different leadership styles were deemed to be effective in one or more of the different societal cultures of the world (each leadership style was considered to represent a *culturally endorsed implicit leadership theory*). There were six underlying dimensions or styles of global leadership.

The researchers drew a number of conclusions (House et al., 2002). They argued that their results showed a picture of subtle, but meaningful, variations in scores around leadership dimensions, and also demonstrated that the charismatic, team-oriented, and participative styles were the most effective leadership styles across cultures. The charismatic dimension (which consisted of such attributes as visionary, inspirational, self-sacrificial, integrity, decisiveness, and performance orientation) appeared to be universally rated as the most important leadership style, but the interpretation of charisma in different societal settings was considered to vary. There was high within-culture agreement with respect to leader attributes and behaviours and two out of six leader behaviour dimensions were viewed universally as contributors to effective leadership. One was viewed nearly universally as an impediment to leadership, and one as nearly universally a contributor. The endorsement of the remaining two varied by culture. In short, there were 21 specific behaviours that were universal, 8 impediment behaviours, and 35 behaviours that depended on the cultural context. Overall, the research supported the argument that leadership is culturally contingent, although the key dimensions of effective leadership are consistent across societal clusters. Charismatic leadership has then been studied at three nested levels by this project: organizational, industry type, and cross-nationally (Erez & Gati, 2004).

Fu et al. (2004) have since reported on a 12-nation study that tested the relationship between three of the GLOBE study cultural variables (in-group collectivism, uncertainty avoidance, and future orientation), individual social beliefs (cynicism, fate control, reward for application, and religiosity), and the perceived effectiveness of different influence strategies (persuasive, assertive, and relationship based). Social beliefs were predictive of influence style and the cultural variables moderated the strength of relationship. Some interest in the impact of cultural factors on leadership continues in studies that are independent of the GLOBE project. For example, Ardichvili and Gasparishvili (2001) surveyed 695 managers in nine manufacturing firms in Russia, Georgia, Kazakhstan, and the Kyrgyz Republic and found differences in cultural values, assumptions about organizational culture, and leadership styles. They noted that despite similarities in economic systems, managerial and organizational structures, assumptions continue to differ across management populations.

RESEARCH ASSUMPTIONS AND METHODOLOGICAL BIASES

In the light of the above work, how should I/O psychologists conducting research currently into any aspect of national culture position their studies? Clearly, the above findings have led to closer questioning of the cultural difference research tradition and this is no longer a dominant perspective. During the review period, we have also seen more conceptual disquiet about many inherited research assumptions. An issue that we have to acknowledge is that much of our work as I/O psychologists (and, indeed, work from other disciplines) is guided by a number of tacit assumptions and methodological biases. Sackmann and Phillips (2004) have provided an insightful review of these. They point out that the way in which researchers conceptualize culture, the research questions they consider it legitimate to ask, and their attempts to identify its effects, are all implicitly influenced by the basic domains and traditions of the fields from which they come, such as anthropology, sociology, psychology, or management. Boyacigiller, Kleinberg, Phillips and Sackmann (2003) delineate three streams of research, each making its own assumptions and emerging within a particular context:

1. *Cross-national comparisons*: Driven by a dominant logic and assumption that 'culture equals nation'. Research (in general) has been guided by a quest to identify '. . . universally applicable dimensions [of national culture] that

would help managers navigate in different countries while doing their work' (Sackmann & Phillips, 2004, p. 372). Studies are therefore rooted in a positivistic paradigm, and universal dimensions of culture have generally been operationalized in large-scale quantitative studies.

2. *Study of intercultural interactions*: Generally initiated on the competitive success of non-US management models (such as the success of Japanese transplant factories in the US and the growth of European and Asian multinational corporations). This stream of research still saw national culture as the fundamental source of identification but argued that '... identification was not ... persistent in the face of cross-national interactions ... instead, culture within organizational settings was seen as emergent and negotiated between interaction partners, hence "socially constructed"' (Sackmann & Phillips, 2004, p. 374). It introduced new assumptions about cultural identification and shifted attention to the nature of bicultural interactions and the characteristics and processes through which cultures are formed. This field has been served principally by anthropologists and ethnographers, not by psychologists, and has resulted in 'thick descriptions' of national culture drawing upon qualitative analyses.

3. *The multiple cultures perspective*: Based on more recent conceptions of organizations operating in a multicultural context, which consider that culture must be a collective, socially constructed phenomenon and that organizations are home to and carriers of several cultures at the levels that include function, organization and business unit, profession and occupational group, ethnic group, project-based network, regional institution, geographical and economic region, ideology, and religion. Developments in information technology have enabled and accelerated the process of globalization, and new communication media have brought a wealth of real-time information from remote cultures thereby changing patterns of problem solving at work. As a result of the processes of globalization within firms '... inter-dependencies and complexity have grown dramatically' (Sackmann & Phillips, 2004, p. 377) and '... individuals may identify with and hold simultaneous membership in several cultural groups' (p. 378).

Table 5.1, based on an amalgam of tables in the review by Sackmann and Phillips (2004), summarizes the contextual influences that have shaped these three streams of research and the challenges facing each stream.

As a general observation, the research discourse in recent years has seen increasing criticism of the cross-national comparison research stream, a call for the intercultural interaction stream to now start to examine more than just bicultural contexts, and an increasing theoretical consensus around the need to see a wider adoption of the multiple cultures perspective.

There is also evidence of a changing focus *within* each of these streams of research over time. For example, an analysis of published and accepted papers in the *Journal of Cross-Cultural Psychology* from 1980 to 1993, compared to 1993 to

Table 5.1 Contextual influences on and challenges facing three streams of research in international management

Perspective/key issues	Cross-national comparison	Intercultural interaction	Multiple cultures
Context driving emergence	Political force • Post World War II Economic forces • Rise of MNC focus on how to conduct business in other countries • Management recognized as means for economic development • US practices = model for other nations Academic research forces • Rise of comparative management • No universal definition of culture • Data collection difficult • Management research a Western (largely US) enterprise Current reinforcers • Globalization • Nation-state as key economic actor • Conservative nature of academe	Economic Forces • Changing balance of global economic power • Dramatic increase in foreign direct investment (e.g., joint ventures, subsidiaries, MNCs)	Political forces • Melting of national boundaries • Separatist movements • Regional independence Economic forces • Increasing globalization • Growing importance of regional economic zones • Increasing strategic alliances within/across boundaries Technological forces • Enhances communications technology Social forces • Growing global movement of people • Increasing workforce diversity • Attention to differences in identity
Theories/assumptions/ frameworks	• Nation-state = 'culture' • Cultural identity is a given, single, immutable individual characteristic • Convergence thesis • Search for universally applicable dimensions	• Culture is socially constructed • National culture/identity of critical importance • Generalized national work culture	• Culture is a collective, socially constructed phenomenon • Organizations = multiplicity of cultures

Research focus	• How do managerial attitudes and behaviours differ across nations?
	• How do national cultural differences affect individual, group, and firm differences be controlled?
		• Organizational culture may be salient
		• Emergent/negotiated culture derived from:
		—organization culture research
		—interpretive paradigm
		—anthropological theories
		—intercultural communication model
		• What is the nature of bicultural interaction and its perceived impact on organizational life?
		• What are the characteristics and processes of culture/formation/evolution/emergence from binational interaction?
			• Individuals may identify with and/or hold membership in many cultures
			• Salience of any cultural group/identity is empirical question
			• Frameworks are
			—a priori
			—empirically derived
			—emergent
			• Many cultures are present within organizations:
			  • Which become salient?
			  • When/why/how does this occur?
			• How do the various cultures interact?
			• How do individuals deal with multiple identities?
			• What are the implications for managerial practice?

Research methods	• Positivistic • Universal categories of culture • Dimensions operationalized as scales • Large-scale quantitative studies	• Interpretive • Anthropological ethnography → thick description • Long-term case study • Primarily qualitative analysis	• Interpretive, inductive methodologies • Seek 'insider's view' • Hybrid, multiple methods • Field-based data collection
Key contributors	• Comparative management: —Farmer & Richman, 1965 —Haire, Ghiselli, & Porter, 1966 —GLOBE project, 1993 —House et al., 1999/2004	Kleinberg, 1989+	• Sociologists focusing on reality, groups, and subcultures (e.g, Berger & Luckmann, 1996) • Industrial anthropologists focusing on subcultures (e.g, Trice & Beyer, 1993)

(Continued)

Table 5.1 (*Continued*)

Perspective/key issues	Cross-national comparison	Intercultural interaction	Multiple cultures
	• Dimensions and constructs —Triandis, 1972 —Hofstede, 1980 (dominant) —Schwartz, 1992 —Smith, Peterson, & Schwartz, 2002 —Trompenaars, 1993 • Country clusters —Ronen & Shenkar, 1985		• Organizational researchers with focus on issues of: —Culture and subcultures in organizational settings (e.g, Martin & Siehl, 1983) —contributors to Sackmann, 1997) —Organizational identity (e.g, contributors to Whetten & Godfrey, 1998) —Professional identity —Social psychologists studying social identity (e.g, Tajfel, 1981)
Contribution to knowledge	• Culture is tractable —Generalizations across national units —Cultural clustering • Cross-national testing of organizational theories, processes, and practices • Motivated development of cultural dimensions and categories • Finite set of cultural dimensions allows other disciplines to use cultural variables • Increasing knowledge of management practice beyond G-7	• Importance of contextual analysis • Process-orientation • Emergent 'negotiated' culture • Attention to intercultural communication in the workplace • 'Thick descriptions' of cultural contexts • Bridge to multiple cultures perspective	• Reveals culture as socially constructed • Focuses on both sensemaking process/content, as well as practical applications • Reveals nature of shared understandings • Appreciative of cultural differences and similarities • Acknowledges complexity of personal identity and organizational life • Recognizes paradoxes in organizational settings

| Challenges to the stream of research | • Continued use of 'nation-state = culture' reinforces assumption of national culture as a given, single, and immutable characteristic of an individual
—Limited focus on certain levels of analysis
—Need to understand 'when culture matters'
• Lack of mid-range theories re: how culture influences behaviour
• Methodological critiques need to be taken seriously and acknowledged in future research
• Underlying influence of colonial theory | • Continued emphasis on national culture as fundamental building block of interaction
• Need for broader comparative base
• Acquiring cross-cultural knowledge
• Research timeframe and costs
• Training in ethnographic perspective and skills
• Publication/career issues | • Recognizes conflicts in organizational and individual identities
• Possibility of achieving synergies by building on similar cultural identities
• Identifies skills needed for work in a multicultural environment
• Methodological variety
• Expand scope of research to address issues such as
—impact on organization performance and effectiveness
—how to develop synergies from cultural commonalities
—appreciating and capitalizing on cultural differences |

Source: Sackmann & Phillips (2004). Contextual influences on culture research. *International Journal of Cross Cultural Management*, **4** (3), 370–390.

2000 (Smith et al., 2001b), examined three types of study: cross-national comparisons; studies comparing two or more cultural groups from within a single nation; and single sample studies. A clear shift in methodology took place between the two historical periods with single nation studies falling from 27.1% to 10.4% of studies and cross-national studies rising from 38.1% to 54.5% of studies. Again, comparing the two time periods, the analysis of topics accepted for publication in cross-cultural (national) psychological research from 1993 to 2000 showed that 28% of papers covered social psychological issues (down from 52% in 1980–1993), 11% of papers were theory based (up from a zero base), 8% examined personality issues (down from 13%), 8% developmental issues (up from 6%), 7% cognition issues (stable), 6% acculturation issues (up from 2%), and 4% psychometric issues (up from 2%). Perhaps the most worrying statistic in this analysis is that from 1993 to 2000, 44% of accepted papers were based on student samples. Organizational studies suffered a higher rejection rate because they tended to be more descriptive in nature. This situation is not atypical of a field that has a strong social psychology element within it, but of course it gives rise to concerns about convenience sampling and a lack of generalizability to more realistic and complex work settings. Since this period we have, however, arguably seen an expansion of cross-cultural psychological research into more applied settings, and a parallel process of more theorizing and better testing in these studies (see in particular the section on Individual Level Studies).

CRITICISMS OF THE CROSS-NATIONAL RESEARCH INHERITANCE

What are the main criticisms of the cross-national stream of work in general (i.e., criticisms that are not just directed at cross-cultural psychological studies but at all contributing disciplines)? Much of the early research in the field was intended to capture and explain observed differences in cross-national samples, and argued that culture was an important explanatory variable in the field of international management. However, as Menon (2004, p. 135) notes: '... national culture has long been an elusive construct, seemingly offering a ready explanation for observed cross-national differences in values and behaviour, and yet very difficult to pin down in terms of definition, structure, or invariant processes that can yield infallible behavioural prescriptions'. Between 2000 and 2002 attention was drawn increasingly to three continuing questions (Koslowsky, Sagie, & Stashevsky, 2002; Menon, 2004):

1. Can we safely assume the existence of single national cultures?
2. Is the influence of culture as an explanatory variable decreasing in the wake of continued globalization?
3. Are there conditions that elicit universal responses from employees regardless of culture?

As noted above, a central premise of the growing critique of work on national culture in the international management field is that, in attempting to categorize cultural groups, it has produced dichotomies—such as individualistic versus collectivistic cultures—that rely on erroneous and increasingly jaundiced assumptions. Categorical approaches also tempt us to view culture as being immutable, monolithic, and able to be captured with scores on a limited set of cultural dimensions. Three points of criticism, which were initially developed throughout the late 1990s, but have become accepted wisdom in the last few years, have emerged. We have seen:

1. A rejection of the homogeneity assumption.
2. Evidence of significant intra-individual variation within cultures.
3. The presence of intracultural and interdomain variation that is falsely attributed to proxy measures of national difference.

The *homogeneity assumption critique* argues that there are significant *within-nation differences on most cultural measures across groups* defined by other social criteria. For example, studies that contrast members of a single collectivist culture with a single individualistic culture, '. . . spawn[s] a lot of misleading generalizations' (Bandura, 2002, p. 275). The individualistic cultures of the USA, Italy, Germany, France, and Britain represent at the least differentiated brands and, within any one of them, multiple brands of individualism may be distinguished, though not easily equated to ethnic groups such as Latinos, African-Americans, and Orientals. In the USA, for example, distinctive Northeast, Midwest, West, and Deep South brands can be identified. The collectivistic systems of Confucianism, Buddhism, and Marxism differ significantly from each other in particular values, meanings, and customs. The review process found a number of studies exploring intranational cultural variation. In a reexamination of differences in cultural orientations of ethnic groups in the USA (over 1500 students), Coon and Kemmelmeier (2001) found significant differences across individualism and collectivism scores between African, Asian, and European Americans. Using secondary statistical data on lifestyle, pace of life, helping behaviour, and demographics in 37 US cities over 17 states, Conway, Ryder, Tweed, and Sokol (2001) found theoretically meaningful regional differences in patterns of collectivism. Similarly, in noting prima facie within-country differences in Belgium, Switzerland, India, Malaysia, and Indonesia, Menon (2004) pointed out that the homogeneity assumption rests on the ability to infer commonalities of core beliefs and assumptions that cut across such ethnic, linguistic, and religious differences within-nation and still maintain explanatory power despite the variety of espoused values and observed behaviours that evidently do differ. Moreover, he concluded:

. . . this distal separation between societal and national commonalities at the level of basic assumptions and observed behaviour partly explains why a growing number of studies have reported that, at a practical level, culture may not be a significant factor in day-to-day business activities or managerial decision making.

(Menon, 2004, p. 137)

The intra-individual variation critique argues that there are differences of communal styles of behaviour *within individuals across classes of relationships* and that these are as important as variation across cultures. Members of a collectivistic culture may be highly communal with in-group but not out-group members, while members of individualistic cultures may be more communal with outgroup members. The reference group is therefore very important (Freeman & Bordia, 2001). Single dimension cultural factors rarely capture the complexity of such individual behaviour. A number of researchers have, for example, identified different varieties of individualism and collectivism (see, for example, Bhagat, Kedia, Harveston, & Triandis, 2002; Triandis, 2001; and also the GLOBE project outlined earlier).

The intracultural and interdomain variability critique, in contrast, argues that decontextualized and non-conditionalized measures of psychological orientation mask intracultural and interdomain *variation that would better be attributed to other processes.* Using nations as proxies for culture and then ascribing psychosocial attributes to all members of that nation means that:

> ... all too often, a selected cultural factor that yields a small difference in group averages is generalised to all individuals in the cultural grouping as though they all believed and behaved alike as dichotomously classified ... readily misattributing effects to traits ascribed to the classification when, in fact, other dynamic processes may be at play.

(Bandura, 2002, p. 276)

Sackmann and Phillips (2004, p. 377) argue that:

> ... a comparison of nations yields insights into national differences that are not necessarily—and are increasingly less likely to be—cultural differences ... the question remains ... how to interpret these differences. Are they indicative of culture at the functional level ... the organizational level ... the regional level ... the national level ... or economic regions transcending national boundaries? If researchers are truly interested in cultural, not national, differences, the cross national comparison perspective and its underlying assumptions will no longer be the most appropriate choice of framework for studying culture in the field of international management.

The cross-national comparison perspective is not without its supporters, however (see, for example, the recent professional dialogue in *Academy of Management Executive* between Hoppe (2004), Bing (2004), and Triandis (2004)). Indeed, some new and insightful work continues to emerge from this perspective. Reflecting some of the previous theoretical criticisms, Smith and Peterson (2005, p. 22) noted '... the field of cross-cultural management continues to struggle with how to conceptualize nations. Nations have been treated as points on a small number of culture dimensions; as complex entities requiring multifaceted ethnographic analysis; as culturally irrelevant political artefacts; or as elements within larger clusters reflecting historical movements of colonization, immigration and other forms of culture spread.' In earlier work—although criticizing some of the specific constructs that have been developed—they remind us that by delineating differences between countries we can use these findings to determine the extent to which organizational psychology findings from Western contexts can be generalized to other settings (Smith et al. 2002). They point out that the past decades have seen considerable progress in the field of cross-cultural psychology and that the work of Hofstede, Trompenaars, and Schwartz led to '. . . the development of a broadly shared framework that conceptualizes the values that underlie the functioning of cultural units as a key to understanding other cultural differences' (Smith et al., 2002, p. 188). Sackmann and Phillips (2004, p. 375), although generally of the view that it is an approach whose time has now passed, concurred with this contribution, acknowledging that the cross-national comparison perspective '. . . demonstrated that the elusive concept of culture can be traced and researched . . . [and] developed a finite set of dimensions for research allowing cross-national testing of theories, processes and practices'.

WHAT IS THE MOST APPROPRIATE LEVEL AT WHICH TO ANALYSE NATIONAL CULTURE?

Cross-national comparisons have, then, mainly focused on values and associated sets of self-concepts and behaviours. In the last few years researchers have re-initiated a debate as to what constitutes the most appropriate level of analysis to capture psychological phenomena in such cross-national studies. Most theories of culture focus on values—and are therefore called mid-level theories as they lie between Schein's (1992) continuum of visibility from behavioural patterns, through values that reflect convictions about the nature of reality, down to basic assumptions about human nature and our relationship to the environment (Erez & Gati, 2004). The work of Hofstede, Inglehart, and Schwartz, for example, lies at the mid-level. Smith et al.'s (2002) work, outlined later, in contrast, operates more at the surface level of behaviours and practices (as does the work of the GLOBE project, detailed earlier). Smith et al. (2002) noted that Hofstede's (1980) definition of culture as a collective programming of the mind conceptualizes culture *as interpretations of behaviours* through *shared meanings* assigned by members of a culture to things and people around them. Broader—more surface level—conceptualizations argue that culture includes *actual differences in behaviour, not just interpretations* of behaviour. Some aspects of this broader view are problematic because '. . . a behaviour that is unambiguously defined in one social context may be defined quite differently in other cultures' (Smith et al., 2002, p. 190). Actual practices, however (admittedly viewed through the way they are interpreted and the actions that follow inside organizations), have more cross-cultural generalizability. Hofstede (2001) reviewed several hundred studies that showed links between one or more of his four dimensions of culture and the frequencies of attitudes, values, and behaviours. A total of 355 significant national culture-level correlations were reported. Smith et al. (2002) criticized this work on two grounds: only a small proportion of the studies had what they deemed to be an adequate range of country sampling (only 27 of the 355 studies drew on data from more than 30 countries); they believed that the review defined and classified culture through behaviours, which, as noted above, they argued cannot be done reliably.

A more supportive analysis of the cross-national comparison approach has been provided by Schwartz and Sagie (2000). They noted that while the level of variation in individual, team, and organizational behaviour is indeed greater in some national cultures than in others, the cultural environment in which we operate means that specific values, norms, attitudes, and practices become more or less dominant and act as a source of shared socialization and social control, thus legitimizing the examination of broad cross-national differences in values. Drawing on the arguments of Schwartz (1999), Smith et al. (2002) stated that values have featured so much because '. . . they can be expressed in a decontextualized manner. Respondents can be asked to report their values without the need to specify what actions might be entailed by adherence to these values given particular circumstances. Individual reports of values can then be used as *indirect indicators* [my emphasis] of the cultural values that prevail across the many contexts to which people are exposed' (p. 189). Behaviours, however, are considered to be too contextualized for researchers to draw any practical implications.

Given the above discussion, *the future research task that remains from within the cross-national comparison perspective* is then to:

- understand *how* generalized values link to specific actions (Smith et al., 2002);
- further investigate *when* such influences actually matter (Sackmann & Phillips, 2004).

Work addressing the first of these issues is reviewed in this section. Work addressing the second issue is broadly picked up in the section examining individual level outcomes associated with cultural differences.

CONTEXTUALIZING NATIONAL CULTURE DIFFERENCES

Drawing on role theory, control theory, and institutional theory, Peterson and Smith (2000) noted that managers rely on a number of sources of guidance that exist beyond the individual when handling events at work. Smith et al.

(2002) tested the proposition that prevailing values lead members of a national culture working in organizations to rely on specific sources of guidance in the process of sensemaking. They developed an *event management theory* to explain this process of sensemaking. They defined a work event as '. . . an occurrence impinging on the awareness of an organization member' (p. 191). As events must be interpreted before a manager determines how to handle them, the manager has to draw upon interpretative schemes (or schemata). These can include a series of internalized representations that act as

> . . . . interpretative structures such as memories, thoughts, and understand-
> ings to which new events can be connected. They can also include view-
> points on events that a manager expects would be taken . . . they can include
> viewpoints perceived to prevail in society in general, due to government, a
> particular religion, or traditional value system.
>
> (Smith et al., 2002, p. 191)

Managers can also use interactions with others and analysis of documents as sources of guidance. In analysing such sources of guidance researchers make the assumption that '. . . reliance on particular sources of guidance influences the types of actual behaviour that then occur' (p. 189). This focus on sources of guidance is a development of early role, control, and institutionalization theories. These theories bring a stronger social cognition influence into the study of national culture. Smith et al. (2002) argued that managers receive guidance from other non-personal sources such as organizational rules and norms and appeal to these sources not just to provide role prescriptions but also to interpret workplace events and problems. Similarly, much of what happens in terms of control inside organizations lies in decisions that change the meanings or undertakings surrounding an event, and these actions are shaped by combinations of personal experience and '. . . more automatic, script and schema-driven actions that are better described as aspects of giving events meaning' (Smith & Peterson, 2005, p. 9).

In their work, Smith and colleagues operationalized their constructs through eight scenarios, each depicting an important organizational event: (1) a vacancy that arises requiring the appointment of a subordinate; (2) a subordinate suddenly deviating from a pattern of having performed at a consistently high level (i.e., having previously done 'good work' and is now doing 'bad work'); (3) machinery needing replacement; (4) a department not providing the resources or (5) the support required; (6) differing opinions within the focal department; (7) a need to introduce new work procedures; and (8) the evaluation of success of these procedures. Respondents were required to evaluate the extent to which the actions they would take were influenced by eight different sources of guidance: (1) formal rules and procedures; (2) unwritten rules as to how things are usually done in the firm; (3) reference to their subordinates; (4) reference to specialists outside the department; (5) reference to other people at the same level; (6) reference to superiors; (7) personal opinions based on their experience and training; and (8) beliefs that are widely accepted in their country. This approach—although more refined in terms of the variety of responses delineated—is reminiscent of the early work of Laurent (1986) on national culture, who argued that the best insights into national culture were created by giving managers common problems and seeing how they solved them. Participants' solutions reveal much about nature of power, status, and perceived roles inside organizations. The approach is also somewhat similar in character to the scenarios and ethical dilemmas adopted by Trompenaars (1993).

Other studies analysed self-reported reliance by managers on sources of guidance, but Smith et al. (2002) argued that these studies generally sampled too few countries to identify which cultural values were associated with reliance on what sources of guidance. Smith et al. studied differences between national cultures by analysing how samples of, on average, 100 middle managers (varying from 38 and 334) in 47 countries reported handling eight specific work events. Their study can be criticized for convenience sampling—managers attending courses at business schools are by no means typical of the national cadre of management. The ethnic concentrations also reflected the location of the various business schools that collected data. However, reliable scales were created for 365 of the 376 measurements, and response bias was statistically controlled for, along with the impact of demographic factors (13 of the 17 demographic variables showed significant relationships and this was later picked in the study by Smith and Peterson (2005)). Individual level data were aggregated to the national level to align with the country level data on value orientations.

In essence, Smith et al. (2002) investigated what percentage of variance in reliance on rules could be accounted for by value orientation scores as measured at the national level—a predictive validity test of their event management theory. They used national scores for nine values derived from the overlapping country scores established by Hofstede (2001), Smith et al. (1996), and Schwartz and Roz (1995), acknowledging that equating culture with nation states was '. . . a rather crude simplification' (p. 189) but arguing that since others have done this, so shall they. These data were then used to test whether these cultural value dimensions predicted the sources of guidance that the managers relied on. Eight of the nine value measures were significantly linked to reliance on vertical sources of guidance (accounting for 46% of variance, primarily due to power distance and mastery values). Reliance on widespread beliefs was associated with five value measures (with power distance and conservatism accounting for 24% of the variance), loyal involvement explained 19% of the variance in reliance on unwritten rules, while utilitarian involvement accounted for 10% of the variance in reliance on specialists.

Smith and Peterson's (2005) publication examined the impact of demographic factors on event management in an extended sample of 7380 middle managers from 60 nations. As a point of methodological departure, it explored ways of dealing with demographic characteristics when undertaking cross-national surveys of organizational behaviour. Smith and Peterson tested whether reliance on sources of guidance was more dependent on patterns of *relational demography* (based on age, gender, and selected patterns of firm ownership and occupational membership) or on national culture values. Relational demography theory argues that team members work best when in similar groupings. Demographic effects were stronger in low power distance and low collectivist countries. In collectivist countries, although role or reciprocal obligations may mean that dissimilar persons work together, because they are linked by collective identity they may still work well. The researchers concluded:

> ... Global institutionalization of subcultures linked to demographic identity is consequential, although weaker than institutionalization based on nation ... match[ing] samples from two or more nations on demographic attributes, such as age or occupational role ... is likely to be helpful but may not be very precise, because the meaning of a given age or a given occupational role may well differ between nations ... the ways in which [such factors] contribute to effects in different locations require examination rather than simple partialling out.
>
> (Smith & Peterson, 2005, pp. 22–23)

In sum, these studies have shown that:

- there is considerable convergent validity among the three most commonly used national values constructs;
- a reliance on the simple polarity of individualism–collectivism should be avoided;
- values predict everyday managerial action (actions defined in terms of sources of guidance they use and indirectly one assumes their interpretative schema);
- reliance on vertical sources of guidance varies more on the basis of prevailing national cultural values than on the basis of managerial demographic attributes;
- cultural awareness programmes would be better served by explaining differences in event management strategies rather than presenting rather decontextualized lists of values orientations;
- research into the success of international joint ventures and mergers could benefit from operationalizing management actions rather than aggregated national level values data.

PROCESSES UNDERPINNING CULTURALLY EMBEDDED BEHAVIOUR

As well as contextualizing cultural value differences in more useful ways, international management researchers have called for a broadening of the scope of cross-cultural analysis to incorporate the social and cognitive processes that underpin culturally embedded behaviour. As societies globalize and become more plural they have to come to terms with phenomena such as *intracultural diversity* and growing *intercultural communalities*. I/O psychologists need to understand work addressing the underlying social and cognitive processes associated with these phenomena (and implicitly, I suggest, study these processes in more detail) for two reasons:

1. It provides a coherent and persuasive critique of and counterbalance to the sometimes overwhelmingly deterministic view of the cultural categorization approach.
2. It highlights models of human functioning that underpin culturally embedded behaviour.

Social-cognitive theory builds on the previous criticisms of the cross-national comparison perspective and supports the view that the homogeneity assumption should be questioned because there is considerable intra-individual and intracultural variability. It also reflects the multiple cultures perspective of Sackmann and Phillips (2004) outlined earlier. Social-cognitive theorists argue that we need to understand:

• how individuals deal with multiple and shifting identities inside organizations;
• how they manage these shifts; and
• what the implications are for the managers who have to deal with this self-management by employees.

Bandura (2002) exemplifies this perspective. He argues that growing levels of globalization and the cultural pluralism of societies mean that we must broaden the scope of cross-cultural analyses. This extension should be directed at:

• understanding the psychosocial determinants of cultural behaviour, and
• the governing mechanisms that regulate them.

How do humans function as individuals, despite the cultural embeddedness of their behaviour? Social-cognitive theory is being used to expand our conception of human agency within cultures and provide greater legitimacy to the study of processes of personal development, adaptation, and change in diverse cultural settings. It '... provides a theoretical framework applicable to both individualistically and collectivistically oriented social systems through its expanded conception of human agency exercised individually, socially mediated and collectively' (Bandura, 2002, p. 278; see also Fernández-Ballesteros, Díez-Nicolás, Caprara, Barbaranelli, & Bandura, 2002). People are producers as well as products of social systems.

Social-cognitive theory draws the attention of international management researchers to two basic capacities (and the specialized mechanisms through which they operate), namely, efficacy beliefs and modelling:

1. *Beliefs about personal efficacy*: Defined as '... the core belief that one has the power to produce desired effects by one's actions' (Bandura, 2002, p. 270). These beliefs represent a central and pervasive mechanism of agency because

they regulate cognitive, motivational, affective, and decisional processes. This assertion needs further empirical support in the area of international management, as the meta-analyses cited by Bandura drew upon a small range of work presented at conferences or research published in the sports psychology area. Nevertheless, Bandura's theory of self-efficacy is now sufficiently established such that it can be drawn upon to support the claim that efficacy beliefs are related to both judgement about personal capabilities and a perception of collective efficacy that resides in the minds of group members and results in people acting in concert on such shared beliefs (Bandura, 2001). Bandura (2002, p. 270) argued that '. . . The relative contribution of individual, proxy and collective modes to the agentic mix may vary cross-culturally. But all of these agentic modes need to be enlisted . . . regardless of the culture in which one happens to reside.' Similarly, how these beliefs are developed and structured, the ways in which they are exercised, and the purposes to which they are put will vary across cultures. However, they have a generalized functional value and allow for flexible adaptation to diverse cultural environments (Earley, 1994).

2. *Modelling capacities*: The capacity to draw upon observational learning enables us to acquire knowledge, attitudes, values, emotional proclivities, and competences through the information that is conveyed to us. This capacity lies at the heart of both culture development and replication.

Social-cognitive theory contends that successful within-culture functioning requires an 'agentic blend' of three different modes of agency (efficacy beliefs):

1. *Direct personal agency*—where in managing our lives we bring our influence to bear directly on our ourselves and on our environment.
2. *Proxy agency*—for those spheres of our life where we have no direct control over the social and institutional practices that affect our everyday life and so rely on others—and must influence others—to act on our behalf and secure personally desired outcomes, i.e., socially interdependent effort.
3. *Collective agency*—where we act in concert with other people to shape our future by pooling knowledge, skills, and resources, forming alliances, and acting in mutual support to secure those things that we cannot accomplish on our own.

There has been some attempt to see whether the structure of such efficacy beliefs is comparable across cultures and develops in the same way. In this connection, the factor structure of children's self-efficacy beliefs previously observed in the USA has been replicated in Italy, Poland, and Hungary (Pastorelli et al., 2001).

Bandura (2002) argued that understanding how these agentic beliefs are brought to bear becomes increasingly important for four reasons: global interconnectedness means that forces operating remotely now produce local effects in cultures; some transnational market forces may be perceived as eroding or undermining valued cultural aspects of life; technological developments, such as the internet, are changing the dynamics and opportunity for personal agency; and mass transnational migrations of people seeking a better life are creating further intracultural diversity and new hybrid cultural forms.

The fundamental contribution of social-cognitive theory is that it offers a potential framework for future investigation of cross-cultural adjustment, adaptation, and acculturation processes. The new context of *intracultural diversity* suggests that this type of research will have some clear practical benefits, especially in the context of:

- personnel selection systems for expatriates and other international employees;
- the concomitant need for HR functions to be able to absorb more culturally diverse workforces even in their domestic markets.

Consider some of the following statistics. In the UK the Chartered Institute of Personnel and Development's Quarterly HR Trends and Indicators survey showed that, by the end of 2004, 28% of employers would be recruiting from abroad, rising to nearly 40% in the case of firms that employ more than 500 employees (Czerny, 2004). In the UK National Health Service, by 2002/2003, 43% of new nurse registrants were from abroad with the vast majority of nurses arriving in London in the last eight years coming from just six countries— the Phillipines, South Africa, Australia, New Zealand, Nigeria, and Ghana. Similarly, in each year from 1993 to 2002, nearly half of all new registrants to the UK General Medical Council were from abroad, increasing to nearly two-thirds by 2003. Employers feel that a migrant workforce can provide not only the necessary skills, but also high levels of dependability and commitment (Sparrow, 2005a). Understanding the personal agency that will be needed by such employees in the context of social-cognitive theory could well be helpful to absorbing new international recruits.

PATTERNS OF CULTURAL CONVERGENCE

As we give renewed attention to the role of personal agency in coping with change in cultures, and as we develop more dynamic and multilevel models of national culture, an issue that re-emerges is the question of the extent of convergence (or not) of cultures across the world. Menon (2004) argued that even if we assume that differences in culture can be better operationalized and have significant explanatory power, we still need to determine whether this explanatory power is consistent over time. Menon (2004, p. 138) asked whether a global work culture is emerging that will lessen the influence of cultural differences, such that '... in a matter of a few generations, a global work culture will prevail' or whether there are '... fundamental, immutable differences in work orientation between cultures that managers can ignore only at their peril'. This question has been around for many years and I suspect will still be being asked in 10 years' time.

The question then of cultural convergence or continued differences has led to a number of different types of study. Some of these are single-country studies that look at generational value-changes *within* the country, from which patterns of convergence and divergence in relation to other cultures are inferred. Other studies focus on a collection of countries that have been subjected to considerable socio-political change—for example, Eastern Europe or Asia—and attempt to assess if there has been any shift in underlying values. In both cases, the unit of analysis is that of generations. Generations are considered to be groups within societies that can be identified on the basis of shared birth years, age, location, or significant life events that occurred at critical stages of their development (Smola & Sutton, 2002). The effects of these historical and social factors are relatively stable over each cohort's lifetime and also serve to distinguish one group from another in terms of important feelings, desires, or stated plans in relation to work. Even within major societies such as the USA, such discussion has been confined to popular articles and has only recently begun to receive attention in the scientific literature (Loughlin & Barling, 2001).

Sparrow and Cooper (2003) noted that *even in the context of single-country studies of generational value-change*, we need to disentangle whether values are influenced more by:

• shared experiences within generations, or
• maturation and development of people over time.

While young employees within any single culture might have different attitudes today as they enter the workforce than the older generation, by the time they themselves are older will they have been socialized back to the same attitudes as the current older generation? Would today's older generation have had similar attitudes when they themselves were younger? Even if there are different attitudes that do seem to reflect novel realities of the contemporary world, if today's older generation were taken back to their youth and were now being released onto the labour market, would they show the same responses as today's younger employees if faced with the same novel situation? Sparrow and Cooper (2003, p. 248) concluded '... unravelling such a range of possible situations with any degree of certainty presents an immense challenge to researchers'.

We tend to think about convergence or continued differences in culture in simplistic ways. However, as another research dialogue outside the field of I/O psychology demonstrates, the same problem has been faced by the comparative HRM researchers. We can learn from this dialogue. Comparative HRM researchers have analysed changes in the adoption of a range of specific tools and practices across countries. In examining changes over time in HR practice between European countries, and attempting to link the pattern of these changes to competing theoretical explanations of what is happening, Mayrhofer, Morley, and Brewster (2004, p. 421) noted that '. . . It is by no means clear what is meant by convergence. Although the general meaning, intuitively, is clear, it becomes more complex at a closer look.' We therefore need a 'more nuanced picture of convergence' (p. 434). Let me borrow their logic to point to the complexity of understanding the issue of cultural convergence. They differentiated between a number of forms of possible convergence. I have substituted value orientations for organizational practice to maintain the analogy:

- *Directional convergence*: When comparing changes in value orientations between two countries, directional convergence exists when the trend (developmental tendency) goes in the same direction. Each country might start with a different proportion of people showing a specific value orientation, and over time the difference in the proportion of people showing that particular value orientation in the two countries might actually have grown larger. However, in both cases, a greater proportion of the population now show the value orientation so it has converged in direction—in this case going up. Similarly, the opposite might apply, with change in a negative direction.
- *Final convergence*: When changes in a value orientation in two different countries point to a common end point (the differences between the countries decrease in magnitude over time), then there is convergence to some final point. However, the direction of the change can vary. The final convergence might be to a point in which in both countries more people share the value orientation, or to a point in which fewer people in both countries end up sharing the value orientation, or to a point in between, where the proportion of people sharing the value orientation ends up higher in one country but lower in the other. All three, however, are examples of final convergence.
- *Stasis*: When there is no change over time in the proportion of people sharing a value and a state of stability thus exists.
- *Divergence*: When the changes in value in two different countries are progressing in truly different directions, one increasing and the other decreasing.

Just in comparing the direction of change in a *single value between two countries* we can see that the reality might convey subtle changes taking place. More to the point, if we study a single country and observe, for example, that there now appear to be a greater proportion of people with individualistic value orientations, to claim that this is evidence of convergence might be highly misleading. If we only study changes of values in a single country, then we might mistakenly think that the increase of the value represents some form of convergence with other countries, but in reality they are on a path of directional convergence and so going in the same direction but actually growing further apart, such are the nuances of studying different patterns of convergence just between one value orientation in two countries. Hence, when we try to make sense of change in several value orientations across numerous countries, the chances of confirming simple patterns of value change must be minimal. As the following examples show, we do not appear to be able to operationalize our studies in ways that might enable such nuanced understanding of patterns of values change to emerge.

Smola and Sutton (2002) attempted to unravel generational changes within the US culture. They replicated a Cherrington, Condie, and England (1979) study that had gathered data on workers' attitudes to jobs, their companies' communities, and work in general in 53 US organizations. In the replication study a snowball sampling technique was used to generate a broadly equivalent sample to the first study. During this time significant shifts had taken place in the US workforce. From 1974 to 1999 the proportion of US employees aged over 25 holding at least a Bachelor degree increased from 16% to 26%. The proportion of female employees had increased from 39% to 49%. Blacks had increased from 10% to nearly 18% of the workforce, and Hispanics from an unrecorded basis to 10% of the workforce. The data from the two surveys were divided into generational cohorts (defined by within-culture time boundaries to delineate groups labelled as traditionals, baby boomers, generation X, and millennials). The replication groups were divided into subgroups so that those who were, for example, 27 in the original study were compared to those who were 52 in the replication. This quasi-longitudinal design revealed true changes in work values that were determined by generational membership and not by age and/or maturation processes. The findings showed an overriding shift away from company loyalty and self-worth associated with jobs.

Two of the research traditions covered earlier in this chapter appear to have also been used as a basis for studies of cultural convergence or divergence: the Meaning of Work International Research Team (MOWIRT) programme; and Schwartz's Value Studies. The MOWIRT view of work values argues that the ordered importance of priority given to work goals can be used as a proxy variable both for work values and the meaning managers attach to their work life. Changing work goals are also a key to understanding managerial responses to reforms and pressures of globalization within countries. National cultural differences and differences in economic ideology and processes of reform both combine in unique ways to explain the way that managers in any one country assign differential orders of importance to 11 work goals (opportunity to learn new things, interesting work, opportunity for promotion, matching of job demands with incumbent competencies, salary level, autonomy in decision making, good social interrelationships, variety of tasks and roles, job security, convenient work hours, and good physical work conditions). Since the original work of Harpaz (1990) and subsequent replication (see, for example, Chatterjee & Pearson, 2000; Lundberg & Peterson, 1994) sporadic work has continued in recent years along this path. In general this work showed relatively little change in priorities and supported the view that the 11 work goals were best treated separately as they were only loosely associated with any higher level composite structures. In a replication of the MOWIRT methodology and extension of the data collection into China and Hong Kong, Westwood and

Lok (2003) gathered new data for 453 Chinese and 893 Hong Kong managers measuring, in addition to the 11 work goals, work centrality and a series of work outcomes. There were many similarities between the two samples and few differences. The two samples demonstrated high work centrality and a proximal location to Japan, work being placed above the family as the dominant life sphere, and a high rating of good interpersonal relationships. The latter could not automatically be linked to collectivisim given that such relations served highly instrumental and pragmatic ends. The researchers noted that unpacking the cause of these changes in shared cultural heritage and different political-economic trajectories was a matter of interpretation as '. . . unfortunately, and this is also true of many cross-cultural or cross-national studies, the MOWIRT study did not properly operationalize such macroeconomic variables . . . this was a flaw in the original design' (Westwood & Lok, 2003, p. 160).

However, Chatterjee and Pearson (2002) argued that the recent context of economic liberalization and Westernized education in Asia could mean that work goal priorities may now be changing in these countries. They too adopted the work goals priorities perspective from the MOWIRT research to their study of the managerial priorities of 1252 senior managers in six Asian countries (India, Mongolia, Singapore, Malaysia, Thailand, and Brunei). Results from data collected during 1996 and 1999 were compared with data collected in the original early 1980s study, prior to the emergence of a global marketplace. The authors acknowledge the different gender ratios and dissimilar sets of respondents in their 1990s data as compared to the original 1980s study. Notable differences were found between the 1980s and 1990s in terms of opportunity to learn new things, promotion, salary, interpersonal relationships, and job security work goals.

> . . . Overall, the data . . . show that there was significant convergence as well as wide divergence across the six countries . . . the work goals of learning new things and interesting work were perceived to be extremely important, the matching of managerial abilities and experience with job demands were of lesser importance, and the two comfort goals of work conditions and convenient work hours were the least important work goals in the six countries.
>
> (Chatterjee & Pearson, 2002, p. 261)

The researchers argued that the findings overall showed significant convergence around a number of work goal items attributed to the process of internalization, coupled also with some divergence of specific work goals in certain countries. However, once again we have the problem that the samples are limited to managers involved with study in business schools or research institutes, and of course such populations are more exposed to a common managerial philosophy.

Continuing problems with current studies on values convergence can be exemplified by the recent analysis by Alexashin and Blenkinsopp (2005) of changes in Russian managerial values. They attempted to test the convergence hypothesis. They did not conduct a longitudinal study but used the same methodology that had been used on previous Russian managerial samples, and demographic profiles were aligned, enabling data to be analysed for 1993, 1996, and 2001. US values were inferred from three previous studies conducted in 1994, 1997, and 1999. The Schwartz Value Survey (measuring the 10 values of power, achievement, hedonism, stimulation, self-direction, universalism, benevolence, tradition, conformity, and security identified by Schwartz and Bardi (2001) and reported earlier in this review) was used in Russian form to enable comparison with the previous studies and time-points. Different patterns of change were found. The researchers adopted the approaches to convergence, stasis, and divergence explained above in their (descriptive) analysis. The patterns, as one would expect, are complex and variable. To take just a few exemplar values, both US and Russian managers showed an increase over time in scores for power, but the Russian scores increased more and the pattern was one of divergence. Both groups showed an increase in scores for achievement, but the Russian managers showed an even larger increase, producing a picture of convergence to a single point. In terms of hedonism, the scores for US managers decreased but increased for the Russians, showing a picture of convergence to a central point. For self-direction, both sets of managers continued to show high scores that were increasing over time, with some (minimal) catching up of the US managers by the Russian managers—close convergence growing a little closer (or stasis?). The researchers wisely pointed out that

> ... the results ... do not invite simple conclusions ... we set out to test whether Russian managerial values might exhibit convergence with what might be deemed the dominant managerial values of the USA, and our findings suggest to some degree this might be the case. However, the test might alternatively be interpreted in terms of whether 'convergence' works ... the results ... appear to indicate that core values within the Russian national culture have remained relatively dominant over the period ... the Russian connotations for sub-dimensions such as achievement and conformance have meanings that are far different from meanings assumed in American or other Western cultures ... This suggests caution in assuming transferability of Western management techniques.
>
> (Alexashin & Blenkinsopp, 2005, p. 441)

Despite measurement of the convergence, stasis, and divergence of values, the ultimate conclusions have to be based upon a within-culture interpretation of what the complex pattern of change is really telling us. This point apart, let us consider more generally the soundness of the evidence base that has been amassed thus far. The following criticisms reflect general weaknesses in the literature and are not intended as a slight on these particular researchers—they have done what most of us would do. I use this study simply because it was the most recent on the topic at the time of going to press. The data are drawn from a convenience sample of 102 senior, middle, and operational Russian managers based in Moscow, St Petersburg, and Cherepovetz. Two of these sites had been used in the previous research, one was new (on the basis that it was a traditional site now exposed to significant international management development). Sixty-nine of the total sample of 102 came from a single company. The results were presented descriptively, such that the complex patterns of change noted above were not tested statistically. If you were a non-Russian firm setting up operations in Russia, would you really bank on there having been values-convergence and therefore a higher chance of more consistent operations on the back of such data and analysis? Clearly, then, when we try to move from demonstrated changes of values, the within-country nature of these types of study makes it very dangerous for us to leap to the kinds of conclusion that we might be tempted to draw.

However, we are not only interested in the study of convergence and divergence. I/O psychologists are especially keen to know whether '... from a managerial standpoint ... similar contextual conditions have similar attitudinal effects, regardless of the cultural context' (Menon, 2004, p. 138). Numerous studies have looked at relevant psychological variables in single countries other than, say, the USA or the UK, so data can be found on organizational citizenship behaviours (OCBs) in, say, Nepal or commitment in, say, Egypt. Such non-Anglo Saxon country studies have used the analysis of key variables to infer the extent to which similar cause–effect patterns emerge between the particular variables under study and in many instances have used the concept of culture to explain the particular pattern found. In this next section, I highlight those studies that, in recent years, have (a) examined the direct impact of national culture on specific work-related outcomes or (b) compared such outcomes across several countries. At the end of the section, I highlight the methodological concerns that cut across some of these studies.

INDIVIDUAL LEVEL STUDIES

What has become known as the *new cultural paradigm research tradition* has treated cultural dimensions as quasi-individual difference characteristics (Clugston, Howell, & Dorfman, 2000; Farh, Earley, & Lin, 1997; Kirkman & Shapiro, 2001; Maznevski, DiStefano, Gomez, Noorderhaven, & Wu, 2002). Earley and Mosakowski (1995) argued that while people from a particular culture can on average share or endorse a given cultural value or belief, and the country can be the single most important determinant of these scores, when values are measured at the individual level there is still enough between-person variability and scale distribution across members from within any single country for their scores on the value orientation to be treated as an important individual difference (i.e., using data from within one country does not produce too restricted a range of scores). Where such measurement of culture is also based on values that are known to operate at the individual level (rather than, for example, using scales that reflect nationally derived cultural constructs that are then converted into questions that individuals might answer), then this new cultural paradigm research approach can find support in the literature.

One question that has been pursued by researchers within the new cultural paradigm tradition has been to investigate which HR practices are values-free, or can be predicted at the individual level by value orientations. Put practically, this question concerns the room for manoeuvre that there might be for International HR Directors in transferring practices abroad. If the *values* of an organization's workforce significantly predict their preference for the nature of HR practices, then it will be more difficult for the organization to transfer them successfully. The organization can change employee attitudes and mindsets to specific practices by communication and educational processes, but employee values tend to be more resistant to change. Preliminary evidence suggests that the answer to this question might be sobering for International HR Directors. In a study of over 400 Taiwanese employees at firms such as Tatung, Mitac, and Acer, Sparrow and Wu (1998) found that 75% of the 'menu' of various HR practices could be predicted by individual level cultural values. A similar proportion was found in a more recent study of Kenyan employees (Nyambegera, Sparrow, & Daniels, 2000).

The next question concerns the strength of effects. How important are individual-level cultural value orientations, especially in relation to other predictive variables? Even if values predict the desirability of a wide range of HR practices, there are lots of other individual factors that might shape the extent to which employees will find specific HR practices desirable or not. By looking at various demographic factors, such as age, service, gender, and grade (e.g., Sparrow & Wu, 1998), and a range of ways of fitting the person to the organization (e.g., Nyambegera et al., 2000), researchers have found that an individual's cultural values by themselves explain from 10% to 16% of the attractiveness (or not) of various HR practices to them. Similarly, cultural values explain about 19% of variance in job involvement and 11% of variance in commitment. To help to scale this impact, where employees work in organizations in which there is a perfect fit between the things they value in the job and these being satisfied within the job, the amount of explained variation in commitment drops to 6%. Cultural values have been found to have about twice as powerful an influence on commitment as satisfaction of valued work features (for further details see Nyambegera et al., 2000; Sparrow & Wu, 1998).

I now briefly review some of the recent studies looking at key psychological constructs such as motivation, job satisfaction, and commitment.

Motivational Dispositions

Mathur, Zhang, and Neelankavil (2001) examined the motivational dispositions of 784 middle managers from China, India, the Philippines, and the USA. Adapting the statistical corrections for possible response bias that is considered necessary for all cross-cultural studies (whereby overall cross-country means are computed and subtracted from individual scores for each item, and then the overall mean for all items is computed separately for each country and subtracted from the scores for dependent variable items separately for each country, as recommended by Aycan et al., 2000), the researchers found that different factors motivated the managers from the four countries, and while there were, of course, differences between the Eastern managers and those from the USA, there were also significant differences between the three Asian countries. China was the most different of all when compared to the USA, and although India and the Philippines exhibited differences to the USA, there were more similarities than differences. D'Iribarne (2002) reported on two case studies of factories in Morocco and Mexico and examined how local values could be used to effect successful change processes. The change management messages had to be positioned in ways that were culturally acceptable to local values, and so a link between values and effectiveness was claimed.

Procedural Justice

Morris and Leung (2000) have provided a review of cross-cultural work on various forms of justice and concluded that different forms of justice—particularly, for example, assessments of distributive justice—can be linked to cultural factors. More recently, however, Murphy-Berman and Berman (2002) examined perceptions of distributive justice among managers in Hong Kong and Indonesia. This study used a convenience sample of 215 students on psychology courses in the two countries. They were presented with distributive justice dilemmas in the form of vignettes (and then attributed justice scores to the actions taken by actors within these scenarios). Scores were also gathered using the 58-item Value Scale of Schwartz (1994) and a 24-item Self-Construal scale, which measure interdependent and dependent beliefs. Although both Indonesia and Hong Kong are collectivist cultures, the value scores differed significantly between the two. Differences in justice assessments were found and it was argued that culture influenced not only the criteria used to evaluate what was fair but also the degree to which what was seen as fair was additionally judged as good or bad. A link between this type of justice vignette and the work of Trompenaars (1993) seems to be evident.

Lam, Schaubroeck, and Aryee (2002) examined the relationship between individual level measures of individualism and power distance and perceived justice, job satisfaction, perceived competence, and absenteeism in a sample of 218 Hong Kong Chinese and 185 US tellers in a bank. While justice perceptions were related to job satisfaction, performance, and absenteeism in both cultures, justice perceptions and the measures of individualism did not differ between the two country cultures, but the effects were of a stronger magnitude among low-power distance individuals. Once cultural measures were applied at the individual level, country effects disappeared. Within the review period two other studies have examined the impact of distributive justice on the adaptation to foreign workplace ideologies of Chinese, Russian, and US managers working in joint ventures, foreign-owned enterprises, and state-owned enterprises (Giacobbe-Miller, Miller, Zhang, & Victorov, 2003) and the link between perceptions of fairness and cultural values of US and Chinese service employees (Tata, Fu, & Wu, 2003).

Identification at Work

Kirpal (2004) reported on the Vocational Identity, Flexibility, and Mobility in the European labour market project funded under the 5th EU Framework Programme. This project attempted to map some of the different ways in which work identities are composed, decomposed, and restructured during times of economic change. Qualitative methods were used (504 employee interviews) to investigate employees in seven countries (Estonia, France, Germany, Czech Republic, Greece, Spain, and the UK). National contexts were extremely important, notably in terms of their labour market operations and the institutional mechanisms to support employees, but the project also identified a general trend towards the individualization of work identities, with individuals being increasingly required to develop a proactive and entrepreneurial work attitude:

> What can also be noticed across all countries is a general trend towards employees needing to develop multi-dimensional (individual and collective) occupational identities that can cope with socio-economic and technological change. In this process, individual employees are increasingly taking the initiative, particularly in the light of the general decline of collective forms of work identities.
>
> (Kirpal, 2004, p. 211)

Commitment

Kirkman and Shapiro (2001) undertook a study of 461 self-managing work team members in two US multinationals covering four countries (Belgium, Finland, the Philippines, and the USA) and examined the impact of culture and a number of mediating factors on organizational commitment and job satisfaction. On the basis of historical studies that had suggested different levels of commitment across cultures (prior to the review period there has been a history of comparisons, for example, between the USA and Japan and demonstration of differences in commitment scores across countries within a multinational), they argued that cultural value–outcome relationships are better understood by identifying the more proximal variables that might account for these, such as employee resistance. An earlier study by Palich, Hom, and Griffeth (1995) had shown that only 2.7% of the variance of commitment scores within a multinational could be attributed to cultural value scores. If more appropriate intervening variables were measured, might clearer affects be demonstrated? To avoid the ecological fallacy problem (see the end of the present section) of using Hofstede's (1980) national level measures to predict individual level variables, Kirkman and Shapiro (2001) used the Cultural Perspectives Questionnaire developed by Maznevski and colleagues, which assesses 11 generic value orientations (validation data on this instrument was later published in Maznevski et al., 2002). They found that collectivism was associated with greater job satisfaction and organizational commitment, but that resistance behaviour (i.e., employee reactions to US-based management initiatives) accounted for much of the variance between cultural values and both satisfaction and commitment. Individual level values had a significant impact on the outcomes—but, ironically, this effect was greater for employees in the USA than for those in Finland or the Philippines.

An important question concerns the relative proximity of cultural values to the behaviour that employees actually exhibit—i.e., do cultural values *work through* more immediate HR concerns (such as there being a fit between the individuals work goals and their job satisfaction) or do they have a direct (and independent or unmediated) influence? This question actually gets at two important issues for the International HR Director. First, if cultural values are mediated by other more immediate factors, then organizations might be able to mollify their influence by working on things like the degree of fit between the employee and the organization. If cultural values impact on HRM independently of other factors, however, then organizations have to cope with the impact that these values will have, regardless. The answer to this first question is as yet unclear. A study by Farh et al. (1997) found that the impact of cultural values could be mediated, while the more recent study by Wu and Sparrow (2000) found that cultural values have an independent and direct impact on commitment.

Vandenberghe, Stinglhamber, Bentein, and Delhaise (2001) undertook a study of 580 employees from 12 countries working for the translation department of the European Commission to test the validity of a multidimensional model of employee commitment. They argued that the handful of previous studies examining commitment across cultures had compared perhaps two or three countries and had not allowed for any conclusions to be drawn about the equivalence of commitment scales across cultures. In their own study they measured a number of different foci of commitment (affective and normative) in relation to the organization as a whole, and the participant's occupation, work group, and to Europe as a project. In addition, a continuance component was assessed in respect of the participants' organizations and their occupations. National scores for cultural variables of power distance, individualism, and masculinity were also derived, reflecting a nested design. Continuance and normative commitment to both the organization and the occupation were indistinguishable, so an eight-factor rather than the hypothesized 10-factor model was found to be the model of choice. Affective bonds to a variety of commitment foci were found to be important predictors of intention to quit. Employees

from more individualistic countries displayed higher levels of continuance commitment to their organization and occupation, and employees from masculine
countries exhibited stronger affective commitment, *but* the relationships between commitment components and intention to quit were consistent across
the cultural dimensions. Vandenberghe et al. argued that conducting the study
in a single organization controlled for the influence of local factors such as reward system, structure, and leadership patterns, thereby making interpretation
of differences across the cultural dimensions safer.

Andolšek and Štebe (2004) used secondary data from the USA, the UK,
East and West Germany, Hungary, Slovenia, and Japan to explore the impact
of personal, organizational, and environmental factors on work values and commitment. They analysed data for 4484 adults from the Work Orientations II
International Social Survey Programme, a continuing annual programme of
cross-national collaboration. The data included measures of affective and continuance commitment and this was tested for each country against variables
such as work values, gender, age, education, employment status, trade union
membership, private or public company, and supervision responsibility. Affective commitment was highest in the USA, followed by Slovenia and then Japan.
Measurement equivalence cannot, however, be assumed with certainty. They
found only mixed support for the idea of universal predictors (age, satisfaction,
insecurity, and high paying jobs appeared to act as universal antecedents to
commitment). However, employees in individualistic countries attached more
importance to job autonomy and employees in collectivistic countries attached
more importance to the opportunity to help others. Andolšek and Štebe (2004,
p. 203) concluded that

... we can confirm that each country has developed some special predictors
of commitment, and three of them are universal: good quality of work, satisfaction with an organization and intrinsic orientation toward work. However,
in most countries these three factors do not explain the whole story. Material
quality of work (job quality, high income) is important in predominantly individualistic countries, while in collectivistic countries post-material quality
of work is decisive.

Commenting on these findings, Menon (2004, p. 139) concluded '... these
nuanced results seem to say that what makes employees like an organization
may differ from country to country, but what affects their likelihood of staying
in an organization is fairly similar across countries'.

Glazer, Daniel, and Short (2004) examined the relationship between
Schwartz's (1992) values and both continuance and affective commitment in a
sample of 1259 nurses from Hungary, Italy, the UK, and the USA. Each commitment component was regressed on four values (openness to change, conservation, self-transcendence, and self-enhancement). The results were compared
across countries, and a pan-cultural mediated regression was conducted to

determine the extent to which country influences values and, in turn, commitment. Continuance commitment was not significantly different across the four nationalities of nurses (this could, of course, reflect an occupational culture), but affective commitment was highest in Hungary and second highest in the USA. The Hungarian scores were significantly higher than those in the UK and Italy. The findings were explained using the distinction between transactional and relational forms of psychological contract (Rousseau & Schalk, 2000). In the more relational psychological contracts of Hungary and Italy, a higher proportion of values correlated with affective commitment. In Hungary and Italy, 10.8% and 9.4% respectively of variance in affective commitment could be predicted by values, falling to 3.1% in the USA and no relationship at all was found in the case of the UK. Openness to change was negatively associated with affective commitment. Continuance commitment was far more weakly predicted by values (2.2% and 2.8% of variance in Hungary and Italy respectively and non-significant relationships in the UK and the USA). This study suggests that international managers need to be flexible when generalizing people's values on the basis of culture value studies (occupation produced some cross-cultural effects here); but values (different patterns) are predictive of different forms of commitment across countries.

Job Satisfaction

Roe, Zinovieva, Dienes, and Ten Horn (2000) asked whether employees from the former communist countries of Eastern Europe resembled Western workers with regard to work motivation and related variables. They examined the antecedents and consequences of job involvement and organizational commitment of 1416 blue- and white-collar workers in Bulgaria, Hungary, and the Netherlands. Quota sampling with respect to gender, age, job level, sector, and geographic region was used and data that was collected in 1994 and 1995 was analysed to test the validity of the Hackman-Oldham job characteristics model across the three countries. Instruments were back-translated. Path analysis was used to test the generic model. This only produced a modest fit to the data, but a better fit was found when testing optimal models for each country separately. Opportunity for growth and esteem were found to be less important in the less individualistic Bulgaria. The distinctiveness of each model was then explained by reference to cultural and economic factors, although this was not assessed directly

Huang and Van de Vliert (2003b, 2004) built on this work. They examined cross-cultural and cross-occupational variations in job satisfaction data from 129,087 respondents from 39 countries surveyed by a multinational company in 2000. They used a multilevel model (see the discussion at the end of this section) to test whether individual level relationships were moderated by country level characteristics. An overall job satisfaction scale was used to create a dependent variable, and independent variables included job level, cultural individualism—operationalized by using country level scores, using Hofstede's (1991) and Triandis's (2001) individualism estimates. Other national level factors such as divorce rate were also used. Extrinsic and intrinsic job motivators were measured and controls introduced for factors such as national wealth, gender, age, tenure, literacy rates, and unemployment levels. Hierarchical linear modelling was used to test for effects across levels. Huang and Van de Vliert found that the individual level relationship between job level and job satisfaction was contingent on cultural individualism. Where employees had little opportunity to use their skills and abilities, blue-collar workers in collectivistic countries were even more satisfied with their jobs than were white-collar workers. Huang and Van de Vliert (2004, p. 343) concluded that '. . . although the evidence provided by this study is far from adequate to reject the universality of the alienation theory, the present findings . . . suggest that the classic alienation theory may rest upon a disputable premise that relies rigidly on observations in individualistic cultural contexts'.

Hui, Au, and Fock (2004) reported on a series of studies to examine cross-cultural variations in empowerment effects. They used secondary data from the World Values Survey II, a large-scale multi-country survey that collected data in 1990 and 1993. Society level data for Hofstede's power distance and wealth levels were entered into hierarchical linear modelling along with individual level data for job autonomy, job satisfaction, and job level and compared 396 frontline hotel employees (and also hotel management students) from Canada and China. This time individual level measures of power distance and customer orientation were used. The cultural variable of power distance was found to consistently moderate the relationship between empowerment/job autonomy and job satisfaction.

Prosocial Behaviour, Organizational Citizenship Behaviours (OCBs), and Trust

Several studies have been conducted within single countries that have tested the relationship between various national culture dimensions and specific behavioural outcomes via proposed intermediate factors. For example, Ramamoorthy and Flood (2004) examined the direct and indirect links between a number of dimensions of individualism and collectivism value orientations on one hand and perceived task interdependency on the other, in terms of their impact on team loyalty and prosocial behaviour in a sample of 204 employees in Irish manufacturing organizations. The results overall indicated that the value orientations had a direct effect on the outcomes with perceptions of task interdependence having only a marginal moderating influence.

A smaller number of studies have compared two or more countries. For example, Kwantes (2003) examined the relationship between organizational commitment and OCBs and withdrawal behaviours in a sample of 319 engineers from US and Indian companies. Affective commitment predicted 8% of

variance in personal industry OCBs for Indian engineers but was not significant in the US sample, and about 10% of variance in individual initiative OCBs
in both countries. Withdrawal behaviours could be predicted in both samples,
but again the forms of commitment had differing relationships across the two
countries. Kwantes (2003, p. 19) concluded: '...support for both emic and
etic aspects of OCBs was found'. Huff and Kelley (2003) examined trust behaviours (propensity to trust, internal trust, external trust, and in-group trust
for ethnic groups) in 1282 bank managers from South Korea, Japan, China,
Taiwan, Hong Kong, Malaysia, and the USA. Contrary to the commonly held
stereotype, individuals from collectivist cultures have greater in-group biases,
resulting in a lower propensity to trust and lower external trust.

Psychological Contract

Reasons to assume that many of the mechanisms of the psychological contract
should operate differently across cultures and countries have been examined
from a theoretical perspective by Sparrow (1998), Rousseau and Schalk (2000),
and Thomas, Au, and Ravlin (2003). The latter note that national culture influences the psychological contract through the zone of negotiability that is
deemed acceptable: 'every society ... sets a zone of negotiability through its
own set of constraints and guarantees ... between societies the zone of negotiability is shaped by societal tolerance for unequal outcomes and ... societal
regulation of employment' (Thomas et al., 2003, p. 286). Building on an earlier analysis of the psychological contract within the single state of Hong Kong
that had showed that Hong Kong managers made little distinction between
different obligations to their employer in contrast to the US literature on the
contract (Westwood, Sparrow, & Leung, 2001), Kickul, Lester, and Belgio
(2004) examined the perceived importance of various psychological contract
obligations, psychological contract breach, and outcome behaviours (satisfaction, commitment, turnover intention, organizational citizenship behaviours)
following breach in a sample of 60 US (part-time MBA students) and 76 Hong
Kong Chinese employees (working in a banking firm). The importance of obligations and breach varied across the two samples, with more importance being
attributed to breach and more negative outcomes, as a consequence, being
reported by the US sample.

Thomas and Au (2002) operationalized measures of horizontal and vertical
individualism and collectivism and job satisfaction, quality of job alternatives,
exit, voice, loyalty, and neglect behaviour and examined responses from 218
New Zealand and Hong Kong managers on executive programmes. Thomas
and Au (2002, p. 321) concluded that '...behavioural responses were contingent on prior job satisfaction and quality of job alternatives in much the
same way in this multicultural sample as in previous single culture studies
...however, culture directly influenced the behavioural responses of exit and
voice, indicating the likelihood of culturally based normative behaviour...for
the exchange relationship'.

More recently, King and Bu (2005) examined the psychological contract from the perspective of 395 new IT recruits (typically 22-year-old graduating undergraduates majoring in computer science, management information systems, and automation) located in the USA and two sites in China (a convergence and high change sector if ever there was one). The motivation for the study was to examine cultural and subcultural patterns of similarity (or not) in expectations of the employment relationship, in the context of the many outsourcing decisions that are now being made in this sector. However, the recent history of high and unexpected costs to foreign employees operating in China due to poor retention of skilled local staff means that organizations have to better understand the psychological contract of local employees. Transactional and relational employer and employee obligations, as drawn from the traditional psychological contract literature, were measured, as were self-efficacy and perceived mobility. Data were adjusted and standardized to account for possible degrees of response acquiescence due to culture biasing using procedures adopted by Hofstede (1980) and Schwartz (1994). The results showed that despite some generic cultural differences, at the subculture level there was more evidence of similarity between the contract as perceived by US and Chinese graduates. Overall, the Chinese and US cohorts held similar beliefs on employer–employee obligations, such as the obligations of the employer to provide high pay, job autonomy, long-term security, financial reward, exciting projects, and opportunities to work on leading-edge technologies—i.e., a global work culture if ever we saw one. Cross-cultural differences still existed in terms of expectations of factors such as rapid career advancement (higher in the USA), having a motivating boss, and completion of assignments on time. More importantly, new IT recruits in the highly foreign exposed Shanghai tended to have beliefs that were closer to the US IT recruits than did the Beijing IT recruits.

Conclusions on Individual Level Studies

Looking across the studies reviewed in this section as a whole, it is clear that our evidence base is still very weak and sporadic. A general conclusion that can be drawn is that where culture has been measured directly at the individual level, then it does appear to predict important outcomes, and where key outcomes have been examined across countries without the specific measurement of culture, then causal factors often appear to have different weightings and occasionally different relationships with each other.

There have been, and continue to be, a number of criticisms made to individual, level research. In many studies (not reviewed here) there is a temptation for authors to examine the relationship between variables in a new country context and then draw upon and infer an assumed national culture explanation for the pattern of findings, even though culture was not operationalized in any way. Even when culture has been assessed in some direct way, or where cross-country differences are used as a proxy for culture, the following notable criticisms have to be addressed (this taxonomy is derived from work by Mathur et al. (2001), Van de Vijver & Poortinga (2002), and Menon (2004)):

1. *Theoretical equivalence in our measurement*: Mathur et al. (2001, p. 264) make the observation that for any one important work-related construct, and certainly for culturally linked antecedents such as values or motivations, problems are caused by researchers '... not because they lack[ed] appropriate instruments but because there was an overabundance of instruments that were tried and are still being tried'. Menon (2004, p. 137) similarly notes: '... the ready availability of "culture scales" makes it easy to add cultural variables to a questionnaire that includes other individual level variables such as job satisfaction and make individual level predictions about cultural effects ... given the typical sample sizes and convenience samples employed by most researchers, it is not surprising to see inconsistent results'. The plethora of different measures for the same cultural or outcome variable make it very hard to equate findings across studies.

2. *Ecological fallacy*: Huang and Van de Vliert (2003a) noted that a common feature of many studies has been to test the moderating effects of national contextual variables—such as individualism and collectivism—at the level of individual workers. This is done by either disaggregating country level measures and assigning each individual a score on the basis of the average score for the nation they come from, or by measuring the individual using instruments designed to assess national level constructs. The first approach falls foul of the ecological fallacy, observed by Hofstede (1980) and attributed to Robinson (1950), whereby national level data are used to predict individual level behaviour, which leads to incorrect estimations of the real effects of the contextual variables.

3. *Contextual determination*: The second approach is an improvement, but still can contain flaws. Where a cross-cultural scale is applied at the individual level only within one country, it is difficult to assume cross-national differences without having data for other countries as well because other contextual variables—for example, wealth or institutional effects—might explain the positioning of individuals on the scale in question.

4. *Structural equivalence of meaning*: The second approach also runs the risk that the construct has a different meaning at the individual level than was the case at the national level. (For a detailed discussion and taxonomy of this last form of error, i.e., problems of structural equivalence and aggregation/disaggregation, see Van de Vijver and Poortinga, 2002).

These issues continue to plague research at the individual level of analysis, as is evidenced by the very situational set of findings that have been reported by the above researchers who have examined cultural antecedents to important work-related outcomes at the individual level. When studies like these use variables that cross levels of analysis, Huang and Van de Vliert (2003a) suggested the use of either two-level correlations or, preferably, hierarchical linear modelling

(HLM), a form of multilevel modelling statistical techniques, capable of relating country level variables to individual level variables, within a unified analysis. HLM and related multilevel modelling procedures are designed to analyse data within a nested structure, and as people are nested within countries, such approaches militate against the ecological fallacy problem by splitting residual variance into individual level and country level estimates. The issue of cross-level construct equivalence is less of a problem because researchers can directly use country level variables in a cross-level model. Finally, multilevel modelling techniques take into account the statistical interdependences of the responses of individuals who share the same national contexts.

Yet we do not only have to contend with problems of ascertaining the equivalence or otherwise of established psychological constructs—many measures of cultural values are themselves notoriously unstable (this reflects the earlier critical view on cross-national comparisons). Once scales are used outside the initial set of countries in which their factor structures were initially established, scale reliabilities often become quite poor. For example, Spector, Cooper, and Sparks (2001) assessed the psychometric properties of the Hofstede (1980) Values Survey Module from samples covering 23 countries. Data for 6737 employees came from the Collaborative International Study of Managerial Stress (CISMS) established in 1996. Sample sizes varied considerably across countries, but Spector et al.'s analysis was very critical of the construct validity of the cultural scales. Internal consistencies at the individual level were poor ('unacceptably low', p. 273) and in the majority of cases failed to reach 0.60. At the country level of analysis only long-term orientation had an acceptable reliability. Spector et al. concluded that

... it seems possible that the assessment of values cross-nationally may be more difficult than the assessment of other types of variables. These values are likely to be broad and multidimensional, making it difficult to capture them with a single short scale ... it is also possible that part of the problem is that value scales may not be as exportable from culture to culture as other types of scales. (p. 279)

For the full debate, see also the replies by Hofstede (2002) and Spector et al. (2001).

UNDERSTANDING CHANGE IN NATIONAL CULTURES: MULTILEVEL FRAMEWORKS

Such statistical refinements apart, Erez and Gati (2004), reflecting the multiple cultures perspective of Sackmann and Phillips (2004), called for a shift in research focus, moving away from approaches that view culture as a stable entity towards approaches that examine dynamic phenomena, and in particular the interplay between different levels of culture: '... very few studies have examined the effect of culture on change, or recognized that culture itself changes over time' (Erez & Gati, 2004). They argued that globalization, as a macro level of culture, produces behavioural change in members of various cultures through top-down structural processes. Reciprocal individual level behavioural changes are also created through bottom-up processes that modify culture at the macro level. Cross-level models, such as the GLOBE project '... identify sources of tension and misfit between levels, but they do not explain the dynamics of culture, where inconsistency between two levels instigates change and cultural adaptation' (Erez & Gati, 2004, p. 589).

We are driven by ecological models of culture change, anchored in ideas within social psychology and anthropology, whereby culture changes by coming into contact with other cultures via international trade, migration, and invasion. Acculturation impacts depend on the extent to which people are attracted to their own culture and the depth of their identification with it (Berry, 1980; Berry, Poortinga, Segall, & Dasen, 1992). Erez and Gati (2004) pointed out that these models focus mainly on the top-down effects of context on culture, but they do not explain how changes at the individual level emerge to become cultural change at the macro level. They cite Chao's (2000) multilevel perspective as providing support for the contention that lower level perceptions and reactions can be shaped by higher level knowledge bases, but note that '... the mechanisms that transmit the effects of higher levels to lower levels and vice versa, were not clearly stated' (Erez & Gati, 2004, p. 589).

As Koslowsky et al. (2002, p. 131) noted:

... Culture implies relative uniformity in attitudes and behaviour across venues within the cultural environment (e.g., country). Yet some extent of uniformity exists across cultural boundaries. In today's increasingly globalized world, culture does not provide the sole explanation for the relative consistency in goals, values, activities, and interactions that take place within and between cultural environments. Universalism accounts for an increased number of these phenomena.

They went on to point out that once we realize that the variance of any important I/O psychology phenomenon across cultural settings—a value, an attitude, or a behaviour—could be explained by different factors, then we have to ask: 'When can we assume that cultural variables account for the variance, and when can it be attributed to universalistic laws?' (p. 132). This is partly addressed by the individual level studies above that attempted to partition change in psychological constructs directly attributable to cultural values. Erez and Gati (2004) noted that cultural commonality—shared meaning systems—can be formed at a number of levels: individual (self-representation), group, organizational, national, and global. These levels exist as a hierarchy, nested one within the other. Each level is interrelated, with top-down socialization processes resulting from ecology, historical events, and cultural diffusion through globalization creating new realities, and creating opportunities for individuals to internalize shared meanings. Erez and Gati (2004) hypothesized that top-down processes first affect the external layer of culture—for example, the behaviours and practices studied by Smith et al. (2002)—which through progressive internalization turn into shared norms and eventually implicit assumptions. Pineda and Whitehead (1997) argued that culture influences the managerial tasks that are carried on inside organizations through a process of first influencing the individual heuristics that are used to manage, which then impact on the managerial activities carried out, and in turn lead to a building of competence around these tasks and the consequent broader establishment of norms.

In the same way that the multiple cultures perspectives points out that within organizations there are multiple cultures, Erez and Gati (2004) argued that under processes of globalization people develop multiple identities—some of which might be driven by a sense of belonging to a (universalistic) global culture, others being driven by local (tribalistic) identities based on socialization processes:

> ... the ability to simultaneously maintain these two types of identity depends on the similarity between the global and local culture ... exposure to the global work environment shapes a global identity. A fit between the global and local identity enables effective adaptation to both environments.
>
> (Erez & Gati, 2004, p. 593)

This aspect of the Erez and Gati model is not well developed, but clearly understanding the dynamics at this individual level is a territory to which psychologists should be able to contribute. The work of Bandura (2002) outlined earlier is perhaps helpful here. I would observe that applying some of this learning to the study of individuals inside those parts of organizations at which top-down and bottom-up processes tend to intersect would form a fascinating area of study now for I/O psychologists. A *de facto* reality in most organizations today is the development of highly interdependent international teams, and perhaps these teams represent the most attractive unit of analysis to evidence (or not) accelerated processes of cultural bridging. Knowledge acquisition and knowledge transfer within teams and other networks should inform our understanding of many of these phenomena. This issue is touched upon in the final sections of this review.

Erez and Gati (2004) also drew attention to Hofstede's assertion that the most effective way of changing 'mental models' (note that for Hofstede national culture was defined as the collective programming of the mind, so 'mental model' is used in this context) is to first change individual behaviours. This is actually an important assertion that needs testing, especially for those interested in helping people in their transition from one culture to another. For cognitive psychologists, cognition is often assumed to precede behaviour, but for management of change scholars it is practise of novel behaviours that creates the mental constructs to make sense of the construct. Bottom-up processes of aggregation create new higher level entities of culture at group, organizational, and national levels. These bottom-up processes must originate in cognition, affect, behaviour, or other individual characteristics, and are transmitted through interactions with others into collective phenomena (Hodgkinson & Sparrow, 2002). In the same way that shared team mental models, synergistic team performance, and team diversity are created as a group property, then so too are new elements in a culture. Erez and Gati (2004) observed that, of course, the top-down processes of structure frequently constrain and define the boundaries that exist between units within a culture, but over time dynamic and sporadic cross-boundary interactions gain more stability: '... hence stable structures emerge from a dynamic process. Because emergent phenomena are based on patterns of interaction, even small changes in individual behaviour or dyadic interactions can yield significant changes in the emergent phenomenon' (Erez & Gati, 2004, p. 591). It is, then, only through these top-down and bottom-up processes that cultures become more dynamic and change (see also Klein & Kozlowski, 2000). Through such reciprocity, facets of global culture can redefine individual level self-concept and identity, and changes in individual cognition can bring down stable cultural institutions. Erez and Gati's model has intuitive appeal and, as with the social cognition theory of Bandura (2002), presents a rather more optimistic view of human agency, but of course there is as yet no real empirical evidence for such causal linkage processes. There are some parallels, however, to the work on competitive enactment and cognitive inertia cited by Hodgkinson and Sparrow (2002).

CONTINUED THEORETICAL CHALLENGES IN THE COMPARATIVE FIELD

The issue of measuring and testing multilevel cultural models is fraught with problems. Aycan (2000) noted that the complexity of organizational life means that variables associated with the individual, organization, and societal context need to be better integrated into theory and research. This statement alone requires a broadening of most psychological theory. The same call was made five years ago in this volume (Smith et al., 2001a). Fischer, Ferreira, Assmar, Redford, and Harb (2005, p. 28) concluded that five years on

... there is little integration of both organizational and socio-cultural variables. Various reviews commented on the fragmented ad hoc and atheoretical state of the field ... research on international and cross-cultural organizational behavior is 'reductionist' in that it fails to acknowledge the complex nature of organizations and the influence of multiple environmental forces that are both internal and external to the organization. Frameworks are needed that incorporate variables at multiple levels in order to paint a fuller and more valid picture of how organizations operate in diverse regions of the world.

They drew attention to many of the theoretical and methodological challenges that remain by taking one example—the issue of organization citizenship behaviour (extra role behaviours) and demonstrating how analysis might benefit by using multilevel frameworks. However, unfortunately, '. . . most often multilevel data are collected at the lowest level (the individual) and then aggregated (at an organizational or country level) for testing of the respective theoretical hypotheses' (Fischer et al., 2005, p. 30).

This criticism could be directed at much of the material covered in this review. Important questions to ask, then, are:

- How might we best formulate appropriate multilevel theories?
- What are the most appropriate data collection and aggregation strategies?
- What are the most appropriate tools for investigating theoretical relationships?

Fischer et al. (2005) argued that the first of these questions requires the identification of appropriate and central variables that then enable the specification of necessary levels, constructs, and processes within a theory. Lachman (1997, p. 318) similarly asked whether culture is '. . . a relevant, significant explanatory factor for the particular observed differences at hand?' Returning to Fischer et al. (2005), they argued that having focused on the specific dependent variable around which a multilevel theory is to be constructed, key questions that have to be asked are:

- Is there empirical evidence that higher level variables are likely to exert an influence on the dependent variable?
- Do work context variables account for more variance in the dependent variable than do within-person variables (for example, attitudes or personality)?
- Are employees in specific cultures more or less likely to demonstrate the dependent variable (for example, OCBs) in question?
- Which specific organization-level practices are most associated with the dependent variable?
- Which dimensions of national culture have the best potential for understanding the organizational behaviour that surrounds the dependent variable in question across cultures?

Having specified the appropriate range of variables across levels, we need to be able to propose the most appropriate relationships and links between them. Fischer et al. (2005) noted that these are typically top-down constructs that have mediating effects on the linkage between variables.

I would point to two additional requirements in considering relationships between variables. The need to:

- incorporate bottom-up linkages (given the discussion of Erez and Gati's (2004) work);
- understand the theories from other fields, such as the resource-based theory of the firm and institutional theory, that are used to explain the linkages between variables.

If we look at the theories driving IHRM, then in recent years a number have come to dominate research in the field (Sparrow & Braun, 2005). These are: resource dependence theory (e.g., Pfeffer & Salancik, 1978) and the resource-based view of the firm (e.g., Barney, 1991) as employed by Morris, Snell, and Wright (2005); the knowledge-based view of the firm (e.g., Tallman & Fladmoe-Lindquist, 2002) and organizational learning theory (e.g., Barkema, Shenkar, Vermeulen, & Bell, 1997) as discussed by Hodgkinson and Sparrow 2002); relational and social capital theory (Lengnick-Hall & Lengnick-Hall, 2005); and institutional theory (e.g., DiMaggio & Powell, 1983) as used by Björkman (2005). I/O psychologists carrying out work at the individual level of analysis have to be increasingly cognizant of these frequently non-psychological theories if they are to be effective researchers in the international management field.

Regarding the issue of variable specification, Koslowsky et al. (2002) explained why this is difficult to accomplish reliably. Two different research goals are being pursued:

1. One research goal is to hypothesize that culture between two or more different groups (nations or societies) *is expected* to show differences on specific organizational measures, to be explained by identifying distinct characteristics within each culture. Where culture is considered to be important, via some evidence base, its inclusion in the research design is justified but on a situational basis (Lachman, 1997).
2. A second research goal is to begin by *hypothesizing universalism*, such that two groups (nations or societies) although different will nonetheless show similar profiles on the same organizational measures, to be explained by a process of internalization of more universal and common elements that underlie the organizational measure. As phenomena are considered to be universal, unless a firm rationale exists to the contrary, *no argument is needed to justify inclusion of culture level variables.*

Sagie and Elizur (1998) argued that we should not take for granted the belief in the universality of organizational behaviour phenomena, so instead *have to test* for the possible presence of cultural determinants before any such assumptions can be made. Only when researchers have demonstrated universality in the face of potential cultural differences can they ignore the possibility that various forms of the phenomena will not be influenced by cultural indicators.

They also warned that it would be unwise to assume relationships among variables or that cause–effect phenomena are the same around the globe. More recently, they argued that the difficulty is that

> ... if a cultural effect is expected and tested empirically, non-significant results are considered to be confirmation of the existence of universalistic factors ... due to the fact that editors in the social science literature are reluctant to publish non-significant findings in their journals, a study where two culturally distinct entities do not differ on one or more attitudes, beliefs, or behaviours is rarely published. Yet such a study may indicate that a measure originally developed in one culture is relevant to another culture.
>
> (Koslowsky et al., 2002, p. 133)

In the final analysis, as argued by Koslowsky et al. (2002), the file draw problem (whereby many non-significant findings in a research area are not reported and so the significant findings that are reported may be attributed to chance, and inferences concerning the existence of an effect or an association between two variables may or may not be true) could ultimately be responsible for the minority of published articles that support a universalistic hypotheses. We could also ask: How many published papers are designed for, or provide in their analysis, a developed multilevel specification? How many referees or editors require it of authors? While much research in the area continues to be published in specialized and sub-field research outlets in which certain methodological assumptions dominate, we are, perhaps, allowed as researchers to continue ignoring these more challenging questions.

The concerns expressed by Sagie and Elizur (1998) and Koslowsky et al. (2002) aside, non-psychologists might argue that the idea above, that we can specify stable multilevel linkages between psychometrically robust and appropriate evidence-based variables, assumes that a somewhat rationalistic and predictive model of cause–effect across multiple levels of analysis actually exists— i.e., that new contexts do not create new patterns of relationships between variables or even new variables. From a more traditional research perspective, the pointers developed by Fischer et al. (2005) in relation to the study of extra-role behaviour are, of course, generalizable and could be applied to most all psychological studies of key processes (motivation, psychological contracting, employee engagement) or outcome behaviours (for example, commitment, identification, involvement).

BEING CLEAR ABOUT FUNCTIONING WITHIN AND BETWEEN LEVELS OF ANALYSIS

I ended the section on individual level studies by noting some of the methodological problems and also some solutions being adopted by researchers pursuing multilevel models. There are a number of other developments that need to occur, not least of which is the specification of a clearer view of *generic human functioning* and linkage between key psychological variables under study (Gelade & Young, 2005). We need this for a number of reasons:

1. The assertion that national culture influences work attitudes and behaviours mainly (but indirectly) through organizational practices (Fischer et al., 2005; Ostroff & Bowen, 2000) suggests that we need to better understand the processes through which organizational culture and organizational practices mediate national culture effects.
2. Bandura's (2002) arguments about the need to incorporate cross-culturally generalizable human functions, such as agency, suggests that we need to develop a more complete functional model that elicits the constructs involved in the organization culture–practice–effectiveness chain.
3. Erez and Gati's (2004) observations that dynamic and two-way (i.e., top-down and bottom-up) processes are involved suggests that this modelling needs to allow for an understanding of *not just* how national culture exerts an influence on work attitudes through its influence on organizational culture and organizational practices (for which we can insert principally HRM practices), but also of how national culture *as enacted within firms and within individuals also creates a bottom-up influence* on the adoption, customization, and redirection of those practices.

Before we can make sense of the different impacts that national culture has on the various constituent elements—HRM practices, leadership, psychological contract, commitment, and so forth—we need to clarify how these elements *generally* relate to and influence each other. It is worth noting that the need to establish such *within-level-of-analysis* linkage is not just a problem that applies to international management researchers—it is, for example, also part of the 'black box' problem in the HRM-organizational performance literature (e.g., Sparrow & Marchington, 1998).

The current evidence of cultural effects consists of a myriad of studies that operationalize single, dual, or multiple organizational psychology variables in the context of a situationally dependent set of cultural variables, which in turn are examined in what are frequently convenience samples of individuals and sets of countries. Studies of this ilk—and we are all guilty of doing this—continue to emerge. We need to clarify what the general model is in order that points of cultural departure can be theorized, if a generic route has ever been conceived to have existed. Figure 5.2 represents an amalgam of three descriptions of this type of functional linkage process, beginning with the initial work of Kopelman, Brief, and Guzzo (1990), but also incorporating Ostroff and Bowen's (2000) analysis and the work of Sparrow (2001).

Within any given cultural context (which impacts on all of the variables depicted in Figure 5.2 at both the organizational and individual level of analysis), *firms that are pursuing globalization strategies* are characterized by cross-border alliances (IJVs and mergers and acquisitions), changes to global knowledge

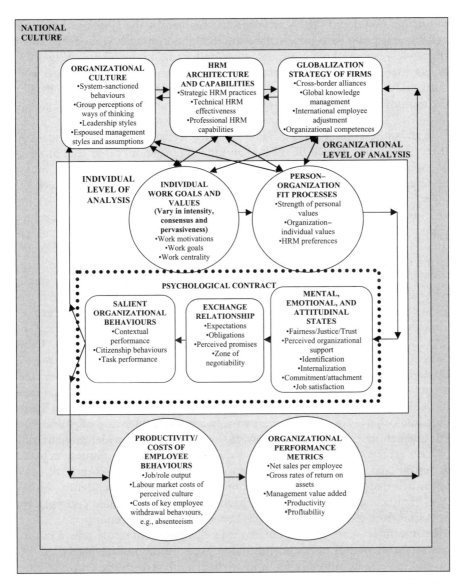

Figure 5.2 An organizational functioning model: Cause–effect linkages within an embedded cultural context

management, changing patterns of international employee adjustment, and the pursuit of specific organizational competences. There is also, within a cultural context, a specific HRM architecture and set of capabilities. This may be seen in terms of the bundles of HRM practices, the technical effectiveness of these practices within the national context, and the professional HRM capabilities of the HR function. Organizational climates and cultures flow from this set of organizational and HRM practices, as reflected by the systems-sanctioned behaviours, group perceptions of ways of thinking, culturally embedded leadership styles, espoused management styles, and assumptions. There are two-way links between all of these organization level contexts and both individual work goals and values and consequent person–organization fit processes (reflecting the top-down and bottom-up processes of change under the context of globalization).

In any one cultural context, organizational effectiveness is also dependent on there being a fit between the person and the organization, often seen in terms of their being some congruence in terms of shared values and also shared preferences for type of HRM. This climate or culture and the fit between the individual and organization then influences a series of mental (cognitive) and emotional (affective) states, such as trust, fairness, perceived organizational support, satisfaction, commitment, motivation, and involvement or identification with the organization. The broad sequential order of these as reflected in the predominantly Western literature is depicted in Figure 5.2. Via the exchange relationship inherent in the psychological contract (which is culturally embedded and dependent upon zones of negotiability) these states then create a series of employee behaviours that are salient to effectiveness, such as: attachment and intention to remain with the organization; performance of the task and contextual performance (organizational citizenship behaviour). These behaviours in turn impact on productivity in a number of ways, both *indirectly*, through problems such as having to cope with the costs of employee disengagement (withdrawal behaviours) and perceived position in the labour market (employer brand), and *directly*, through task competence and role capability. These outcome behaviours again have a two-way impact, influencing organizational effectiveness but also enacting upwards to influence the wider globalization process via the organizational cultures that they create. With all these in place, organizational productivity can be improved, and the flow can then be directed towards broader aspects of organizational effectiveness. Dependent upon the level of organizational effectiveness (itself a culturally embedded concept), the pressures from globalization changes become more or less intense.

In sum, it is clear that our current evidence base represents only a limited test of the myriad of potential cultural impacts on the underlying HRM–I/O psychology–organizational effectiveness chain implied by the theoretical framework depicted in Figure 5.2.

ADJUSTMENT PROCESSES AND INTERCULTURAL COMPETENCE

Traditionally, I/O psychologists have devoted most of their research attention within the study of international management processes to the management of international workforces and, within this topic area, to the management of

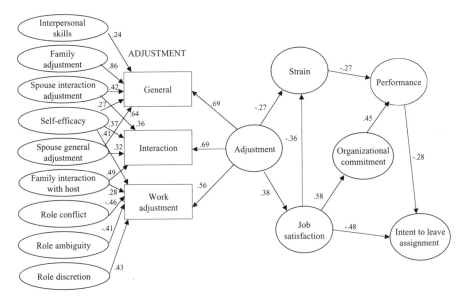

Figure 5.3 Model of expatriate outcomes
Source: Hechanova, R., Beehr, T.A., & Christiansen, N.D. (2003). Antecedents and consequences of employees' adjustment to overseas assignment: A meta-analytic review. *Applied Psychology: An International Review*, **52** (2), 213–236.

expatriates. Processes of adjustment have been examined from the perspective of lead international managers (such as expatriates) and this work has then been used to influence organizations' selection, assessment, and training activities in the field of international management. Hechanova, Beehr, and Christiansen (2003) applied meta-analytic methods to research on expatriate adjustment. Based on 42 empirical studies covering 5210 expatriates, a number of important predictive relationships were reliably identified, as shown in Figure 5.3.

Graf (2004) pointed out that global relocation surveys suggest that, world wide, the number of international assignees is expected to continue increasing, but that on a broad measure of failure (breaking off the assignment or the expatriate did not achieve the goals of the company), failure rates remain surprisingly high. Intercultural competence has been widely recognized as an important factor for international cooperation between companies. An important question, however, is whether intercultural competencies are culture-bound or culture-free.

Graf (2004) reported on two psychometric analyses in the USA and Germany to examine this question. The first of their studies sampled 188 US and 179 German management students of similar age and education and assessed intercultural competence using five instruments. The second study examined 177 employees in four large-scale insurance companies, two in the USA and two in Germany using three of the instruments. Measures included the Behavioural Assessment Scale for Intercultural Communication

Effectiveness, the Intercultural Sensitivity Scale, and the Interpersonal Competence Questionnaire, the Social Problem Solving Inventory, and the Self-Monitoring Scale. Nation (as a proxy of national culture) was found to be a significant independent variable in both the undergraduate and workforce samples, impacting upon several intercultural competencies. However, compared to score differences within each country, cross-country differences were only modestly significant: '. . . the intercultural differences of the assessed intercultural competencies were moderate in comparison with the evaluated intracultural differences' (Graf, 2004, p. 1142). Compared to the other factors tested (gender cultures and organizational cultures), national culture had a smaller effect. The conclusion was that '. . . intercultural competencies may be culture-general as far as the two national cultures are concerned. Conceptually, the studies supply some first evidence that a general model of intercultural competencies might be justified' (Graf, 2004, p. 1140).

As noted at the outset, one of the challenges in writing this review is to delineate both the range of topics to cover and academic disciplines upon which to draw, for as the international management field continues to mature it is beginning to import major conceptual, empirical, and methodological debates from the various disciplines that contribute to it. Thus, for example, when analysing the role of cross-cultural adjustment and expatriate management, we now see researchers looking, for example, at fundamental processes of person–organization fit from I/O psychology, sensemaking from the field of management cognition, and identification from the field of social psychology. In seeking to apply such a disparate array of concepts, data, and research methods for the advancement of international management, we need to carefully consider how we might apply what we know about these processes and methods from what is essentially relatively 'pure disciplinary research' to the international context in order to genuinely add value to international management research, rather than build a coherent understanding of international management and then comment on what this might mean for research on, for example, person–organization fit, sensemaking, and identification.

As an example of work that draws upon generic I/O processes, Van Vianen, de Pater, Kristof-Brown, and Johnson (2004) have used the lens of person–environment fit theory to reconsider the process of adjustment. As seen above, cross-cultural adjustment has been viewed along three dimensions: adjustment to the general environment; interactions with host country nationals; and work adjustment (see also Black, Mendenhall, & Oddou, 1991). However, researchers investigating diversity in workgroups have differentiated surface level aspects of culture (characteristics such as age and gender that are easily visible) and deeper level aspects of culture (beliefs and values), with the latter only being learned through extended individualized interaction and information gathering. Individuals make an initial assessment of surface level diversity to categorize others as being similar or dissimilar, then recategorize them on the basis of surfaced deep-level differences. In a two-wave longitudinal field study,

Van Vianen et al. (2004) monitored 208 expatriates (falling to 134 by time 2) in four multinationals over a three-month period. They measured cross-cultural adjustment, cultural novelty (to assess surface level differences in culture), and used Schwartz's (1992) scale of basic values to measure deep-level differences (discussed earlier in this chapter). They measured perceptions of host country values (and found that the average intraclass correlation of these assessments and actual national values was $r = 0.43$). As expected, surface level cultural differences were related to adjustment to general living conditions, while controlling for family situation, tenure, and previous assignment experience, thus indicating that adjustment to new living conditions is difficult when differences are easily visible. In contrast, interaction adjustment and work adjustment were not predicted by surface level differences but were predicted by differences in underlying value structure. Intriguingly, misfit in specific values created problems. Differences in openness to change, conservation, and self-enhancement had no impact, but self-transcendence values did create adjustment problems. Of course, no causal links can be assumed, as poorly adjusted expatriates might just report greater value differences between themselves and host locals, but the study as claimed does help to advance Black et al.'s (1991) framework by identifying unique values-fit antecedents to each form of adjustment.

MUTUAL ADJUSTMENT PROCESSES AMONG A MORE DIVERSE SET OF INTERNATIONAL EMPLOYEES

One of the issues that has led to a recent resurgence of interest in the topic of expatriate adjustment has been the realization that the need to understand the impact of internationalization (and associated requirements to manage adjustment processes associated with cross-cultural working) now applies to a much broader population of employees (Sparrow, 2005b). Briscoe and Schuler (2004, p. 223) noted that: '... the tradition of referring to all international employees as expatriates—or even international assignees—falls short of the need for international HR practitioners to understand the options available ... and fit them to evolving international business strategies'. In terms of global workforce planning researchers prefer now to talk about international employees (IEs) rather than the more traditional idea of expatriates and categorization of international assignee, parent country national, host country national, or third country national (Briscoe & Schuler, 2004). Mayerhofer, Hartmann, Michelilitsch-Riedl, and Kollinger (2004) used the term 'flexpatriates' to cover those employees who travel for brief assignments away from home and across national borders. IEs include international commuters, employees on long-term business trips, assignees on short-term or intermediate-term foreign postings, permanent transferees or permanent cadre, international transferees (moving from one subsidiary to another), immigrants, returnees, contract expatriates, and virtual IEs in cross-border project teams (Briscoe & Schuler, 2004). The key question is whether or not such employee categories all need to have the same depth of cross-cultural skills or the same type of international mindset, and what might be the impact on organizational effectiveness if such attributes are present or missing.

To answer these questions we have to rely primarily on a priori theory, since there is little empirical investigation of the new more diverse types of international employee. From a theoretical perspective, expatriate adjustment models can be classified as being driven by assumptions about learning, stress-coping, development, and personality (Mendenhall, Kühlman, Stahl, & Osland, 2002). Mendenhall et al. summarized these assumptions as follows:

1. Learning models assume that since expatriate adjustment has to do with learning new skills and techniques of adaptation, the impact of the 'other' culture can be seen as a change in behavioural reinforcement contingencies. The major task facing expatriates is to adjust their social skills such that they can learn the salient characteristics of the new environment in terms of new roles, rules, and norms of social interaction. Cross-cultural training is designed on the principle that the rules and values of a new culture have to be learned (and a repertoire of cognitive and behavioural schemata and responses developed) before adjustment can take place.

2. Stress-coping models are based on the assumption that feelings of anxiety, confusion, and disruption associated with culture shock are akin to individual stress reactions under conditions of uncertainty, information overload, and loss of control. The adjustment reaction is characterized by a variety of symptoms of psychological distress associated with any critical life event. Stress management (coping strategies), rather than stress avoidance, is necessary in order for expatriates to engage in necessary behaviours.

3. Developmental models tend to highlight phases of adjustment (for example, contact, disintegration, reintegration, autonomy, and independence) that reflect progressive stages of cultural awareness. Individuals undertake adaptive activities only when environmental challenges threaten their internal equilibrium. Processes of periodic (rather than linear) disintegration, regrouping/regeneration then higher maturation (progressive intercultural sensitivity often also associated with global leadership competence) are a consequence of exposure to other cultures.

4. Personality-based models imply that such development can in part be predicted by a set of generalizable attitudes and traits, such as adaptation, cross-cultural and partnership skills, or personality variables that are associated with model cross-cultural collaborators. The importance of these prerequisites depends on the nature of the position and task variables, firm characteristics, and contingent features of the host country. Empirical support is, however, still weak, and again there may be contradictions between

what is required for interaction adjustment (i.e., social) and work (i.e., task) adjustment.

Based on their review of the international management literature, however, Mendenhall et al. (2002, p. 169) noted that '. . . most empirical research in the field examines the expatriation process from a one-sided perspective, focusing solely on accounts of expatriate managers. Few empirical studies have included the host country perspective.' They argued that researchers have commonly regarded expatriate adjustment as a unidirectional process of one individual adjusting to a foreign environment. This results in a limited view of expatriate adjustment processes. If we are to move beyond this, we need more research that:

- employs longitudinal designs;
- includes the host country perspective on the determinants, processes, and outcomes of adjustment;
- examines what occurs when two diverse groups begin interacting with one another.

Building on the insights of this critique, Sparrow (2005b) argued that we must see adjustment as part of a process of *mutual adjustment*. This is, of course, a call for research from an intercultural interaction perspective—which Sackmann and Phillips (2004, p. 375) believe '. . . has demonstrated the importance of contextual analysis and process orientation in cultural research . . . [and] the resulting thick descriptions reveal insights about the emergence and negotiation of culture and shed light on issues of intercultural communication in the workplace'—but with a new modification. The need to understand mutual adjustment processes (and by this I mean multiple mutualities between team members of several different nationalities) is important for four reasons:

1. On their assignment expatriates increasingly have to cooperate with host country nationals, and therefore frequently have to rely on their assistance (Zimmermann, Holman, & Sparrow, 2003). Moreover, expatriates often have to work as part of an international team both within the subsidiary, and across different countries.
2. As seen in the new IE categorizations, not all employees on foreign assignment today can be considered as traditional expatriates.
3. As noted by Erez and Gati (2004), teams represent the most attractive unit of analysis to evidence (or not) accelerated processes of cultural bridging.
4. As observed by Sackmann and Phillips (2004, p. 377), though '. . . [the intercultural interaction perspective] still maintains that national culture is fundamental to interaction and the basis from which non-national cultural groupings emerge, its hitherto bicultural focus could be extended to multicultural interactions'.

If we are to better facilitate coping, we first need to refine our understanding of the skills that are needed to effectively navigate, work, and manage in cross-cultural contexts that demand the maintenance of partial and multiple identities. We need, then, to see studies conducted in more realistic, multicultural contexts and focus investigation on the variables that help groups to deal with particular settings.

A recent attempt to respond to this challenge can be seen in the study by Zimmermann and Sparrow (in press). They argued that differences between members in international teams tend to focus on understanding of work practices (reflecting the work outlined earlier on differences in recipe knowledge across nationalities) and also in the interaction styles associated with cultural differences. These differences may cause difficulties in cross-cultural collaboration, requiring mutual adjustments if the team is to function well. Adjustment processes should not, then, be examined in the isolated context of an expatriate, but should be understood as a dynamic, complex series of mutual interactions. In order to understand mutual adjustment we need to study the process by which members of different nationalities achieve a fit and reduced conflict between each other, with regard to their differences in work practices and interaction styles. In the Zimmermann and Sparrow (in press) study, a total of 116 managers in 11 binational teams were investigated over a period of one year in two German companies: a bank and an electronics company. The teams consisted of four different combinations of nationalities, allowing for an understanding of German to English, German to Japanese, German to Indian, and German to Austrian adjustments. At the bank, two German–English teams took part, which were responsible for international business management and for implementing IT systems, respectively. In the electronics company, five German–Indian, two German–Japanese, and two German–Austrian teams were examined. They were tasked with developing software functions for electronic control units to be used in car engines. The findings from in-depth interviews and team observations revealed the mechanisms of mutual adjustment at the level of cognitive processes, attitudes, and behaviours of team members. The study also highlighted the special importance of the interaction processes that were identified as the 'internal adjustment components', namely, certain types of communication, a change of views through different information sources, evaluations of differences, adjustment attitudes, and teaching and control. Once more, this is ripe territory for further exploration and theoretical development.

Others, however, have argued that the lens of adjustment is perhaps not the most appropriate one to use. Although it represents a multilevel theory, it is too rationalistic in its assumptions. For example, Cerdin (2003) has argued that while explorations of the traditional adjustment model have brought a degree of theoretical rigour to what was generally descriptive research, models of adjustment from all four of the above perspectives are still somewhat mechanistic. The main critique is that these models tend to focus on an image of expatriation at only one point of time. A more holistic view of the experience of expatriation is needed and, according to Cerdin and Dubouloy (2004), this can be afforded by a psychoanalytical perspective. Noting Cerdin's (2002) earlier work on the motivations for assignment of French expatriates, they argued that the rather pure work-driven and career-oriented motives ascribed to expatriation often have little to do with the factors that really drive international managers. They drew attention to positive and negative reasons, such as desires for escape, people in search of their own identity, and narcissistic behaviours, and drew parallels between the U-curve cultural adjustment process and personal maturation processes. Such an approach can help to delve beneath the discrepancy between the reasons we give for our actions and the real motives that drive them—and in their work Cerdin and Dubouloy (2004) drew attention to earlier work by Schneider and Asakawa (1995) and Gabriel (2002)—and applied the analysis to a sample of 15 French expatriates, delving into their family histories, life events, and experiences pre-, during, and post-expatriation. Their analysis was used to make recommendations to organizations on how better to negotiate the reasons for assignment and manage the risks associated with individuals, and how to ensure the developmental space on assignments necessary for managers to acquire appropriate and more accurate self-perceptions.

We can then see a number of new avenues of research opening up in the area of expatriate and IE adjustment. However, one final area to which I draw attention under the topic of the international adjustment of expatriates is the question of what makes an international manager valuable to an organization. Suutari (2002) noted that the capacity for cross-border leadership has to be built through the traditional international management staffing systems and applied to all employees in the firm, because firms cannot just be reliant on a cadre of expatriates. A much broader proportion of the workforce is now exposed to situations where international management competencies are needed. When advising on the nature of these staffing systems, I/O psychologists have traditionally focused on those human capabilities they can help to develop—but in today's organizations the selection of these managers is not just a question of their individual competencies (human capital) but also of the other forms of capital that they possess—social and political. Harvey and Novicevic (2004, p. 1173) noted that global leaders '... have to possess a complex amalgamation of technical, functional, cultural, social and political competencies to navigate successfully the intricacies of changing cross-border responsibilities'. They made a distinction between social capital and political capital, and used political influence theory to understand the importance of the capital that global leaders accumulated during global assignments. Social capital leads to trust. Political capital leads to legitimacy. Human capital leads to competencies. Cultural capital leads to social inclusion and acceptance. Social capital is typically reflected in the standing the manager has in the organization and his or her concomitant ability to use that standing to influence others. It is used to help to build on and meld the many cultural norms that exist in a foreign subsidiary. However, global leaders also have to accumulate political capital—including reputational capital (i.e., being known in the network for getting things done) and representative capital (the capacity to effectively build constituent support and acquire legitimacy by using traditional forms of power)—thereby being in a position to remove obstacles to cooperation. Such capital serves a key role in reducing dysfunctional conflicts.

Therefore, a potentially important new direction for practising I/O psychologists is to advise firms on how they can use expatriation and inpatriation processes to develop and exploit different forms of capital. Human capital and cultural capital are important but are of lower value (they can be imitated and developed by other firms) relative to social and political capital. The latter clearly add greater value because they are more difficult to develop and/or imitate. Harvey and Novicevic (2004, p. 1185) concluded '. . . further research should examine both the value and related costs (i.e., net value) of developing and using the corporate HR adaptive capacity to develop global leaders through appropriate design and efficient administration of global assignments'. The implication of this is that we need more psychological research that focuses on new assessment methods that are more closely aligned to the strategic requirement of knowledge transfer and the development of an international mindset. Building an international mindset provides a fundamental basis for overcoming inadequate political and social capital development.

INTERNATIONAL MINDSETS AND GLOBAL KNOWLEDGE TRANSFER

Søderberg and Holden (2002) noted that the management of multiple cultures (as discussed earlier in this review) requires that we understand knowledge transfer, organizational learning, and networking. I also noted earlier that Erez and Gati (2004) drew attention to the importance of the role of teams and networks in their model of bottom-up and top-down processes of cultural change. The topic of global knowledge management has received much analysis of late, and within this field of study there are some interesting lines of enquiry for I/O psychologists. In this, the penultimate, section I draw attention to just a few areas that I believe constitute the more fruitful areas for new psychological research. Sparrow (2005c) has recently examined how each of five main forms of global knowledge management (centres of excellence, managing systems and technology-driven approaches to global knowledge management systems, capitalizing on expatriate advice networks, coordinating international management teams, and developing communities of practice or global expertise networks) contributes to three knowledge-based capabilities:

- Knowledge acquisition and creation: that is, the generation of new knowledge fundamental to the long-term viability of the enterprise.

- Knowledge capture and storage: that is, creation of an inventory of knowledge so that the organization knows what knowledge it possesses, and where it resides and the maintenance of current knowledge in usable form so that it remains valuable.
- Knowledge diffusion and transfer: that is, ensuring the subsequent mobilization and flow of knowledge within the organization in order to create knowledge-based value.

It is well beyond the scope of this review to detail all the work that this entails for I/O psychologists, but I draw attention to some of the most immediate contributions that could be made. The first and arguably most significant contribution that could be made by I/O psychologists is in respect of the development of international mindsets, which, as noted above, is becoming increasingly central to the successful accumulation of social and political capital.

But what exactly is implied by this, above and beyond the building of social and political capital per se? The earliest debates on international management strategy argued that strategic capability is ultimately dependent on the 'cognitive processes' of international managers and the ability of firms to create a 'matrix in the minds of managers' or a transnational mentality (Bartlett & Ghoshal, 1989, p. 195). There are two aspects or components to this mentality (but, as noted later, there is considerable debate about the level of connectivity between the two):

- attitudinal/values
- cognitive structures.

The first component has been described as representing an 'attitudinal attribute' of an international orientation. This attitude is assumed to correlate with both the extent and quality of international experience. Researchers have attempted to develop measures that correspond to the core dimensions of a manager's thinking about international strategy and international organization and have then shown how this mindset changes over time. As an example of this kind of work, Murtha, Lenway, and Bagozzi (1998) conducted a study of cognitive change towards a more global mindset in 410 managers over a three-year period within a single multinational organization. They identified a core value-set or logic that was associated with global operations.

Global managers also need to have an effective *mental model of how knowledge and information are shared* across the people with whom they need to interact if they are to deliver an important global business process, product, or service (Hodgkinson & Sparrow, 2002). In this regard, expatriates have been seen as an important mechanism for knowledge capture and transfer inside global firms. Recently we have seen both more empirical study and detailed theorizing about this phenomenon. Theoretical work includes the application of knowledge transfer theory to the topic of expatriation (Bonache & Brewster,

2001) and modelling of how expatriates help to diffuse HRM practices across international borders (Cerdin, 2003). Empirical work has also examined:

- the spread of tacit knowledge within top management teams through 'advice networks' (Athanassiou & Nigh, 2000);
- the factors that mitigate against the international transfer of knowledge through expatriates (Smale & Riusala, 2004);
- the 'social capital' that accrues to international managers as a consequence of their boundary spanning roles (Kostova & Roth, 2003); and
- knowledge sharing through interpersonal cross-border relationships (Makela, 2004).

Attention has focused on the role played by both social networks and the superior cognitive processes characteristic of successful expatriates. As researchers, we need richer and more complex tools to help expatriates and domestic members of international teams to be effective. Athanassiou and Nigh (1999, 2000, 2002) argued that this means conceptualizing, measuring, and analysing the complexity of interpersonal processes within global firms by using new research methods.

For many years researchers such as Sackmann (1991, 1992) and Zack (1999) have argued that we have to better understand different kinds of cultural knowledge:

- declarative (or dictionary) knowledge, concerning the way that managers define what something is, i.e., the means by which they classify objects;
- directory (or process or procedural) knowledge, concerning the information that describes how things are done;
- prescriptive (or recipe) knowledge, concerning information about how things should *preferably* be done;
- axiomatic knowledge, reflective of fundamental beliefs and attributed causes (why something happens) that cannot be reduced any further.

By implication, an international mindset must display insight into each of these forms or types of knowledge. Not surprisingly, research at the individual level tends to demonstrate the deep persistence of nationality and considerable stickiness in the transfer of knowledge from one culture to another. First, even within an apparently like-minded cadre, team, or network there are often different logics at play. For example, when HR professionals are asked about the perceived relevance of specific HR practices to the competitive advantage of their firms, there is a clear imprint of nationality. Sparrow and Budhwar (1997) analysed the practices that HR professionals from around the world rated as contributing to the competitive advantage of their firms. Analysis of the responses across the 13 countries showed that respondents 'packaged' HR practices into a series of *recipes* (prescriptions of how they believed things should be done). These recipes concerned: the range of practices that created a sense of empowerment through changes to organization structure; the range of practices that accelerated the pace at which HR could be developed within the firm; the practices to develop an employee welfare; an efficiency orientation; and a long-term perspective. The recipes were the product of a complex range of causal factors including such things as the role of the state, financial sectors, national systems of education and training, labour relations systems, and the influence of cultural value orientations (Whitley, 1999), but clearly HR managers had created their unique logics of action that guide management practice in each country. The challenge for I/O psychologists is to understand which parts of the *recipe knowledge* adopted can be influenced by individual level factors or, more to the point, changed once the manager operates outside the context of his or her indigenous national business system (Sparrow, 2005b).

A second and equally complex problem is that even when managers apparently agree about the importance and relevance of a particular practice or intervention, there may in practice be very different cognitive maps within the group about the resultant cause-and-effect processes inherent in any intervention. Their axiomatic knowledge, or beliefs, is reflective of very different assumptions about fundamental cause and effect relationships. There are, for example, marked differences in perceptions around any best practice, i.e., why such a practice might be important and the particular outcomes anticipated. To explore this, Budhwar and Sparrow (2002b) examined the revealed cognitive maps of 48 British and Indian HR professionals around the issues of integration of HR with the wider business strategy and devolvement of HR to line managers, using a visual card sort approach (Daniels, Chernatony, & Johnson, 1995). Analysis of the participants' causal belief structures, using transcribed data from the interviews, which was submitted to the CMAP-2 computer package (Laukkenan, 1994, 1998), identified 571 natural language units—303 from Indian managers and 268 from British managers—for the two themes of which there were 432 standard causal units shared by both Indian and British managers. The study showed that at a 'macro' level managerial thinking about the topic of HRM, especially with regard to strategic concepts such as integration and devolvement, was converging. However, at a 'micro' level there was still a strong divergence in managerial thinking about HRM practices. Although in surveys both sets of HR professionals had rated these policies as being extremely important, when cognitive mapping techniques were used to reveal why they were important and what the assumed cause-and-effect outcomes would be, the professionals in the two countries were working to fundamentally different logics.

Understanding that there are different logics at play, and unravelling the content of these, are clearly just the first contributions that I/O psychologists can make at this level. In the context of global management, Baba, Gluesing, Ratner, and Wagner (2004) argued that we now must consider deeper issues. Does the evidence suggest that *knowledge* (procedural, directory, and recipe) and *beliefs* (i.e., axiomatic knowledge) should be considered as separate entities, or must they be viewed as intertwined? There are competing views on this question among the cognitive scientists, let alone among international management researchers. Work on team cognition considers that knowledge and belief can be separated out from each other, such that knowledge may be considered as objective and beliefs as more subjective (e.g., Wiersema & Bantel, 1992). Set against this, a more social-constructionist perspective considers that all four forms of knowledge noted above *are built into cognitive structures*. The latter perspective assumes that there are complex networks of associations between cognitive schemata that reflect actual experience and memory. These cognitive structures are then connected to beliefs, and the beliefs in turn are 'validated' by cultural experiences.

This is not just some quaint academic debate. Depending on the answer, firms might be advised by I/O psychologists to adopt very different tools, techniques, processes, and mechanisms. Baba et al. (2004) demonstrated this by questioning the efficacy of globally distributed teams as a vehicle for knowledge sharing. While global teams have created an explosion in the quantity and complexity of interrelationships among the various national systems that exist inside international firms, their study challenges some assumptions about the performance gains that might arise from this coordinating mechanism. Baba et al. examined the process through which the cognitive structures of globally distributed team members became more similar to one another over time, using a longitudinal and ethnographic research method. They studied six teams in a US manufacturing multinational from 1993 to 2001, reporting the findings of having tracked one of these teams over a 14-month period, a 20-person team operating across one US and six European and Asian sites. Their findings showed that four things were necessary for effective change in cognitions—all of which they argued were missing from global teams (thereby reinforcing the persistence of cognitive differences):

(1) observation of others at work;
(2) conversations that include joint problem solving;
(3) testing of ideas; and
(4) resolving of discrepancies.

They showed that beliefs about overall business models were culturally grounded. These beliefs were mutually contradictory, which meant that team members rejected certain aspects of knowledge held by others (especially declarative and procedural types of knowledge). Knowledge-sharing processes in themselves do not produce shared cognitions; rather, team members have to undergo separate but parallel learning experiences in a common context. Hidden knowledge in remote sites has to be surfaced, often by third party mediators or knowledge brokers. Issues of self-interest and power (historical, cultural, and linguistic issues can be exploited by team leaders to further their own agendas) have to be shifted towards more collaborative and task-interdependent work processes. In a cross-cultural context, sharing of knowledge has to include the beliefs upon which evaluative knowledge is based. Using a biological and genetic metaphor, Baba et al. (2004) argued that evaluative knowledge acts as a control gene that regulates whether other forms of more structural knowledge will be switched on (accepted and integrated into the team's cognitive structure) or switched off (rejected). It would be nice to see a more rigorous testing of such propositions.

In effect, in order to facilitate better global management, I/O psychologists have to help top teams and those individuals involved in the eventual execution of a global strategy to understand the basis of their views. This requires the development of what Martin and Beaumont (2001) and previous researchers have called strategic discourses inside firms—institutional changes that serve to 'sediment' messages about any particular change into the mindset of local employees and habitualize other parts of the firm towards a new strategy.

CONCLUDING REMARKS

The relative lack of existing knowledge from a comparative perspective and the need to address some of the methodological issues discussed throughout this review has become more pressing, for we now find that as the IHRM field has advanced, two developments have occurred, opening up new areas of investigation for I/O psychologists:

1. There has begun to be some convergence of interests between the fields of IHRM and CHRM. Although originally CHRM and IHRM were distinct fields of study, the increasing reliance by firms on strategic partnerships and joint ventures, coupled with a trend towards a localization of management, has made it more important to understand *how HRM is delivered in different country contexts*. Consequently, there has been a degree of convergence in thinking and also theorizing within the CHRM and IHRM fields (Budhwar & Sparrow, 2002a).

2. More attention is being given to the strategic nature of IHRM activity. Firms have continued to globalize at a rapid pace. Information and communication technologies are transforming organizational structures and business processes, further breaking down organizational and geographic boundaries. The advent of the internet, e-commerce, and e-enablement of management is further increasing the international flow of goods and services and, therefore, the pace at which internationalization is impacting on the conduct of HRM. Businesses, whether large or small, are finding competition increasing at rapid rates as more and more competitors enter traditional markets. Organizations are realizing that attention to foreign markets and competitors have become central to survival. This has provided a new lease of life to the work of I/O psychologists, where rigorous research can contribute fundamental knowledge that might facilitate internationalization strategies.

Søderberg and Holden (2002, p. 111) are among many contemporary commentators who believe that the time has now come to move beyond a cross-cultural management perspective. They argued

> ... the thinking which still takes the nation-state as point of departure [does] not fully resonate with the interactions of transnational corporations and organizations in a still more globalized economy. At the same time it seems that many engaged in cross-cultural management, teaching and training are lagging behind the changes in the world economy and in the nature of management work.

They noted that there have been calls for a more dynamic research agenda for a while. This resonates with the remarks of Segalla, Fischer, and Sandner (2000, p. 42), who criticized '... *the cross-cultural knowledge industry* for its slowness to develop new, business-specific information useful to current problems that ... firms face ... [such as] cross-border integration problems associated with international mergers, acquisitions, joint ventures and alliances'. As observed by Bartholomew and Adler (1996, p. 26): '... the academic community, by itself, has remained primarily dedicated to single culture and comparative research which, while still necessary, is no longer sufficient—and therefore no longer as relevant—for the competitive environment of today's transnational firm'.

In concluding this review I turn finally to outline some of the globalization processes that warrant study and highlight some of the relevant work in areas that seem particularly attractive to I/O psychologists, notably the study of international mindset, global knowledge transfer, and adjustment processes in IEs. IHRM is a rapidly changing field and we have seen very significant developments taking place *within* international firms, which in turn help to set the context for much psychological work within the realm of international management. For example, in 2001 the UK's Chartered Institute of Personnel and Development commissioned research to study the impact of globalization on the HR profession, with the project reporting in 2004 (see Brewster, Sparrow, & Harris, 2005; Sparrow, Brewster, & Harris, 2004). One of the central findings of the research was that an underlying shift in global thinking can be seen in the actions of several leading multinational and domestic firms. They are being driven by the need to remain innovative in what may be contracting and rationalizing markets or markets that are being shaken up by new entrants and new competitive behaviours. Initiatives aimed at improving temporal, functional, or financial flexibility are being introduced side by side with integrated programmes intended to link work practices to the need to deliver radical cost improvements. In increasing flexibility, firms also want to change the nature of employee identification and their sense of involvement, and this changed identity knows few national borders. IHR functions are increasingly being required to help their firms to manage a number of changes (for each change, I note some areas of attention for

I/O psychologists in brackets), namely:

- the consequences of global business process redesign, the pursuit of a global centre of excellence strategy, and the global redistribution and relocation of work that this often entails (reactions to downsizing and job insecurity in different cultural contexts, dynamics of the psychological contract across cultures);
- the absorption of acquired businesses, merging of existing operations on a global scale, the staffing of strategic integration teams, and attempts to develop and harmonize core HR processes within these merged businesses (the cross-cultural applicability of merger syndrome, bereavement, and work role transition theory);
- the rapid start-up of international operations and requirement to oversee organizational development as they mature through different stages of the business life cycle and the changing capabilities of international operations with associated needs for the up-skilling of local operations and greater complexity of international job roles (the cognitive components of international mindset and global leadership);
- the need to capitalize on the potential that technology affords for the delivery of HR through shared services, on a regional and global basis, while also ensuring that local social and cultural insights are duly considered when it is imperative to do so (the impact of culture on the various linkages outlined in Figure 5.2 that create organizational effectiveness);
- learning about operating through formal or informal global HR networks, acting as knowledge brokers across international operations, and avoiding a 'one best way' HR philosophy (work on knowledge management processes within networks, the social and political capital of international managers, the international management teams, and mutual adjustment processes);
- offering a compelling value proposition to the employees of the firm, and understanding and then marketing the brand that the firm represents across global labour markets that in practice have different values and different perceptions (the impact of culture on motivation, cross-cultural differences in employee engagement behaviours, generational changes in values, and person–organization fit processes).

Sparrow et al. (2004) drew two key conclusions about the role of the HR function in international firms. First, the added value of the HR function in an international firm lies in its ability to manage the delicate balance between overall coordinated systems and sensitivity to local needs, including cultural differences, in a way that aligns with both business needs and senior management philosophy. Second, there is a distinction to be made now between IHRM and global HRM. Traditionally, IHRM has been about managing an international workforce—the expatriates, frequent commuters, cross-cultural team members, and specialists involved in international knowledge transfer. Global HRM, in contrast, is not simply about covering these staff around the world. It now concerns managing IHRM activities through the application of global rule-sets.

In the context of these developments inside organizations, once we begin to adopt multilevel theories in the field of international management, we not only need to understand the linkages between variables that operate across different levels of analysis, but we also need to relate our analyses to the dominant theories and perspectives of each level. I have argued that psychologists carrying out work at the individual level of analysis have to be cognizant of these frequently non-psychological theories if they are to be effective researchers in the international management field. I also noted that there are dynamic processes taking place inside organizations that are largely the result of globalization processes and have related this to Erez and Gati's (2004) call to incorporate both top-down and bottom-up culture change processes in our research. These processes of globalization (and the blocks to such processes) need to be incorporated into our theorizing. Moreover, some of these processes also warrant specific study as new lines of enquiry by I/O psychologists, for we can make some powerful contributions to understanding their effects.

REFERENCES

Alexashin, Y. & Blenkinsopp, J. (2005). Changes in Russian managerial values: A test of the convergence hypothesis. *International Journal of Human Resource Management*, **16** (3), 427–444.

Andolšek, D.M. & Štebe, J. (2004). Multinational perspectives on work values and commitment. *International Journal of Cross Cultural Management*, 4 (2), 181–209.

Ardichvili, A. & Gasparishvili, A. (2001). Socio-cultural values, internal work culture and leadership styles in four post-communist countries: Russia, Georgia, Kazakhstan and the Kyrgyz Republic. *International Journal of Cross Cultural Management*, 1 (2), 227–242.

Ashkanasy, N.M., Trevor-Roberts, E., & Earnshaw, L. (2002). The Anglo Cluster: legacy of the British empire. *Journal of World Business*, 37, 28–39.

Athanassiou, N. & Nigh, D. (1999). The impact of company internationalisation on top management team advice networks: A tacit knowledge perspective. *Strategic Management Journal*, 19 (1), 83–92.

Athanassiou, N. & Nigh, D. (2000). Internationalisation, tacit knowledge and the top management team of MNCs. *Journal of International Business Studies*, 31 (3), 471–488.

Athanassiou, N. & Nigh, D. (2002). The impact of the top management team's international business experience on the firm's internationalisation: Social networks at work. *Management International Review*, 42 (2), 157–182.

Aycan, Z. (2000). Cross-cultural industrial and organizational psychology: contributions, past developments and future directions. *Journal of Cross-Cultural Psychology*, 31, 110–128.

Aycan, Z., Kanungo, R.N., Mendonca, M., Yu, K., Deller, J., Stahl, G., & Kurshid, A. (2000). Impact of culture on human resource management practices: A 10 country comparison. *Applied Psychology: An International Review*, 49 (1), 192–221.

Baba, M.L., Gluesing, J., Ratner, H., & Wagner, K.H. (2004). The contexts of knowing: Natural history of a globally distributed team. *Journal of Organisational Behaviour*, 25 (5), 547–587.

Bandura, A. (2001). Social cognitive theory: An agentic perspective. *Annual Review of Psychology* (Vol. 52, pp. 1–26). Palo Alto, CA: Annual Reviews Inc.

Bandura, A. (2002). Social cognitive theory in cultural context. *Applied Psychology: An International Review*, 51 (2), 269–290.

Barkema, H.G., Shenkar, O., Vermeulen, F., & Bell, J.H.J. (1997). Working abroad, working with others. How firms learn to operate international joint ventures. *Academy of Management Journal*, 40 (2), 426–442.

Barney, J.B. (1991). Firm resources and sustained competitive advantage. *Journal of Management*, 17, 99–120.

Bartholomew, S. & Adler, N. (1996). Building networks and crossing borders: The dynamics of knowledge generation in a transnational world. In P. Joynt & M. Warner (Eds), *Managing across cultures: Issues and perspectives* (pp. 7–32). London: International Thomson.

Bartlett, C.A. & Ghoshal, S. (1989). *Managing across borders: The transnational solution.* Boston, MA: Harvard Business School Press.

Berger, P.L. & Luckmann, T. (1996). *The social construction of reality.* New York: Doubleday.

Berry, J.W. (1980). Social and cultural change. In H.C. Triandis & R.W. Brislin (Eds), *Handbook of cross cultural psychology* (Vol. 5, pp. 211–280). Boston: Allyn & Bacon.

Berry, J.W., Poortinga, Y.H., Segall, M.H., & Dasen, P.R. (1992). *Cross-cultural psychology: Research and application.* New York: Cambridge University Press.

Bhagat, R.S., Kedia, B.L., Harveston, P.D., & Triandis, H.C. (2002). Cultural variations in the cross-border transfer of organizational knowledge: An integrative framework. *Academy of Management Review*, 27 (2), 204–221.

Bing, J.W. (2004). Hofstede's consequences: The impact of his work on consulting and business practices. *Academy of Management Executive*, 18 (1), 80–87.

Björkman, I. (2005). International human resource management research and institutional theory. In I. Björkman & G. Stahl (Eds), *Handbook of research into international HRM*. London: Edward Elgar.

Black, J.S., Mendenhall, M., & Oddou, G. (1991). Toward a comprehensive model of international adjustment: An integration of multiple theoretical perspectives. *Academy of Management Review*, 16, 291–317.

Bonache, J. & Brewster, C. (2001). Knowledge transfer and the management of expatriation. *Thunderbird International Business Review*, 43 (1), 145–168.

Boyacigiller, N.A., Kleinberg, J., Phillips, M.E., & Sackmann, S. (2003). Conceptualising culture: Elucidating the streams of research in international cross-cultural management. In B.J. Punnett & O. Shenkar (Eds), *Handbook of international management research* (2nd edn, pp. 99–167). Ann Arbor, MI: University of Michigan Press.

Brewster, C., Sparrow, P.R., & Harris, H. (2005). Towards a new model of globalising human resource management. *International Journal of Human Resource Management*, 16 (6), 953–974.

Briscoe, D. & Schuler, R.S. (2004). *International human resource management* (2nd edn). New York: Routledge.

Budhwar, P.S. & Sparrow, P.R. (2002a). An integrative framework for understanding cross national human resource management principles. *Human Resource Management Review*, 10 (7), 1–28.

Budhwar, P.S. & Sparrow, P.R. (2002b). Strategic HRM through the cultural looking glass: Mapping the cognition of British and Indian managers. *Organisation Studies*, 23 (4), 599–638.

Cerdin, J.-L. (2002). *L'expatriation* (2nd edn). Paris: Editions d'Organization.

Cerdin, J.-L. (2003). International diffusion of HRM practices: The role of expatriates. *Beta: Scandinavian Journal of Business Research*, **17** (1), 48–58.

Cerdin, J.-L. & Dubouloy, M. (2004). Expatriation as a maturation opportunity: A psychoanalytical approach based on 'copy and paste'. *Human Relations*, **57** (8), 957–981.

Chao, G.T. (2000). Multilevel issues and culture: An integrative view. In K.J. Klein & S.W.J. Kozlowski (Eds), *Multilevel theory, research and methods in organizations: Foundations, extensions and new directions*. San Francisco: Jossey-Bass.

Chatterjee, S.R. & Pearson, C.A.L. (2000). Indian managers in transition: Orientations, work goals, values and ethics. *Management International Review*, **40** (1), 81–95.

Chatterjee, S.R. & Pearson, C.A.L. (2002). Work goals of Asian managers: Field evidence from Singapore, Malaysia, India, Thailand, Brunei and Mongolia. *International Journal of Cross Cultural Management*, **2** (2), 251–268.

Cherrington, D.J., Condie, S.J., & England, J.L. (1979). Age and work values. *Academy of Management Journal*, **22**, 617–623.

Clugston, M., Howell, J.P., & Dorfman, P.W. (2000). Does cultural socialization predict multiple bases and foci of commitment? *Journal of Management*, **26**, 5–30.

Conway III, L.G., Ryder, A.G., Tweed, R.G., & Sokol, B.W. (2001). Intranational cultural variation: Exploring further implications of collectivism within the United States. *Journal of Cross-Cultural Psychology*, **32** (6), 681–697.

Coon, H.M. & Kemmelmeier, M. (2001). Cultural orientations in the United States: (Re) examining differences among ethnic groups. *Journal of Cross-Cultural Psychology*, **32** (3), 348–364.

Czerny, A. (2004). UK's foreign trawl continues. *People Management*, **10** (20), 7.

Daniels, K., Chernatony, K.L., & Johnson, G. (1995). Validating a method for mapping managers' mental models of competitive industry structures. *Human Relations*, **48**, 975–991.

DiMaggio, P.J. & Powell, W.W. (1983). The iron cage revisited: Institutional isomorphism and collective rationality in organizational fields. *American Sociological Review*, **48**, 147–160.

D'Iribarne, P. (2002). Motivating workers in emerging countries: Universal tools and local adaptations. *Journal of Organizational Behavior*, **23** (3), 243–257.

Dowling, P.J., Welch, D.E., & Schuler, R.S. (1998). *International human resource management. Managing people in a multinational context*. Cincinnati: South-Western College Publishing.

Earley, C. (1994). Self or group? Cultural effects of training on self-efficacy and performance. *Administrative Science Quarterly*, **39**, 89–117.

Earley, P.C. & Mosakowski, E. (1995). A framework for understanding experimental research in international and intercultural context. In B.J. Punnett & O. Shenkar (Eds), *Handbook of international management research* (pp. 83–114). London: Blackwell.

Erez, M. & Gati, E. (2004). A dynamic, multi-level model of culture: From the micro level of the individual to the macro level of a global culture. *Applied Psychology: An International Review*, **53** (4), 583–598.

Farh, J.L., Earley, P.C., & Lin, S.C. (1997). Impetus for action: A cultural analysis of justice and organizational citizenship behavior in Chinese society. *Administrative Science Quarterly*, **42**, 421–444.

Farmer, R.N. & Richman, B.N. (1965). *Comparative management and economic progress*. Homewood, IL: Irwin.

Fernández-Ballesteros, R., Díez-Nicolás, J., Caprara, G.V., Barbaranelli, C., & Bandura, A. (2002). Determinants and structural relation of perceived personal efficacy to perceived collective efficacy. *Applied Psychology: An International Review*, **51**, 107–125.

Fischer, R., Ferreira, M.C., Assmar, M.L., Redford, P., & Harb, C. (2005). Organizational behaviour across cultures: Theoretical and methodological issues for developing multi-level frameworks involving culture. *International Journal of Cross Cultural Management*, **5** (1), 27–48.

Freeman, M.A. & Bordia, P. (2001). Assessing alternative models of individualism and collectivism: A confirmatory factor analysis. *European Journal of Personality*, **15**, 105–121.

Fu, P.P., Kennedy, J., Tata, J., Yukl, G., Bond, M.H., Peng, T.K. et al. (2004). The impact of societal cultural values and individual social beliefs on the perceived effectiveness of managerial influence strategies: A meso approach. *Journal of International Business Studies*, **35**, 284–305.

Gabriel, Y. (2002). Organizations, management and psychoanalysis: An overview. *Journal of Managerial Psychology*, **5**, 348–65.

Gelade, G.A. & Young, S. (2005). Test of a service profit chain model in the retail banking sector. *Journal of Occupational and Organizational Psychology*, **78** (1), 1–22.

Giacobbe-Miller, J.K., Miller, D.J., Zhang, W., & Victorov, V.I. (2003). Country and organizational-level adaptation to foreign workplace ideologies: A comparative study of distributive justice values in China, Russia and the United States. *Journal of International Business Studies*, **34**, 389–406.

Glazer, S., Daniel, S.C., & Short, K.M. (2004). A study of the relationship between organizational commitment and human values in four countries. *Human Relations*, **57** (3), 323–345.

Graf, A. (2004). Screening and training inter-cultural competencies: Evaluating the impact of national culture on inter-cultural competencies. *International Journal of Human Resource Management*, **15** (6), 1124–1148.

Haire, M., Ghiselli, E.E., & Porter, L. (1966). *Managerial thinking: An international study*. New York: John Wiley & Sons.

Harpaz, I. (1990). The importance of work goals: An international perspective. *Journal of International Business Studies*, **21** (1), 75–93.

Harvey, M. & Novicevic, M.M. (2004). The development of political skill and political capital by global leaders through global assignments. *International Journal of Human Resource Management*, **15** (7), 1173–1188.

Hechanova, R., Beehr, T.A., & Christiansen, N.D. (2003). Antecedents and consequences of employees' adjustment to overseas assignment: A meta-analytic review. *Applied Psychology: An International Review*, **52** (2), 213–236.

Hodgkinson, G.P. & Sparrow, P.R. (2002). *The competent organization: A psychological analysis of the strategic management process*. Buckingham, UK: Open University Press.

Hofstede, G.H. (1980). *Culture's consequences: International differences in work-related values*. Beverly Hills, CA: Sage.

Hofstede, G. (1991). *Cultures and organizations: Software of the mind*. London: McGraw-Hill.

Hofstede, G.H. (1994). Management scientists are human. *Management Science*, **40**, 4–13.

Hofstede, G.H. (2001). *Culture's consequences: Comparing values, behaviours, institutions and organizations across nations*. Thousand Oaks, CA: Sage.

Hoppe, M.H. (2004). Introduction: Geert Hofstede's culture's consequences: International differences in work-related values and an interview with Geert Hofstede. *Academy of Management Executive*, **18** (1), 73–79.

House, R.J. et al. (2004). *Culture, leadership and organization: A globe study of 62 societies.* Thousand Oaks, CA: Sage.

House, R.J., Hanges, P.J., Ruiz-Quintanilla, S.A., Dorfman, P.W., Javidan, M., Dickson, M., Gupta, V., & GLOBE (1999). Cultural influences on leadership and organizations: Project GLOBE. In W.F. Mobley, M.J. Gessner, & V. Arnold (Eds), *Advances in global leadership* (Vol. 1, pp. 171–233). Stanford, CT: JAI Press.

House, R.J., Javidan, M., Hanges, P., & Dorfman, P. (2002). Understanding cultures and implicit leadership theories across the globe: An introduction to project GLOBE. *Journal of World Business*, **37**, 3–10.

Huang, X. & Van de Vliert, E. (2003a). Comparing work behaviours across cultures: A cross-level approach using multilevel modelling. *International Journal of Cross Cultural Management*, **3** (2), 167–182.

Huang, X. & Van de Vliert, E. (2003b). Where intrinsic job satisfaction fails to work: National moderators of intrinsic motivation. *Journal of Organizational Behavior*, **24** (2), 159–170.

Huang, X. & Van de Vliert, E. (2004). Job level and national culture as joint roots of job satisfaction. *Applied Psychology: An International Review*, **53** (3), 329–348.

Huff, L. & Kelley, L. (2003). Levels of organizational trust in individualist versus collectivist societies: A seven-nation study. *Organization Science*, **14** (1), 81–90.

Hui, M.K., Au, K., & Fock, H. (2004). Empowerment effects across cultures. *Journal of International Business Studies*, **35**, 46–60.

Inglehart, R., Basanez, M., & Moreno, A. (1998). *Human values and beliefs: A cross-cultural sourcebook.* Ann Arbor, MI: University of Michigan Press.

Kickul, J., Lester, S.W., & Belgio, E. (2004). Attitudinal and behavioural outcomes of psychological contract breach: A cross cultural comparison of the United States and Hong Kong Chinese. *International Journal of Cross Cultural Management*, **4** (2), 229–252.

Kim, K., Park, J.-H., & Prescott, J.E. (2003). The global integration of business functions: A study of multinational businesses in integrated global industries. *Journal of International Business Studies*, **34**, 327–344.

King, R.C. & Bu, N. (2005). Perceptions of the mutual obligations between employees and employers: A comparative study of new generation IT professionals in China and the United States. *International Journal of Human Resource Management*, **16** (1), 46–64.

Kirkman, B.L. & Shapiro, D.I. (2001). The impact of cultural values on job satisfaction and organizational commitment in self-managing work teams: The mediating role of employee resistance. *Academy of Management Journal*, **44** (3), 557–569.

Kirpal, S. (2004). Researching work identities in a European context. *Career Development International*, **9** (3), 199–221.

Klein, K.J. & Kozlowski, S.W.J. (Eds) (2000). *Multilevel theory, research and methods in organizations: Foundations, extensions and new directions.* San Francisco: Jossey-Bass.

Kleinberg, M.J. (1989). Cultural clash between managers: America's Japanese firms. In S.B. Prasad (Ed.), *Advances in international comparative management* (Vol. 4, pp. 221–244). Greenwich, CT: JAI Press.

Kopelman, R.E., Brief, A.P., & Guzzo, R.A. (1990). The role of climate and culture in productivity. In B. Schneider (Ed.), *Organizational climate and culture.* San Francisco: Jossey-Bass.

Koslowsky, M., Sagie, A., & Stashevsky, S. (2002). Introduction: Cultural relativism and universalism in organizational behaviours. *International Journal of Cross Cultural Management*, **2** (2), 131–135.

Kostova, T. & Roth, K. (2003). Social capital in multinational corporations and a micro–macro model of its formation. *Academy of Management Review*, **28** (2), 297–317.

Kwantes, C.T. (2003). Organizational citizenship and withdrawal behaviours in the USA and India: Does commitment make a difference? *International Journal of Cross Cultural Management*, **9** (1), 5–26.

Lachman, R. (1997). Taking another look at the Elephant: Are we still (half) blind? Comments on the cross-cultural analysis of achievement motivation by Sagie et al. (1996). *Journal of Organizational Behavior*, **18**, 317–321.

Lam, S.S.K., Schaubroeck, J., & Aryee, S. (2002). Relationship between organizational justice and employee work outcomes: A cross-national study. *Journal of Organizational Behavior*, **23** (1), 1–12.

Laukkanen, M. (1994). Comparative cause mapping of organizational cognitions. *Organization Science*, **5**, 322–343.

Laukkanen, M. (1998). Conducting causal mapping research: Opportunities and challenges. In C. Eden & J.-C. Spender (Eds), *Managerial and organizational cognition*. London: Sage.

Laurent, A. (1986). The cross-cultural puzzle of international human resource management. *Human Resource Management*, **25** (1), 91–102.

Lengnick-Hall, M.L. & Lengnick-Hall, C. (2005). International human resource management research and social network/social capital theory. In I. Björkman & G. Stahl (Eds), *Handbook of research into international HRM*. London: Edward Elgar.

Lin, N. (2001). Building a network theory of social capital. In N. Lin, K. Cook, & R.S. Burt (Eds), *Social capital: Theory and research* (pp. 3–29). New York: Aldine de Gruyter.

Loughlin, C. & Barling, J. (2001). Young worker's work values, attitudes and behaviors. *Journal of Occupational and Organizational Psychology*, **74** (4), 543–558.

Lundberg, C.D. & Peterson, M.F. (1994). The meaning of working in the US and Japanese local governments at three hierarchical levels. *Human Relations*, **47** (12), 1459–1487.

Makela, A.K. (2004). *The social capital of expatriates and repatriates: Knowledge sharing through interpersonal cross-border relationships.* Paper presented at EIASM Workshop on Expatriation, Brussels, 18–19 October.

Martin, G. & Beaumont, P. (2001). Transforming multinational enterprises: Towards a process model of strategic human resource management change. *International Journal of Human Resource Management*, **12** (8), 1234–1250.

Martin, J. & Siehl, C. (1983). Organizational culture and counter-culture: An uneasy symbiosis. *Organizational Dynamics*, **12** (2), 52–64.

Mathur, A., Zhang, Y., & Neelankavil, J.P. (2001). Critical managerial motivational factors: A cross cultural analysis of four culturally divergent countries. *International Journal of Cross Cultural Management*, **1** (3), 251–267.

Mayerhofer, H., Hartmann, L.C., Michelilitsch-Riedl, G., & Kollinger, I. (2004). Flex-patriate assignments: A neglected issue in global staffing. *International Journal of Human Resource Management*, **15** (8), 1371–1389.

Mayrhofer, W., Morley, M., & Brewster, C.B. (2004). Convergence, stasis, or divergence? In C.B. Brewster, W. Mayrhofer, & M. Morley (Eds), *Human resource management in Europe: Evidence of convergence?* (pp. 415–436). London: Elsevier Science.

Maznevski, M.L., DiStefano, J.J., Gomez, C.B., Noorderhaven, N.G., & Wu, P.C. (2002). Cultural dimensions at the individual level of analysis: The cultural orientation framework. *International Journal of Cross Cultural Management*, **2** (3), 275–298.

Mendenhall, M.E., Kühlman, T.M., Stahl, G., & Osland, J.S. (2002). Employee development and expatriate assignments. In M.J. Gannon & K.L. Newman (Eds), *Handbook of cross-cultural management*. London: Blackwell.

Menon, S.T. (2004). Introduction to ISSWOV Special Section: Culture's consequences for 21st century research and practice. *International Journal of Cross Cultural Management*, 4 (2), 135–140.

Morris, M.W. & Leung, K. (2000). Justice for all? Progress in research on cultural variation in the psychology of distributive and procedural justice. *Applied Psychology: An International Review*, 49 (1), 100–132.

Morris, S.S., Snell, S.A., & Wright, P.M. (2005). A resource-based view of international human resources: Towards a framework of integrative and creative capabilities. In I. Björkman & G. Stahl (Eds), *Handbook of research into international HRM*. London: Edward Elgar.

Morrison, A.J. (2000). Developing a global leadership model. *Human Resource Management*, 39 (2/3), 117–131.

Murphy-Berman, V. & Berman, J.J. (2002). Cross-cultural differences in perceptions of distributive justice: A comparison of Hong Kong and Indonesia. *Journal of Cross-Cultural Psychology*, 33 (2), 157–170.

Murtha, T.P., Lenway, S.A., & Bagozzi, R.P. (1998). Global mind-sets and cognitive shift in a complex multinational corporation. *Strategic Management Journal*, 19, 97–114.

Nyambegera, S., Daniels, K., & Sparrow, P.R. (2001). Why fit doesn't always matter: The impact of HRM and cultural fit on job involvement of Kenyan employees. *Applied Psychology: An International Review*, 50 (1), 109–140.

Nyambegera, S., Sparrow, P.R., & Daniels, K. (2000). The impact of cultural value orientations on individual HRM preferences in developing countries: Lessons from Kenyan organizations. *International Journal of Human Resource Management*, 11 (4), 639–663.

Ostroff, C. & Bowen, D.E. (2000). Moving HR to a higher level: HR practices and organizational effectiveness. In J.K. Klein & S.W.J. Kozlowski (Eds), *Multilevel theory, research and methods in organizations: Foundations, extensions and new directions* (pp. 211–266). San Francisco: Jossey-Bass.

Palich, L.E., Hom, P.W., & Griffeth, W. (1995). Managing in the international context: Testing the cultural generality of sources of commitment to multinational enterprises. *Journal of Management*, 21, 671–690.

Pastorelli, C., Caprara, G.V., Barbaranelli, C., Rola, J., Rorza, S., & Bandura, A. (2001). Structure of children's perceived self-efficacy: A cross-national study. *European Journal of Psychological Assessment*, 17, 87–97.

Peterson, M.F. & Smith, P.B. (2000). Meanings, organization and culture: Using sources of meaning to make sense of organizational events. In N. Ashkanasy, C.P.M. Wilderom, & M.F. Peterson (Eds), *Handbook of organizational culture and climate* (pp. 101–116). Thousand Oaks, CA: Sage.

Pfeffer, J. & Salancik, G. (1978). *The external control of organizations: A resource dependence perspective*. New York: Harper & Row.

Pineda, R.C. & Whitehead, C.J. (1997). The effects of ethnic group culture on managerial task activities. *Group and Organization Management*, 22 (1), 31–52.

Ramamoorthy, N. & Flood, P.C. (2004). Individualism/collectivism, perceived task interdependence and teamwork attitudes among Irish blue-collar employees: A test of the main and moderating effects. *Human Relations*, 57 (3), 347–366.

Robinson, W.S. (1950). Ecological correlations and behavior of individuals. *American Sociological Review*, 15, 351–357.

Roe, R., Zinovieva, I.L., Dienes, E., & Ten Horn, L.A. (2000). A comparison of work motivation in Bulgaria, Hungary, and the Netherlands: Test of a model. *Applied Psychology: An International Review*, 49 (4), 658–687.

Ronen, S. & Shenkar, O. (1985). Clustering countries on attitudinal dimensions: A review and synthesis. *Academy of Management Review*, 10 (3), 434–454.

Rousseau, D.M. & Schalk, R. (Eds) (2000). *Psychological contracts in employment: Cross-national perspectives*. Thousand Oaks, CA: Sage.

Sackmann, S.A. (1991). *Cultural knowledge in organisations: Exploring the collective mind.* Newbury Park, CA: Sage.

Sackmann, S.A. (1992). Culture and sub-cultures: An analysis of organisational knowledge. *Administrative Science Quarterly*, 37, 140–161.

Sackmann, S.A. (Ed.) (1997). *Cultural complexity in organizations: Inherent contrasts and contradictions.* Newbury Park, CA: Sage.

Sackmann, S.A. & Phillips, M.E. (2004). Contextual influences on culture research: Shifting assumptions for new workplace realities. *International Journal of Cross Cultural Management*, 4 (3), 370–390.

Sagie, A. & Elizur, D. (1998). Taking another look at cross-cultural research: Rejoinder to Lachman (1997). *Journal of Organizational Behavior*, 19, 421–427.

Schein, E.H. (1992). *Organizational culture and leadership.* San Francisco: Jossey-Bass.

Schneider, S.C. & Asakawa, K. (1995). American and Japanese expatriate adjustment: A psychoanalytic perspective. *Human Relations*, 48, 1109–1127.

Schwartz, S.H. (1992). Universals in the content and structure of values: Theoretical advances and empirical tests in 20 countries. In M.P. Zanna (Ed.), *Advances in experimental social psychology* (pp. 1–65). San Diego, CA: Academic Press.

Schwartz, S.H. (1994). Beyond individualism/collectivism: New cultural dimensions of values. In U. Kim, H.C. Triandis, C. Kagitcibasi, S.C. Choie, & G. Yoon (Eds), *Individualism and collectivism: Theory, method and applications* (pp. 85–119). Thousand Oaks, CA: Sage.

Schwartz, S.H. (1999). Cultural value differences: Some implications for work. *Applied Psychology: An International Review*, 48, 23–48.

Schwartz, S.H. & Bardi, A. (2001). Value hierarchies across cultures: Taking a similarity perspective. *Journal of Cross-Cultural Psychology*, 32 (3), 268–290.

Schwartz, S.H. & Roz, M. (1995). Values in the West: A theoretical and empirical challenge to the individualism–collectivism cultural dimension. *World Psychology*, 1, 91–122.

Schwartz, S.H. & Sagie, G. (2000). Value consensus and importance: A cross-national study. *Journal of Cross-Cultural Psychology*, 32, 465–497.

Segalla, M., Fischer, I., & Sandner, K. (2000). Making cross-cultural research relevant to European corporate integration: Old problem—new approach? *European Management Journal*, 18 (1), 38–51.

Smale, A. & Riusala, K. (2004). *Predicting stickiness factors in the international transfer of knowledge through expatriates.* Paper presented at EIASM Workshop on Expatriation, Brussels, 18–19 October.

Smith, P.B., Fischer, R., & Sale, N. (2001a). Cross-cultural industrial and organizational psychology. In C.L. Cooper & I.T. Robertson (Eds), *International review of industrial and organizational psychology* (Vol. 16, pp. 147–194). New York: John Wiley & Sons.

Smith, P.B., Harb, C., Lonner, W.J., & Van de Vijver, F.J.R. (2001b). *The Journal of Cross-Cultural Psychology* between 1993 and 2000: Looking back and looking ahead. *Journal of Cross-Cultural Psychology*, 32 (1), 9–17.

Smith, P.B. & Peterson, M.F., with Ahmad, A.H., Akande, D., Anderson, J.A. et al. (2005). Demographic effects on the use of vertical sources of guidance by managers in widely differing cultural contexts. *International Journal of Cross Cultural Management*, 5 (1), 5–26.

Smith, P.B., Peterson, M.F., & Schwartz, S.H. with Ahmad, A.H., Akande, D., Andersen, J.A. et al. (2002). Cultural values, sources of guidance, and their relevance to managerial behaviour: A 47-nation study. *Journal of Cross-Cultural Psychology*, 33 (2), 188–208.

Smith, P.B., Peterson, M.F., & Wang, Z.M. (1996). The manager as mediator of alternative meanings. *Journal of International Business Studies*, 27, 115–137.

Smola, K.W. & Sutton, C.D. (2002). Generational differences: Revisiting generational work values for the new millennium. *Journal of Organizational Behavior*, 23, 363–382.

Søderberg, A.-M. & Holden, N. (2002). Rethinking cross cultural management in a globalising business world. *International Journal of Cross Cultural Management*, 2 (1), 103–121.

Sparrow, P.R. (1998). Re-appraising psychological contracting: Lessons for employee development from cross-cultural and occupational psychological research. *International Studies in Management and Organization*, 28 (1), 30–63.

Sparrow, P.R. (2001). Developing diagnostics for high performance organization cultures. In S. Cartwright, C. Cooper, & C. Earley (Eds), *International handbook of culture and climate*. New York: John Wiley & Sons.

Sparrow, P.R. (2005a). *International recruitment, selection and assessment*. London: Chartered Institute of Personnel and Development.

Sparrow, P.R. (2005b). Global human resource management. In P.R Jackson & M. Shams (Eds), *Developments in work and organizational psychology*. London: Elsevier Science.

Sparrow, P.R. (2005c). Knowledge management in global organizations. In I. Björkman & G. Stahl (Eds), *Handbook of research into international HRM*. London: Edward Elgar.

Sparrow, P.R. & Braun, W. (2005). Human resource strategy in international context. In M.M. Harris (Ed.), *Handbook of research in international human resource management*. New York: Lawrence Erlbaum.

Sparrow, P.R., Brewster, C., & Harris, H. (2004). *Globalising human resource management*. London: Routledge.

Sparrow, P.R. & Cooper, C.L. (2003). *The employment relationship: Key challenges for HR*. London: Butterworth-Heinemann.

Sparrow, P.R. & Marchington, M. (1998). *HRM: The new agenda*. London: Prentice-Hall.

Sparrow, P.R. & Wu, P.C. (1998). How much do national value orientations really matter? Predicting HRM preferences of Taiwanese employees. *Employee Relations: the International Journal*, 20 (1), 26–56.

Spector, P.E., Cooper, C.L., & Sparks, K. with Bernin, P., Büssing, A., Dewe, P. et al. (2001). An international study of the psychometric properties of the Hofstede Values Survey Module 1994: A comparison of individual and country/province level results. *Applied Psychology: An International Review*, 50 (2), 269–281.

Spini, D. (2003). Measurement equivalence of 10 value types from the Schwartz Value Survey across 21 countries. *Journal of Cross-Cultural Psychology*, 34 (1), 3–23.

Suutari, V. (2002). Global leader development: An emerging research agenda. *Career Development International*, 7 (4), 218–233.

Tajfel, H. (1981). *Human groups and social categories: Studies in social psychology*. New York: Cambridge University Press.

Tallman, S. & Fladmoe-Lindquist, K. (2002). Internationalization, globalization and capability-based strategy. *California Management Review*, 45 (1), 116–135.

Tata, J., Fu, P.P., & Wu, R. (2003). An examination of procedural justice principles in China and the US. *Asia Pacific Journal of Management*, 20 (2), 205–215.

Thomas, D.C. & Au, K. (2002). The effect of cultural differences on behavioral responses to low job satisfaction. *Journal of International Business Studies*, **33** (2), 309–326.

Thomas, D.C., Au, K., & Ravlin, E.C. (2003). Cultural variation and the psychological contract. *Journal of Organizational Behavior*, **24** (5), 451–462.

Triandis, H.C. (1972). *The analysis of subjective culture*. New York: John Wiley & Sons.

Triandis, H.C. (2001). Individualism–collectivism and personality. *Journal of Personality*, **69** (6), 907–924.

Triandis, H.C. (2004). The many dimensions of culture. *Academy of Management Executive*, **18** (1), 88–93.

Trice, H.M. & Beyer, J.M. (1993). *The cultures of work organizations*. Englewood Cliffs, NJ: Prentice-Hall.

Trompenaars, F. (1993). *Riding the waves of culture: Understanding diversity in global business*. Chicago, IL: Irwin.

Trompenaars, F. & Hampden-Turner, C. (1998). *Riding the waves of culture: Understanding diversity in global business* (2nd edn). New York: McGraw-Hill.

Vandenberghe, C., Stinglhamber, F., Bentein, K., & Delhaise, T. (2001). An examination of the cross-cultural validity of a multidimensional model of commitment in Europe. *Journal of Cross-Cultural Psychology*, **32** (3), 322–347.

Van de Vijver, F.J.R. & Poortinga, Y.H. (2002). Structural equivalence in multilevel research. *Journal of Cross-Cultural Psychology*, **33**, 141–156.

Van Vianen, A.E.M., de Pater, I.E., Kristof-Brown, A.L., & Johnson, E.C. (2004). Fitting in: Surface- and deep-level cultural differences and expatriates' adjustment. *Academy of Management Journal*, **47** (5), 697–709.

Werner, S. (2002). Recent developments in international management research: A review of 20 top management journals. *Journal of Management*, **28** (3), 277–305.

Westwood, R. & Lok, P. (2003). The meaning of work in Chinese contexts: A comparative study. *International Journal of Cross Cultural Management*, **3** (2), 139–166.

Westwood, R., Sparrow, P.R., & Leung, A. (2001). Challenges to the psychological contract in Hong Kong. *International Journal of Human Resource Management*, **12** (4), 621–651.

Whetten, D.A. & Godfrey, P.C. (Eds) (1998). *Identity in organizations*. Thousand Oaks, CA: Sage.

Whitley, R.D. (1999). *Divergent capitalisms: The social structuring and change of business systems*. Oxford: Oxford University Press.

Wiersema, M.F. & Bantel, K.A. (1992). Top team demography and corporate strategic change. *Academy of Management Journal*, **35**, 91–121.

Wu, P.C. & Sparrow, P.R. (2002). *Influence of cultural values and work value/job satisfaction fit on organizational commitment*. Paper presented at US Academy of Management Conference, August, Denver.

Zack, M. (1999). Managing codified knowledge. *Sloan Management Review*, Summer: 45–58.

Zimmermann, A., Holman, D., & Sparrow, P.R. (2003). Unravelling adjustment mechanisms: Adjustment of German expatriates to intercultural interactions, work, and living conditions in the People's Republic of China. *International Journal of Cross Cultural Management*, **3** (1), 45–66.

Zimmermann, A. & Sparrow, P.R. (in press). Mutual adjustment processes in international teams: Lessons for the study of expatriation. *International Studies in Management and Organisation*.

Chapter 6

WOMEN IN MANAGEMENT: AN UPDATE ON THEIR PROGRESS AND PERSISTENT CHALLENGES

Karen S. Lyness and Jolie M.B. Terrazas
Department of Psychology, Baruch College,
City University of New York, USA

In recent years significant numbers of women have moved into management positions in many countries. For example, in private sector organizations in the USA the proportion of women managers and officials has increased from 29% in 1990 to 36% in 2002 (United States Equal Employment Opportunity Commission, 2004). Also, recent international data indicated that women generally held between 20% and 40% of managerial jobs in most countries where data were available, and that women held a larger share of managerial jobs in North America, South America, and Eastern Europe than in East Asia, South Asia, and the Middle East (International Labour Office, 2004). Nevertheless, in almost all of these countries women were still notably under-represented in managerial jobs in comparison to their proportion in the overall labor market (International Labour Office, 2004).

As women have moved into management positions, researchers have compared experiences, behaviors, and attitudes of women and men managers, and have also examined glass ceiling barriers that continue to impede women's advancement into senior level management positions. In this chapter we summarize recent literature about women in management, with a focus on their progress and how women managers' experiences compare to those of their male counterparts. In addition, we describe persistent challenges for women managers, such as societally based stereotypes and assumptions, male-dominated management hierarchies, limited job opportunities, and difficulties associated with managing competing demands from family and other non-work responsibilities. In trying to understand why women's progress in advancing into senior management positions has been so slow, we think that it is important to examine whether women are perceived to have key characteristics, such as leadership

International Review of Industrial and Organizational Psychology, 2006, Volume 21
Edited by G.P. Hodgkinson and J.K. Ford. © 2006 John Wiley & Sons, Ltd.

ability, that are needed to succeed as senior managers. We will review recent theories and empirical studies that are relevant to these issues, followed by a consideration of national culture variables that are related to women's management experiences and advancement. In addition, we will review facilitators of women's advancement that might offset some of the gender-related challenges they face. Finally, we conclude with ideas about future research that is needed to further our understanding of these issues.

WOMEN'S PROGRESS IN ATTAINING MANAGEMENT POSITIONS

As we noted earlier, women's representation in managerial jobs has not always kept pace with their representation in the overall workforce in most countries (International Labour Office, 2004). International statistics indicated that the USA might be an exception to this pattern, because women made up about 47% of the labor force in 2002, and women also held 46% of the managerial, legislative, and administrative jobs (ISCO-1968, Major group 2, Table 2C) (International Labour Office, 2003). However, more detailed US data that included separate statistics for management positions shows that although women made up 46.5% of the labor force in 2004, they held less than 37% of the management positions (United States Department of Labor Bureau of Labor Statistics, 2004). These data suggest that, based on more specific information, women's representation in US management positions is lower than their proportion in the labor force.

In most other industrialized countries there is a noticeable gap between women's representation in the workforce and their representation in managerial and related positions. For example, in Canada women made up 46% of the labor force, but held only 35% of managerial positions in 2001 (Statistics Canada, 2002). Similar trends are evident in European countries where women's representation in the labor force was generally larger than their representation within the ranks of senior officials, managers, and legislators (ISCO-88, Major group 1, Table 2C) (International Labour Office, 2003). For instance, in 2002 women's representation in the labor force compared to their representation among managerial and related jobs was 45% versus 31% for the UK, 48% vs 31% for Sweden, 43% vs 26% for the Netherlands, and 38% vs 21% for Italy (ISCO-88, Major group 1, Table 2C) (International Labour Office, 2003). In addition, women comprised 44% of the total labor force in Australia but held only 35% of the managerial and related jobs in 2002 (ISCO-88, Major group 1, Table 2C) (International Labour Office, 2003). Among industrialized countries, one of the largest gender gaps is in Japan, where women made up 41% of the workforce but held less than 9% of the administrative and managerial positions in 2001 (ISCO-1968, Major group 2,

Table 2C) (International Labour Office, 2003). These statistics show that although women represent close to half of the labor force in many industrialized countries, their representation in managerial and related jobs is generally much smaller. Moreover, even among industrialized countries, there is considerable variation in the proportion of managerial jobs held by women.

Vertical Segregation of Management Jobs and 'Glass Ceilings'

A close examination suggests that even though women have made some progress at moving into management, they are still not comparably represented across all types of management jobs. In particular, there is evidence of vertical and horizontal segregation of management positions in many countries. Vertical segregation refers to the fact that when women attain management positions, they are typically found in low or middle levels of the management hierarchy, and the majority of senior level management positions are still held by men (e.g., Blau, Ferber, & Winkler, 2002; International Labour Office, 2004; Jacobs, 1999). This is often referred to as the 'glass ceiling' for women, suggesting that there is an invisible but impenetrable barrier preventing women from advancing to senior management levels (e.g., Lyness, in press; Morrison & von Glinow, 1990).

For example, in the USA although women held 36% of the private-sector management jobs in 2002 (United States Equal Employment Opportunity Commission, 2004), in Fortune 500 companies women held less than 16% of the corporate officer positions and only about 1% of Chief Executive Officers were women (Catalyst, 2002). In Canada women held 35% of managerial positions but only 23% of senior management positions in 2001, although these proportions represented a considerable increase from 1994 when women held only 12% of managerial positions and less than 2% of senior management positions (Statistics Canada, 2002). Similar patterns are found in most European countries; for instance, in the UK the number of female directors in FTSE 100 companies increased from 84 in 1999 to 101 in 2003 (International Labour Office, 2004). However, in 2003 there were only 17 female executive directors in these top 100 British companies, and 32 of these companies still had no women directors (International Labour Office, 2004).

Horizontal Segregation of Management Jobs and 'Glass Walls'

In addition to vertical gender segregation of management positions, there is also horizontal occupational segregation by gender, especially in large, private-sector organizations. Generally, the higher status and more powerful management jobs are held by men, with women concentrated in the lower status and less powerful positions (Blau et al., 2002; Ragins & Sundstrom, 1989). Also, jobs typically held by women tend to have more limited opportunities for promotion or mobility (Baron, Davis-Blake, & Bielby, 1986), leading to the term 'glass walls' as a way to describe barriers to women's horizontal mobility, and especially to their ability to move laterally into more powerful positions. US research has shown that within the same level of management, line jobs that are higher in power, status, and promotion opportunities are more likely to be held by men, and women are more likely to be found in staff specialist or support positions (Baron et al., 1986; Blau et al., 2002; Jacobs, 1999; Ragins & Sundstrom, 1989). Furthermore, Lyness and Schrader's (in press) research about mobility patterns among senior US corporate managers showed that, among staff managers, women were less likely than men to move into line positions. These findings have important implications for women's careers because line management experience is generally needed for advancement to the highest level corporate management positions (e.g., Wellington, Kropf, & Gerkovich, 2003).

US patterns of occupational gender segregation appear to hold in other countries as well, where managerial women are often concentrated in 'traditionally female' jobs in education, health services, finance and banking, communication, and personnel (Omar & Davidson, 2001). Interestingly, there is also global evidence of vertical segregation in occupations dominated by women, with men more likely than women to hold the more senior and better compensated positions (International Labour Office, 2004). Taken together, these global findings suggest that although women have undeniably made progress at moving into managerial jobs, their progress can best be characterized as 'slow, uneven, and sometimes discouraging' (International Labour Office, 2004, p. 13).

THEORETICAL FRAMEWORKS ABOUT WOMEN IN MANAGEMENT

Despite obstacles, such as vertical and horizontal gender segregation, women have made notable progress in moving into management positions, and their progress is reflected in the changing emphasis of literature about women in management. Early studies and review articles tended to focus on organizational and societal barriers that made it difficult for women to attain any type of management job. For instance, in an early research review, Terborg (1977) discussed the role of societal norms in perpetuating a 'male managerial model' which both served to undermine women's self-confidence about entering managerial careers and led to hiring discrimination against female applicants for management positions.

In more recent years scholars have developed a substantial body of literature about gender differences in managerial experiences and persistent glass ceiling barriers that make it more difficult for women than men to advance to senior level positions. Commonly mentioned theoretical explanations have focused on a variety of factors at different levels of analysis to explain differences in women's and men's managerial experiences as well as gender gaps in career advancement (e.g., Burke & McKeen, 1992; Fagenson, 1990; Lyness, 2002; Morrison & von Glinow, 1990; Perry, Davis-Blake, & Kulik, 1994; Powell, 1999).

For example, person-centered theories focus on individual level differences in attributes of women and men to explain gender differences in career outcomes. These theories suggest, for instance, that gender gaps in career advancement are due to deficiencies in women's human capital, qualifications, or other attributes in comparison to those of their male counterparts (e.g., Ward, Orazem, & Schmidt, 1992). Some scholars concluded years ago, however, that there was less empirical support for most person-centered theories than for various types of external barriers as explanations for the gender gap in managerial career outcomes (e.g., Morrison & von Glinow, 1990). For example, evidence refuting the person-centered explanations comes from longitudinal studies of comparably qualified MBA-program graduates where men and women often started out in similar positions, but over time the women fell behind in career advancement and compensation, suggesting that the women may have encountered greater organizational barriers than their male counterparts (e.g., Cox & Harquail, 1991; Olson, Frieze, & Good, 1987; Schneer & Reitman, 1994). Also, a recent 24-country examination of personality traits concluded that differences between men and women were small relative to the amount of individual variation within genders (Costa, Terracciano, & McCrae, 2001). Nevertheless, researchers continue to investigate personal attributes to explain gender differences in managerial experiences and outcomes (e.g., Tharenou, 2001).

Other theoretical approaches focus on various types of situational barriers that women encounter as explanations for observed gender differences in career outcomes. Examples include: (1) theories that focus on cognitive processes, such as gender stereotypes, that can lead to gender bias against women when organizational selection or promotion decisions are made (e.g., Heilman, 1995); (2) theories that focus on structural barriers in organizations that impede women's mobility and advancement, such as horizontal and vertical gender segregation of jobs and male domination of organizational power structures (e.g., Kanter, 1977a; Ragins & Sundstrom, 1989); and (3) theories about the larger societal and institutional context, such as widely shared cultural values or norms that prescribe different roles and behaviors for women than for men, and that in turn influence the cultures, values, and norms of organizations within those societal contexts (e.g., Acker, 1990).

Interactions of variables across different levels of analysis can also moderate or exacerbate the likelihood of gender differences in outcomes. For instance, Perry et al. (1994) proposed that gender stereotypes are more likely to influence organizational selection decision making (a cognitive process) when the job being filled has traditionally been held primarily by one gender, as would be the case when jobs are segregated by gender (a characteristic of organizational structure).

SIMILARITIES IN FEMALE AND MALE MANAGERS

Although there is evidence of vertical and horizontal gender segregation of managers, within the last 10 to 15 years women have moved into managerial positions in sufficient numbers to permit researchers to study more comparable samples of male and female managers or executives than were available in the past. This has allowed researchers to better isolate the effects of gender when comparing career outcomes and experiences of women managers to those of their male counterparts. In particular, researchers have either conducted field studies using carefully matched samples of male and female managers or else studied large enough groups of female and male managers to use statistical controls for important characteristics that may covary with gender, such as age, organizational tenure, and hierarchical level. In some instances these studies of more comparable managerial samples have failed to find gender differences that were observed in earlier research comparing less similar groups of male and female managers. It is likely that participants in the earlier studies differed in the types of jobs they held as well as their human capital, organizational tenures, hierarchical levels, or other characteristics that might have explained observed gender differences in career outcomes, behaviors, or work attitudes.

For instance, when Lyness and Thompson (1997) compared samples of women and men executives who were carefully matched on hierarchical level, job type, age, and organizational performance ratings, these researchers did not find significant gender differences in organizational rewards, such as base pay and performance bonuses, whereas many prior studies had found higher pay for male than female managers or executives (e.g., Judge, Cable, Boudreau, & Bretz, 1995; Stroh, Brett, & Reilly, 1992). Lyness and Thompson suggested that their results may not have shown the gender pay gap that has been frequently reported in prior studies because their study compared executives from the same organization who were better matched on salient organizational characteristics related to pay than was possible in prior studies of broader groups of managers or employees drawn from many organizations. Also, Lyness and Thompson's study of matched samples of executives did not find gender differences in important work attitudes, such as organizational commitment, job involvement, and job satisfaction. However, it is important to keep in mind that research on matched samples of male and female executives does not address the possibility that other women continue to encounter organizational barriers that make it difficult for them to reach the elite positions held by women in the Lyness and Thompson (1997) study.

Recent studies have found other similarities among matched samples of men and women that contradict findings of earlier research. For instance, Lyness and Thompson (2000) found more similarities than differences in developmental experiences associated with advancement for similarly successful female and male executives whereas earlier studies showed greater gender differences in developmental experiences, such as men being more likely than women to report opportunities to start up new businesses or to turn around businesses that were in trouble (e.g., Ohlott, Ruderman, & McCauley, 1994; Van Velsor & Hughes, 1990). Also, studies in the USA and Australia found that matched samples of female and male managers did not differ in self-reported masculinity scores, which were associated with some measures of career advancement (Kirchmeyer, 2002; Tharenou, 2001), and a study in the Netherlands found that women and men middle managers expressed similar preferences for 'masculine' organizational cultures (Van Vianen & Fischer, 2002). Lubatkin and Powell's (1998) study of Hungarian managers found that respondents' work attitudes and values did not differ by gender but were related to their management level and whether they worked in private-sector or public-sector organizations.

Furthermore, Lyness and Judiesch (2001) conducted a longitudinal study of voluntary turnover among 26,359 managers and found lower turnover rates for women managers than for their male counterparts. This finding is contrary to prior research among broader groups of managers and professionals showing that women generally had higher rates of turnover or employment disruptions than men (e.g., Schneer & Reitman, 1990; Stroh, Brett, & Reilly, 1996; Tharenou, 1999). The finding that female managers' voluntary turnover rates were no higher than those of male managers is important for correcting mistaken or outdated stereotypic assumptions that women are more likely to quit their jobs for family responsibilities or other reasons, because these beliefs could lead to discrimination against women by organizational decision makers in hiring, promotion, or other employment decisions. Taken together, these research studies underscore the need to study women and men in comparable management jobs in order to shed light on gender differences by controlling for other relevant factors.

PERSISTENT CHALLENGES FOR WOMEN IN MANAGEMENT

Although women have undoubtedly made progress in moving into managerial positions, recent research suggests that there remain some persistent challenges for women managers, particularly as they move into organizational functions or hierarchical levels that have been traditionally dominated by men. In fact, it is interesting to note that even some of the most recent studies have identified challenges to women's advancement, such as gender stereotypes, limited job opportunities, negative consequences associated with token representation, and challenges of managing both work and family responsibilities, that are similar to some challenges for women that were reported over 30 years ago.

Gender Stereotypes

Research showing that attributes of successful middle managers are believed to be more similar to many stereotypic attributes of men (e.g., assertive, forceful, and ambitious) than to stereotypic attributes of women dates back to Schein's

(1973, 1975) early studies of managers' perceptions about these issues. In addition, this stream of research led to Heilman's (1983) theory about bias against women in selection for managerial positions due to a perceived lack of fit between women's attributes and managerial job requirements.

More recently, researchers have addressed questions about whether women's increased representation in management roles has made a difference in these widely held beliefs about stereotypic masculine requirements of management jobs. There is some evidence that although US business students continue to perceive a good manager as having predominantly masculine characteristics, student ratings of these attributes in 1999 reflected somewhat less emphasis on masculine characteristics than was found in comparable student ratings collected in 1976 and 1977 (Powell, Butterfield, & Parent, 2002). These findings suggest that women's progress in attaining management positions may have had some effect on general beliefs about gender-related managerial attributes. However, other studies conducted with US managers revealed gender differences in perceptions of managerial attributes, suggesting that women managers' beliefs may have changed more than those of their male counterparts. In fact, research has found that male managers continued to describe successful managers as more similar to men than to women (Brenner, Tomkiewicz, & Schein, 1989; Heilman, Block, Martell, & Simon, 1989), but female managers reported that successful managers had some characteristics in common with both men and women (Brenner et al., 1989).

Despite some reported changes in these beliefs, there is evidence that gender stereotypes still appear to be a key obstacle to women's advancement into senior management. For example, recent Catalyst surveys of female executives found that 'stereotypes and preconceptions of women's roles and abilities' was the most commonly reported barrier to career advancement for women in surveys of European and Canadian respondents, and this issue was the third most commonly reported barrier among US respondents (Catalyst, 2003; Catalyst & The Conference Board, 2002; Catalyst & The Conference Board of Canada, 1998). These Catalyst survey findings are consistent with studies showing that male managers continued to hold traditional beliefs about stereotypic masculine attributes of successful managers (Brenner et al., 1989; Heilman et al., 1989). Since men are more likely than women to hold key organizational decision-making roles, these stereotypic beliefs could influence their decisions about female candidates for promotions and other job opportunities.

Limited Job Opportunities

According to Doeringer and Piore's (1971) dual labor market model, organizations have primary jobs with important responsibilities, high pay, and good promotional opportunities, and secondary jobs that are less important, offer lower pay, and have more limited promotional opportunities. As we discussed earlier, structural barriers to women's advancement, including vertical and horizontal segregation of management positions and male-dominated power structures, make it difficult for women to obtain the best jobs in an organization. Thus, men are typically concentrated in the primary jobs that offer better advancement and other opportunities, and women are typically concentrated in the secondary jobs (Blau et al., 2002).

These challenges persist, as was shown by recent Catalyst surveys where 'lack of general management or line experience' was the most commonly reported advancement barrier among female executives in the USA and was among the top three most commonly reported barriers for respondents in Canada and Europe (Catalyst, 2003; Catalyst & The Conference Board, 2002; Catalyst & The Conference Board of Canada, 1998). Moreover, 'lack of general management or line experience' was also the most commonly reported barrier to women's advancement according to Chief Executive Officers who were included in the US and Canadian Catalyst studies. In addition to structural barriers, another possible explanation for women's difficulties in getting line jobs, particularly at upper levels of management, is related to perceived requirements of these jobs. Because line jobs are high in status and power, and involve directing essential organizational activities, these jobs are likely to be perceived as requiring stereotypic male attributes, such as forcefulness and achievement orientation; thus, there may be a greater perceived lack of fit between female attributes and requirements of line jobs than requirements of staff support jobs (Lyness & Heilman, in press).

Lyness and Schrader's recent (in press) research examining job moves of senior US managers shed further light on gender differences in career paths that might be related to glass ceiling barriers. This study focused on an elite sample of senior managers who had been selected for new positions that were announced in the *Wall Street Journal* (the leading US business newspaper). The research findings suggested that there were important gender differences in mobility patterns, such that the women's new jobs were generally more similar to their previous jobs than was true for the men. For example, women's new positions were less likely than men's new jobs to involve a promotion in management level or a move to a new company. Also, among staff managers, women were less likely than men to move to line positions or to different functional areas. Because prior research has shown that organizational advancement is related to having a wide variety of managerial jobs and developmental experiences (Lyness & Thompson, 2000; McCauley, Ruderman, Ohlott, & Morrow, 1994), the women's more limited mobility in the Lyness and Schrader study raises questions about whether these senior women were falling behind their male counterparts in career development and preparation for further career advancement.

Negative Consequences Associated with Token Representation of Women

In her seminal (1977a, 1977b) research, Kanter identified important negative consequences for women that occurred when there were skewed sex ratios in organizational units with only token numbers (15% or less) of women. Kanter's findings could still apply to today's women who work in traditionally male-dominated organizational areas, such as senior management and line management jobs. According to Kanter, women's token status affects their interactions with the dominant group (i.e., men). This leads to negative consequences for the token women, such as exclusion from informal interactions with men and heightened performance pressures due to their visibility. Consistent with this early research, recent Catalyst surveys of female executives in both the USA (Catalyst, 2003) and Canada (Catalyst & The Conference Board of Canada, 1998) found that exclusion from informal networks with male peers was among the most commonly reported barriers to women's advancement, but this issue was not among the top barriers reported by female executives in Europe (Catalyst & The Conference Board, 2002). Other US research has found that women executives reported being excluded from networks with their male peers (Davies-Netzley, 1998; Lyness & Thompson, 2000), and that informal networks were more useful to male managers than female managers for getting promoted (Forret & Dougherty, 2004; Kirchmeyer, 1998).

Moreover, 'consistently exceeding performance expectations' was among the most frequently identified advancement strategies of female executives responding to Catalyst surveys in the USA, Canada, and Europe. It is possible that, based on Kanter's theory, high performance is particularly critical for female executives because they must cope with greater visibility and performance pressures than is true for their male peers.

Earlier we discussed areas where the matched male and female executive samples in the Lyness and Thompson (1997) research did not differ, but this study also found some important gender differences. For example, consistent with Kanter's tokenism research, women at the highest executive levels (where there were the fewest women) reported greater obstacles, such as lack of personal support and not fitting the corporate culture, than did women at lower hierarchical levels (where there were more women), but there was no relationship between hierarchical level and perceived obstacles for male executives (Lyness & Thompson, 1997). Other US research found that in organizations with fewer women in senior management, gender roles were perceived more stereotypically than in organizations with more women in senior management (Ely, 1995), and that, compared to men, women at higher levels in a male-dominated management hierarchy were less likely to be promoted than women at lower levels (Lyness & Judiesch, 1999). Tharenou's (2001) longitudinal study of matched samples of female and male Australian managers found that women were less likely to advance into lower and middle levels of management in organizations where management hierarchies were dominated by men. Women in these male-dominated organizations were also more likely than men to fall to lower management levels over time, all of which suggested that there was a cumulative advancement disadvantage for women compared to men in male-dominated organizations.

There is also research evidence indicating that when women are in management jobs traditionally held by men or in male-dominated work groups, they receive lower performance ratings than women in other types of jobs or more balanced work groups. For instance, research about Israeli military officers in non-combat jobs found that women's performance ratings were higher in work groups with a greater proportion of women whereas men's ratings were not related to the gender composition of their work groups (Pazy & Oron, 2001). In addition, a study of US upper level managers found that women in line management jobs received lower performance ratings than women in staff support or specialist management jobs, or than men in either line or staff management jobs (Lyness & Heilman, in press).

Combining Work with Family Responsibilities

Another persistent challenge for many women managers is how to combine their work and family responsibilities. As Kanter (1977a) noted, organizations often expect total dedication from their managers, and these pressures can exclude many women from managerial positions. Since Kanter conducted her research, a great deal of attention has been given to conflicts between work and family roles, particularly for women (see Greenhaus & Parasuraman, 1999, for a review).

Researchers continue to examine these issues as well as relationships between work–family conflict and women's careers. For example, Simpson's (1998) study of British managers found that women with children were likely to report that work–family conflict was a source of pressure. In addition, Simpson reported that work–family conflict was particularly difficult for women managers who worked in male-dominated organizations and for women in senior levels of management as they felt pressure to work long hours in order to visibly demonstrate their organizational commitment (Simpson, 1998), suggesting that work–family conflict may have been exacerbated by the pressures associated with being token women in these work settings.

On the other hand, research by Dreher (2003) suggested that there may be a positive linkage between organizational work–family support and women's advancement. Specifically, Dreher's study of US organizations found positive relationships between the percentage of women managers in the 1980s and whether the organizations had work–life programs in 1994, which was in turn related to the percentage of women in senior management in 1999.

The challenge of managing work and family responsibilities for women was underscored by European research showing that no matter how many hours women managers worked, they still took primary responsibility for childrearing and household tasks (Linehan & Walsh, 2000). Also, Kirchmeyer's (2002) longitudinal research with mid-career graduates of a US MBA program found that marriage and children were negatively related to measures of managerial success (i.e., income and promotions) for women but positively related to success for men. A possible explanation is provided by longitudinal research showing that US managers who took leaves of absence for family or other reasons received fewer subsequent promotions and smaller salary increases than managers who had not taken leaves of absence, and that the majority of leaves were taken by women (Judiesch & Lyness, 1999). Perhaps as a way of avoiding conflicts between work and family, research has also found that US and British female managers and executives were less likely than their male counterparts to be married or have children (e.g., Kirchmeyer, 2002; Lyness & Thompson, 1997; Omar & Davidson, 2001).

Nevertheless, not all research has found negative relationships between family involvement and women's careers. In fact, Barnett and Hyde's (2001) expansionist theory suggests that there can be benefits to having multiple roles, and that there can be positive spillover between work and family roles. Consistent with this recent theoretical development, Tharenou's (1999) study of Australian managers and professionals found that married women and men advanced more than single, childless respondents. In addition, Ruderman, Ohlott, Panzer, and King's (2002) research discovered many benefits of multiple roles for managerial women, including positive relationships of multiple roles to reported life satisfaction and self-esteem, as well as to development of their interpersonal and managerial skills.

ADVANCEMENT OF WOMEN INTO SENIOR MANAGEMENT

A possible distinction between lower levels of management, where women have made considerable progress at increasing their representation, and more senior levels, where women are still not well represented, is that senior management positions may have different requirements. These requirements include functioning in leadership roles and making strategic decisions, which may not be as necessary for success in lower level management positions. Thus, possible explanations for women's slow progress into senior management positions are that women might not be well accepted as leaders or they might not be perceived to have other attributes necessary for effectiveness in senior management roles. Several recent theories have offered different explanations for women's slow advancement to senior management positions.

Theories Related to Advancement of Women into Senior Management

Building on her earlier (1983) theory about the perceived lack of fit between stereotypic attributes of women and requirements of management roles, Heilman (2001) more recently argued that both descriptive and prescriptive aspects of gender stereotypes can result in lower evaluations of women managers and undermine their career advancement. Descriptive aspects of stereotypes refer to beliefs that men possess agentic attributes (e.g., forceful, independent, and decisive) whereas women possess communal attributes (e.g., kind, helpful, and concerned about others), and that there is a better perceived fit between requirements of senior management jobs and agentic attributes than communal attributes. This perceived job–gender incongruence results in selection bias against women because they are expected to be less likely than men to succeed in senior management positions.

Furthermore, Heilman (2001) argued that gender stereotypes are also prescriptive in that they play an important role in shaping beliefs about how men and women should behave. Thus, based on these prescriptive stereotypic norms, when women display agentic behaviors, as may be required for successful performance in senior management jobs, these women's counternormative behaviors can result in disapproval and negative evaluations because they are not behaving as women should. In other words, if women perform as competent senior managers, they may be penalized and disliked for being unfeminine. This dilemma has been referred to as the 'femininity–competence double bind' (Jamieson, 1995; Lyness, 2002) and helps to explain why successful women have reported that career advancement for women may require that they develop a style with which men are comfortable (Ragins, Townsend, & Mattis, 1998). These findings are also consistent with laboratory research showing that men resist being influenced by competent women unless these women temper their competence with warmth and communal behaviors (see Carli, 2001, for a review of this literature).

There is also research evidence showing that requirements of upper level management jobs may be perceived as more masculine than requirements for management jobs at lower levels. Recent research with US business students found that both men and women perceived specific upper management roles, such as strategic decision making, delegating, and resource allocation, to be more masculine than feminine (Atwater, Brett, Waldman, DiMare, & Hayden, 2004), thus supporting Heilman's contention that men are likely to be perceived as a better fit than women with these senior management role requirements. Other research with US managers found some evidence of same-gender bias in judgments about the likelihood that men or women managers would engage in various effective leadership behaviors, but, consistent with the Atwater research, both genders reported that men would be more likely than women to delegate (Martell & DeSmet, 2001). Given the prevalence of men in current senior management positions, evidence of same-gender bias in male managers' beliefs about who would engage in effective leadership behaviors also supports Heilman's contentions about biased perceptions on the part of organizational decision makers that could make it more difficult for women than men to be promoted into senior leadership roles.

Eagly and Karau's (2002) role congruity theory has some similarities to Heilman's theory, but more directly addresses the issue of bias against women as leaders by arguing that communal attributes associated with stereotypic perceptions of the female gender role are inconsistent with agentic qualities generally believed to be needed for success as a leader. According to Eagly and Karau, this perceived incongruity makes it more difficult for women to be selected for leadership roles and less likely that women will be perceived as successful leaders. Moreover, these scholars pointed out that the degree of perceived incongruity is greater for masculine leadership roles, as would be the case for most senior management positions, than for leadership roles in more female-dominated settings. In addition, Eagly and Karau argued that men might be particularly reluctant to promote women to positions where they have power over other people.

Whereas Heilman's (2001) and Eagly and Karau's (2002) theories focused on various aspects of job–gender incongruity, Glick and Fiske's (1996, 2001) theory about ambivalent sexism offers an updated and more complex explanation about prejudice against women that may also be related to gender differences in career outcomes. According to Glick and Fiske's theory, there are two different but related types of sexism: (1) hostile sexism, which is based on the perception that women seek to control men, and results in grudging respect but negative emotions toward women because they are viewed as a competitive threat to men, and (2) benevolent sexism, which is based on perceptions that women possess idealized, communal characteristics, and leads to more positive views about women but also to paternalistic stereotypes, such that women are viewed as best suited for traditional gender roles, whereas men are believed to be best suited for high status roles. Thus, for different reasons, both hostile and benevolent sexist beliefs on the part of organizational decision makers could result in bias against women when selection or promotion decisions are made to fill high status positions, such as senior management jobs.

Glick and Fiske's two types of sexism appear to be related to key concepts in the theories developed by Heilman (2001) and Eagly and Karau (2002). Benevolent sexism is based on traditional communal stereotypes about women and agentic stereotypes about men, leading to beliefs that men are best suited for high status jobs. This perspective is consistent with Heilman's (2001) views that descriptive gender stereotypes result in perceptions that men are a better fit than women with agentic requirements of senior management jobs. Similarly, Glick and Fiske's concept of benevolent sexism is consistent with Eagly and Karau's (2002) views that there is a perceived inconsistency between women's communal qualities and agentic attributes needed for successful leadership. In addition, both Heilman's gender stereotype theory and Eagly and Karau's role congruity theory described penalties for women who violate communal gender role prescriptions by exhibiting agentic attributes. These penalties may be at least partly due to perceptions of these women as a competitive threat, which is consistent with Glick and Fiske's concept of hostile sexism.

Although these theories suggest that women who violate gender role prescriptions will be penalized or disliked, other research has found that there may also be costs for women managers who adapt their behavior to fit gender role prescriptions. For example, Simpson and Stroh (2004) surveyed US managers about their emotional expression at work, and found that women were more likely than men to conform to feminine norms of displaying positive feelings but suppressing negative feelings. Moreover, Simpson and Stroh's study also found that women who conformed to feminine norms of emotional expression paid a price in that they reported feeling personally inauthentic at work, and these types of feelings were shown in other research to be antecedents of negative outcomes, such as stress and depression (e.g., Erickson & Wharton, 1997).

Finally, from the perspective of a sociologist, Foschi (1992, 1996, 2000) developed a theory about double standards for evaluation that offers a different explanation for bias against women when decisions are made about promotion to senior management positions. According to Foschi's theory, members of various demographic groups are evaluated based on their status in society, with higher status groups, such as men, generally expected to be more competent than lower status groups, such as women. Because of these varying expectations, different standards are used to scrutinize equal performance by men and women in order to judge their competence. Specifically, Foschi contended that performance of lower status groups (e.g., women) is assessed by stricter standards than similar performance by higher status groups (e.g., men), particularly when the status characteristic (i.e., gender) is perceived to be relevant to task performance, as would be the case for senior management jobs that are perceived to require masculine attributes. When women and men have similar performance records at lower levels of management, this theory predicts that men will be perceived as more competent, and thus more likely to be chosen for senior management positions.

Furthermore, Foschi (2000) explained that the use of double standards is a subtle exclusionary practice that can operate even when performance evaluations are unbiased. In other words, Foschi's theory suggests that gender bias occurs in the way performance evaluations are used to make judgments about the relative competence of women and men, and thus could occur even if the original evaluations of their performance were made without gender bias against women. However, according to Heilman's (2001) theory about gender stereotypes and Eagly and Karau's (2002) theory about role incongruity, it is possible that performance evaluations are also biased against women when evaluators believe that jobs require agentic attributes, thus compounding the sources of gender bias against women if double standards are also used to evaluate their competence. Support for predictions based on Foschi's theory comes from Lyness and Heilman's (in press) longitudinal research about upper level managers showing that stricter and less flexible standards were used in making promotion decisions about women managers than their male counterparts.

Empirical Studies about Women in Leadership Roles

Earlier we suggested that functioning in leadership roles is likely to be a critical requirement of most senior management positions, and a number of studies have examined gender differences in leadership ability as a possible explanation for women's difficulties in attaining senior management positions. One of the most comprehensive examinations of this question was conducted by Eagly, Johannesen-Schmidt, and Van Engen (2003), who carried out a meta-analysis of 45 prior studies comparing leadership styles of women and men working in a variety of settings, including business, educational, and government organizations. Based on current theories and research about the relative effectiveness of different leadership styles, the researchers were interested in determining whether differences in women's and men's leadership styles could explain gender gaps in advancement to leadership positions. Eagly et al.'s findings indicated that there were gender differences in leadership styles, with women more likely than men to exhibit behaviors associated with the transformational leadership style and the contingent rewards aspect of the transactional leadership style. More importantly, Eagly et al. noted that, based on prior meta-analytic leadership research (DeGroot, Kiker, & Cross, 2000; Lowe, Kroeck, & Sivasubramaniam, 1996), the leadership styles more commonly used by women were more effective than the leadership styles more commonly used by men. Consistent with the theories by Heilman (2001) and Eagly and Karau (2002) about gender role prescriptions, Eagly et al. (2003) pointed out that women might use the transformational and contingent reward leadership styles because these approaches include communal behaviors that are consistent with traditional female gender roles. In addition, Eagly et al. (2003) noted that women in leadership positions may be on average more competent than men in similar jobs because incompetent women would be more quickly removed than incompetent men from leadership roles due to stricter standards and less leniency in evaluating women than men (Foschi, 2000). The Eagly et al. meta-analytic findings are important because they suggest that, based on their more frequent use of effective leadership styles, women are no less qualified than men for leadership roles, such as senior management positions.

In an earlier meta-analytic study comparing women and men leaders in organizational settings as well as controlled laboratory studies, Eagly, Karau, and Makhijani (1995) concluded that in general women and men did not differ in their effectiveness as leaders. However, more detailed analyses revealed that context was related to ratings of leadership effectiveness, with leaders of each gender receiving higher effectiveness ratings in leadership roles that were perceived to be gender-congruent. For example, men were evaluated more favorably than women in male-dominated settings, such as military organizations, and women were evaluated more favorably in more gender-balanced settings, such as educational and social service organizations. It should be noted, however, that the finding that men were evaluated more favorably than women in male-dominated settings is somewhat inconsistent with the more recent Eagly et al. (2003) meta-analytic research showing that women tended to make greater use than did men of more effective leadership styles.

Gardiner and Tiggemann (1999) extended this line of research by examining Australian middle level female and male managers holding similar positions to see if their leadership styles varied depending on whether they worked in male-dominated industries (e.g., automotive, information and technology, or accounting) or female-dominated industries (e.g., early childhood education or nursing). These researchers found that women managers in female-dominated industries used a more feminine, interpersonally oriented leadership style than did men in these settings, which may help to explain Eagly et al.'s (1995) findings that women leaders were considered to be more effective in gender-congruent settings than in male-dominated settings. On the other hand, Gardiner and Tiggemann found that women and men in male-dominated organizations did not differ in their use of an interpersonally oriented leadership style, but that women showed a higher level of task orientation than men. This finding led the researchers to conclude that the women had adapted to masculine norms in male-dominated industries by displaying a more stereotypically masculine leadership style than women working in female-dominated industries. Although these results suggest that organizational gender composition may be related to women's leadership styles, the authors did not collect data regarding the perceived effectiveness of the women's or men's leadership. Nevertheless, taken together, the empirical research and meta-analytic studies suggest that women are no less qualified than men for leadership roles, such as those associated with senior management positions.

CROSS-CULTURAL RESEARCH

As we discussed earlier, women have made progress in recent years at moving into management positions in many countries. This raises interesting questions about whether there are cross-cultural differences in perceptions of women as managers, and whether gender stereotypes and perceptions of women managers have changed in countries where women have entered the managerial ranks in greater numbers. Another important question that can best be addressed with cross-cultural research is whether characteristics of national cultures are related to women managers' experiences or career outcomes. Unfortunately relatively few cross-national studies have been conducted to shed light on these issues, but we will review some of the available findings.

Gender Stereotypes

As we discussed earlier, several studies have found that stereotypic masculine attributes are perceived to be a better fit than stereotypic female attributes with requirements of management positions (e.g., Schein, 1973, 1975). However, more recent research in the USA found that although male managers continued to endorse the 'think manager–think male' model, female managers reported resemblance of good manager attributes to some characteristics of both men and women (Brenner et al., 1989).

Schein and her colleagues replicated this research with management students in the UK, Germany, Japan, and China, to see if the 'think manager–think male' beliefs held across other cultures (Schein, 2001; Schein & Mueller, 1992; Schein, Mueller, Lituchy, & Liu, 1996). These studies found that both men's and women's ratings of male attributes strongly resembled their ratings of managerial attributes. However, there was also some variability in resemblance of women's ratings of female attributes to managerial attributes, ranging from close to zero in Japan to more moderate similarities in the UK (Schein, 2001; Schein & Mueller, 1992; Schein et al., 1996). Schein and her colleagues interpreted the variations in women's ratings as reflecting cross-national differences in perceived opportunities and actual representation of women in management positions. In other words, in countries such as the UK, where women were more likely to hold management positions, women's beliefs about requisite managerial attributes included more stereotypic female attributes than in countries such as Japan, where women were less likely to hold managerial positions. However, women in all of these countries reported more congruence of male attributes rather than female attributes to those of managers, leading the researchers to conclude: 'Overall, the results lend strong support to the view that "think manager–think male" is a global phenomenon, especially among males' (Schein et al., 1996, p. 39).

National Cultures

Several cross-cultural studies have found evidence that various characteristics of national cultures are related to important outcomes for women in the workforce. For example, Hofstede's (1980) seminal research about national culture values identified a key cultural dimension that he labeled 'masculinity/femininity,' which refers to beliefs about 'whether the biological differences between the sexes should or should not have implications for their roles in social activities' (p. 261).

The more recent Project GLOBE research in 62 cultures by House and his colleagues extended the Hofstede work and collected ratings from 17,000 middle level managers about actual practices as well as shared values (i.e., beliefs about what 'should be') in both their organizations and societies (House, Hanges, Javidan, Dorfman, & Gupta, 2004). These researchers measured nine dimensions of societal cultures, including two separate gender-related dimensions: (1) gender egalitarianism, which refers to 'beliefs about whether members' biological sex should determine the roles that they play in their homes, business organizations and communities' (Emrich, Denmark, & Den Hartog, 2004, p. 347), and (2) assertiveness, which refers to 'beliefs as to whether people are or should be encouraged to be assertive, aggressive, and tough, or non-assertive, non-aggressive, and tender in social relationships' (Den Hartog, 2004, p. 395). The GLOBE assertiveness dimension was significantly correlated with Hofstede's masculinity/femininity dimension, and both dimensions reflect a continuum from stereotypic masculine (i.e., assertive) to stereotypic feminine (i.e., non-assertive) societal values and practices (Hanges & Dickson, 2004, p. 140). However, the GLOBE gender egalitarianism dimension was not found to be significantly related to Hofstede's masculinity/femininity dimension (Hanges & Dickson, 2004, p. 140).

In addition, House and his colleagues found important relationships of societal values and practices to values and practices of organizations within those societies. This research underscores the importance of taking into account the national context, which is often ignored in studies about women in management, most of which have been conducted in single countries, especially the USA, the UK, and Australia. As Omar and Davidson (2001) explained, the status of women and men in their organizations should be considered within the societal context where those status differentials or equalities originated.

The importance of societal culture was illustrated by Bajdo and Dickson's (2001) research using GLOBE data from 3544 managers in 32 countries to examine the relationship between managers' ratings of their organizations' cultures and the percentage of women in management. Bajdo and Dickson found that although their respondents' ratings of several different cultural dimensions were related to the percentage of women managers in their organizations, ratings of organizational practices reflecting the gender egalitarianism dimension had the strongest positive relationship to the percentage of women managers in respondents' organizations. Interestingly, Bajdo and Dickson also found that respondents' ratings of actual organizational practices were more strongly related to women's advancement than were ratings of organizational values.

Further support for the importance of considering national culture in understanding the work environment for women was provided by Glick et al.'s (2000) cross-cultural research in 19 countries, including countries from North and South America as well as Europe, Africa, and Asia. These researchers found negative relationships between national gender equality, measured with two indices developed by the United Nations (UN), and both hostile and benevolent sexism, particularly as measured by male respondents' scores. These results showed that men's sexism scores were negatively related to both the UN Gender Empowerment Measure, which reflects women's national representation in high status jobs, such as managers and parliament members, and the UN Gender-Related Development Index, which reflects gender equality in overall standard of living. The authors explained that both types of sexism could undermine women's advancement, but that the effects of benevolent sexism may be more subtle and covert. Hostile sexism may lead to overt behaviors that provoke criticism, but benevolent sexism may also undermine women's attempts to achieve equality by reinforcing their conformity to traditional gender roles.

Work and Family Responsibilities

Based on case studies conducted in the USA, the UK, Sweden, and Australia, Haas, Hwang, and Russell (2000) concluded that there were important relationships between national contexts and organizational practices related to work and family issues. For example, governmental regulations can mandate that employers must offer benefits that help managers to balance their work and family responsibilities, as in the case of Sweden where employers must provide paid family leave to their employees (Björnberg, 2000). However, in other countries, such as the UK, with less governmental regulation of policies related to parental leave and childcare, there is more variation in benefits across employers (Brannen & Lewis, 2000; Den Dulk, 2002).

Lyness and Kropf (2005) suggested that national gender equality, defined as the extent to which national cultures support women's development and achievements, and recognize the importance of including women in all aspects of life (United Nations Development Programme, 2001), is likely to be related to organizational policies and practices that affect managers' work–family balance. They investigated these issues in 20 European countries, and found some support for predicted positive relationships between national gender equality, measured with UN Gender-Related Development Index scores for respondents' countries, and survey measures of respondents' perceptions about their organizations' work–family supports as well as their own individual work–family balance. Moreover, among respondents employed by multinational organizations and working in host countries outside the organizational headquarters country, Lyness and Kropf found that both the headquarters country culture and the local host country culture were related to organizational practices and managers' work–family balance. In addition, their data showed that the proportion of women in an organization's senior management was related to supportiveness of the organizational culture for work–family balance. The researchers interpreted these findings as showing that 'inclusion of women in critical societal or organizational roles may help to temper otherwise male-gendered organizational cultures, resulting in cultures that are more supportive of employees' needs to balance work and family' (Lyness & Kropf, 2005, p. 55).

ADVANCEMENT OF WOMEN IN MANAGEMENT

As can be seen in the previous sections of this chapter, there are many empirical studies and theories about obstacles to women's advancement. In addition, there is some evidence that contextual factors, such as societal values related to gender equality and organizations with greater proportions of women in powerful positions, can play a key role in facilitating women managers' advancement. Other US research has shown that women are more likely to hold top management jobs in organizations with greater representation of women in lower level management, higher management turnover, and greater emphasis on internal development and promotion of employees (Goodman, Fields, & Blum, 2003).

In addition, some studies have examined specific strategies that women managers have used to facilitate their advancement. It is interesting to note that several of these advancement strategies appear to be targeted at some of the challenges for women managers that have been reviewed in this chapter. For example, one of the most frequently mentioned advancement strategies for female executives is having a good track record of successful performance (e.g., Lyness & Thompson, 2000; Ragins et al., 1998), which may be particularly important for enabling women to overcome other people's perceptions about women's lack of fit with agentic requirements of managerial jobs.

Another important strategy that has been identified in studies of successful women managers and executives is developing various types of relationships, which also includes related strategies of networking, and obtaining mentors or sponsors (e.g., Davies-Netzley, 1998; Ibarra, 1997; Lyness & Thompson, 2000; Ragins et al., 1998). Relationships are important for enabling women to overcome social isolation, as well as for gaining organizational sponsorship, career guidance, and emotional support. Also, relationships may help competent women to be perceived as likable and to offset potential penalties associated with exhibiting agentic behaviors that violate traditional feminine stereotypes. Other evidence that successful US female executives may focus on avoiding penalties for violating traditional gender role prescriptions comes from Catalyst surveys reporting that 'developing a style with which male managers are comfortable' was among the most commonly reported advancement strategies in both 1996 and 2003 (Catalyst, 1996, 2003).

CONCLUSIONS AND SUGGESTIONS FOR FUTURE RESEARCH

As shown by our review of international statistics about gender composition of management jobs, women have made notable progress at moving into management positions and have even made progress in advancing to senior levels in some management hierarchies. However, there is also evidence that women's representation in managerial and related positions is smaller than their representation in the overall workforce in most countries. In addition, women's advancement appears to be hampered by vertical and horizontal gender segregation, particularly in large, private-sector organizations, where men typically still hold most of the jobs that are highest in power, status, and promotional opportunities.

Our review of the recent literature suggests that women managers face a number of persistent challenges, such as gender stereotypes, limited job opportunities, lack of culture fit, exclusion from informal networks with male peers, and difficulties associated with trying to balance work and family responsibilities. The current literature also suggests that women continue to come up against glass ceiling barriers that make it difficult for them to advance to senior management. Some recent theories have offered explanations for these glass ceiling barriers, such as suggesting that women's organizational advancement is hampered by perceived incongruities between stereotypic communal female attributes and requirements of senior management jobs or leadership roles (Eagly & Karau, 2002; Heilman, 2001).

Consistent with Kanter's (1977b) research on tokenism, women managers appear to be most likely to face challenges when they work in male-dominated work settings, such as senior management or jobs traditionally held by men. Some evidence to substantiate the persistent nature of these challenges comes from the fact that many of the most frequently reported advancement strategies used by female executives seem to correspond to gender-related obstacles that women face. For example, social isolation has been identified as a challenge for women, and this obstacle might be at least partially overcome by developing relationships with other people, which successful female executives have often reported as a key strategy for their career advancement. In addition, executive women also apparently have to negotiate a femininity–competence double bind, which requires them to walk a narrow line between doing what their jobs require without violating prescriptive feminine norms. More organizational research is needed to enhance our understanding of exactly how women managers can successfully navigate gender-related challenges, with a particular focus on identifying the specific underlying processes that are involved and factors, in addition to gender composition of management hierarchies, that might be important moderating variables.

Although women appear to have faced greater challenges than men in attaining management jobs, there is also some indication that once women move into management positions, their attitudes and behaviors are more similar in some respects to those of male managers than was previously thought. In particular, some recent studies, such as Lyness and Thompson's (1997, 2000) research comparing more similar samples of male and female managers than were available in previous research, have suggested that some of the earlier observed gender differences might have been due to gender differences in other characteristics, such as job type, organizational level, or human capital. Moreover, Eagly et al.'s (2003) meta-analytic research, showing that women were more likely than men to use the most effective leadership styles, suggests that women may be no less qualified than their male counterparts to hold leadership positions. One possible interpretation of these recent findings is that they are more consistent with situational theories, which suggest that women's limited advancement is due to various external barriers that they face, rather than with person-centered theories, which suggest that women lack critical attributes, such as leadership ability, that are required for senior management positions.

Additional insights about progress and challenges for women in management come from recent cross-cultural research that has identified gender-related societal values and practices that are related to values and practices of organizations within those societies (House et al., 2004). The importance of cross-cultural research for understanding issues for managerial women was illustrated by cross-national studies showing that women's advancement was positively related to organizational practices reflecting gender egalitarianism (Bajdo & Dickson, 2001) and negatively related to sexist beliefs (Glick et al., 2000). Cross-cultural research also shed light on the importance of considering national context in examining work–family issues, as there were positive relationships between the degree of national gender equality, organizational support for work–family balance, and managers' reported work–family balance (Lyness & Kropf, 2005). These studies underscore the importance of societal values for influencing organizational values and practices that can facilitate or impede women's advancement.

It appears that much more is known about persistent gender-related challenges for women managers than how to remedy these problems. Thus, it would be useful to learn more about characteristics of organizations and cultures where women experience better advancement opportunities and fewer challenges. Recent studies showing fewer observed gender differences when more similar samples of managers are examined also suggest that it is very important for future research to be conducted with comparable samples of women and men managers to rule out alternative explanations for observed gender differences. Some intriguing research has suggested that women may use particularly effective leadership styles (Eagly et al., 2003), and more such studies are needed, particularly at executive levels in business organizations where there has been relatively little previous research about these issues. Finally, findings from cross-cultural research suggest that examining variations in national contextual variables can help us to identify both challenges and factors related to advancement for women managers. We hope that more cross-national studies will be conducted in the future not only to enhance our understanding of these issues but also to seek remedies for persistent gender-related challenges for women managers.

REFERENCES

Acker, J. (1990). Hierarchies, jobs, bodies: A theory of gendered organizations. *Gender and Society*, 4, 139–158.

Atwater, L.E., Brett, J.F., Waldman, D., DiMare, L., & Hayden, M.V. (2004). Men's and women's perceptions of the gender typing of management subroles. *Sex Roles*, 50, 191–199.

Bajdo, L.M. & Dickson, M.W. (2001). Perceptions of organizational culture and women's advancement in organizations: A cross-cultural examination. *Sex Roles*, 45, 399–414.

Barnett, R.C. & Hyde, J.S. (2001). Women, men, work, and family: An expansionist theory. *American Psychologist*, **56**, 781–796.

Baron, J.N., Davis-Blake, A., & Bielby, W.T. (1986). The structure of opportunity: How promotion ladders vary within and among organizations. *Administrative Science Quarterly*, **31**, 248–273.

Björnberg, U. (2000). Equality and backlash: Family, gender, and social policy in Sweden. In L.L. Haas, P. Hwang, & G. Russell (Eds), *Organizational change and gender equity: International perspectives on fathers and mothers at the workplace* (pp. 57–75). Thousand Oaks, CA: Sage.

Blau, F.D., Ferber, M.A., & Winkler, A.E. (2002). *The economics of women, men, and work* (4th edn). Upper Saddle River, NJ: Prentice-Hall.

Brannen, J. & Lewis, S. (2000). Workplace programmes and policies in the United Kingdom. In L.L. Haas, P. Hwang, & G. Russell (Eds), *Organizational change and gender equity: International perspectives on fathers and mothers at the workplace* (pp. 99–115). Thousand Oaks, CA: Sage.

Brenner, O.C., Tomkiewicz, J., & Schein, V.E. (1989). The relationship between sex role stereotypes and requisite management characteristics revisited. *Academy of Management Journal*, **32**, 662–669.

Burke, R.J. & McKeen, C.A. (1992). Women in management. In C.L. Cooper & I.T. Robertson (Eds), *International review of industrial and organizational psychology* (Vol. 7, pp. 246–283). New York: John Wiley & Sons.

Carli, L.L. (2001). Gender and social influence. *Journal of Social Issues*, **57**, 725–741.

Catalyst (1996). *Women in corporate leadership: Progress and prospects*. New York: Catalyst.

Catalyst (2002). *2002 Catalyst census of women corporate officers and top earners of the Fortune 500*. New York: Catalyst.

Catalyst (2003). *Women in US corporate leadership: 2003*. New York: Catalyst.

Catalyst & The Conference Board (2002). *Women in leadership: A European business imperative*. New York: Catalyst & The Conference Board.

Catalyst & The Conference Board of Canada (1998). *Closing the gap: Women's advancement in corporate and professional Canada*. New York: Catalyst & The Conference Board of Canada.

Costa, P.T., Jr, Terracciano, A., & McCrae, R.R. (2001). Gender differences in personality traits across cultures: Robust and surprising findings. *Journal of Personality and Social Psychology*, **81**, 322–331.

Cox, T.H. & Harquail, C.V. (1991). Career paths and career success in the early career stages of male and female MBAs. *Journal of Vocational Behavior*, **39**, 54–75.

Davies-Netzley, S.A. (1998). Women above the glass ceiling: Perceptions of corporate mobility and strategies for success. *Gender and Society*, **12**, 339–355.

DeGroot, T., Kiker, D.S., & Cross, T.C. (2000). A meta-analysis to review organizational outcomes related to charismatic leadership. *Canadian Journal of Administrative Sciences*, **17**, 356–371.

Den Dulk, L. (2002). *Organizational responses to work–family issues in Europe: A cross-national comparison*. Paper presented at the 17th Annual Conference of the Society for Industrial and Organizational Psychology, Inc., Toronto, Canada.

Den Hartog, D.N. (2004). Assertiveness. In R.J. House, P.J. Hanges, M. Javidan, P.W. Dorfman, & V. Gupta (Eds), *Culture, leadership, and organizations: The GLOBE study of 62 societies* (pp. 395–436). Thousand Oaks, CA: Sage.

Doeringer, P.B. & Piore, M.J. (1971). *Internal labor markets and manpower analysis*. Lexington, MA: D.C. Heath.

Dreher, G.F. (2003). Breaking the glass ceiling: The effects of sex ratios and work–life programs on female leadership at the top. *Human Relations*, **56**, 541–562.

Eagly, A.H., Johannesen-Schmidt, M.C., & Van Engen, M.L. (2003). Transformational, transactional, and laissez-faire leadership styles: A meta-analysis comparing women and men. *Psychological Bulletin*, **129**, 569–591.

Eagly, A.H. & Karau, S.J. (2002). Role congruity theory of prejudice toward female leaders. *Psychological Review*, **109**, 573–598.

Eagly, A.H., Karau, S.J., & Makhijani, M. (1995). Gender and the effectiveness of leaders: A meta-analysis. *Psychological Bulletin*, **117**, 125–145.

Ely, R.J. (1995). The power in demography: Women's social constructions of gender identity at work. *Academy of Management Journal*, **38**, 589–634.

Emrich, C.G., Denmark, F.L., & Den Hartog, D.N. (2004). Cross-cultural differences in gender egalitarianism: Implications for societies, organizations, and leaders. In R.J. House, P.J. Hanges, M. Javidan, P.W. Dorfman, & V. Gupta (Eds), *Culture, leadership, and organizations: The GLOBE study of 62 societies* (pp. 343–394). Thousand Oaks, CA: Sage.

Erickson, R.J. & Wharton, A.S. (1997). Inauthenticity and depression: Assessing the consequences of interactive service work. *Work and Occupations*, **24**, 188–213.

Fagenson, E.A. (1990). At the heart of women in management research: Theoretical and methodological approaches and their biases. *Journal of Business Ethics*, **9**, 267–274.

Forret, M.L. & Dougherty, T.W. (2004). Networking behaviors and career outcomes: Differences for men and women? *Journal of Organizational Behavior*, **25**, 419–437.

Foschi, M. (1992). Gender and double standards for competence. In C.L. Ridgeway (Ed.), *Gender, interaction, and inequality* (pp. 181–207). New York: Springer-Verlag.

Foschi, M. (1996). Double standards in the evaluation of men and women. *Social Psychology Quarterly*, **59**, 237–254.

Foschi, M. (2000). Double standards for competence: Theory and research. *Annual Review of Sociology*, **26**, 21–42.

Gardiner, M. & Tiggemann, M. (1999). Gender differences in leadership style, job stress and mental health in male- and female-dominated industries. *Journal of Occupational and Organizational Psychology*, **72**, 301–315.

Glick, P. & Fiske, S.T. (1996). The ambivalent sexism inventory: Differentiating hostile and benevolent sexism. *Journal of Personality and Social Psychology*, **70**, 491–512.

Glick, P. & Fiske, S.T. (2001). An ambivalent alliance: Hostile and benevolent sexism as complementary justifications for gender inequality. *American Psychologist*, **56**, 109–118.

Glick, P., Fiske, S.T., Mladinic, A., Saiz, J.L., Abrams, D., Masser, B. et al. (2000). Beyond prejudice as simple antipathy: Hostile and benevolent sexism across cultures. *Journal of Personality and Social Psychology*, **79**, 763–775.

Goodman, J.S., Fields, D.L., & Blum, C.T. (2003). Cracks in the glass ceiling: In what kinds of organizations do women make it to the top? *Group and Organization Management*, **28**, 475–501.

Greenhaus, J.H. & Parasuraman, S. (1999). Research on work, family and gender: Current status and future directions. In G.N. Powell (Ed.), *Handbook of gender and work* (pp. 391–412). Thousand Oaks, CA: Sage.

Haas, L.L., Hwang, P., & Russell, G. (2000). *Organizational change and gender equity: International perspectives on fathers and mothers at the workplace*. Thousand Oaks, CA: Sage.

Hanges, P.J. & Dickson, M.W. (2004). The development and validation of the GLOBE culture and leadership scales. In R.J. House, P.J. Hanges, M. Javidan, P.W. Dorfman, & V. Gupta (Eds), *Culture, leadership, and organizations: The GLOBE study of 62 societies* (pp. 122–151). Thousand Oaks, CA: Sage.

Heilman, M.E. (1983). Sex bias in work settings: The lack of fit model. In B.M. Staw & L.L. Cummings (Eds), *Research in organizational behavior* (Vol. 5, pp. 269–298). Greenwich, CT: JAI Press.

Heilman, M.E. (1995). Sex stereotypes and their effects in the workplace: What we know and what we don't know. *Journal of Social Behavior and Personality*, **10**, 3–26.

Heilman, M.E. (2001). Description and prescription: How gender stereotypes prevent women's ascent up the organizational ladder. *Journal of Social Issues*, 57, 657–674.
Heilman, M.E., Block, C.J., Martell, R.F., & Simon, M.C. (1989). Has anything changed? Current characterizations of men, women, and managers. *Journal of Applied Psychology*, 74, 935–942.
Hofstede, G. (1980). *Culture's consequences: International differences in work-related values* (Vol. 5). Newbury Park, CA: Sage.
House, R.J., Hanges, P.J., Javidan, M., Dorfman, P.W., & Gupta, V. (Eds) (2004). *Culture, leadership, and organizations: The GLOBE study of 62 societies*. Thousand Oaks, CA: Sage.
Ibarra, H. (1997). Paving an alternative route: Gender differences in managerial networks. *Social Psychology Quaterly*, 60, 91–102.
International Labour Office (2003). *Yearbook of labour statistics*. Geneva, Switzerland: International Labour Office.
International Labour Office (2004). *Breaking through the glass ceiling: Women in management*. Geneva, Switzerland: International Labour Office.
Jacobs, J.A. (1999). The sex segregation of occupations: Prospects for the 21st century. In G.N. Powell (Ed.), *Handbook of gender and work* (pp. 125–139). Thousand Oaks, CA: Sage.
Jamieson, K.H. (1995). *Beyond the double bind: Women and leadership*. New York: Oxford University Press.
Judge, T.A., Cable, D.M., Boudreau, J.W., & Bretz, R.D., Jr (1995). An empirical investigation of the predictors of executive career success. *Personnel Psychology*, 48, 485–519.
Judiesch, M.K. & Lyness, K.S. (1999). Left behind? The impact of leaves of absence on managers' career success. *Academy of Management Journal*, 42, 641–651.
Kanter, R.M. (1977a). *Men and women of the corporation*. New York: Basic Books.
Kanter, R.M. (1977b). Some effects of proportions on group life: Skewed sex ratios and responses to token women. *American Journal of Sociology*, 82, 965–990.
Kirchmeyer, C. (1998). Determinants of managerial career success: Evidence and explanation of male/female differences. *Journal of Management*, 24, 673–692.
Kirchmeyer, C. (2002). Gender differences in managerial careers: Yesterday, today, and tomorrow. *Journal of Business Ethics*, 37, 5–24.
Linehan, M. & Walsh, J.S. (2000). Work–family conflict and the senior female international manager. *British Journal of Management*, 11, S49–S58.
Lowe, K.B., Kroeck, K.G., & Sivasubramaniam, N. (1996). Effectiveness correlates of transformational and transactional leadership: A meta-analytic review of the MLQ literature. *Leadership Quarterly*, 7, 385–425.
Lubatkin, M. & Powell, G. (1998). Exploring the influence of gender on managerial work in a transitional, Eastern European nation. *Human Relations*, 51, 1007–1031.
Lyness, K.S. (2002). Finding the key to the executive suite: Challenges for women and people of color. In R. Silzer (Ed.), *The 21st century executive: Innovative practices for building leadership at the top* (pp. 229–273). San Francisco: Jossey-Bass.
Lyness, K.S. (in press). The glass ceiling. In J.H. Greenhaus & G.A. Callanan (Eds), *Encyclopedia of career development*. Thousand Oaks, CA: Sage.
Lyness, K.S. & Heilman, M.E. (in press). When fit is fundamental: Performance evaluations and promotions of upper-level female and male managers. *Journal of Applied Psychology*.
Lyness, K.S. & Judiesch, M.K. (1999). Are women more likely to be hired or promoted into management positions? *Journal of Vocational Behavior*, 54, 158–173.
Lyness, K.S. & Judiesch, M.K. (2001). Are female managers quitters? The relationships of gender, promotions, and family leaves of absence to voluntary turnover. *Journal of Applied Psychology*, 86, 1167–1178.

Lyness, K.S. & Kropf, M.B. (2005). The relationships of national gender equality and organizational support with work–family balance: A study of European managers. *Human Relations*, **58**, 33–60.

Lyness, K.S. & Schrader, C.A. (in press). Moving ahead or just moving? An examination of gender differences in senior corporate management appointments. *Group and Organization Management*.

Lyness, K.S. & Thompson, D.E. (1997). Above the glass ceiling? A comparison of matched samples of female and male executives. *Journal of Applied Psychology*, **82**, 359–375.

Lyness, K.S. & Thompson, D.E. (2000). Climbing the corporate ladder: Do female and male executives follow the same route? *Journal of Applied Psychology*, **85**, 86–101.

Martell, R.F. & DeSmet, A.L. (2001). A diagnostic-ratio approach to measuring beliefs about the leadership abilities of male and female managers. *Journal of Applied Psychology*, **86**, 1223–1231.

McCauley, C.D., Ruderman, M.N., Ohlott, P.J., & Morrow, J.E. (1994). Assessing the developmental components of managerial jobs. *Journal of Applied Psychology*, **79**, 544–560.

Morrison, A.M. & von Glinow, M.A. (1990). Women and minorities in management. Special Issue: Organizational psychology. *American Psychologist*, **45** (2), 200–208.

Ohlott, P.J., Ruderman, M.N., & McCauley, C.D. (1994). Gender differences in managers' developmental job experiences. *Academy of Management Journal*, **37**, 46–67.

Olson, J.E., Frieze, I.H., & Good, D.C. (1987). The effects of job type and industry on the income of male and female MBAs. *Journal of Human Resources*, **22**, 532–541.

Omar, A. & Davidson, M.J. (2001). Women in management: A comparative cross-cultural overview. *Cross Cultural Management*, **8** (3/4), 35–67.

Pazy, A. & Oron, I. (2001). Sex proportion and performance evaluation among high-ranking military officers. *Journal of Organizational Behavior*, **22**, 689–702.

Perry, E.L., Davis-Blake, A., & Kulik, C.T. (1994). Explaining gender-based selection decisions: A synthesis of contextual and cognitive approaches. *Academy of Management Review*, **19**, 786–820.

Powell, G.N. (1999). Reflections on the glass ceiling: Recent trends and future prospects. In G.N. Powell (Ed.), *Handbook of gender and work* (pp. 325–345). Thousand Oaks, CA: Sage.

Powell, G.N., Butterfield, D.A., & Parent, J.D. (2002). Gender and managerial stereotypes: Have the times changed? *Journal of Management*, **28**, 177–193.

Ragins, B.R. & Sundstrom, E. (1989). Gender and power in organizations. *Psychological Bulletin*, **105**, 51–88.

Ragins, B.R., Townsend, B., & Mattis, M. (1998). Gender gap in the executive suite: CEOs and female executives report on breaking the glass ceiling. *Academy of Management Executive*, **12** (1), 28–42.

Ruderman, M.N., Ohlott, P.J., Panzer, K., & King, S.N. (2002). Benefits of multiple roles for managerial women. *Academy of Management Journal*, **45**, 369–386.

Schein, V.E. (1973). The relationship between sex role stereotypes and requisite management characteristics. *Journal of Applied Psychology*, **57**, 95–100.

Schein, V.E. (1975). Relations between sex role stereotypes and requisite management characteristics among female managers. *Journal of Applied Psychology*, **60**, 340–344.

Schein, V.E. (2001). A global look at psychological barriers to women's progress in management. *Journal of Social Issues*, **57**, 675–688.

Schein, V.E. & Mueller, R. (1992). Sex role stereotyping and requisite management characteristics: A cross cultural look. *Journal of Organizational Behavior*, **13**, 439–447.

Schein, V.E., Mueller, R., Lituchy, T., & Liu, J. (1996). Think manager–think male: A global phenomenon? *Journal of Organizational Behavior*, **17**, 33–41.

Schneer, J.A. & Reitman, F. (1990). Effects of employment gaps on the careers of MBAs: More damaging for men than for women? *Academy of Management Journal*, 33, 391–406.

Schneer, J.A. & Reitman, F. (1994). The importance of gender in mid-career: A longitudinal study of MBAs. *Journal of Organizational Behavior*, 15, 199–207.

Simpson, P.A. & Stroh, L.K. (2004). Gender differences: Emotional expression and feelings of personal inauthenticity. *Journal of Applied Psychology*, 89, 715–721.

Simpson, R. (1998). Presenteeism, power, and organizational change: Long hours as a career barrier and impact on the working lives of women managers. *British Journal of Management*, 9, S37–S50.

Statistics Canada (2002). *Women in Canada: Work chapter updates.* Retrieved February 20, 2005, from http://collection.nlc-bnc.ca/100/201/301/statcan/women_can_work/89F0133XIE01001.pdf.

Stroh, L.K., Brett, J.M., & Reilly, A.H. (1992). All the right stuff: A comparison of female and male managers' career progression. *Journal of Applied Psychology*, 77, 251–260.

Stroh, L.K., Brett, J.M., & Reilly, A.H. (1996). Family structure, glass ceiling, and traditional explanations for the differential rate of turnover of female and male managers. *Journal of Vocational Behavior*, 49, 99–118.

Terborg, J.R. (1977). Women in management: A research review. *Journal of Applied Psychology*, 62, 647–664.

Tharenou, P. (1999). Is there a link between family structures and women's and men's managerial career advancement? *Journal of Organizational Behavior*, 20, 837–863.

Tharenou, P. (2001). Going up? Do traits and informal social processes predict advancing in management? *Academy of Management Journal*, 44, 1005–1017.

United Nations Development Programme (2001). *Human development report 2001: Making new technologies work for human development.* New York: Oxford University Press.

United States Department of Labor Bureau of Labor Statistics (2004). *Labor force statistics from the Current Population Survey, Table 11 Employed persons by detailed occupation, sex, race, and Hispanic or Latino ethnicity.* Retrieved 2/20, 2005, from http://www.bls.gov/cps/cpsaat11.pdf.

United States Equal Employment Opportunity Commission (2004). *Glass ceilings: The status of women as officials and managers in the private sector.* Retrieved February 20, 2005, from http://www.eeoc.gov/stats/reports/glassceiling/index.pdf.

Van Velsor, E. & Hughes, M.W. (1990). *Gender differences in the development of managers: How women managers learn from experience* (Technical report No. 145). Greensboro, NC: Center for Creative Leadership.

Van Vianen, A.E.M. & Fischer, A.H. (2002). Illuminating the glass ceiling: The role of organizational culture preferences. *Journal of Occupational and Organizational Psychology*, 75, 315–337.

Ward, P.A., Orazem, P.F., & Schmidt, S.W. (1992). Women in elite pools and elite positions. *Social Science Quarterly*, 73, 31–45.

Wellington, W., Kropf, M.B., & Gerkovich, P.R. (2003). What's holding women back? *Harvard Business Review*, 81 (6), 18–19.

Chapter 7

ADVANCES IN THE SCIENCE OF PERFORMANCE APPRAISAL: IMPLICATIONS FOR PRACTICE

Gary P. Latham and Sara Mann

Rotman School of Management, University of Toronto, Canada

There have been at least five reviews of the literature on performance appraisal. Two appeared in this series 20 years ago (Latham, 1986) and 13 years ago (Latham, Skarlicki, Irvine, & Siegel, 1993). A third review was conducted five years later by Arvey and Murphy (1998). The fourth and fifth interrelated reviews by Fletcher (2001) and Fletcher and Perry (2001) appeared five years ago.

The topics focused on in the first two time periods are re-examined in the present chapter. They include legal issues affecting performance appraisals, performance criteria, and the scales that can be used for assessing people on them, possible sources of an appraisal, objectivity/accuracy of appraisers, and ways of bringing about and sustaining a person's performance effectiveness. The literature on legal issues in the first two time periods was restricted primarily to North American organizations. This is no longer the case in this new millennium. The present chapter describes legislation affecting performance appraisals conducted in Asia, Australia, Europe, and Latin America. Contrary to the conclusions reached in the two earlier reviews, there is now evidence that appraisers do discriminate against people on the basis of demographic variables. As a result of Bommer, Johnson, Rich, Podsakoff, and MacKenzie's (1995) meta-analysis revealing the convergent validity of hard versus soft criteria, the debate around the use of these two performance measures in the first two time periods has ended. The current focus is on the identification and measurement of employee behaviors, particularly those that are task related, which impact an organization's effectiveness. The focus on different methods of job analysis that occupied the attention of researchers in the 1980s disappeared in the 1990s and has not been resurrected. This domain has been mastered. User reactions to appraisals were only touched upon in the 1980s–1990s,

International Review of Industrial and Organizational Psychology, 2006, Volume 21
Edited by G.P. Hodgkinson and J.K. Ford. © 2006 John Wiley & Sons, Ltd.

when the emphasis was on psychometric concerns regarding the scales used for making appraisal decisions. The converse is true in the present time period. We know how to build reliable and content valid appraisal scales. We are currently discovering how to get people to like them so much that they will use them. This is necessitated by the fact that many managers are so uncomfortable conducting appraisals that they give uniformly high ratings to their employees (Tziner & Murphy, 1999). The employees who are on the receiving end of the appraisal express dissatisfaction with both the decisions made as a result of a performance assessment and the process of performance assessment. As Bowman (1999, p. 557) wryly observed, a performance appraisal is 'given by someone who does not want to give it to someone who does not want to get it.'

With regard to sources of appraisal, the primary focus of research in the 1980s was on supervisory, peer, and self-appraisals. In the 1990s, upward feedback from subordinates was also being studied. No mention was made in either time period on the use of multisources commonly referred to as 360-degree feedback. Research on this latter topic has subsequently blossomed in North America and the United Kingdom (Fletcher, 2001). Research on cognitive information processes as a way to improve appraiser accuracy, relative to the two earlier time periods, has decreased significantly. There is general agreement that this research stream was not productive (e.g., Arvey & Murphy, 1998; Fletcher, 2001). As Fletcher and Perry (2001) noted, the findings from the voluminous laboratory experiments on this subject did not take into account the motives of appraisers, and how these motives affect appraisal decisions. With regard to the theoretical frameworks guiding appraisal research, attribution theory is no longer used. Researchers continue to draw upon goal setting and organizational justice theories. Finally, the perennial debate on whether the developmental aspects of a performance appraisal should be temporally separated from those that are evaluative has subsided. This is the result of a monumental shift in the attention of researchers from the discrete performance appraisal to ongoing performance management where coaching is inherent in the process. Thus this may be the last review of the literature where performance appraisal is in the title. The present chapter concludes with a research agenda for performance management based on findings from ongoing research in the motivation and decision-making fields of industrial and organizational (I/O) psychology as well as those in clinical/counseling psychology. These issues have not been discussed in previous literature reviews.

LEGAL ISSUES

Because organizations have become increasingly global in the twenty-first century, it has become important for organizational decision makers to be aware of and sensitive to legislation and court decisions governing performance appraisal, both of which reflect a country's culture. In doing so, Latham and

McCauley (2005) predicted that, as this new millennium progresses, there will be a shift in emphasis from the twentieth-century focus on diversity issues within a country regarding an employee's race, sex, or age to organizational leaders having to take into account differences among countries regarding employee ethnicity, national origin, and political ideology. For example, Fletcher and Perry (2001) observed that the purpose of performance appraisals varies across cultures. In individualistic, low-power cultures typified by Canada and the USA, appraisals are often used to differentiate among employees for making pay and promotion decisions. Employees expect and are expected to participate in the appraisal process. In collectivistic, high-power cultures typified by many countries in Asia and Latin America, the developmental aspects of appraisals are emphasized relative to the evaluative so as to increase organizational commitment. Employees neither expect nor are they expected to be involved in this process. Hence, performance appraisals are likely to be most effective and accepted when a country's cultural values are taken into account in their design and implementation (Erez, 1994). But, despite the large shadow that the law casts on this domain, there is an absence of empirical research on the role that cultural differences actually play in performance appraisals (Fletcher & Perry, 2001).

The need for this research is evidenced by the fact that people in the United States, a culturally diverse society, have become increasingly aware of their legal rights. Martin, Bartol, and Kehoe (2000) reported a 100% increase in the number of discrimination cases filed in 1999 over the number filed in 1995. Moreover, these court cases usually involved complaints regarding a performance appraisal (Arvey & Murphy, 1998). Werner and Bolino (1997) updated the findings of Feild and Holley (1982) on ways that organizations are likely to win a court case. Emphasis is given by the US courts to evidence of fairness and due process—subjects that are discussed in more detail in a subsequent section. Issues that are of lesser importance to the court include the type of appraisal scale and evidence of validity.

Legal concerns pertaining to performance appraisal are by no means restricted to North America (Woodford & Maes, 2002). For example, Head, Haug, Krabbenhoft, and Ma (2000) reported that in Latin America, countries such as Panama, Nicaragua, Bolivia, and Argentina have outlawed discrimination based on political opinion. However, in Chile, Guatemala, and Paraguay no groups are protected and employment discrimination can occur openly. In Asia, India prohibits discrimination on the grounds of religion, race, caste, sex, and place of birth or residence (Jain, Sloan, & Horowitz, 2003).

Western-oriented countries have passed legislation that is more similar than different from the USA. For example, Australia has comprehensive anti-discrimination legislation that prohibits the use of gender, sexual preference, age, marital status, child or elder care responsibilities, race, religion, political belief, pregnancy, physical features, industrial activity, and impairment in any and all aspects of employment decision making, including recruitment, selection, performance appraisal, training, compensation, and separation (Bennington & Roberts-Calvert, 1998; Bennington & Wein, 2000). As of 1994, legislation in South Africa provides equal opportunity to all citizens regardless of color, gender, religion, political opinion, or sexual orientation (Jain et al., 2003). In 1996, legislation in Northern Ireland was passed prohibiting employment discrimination on the basis of religion, political opinion, color, nationality, race, and ethnic or national origin (Jain et al., 2003). Similarly, the Race Relations Act in Britain outlaws direct and indirect discrimination on the grounds of race, color, and nationality, including citizenship or ethnic or national origins, but not on religious grounds (Jain et al., 2003). The European Union (EU) has not passed new legislation affecting performance appraisals. Instead the EU has kept in place the local labor laws of the 15 member countries (Claus, 2003).

APPRAISER BIAS

Is the concern of legislators and the courts justified regarding the fairness of an employee's performance appraisal? The empirical literature suggests that the answer is 'Yes.'

Lance (1994) found that 'ratings were stronger reflections of raters' overall biases than of true performance factors' (p. 768). A massive study involving over 4000 managers where there were appraisals from at least two supervisors, two peers, two subordinates, plus self-appraisals, indicated that individual rater effects account for over half of the rating variance (Scullen, Mount, & Goff, 2000).

A field study involving the US Army showed that the person's knowledge and ability explained only 13% of the variance in an appraisal from a supervisor, and just 7% in appraisals from peers. Future research should focus on the extent to which this is due to supervisors and peers weighting issues of interpersonal facilitation skills and trust as more important than a person's current knowledge and ability. If this is true, the appraisals reflect important variance on the relationship aspects of a person's job. Support for this hypothesis can be inferred from the research on the multidimensions of performance discussed subsequently in this chapter.

A review of the literature revealed that the supervisor's positive regard for a subordinate resulted in leniency and halo errors, and less inclination to punish poor performance (Lefkowitz, 2000). Studies in the private sector have found that the perceived similarity of the subordinate by the supervisor inflates the appraisal (Wayne & Liden, 1995). This is especially true with regard to perceived similarities regarding extroversion, conscientiousness, and emotional stability (Strauss, Barrick, & Connerley, 2001). In short, to the extent that appraisers viewed an employee as similar to themselves, they tended to like the person more, and consequently, gave the person a higher rating. Again, research is needed on the extent to which appraisers are focusing on the interpersonal facilitation skills required of a person to be effective in today's team-driven organizations rather than on traditional performance metrics (e.g., goals set vs goals attained) that are often affected by factors beyond a person's control (e.g., the economy).

A person's appraisal is also affected by gender, a finding that does not go unnoticed by the courts. A review of objective and subjective indicators of performance as a leader revealed that men are usually evaluated as more effective than women (Eagly, Karau, & Makhijani, 1995). That this finding, at least in part, reflects discrimination is suggested by the fact that even when the sexes engaged in equivalent leadership behavior, women were devalued when leadership roles required a 'masculine' leadership style, and the appraisers were male (Eagly, Makhijani, & Klonsky, 1992).

A subsequent review of leadership perceptions in the military revealed preferential ratings for men in training groups primarily where there was a 'token' woman; this typically was not found in groups where there were several women (Biernat, Crandall, Young, Kobrynowicz, & Halpin, 1998). Token status exacerbates less positive evaluations of women than men, because tokens receive considerable attention that increases the pressure on them to perform well (Biernat et al., 1998).

Boldry, Wood, and Kashy (2001) found that sex proportion is a factor affecting rating accuracy. The respondents, only 27 of whom were female, reported that men possess the motivation and leadership qualities necessary for effective performance, whereas women possess feminine attitudes that impair effective performance. Yet there were no sex differences on any performance measure (i.e., grades, rank, physical training scores). The authors concluded: 'Overall, these results indicate that sex differences in evaluations do not reflect a kernel of truth as represented by sex differences in performance or by sex differences in self ratings' (p. 702). These findings link the lower evaluations of women to general gender stereotypes and show that these stereotypes extend to perceived motivation as well as leadership.

In a study of over 3000 high-ranking military officers (majors, lieutenant-colonels) in Israel, five variables were analyzed, namely, overall performance, advancement prospects, analytic competence, operational competence, and interpersonal relations (Pazy & Oron, 2001). The results showed that the performance of women was rated higher than that of men when the women constituted a higher proportion than the men. Sex proportion appears to be a contextual variable of importance in explaining gender-related influences on performance evaluations (Bartol, 1999). Increasing the representation of women in mixed groups increases their positive appraisals. The authors concluded that under-representation of women in military units, even at very high ranks, has a deleterious effect on the performance appraisals they receive. These findings are similar to those obtained by Kraiger and Ford (1985) regarding the evaluations of African-Americans.

In a field study of 1268 managerial employees, Landau (1995) found that controlling for age, education, tenure, salary grade, functional area, and satisfaction with support for one's career, both race and gender were related to appraisals of one's promotion potential. Females were rated lower than males, and blacks and Asians were rated lower than whites. Just as it has been found that both black and white appraisers assessed the performance of black employees as lower than that of white employees, Dewberry (2001) reported similar effects for ethnic minority vs white comparisons in the United Kingdom.

A meta-analysis by Bowen, Swim, and Jacobs (2000) provides a ray of optimism with regard to these findings. They found no evidence of gender bias in performance ratings when all the raters are not male, and when the appraisal instrument is not gender-typed, that is, contains no male or female stereotypes of performance.

In a field study of entry level employees in accounting firms, Saks and Waldman (1998) found that when work experience, in terms of the number of previously held jobs and a person's grade point average, is controlled, there is no relationship between age and performance evaluations. Gordon and Arvey (2004) conducted a meta-analytic review of age discrimination research on job incumbents that provides still another ray of hope in this area. Their results suggest that age bias is less of a problem today than it was in previous decades. The greater and more relevant the information that is provided regarding an employee, and the greater and more relevant the experience of the raters, the less evidence of age bias.

Gilbert, Hannan, and Lowe (1998) found that people who smoke are rated lower than non-smokers on professional comportment, working with others, and dependability. This is likely the result of smokers losing production time as a result of leaving for designated smoking areas, and due to rater bias against those who smoke.

A person's reputation also plays a role in decisions regarding rewards that are to be administered. Johnson, Erez, Kiker, and Motowidlo (2002) found that a helpful person who has a good reputation received more rewards than did a helpful person who has a bad reputation. An unhelpful person, with a good reputation, did not receive more rewards than an unhelpful person with a bad reputation. These findings suggest that when a person is unhelpful, a good reputation does not help. But when a person's performance is helpful, a bad reputation continues to adversely affect the rewards that are subsequently administered despite the person's good performance.

The motivation attributed by a supervisor to an employee also affects appraisals of that person's performance. In a laboratory experiment, Pelletier and Vallerand (1996) found that even when there are no differences in job performance among subordinates, supervisors evaluate an employee's performance more positively when they believe that the subordinate is motivated to perform the task for intrinsic rather than extrinsic reasons. In short, a performance appraisal is influenced not only by the performance demonstrated by an employee, but also by what a supervisor perceives the motivation of the employee to be.

DeVoe and Iyengar (2003) also examined the relationship, in three different cultures, between a manager's perception of an employee's motivation and the subsequent performance appraisal. North American managers perceived their employees as being more extrinsically than intrinsically motivated. Perceptions of intrinsic motivation resulted in a high performance appraisal. Asian managers perceived their subordinates as being motivated by both factors, and their perceptions affected performance appraisals positively. Latin American managers perceived their employees as being more intrinsically motivated, and only their perceptions of an employee's intrinsic motivation correlated significantly with an employee's performance appraisal.

In short, legislation and court decisions alone are not eliminating bias in performance appraisals. This does not bode well for organizations whose leaders must find ways to minimize rigidity, insensitivity in interactions, and intolerance among different ethnic groups (Latham & McCauley, 2005). The solutions to this problem may be at least three-fold, namely, find ways to increase user acceptance of the appraisal process, base appraisal decisions on multi-sources, and train appraisers not only to be objective, but to coach employees on a year-round basis. Research is now needed to test the effect of this treatment intervention on perceived fairness in performance evaluations. Advances that have been made on the individual components of this proposed 'treatment package' are reviewed below.

THE APPRAISAL SCALE AND USER REACTIONS

An organization's strategic plan often fails because little or no attention is given to how it should be operationalized behaviorally in the field (Latham & Latham, 2000). An appraisal scale that specifies what an employee must start doing, stop doing, or continue doing becomes a diagnostic instrument that facilitates self-management, as well as coaching by others of an employee. Such an instrument becomes highly relevant for the employee and the appraiser(s) because it specifies the behaviors necessary for the strategic plan to succeed. As a result, such an instrument is difficult to attack in a court of law. Hence the importance of job analysis for identifying critical behaviors cannot be overemphasized. Cronshaw (1998) argued the merits of a future-oriented analysis where the emphasis is on the anticipation of behaviors that will become necessary for the effective implementation of an organization's strategy.

Failure to develop appraisal scales that operationalize behaviorally what must be done to implement an organization's strategy probably explains Fletcher's (2001) finding. He reported that most organizations in the United Kingdom remain dissatisfied with their appraisal systems, not only because these systems cannot be shown to be psychometrically valid, but because they are not perceived as a means for developing and motivating people. Hence legal challenges initiated by employees to an appraisal that adversely affects them should not be surprising.

In short, a primary reason for the frequent failure of a performance appraisal to bring about a positive change in a person's behavior is that the appraisal instrument often measures the 'wrong things.' In Australia, a study of more than 400 Army officers revealed that a substantial proportion reported concerns regarding the utility of the appraisal instrument as a device for accurately assessing work performance and promotion potential (Salter, 1996).

Job analysis methods for correcting the issues described above were developed in the past century. The emphasis now needs to shift from science to practice regarding the measurement of an employee's performance. Hence little attention is currently being given by researchers to the development of additional job analysis techniques.

Attention continues to be given to what constitutes performance effectiveness. Conway (1996, 1999), using factor analysis and a multitrait–multirater database, found that employee performance should be defined as either task or contextual. The latter is often referred to as organizational citizenship behavior or OCB (Organ, 1997). Van Scotter and Motowidlo (1996) found that OCB can be further dichotomized in terms of interpersonal facilitation and job dedication. However, from a practical standpoint, OCB can be treated as an aggregate construct. A meta-analysis revealed that the two dimensions are not only highly correlated, but that there are no meaningful differences in their relationships with such measures as job satisfaction, organizational commitment, or conscientiousness (LePine, Erez, & Johnson, 2002). Rotundo and Sackett (2002) found that job performance has three dimensions, namely, task performance, OCB, and counterproductive performance. An appraisal instrument should assess people on each of these three factors in relation to an organization's strategy.

Similar to the decrease in research emphasis on the development of new methods of job analysis, there has been a decrease in emphasis by researchers on the development of new appraisal instruments. An exception to this statement is an innovative approach to the development of an appraisal instrument that was tested in a laboratory experiment by Borman et al. (2001). They found that a computerized adaptive rating scale (CARS) had higher interobserver reliability and accuracy than a behaviorally anchored rating scale (BARS). In brief, this appraisal format presents the appraiser with two behavioral statements associated with a given dimension of performance, one reflecting 'below average' and the other 'above average' performance. Depending on which of two statements the appraiser chooses as describing the ratee, the computer selects two additional behavioral statements; one with a scaled effectiveness level above, and one below the effectiveness value of the statement chosen initially. A ratee's 'true' level of effectiveness is determined by these iterative paired comparisons. User reactions in field settings to CARS have yet to be tested.

There is evidence suggesting that the number of categories, three vs five, that an organization allows for describing a person's performance affects motivation and perceptions of fairness. Bartol, Durham, and Poon (2001), in a laboratory experiment, found that the number of performance categories was positively related to (a) the person's self-efficacy for attaining the next higher rating category, (b) higher goals being set, and (c) higher performance, with five being superior to three.

Jack Welch, the former CEO of the General Electric Company, argued that: 'A company that bets its future on its people must remove the lower 10%, and keep removing it every year—always raising the bar of performance...' (General Electric Company, 2000, p. 4). Through the use of a simulation, Scullen, Bergey, and Aiman-Smith (2005) investigated the effect of this forced distribution rating system on the performance of a workforce. They found that there is indeed a noticeable improvement in the first several years. However, their findings also show that eventually each time a company improves its workforce by replacing an employee with a new hire, it becomes more difficult to do so again. This is because an organization eventually reaches the point where its poorest employees are as capable as its best applicants. Employees at Microsoft, Conoco, Ford, Goodyear, and General Motors have filed class-action law suits in the USA claiming that this appraisal system resulted in discrimination against blacks, women, older employees, and non-citizens (Scullen et al., 2005).

With the emphasis that the courts place on the concept of fairness in appraising employees, Sulsky and Keown (1998) concluded, after reviewing the appraisal literature, that research emphasis needs to be placed on ways to improve user reactions to the appraisal process. Mayer and Davis (1999), in a longitudinal field study, found that trust in top management increased significantly when a new performance appraisal system was introduced to replace one that was viewed by the employees as inaccurate and not allowing for performance-related rewards. Similarly, in an empirical study involving the US Air Force's use of BARS, Hedge and Teachout (2000) argued that psychometric considerations regarding the reliability and validity of appraisals will always need to be taken into account, but they are not sufficient criteria for evaluating an appraisal system. Critical to the implementation and ongoing use of appraisals is user acceptance. Trust, as well as perceptions of situational constraints, predicted the motivation to rate others, as well as the motivation to rate them accurately. Trust was defined as perceptions of whether people adhere to the rules when making appraisals, whether the appraisals are accurate, and whether the appraisals reflect favoritism. Situational constraints include the absence, or lack of clarity, of a technical manual for conducting performance appraisals.

A meta-analysis by Cawley, Keeping, and Levy (1998) revealed that the employee's motivation to improve performance, employee satisfaction with the appraisal system as a whole, as well as with the appraisal session itself, is high if the person is allowed to participate in the appraisal process. Participation that results in perceptions by employees that their viewpoints were taken into account in administrative decisions has a greater impact on their satisfaction than participation for the purpose of influencing the end result. In short, allowing employees 'voice' influences their perceptions of fairness. Consistent with these findings, Kleingeld, Van Tuijl, and Algera (2004), in a field study involving employees of a Dutch supplier of office equipment, found that implementing a performance management system that involves employee participation can lead to a significant increase in performance. In addition, they found that employee satisfaction with the program, and the perceived usefulness of the feedback, were significantly higher when the performance appraisal system included employee participation.

In their review of the literature on user reactions to different appraisal instruments, Tziner and Kopelman (2002) reported that an appraisal system is often abandoned if it fails to elicit positive reactions from the user. Behavioral Observation Scales or BOS (Latham & Wexley, 1994) were found to be superior to other appraisal instruments in terms of eliciting favorable attitudes. They concluded that this is because, relative to other instruments such as BARS and trait scales, BOS convey precisely what an individual 'must do,' feedback is perceived as factual, objective, and unbiased; and BOS feedback is conducive to setting specific high goals that are job related. Users preferred trait scales over BARS (see also Bernardin, 2005). In addition, Varma, DeNisi, and Peters (1996) found that bias in ratings is reduced when the appraisal instrument requires appraisals based on observable behavior. The bias of the appraiser, as noted earlier, continues to plague appraisal decisions.

SOURCES OF APPRAISAL

A critical component of any appraisal system is the appraiser (Sulsky & Keown, 1998). Thus, once the decision has been made as to the appraisal instrument that is acceptable to stakeholders, the issue remains as to who should use it. Who should do the appraisal? Is the answer supervisors, peers, subordinates, the employees themselves, or all of the above?

Supervisory Appraisals

Walker and Smither (1999) found that a subordinate's performance increases significantly more in those years in which the supervisor holds appraisal meetings than in the years where such meetings do not take place. This finding indicates that in spite of the biases that can enter into an appraisal, sitting with and talking to an individual is a worthwhile process for bringing about a subsequent improvement in a person's performance.

There are data that suggest that supervisors spend less than 1% of their time observing their subordinates (Komaki & Desselles, 1994). Appraisal errors are highly likely when an observer has limited opportunity to observe an employee. Consequently, another reason why appraisals can fail to improve a person's performance is employee hostility toward the supervisor. Difficulty in answering satisfactorily such questions as: 'On what basis are you able to evaluate me?' undermines the credibility of the source.

Hence it would appear that supervisors, rather than being the primary source for observing an employee's performance, should be held accountable primarily for collecting data for appraising an individual from multiple sources, and then making the final appraisal decision based on these multiple sources of information. Administrative and developmental decisions based on multiple sources are likely to have high credibility in the courtroom as well as in the court of public opinion. Moreover, multiple sources of feedback increase the probability that the person will take positive action as a result of the feedback (Smither, London, Flautt, Vargas, & Kucine, 2003). Sources of an appraisal, in addition to supervisors, include an employee's peers, subordinates, as well as self.

Peer Appraisals

Greguras and Robie (1998) found that peers are the most reliable source of performance information followed by subordinates and superiors, respectively. They concluded that 'although reliability does not necessitate validity, these results suggest that researchers and practitioners may be well advised to seek, and perhaps weight more heavily information from peers and subordinates' (p. 964).

In a laboratory experiment involving the use of BOS, anonymous peer appraisals increased a person's interpersonal effectiveness (Dominick, Reilly, & McGourty, 1997). In a study involving MBA students working in project teams, peer appraisals increased group cohesion, openness of communication, task motivation, and group satisfaction (Drusket & Wolff, 1999). These findings are consistent with Conway's (1999) study of managers. Peers tend to give more emphasis to interpersonal skills than to task performance in making overall performance ratings, whereas the converse is true for supervisors. It was found that a subsequent improvement in performance resulting from peer feedback is especially likely if the person scores highly on conscientiousness and openness to experience.

In a study of the Special Forces in the US Army, peer rankings predicted final training outcomes better than did ratings from the staff. Again, it was found that peers placed significantly more importance on interpersonal performance and motivation than did the staff, and they placed significantly less importance on task performance (Zazanis, Zaccaco, & Kilcullen, 2001). Fletcher (2001) concluded that peers are the optimal source for assessments of a person's OCB.

Anonymous peer appraisals are becoming increasingly accepted as teams are becoming critical to the way that work is accomplished (Cohen & Bailey, 1997).

Moreover, teams are expected to be self-managing groups (Druskat & Wolff, 1999). Thus the people who comprise the teams are responsible for appraising and coaching one another.

Bettenhausen and Fedor (1997) reported that one's relationship with one's supervisor has little effect on one's perspective regarding peer appraisals. In contrast, only those with good coworker relationships supported their use, even when they are used for developmental rather than administrative purposes.

Among the reasons peer appraisals have been found to be unacceptable in previous studies is that inadequate appraisal instruments were used, namely, global trait-like measures. A robust finding in the behavioral sciences is that negative outcomes are perceived as particularly unfair when they are not adequately explained; they are perceived as fair when they are accompanied by an informative explanation (Greenberg, 2000). Consequently, Latham and Seijts (1997) looked at whether the type of appraisal instrument, namely, BOS, BARS, trait scales, or a blank sheet of paper that is used to provide feedback to managers, affects satisfaction with a peer appraisal. The results supported the hypothesis that peer appraisals are viewed as most useful and most fair when based on either BOS or a blank sheet of paper. Use of the latter, however, is likely to be problematic in a court of law as it invites idiosyncratic decisions on the part of appraisers that may not be job related.

Subordinate Appraisals

Atwater, Roush, and Fischthal (1995) found that anonymous feedback from subordinates promotes positive changes in a leader's behavior. Moreover, the study showed that leaders who receive feedback from subordinates that is more negative than their own self-evaluation show the greatest level of subsequent improvement.

Smither et al. (1995) obtained similar results in a study involving managers who were assessed on BOS. The greatest improvement was observed on the part of those managers whose self-evaluation was initially higher than the evaluation they received from their subordinates. These changes in behavior on the part of managers were not only positive, but they were shown to be sustainable over time (Reilly, Smither, & Vasilopoulos, 1996; Walker & Smither, 1999).

Heslin and Latham (2004), in a study of an Australian professional services firm, found that upward feedback from subordinates improves the performance of managers. Two key moderators are the manager's self-efficacy, that is, the 'belief that I can change,' as well as a learning goal orientation, that is, a focus on performance improvement rather than 'one's score.'

As is the case with peers, subordinate evaluations must be anonymous. Antonioni (1994) found, not surprisingly, that subordinates who were not allowed anonymity viewed the process more negatively than those who were anonymous, so much so that many non-anonymous raters refused to provide appraisals. Those subordinates who continued to give appraisals were significantly more lenient in their appraisals than their anonymous counterparts.

The purpose of an appraisal affects the assessments given by subordinates. Greguras, Robie, Schleicher, and Goff (2003) found that the quality of subordinate ratings is significantly better when they are to be used for developmental rather than for administrative purposes. However, Smither and Walker (2004) found that people who receive more favorable narrative comments from their direct reports also received a more favorable annual review from their supervisor. And Ostroff, Atwater, and Feinberg (2004) found that subordinate, in addition to peer, evaluations were related to a supervisor's overall evaluation of an employee. This may reflect the fact that supervisors become knowledgeable of a person's performance by listening to what others have observed.

Self-appraisals

That agreement between a self-appraisal and appraisals from other sources is usually lacking was shown in a meta-analysis by Beehr, Ivanitskaya, Hansen, Erofeev, and Gudanowski (2001) of over 2000 employees who received supervisor, peer, and self-appraisals. Moreover, self-appraisals had the least predictive validity regarding a person's future performance.

Although employees generally rate their performance more favorably than do their supervisors, Korsgaard, Meglino, and Lester (2004), in a study of employees at a healthcare claims center in the Midwestern US, found that this depends on an employees' self vs other orientation. Individuals who emphasize others rather than oneself place importance on fitting in with peers, and gaining a sense of belonging. Moreover, the self-ratings by other-oriented individuals not only showed greater agreement with ratings provided by their supervisor, but in addition had less leniency relative to their supervisor's appraisals of them.

These findings are consistent with previous cross-cultural studies. Markus and Kitayama (1991) found that Asians exhibit less leniency bias in their self-ratings. They also found that individuals from Eastern cultures are more likely to exhibit a greater discrepancy between their actual and ideal self. They concluded that individuals from Eastern cultures are more likely to accept information about their poor performance than employees in the West. Japanese employees, for example, are encouraged to focus on self-criticism as a way of improving their performance.

The effect of a person's self-esteem on self-ratings was examined in a laboratory study involving undergraduate students. Bernichon, Cook, and Brown (2003) found that individuals with high self-esteem tend to seek self-verifying feedback, even if it is negative. Low self-esteem individuals tend to seek positive feedback, even if it is non-self-verifying.

Ostroff et al. (2004) examined the relative importance of a number of demographic and contextual variables on self-other agreement. In a field study involving over 4000 US managers across 650 organizations, they found that women, whites, younger managers, those with less experience, and those with higher education tend to show agreement between self-ratings and ratings from others. Over-raters tended to be men, older managers, non-whites, those with a lower education, those in service-oriented functional areas, and those who supervise a large number of employees.

The importance of agreement between one's self-appraisal and appraisals by others was shown in a study by Fletcher (1997). People whose self-appraisals are relatively aligned with the appraisals they receive from others are usually high performers. This, Fletcher concluded, is due to their 'self-awareness' regarding their ability.

The extent to which self-monitoring and attitudes affect rating accuracy was subsequently examined. Miller and Cardy (2000) found that the self-ratings of self-monitoring individuals are higher than their low self-monitoring counterparts. Furthermore, they found that there is higher agreement with other sources of appraisals for low self-monitoring than for high self-monitoring individuals. Subsequently, Jawahar (2001), in a field study involving university employees, found that rating accuracy is higher for low rather than for high self-monitors. In short, self-monitoring significantly influences rating accuracy such that one's accuracy declines with increasing levels of self-monitoring.

Mann and Budworth (2005) found that at least three variables affect the extent to which there is agreement between self- and peer appraisals of counterproductive behavior in groups of undergraduate students who worked together for 12 weeks. Consistent with Rotundo and Sackett (2002), they defined counterproductive behavior as voluntary behavior that harms the well-being of the group. They found that agreement increases to the extent that self and peers score similarly on a measure of conscientiousness, have common beliefs as to what constitutes integrity, and engage in similar levels of counterproductive behavior.

Schrader and Steiner (1996) found that an effective way to improve agreement between self- and supervisory assessments of performance is to use explicit absolute criteria rather than internal comparisons with self, or relative comparisons with others. For example, in a study involving over 3000 supervisors, 12,000 peers, and nearly 3000 subordinates, relative agreement among sources was obtained when a 48-item behaviorally oriented appraisal instrument was used (Facteau & Craig, 2001).

Multisource Feedback

Rather than choosing only one of the above sources of appraisal, 90% of Fortune 1000 firms now collect feedback from multisources (Atwater & Waldman, 1998). While some organizations use multisource feedback for developmental purposes only, others use them for making administrative decisions regarding compensation, job placement, and promotion (London & Smither, 1995). A survey of 100 organizations in Canada revealed that over half were either using a multisource system, or were considering using it in the near future (Brutus & Derayeh, 2002). Basing an appraisal of a person on information from the above sources is referred to in the literature as 360-degree feedback because it provides a relatively complete picture of an employee's performance.

In the Psycinfo database, there are no references to 360-degree feedback prior to 1990, and only four citations between 1990 and 1995, namely four unpublished doctoral dissertations. Since 1995 there have been at least 89 studies on input from multisources, namely, supervisor, peers, subordinates, and, in many instances, self (Bracken, Timmreck, & Church, 2001). This is likely because input from multisources takes into account the 'multidimensional nature of jobs as seen by different constituencies' (London & Smither, 1995, p. 804). It takes into account the fact that different populations (e.g., peers, subordinates) have different opportunities to observe different aspects of a person's performance (Murphy & Cleveland, 1995). Similarly, Borman (1997) argued that appraisers from different populations (e.g., supervisors vs subordinates) attach different weights to the same aspects of performance that they observe as a result of their different organizational perspectives. Thus collecting appraisals from multisources provides an integrated, holistic view of an employee, thereby offsetting the drawbacks of an appraisal from only a single vantage point (e.g., supervisor). Moreover, 360-degree feedback is consistent with the organizational environment in this new millennium, one that is increasingly filled with novel, ill-defined problems. As Latham and McCauley (2005) observed, tomorrow's issues are unlikely to lend themselves to rapid solutions by assigning them to a single leader. Multiple perspectives and expertise will have to be brought to bear, especially due to the multiple stakeholders who will claim a stake in these complex issues. Hence the collective perspective of multiple individuals will often be required on performance-related decisions.

Bailey and Fletcher (2002) conducted a study of 104 managers where input was collected from at least one supervisor, three subordinates, as well as a self-assessment. There was agreement among sources on the manager's competence, developmental needs, and between the manager's self-evaluation and the evaluations the manager received from others. Agreement among multiple sources of an appraisal is evidence of convergent validity or accuracy (Bozeman, 1997).

With regard to interobserver reliability within populations of appraisers, peers have the highest, followed by subordinates and supervisors (Greguras & Robie, 1998). Thus there is benefit in treating each appraisal source as a measure of a different aspect of an employee's performance for determining developmental goals, and/or making an administrative decision (e.g., promotion).

Intersource agreement among populations, however, is not necessarily to be expected (Murphy & Cleveland, 1995). This is because each source of appraisal (e.g., peers, subordinates) often observes an employee in different contexts (Bozeman, 1997). The correlations among ratings made by a supervisor, peer, subordinate, and self range from a high of 0.79 (supervisor–peer) to a low of 0.14 (subordinate–self). Disagreement in conclusions are especially likely if different appraisal instruments are designed to assess those aspects of the job that a specific population (e.g., subordinates) is most likely to observe the employee performing on an ongoing basis (Facteau & Craig, 2001). Thus a person's appraisal may differ across populations (supervisor/subordinates) because of actual differences in the type of behaviors that are observed. Hence, Atwater, Ostroff, Yammarino, and Fleenor (1998) argued the importance of taking into account multiple appraisal sources in assessing and explaining a person's effectiveness.

Bailey and Fletcher (2002), cited earlier, were among the first to examine how well multisource ratings predict a person's subsequent performance. They found that over a two-year period both employees' and managers' assessments of managerial competence increased while perceived developmental needs decreased. Atkins and Wood (2002) used performance in an assessment center as a proxy for performance on the job. The average of supervisor, peer, and subordinate ratings predicted performance, as did the supervisor ratings alone. With respect to self-ratings, those who rated themselves most highly tended to be the poorest performers. Conversely, those who rated themselves in the midrange of the scale were more likely to be higher performers than those who rated themselves at the top or bottom ends of the scale. In other words, highly competent employees underestimated their abilities while less competent employees tended to overestimate their abilities relative to others. Atkins and Wood urged caution in the use of self-ratings in a 360-degree feedback program. They suggested that self-ratings should not be interpreted as reflecting actual competency levels, and should not be included in aggregations of ratings for evaluation purposes.

With respect to user reactions, Maurer, Mitchell, and Barbeite (2002) found that positive attitudes toward the system is dependent upon a positive relationship between peer and subordinate ratings and peer–self agreement, such that the more different peer ratings are compared to self-ratings, the more favorable ratee attitudes are toward the system. Other predictors of positive attitudes toward a 360-degree appraisal include a work context that involves people who are supportive of skill development, and beliefs by the feedback recipients that it is not only possible for them to improve their skills, but that they are capable of doing so.

No appraisal method is above criticism. A consulting firm, Watson Wyatt (2002), reported that 360-degree feedback can lead to a 10.6% decrease in corporate shareholder value. This finding may reflect a failure by these firms to take into account individual and contextual factors that affect receptivity to 360-degree feedback. Funderburg and Levy (1997) found that organizations who have individuals with high self-esteem, internal locus of control, individuals who report to autocratic leaders, and individuals who work in an environment that encourages seeking feedback have a positive attitude toward 360-degree appraisals. The finding regarding people with autocratic leaders reacting favorably to 360-degree feedback is ironic. It may reflect the fact that those with highly participatory leaders receive feedback on an ongoing basis and hence perceive less need for information from multisources.

In an essay, Ghorpade (2000) worried that the use of multiple sources of an appraisal may nevertheless fail to take into account situational factors that adversely affect a person's performance. Hence, more information through the use of multisources would not necessarily yield superior feedback. Empirical research suggests otherwise.

Church (2000) found that managers who received more favorable multi-source feedback had lower employee turnover and higher service quality in their workgroups. In addition, Church found that multisource ratings (e.g., supervisors, peers, and subordinates) accurately distinguished between high- and low-performing managers as assessed by independent measures. Erikson and Allen (2003) found that multisource feedback ratings were related posi-tively with retail store revenue, gross margin, and sales of accessories.

Smither, London, and Reilly (2005) presented a theoretical framework and reviewed empirical evidence suggesting that an improvement in performance resulting from multisource feedback is moderated by a number of variables. These variables include a person's perception that there is a need to alter one's behavior, belief that the change is feasible, and goal setting based on this feed-back.

In summary the literature suggests that 360-degree feedback should be used if: (a) the appraisal instrument is based on the core behaviors directly relevant to the organization; (b) peer and subordinate appraisals are anonymous; (c) the organizational environment encourages seeking feedback; and (d) appraisers are trained in conducting appraisals. The latter topic is discussed next.

TRAINING APPRAISERS

The importance of training appraisers is further evident in a study of auto-mobile salespeople. Pettijohn, Pettijohn, and d'Amico (2001) reported that job satisfaction was due in part to appraisal-related factors. Specifically, they found that—to the extent that there are clear criteria, the criteria meet the employee's approval, and the resulting appraisal of the person on these criteria is perceived as fair—job satisfaction increases. This finding is supported by another study that shows that a poorly implemented performance appraisal system increases employee 'burnout' (Gabris & Ihrke, 2001). A study involv-ing the Australian government showed that important predictors of employee acceptance or rejection of the appraisal program is satisfaction with their super-visor, the feedback anticipated by the employee, and anticipated consequences of the appraisal (Langan-Fox, Waycott, Morizzi, & McDonald, 1998).

Further evidence of the need for training on ways to increase objectivity and accuracy in making assessments of people is the finding that personality differ-ences among appraisers can affect an employee's appraisal. Kane, Bernardin,

Villanova, and Peyrefitte (1995) found that leniency in ratings is a relatively stable characteristic of a rater. Bernardin, Cooke, and Villanova (2000), in a laboratory study involving undergraduate students, found that two of the Big Five personality factors predict leniency ratings. People who scored highly on agreeableness tended to provide more elevated ratings of a peer's performance on group exercises, whereas individuals who scored highly on conscientiousness rated peers relatively low.

Even an appraiser's mood can affect rating accuracy. Freid, Levi, Ben-David, Tiegs, and Avital (2000), in a field study conducted in the USA and Israel, found that negative mood predisposition was negatively associated with performance ratings of employees whereas a positive mood predisposition was unrelated to performance ratings of employees.

Not surprisingly, organizational politics affect appraisals. Tziner (1999), in a field study of police officers, found a negative relationship between an appraiser's self-efficacy as a rater and the effect of political considerations. People who perceive themselves as insufficiently skilled as raters tend to remove themselves from the uncomfortable situation of appraising others by invoking political considerations and distorting the results of the performance appraisal. This reflects the raters' desire to avoid giving performance ratings that might antagonize employees or provoke their resentment. Tziner, Latham, Price, and Haccoun (1996) have developed a 25-item scoring instrument to measure perceptions of the extent to which performance appraisals are affected by organizational politics.

Uggerslev and Sulsky (2002) found that supervisors take into account information from an employee's coworkers when making an appraisal. But, they do so only when it is consistent with their own observations, and they do so primarily when the information is positive.

A final reason for training appraisers can be found in a field study conducted in Canada, Israel, and the USA. Tziner, Murphy, and Cleveland (2001) found that an appraiser's self-efficacy for making accurate ratings as well as confidence, trust, and comfort level with the appraisal process accounted for significant variance in raters' tendency to differentiate among employees and to differentiate their ratings in accordance with the different dimensions of performance on which an employee was being assessed.

Rater Accuracy

Training that allows people to evaluate actors presented on videotape receive feedback as to their rating accuracy, and to practice, practice, practice increases objectivity and minimizes leniency, halo, and similar to me biases (Cardy & Keefe, 1994; Latham, Wexley, & Pursell, 1975; Noonan & Sulsky, 2001; Schleicher & Day, 1998; Sulsky & Keown, 1998; Woehr & Huffcutt, 1994). This training teaches appraisers (a) the relevant performance criteria for evaluating people, (b) the relevant job behaviors, and (c) ways to effectively minimize errors in judgment when using the appraisal instrument. In addition, Keown-Gerrard and Sulsky (2001) found that this training is highly effective when it includes context-specific issues relevant to the organization and/or job, particularly situational constraints that inhibit or interfere with a person's performance. Further research in this area is not likely to be needed. Findings from this research can be put into practice.

DeNisi and Peters (1996) conducted the only field study of cognitive processes on performance appraisals. They found that structured diary keeping and structured recall results in raters having more positive reactions to the appraisal process, having better recall of performance information, and producing ratings that are less elevated. Structured recall involves asking raters to recall performance incidents and then to record them according to a given format. Organizing information according to persons, rather than according to task dimensions, was better for both ratings and recall. Organizing information according to persons involves recalling incidents for one subordinate and then moving on to the next employee. Raters using this format reported that their ratings were more fair and accurate. As Arvey and Murphy (1998) noted, no direct measurement of the proposed cognitive processes was assessed in this study, but the implications for practice are straightforward.

Similarly, Jelley and Goffin (2001) found that priming a rater improves the accuracy of performance ratings. The experiment involved undergraduate students making a global performance rating of their lecturers on dimensions such as clarity and enthusiasm. This was followed by a request for them to assess these same lecturers on the specific behaviors that define these two performance criteria. Replications in the field are now needed.

Tests of Dweck's (1999) implicit person theory (IPT) have been restricted largely to children. Her findings show that entity theorists believe that personal attributes of an individual are largely fixed. This leads them to quickly form strong impressions of others that they resist revising, even in light of contradictory information. Incrementalists, on the other hand, appreciate the dynamic and personal determinants of behavior, and thus reconsider their initial impressions after receiving new information. Based on Dweck's findings, Heslin, Latham, and VandeWalle (2005) examined the extent to which the IPT of managers affects their appraisals of others. They found that the extent to which managers hold an incremental IPT is positively related to their recognition of both good and poor performance, relative to the employee's behavior they initially observed. The judgments of managers with entity theorist beliefs are anchored by their prior impressions of an employee.

The authors then adapted Aronson's (e.g., Pratkanis & Aronson, 2001) self-persuasion techniques to train managers with entity beliefs to adopt an incremental IPT. The long-term benefit of this training was shown in a six-week follow-up study. Those entity theorists who were randomly assigned to the training condition acknowledged an actual improvement in an employee's performance relative to their counterparts in the control group.

PERFORMANCE MANAGEMENT

The present review shows that significant advances have been made by behavioral scientists in the past century regarding the development and implementation of performance appraisal systems. A primary objective of doing an appraisal is to inculcate in employees the desire for continuous improvement. The attainment of this objective, however, is hampered by the fact that appraisals are done on a discrete basis. That is, they are usually done quarterly, bi-annually, or annually. Currently, there is a major shift in emphasis from performance appraisal to performance management, from being a performance appraiser to becoming a performance coach (Cederblom & Pemerl, 2002). The shift is from a discrete activity to one that is an ongoing process. The shift is from being solely an evaluator of people to, in addition, being a developer of people.

In a study of 400 companies, Campbell, Garfinkel, and Moses (1996) found that cyclical year-round performance management (i.e., feedback, analyzing results, goals) effectively increases organizational performance. In a study of executive coaching in a public sector municipal agency, Olivero, Bane, and Kopelman (1997) found that those who received coaching that included goal setting, collaborative problem solving, practice, feedback, and evaluation of end results increased their productivity dramatically. Consistent with these findings, Smither et al. (2003), in a field study of over a thousand senior managers, found that those who worked with an executive coach, in an organization that uses a multisource feedback system, were more likely than other managers to set specific high goals, and to seek feedback on ways to improve their performance from their supervisors. This led to an improvement in the ratings they received from their direct reports as well as from their supervisor.

Luthans and Peterson (2003), in a field study within a small manufacturing company, found that a way to improve the effectiveness of a 360-degree system is to combine it with coaching that focuses on enhancing self-awareness and performance management. The combination of feedback and coaching resulted in improved manager and employee satisfaction, increased commitment to the organization, reduced intentions to quit, and indirectly increased the firm's performance.

In short, coaching appears to be a powerful catalyst for bringing about a relatively permanent improvement in a person's behavior (Kalinauckas & King, 1995), because a coach challenges employees on a day-to-day basis, to instill in them the confidence that they can expand their abilities to attain desired goals (Ellinger, Watkins, & Bostrom, 1999). Hence, communication skills are a core competency of an effective coach (Richardson, 1998) especially with regard to conveying knowledge as well as expectations to others (Tyler, 1997). The question that has yet to be answered is, who is an ideal coach? Is it the person's supervisor, peers, an external agent, or oneself?

Hall, Otazo, and Hollenbeck (1999) defined a coach in an organizational setting as a person who works with others to develop and implement strategies to improve their performance. Typically, the coach is not the employee's supervisor and hence does not provide, and is not solicited for, input regarding the organization's formal reward system for the employee. For example, a global consulting firm, with offices in such countries as Australia, Canada, and the United Kingdom, uses self as well as peer coaching due to the fact that it is a partnership, and the partners work alone as well as in teams on assignments. The emphasis is on increasing the person's interpersonal skills within the firm as well as with the client in order to increase the firm's revenue. A nuclear power plant in Canada uses an external agent to coach its key managers on ways to increase their interpersonal skills, especially team playing, as does an investment bank in the USA.

Despite the voluminous practitioner literature on the value of coaching, there are few or no empirical studies that have evaluated the effectiveness of this practice on the subsequent performance of others. Moreover, there is little or no empirical evidence as to who is most effective as a coach. Theoretical and empirically derived frameworks, however, do exist for guiding research on this topic. For example, evidence suggestive of the effectiveness of self-coaching can be inferred from Aronson's (1999a, 1999b) self-persuasion theory. The theory states that self-persuasion strategies produce more powerful and long-lasting effects than do alternative sources. Attitude and behavior change induced from others is relatively short term, especially when there is a strong emotional component (e.g., an adverse effect on one's job or career). With self-persuasion, there is no direct attempt from others to convince anyone to do anything. Hence, the theory states that self-persuasion allows individuals to convince themselves of the desirability of a behavior or behaviors. The empirical data in support of this theory, however, have been limited to social psychology experiments involving such diverse areas as use of condoms by teenagers (Aronson, Fried, & Stone, 1991; Stone, Aronson, Crain, Winslow, & Fried, 1994), and energy and water conservation among adults (Dickerson, Thibodeau, Aronson, & Miller, 1992). With the exception of the study by Heslin et al. (2005) described earlier, there are few or no studies of the effect of self-persuasion in organizational settings.

Further evidence suggesting the efficacy of self-coaching as a self-regulatory technique comes from Meichenbaum (1977), a clinical psychologist who developed a method for changing a person's dysfunctional to functional self-talk. Millman and Latham (2001) effectively adapted this methodology for training displaced managers to use this verbal self-guidance (VSG) technique to successfully obtain re-employment. In two subsequent studies, Brown and Latham (in press) found that VSG increased a person's team-playing behavior within a group, and Brown (2003) found that it increases both collective efficacy as well as a team's performance.

Evidence suggesting the effectiveness of peers as coaches can be inferred from Festinger's (1954) social comparison theory. The theory states that the drive for self-comparison is a force acting on a person to belong to a group. On subjective criteria (e.g., team playing), people assess their ability in comparison to others. 'Given a range of possible persons for comparison, someone close to one's ability or opinion will be chosen for comparison ... Those with whom one does not compare oneself are different kinds of people or members of different groups' (Festinger, 1954, p. 121).

Support for the use of peers as coaches can also be found in sociotechnical systems theory (Trist, 1977). The theory states that it is the group who should monitor the individual's contribution. Productivity is fostered by the group allocating tasks and other rewards and punishments to control what the group considers to be a fair contribution by a group member (Emery & Thorsrud, 1976). Little, if anything, however, has been published in the sociotechnical literature on the effectiveness of peers in increasing the performance of a colleague.

Support for the use of an external agent as a coach can be inferred from the social psychology literature on persuasion. For example, Cialdini (2001) argued that authority is a key determinant of another person's attitudes and actions. He argued further that a person can harness the power of authority by touting experience, expertise, and credentials. People value the expertise of authorities because it helps them to choose both quickly and well. Expertise refers to the extent to which a person is perceived to be a source of valid assertions, especially with regard to the task that is being performed. The higher the perceived source credibility, the higher the likelihood that behavior will change as a result of it (Hovland & Weiss, 1951). There is a positive relationship between the credibility of the source of delivery and information retention (Zagona & Harter, 1966), feedback acceptance (Halperin, Snyder, Shenkel, & Houston, 1976), feedback favorability (Albright & Levy, 1995), intention to use feedback (Bannister, 1986), and performance in a laboratory setting (Northcraft & Earley, 1989). Thus on the basis of the social psychology literature, one can infer that the use of an external agent as a coach is effective in bringing about a desired behavior change in others.

An initial step to providing an answer to the above question was taken by Sue-Chan and Latham (2004). Two studies in two different continents using two different dependent variables examined the relative effectiveness of external, peer, and self-coaches on the performance of participants in two MBA programs. The first study involved MBA students in Canada. Those who were coached by an external coach exhibited higher team-playing behavior than did those who were coached by peers. The second study involved EMBA managers in Australia. Those who were coached by an external person or who were self-coached had significantly higher grades than those who were coached by a peer. In both studies, an external coach was perceived to have higher credibility than peers. In the second study, self-coaching was perceived to be more credible than coaching from peers. Satisfaction with the coaching process was highest among the managers who had an external coach.

Future research should examine the effect of peers serving as coaches in work contexts where the peer has as much or more expertise than the person who is being coached. In such a context, a peer who is viewed as an expert is likely to be a much more credible coach than was the case in the two present studies. That peers in the two present studies were not effective coaches appears to have been due to their perceived lack of expertise.

Participants in the self-coaching condition in the first study stated that they had difficulty identifying which behaviors to improve on in the future. The Australians who coached themselves, however, reported that the process was effective. As one Australian manager noted, 'self-coaching raised my awareness of "positive" and "bad" behaviors.' Thus, the contrary findings of the present two studies suggest a boundary condition for Aronson's (1999a, 1999b) theory of self-persuasion, namely, the extent to which the person possesses the knowledge and ability to perform the task. In all of Aronson's studies of self-persuasion, the person already possessed the requisite knowledge and skill to make the behavior change. The issue confronting the individual was primarily one of motivation to do so. The students in Canada lacked the knowledge and skill necessary to improve themselves as team players. The Australians were experienced managers from industry. They had little difficulty in coaching themselves using the behavioral appraisal instrument provided to them for attaining a high grade. Studies are now needed to compare the self-coaching effects of VSG training with Aronson's self-persuasion techniques alone and in combination.

The movement away from performance appraisal to performance management necessitates managers enlarging their role to include the coaching of employees. In a longitudinal field study, Heslin, VandeWalle, and Latham (2005) found that a manager's IPT predicts employee ratings of their coaching behavior. That is, managers who hold incremental beliefs coached their subordinates. A second study showed that managers with entity beliefs who were trained to adopt incremental beliefs provided more improvement suggestions of higher quality than their colleagues in the control group. It would appear that IPT is a state that is malleable rather than relatively fixed.

Feedback

Regardless of who serves in the role of coach, feedback is central to the effectiveness of the performance management process. Yet a meta-analysis by Kluger and DeNisi (1996) on the effect of feedback showed that in one-third of the interventions, feedback decreased rather than increased performance. However, when feedback is delivered in an informational rather than in a controlling way, a person's subsequent performance improves (Zhou, 1998). In addition, for feedback to bring about a positive change in behavior, it must: (a) focus on the behavior rather than the person; (b) be selective so as not to overwhelm the person; (c) focus on the behavior that is desired, and the way to demonstrate it; and (d) be the basis for setting specific high goals (DeNisi & Kluger, 2000).

Nease, Mudgett, and Quinones (1999) found that people who have high self-efficacy on the requisite tasks disregard repeated negative feedback. Not surprisingly, those with low self-efficacy did not reject feedback that was repeatedly negative.

Brett and Atwater (2001), in a study involving graduate students, found that negative feedback, which was lower than the person expected, was not viewed as accurate or useful. Not surprisingly, it led to feelings of anger and discouragement. High ratings, however, were not related to positive reactions, but only to the absence of negative reactions. These feelings suggest that people who may need feedback the most because they are not performing well are not receptive to it.

Lam, Yik, and Schaubroeck (2002) examined the effects of performance appraisal feedback on job and organizational attitudes of tellers in a large international bank. An employee's negative affectivity moderated the relationship between the receipt of favorable feedback and subsequent job attitudes. That is, there was an improvement in an employee's attitude following favorable feedback that persisted for six months among tellers who scored low on a measure of negative affectivity. This did not occur for those who were high on negative affectivity.

Smither and Walker (2004), in a study of 176 managers, found that those who received favorable comments tended to improve more than managers who received unfavorable comments. Contrary to expectations, behavior/task-oriented comments did not lead to greater improvement than did trait-focused comments. In addition, those who received fewer unfavorable comments improved more than did other managers. With respect to the specificity of the feedback, Goodman, Wood, and Hendrickx (2004) found that the more systematic a person is in the exploration process, the less confounded the information obtained, and the more beneficial the feedback for performance.

Frese (2005) has shown that people can be easily taught through instructions to embrace negative feedback by framing errors as beneficial to the learning process, and to be resilient subsequent to making an error, through systematic exploration. Future research should examine the effect of setting specific high-learning goals in the context of error management training.

The impersonal nature of communicating via e-mail appears to increase the objectivity of an appraisal, but it lessens the sensitivity and tact of the appraiser (Weisband & Atwater, 1999). Sensitivity and tact in giving feedback is critical for bringing about a change in behavior regardless of the medium by which it is communicated. For example, Seifert, Yukl, and McDonald (2003) found that having a competent, supportive facilitator present when feedback is provided, vs receiving only a printed feedback report, increases the perceived utility of the feedback, and results in more behavior change.

Employees should be encouraged to seek feedback. Seeking feedback has been found to increase an employee's understanding of where performance improvement is needed, and hence it increases goal commitment (London, Smither, & Adsit, 1997; Walker & Smither, 1999). Moreover, appraisers engage in fairer behavior when interacting with and justifying an appraisal decision with an assertive rather than an unassertive employee (Korsgaard, Roberson, & Rymph, 1998).

Goal Setting

Feedback in the absence of goal setting has little or no effect on behavior (Locke & Latham, 2002), because feedback is only information; its effect on action depends on how it is appraised by the recipient, and what decisions are made with respect to it. For feedback to improve behavior, specific high goals must be set (Latham, Locke, & Fassina, 2002), because goal setting affects choice, effort, and persistence. A meta-analysis revealed a strong relationship between goal commitment and a person's performance (Klein, Wesson, Hollenbeck, & Alge, 1999).

The importance of goal commitment was also shown in a field study by Renn (2003) involving rehabilitation counselors of a state agency. Feedback had a positive relationship with work performance only for those individuals with high goal commitment; it had a negative relationship with performance for those with lower goal commitment.

A key variable for bringing about goal commitment is to focus on outcome expectancies (Klein et al., 1999; Latham, 2001). That is, getting people to see the relationship between what they do or fail to do and the outcome they can expect. Employees who do not see the link between improving their performance and an improvement in their appraisal have little or no motivation to change their behavior (Boswell & Boudreau, 2002). This finding provides additional evidence for the necessity of training appraisers on ways to improve the accuracy of their evaluations.

The importance of goal-setting theory was explained by Locke and Latham (1990). Relative to exhorting people to 'do their best,' the assignment of a specific high goal increases performance by 0.42 to 0.80 standard deviations. A meta-analysis by O'Leary-Kelly, Martocchio, and Frink (1994) found an average standard deviation difference of 0.91 in the performance of teams *with* vs *without* a specific high goal.

Recent research on goal setting shows that when the person has the requisite knowledge and skill, specific high outcome goals should be set; when the person lacks the requisite knowledge and skill, specific high-learning goals should be set (Seijts & Latham, 2001, 2005; Winters & Latham, 1996). For example, a golfer with a low handicap might set an outcome goal of 68. A golfer with a high handicap might set a specific high goal of discovering (learning) six ways to lower the handicap. The focus of learning goals is on the process or procedure for attaining the outcome rather than on the outcome itself. These findings have yet to be studied in the context of performance appraisals.

Behaviorally set goals should be set when they are based on an appraisal instrument derived from a job analysis. In such cases, the behavioral items on the appraisal instrument removes the necessity of discovering the requisite knowledge or behavior for performing tasks effectively (Brown & Latham, 2002). When the environment is inherently unstable, proximal or sub-goals should be set in addition to a distal goal (Latham & Seijts, 1999) because, in highly dynamic situations, it is important to actively search for feedback and react quickly to it (Frese & Zapf, 1994). In addition, Dorner (1991) has found that performance errors on a dynamic task are often due to deficient decomposition of a goal into proximal goals. Proximal goals can increase what Frese and Zapf (1994) call error management. Errors provide information to employees as to whether their picture of reality is congruent with goal attainment. There is an increase in informative feedback when proximal or sub-goals are set relative to setting a distal goal only.

In addition to being informative, the setting of proximal goals can also be motivational relative to a distal goal that is far into the future. The attainment of proximal goals increases commitment, through enactive mastery, to attain the distal goal (Bandura, 1997). These findings regarding learning as well as proximal goals have yet to be examined within the context of performance appraisals.

Tziner, Joannis, and Murphy (2000), however, compared three appraisal instruments to determine the extent to which they facilitate goal setting. Goals set with BOS were more specific than those established on the basis of BARS or trait scales.

Organizational Justice

Regardless of how well feedback is delivered, and how goals based on this feedback are set, few things demoralize a person or team faster than feelings of jealousy, perceptions of favoritism, or beliefs that someone is unfairly getting a 'better deal' than someone else. Organizational justice theory states that in addition to being fair, decision makers must be seen as being fair (Greenberg, 2000). Providing the logic or rationale for decisions increases perceptions of fairness.

Evidence presented as to the validity of appraisal decisions increases perceptions of procedural justice; providing feedback that has taken into account the employee's input increases perceptions of interactional justice as well as the belief that one's voice has been heard (Erdogan, Kraimer, & Liden, 2001). As noted earlier, a meta-analysis involving over 6000 employees found that allowing employees a voice in the appraisal process increases employee satisfaction with the appraisal, perceived fairness of the appraisal, perceived usefulness of the appraisal, and the employee's motivation to improve as a result of the appraisal (Cawley et al., 1998).

Taylor, Tracy, Renard, Harrison, and Carroll (1995) examined the differences in outcomes resulting from a 'traditional' appraisal vs one that is based on 'due process.' The latter is defined as giving people adequate notice of their appraisal (e.g., explaining the standards in advance, seeking self-appraisals, giving feedback on an ongoing basis), fair hearing (adequate observations of the person's performance, granting an opportunity to explain self-evaluations), and judgment based on evidence (e.g., consistent application of standards, opportunity to appeal). Employees who were appraised in the due process condition perceived their appraisal system to be more fair and accurate than those in the traditional condition. This occurred despite the fact that employees in the due process condition had lower evaluations than those who received a traditional appraisal. This suggests that training appraisers in the principles of organizational justice is also an effective way of minimizing leniency error. Levy and Williams (1998) found that perceived system knowledge—that is, the extent to which individuals perceive that they understand the objectives of the appraisal system, how the appraisal process works, and the goals of the process—predicts user reactions, perceptions of fairness, job satisfaction, and organizational commitment. Lam and Schaubroeck (1999), in a field study of front-line supervisors in Hong Kong, compared outcome-focused appraisals with process-focused appraisals, that is, one that provides information on the manner in which an individual implements the organization's strategy. Process-focused appraisals had a more positive impact on satisfaction with the appraisal, perceived accuracy of the appraisal, and expectations of performance improvement.

MOTIVATING APPRAISERS

For appraisers to be motivated to take appraisals seriously, they must see the relationship between doing so and desirable outcomes for themselves, and the organization (Latham & Latham, 2000). They must see the relationship between the performance appraisal and other human resource systems including staffing, training, and, as emphasized throughout this chapter, the effective implementation of the organization's strategic plan. Additional research is needed on outcome expectancies. A maxim attributed to the late Mason Hare is 'that which gets measured gets done.' Hence many organizations have embraced a balanced scorecard (Kaplan & Norton, 1993). PriceWaterhouseCoopers, for example, places equal weighting on client (revenue generated from new and existing clients; client satisfaction), people (coaching and developing staff), and firm (service on committees crucial to the ongoing reinvention of the firm's business strategy necessary to ensure its success in a local and global marketplace).

NEW FRONTIERS

What are the next steps for making significant advances in the effectiveness of performance management? The answers may lie in the fields of decision making, motivation, and clinical counseling psychology, because there are at least two interrelated reasons for conducting performance appraisals of people—namely, to make developmental decisions regarding the ongoing improvement of an employee's performance, and to make administrative decisions regarding retaining, promoting, transferring, paying, and/or terminating the person based on the extent to which the person's performance is contributing to an organization's strategy. These are unarguably important decisions, yet the knowledge accumulated from theory and empirical research in the area of decision making has been largely ignored in the context of performance appraisals. There is at least one study that suggests that it is a mistake to continue doing so.

Latham and Budworth (2005) found that managers make an anchoring error in their appraisals of others. In a laboratory experiment, those who were randomly assigned to a condition where they were told how good they were subsequently rated a hypothetical employee shown on a videotape significantly higher than those managers who were told that they were poor performers. A field study, involving a manufacturing company, showed that there is a significant correlation between the performance rating that a manager receives and the rating the manager subsequently gives to his or her direct reports. Further research would appear necessary on the dangers of anchoring and other decision-making errors (e.g., satisficing, saliency, escalation to commitment, hindsight bias) as well as on ways to overcome them.

Motivation

Performance management involves coaching people in ways that will motivate them to improve their performance. Latham and Pinder (2005) reviewed the literature on motivation in the workplace. The study of traits has recaptured the attention of researchers. For example, Baum, Locke, and Smith (2001) showed that the relationship between personality and performance is mediated by situationally specific goals and self-efficacy. Ways of setting goals and building self-efficacy should become the mainstay of the coaching process. The former is a strong variable that masks individual differences (Locke & Latham, 2002).

In a study of more than 19,000 participants in 25 countries, Scholz, Dona, Sud, and Schwarzer (2002) found a high degree of consistency in the psychometric properties of measures of self-efficacy, a variable key to goal commitment and self-regulation. Steers and Sanchez-Runde (2002) developed a conceptual model that has yet to be empirically tested regarding leading across diverse cultures. The model focuses on self-efficacy beliefs, work motivation levels and goals, as well as the nature of incentives and disincentives to perform well, and the extent to which societal culture is a moderator.

Seijts, Latham, Tasa, and Latham (2004) discovered that goal orientation is more properly treated as a state rather than a stable individual difference variable. Hence, coaches can inculcate a learning goal orientation in employees in addition to setting specific high-learning goals. A promotion focus (Higgins, 1999) is conceptually similar to a learning goal orientation. Erez, Kaplan, and Van-Dijk (2004) found that it too is a malleable state rather than a stable trait.

Research is needed on whether there are incremental increases in an employee's performance when a specific high-learning goal is set, and a learning goal orientation as well as a promotion focus is conveyed by one's coach.

Significant findings in social psychology regarding implementation intentions and automotive goals should be investigated within the context of performance management. Social psychologists are currently examining the variety of ways in which goals may be automatically activated in everyday settings, and how goal priming may affect the goals a person pursues. Specifically, they are examining aspects of the environment that might cause a person to spontaneously rather than purposefully pursue a goal. In addition, they are examining how a person's self-regulation system deals with the variety of goals that may be primed by one's environment.

Bargh and his colleagues primed goals by taking advantage of their associations to semantically related words. Shah (2005) examined two other associations: (1) goals associated with those things that help to bring about their attainment, that is, instrumental goal priming; and (2) goal association with other individuals, that is, interpersonal goal priming.

A particular goal is often pursued in particular settings, and while one is engaging in specific behaviors or activities, the goal may become associated with such settings. The instrumental or means–goal association is not dependent on the semantic relation of the means and goal, but rather on their perceived functional relationship—that is, said Shah, the degree to which the means is seen as facilitating the attainment of one's goal. The stronger the association, the higher the likelihood that encountering the setting, or the means to attain it, will automatically lead to the pursuit of that goal. In short, Shah has argued that surrounding a person with various means to attain a specific goal is likely to move that goal to the center of a person's attention, thus enhancing that individual's commitment to attaining it.

In addition to semantic and instrumental goal priming, a third source of goal priming is the people who are significant to an individual. Shah (2003a) found that when people are presented the name of a close significant other subliminally, that is, a person who would want them to do well on the task, the salience of the task goal increases, as does persistence and actual performance. Shah also found that priming a significant other decreases pursuit of the goal if the significant other does not support the goal, or is strongly associated with the pursuit of a different or unrelated goal.

In still another study, Shah (2003b) found that a significant other affects how a goal is consciously perceived and expressed by the person who is pursuing it. A significant other 'automatically' affects the perceived difficulty and value of a goal, and how the person feels emotionally about success and failure regarding goal attainment.

Interpersonal goal priming even affects subsequent social interactions. Fitzsimons and Shah (2005) subliminally presented words that were designed to prime a goal to achieve academically. People, randomly assigned to an experimental group, relative to their counterparts in the control group, reported feeling significantly closer to those specific significant others who could help them to attain the goal. In addition, they indicated that they intended to spend less time with those significant others who they perceived as not facilitating academic success. In short, the environment contains inanimate signs, signals, or cues that can 'prime' or trigger the automatic pursuit of our goals. This is both an exciting and frightening finding. How many of us will want our bosses to master the implementation of these techniques?

Clinical/Counseling Psychology

I/O psychology has a long history of successfully adapting methodology from experimental as well as social psychology for studying and resolving issues in the workplace. Latham and Heslin (2003) have stressed the potential pay-offs for adapting theoretical frameworks and methods from clinical/counseling psychology. The payoffs would appear to be particularly large for increasing the effectiveness of performance management. For example, Meichenbaum's (1977) technique for teaching people to become aware of their internal dialogue and its effect on their effort and behavior was discussed earlier (Brown, 2003; Brown & Latham, in press; Millman & Latham, 2001). VSG should be investigated as a means for ongoing coaching of self.

Ellis's (1999) rational emotive therapy (RET) has been shown in clinical settings to be effective in overcoming problems due to anxiety, anger, and procrastination. RET teaches people to set realistic personal goals, and in the face of failures to redirect their cognitive and emotional energy toward developing new strategies for attaining them. RET is also effective for overcoming a desire for perfection. This methodology should be easily adaptable to performance management in the workplace.

Seligman's (1998) training technique, based on attribution theory for overcoming learned helplessness and instilling optimism in the face of repeated failures, also warrants investigation in the context of performance management. His techniques for effectively disputing one's dysfunctional beliefs include: (a) examining and questioning the evidence for their validity; (b) focusing on changeable, specific, and non-personal causes of the negative actions one experiences, rather than making attributions to permanent, pervasive, and personal causes; (c) avoiding catastrophizing the implications of one's negative attributes; and (d) distracting oneself from recurring self-defeating thoughts. This methodology is also applicable to the workplace.

Bordin's (1994) working alliance focuses on straightforward ways of enhancing the relationship between the therapist and the client. The emphasis is on steps for ensuring a mutual understanding and agreement between the two parties regarding the goal or goals of therapy, and the tasks to be pursued to attain the goal(s). These principles would appear to be highly applicable for a supervisor, team leader, or external coach working with people in organizational settings.

An inherent danger in coaching that is seldom, if ever, discussed, let alone studied in the I/O or human resource management (HRM) literature, is the dysfunctional attachment that can occur between an employee and the coach or supervisor. Bowlby's (1979) attachment theory explains how different attachment styles systematically influence how people seek and process feedback, interact with and evaluate others, and regulate their emotions. The theory suggests that an avoidant or anxious–ambivalent attachment style on the part of a supervisor or coach may result in that person encoding less information about an employee (Fraley, Garner, & Shaver, 2000) and being less able to describe an employee's behavior objectively than those with a secure attachment style. His findings have yet to be applied to the field of performance management, but nevertheless have strong implications for who should and should not take on a coaching role.

CONCLUSIONS

Science has informed practice.

1. We know how to conduct a job analysis to develop an appraisal instrument that is reliable, valid, and legally defensible. We know how to develop appraisal instruments that facilitate goal setting.
2. The reliability and validity of different sources of appraisal are known. There is growing acceptance in organizations of the importance of using multisources for an appraisal.
3. Ways of gaining user acceptance of the appraisal system/process have been identified.
4. We know how to train appraisers so that their objectivity/accuracy increases. We also know that political factors may override the goal for accuracy.
5. We know that performance management, defined as year-round coaching of an employee, is more likely to inculcate a desire for continuous improvement, and to bring about and sustain a significant increase in an employee's behavior than an annual or even a quarterly appraisal.
6. There are three theoretical frameworks to draw upon in the practice of performance appraisal/management: goal setting with regard to the importance of setting specific high-performance, learning, or behavioral goals; social cognitive with regard to increasing self-efficacy; and organizational justice with regard to minimizing findings of favoritism, exploitation, or injustice.

Practice is informing science on areas requiring research:

1. Appraiser bias remains an issue. It is likely to become a bigger issue as global companies bring together employees with different ethnic backgrounds who live in countries with different political ideologies.
2. The effect of cultural context on effective ways of appraising and coaching employees needs to be investigated.

3. Additional information is needed on who is the ideal coach. Is it someone external to the organization, the supervisor, peers, or oneself? The answers may vary as a function of context, including societal culture. The answer may be multiple sources.

4. The study of proximal vs distal goals, and learning vs behavioral vs performance outcome goals, should be studied within the context of performance appraisal/management.

5. Adapting theories and research findings from the fields of decision making and motivation as well as clinical-counseling psychology should accelerate discoveries of ways of improving the performance management process in organizational settings.

6. Technology needs to be studied as a moderator with regard to all of the above. Large, geographically dispersed groups of people, connected only by their use of communication technology such as mobile phones, text messaging, two-way pagers, and e-mail, can already be drawn together at a moment's notice, like schools of fish, to perform some collective action. In virtual teams spanning global organizations, how will this technology facilitate or inhibit performance appraisal/management?

ACKNOWLEDGMENTS

The authors thank Drs Richard Arvey, Lorne Sulsky, and Maria Rotundo for their helpful comments on this chapter. Preparation for this chapter was supported in part by an SSHRC grant to, and funding from, the Canadian Forces for the first author.

REFERENCES

Albright, M.D. & Levy, P.E. (1995). The effects of source credibility and performance rating discrepancy on reactions to multiple raters. *Journal of Applied Social Psychology*, **25**, 577–600.

Antonioni, D. (1994). The effects of feedback accountability on upward appraisal ratings. *Personnel Psychology*, **47**, 349–356.

Aronson, E. (1999a). *The social animal* (8th edn). New York: Freeman.

Aronson, E. (1999b). The power of self-persuasion. *American Psychologist*, **54**, 875–884.

Aronson, E., Fried, C., & Stone, J. (1991). Overcoming denial and increasing the intention to use condoms through the induction of hypocrisy. *American Journal of Public Health*, **81**, 1636–1638.

Arvey, R.D. & Murphy, K.R. (1998). Performance evaluation in work settings. *Annual Review of Psychology*, **49**, 141–168.

Atkins, P.W.B. & Wood, R.E. (2002). Self- versus others' ratings as predictors of assessment center ratings: Validation evidence for 360-degree feedback programs. *Personnel Psychology*, **55**, 871–904.

Atwater, L., Ostroff, C., Yammarino, F.J., & Fleenor, J.W. (1998). Self–other agreement: Does it really matter? *Personnel Psychology*, 51, 577–598.

Atwater, L., Roush, P., & Fischthal, A. (1995). The influence of upward feedback on self- and follower ratings of leadership. *Personnel Psychology*, 48, 35–59.

Atwater, L.E. & Waldman, D.A. (1998, May). Accountability in 360 degree feedback. *HR Magazine*, 96–104.

Bailey, C. & Fletcher, C. (2002). The impact of multiple source feedback on management development: Findings from a longitudinal study. *Journal of Organizational Behavior*, 23, 853–867.

Bandura, A. (1997). *Self-efficacy.* New York: Freeman.

Bannister, B.D. (1986). Performance outcome feedback and attributional feedback: Interactive effects on recipient responses. *Journal of Applied Psychology*, 71, 203–210.

Bartol, K.M. (1999). Gender influences on performance evaluations. In G.N. Powell (Ed.), *Handbook of gender and work.* Thousand Oaks, CA: Sage.

Bartol, K.M., Durham, C.C., & Poon, J.M.L. (2001). Influence of performance evaluation rating segmentation on motivation and fairness perceptions. *Journal of Applied Psychology*, 86, 1106–1119.

Baum, J.R., Locke E.A., & Smith, K.G. (2001). A multidimensional model of venture growth. *Academy of Management Journal*, 44, 292–303.

Beehr, T.A., Ivanitskaya, L., Hansen, C.P., Erofeev, D., & Gudanowski, D.M. (2001). Evaluation of 360 degree feedback ratings: Relationships with each other and with performance and selection predictors. *Journal of Organizational Behavior*, 22, 775–788.

Bennington, L. & Roberts-Calvert, B. (1998). Antidiscrimination legislation and HRM practice. In M. Patrickson & L. Hartmann (Eds), *Managing an ageing workforce.* Sydney, Australia: Woodslane Publishing.

Bennington, L. & Wein, R. (2000). Anti-discrimination legislation in Australia: Fair, effective, efficient or irrelevant? *International Journal of Manpower*, 21, 21–33.

Bernardin, H.J. (2005). Behavioral observation scales. In S. Cartwirght (Ed.), *Human resource management. V: The Blackwell Encyclopedia of Management* (2nd edn). Malden, MA: Blackwell.

Bernardin, H.J., Cooke, D.K., & Villanova, P. (2000). Conscientiousness and agreeableness as predictors of rating leniency. *Journal of Applied Psychology*, 85, 232–234.

Bernichon, T., Cook, K.E., & Brown, J.D. (2003). Seeking self-evaluative feedback: The interactive role of global self-esteem and specific self-views. *Journal of Personality and Social Psychology*, 84, 194–204.

Bettenhausen, K.L. & Fedor, D.B. (1997). Peer and upward appraisals: A comparison of their benefits and problems. *Group and Organization Management*, 22, 236–263.

Biernat, M., Crandall, C.S., Young, L.V., Kobrynowicz, D., & Halpin, S.M. (1998). All that you can be: Stereotyping of self and others in a military context. *Journal of Personality and Social Psychology*, 75, 301–317.

Boldry, J., Wood, W., & Kashy, D.A. (2001). Gender stereotypes and the evaluation of men and women in military training. *Journal of Social Issues*, 57 (4), 689–705.

Bommer, W.H., Johnson, J.L., Rich, G.A., Podsakoff, P.M., & MacKenzie, S.B. (1995). On the interchangeability of objective and subjective measures of employee performance: A meta-analysis. *Personnel Psychology*, 48, 587.

Bordin, E.S. (1994). Theory and research on the therapeutic working alliance. *Psychotherapy: Theory, Research and Practice*, 16, 252–260.

Borman, W.C. (1997). 360° ratings: An analysis of assumptions and a research agenda for evaluating their validity. *Human Resource Management Review*, 7, 299, 315.

Borman, W.C., Buck, D.E., Hanson, M.A., Motowidlo, S.J., Stark, S., & Drasgow, F. (2001). An examination of the comparative reliability, validity and accuracy of performance ratings made using computerized adaptive rating scales. *Journal of Applied Psychology*, **86**, 965–973.

Boswell, W.R. & Boudreau, J.W. (2002). Separating the developmental and evaluative performance appraisal uses. *Journal of Business and Psychology*, **16**, 391–412.

Bowen, C.C., Swim, J.K., & Jacobs, R.R. (2000). Evaluating gender biases on actual job performance of real people: A meta-analysis. *Journal of Applied Social Psychology*, **30**, 2194–2215.

Bowlby, J. (1979). *The making and breaking of affectional bonds*. London: Tavistock.

Bowman, J.S. (1999). Performance appraisal: Verisimilitude trumps veracity. *Public Personnel Management*, **28**, 557–594.

Bozeman, D.P. (1997). Interrater agreement in multi-source performance appraisal: A commentary. *Journal of Organizational Behavior*, **18**, 313–316.

Bracken, D.W., Timmreck, C.W., & Church, A.H. (Eds) (2001). *The handbook of multisource feedback*. San Francisco: Jossey-Bass.

Brett, J.F. & Atwater, L.E. (2001). 360° feedback: Accuracy, reactions, and perceptions of usefulness. *Journal of Applied Psychology*, **86**, 930–942.

Brown, T.C. (2003). The effect of verbal self-guidance training on collective efficacy and team performance. *Personnel Psychology*, **56**, 935–964.

Brown, T.C. & Latham, G.P. (2002). The effects of behavioural outcome goals, learning goals, and urging people to do their best on an individual's teamwork behaviour in a group problem solving task. *Canadian Journal of Behavioural Science*, **34**, 276–285.

Brown, T.C. & Latham, G.P. (in press). The effect of training in verbal self-guidance on performance effectiveness in a MBA program. *Canadian Journal of Behavioural Science*.

Brutus, S. & Derayeh, M. (2002). Multisource assessment programs in organizations: An insider's perspective. *Human Resource Development Quarterly*, **13**, 187–202.

Campbell, J.D., Garfinkel, R.B., & Moses, L. (1996). Strategies for success in measuring performance. *HR Magazine*, **41**, 98.

Cardy, R.L. & Keefe, T.J. (1994). Observational purpose and evaluative articulation in frame-of-reference training: The effects of alternative processing modes on rating accuracy. *Organizational Behavior and Human Decision Processes*, **57**, 338–357.

Cawley, B.D., Keeping, L.M., & Levy, P.E. (1998). Participation in the performance appraisal process and employee reactions: A meta-analytic review of field investigations. *Journal of Applied Psychology*, **83**, 615–631.

Cederblom, D. & Permerl, D.E. (2002). From performance appraisal to performance management. One agency's experience. *Public Personnel Management*, **31**, 131–140.

Church, A.H. (2000). Do higher performing managers actually receive better ratings? A validation of multirater assessment methodology. *Consulting Psychology Journal: Practice and Research*, **52**, 99–116.

Cialdini, R.B. (2001). The science of persuasion. *Scientific American*, **284**, 76–81.

Claus, L. (2003). Similarities and differences in human resource management in the European Union. *Thunderbird International Business Review*, **45**, 729–755.

Cohen, S.G. & Bailey, D.E. (1997). What makes teams work: Group effectiveness research from the shop floor to the executive suite. *Journal of Management*, **23**, 239–290.

Conway, J.M. (1996). Analysis and design of multitrait–multirater performance appraisal studies. *Journal of Management*, **22**, 139–162.

Conway, J.M. (1999). Distinguishing contextual performance from task performance for managerial jobs. *Journal of Applied Psychology*, **84**, 3–13.

Cronshaw, S.F. (1998). Job analysis: Changing nature of work. *Canadian Psychology*, **39**, 5–13.

DeNisi, A.S. & Kluger, A.N. (2000). Feedback effectiveness: Can 360-degree appraisals be improved? *Academy of Management Executive*, **14**, 129–139.

DeNisi, A.S. & Peters, L.H. (1996). Organization of information in memory and the performance appraisal process: Evidence from the field. *Journal of Applied Psychology*, **81**, 717–737.

DeVoe, S.E. & Iyengar, S.S. (2003). Managers' theories of subordinates: A cross-cultural examination of manager perceptions of motivation and appraisal of performance. *Organizational Behavior and Human Decision Processes*, **93**, 47–61.

Dewberry, C. (2001). Performance disparities between whites and ethnic minorities: Real differences of assessment bias? *Journal of Occupational and Organizational Psychology*, **74**, 656–673.

Dickerson, C.A., Thibodeau, R., Aronson, E., & Miller, D. (1992). Using cognitive dissonance to encourage water conservation. *Journal of Applied Social Psychology*, **22**, 841–854.

Dominick, P.G., Reilly, R.R., & McGourty, J.W. (1997). The effects of peer feedback on team member behaviour. *Group and Organization Management*, **22**, 508–520.

Dorner, D. (1991). The investigation of action regulation in uncertain and complex situations. In J. Rassmussen, G. Brehmer, & J. Leplat (Eds), *Distributed decision making: Cognitive models for cooperative work*. New York: John Wiley & Sons.

Druskat, V.U. & Wolff, S.B. (1999). Effects and timing of developmental peer appraisals in self-managing work groups. *Journal of Applied Psychology*, **84**, 58–74.

Dweck, C.S. (1999). *Self theories: Their role in motivation, personality, and development*. Philadelphia: Psychology Press.

Eagly, A.H., Karau, S.J., & Makhijani, M.G. (1995). Gender and the effectiveness of leaders: A meta-analysis. *Psychological Bulletin*, **117**, 125–145.

Eagly, A.H., Makhijani, M.G., & Klonsky, B.G. (1992). Gender and the evaluation of leaders: A meta-analysis. *Psychological Bulletin*, **111**, 3–22.

Ellinger, A.D., Watkins, K.E., & Bostrom, R.P. (1999). Managers as facilitators of learning in learning organizations. *Human Resource Development Quarterly*, **10**, 105–125.

Ellis, A. (1999). Early theories and practices of rational emotive behaviour therapy and how they have been augmented and revised during the last three decades. *Journal of Rational-Emotive and Cognitive Behavior Therapy*, **17**, 69–93.

Emery, F.E. & Thorsrud, E. (1976). *Democracy at work*. Leiden, The Netherlands: Martinus Nijhoff.

Erdogan, B., Kraimer, M.L., & Liden, R.C. (2001). Procedural justice as a two-dimensional construct: An examination in the performance appraisal account. *Journal of Applied Behavioral Science*, **37** (2), 205–222.

Erez, M. (1994). Toward a model of cross-cultural industrial and organizational psychology. In H.C. Triandis & M.D. Dunnette (Eds), *Handbook of industrial and organizational psychology* (Vol. 4, pp. 559–607). Palo Alto, CA: Consulting Psychologists Press.

Erez, M.E., Kaplan, E., & Van-Dijk, D. (2004). *Goal setting and regulatory focus: An integrative approach*. Paper presented at the annual meeting of the Society for Industrial and Organizational Psychology, Chicago.

Erikson, A. & Allen, T. (2003). *Linking 360° feedback to business outcome measures*. Paper presented at the annual meeting of the Society for Industrial and Organizational Psychology, Orlando, FL.

Facteau, J.D. & Craig, S.B. (2001). Are performance appraisal ratings from different rating sources comparable? *Journal of Applied Psychology*, **86**, 215–227.

Feild, H.S. & Holley, W.H. (1982). The relationship of performance appraisal system characteristics to verdicts in selected employment discrimination cases. *Academy of Management Journal*, **25**, 392–406.

Festinger, L. (1954). A theory of social comparison processes. *Human Relations*, 7, 117–140.

Fitzsimons, G. & Shah, J.Y. (2005). Instrumentality yours: How goal pursuits automatically affect social relations. Unpublished manuscript, Stanford University, Stanford, CA.

Fletcher, C. (1997). Self-awareness—A neglected attribute in selection and assessment? *International Journal of Selection and Assessment*, 5, 183–187.

Fletcher, C. (2001). Performance appraisal and management: The developing research agenda. *Journal of Occupational and Organizational Psychology*, 74, 473–487.

Fletcher, C. & Perry, E.L. (2001). Performance appraisal and feedback: A consideration of national culture and a review of contemporary research and future trends. In N.D. Anderson et al. (Eds), *Handbook of industrial, work and organizational psychology*. London: Sage.

Fox, S., Ben-Nahum, Z., & Yinnon, Y. (1989). Perceived similarity and accuracy of peer ratings. *Journal of Applied Psychology*, 74, 781–786.

Fraley, R.C., Garner, J.P., & Shaver, P.R. (2000). Adult attachment and the defensive regulation of attention and memory: Examining the role of preemptive and postemptive defensive processes. *Journal of Personality and Social Psychology*, 79, 816–826.

Freid, Y., Levi, A.S., Ben-David, H.A., Tiegs, R.B., & Avital, N. (2000). Rater positive and negative mood predispositions as predictors of performance ratings of ratees in simulated and real organizational settings. *Journal of Organizational and Occupational Psychology*, 73, 373–378.

Frese, M. (2005). Grand theories and midrange theories. Cultural effects on theorizing and the attempt to understand active approaches to work. In K.G. Smith & M. Hitt (Eds), *The Oxford handbook of management theory: The process of theory development*. Oxford, UK: Oxford University Press.

Frese, M. & Zapf, D. (1994). Action as the core of work psychology: A German approach. In H.C. Triandis, M.D. Dunnette, & L.M. Hough (Eds), *Handbook of industrial and organizational psychology* (2nd edn). Palo Alto, CA: Consulting Psychologists Press.

Funderburg, S.A. & Levy, P.E. (1997). The influence of individual and contextual variables on 360-degree feedback system attitudes. *Group and Organization Management*, 22 (2), 210–235.

Gabris, G.T. & Ihrke, D.M. (2001). Does performance appraisal contribute to heightened levels of employee burnout? The results of one study. *Public Personnel Management*, 30, 157–172.

General Electric Company (2000). *GE 2000 Annual Report*.

Ghorpade, J. (2000). Managing five paradoxes of 360-degree feedback. *Academy of Management Executive*, 14, 140–151.

Gilbert, G.R., Hannan, E.L., & Lowe, K.B. (1998). Is smoking stigma clouding the objectivity of employee performance appraisal? *Public Personnel Management*, 27 (3), 285–300.

Goodman, J.S., Wood, R.E., & Hendrickx, M. (2004). Feedback specificity, exploration, and learning. *Journal of Applied Psychology*, 89, 248–262.

Gordon, R.A. & Arvey, R.D. (2004). Age bias in laboratory and field settings: A meta-analytic investigation. *Journal of Applied Social Psychology*, 34, 468–492.

Greenberg, J. (2000). Promote procedural justice to enhance acceptance of work outcomes. In E. Locke (Ed.), *Handbook of principles of organizational behavior*. Oxford, UK: Blackwell.

Greguras, G.J. & Robie, C. (1998). A new look at within-source interrater reliability of 360-degree feedback ratings. *Journal of Applied Psychology*, 83, 960–968.

Greguras, G.J., Robie, C., Schleicher, D.J., & Goff, M. (2003). A field study of the effects of rating purpose on the quality of multi-source ratings. *Personnel Psychology*, 56, 1–21.

Hall, D.T., Otazo, K.L., & Hollenbeck, G.P. (1999). Behind closed doors: What really happens in executive coaching. *Organizational Dynamics*, 27, 39–53.

Halperin, K., Snyder, C.R., Shenkel, R.J., & Houston, B.K. (1976). Effects of source status and message favorability on acceptance of personality feedback. *Journal of Applied Psychology*, 61, 85–88.

Head, T., Haug, R., Krabbenhoft, A., & Ma, C. (2000). Issues and trends in international business law: Implications for OD consultants. *Organization Development Journal*, 18, 62–73.

Hedge, J.W. & Teachout, M.S. (2000). Exploring the concept of acceptability as a criterion for evaluating performance measures. *Group and Organization Management*, 25, 22–44.

Heslin, P. & Latham, G.P. (2004). The effect of upward feedback on managerial behavior. *Applied Psychology: An International Review*, 53, 23–38.

Heslin, P.A., Latham, G.P., & VandeWalle, D. (2005). Implicit person theory and performance appraisal. *Journal of Applied Psychology*, 90, 842–856.

Heslin, P.A., VandeWalle, D., & Latham, G.P. (2005). *Keen to help: Managers implicit person theory and their subsequent employee coaching*. Paper presented at the Annual Meeting of the Academy of Management, Honolulu.

Higgins, E.T. (1999). Persons or situations: Unique explanatory principles or variability in general principles? In D. Cervone & Y. Shoda (Eds), *The coherence of personality: Social cognitive biases of consistency, variability and organization* (pp. 61–93). New York: Guilford Press.

Hovland, C. & Weiss, W. (1951). The influence of source credibility on communication effectiveness. *Public Opinion Quarterly*, 15, 635–650.

Jain, H.C., Sloan, P.J., & Horowitz, F.M. (2003). *Employment equity and affirmative action: An international comparison*. Armonk, NY: Sharpe.

Jawahar, I.M. (2001). Attitudes, self-monitoring and appraisal behaviors. *Journal of Applied Psychology*, 86, 875–883.

Jelley, R.B. & Goffin, R.D. (2001). Can performance-feedback accuracy be improved? Effects of rater priming and rating-scale format on rating accuracy. *Journal of Applied Psychology*, 86, 134–144.

Johnson, D.E., Erez, A., Kiker, D.S., & Motowidlo, S.J. (2002). Liking and attributions of motives as mediators of the relationships between individuals' reputations, helpful behaviors and raters' reward decisions. *Journal of Applied Psychology*, 87, 808–815.

Kalinauckas, P. & King, H. (1995). Coaching gets to parts that other methods cannot reach. *People Management*, 1, 51.

Kane, J.S., Bernardin, H.J., Villanova, P., & Peyrefitte, J. (1995). Stability of rater leniency: Three studies. *Academy of Management Journal*, 38, 1036–1051.

Kaplan, R.S. & Norton, D.P. (1993). Putting the balanced scorecard to work. *Harvard Business Review*, Sept–Oct, 134–147.

Keown-Gerrard, J.A. & Sulsky, L.M. (2001). The effects of task information training and frame-of-reference training with situational constraints on rating accuracy. *Human Performance*, 14, 305–320.

Klein, H.J., Wesson, M.J., Hollenbeck, J.R., & Alge, B.J. (1999). Goal commitment and the goal-setting process: Conceptual clarification and empirical synthesis. *Journal of Applied Psychology*, 84, 885–896.

Kleingeld, A., Van Tuijl, H., & Algera, J.A. (2004). Participation in the design of performance management systems: A quasi-experimental field study. *Journal of Organizational Behavior*, 25, 831–851.

Kluger, A.N. & DeNisi, A. (1996). The effects of feedback interventions on performance: A historical review, a meta-analysis, and a preliminary feedback intervention theory. *Psychological Bulletin*, **119**, 254–284.

Komaki, J.L. & Desselles, M.L. (1994). *Supervision reexamined: The role of monitors and consequences*. Boston: Allen & Unwin.

Korsgaard, M.A., Meglino, B.M., & Lester, S.W. (2004). The effect of other orientation on self-supervisor rating agreement. *Journal of Organizational Behavior*, **25**, 873–891.

Korsgaard, M.A., Roberson, L., & Rymph, R.D. (1998). What motivates fairness? The role of subordinate assertive behavior on manager's interactional fairness. *Journal of Applied Psychology*, **83** (5), 731–744.

Kraiger, K. & Ford, J.K. (1985). A meta-analysis of ratee race effects in performance ratings. *Journal of Applied Psychology*, **70**, 56–65.

Lam, S.S.K. & Schaubroeck, J. (1999). Total quality management and performance appraisal: An experimental study of process versus results and group versus individual approaches. *Journal of Organizational Behavior*, **20**, 445–457.

Lam, S.S.K., Yik, M.S.M., & Schaubroeck, J. (2002). Responses to formal performance appraisal feedback: The role of negative affectivity. *Journal of Applied Psychology*, **87**, 192–201.

Lance, C.E. (1994). Test of a latent structure of performance ratings derived from Wherry's (1952) theory of ratings. *Journal of Management*, **20**, 757–771.

Landau, J. (1995). The relationship of race and gender to managers' ratings of promotion potential. *Journal of Organizational Behavior*, **16**, 391–400.

Langan-Fox, J., Waycott, J., Morizzi, M., & McDonald, L. (1998). Predictors of participation in performance appraisal: A voluntary system in a blue-collar work environment. *International Journal of Selection and Assessment*, **6** (4), 249–260.

Latham, G.P. (1986). Job performance and appraisal. In C. Cooper & I. Robertson (Eds), *Review of industrial and organizational psychology*. Chichester, UK: John Wiley & Sons.

Latham, G.P. (2001). The importance of understanding and changing employee outcome expectancies for gaining commitment to an organizational goal. *Personnel Psychology*, **54**, 707–716.

Latham, G.P. & Budworth, M. (2005, April). *Anchoring the subsequent appraisal of others on one's own performance appraisal*. Paper presented at the annual meeting of the Society for Industrial and Organizational Psychology, Los Angeles, California.

Latham, G.P. & Heslin. P. (2003). Training the trainee as well as the trainer: Lessons to be learned from clinical psychology. *Canadian Psychology*, **44**, 218–231.

Latham, G.P. & Latham, S.D. (2000). Overlooking theory and research in performance appraisal at one's peril: Much done, more to do. In C. Cooper & E.A. Locke (Eds), *International review of industrial and organizational psychology*. Chichester, UK: John Wiley & Sons.

Latham, G.P., Locke, E.A., & Fassina, N.E. (2002). The high performance cycle: Standing the test of time. In S. Sonnentag (Ed.), *The psychological management of individual performance: A handbook in the psychology of management in organizations* (pp. 201–228). Chichester, UK: John Wiley & Sons.

Latham, G.P. & McCauley, C.D. (2005). Leadership in the private sector: Yesterday versus tomorrow. In C. Cooper (Ed.), *The twenty-first century manager*. Oxford, UK: Oxford University Press.

Latham, G.P. & Pinder, C.C. (2005). Work motivation theory and research at the dawn of the twenty-first century. *Annual Review of Psychology*, **56**, 485–516.

Latham, G.P. & Seijts, G.H. (1997). The effect of appraisal instrument on managerial perceptions of fairness and satisfaction with appraisals from their peers. *Canadian Journal of Behavioural Science*, **29**, 275–282.

Latham, G.P. & Seijts, G.H. (1999). The effects of proximal and distal goals on performance on a moderately complex task. *Journal of Organizational Behavior*, 20, 421–429.

Latham, G.P., Skarlicki, D., Irvine, D., & Siegel, J. (1993). The increasing importance of performance appraisals to employee effectiveness in organizational settings in North America. In C. Cooper & I. Robertson (Eds), *International review of industrial and organizational psychology* (pp. 87–132). Chichester, UK: John Wiley & Sons.

Latham, G.P. & Wexley, K.N. (1994). *Increasing productivity through performance appraisal* (2nd edn). Reading, MA: Wesley.

Latham, G.P., Wexley, K.N., & Pursell, E.D. (1975). Training managers to minimize rating errors in the observation of behavior. *Journal of Applied Psychology*, 60, 550–555.

Lefkowitz, J. (2000). The role of interpersonal affective regard in supervisory performance ratings: A literature review and proposed causal model. *Journal of Occupational and Organizational Psychology*, 73, 67–85.

Lefkowitz, J. & Battista, M. (1995). Potential sources of criterion bias in supervisor ratings used for test validation. *Journal of Business and Psychology*, 9, 389–414.

LePine, J.A., Erez, A., & Johnson, D.E. (2002). The nature and dimensionality of organizational citizenship behavior: A critical review and meta-analysis. *Journal of Applied Psychology*, 87, 52–65.

Levy, P.E. & Williams, J.R. (1998). The role of perceived system knowledge in predicting appraisal reactions, job satisfaction and organizational commitment. *Journal of Organizational Behavior*, 19, 53–65.

Locke, E.A. & Latham, G.P. (1990). *A theory of goal setting and task performance*. Englewood Cliffs, NJ: Prentice-Hall.

Locke, E.A. & Latham, G.P. (2002). Building a practically useful theory of goal setting and task motivation: A 35-year odyssey. *American Psychologist*, 57, 705–717.

London, M. & Smither, J.W. (1995). Can multi-source feedback change perceptions of goal accomplishment, self-evaluations, and performance-related outcomes? Theory-based applications and directions for research. *Personnel Psychology*, 48, 803–839.

London, M., Smither, J.W., & Adsit, D.J. (1997). Accountability: The Achilles' heel of multisource feedback. *Group and Organization Management*, 22, 162–184.

Luthans, F. & Peterson, S.J. (2003). 360-degree feedback with systematic coaching: empirical analysis suggests a winning combination. *Human Resource Management*, 42, 243–256.

Mann, S.L. & Budworth, M.H. (2005). *Self and peer rater agreement of counterproductive performance*. Paper presented at the annual meeting of the Society for Industrial and Organizational Psychology, Los Angeles.

Markus, H.R. & Kitayama, S. (1991). Culture and the self: implications for cognition, emotion and motivation. *Psychological Review*, 98, 224–253.

Martin, D., Bartol, K., & Kehoe, P. (2000). The legal ramifications of performance appraisal: The growing significance. *Public Personnel Management*, 29, 379–406.

Maurer, T.J., Mitchell, D.R.D., & Barbeite, F.G. (2002). Predictors of attitudes toward a 360° feedback system and involvement in post-feedback management development activity. *Journal of Occupational and Organizational Psychology*, 75, 87–107.

Mayer, R.C. & Davis, J.H. (1999). The effect of the performance appraisal system on trust for management: A field quasi-experiment. *Journal of Applied Psychology*, 84, 123–136.

Meichenbaum, D. (1977). *Cognitive behavior modification: An integrative approach*. New York: Plenum Press.

Miller, J.S. & Cardy, R.L. (2000). Self-monitoring and performance appraisal: Rating outcomes in project teams. *Journal of Organizational Behavior*, 21, 609–626.

Millman, Z. & Latham, G.P. (2001). Increasing reemployment through training in verbal self-guidance. In M. Erez, U. Kleinbeck, & H. Thierry (Eds), *Work motivation in the context of a globalizing economy*. Mahwah, NJ: Lawrence Erlbaum.

Murphy, K.R. & Cleveland, J.N. (1995). *Understanding performance appraisal: Social, organizational, and goal-based perspectives*. Thousand Oaks, CA: Sage.

Nease, A.A., Mudgett, B.O., & Quinones, M.A. (1999). Relationships among feedback sign, self-efficacy, and acceptance of performance feedback. *Journal of Applied Psychology*, 84, 806–814.

Noonan, L.E. & Sulsky, L.M. (2001). Impact of frame-of-reference training on alternative training effectiveness criteria in a Canadian military sample. *Human Performance*, 14, 3–26.

Northcraft, G.B. & Earley, P.C. (1989). Technology, credibility, and feedback use. *Organizational Behavior and Human Decision Processes*, 44, 83–96.

O'Leary-Kelly, A., Martocchio, J., & Frink, D. (1994). A review of the influence of group goals on group performance. *Academy of Management Journal*, 37, 1285–1301.

Olivero, G., Bane, K.D., & Kopelman, R.E. (1997). Executive coaching as a transfer of training tool: Effects on productivity in a public agency. *Public Personnel Management*, 26, 461–469.

Organ, D. (1997). Organizational citizenship behavior: It's construct clean-up time. *Human Performance*, 10, 85–98.

Ostroff, C., Atwater, L.E., & Feinberg, B.J. (2004). Understanding self–other agreement: A look at rater and ratee characteristics, context and outcomes. *Personnel Psychology*, 57, 333–375.

Pazy, A. & Oron, I. (2001). Sex proportion and performance evaluation among high-ranking military officers. *Journal of Organizational Behavior*, 22, 689–702.

Pelletier, L.G. & Vallerand, R.J. (1996). Supervisors' beliefs and subordinates' intrinsic motivation: A behavioral confirmation analysis. *Journal of Personality and Social Psychology*, 71, 331–340.

Pettijohn, C.E., Pettijohn, L.S., & d'Amico, M. (2001). Characteristics of performance appraisals and their impact on sales force satisfaction. *Human Resource Development Quarterly*, 12, 127–146.

Pratkanis, A. & Aronson, E. (2001). *Age of propaganda: The everyday use and abuse of persuasion*. New York: Freeman.

Reilly, R.R., Smither, J.W., & Vasilopoulos, N.L. (1996). A longitudinal study of upward feedback. *Personnel Psychology*, 49, 599–612.

Renn, R.W. (2003). Moderation by goal commitment of the feedback–performance relationship: Theoretical explanation and preliminary study. *Human Resource Management Review*, 13, 561–580.

Richardson, L. (1998). Five-minute sales coaching. *Training and Development*, 52, 53–57.

Rotundo, M. & Sackett, P.R. (2002). The relative importance of task, citizenship and counterproductive performance to global ratings of job performance: A policy-capturing approach. *Journal of Applied Psychology*, 87, 66–80.

Saks, A.M. & Waldman, D.A. (1998). The relationship between age and job performance evaluations for entry-level professionals. *Journal of Organizational Behavior*, 19, 409–419.

Salter, J.S. (1996). Officer attitude and opinion survey: Career management and job performance issues. *Australian Army First Psychological Research Unit Report*, May, 20.

Schleicher, D.J. & Day, D.V. (1998). A cognitive evaluation of framework-of-reference rater training: Content and process issues. *Organizational Behavior and Human Decision Processes*, 73, 76–101.

Scholz, U., Dona, B.G., Sud, S., & Schwarzer R. (2002). Is general self-efficacy a universal construct? Psychometric findings from 25 countries. *European Journal of Psychological Assessment*, **18**, 242–251.

Schrader, B.W. & Steiner, D.D. (1996). Common comparison standards: An approach to improving agreement between self and supervisory performance. *Journal of Applied Psychology*, **81**, 813–820.

Scullen, S.E., Bergey, P.K., & Aiman-Smith, L. (2005). Forced distribution rating systems and their improvement of workforce potential: A baseline simulation. *Personnel Psychology*, **58**, 1–32.

Scullen, S.E., Mount, M.K., & Goff, M. (2000). Understanding the latent structure of job performance ratings. *Journal of Applied Psychology*, **85** (6), 956–970.

Seifert, C.F., Yukl, G., & McDonald, R.A. (2003). Effects of multi-source feedback and a feedback facilitator on the influence behavior of managers toward subordinates. *Journal of Applied Psychology*, **88**, 561–569.

Seijts, G.H. & Latham, G.P. (2001). The effect of learning, outcome, and proximal goals on a moderately complex task. *Journal of Organizational Behavior*, **22**, 291–307.

Seijts, G.H. & Latham, G.P. (2005) Learning versus performance goals: When should each be used? *Academy of Management Executive*, **19**, 124–131.

Seijts, G.H., Latham, G.P., Tasa, K., & Latham, B.W. (2004). Goal setting and goal orientation: An integration of two different yet related literatures. *Academy of Management Journal*, **47**, 227–239.

Seligman, M.E.P. (1998). *Learned optimism*. New York: Pocket Books.

Shah, J. (2003a). Automatic for the people: How representations of significant others implicitly affect goal pursuit. *Journal of Personality and Social Psychology*, **84**, 661–681.

Shah, J. (2003b). The motivational looking glass: How significant others implicitly affect goal appraisals. *Journal of Personality and Social Psychology*, **85**, 424–439.

Shah, J.Y. (2005). The automatic pursuit and management of goals. *Current Directions in Psychological Science*, **14**, 10–13.

Smither, J.W., London, M., Flautt, R., Vargas, Y., & Kucine, I. (2003). Can working with an executive coach improve multisource feedback ratings over time? A quasi-experimental field study. *Personnel Psychology*, **56**, 23–44.

Smither, J.W., London, M., & Reilly, R.R. (2005). Does performance improve following multisource feedback? A theoretical model, meta-analysis, and review of empirical findings. *Personnel Psychology*, **58**, 33–66.

Smither, J.W., London, M., Vasilopoulos, N.L., Reilly, R.R., Millsap, R.E., & Salvemini, N. (1995). An examination of the effects of an upward feedback program over time. *Personnel Psychology*, **48**, 1–34.

Smither, J.W. & Walker, A.G. (2004). Are the characteristics of narrative comments related to improvement in multirater feedback ratings over time? *Journal of Applied Psychology*, **89**, 575–581.

Steers, R.M. & Sanchez-Runde, C.J. (2002). Culture, motivation, and work behavior. In M.J. Gannon and K.L. Newman (Eds), *The Blackwell handbook of principles of cross-cultural management*. Bodmin, UK: MPG Books.

Stone, J., Aronson, E., Crain, A.L., Winslow, M.P., & Fried, C.B. (1994). Inducing hypocrisy as a means of encouraging young adults to use condoms. *Personality and Social Psychology Bulletin*, **20**, 116–128.

Strauss, J.P., Barrick, M., & Connerley, M. (2001). An investigation of personality similarity effects (relational and perceived) on peer and supervisor ratings and the role of familiarity and liking. *Journal of Occupational and Organizational Psychology*, **74** (5), 637–657.

Sue-Chan, C. & Latham, G.P. (2004). The relative effectiveness of external, peer and self-coaches. *Applied Psychology: An International Review*, **53**, 260–278.

Sulsky, L.M. & Keown, J.L. (1998). Performance appraisal in the changing world of work: Implications for the meaning and measurement of work performance. *Canadian Psychology*, **39** (1–2), 52–59.

Taylor, M.S., Tracy, K.B., Renard, M.K., Harrison, J.K., & Carroll, S.J. (1995). Due process in performance appraisal: A quasi-experiment in procedural justice. *Administrative Science Quarterly*, **40**, 495–523.

Trist, E.L. (1977). Collaboration in work settings. *Journal of Applied Behavioral Science*, **13**, 268–278.

Tyler, K. (1997). Prepare managers to become career coaches. *HRMagazine*, **42**, 98–101.

Tziner, A. (1999). The relationship between distal and proximal factors and the use of political considerations in performance appraisal. *Journal of Business and Psychology*, **14**, 217–231.

Tziner, A., Joannis, C., & Murphy, K.R. (2000). A comparison of three models of performance appraisal with regard to goal properties, goal perception and ratee satisfaction. *Group and Organization Management*, **25**, 175–190.

Tziner, A. & Kopelman, R.E. (2002). Is there a preferred performance rating format? A non-psychometric perspective. *Applied Psychology: An International Review*, **51**, 479–503.

Tziner, A., Latham, G.P., Price, B.S., & Haccoun, R. (1996). Development and validation of a questionnaire for measuring perceived political considerations in performance appraisal. *Journal of Organizational Behavior*, **17**, 179–190.

Tziner, A., Murphy, K.R., & Cleveland, J.N. (2001). Relationships between attitudes towards organizations and performance appraisal systems and rating behaviors. *International Journal of Selection and Assessment*, **9**, 226–239.

Uggerslev, K.L. & Sulsky, L.M. (2002). Presentation modality and indirect performance information: Effects on ratings, reaction and memory. *Journal of Applied Psychology*, **87**, 940–950.

Van Scotter, J.R. & Motowidlo, S.J. (1996). Interpersonal facilitation and job dedication as separate facets of contextual performance. *Journal of Applied Psychology*, **81**, 525–531.

Varma, A., DeNisi, A.S., & Peters, L.H. (1996). Interpersonal affect and performance appraisal: A field study. *Personnel Psychology*, **49**, 341–361.

Walker, A.G. & Smither, J.W. (1999). A five-year study of upward feedback: What managers do with their results matters. *Personnel Psychology*, **52**, 393–423.

Watson Wyatt (2002). *Human Capital Index: Human capital as a lead indicator of shareholder value*. Washington, DC: Author.

Wayne, S.J. & Liden, R.C. (1995). Effects of impression management on performance ratings: A longitudinal study. *Academy of Management Journal*, **38**, 232–260.

Weisband, S. & Atwater, L. (1999). Evaluating self and others in electronic and face-to-face groups. *Journal of Applied Psychology*, **84** (4), 632–639.

Welch, J. & Byrne, J.A. (2001). *Jack: Straight from the gut*. New York: Watner Books.

Werner, J.M. & Bolino, M.C. (1997). Explaining US courts of appeals decisions involving performance appraisal: Accuracy, fairness, and validation. *Personnel Psychology*, **50**, 1–24.

Winters, D. & Latham, G.P. (1996). The effect of learning versus outcome goals on a simple versus a complex task. *Group and Organization Management*, **21**, 236–250.

Woehr, D.J. & Huffcutt, A.I. (1994). Rater training for performance appraisal: A quantitative review. *Journal of Occupational and Organizational Psychology*, **67**, 189–205.

Woodford, K. & Maes, J.D. (2002). Employee performance evaluations: Administering and writing them correctly in the multi-national setting. *Equal Opportunities International*, **21**, 1–8.

Zagona, S.V. & Harter, R. (1966). Credibility of source and recipient's attitude: Factors in the perception and retention of information on smoking behavior. *Perceptual and Motor Skills*, **23**, 155–168.

Zazanis, M.M., Zaccaco, S.J., & Kilcullen, R.N. (2001). Identifying motivation and interpersonal performance using peer evaluations. *Military Psychology*, **13**, 73–88.

Zhou, J. (1998). Feedback valence, feedback style, task autonomy, and achievement orientation: Interactive effects on creative performance. *Journal of Applied Psychology*, **83**, 261–276.

Chapter 8

QUALITATIVE METHODS IN INDUSTRIAL AND ORGANIZATIONAL PSYCHOLOGY

Catherine Cassell
Manchester Business School, University of Manchester, UK
and
Gillian Symon
Department of Organizational Psychology, Birkbeck, University of London, UK

The last 25 years have seen calls for the increased utilization of qualitative methods within the organization sciences (Boje, 2001; Crompton & Jones, 1988; Prasad & Prasad, 2002; Reason & Rowan, 1981; Van Maanen, 1979). Some have argued the case for qualitative methods in industrial and organizational (I/O) psychology specifically (e.g, Fryer, 1991; Lee, Mitchell, & Sablynski, 1999; Symon, Cassell, & Dickson, 2000). Advocates of qualitative research have presented it as potentially enhancing our understanding of key issues within I/O psychology, particularly given the increasingly complex substantive topics with which we are faced (Bartunek & Seo, 2002; Johnson & Cassell, 2001; Lee et al., 1999; Locke & Golden-Biddle, 2002). Indeed, King (2000) asserts that there are 'some organizational phenomena that seem especially suited to qualitative examination' (King, 2000, p. 590). Despite these claims and arguments, however, Spector (2001, p. 11) has observed that the methodological emphasis of I/O psychology has remained resolutely quantitative:

> Industrial/organizational psychology is a quantitative science, and most of our research follows in this tradition. Recent advances in qualitative methods (Cassell & Symon, 1994) have seen only occasional use in our field to date, but can be found more often in other social sciences.

Similarly, Locke and Golden-Biddle (2002) argue that I/O psychology 'has not as yet taken full advantage' (p. 100) of qualitative research, and Anderson

International Review of Industrial and Organizational Psychology, 2006, Volume 21
Edited by G.P. Hodgkinson and J.K. Ford. © 2006 John Wiley & Sons, Ltd.

(1998) has recorded considerable disappointment in the failure of the field to change or develop with respect to adopting new approaches, including qualitative ones.

Our main aim in this chapter is to review current practice with respect to qualitative research methods in I/O psychology including: the extent to which such methods are reported in relevant journals; potential insights to be gained from such methods; problems with conducting qualitative research in I/O psychology; other available sources of qualitative work; and suggestions for future work in the area. We begin by attempting a definition of 'qualitative research' but highlight the difficulties and debates inherent in this endeavour. While recognizing the problems, we conclude that qualitative research is probably interpreted within our discipline as research approaches that do not seek to quantify data. In preparation for our review of current practice, we then trace something of the history of the development of the discipline with respect to research methods. This suggests a focus on quantitative methods of assessment and research as fulfilling particular disciplinary objectives and goals. Recent reviews of published articles in I/O psychology journals conducted by other researchers are outlined before we present our own analysis of contemporary published work, covering the period 2000–2004 (updating previous reviews). This analysis seems largely to support the views of Spector (2001) and Locke and Golden-Biddle (2002), as outlined above. However, we examine in detail some specific papers that illustrate the different perspectives that have been taken on qualitative research in I/O psychology in very recent years, and we suggest other sources of qualitative research work in areas relevant to I/O psychology. We conclude with a consideration of the key challenges for, and future potential of, the development of I/O psychology in this area.

DEFINING QUALITATIVE RESEARCH

Defining qualitative research is not as straightforward as it might seem because there are so many varieties of approach subsumed under the heading 'qualitative'. However, Holloway and Todres (2003) argue that many elements of qualitative research are shared between different approaches and that:

> such an overlap of epistemological, aesthetic, ethical and procedural concerns can encourage a fairly generic view of qualitative research—a 'family' approach in which the similarities are considered more important than the differences, and where the notion of *flexibility* becomes an important value and quest. (p. 346)

In a similar fashion, Cassell and Symon (1994b) suggest that rather than seeking an all-embracing definition of qualitative methods it is perhaps more helpful to outline the key characteristics that qualitative methods share. They outline six such characteristics. First, that qualitative research is generally *non-restrictive*, in that it is usually the case that qualitative research is less likely to impose a priori classifications on the data. Second is a focus on *subjectivity*. It is often argued that one of the cornerstones of the qualitative approach is its acceptance of the inherent subjectivity of the research endeavour (Bryman, 1988). It is the view of the world as the organizational actors perceive it that is of explanatory value and interest (Locke & Golden-Biddle, 2002). Third, they suggest that qualitative research is *context-dependent*. In one sense, this implies that qualitative research should be conducted in naturalistic settings, that is, on location in organizations rather than in laboratories or other artificially constrained settings (Lincoln & Guba, 1984; Marshall & Rossman, 1989). It also suggests that context should be taken into account as formative in our explanations rather than as background noise which needs to be controlled. Another key characteristic is that of taking a *holistic perspective*. An important characteristic of qualitative approaches is that they seek to provide a holistic view of the situations or organizations that researchers are trying to understand (Bogdan & Taylor, 1975; Patton, 1980). In this context, the individuals or organizations are not reduced to an isolated variable but are, rather, seen as part of a whole (Symon, 2000a). The final characteristic is that those contributing to the research are treated as *participants not subjects*. Because such methods take place in the original setting of the research participant, Kirk and Miller (1986) suggest that qualitative researchers are engaged in interacting with people in their own language and on their own terms, as would be expected on someone else's territory.

In addition to this analysis, some authors have suggested that a key defining characteristic of qualitative research is that it takes a 'critical' approach. On the one hand, there are those who argue that qualitative researchers are 'critical' of other methodological approaches. Holloway and Todres (2003) refer to qualitative researchers as generally having a 'critical stance towards positivist perspectives' as a result of their 'disappointment with the opportunities that those perspectives present in capturing lived experience' (p. 345). Such dissatisfaction with more traditional research designs has led others to argue for the wider application of qualitative methods within the I/O psychology field (e.g., Hollway, 1991; King, 2000; Symon et al., 2000). Alternatively, some writers argue that a key purpose of qualitative research is to take a political perspective (e.g., Alvesson & Skoldberg, 2000): the focus is upon recognizing the subjective nature of the research process and on how the knowledges we produce as a result of research may bring about social change. Although most I/O psychologists would argue that the purpose of their endeavours is to bring about valued organizational change, some qualitative work differs from mainstream I/O psychology in having an ideological base and recognizing the subjectivity of this goal (e.g., whose values are supported in the change?, the changes are for whose benefit?). Such work may be informed by the perspectives of feminist-standpoint research (Griffin, 1995), intervention research (Fryer & Feather,

1994), and critical theory (Alvesson & Deetz, 2000). However, as Lee et al. (1999, p. 168) suggest:

> Most organizational and vocational psychologists are likely taught that the scientific enterprise should be, as far as possible, 'objective, dispassionate and fair'. Many qualitative researchers applaud this intention, yet may also find it unrealistic. Instead they believe the scientific process (and the empirical world itself) is, in reality, subjective, passionate and inherently unfair.

On the face of it, an obvious and shared characteristic of qualitative approaches might be that they do not seek to quantify phenomena: 'in the act of analysis, qualitative researchers work with verbal language rather than numerical language as indicators of the phenomenon of interest' (Locke & Golden-Biddle, 2002, p. 100). However, some researchers may conduct qualitative research but then go on to quantify their data (e.g., counting frequencies of interview responses, and using statistical techniques to compare groups). This raises the issue of whether non-numerical data are, in fact, defining characteristics or, alternatively, whether these researchers are conducting 'pure' qualitative research? The answer to this probably lies in the underlying assumptions and beliefs about research as knowledge production (epistemology): those who then seek to quantify the outputs of their qualitative research may be working within a positivist paradigm (what Prasad and Prasad (2002) describe as 'qualitative positivism', p. 6), which seeks to 'parsimoniously explain and predict behaviour' (Johnson, Buehring, Cassell, & Symon, 2005, p. 13).

As a consequence of this observation, we have argued elsewhere that whether research is defined as 'qualitative' or 'quantitative' is something of a 'red herring' (Symon & Cassell, 1998, p. 3). Similarly, Morgan and Smircich (1980) describe the distinction as 'a somewhat crude and over-simplified dichotomization' (p. 491). What is more pertinent is the epistemological tradition within which the research is carried out. The assumption here is that in understanding particular research practices it is important to appreciate a variety of ontological and epistemological stances. These stances in relation to organizational research are summarized in the various meta-theories of writers such as Burrell and Morgan (1979), Guba and Lincoln (1994) and Alvesson and Deetz (2000). Whereas most of the quantitative studies reported in I/O psychology might be underpinned by a positivist or modernist paradigm, qualitative methods might be informed by all possible epistemological positions, such as postmodernism, interpretivism, and social constructionism, *including* positivism (Gephart, 1999). Thus Morgan and Smircich (1980, p. 498) point out that:

> ... any given technique often lends itself to a variety of uses according to the orientation of the researcher. For example, participant observation in the hands of a positivist may be used to document the number and

length of interactions within a setting, but in the hands of an action theorist may be used to explore the realms of subjective meaning of those
interactions.

It might, therefore, be more useful with respect to qualitative methods to
distinguish between them according to the underlying epistemological assumptions of the study, rather than the nature of the data collected. To group them
altogether as 'qualitative' can be more confusing than helpful and disguises
some very important differences. Indeed, Dachler (1997) suggests that this
practice of labelling research 'qualitative' merely to distinguish it from quantitative serves to privilege the quantitative. As long as qualitative methods are
labelled in this way, they will always be perceived as an adjunct to quantitative research, rather than forming a distinct perspective based on different
underlying epistemological assumptions and following different research goals.
Additionally, this practice puts the emphasis very much on the method (and
its 'technical' qualities), rather than, for example, the underlying assumptions
of the researcher or the context of the research.

On the other hand, Hoshmand (1999, p. 15) argues that:

Philosophical and procedural differences among qualitative approaches have
made it difficult for qualitative researchers to forge a unified proposal and to
establish the place of qualitative inquiry in psychology in particular and in
the social sciences in general.

Hoshmand advocates that qualitative researchers form a 'community'
around particular characteristics (she recommends action research and critical hermeneutics) in order to pursue and strengthen the credibility of the
research.

Given these debates, we can see that defining 'qualitative research' is not necessarily a straightforward process. However, the generic term is well used within
social science disciplines. Our intention here is to bring these debates regarding
definition to the reader's attention rather than providing any resolutions. Such
debates characterize the lively nature of discussions about qualitative research
shared by qualitative researchers, who are not in themselves a homogeneous
group. Suffice it to say that the most valuable strategy in this context is for the
researcher to be explicit about the definition being used and the philosophical
assumptions underlying the work.

For the purpose of this chapter, and in the interests of pragmatism, we will
use the term in its conventional sense within the I/O psychology field: that is,
to represent those techniques of data collection and analysis that rely on non-
numerical data. In defining 'qualitative' in this way, we seek to be inclusive of a
range of techniques that focus on textual data or visual images, while excluding
techniques specifically involving quantification processes. We recognize that

there are some who would dispute our definition, but it is offered in the context of the problems outlined above.

THE HISTORY OF RESEARCH METHODS IN I/O PSYCHOLOGY

In assessing the current role and status of qualitative methods in I/O psychology, it is important to consider the historical context within which the discipline has developed.

> ... methodology helps legitimate and elevate a discipline or practice among other enterprises and social practices. Metaphorically, it is the armed wing of science.
>
> (Seale, Gobo, Gubrium, & Silverman, 2004, p. 7)

An important element of the development of I/O psychology has been the ability of work psychologists to measure aspects of human behaviour in a credible manner. Hollway (1991), in her critical account of the history of work psychology, argues that a focus on measurement is a key theme running through the history of the development of the I/O psychology discipline, starting with scientific management in the early 1900s. She suggests that interviewing (as a qualitative data collection technique) within I/O psychology emerged around the same time as the view of the sentimental worker underlying human relations. She highlights that the benefits from interviews were far wider than collecting quality research data, but also formed the basis for designing interventions, as suggested by evidence from the Hawthorne studies. What is interesting about the interview method in this context is the assumption that the data collected are valid, reliable, and indeed can be acted upon. The collection of qualitative data was a key part of the Hawthorne studies overall. At that time, qualitative research (certainly in the guise of interview studies) was seen to be acceptable.

However, Hollway describes the two developing traditions within I/O psychology of 'fitting the man to the job' and 'fitting the job to the man' as both requiring methods of screening individuals which rely upon the measurement of work environments and their impact, and the increasingly sophisticated development of psychometric testing. These developments are largely based on quantitative assessments. In addition, she argues that during the Second World War there was a growing interest in attitude surveys, due to the ongoing interest in assessing the state of public morale. Interest in such surveys developed rapidly, and the (quantitative) survey clearly has had a key role in I/O psychology research ever since. From her historical analysis, Hollway (1991) has argued that in the early to mid part of the last century at least, I/O psychology has apparently chosen a quantitative path of methodological development.

This interpretation is supported by the review presented by Austin, Scherbaum, and Mahlman (2002). Billed as a 'History of research methods in industrial and organizational psychology', the assumption is that such a history is one of psychometrics and the development of attitude measures. They argue that in the formative years of I/O psychology, researchers were trained in experimental psychology and their interpretation of the Hawthorne studies is that they 'marked a shift towards studying social forces at work using "quasi-experimental" designs' (p. 13). Dividing the last century into three distinct eras, and in a similar fashion to Hollway, they illustrate how each era has provided opportunities for I/O psychologists to develop further (quantitative) measures. For example, the great depression and the Second World War provided opportunities for the development of job analysis instruments, and the civil rights era of the 1960s with its emphasis on equal opportunities and affirmative action led to the emergence of test fairness and adjustment models. Austin et al.'s depiction of the history of I/O psychology differs somewhat from Hollway's—particularly in their interpretation of the early years of the emerging discipline—but otherwise follows a similar argument in indicating how, on the whole, I/O psychologists have used the opportunities of different eras to develop more sophisticated (quantitative) measuring instruments.

In the same volume as Austin et al.'s historical review of research methods in I/O psychology, Locke and Golden-Biddle (2002) provide a similar historical analysis of the development of qualitative research specifically. They suggest that this has its roots in anthropology and sociology, and overall their account depicts a research approach developing *outside* I/O psychology, rather than, as in Austin et al.'s account, being intimately tied up with the development of the discipline itself. Indeed, they suggest that qualitative research within I/O psychology has 'increasingly looked to the humanities for informing schools of thought and practice approaches to study life at work' (p. 115).

We would argue that this focus on quantitative measurement within I/O psychology has been underpinned by a positivist epistemology. Johnson and Cassell (2001) argue that 'positivism has been crucial to the development, security and credibility of work psychology as a discipline' (p. 128). One of the key underlying assumptions of positivism is the methodological unity between the natural and social sciences; therefore I/O psychologists have traditionally mirrored the methods in use in the natural sciences (Behling, 1980). This methodological unity not only provides guidelines for the appropriate conduct of research within the discipline, but also serves to provide credibility for I/O psychology as a true and proper science. In I/O psychology efforts to legitimize psychology as a scientific endeavour (in the positivist sense) have been translated as the search for the 'natural (field) experiment' or the adoption of 'quasi-experimental' techniques (Cook & Campbell, 1979). An I/O psychology discipline underpinned by positivism is based on the notion of an objective truth existing 'out there', discoverable by 'scientific' methods. Therefore research practices must be seen as untainted by subjectivity, and controlled and narrowly focused to get to and dissect that truth. Consequently value is placed in psychology on research that is perceived to be methodologically rigorous. This is usually equated with quantitative approaches that are constructed as 'hard' and scientific, and clearly has implications for the use of qualitative methods when useful and appropriate knowledge is constructed as being produced by orthodox techniques. Consequently, even in relation to qualitative research methods, 'some scholars . . . have suggested that while psychology in general has moved towards embracing interview- and fieldwork-based research, it has done so largely within the modernist paradigm' (Locke & Golden-Biddle, 2002, p. 114).

What we can note from this brief analysis of the history of the development of research methods within I/O psychology is that qualitative methods are not new to I/O psychology but over the decades may have become sidelined in favour of quasi-experiments and psychometric measures. This may be because of a continuing association of I/O psychology with the research designs and methods of the natural sciences and, consequently, a commitment to the goals of positivist research. However, in recent years, qualitative research has come to the fore within social psychology and organizational sciences more widely. We therefore turn our attention to the more contemporary use of research methods to discover if, in keeping with this broader trend, qualitative methods have also become more prevalent within the I/O psychology field.

CHARTING THE CONTEMPORARY USE OF QUALITATIVE RESEARCH WITHIN I/O PSYCHOLOGY

During the last 30 years, psychology in general has seen a number of challenges to the dominance of positivism and what have been termed 'new paradigms' have emerged (e.g., Smith, Harré, & Van Langenhove, 1995). The origins of these challenges are located in critiques of social psychology that emerged in the 1970s where Shotter (1975) questioned the epistemological authority underpinning experimental research, and others (e.g., Henriquez, Hollway, Urwin, Venn, & Walkerdine, 1984) challenged the whole notion of the concept of the 'subject' upon which psychology is based. Indeed, Smith et al. (1995, p. 2) suggest that the impact of this dissatisfaction is that psychology has clearly moved away from the 'hegemony of the laboratory experiment in the last twenty years'. Within the United Kingdom this was accompanied by the emergence of new initiatives in qualitative methods, stimulated by *The Future of Psychological Sciences Report* (BPS, 1988). For example, a symposium sponsored by the Scientific Affairs Board of the British Psychological Society (BPS) at the 1992 London conference argued that researchers needed to pay much more attention to qualitative methods (Henwood & Nicolson, 1995).

However, despite this increasing interest in qualitative methods in general psychology during the 1990s, this did not seem to reach published work within the I/O psychology field. Although there were some moves towards raising the profile of qualitative methods, most notably with the publication of textbooks providing advice for researchers on how to use qualitative methods in their research (e.g., Cassell & Symon, 1994a; Lee, 1999; Symon & Cassell, 1998), very little qualitative research was being published in I/O psychology journals at this time. Sackett and Larson (1990) reviewed the various strategies and tactics used within I/O psychology research through an empirical study of the research methods used in every article published in the years 1977, 1982, and 1987 in three journals: the *Journal of Applied Psychology*; *Organizational Behavior and Human Decision-Making Processes*; and *Personnel Psychology*. Contrary to assertions by Smith et al. (1995) about the demise of the experiment, they argued that:

The field of I/O psychology has changed dramatically over the past several decades in the extent to which experimentation has been used as a research methodology. Twenty-five years ago experimental studies performed on work-related topics were still relatively uncommon, especially if they were done in a laboratory. Today, by contrast they are one of the field's most frequently reviewed methodologies.

(Sackett & Larson, 1990, p. 443)

In their review of the literature, Sackett and Larson found that 50% of the empirical studies examined used some form of experimental design, but only 13% of those were actually conducted in the field. This compares to 18% of studies that used archival data, 36% of studies using questionnaires, and only 3% interview studies. They concluded that the published literature is dominated by two kinds of studies. The first is short-term laboratory experiments, using college students as experimental subjects; the second is questionnaire surveys of employees, where self-report measures are used. At a similar time, Schaubroeck and Kuehn (1992) presented a review of research designs utilized in studies published in what they considered the 'top' work psychology journals over the period 1989–1990. Their review covered 170 articles published during those two years in the *Journal of Applied Psychology*, *Personnel Psychology*, and *Organizational Behavior and Human Decision-Making Processes*. Coming from an overtly positivist perspective, they concluded that such journals had given little space to qualitative studies which were, at any rate, of 'marginal value' (p. 119). Additionally, a brief evaluation of studies published in the dominant UK organizational psychology journal, the *Journal of Occupational and Organizational Psychology*, from 1990 to 1998 indicated that about 3% of the studies were 'qualitative' (Symon & Cassell, 1999).

Previous reviews indicate, therefore, that although there may be an increased use of and interest in qualitative methods within the I/O psychology domain, this has not necessarily been reflected in any outputs. The reviews described above, however, are rather dated. An up-to-date analysis is required and it is to this task that we now turn.

REVIEW OF CURRENT RESEARCH METHODS IN USE IN I/O PSYCHOLOGY

In order to investigate the *current* uses of qualitative research in I/O psychology, we conducted a review of journal output similar to those recorded above. Specifically we examined the published output of five key journals in the field. The journals concerned were the *Journal of Applied Psychology*, *Personnel Psychology*, *European Journal of Work and Organizational Psychology*, *Journal of Organizational Behavior*, and the *Journal of Occupational and Organizational Psychology*. We realize that in choosing these journals we are omitting some important publications. Our rationale for focusing on these particular journals was as follows. First, we wanted to consider only general I/O psychology journals, as opposed to those dealing with specialist areas of application, such as personnel selection, engineering psychology/human factors, and stress research, as the more specialist journals in areas such as these tend to favour particular research methods (typically questionnaires and/or laboratory methods). Second, with one notable exception, we excluded journals that publish articles falling within the purview of I/O psychology but whose remit lies beyond the boundaries of this particular field. (Thus, for example, we excluded a number of journals falling within organization theory and/or management research more broadly.[1]) In summary, in conducting this review, we wanted to examine publications that were specifically within the focal domain of I/O psychology but had a broad remit, covering various aspects of the discipline. We also wanted to concentrate on those journals that could be regarded as both high status and commanding a wide and international audience of readers. Our reasoning here is that these can be regarded as perhaps the most influential publications, certainly within academic I/O psychology, and therefore likely to be shaping ideas of accepted practice within I/O psychology research. An examination of these journals should therefore enable us to present a preliminary analysis of what is happening in the field as a whole.

We examined the articles published in these journals between January 2000 and December 2004. In each case we categorized the articles according to the following criteria:

• Type of paper (review or empirical)
• The research design employed
• Predominant methods of data collection and analysis
• Location of first author.

Such a review is more complex than it appears. As suggested earlier, the definition of 'qualitative' is problematic; consequently, identifying papers as

---

[1] The *Journal of Applied Psychology* covers a wider remit than I/O psychology per se; however, it is a recognized leader in the field and is regularly included in other reviews, hence its inclusion here.

'qualitative' is similarly difficult. In accordance with the conclusions reached earlier, we categorized papers as 'qualitative' if there was no quantification of data in the paper. This is quite a rigorous definition, excluding studies that may have transformed qualitative data gathered using qualitative methods (such as interviews) into quantitative data for statistical analysis, or studies that may have used both qualitative and quantitative data. We do, however, describe some specific papers of these kinds in more detail as illustration of these types of approaches.

In detail, the review process entailed, first, reading through the abstract of the article. We then categorized papers according to whether they were reviews or empirical studies. Within the review category we included commentaries, contributions to debates, and reviews of particular methodological approaches. All other papers were categorized as empirical. Where it was not possible to categorize the empirical articles on the basis of the abstract alone (which was frequently the case), we then examined the methodology sections (i.e., research design, data collection, and data analysis) for all studies included in the paper. We also took note of the wording of the research questions (qualitative studies tend to address broad research questions, while quantitative studies address hypotheses). Where a variety of similar methods were used in the same study or the article included more than one study, using different methods, we categorized the article according to the predominant method of data collection and analysis employed. The empirical papers were categorized according to seven potential designs/methods:

- questionnaires (including attitude surveys, structured interviews, and psychometrics);
- experimental and quasi-experimental designs;
- statistical meta-analysis;
- simulations (including vignettes and role plays);
- performance measures;
- other quantitative (e.g., experience sampling, computer modelling, and utility analysis); and
- 'pure' qualitative (as outlined earlier).

Geographical Distribution of First Authors

We begin by considering the geographical distribution of first authors (see Table 8.1). By identifying the geographical location of first authors, we hoped to get some idea of the extent of the international contribution to the field of I/O psychology in general. In multi-authored papers, clearly authors may come from different countries. However, although we recognize that authorship is sometimes alphabetical, we took the view that *first* authors are usually those who have contributed most to the research itself, particularly in the presentation of that research.

Table 8.1   Location of first authors in five I/O journals over the period 2000–2004

Country	JAP^1	$JOOP^2$	$EJWOP^3$	PP^4	JOB^5	Total
Australia	11	12	2	2	14	41
Austria	2					2
Belgium	1	3	3	2	4	13
Canada	15	11	1	4	17	48
China				1	1	2
Denmark			3			3
Finland	1	2	5		4	12
France				1	1	2
Germany	6	2	17		5	30
Hong Kong	11	2		1	8	22
India			1			1
Ireland			4			4
Israel	8	5	3	3	13	32
Italy	1					1
Korea					1	1
Malaysia		1				1
Netherlands	11	15	23	4	17	70
New Zealand	1	2	1		2	6
Nigeria					1	1
Norway	1	1	3			5
Singapore	3				3	6
Spain	2	2	4	1	1	10
Sweden	2	1	5		1	9
Taiwan	1	1			1	3
Turkey		1				1
UK	13	52	32	2	7	106
USA	398	45	7	113	161	724
Total no. of papers	488	158	114	134	262	1156

[1] *Journal of Applied Psychology.*
[2] *Journal of Occupational and Organizational Psychology.*
[3] *European Journal of Work and Organizational Psychology.*
[4] *Personnel Psychology.*
[5] *Journal of Organizational Behavior.*

As the *Journal of Applied Psychology* (JAP) is an American Psychological Association journal, it is perhaps not surprising that by far the majority of the contributors come from the USA (82%). However, given that this journal is also one of the top rated within I/O psychology research, and is seen as a key outlet for I/O psychology research (Anderson, Herriot, & Hodgkinson, 2001), these figures are significant in revealing the dominance of North American approaches within the discipline more generally. The same can be said for *Personnel Psychology* (PP), another highly rated journal, where contributions from outside the USA make up only 15.7% of the sample. The *Journal of Organizational Behavior* (JOB) is argued to have a more international remit

(Peterson, 2001) and authors from outside the USA make up 38.6% of the contributors. It might be expected that the UK-based *Journal of Occupational and Organizational Psychology* (*JOOP*) would have more UK contributors than any other, but the work of North Americans is again notable (28% from the USA and 7% from Canada). Most contributors to the *European Journal of Work and Organizational Psychology* (*EJWOP*) are from the UK (28%) and the Netherlands (20%). One conclusion to draw from Table 8.1 would seem to be the dominance of North American work in certain key journals within the I/O psychology field. However, there are other issues to consider. For instance, we should recognize that this may be as a result of examining journals that publish only in the English language. Where there are multiple authors, the first author may be from North America simply because of the language requirements. In addition, there are proportionally more relevant academics in the USA than in other countries. On the other hand, these journals are regarded as the most prestigious and the fact that they are dominated by North American and (to a lesser extent) British academics is significant—a state of affairs that has not gone unrecognized. Berry (1996) argues that researchers outside North America feel pressure to publish in North American journals and consequently may adopt the favoured research designs and methods of that continent. In an article specifically addressing this phenomenon, Peterson (2001) reports a personal communication from Heller observing that this situation is likely to continue as Europe moves towards more research evaluation processes based on US practices. While we shall discuss this conclusion in more detail in a later section, Peterson (2001, p. 64) suggests that 'the influence of US theories, methods preferences, scholars, academic organizations and journals in OB research is a part of the field's global institutional context that is both well recognized and often resented'. Seeing this dominance as an outcome of the US scholars' better access to support for research, he also concludes that times are changing and that 'the period of the hegemony of US journals may eventually pass...' (p. 78).

Types of Paper and Research Design Utilized

Table 8.2 outlines the types of paper that each of the journals publish. From this table it is clear that by far the majority of papers in each case are empirical, though more reviews and commentaries can be found in *JOOP* than in the other journals (27% of the total number). *JOOP*, *EJWOP*, and *JOB* have more theoretical reviews and commentary papers than either *JAP* or *PP*. Seven of the theoretical reviews in *JAP*, for example, came from a special issue on theoretical models and conceptual analyses.

Table 8.3 presents the findings of our analysis of research methods utilized in the journals reviewed.

From this table it appears that very few 'purely' qualitative papers were published in most of the journals surveyed over the specified period. *JAP* and

Table 8.2   Numbers of reviews and empirical studies published in five I/O psychology journals over the period 2000–2004

Articles	JAP^1	$JOOP^2$	$EJWOP^3$	PP^4	JOB^5	Total
Reviews/Editorials/Commentaries and Debates	9	43	21	14	43	130
Empirical papers	479	115	93	120	219	1026
Total no. of papers	488	158	114	134	262	1156

[1] *Journal of Applied Psychology.*
[2] *Journal of Occupational and Organizational Psychology.*
[3] *European Journal of Work and Organizational Psychology.*
[4] *Personnel Psychology.*
[5] *Journal of Organizational Behavior.*

PP are generally dominated by questionnaire and experimental designs. In both cases the analysis of performance data and papers based on meta-analyses were the next prevalent. In the remaining three journals, the predominant method utilized was the questionnaire. Indeed, all the journals are similar with regard to their reliance on questionnaire methods.

There were 13 qualitative papers published in *EJWOP* during the five-year period encompassed by this review. However, a closer inspection reveals that

Table 8.3   Research designs/methods utilized in five I/O psychology journals over the period 2000–2004

	JAP^1	$JOOP^2$	$EJWOP^3$	PP^4	JOB^5	Total
Questionnaires (Attitude surveys/ Psychometrics/Structured interviews)	221	86	71	52	165	595
Experiments/Quasi-experiments	146	5	1	25	11	188
Performance ratings/Measures	43	12	1	15	7	78
Meta-analysis	49	5	2	11	5	72
Vignettes/Role plays/Simulations	11	4	2	3	5	25
Other quantitative	9	3	3	12	17	44
'Pure' qualitative			13*	2	9	24
Total no. of empirical papers	479	115	93	120	219	1026

[1] *Journal of Applied Psychology.*
[2] *Journal of Occupational and Organizational Psychology.*
[3] *European Journal of Work and Organizational Psychology.*
[4] *Personnel Psychology.*
[5] *Journal of Organizational Behavior.*
* Includes eight papers from special issues on qualitative methods and relational constructionism.

eight of these papers came from special issues of the journal: one a special issue on qualitative methods in I/O psychology that came out in 2000, and one a special issue on relational constructionist approaches to organizational learning (which also accounts for five of the theoretical review papers). Nine 'purely' qualitative studies were published in *JOB*, four of these from a special issue on electronic working. A tentative conclusion might be that qualitative studies are more likely to be included within special issues assembled by guest editors. We can only speculate about the reasons for this, which may include a greater likelihood that authors will submit qualitative pieces to special issues. It may be that special issues can act as primers for further contributions in the normal issues of the journal concerned. On the other hand, it may just act to confirm the suspicion that qualitative research is in some way 'unusual' and to keep such research segregated.

Where qualitative methods of data collection such as interviews were utilized these were often either supplemented by quantitative data, or, more usually, used to generate constructs that were then quantified through a process of content analysis. So it would seem that in the few cases of qualitative work being reported in I/O psychology research, such methods are mainly used as a precursor to quantitative analysis. Indeed, sometimes it was claimed that a mixture of qualitative and quantitative methods were used (usually questionnaires and interviews) but then only the quantitative data were fully analysed and reported. Lee (1999) suggests that there are advantages to organizational researchers of the 'two-phase design' strategy, in particular that it enables researchers to capitalize on the different strengths of two traditionally separate research orientations. However, in most cases, it would seem that where this occurs the qualitative element is a minor part of the overall research design.

Detailed Analysis of a Selection of Empirical Papers

Frequencies of research designs provide only a small insight into how qualitative methods are being used in the I/O psychology journals reviewed. To enhance our understanding, we need to look in more depth at particular types of design involving some form of qualitative data. In the section that follows we therefore look at two papers from each of the different designs in which qualitative methods were used. First, we examine two papers where the qualitative element precedes some quantification process. Second, we consider two papers where both qualitative and quantitative techniques are used, and, third, we consider two purely qualitative papers. These papers have been selected to illustrate the characteristics of these different approaches.

Qualitative data leading to quantification

The first example of how qualitative research is transformed comes from the *Journal of Applied Psychology*. Bligh, Kohles, and Meindl (2004), in their paper entitled 'Charting the language of leadership: A methodological investigation of President Bush and the crisis of 9/11', suggest that their choice of a qualitative approach (namely rhetorical analysis) has the opportunity to provide new insights into the phenomenon of leadership:

> Despite the multitude of studies devoted to leadership, many researchers continue to use traditional survey methodologies. This reliance on purely quantitative methodologies has limited new insights into and developments into the leadership process, particularly as it is affected by the social psychological and contextual variables that surround it. (p. 562)

They suggest that their methodology of 'dictionary based content analysis' enables the reliable and systematic study of the linguistic-based elements of the leadership relationship. This paper is interesting in that the authors clearly have a positivist orientation in terms of the conduct of their qualitative research and regularly reassure the reader that the analysis is rigorous, reliable, and, indeed, 'completely impartial' (p. 563) in its approach. In other areas of rhetorical analysis, informed by constructivist approaches (e.g., Symon, 2000b), it is seen as important for the researchers to critique their own position in relation to the account they are providing. In this paper, however, it is argued that using computer-aided data analysis exempts the analytic process from any undue influence of the coder. The package used in this case is DICTION, a program specifically designed to examine the 'linguistic elements of political leaders'. The program was used to analyse 74 of President Bush's major speeches and radio addresses, with a focus on six constructs: optimism, collectives, faith, patriotism, aggression, and ambivalence. Through univariate and covariate analyses in respect of each of the dependent variables, the authors demonstrate that the President's rhetoric changed after the crisis of 9/11. The authors suggest that 'this methodology is ideal for a "before and after" approach that helps elucidate changes in leadership processes in response to environmental contingencies' (p. 568).

The Bligh et al. article is an example of how, when qualitative methods are used in the journals listed above (albeit rarely), the qualitative data collected are then quantified and subjected to statistical analysis. Given the quantitative nature of the analysis we categorized this under 'Other Quantitative'.

The second example of work in this tradition is also taken from the *Journal of Applied Psychology*. Bateman, O'Neill, and Kenworthy-U'Ren (2002) interviewed 75 top managers from three countries to develop a taxonomy of managerial goals, and through a content analysis of the interview transcripts produced a total of 2182 goals. In justifying the use of a qualitative approach the authors argue:

> Because goals constitute a broad domain of incompletely documented phenomena, our approach was inductive. We allowed categories to emerge

naturally from field interviews rather than be contaminated or constrained by prior work and a priori assumptions. We collected, coded, and analysed the qualitative data until clear patterns emerged and further such efforts added little new information, insight, or refinement. (p. 1136)

The goals derived from the interviews were classified into different categories by four independent coders and levels of interrater reliability were calculated. Ten goal categories were produced which provided the new taxonomy. A number of statistical tests were then performed to see if a series of predictions regarding the nature of managerial goals could be upheld. These focused on issues such as individual and national differences in managerial goals. In critiquing their own research the authors, as with the Bligh et al. paper, use criteria from the positivist paradigm. They suggest that the problems with their study emerge from issues to do with bias in relation to coding in the content analysis, and the lack of performance or behavioural data to support the findings.

There are a number of similarities in the ways in which qualitative data are being used in these examples. First, they are used as a means of providing an initial exploration of the type of issues that might be worthy of investigation, or the key concepts of significance to individuals. Second, in each case, content analysis is the analytic procedure of choice, most probably because of the potential it offers for further quantification. Third—an important issue for qualitative researchers generally—all of these authors critique their own work using the criteria for assessment that are associated with traditional positivist approaches, such as reliability and validity. This is a point we shall return to later, when we discuss the various criteria in use for assessing the quality of qualitative research; however, at this stage, it is worth noting that in each of the articles outlined, reliability coefficients designed to test the robustness of the coding process were used. It would seem that when qualitative research is published, it needs to follow the procedural checks of reliability and validity that are used by quantitative researchers. Thus, overall, we would argue that in the majority of cases, where qualitative research is published in these journals, a modernist approach has been adopted (Locke & Golden-Biddle, 2002).

Multimethod designs

A further way in which qualitative methods are utilized, in a minority of cases, is as part of a multimethod design, where both qualitative and quantitative techniques are used to provide different types of data about the same phenomenon under investigation. This approach can be used when authors recognize that different methods produce different types of insights and can therefore be complementary. It is also useful when authors are keen to triangulate their findings, through using data from a range of techniques. This may be particularly pertinent to case study research.

In the first case (from the *Journal of Organizational Behavior*), we provide an example where qualitative data were used to elucidate an initial quantitative data set. Zweig and Webster (2002) set out to investigate employees' reactions to electronic 'awareness monitoring systems' (in this case, in-office video links) meant to enhance collaboration at a distance. The researchers began by formulating a theoretical (causal) model of the potential predictors of acceptance of these kinds of technologies, and as a consequence derived some specific hypotheses for testing. A sample of 612 participants were provided with scenarios (in which the characteristics of the technology were systematically varied) and asked to respond to various scale measures (which tapped the variables of interest). Through Structural Equation Modelling, the resultant data were seen to support the model and indicate predictors of acceptance. In their second qualitative study (five focus groups), they went on to 'move beyond an understanding of how the variables in the model are related to discover why the relationships exist'; to uncover other variables not in the model; and 'to help generate both theoretical and practical suggestions for future research . . .' (p. 618). The transcripts of the focus groups were coded both inductively and deductively, interrater agreements were calculated, and frequencies of categories were computed. Most importantly, these qualitative data not only indicated reasons *why* identified variables were considered important, but they also highlighted potential contingencies and areas of disagreement between participants. The qualitative data also suggested a new aspect (psychological boundary violations) that was not considered in the original model (which had been derived from existing literature). On the basis of the qualitative data, Zweig and Webster were able to suggest a variety of new avenues for research and practice (in the design and implementation of such technologies).

Our second example focuses on a paper (from the *Journal of Occupational and Organizational Psychology*) where both qualitative and quantitative data are used to provide different insights into the same phenomenon. Mackenzie-Davey and Arnold (2000) present data from two different sources to shed light on the personal change that individuals experience when starting work at the early stages of their career. The first source of data was a questionnaire survey of a large number of graduates, which was administered twice, with a year-long interval. Questions focused on the extent to which individuals felt they had changed as a result of starting work, and included issues such as changes in values, career goals, personality, and attitudes. The questionnaire also had an open-ended element, and responses to the open-ended section were content analysed. The second source of data for the study came from nine interviews with women who had rated themselves as having changed 'a great deal' on the original questionnaire. Accounts of personal change and identity were explored through these interviews. The interview data were analysed through a focus on the discourses of personal change that emerged from the transcripts. In this context, the key advantage of using both qualitative and quantitative techniques together was that it enabled the authors to comment on both the amount of change individuals felt they had experienced, as deduced from the survey data, plus the processes of change that they felt had occurred, and how they felt about those changes, from the interview data. The authors point to some of the difficulties inherent in mixing methods in this way. A particularly interesting comment made by the authors is that rather than the use of quantitative and qualitative methods encouraging some form of triangulation of the data, the use of multiple methods of investigation actually led to 'rich, messy and even contradictory' data (p. 480). A paper such as this also highlights some of the problems in attempting to categorize papers as either qualitative or quantitative as we have sought to do. Clearly there is quantitative analysis in this paper with the use of analytic statistics such as chi-squared and significance testing, therefore it cannot be categorized as a purely qualitative paper. However, the role of the qualitative data is key to the analysis presented. In the review generally it was rare to find articles such as these where the qualitative data analysis were presented separately as an additional source of information in the write-up.

These two papers illustrate how qualitative and quantitative methods can be combined. In both cases, the authors claim that this combination provides a particularly distinctive focus and creates new insights into the phenomena under investigation. Within both papers we see an element of positivism in the way the qualitative data are treated and critiqued. In both papers, for example, interrater reliabilities were calculated for the content analysis parts. This implies a realist epistemology: that there is a true form of categorization, and that each rater, if trained sufficiently, will be able to code a segment of transcript identically and replicably. In the Mackenzie-Davey and Arnold paper, the authors refer to these epistemological issues specifically, suggesting that combining methods from different paradigms can create difficulties for the researchers concerned—for example, paradigm incommensurability (Burrell & Morgan, 1979). Where one approach is based on the notion of a constructed social reality (e.g., discourse analysis) and the other on a reality existing independently of humanity (e.g., questionnaire, content analysis), combining the two appears deeply problematic. While there is an ongoing debate about the constraints of paradigm incommensurability (Burrell & Morgan, 1979; Hassard, 1991; Jackson & Carter, 1991), in this context it is interesting to consider its effects in terms of the demands that are placed on qualitative researchers to account for and explain their work. It is possible that a greater range of potential epistemological tensions and difficulties can arise when seeking to conduct multimethodological work combining quantitative and qualitative approaches. This may partially explain the lack of such work in the journals we reviewed. However, this speculation needs to be explored further.

Purely qualitative

Table 8.3 indicates that there is very little published work that is 'purely' qualitative. Where qualitative methods are reported we have further classified them according to type in Table 8.4.

From Table 8.4 we can see that both interviews and case studies are the most often reported qualitative methods. However, again it is sometimes difficult to classify techniques. A case study, for example, may cover a range of qualitative methods of both data collection and analysis. Some authors may have utilized a combination of separate techniques and called the overall design a 'case study'. Others may have used a combination of techniques and simply referred to a 'multimethod approach' (even though being utilized in the same organization). We tended to be guided by the authors' own categorization here.

Considering some of these studies in more detail illustrates the potential insights that qualitative research can provide into some key areas of I/O psychology. While we are not suggesting that the studies we describe are above criticism in terms of their design and execution, our purpose is to illustrate rather than critique. Here we concentrate on the features that differentiate the studies from quantitative studies and the insights claimed to have been drawn.

Länsisalmi, Peiró, and Kivimäki (2000) examine collective definitions of stress and coping within an organizational environment. The paper (published in the *European Journal of Work and Organizational Psychology*) presents a case study in that the focus is a particular multinational company, but data were collected from three separate divisions. They suggest that using qualitative methods in this context is appropriate because of their aims to *develop* rather than *test* theory. The researchers conducted 63 interviews with individuals, followed by a series of 32 group interviews using the critical incident technique. Given that individuals may have very different experiences in this context, one could argue that variability would not have been apparent if the data had been collected using a questionnaire consisting of standardized items. In addition, the researchers used a range of other qualitative techniques such as participant observation and analysis of company documentation. These methods were designed to assess collective definitions of well-being and sources of stress which, as the authors found, differed across the various divisional cultures. Rather than content analysis, Länsisalmi et al. used grounded theory

Table 8.4 Type of qualitative design/method utilized in 'pure' qualitative articles identified

Type of qualitative study	Frequency
Case study	10
Interviews	4
Discourse analysis	2
Narrative	2
Method combination	2
Co-/emancipatory research	2
Focus groups	1
Repertory grid	1
Total	24

(Glaser & Strauss, 1967) in order to develop theory in this area. The authors found that definitions of well-being did vary across the different cultures with regard to the extent to which the emphasis was upon work or other life domains as sources of well-being. They concluded that stress experiences and coping strategies do have collective properties that are influenced by the organizational cultures of the divisions, and that the use of qualitative methods in this context enabled a clearer understanding of the role of coping in the stress/health relationship than would have been possible through the quantification of stress reactions. This identification and development of the concept of an important *collective* element to coping with stress at work represents a key theoretical contribution to the field of stress research.

Our second example comes from the *Journal of Organizational Behavior*. Ford and Locke (2002) explore the introduction of a 'paid time off' (PTO) scheme in a specific organization. From their analysis of existing literature, they conclude that a scheme of this sort does 'not exist as an objective entity; rather, it is an occasion for, and the product of, sensemaking' (p. 492). As a consequence, their approach to understanding the operation of a PTO scheme is to explore how different employees make sense of the scheme and how this affects what they do with respect to the scheme. Symbolic interactionism provides the underlying metatheoretical stance, and a typology of self-conceptions from Gephart (1993, 1997), referenced by Ford and Locke (2002, p. 493), provides a conceptual framework. Rather than specific hypotheses, a number of broad research questions guided the data collection (e.g., 'What sensemaking resources were relevant to how organization members understood and implemented the PTO benefit?' (p. 493)). Given the objectives, the researchers required an in-depth, longitudinal study of a specific organization introducing such a policy. Their methods included individual interviews, access to archival sources, and participant observation. In the latter case, Ford and Locke are clear about the researcher's role in the research: not as 'objective bystander' but as an adviser to the organization. This role is seen as enhancing the depth and variety of information available to the research team. In identifying the interview sample, and unlike most positivist research, which would specify the required sample up front, Ford and Locke began with opportunistic sampling, but moved to a more purposive sampling strategy as they were able to identify specific individuals utilizing the PTO scheme in specific ways, i.e., 'sampling for maximum variation in use of PTO' (p. 495). As with Länsisalmi et al. (2000), a grounded theory approach to analysis was adopted and detail is provided as to the unfolding categorization scheme. The two researchers describe their process of working closely together in an iterative manner to 'understand' their data and no specific forms of reliability 'tests' are reported: the description itself makes the process clear and allows judgement of the quality of that process. As the analysis progressed, initial themes were replaced by others, as more insight was gained, and Gephart's typology both informed the scheme and yet required modification in the light of the data (i.e., a combination of inductive and deductive analysis). Ford and Locke conclude that the study provides insights into why PTO schemes may be problematic in operation, specifically in the (different) self-conceptions that managers and employees bring to the sense-making process. Such an analysis, they claim, reveals managers not as simply agents of capitalism but 'trapped in their own categorization schemes' (p. 507) and the symbolic interactionist approach as providing 'insight into how small structures—day to day dealings—have large consequences' (p. 507). They see their study as a 'starting point' (p. 507) in a relatively unexplored field but do not conclude by deriving testable propositions or suggesting that the ideas need testing through surveys or experimental methods.

We can see a number of similarities across these papers. First, there is a focus on the meanings *for the participants* that are associated with such concepts as 'paid time off work' and 'stress'. The in-depth analysis provided enables us to see how these meanings influenced individual behaviour around these issues. Such subjective meanings are hard to identify from quantitative assessments. Second, context is seen as important in explaining the outcomes (both focus on particular case organizations). Third, while previous theory was taken into account in the analysis it did not determine it and was indeed challenged by it. Fourth, the researchers describe in detail their processes of analysis: the emergent nature of their conclusions, which were deeply embedded in the data, and their intense collaboration in the analysis process, allowing readers to come to their own conclusions about the potential usefulness of the results, rather than this being obscured by a simple set of statistics. While they are not unproblematic (both suffer from some lack of reflexivity and are open to accusations of 'finding what they were looking for', as is the case with much questionnaire data reported), these purely qualitative studies clearly provide some thought-provoking insight into the phenomena of interest.

Potential Problems of the Review

The overall conclusion from our review is that there is very little purely qualitative work. This finding supports other observations in this area (e.g., Bartunek & Seo, 2002; Sackett & Larson, 1990; Symon & Cassell, 1999). However, we should consider whether the findings we present here are an arte-fact of our review process: are our criteria for defining research as qualitative too rigorous and exclusive? Has our selection of relevant journals been too narrow? We have already explained our review criteria but these are still relevant issues that need to be raised. We should also acknowledge the possibility that there is simply a dissemination lag and that the increased interest in qualitative re-search noted earlier has not yet filtered through to the journals incorporated in our review. Perhaps another five years will paint a very different picture. On the other hand, from when should we delimit a potential period of change: 1970s with the 'crisis' in social psychology (30 years ago)?; 1979 with the publication of Van Maanen's special edition of *Administrative Science Quarterly* (25 years ago)?; 1988 with the publication of the *Future of Psychological Sciences Report* in the UK (17 years ago?); 1994 with the publication of Cassell and Symon's textbook on qualitative organizational research methods (10 years ago)? If any of these events prompted a shift to qualitative methods, the effects have not been seen in journal outputs.

We should also consider the possibility that I/O psychology researchers may be choosing not to submit their work to journals in the I/O psychology field, preferring instead to present their work in the management arena. Given the potential applications of I/O psychology research to the management field, this would not be surprising.

Larsson and Lowendahl (1996) conducted a meta-analytic review of the espoused and actual applications of qualitative methods in management research. The journals that formed the basis of their review were *Academy of Management Journal, Administrative Science Quarterly, Organization Science*, and *Strategic Management Journal*. When assessing the articles published between 1984 and 1994 they concluded that just 12 studies during that period could be classed as qualitative. Bearing in mind the length of the period, and the number of journals covered, it would seem that qualitative methods have also not been particularly prevalent in the management field. It could be, however, that things have progressed somewhat since 1994. Lee et al. (1999) conducted another review of more specific relevance to I/O psychologists. Their review, in the *Journal of Vocational Behavior*, has the intention of 'inspiring' I/O psychology researchers to use qualitative methods more regularly in their work. Their review covered what they describe as 'the major journals in organizational and vocational psychology' (p. 162) over the period 1988–1998, which included the following: *Administrative Science Quarterly, Journal of Vocational Behavior, Academy of Management Journal, Organization Science*, and *Personnel Psychology*. We should note here that we would regard at least three of these journals as management/organization studies journals rather than specifically I/O psychology journals. From this review, they identified 33 papers that used qualitative techniques (as they do not indicate how many articles were reviewed altogether, it is not clear what proportion of the total this represents). However, they themselves conclude that few qualitative studies have been published. These reviews, too, thus seem to indicate a dearth of qualitative research in the wider organization studies and management journals.

Making Sense of the Review Findings

The conclusion from this review is that there appears to be very little qualitative research published in the I/O psychology field specifically. The question then becomes why this might be the case. Some qualitative researchers have argued that these journals, regarded by many as the top journals in the field, are hostile to qualitative research, but the editors of these and related journals have responded by arguing that this is not the case (see, e.g., West, Arnold,

Corbett, & Fletcher, 1992). Indeed, the argument may be that qualitative research articles are simply not submitted to these journals. This may be a self-fulfilling prophecy, in that qualitative researchers do not see qualitative work appearing in these journals so do not submit their work to these outlets. This apprehension continues despite overt and covert encouragement by the editors of some of these journals (e.g., Bartunek & Seo, 2002; Sparrow, 1999). The unfortunate consequence of this situation, whatever its cause, is that the two approaches, quantitative and qualitative, get ever more divergent. In addition, as we have suggested, the journals reviewed here rank among the more important in the I/O field, encouraging an association between quantitative research and status.

Symon and Cassell (1999) argue that this lack of visibility for qualitative methods arises from difficulties in opposing the current dominant practice. They identify a number of different barriers to the publication of qualitative research, including: (1) getting research past epistemological gatekeepers (journal editors and reviewers, conference committees); (2) conforming to journal editorial criteria and constraints of other presentations, which have probably been set up with quantitative studies in mind; (3) the pressure to justify research methods according to (sometimes) inappropriate (positivist) criteria; and (4) the lack of exposure to alternatives in I/O psychology publications and on I/O psychology courses. These arguments suggest a reason for why qualitative methods are not being used by researchers without attributing the cause to something inherent in the techniques themselves. Additionally, they provide an account for why qualitative researchers are not publishing in the best journals that does not locate the problem with the researcher. It is not that qualitative research and those who conduct it are inherently weaker, but rather that judgements of 'good practice' in research cannot be made without reference to the social and political context. We shall explore these issues in more detail later, when we consider the challenges facing the development of qualitative methods in I/O psychology in the future.

ALTERNATIVE SOURCES OF QUALITATIVE RESEARCH IN I/O PSYCHOLOGY

So far we have considered the scope and extent of use of qualitative research through a focus on its distribution within I/O psychology and management/organization journals. However, journals that focus on qualitative research specifically have emerged in recent years (e.g., *Qualitative Research*, *Qualitative Inquiry*) and 2004 saw the publication of the first issue of the journal *Qualitative Research in Psychology*. These are not oriented to organizational or work research specifically, and, indeed, their publication could further indicate the widening divide between qualitative and quantitative work.

More strikingly, the last 15 years have seen the publication of a number of textbooks that provide readers with advice on how to use qualitative research methods. Seale et al. (2004), in an analysis of the catalogues produced by the academic publisher Sage Publications, conclude that there has been an 'explosion of texts' (p. 1) from a mere 10 in the 1980s to over 130 in the period 1995–2002. Overall, most of these publications are 'general' qualitative research texts, rather than specific to organizational research (e.g., Denzin & Lincoln, 2000; Flick, Von Kardoff, & Steinke, 2004; Seale et al., 2004; Silverman, 2000). Such publications cover a number of underlying meta-theories as well as specific methods and analysis techniques. Other 'general' texts may focus on techniques of qualitative data *analysis* specifically (e.g., Bryman & Burgess, 1994; Coffey & Atkinson, 1996; Miles & Huberman, 1994; Silverman, 2001). In-depth presentations of specific research methods include action research (e.g., McNiff, 2000), ethnography (e.g., Brewer, 2000), case studies (e.g., Yin, 2003), interviewing (e.g., Kvale, 1996), and narrative analysis (e.g., Czarniawska, 2004). Specific forms of qualitative data analysis are also covered, such as thematic analysis (e.g., Boyatzis, 1998), grounded theory (e.g., Locke, 2003), discourse analysis (e.g., Phillips & Hardy, 2002), and computer-assisted analysis (e.g., Gibb, 2002). Texts are available which advise on how to design qualitative research (e.g., Creswell, 1998; Marshall & Rossman, 1989) and how to write it up (e.g., Golden-Biddle & Locke, 1997).

With respect to organizational research, there is the annual series *Advances in Qualitative Research in Organizations* and the textbooks of Lee (1999), Cassell and Symon (1994a, 2004), and Symon and Cassell (1998). These publications focus on organizational research per se, and are produced by I/O psychologists specifically.

Lee's (1999) goals are not only to advocate the use of qualitative methods but to 'make the traditionally quantitative researcher comfortable with qualitative methods and the traditionally qualitative researcher comfortable with categorical data analysis' (p. 5). The contents of his book comprises chapters on specific and generic techniques for qualitative research, plus chapters covering issues of reliability and validity. Methods covered include the hermeneutic interpretation of company documents; the job analysis interview; protocol analysis; and audio-visual data. Specifically there is a focus on how qualitative research can be conducted in a 'rigorous' manner, in line with a set of criteria presented for good practice in qualitative research.

Cassell and Symon's three edited texts take a somewhat different approach (Cassell & Symon, 1994a, 2004; Symon & Cassell, 1998). In their first book they suggest that their aims are to: first, document the variety of qualitative methods currently used by occupational and organizational psychologists; second, to provide the researcher and the practitioner with an overview of a range of methods, together with examples of how they are currently being used in practice; and, third, to try to raise the profile of qualitative methods within the discipline. In their third edited volume, *Essential Guide to Qualitative Methods in Organizational Research*, they also suggest that their intention is to enable researchers to claim some legitimacy for the techniques they use. Each of the 29 chapters is authored by researchers who have particular experience of using the method concerned. Examples embrace a number of different ways of conducting interviews (including electronic interviews; repertory grid interviews; critical incident technique; life histories and cognitive mapping techniques) and a variety of other methods of both data collection and analysis (e.g., qualitative research diaries, stories, pictorial representation, conversation analysis, hermeneutic understanding). It is worth noting that, in comparison to Table 8.4 (in which methods reported in the journals reviewed are presented), there is a far greater range of methods presented in textbooks, indicating that researchers may not be using or exposed to the full range of qualitative methods available

KEY CHALLENGES FOR THE DEVELOPMENT OF QUALITATIVE METHODS WITHIN I/O PSYCHOLOGY

So far, we have explored the extent to which qualitative methods have been used by I/O psychology researchers. In this penultimate section we consider some of the key challenges for I/O psychology as a discipline, with regard to the further development of research using qualitative techniques. In particular we outline three key challenges that have emerged from this review. These are intimately related and suggest some potential ways forward for the development of I/O psychology in relation to qualitative methods.

A clear conclusion has been that little purely qualitative research has been published within the key journals in the field. Specifically, from this review, we have argued that there may be a number of additional factors that impact on the potential widespread uptake of qualitative research within the discipline. These factors are not intrinsic to the methods themselves, but rather emerge from the political and organizational context within which I/O psychology research takes place. Therefore the first challenge we consider is that of outlining and investigating the impact of some of these contextual factors. Second, a point that has emerged repeatedly is that of the criteria we use to assess the quality of qualitative research. We have argued that qualitative research may sometimes be assessed inappropriately as a result of applying quality criteria from one broadly defined epistemological approach, such as positivism, to qualitative research that adopts another (again broadly defined) epistemological approach, such as social constructionism. Therefore, we address quality criteria in the context of alternative epistemological approaches as the second challenge. Third, and finally, we address the challenge of reflexivity, and argue that the critical appraisal of our research practices is an important process for all I/O psychologists.

Contextual Issues

In seeking to explain the current dearth of qualitative research papers in prestigious and widely read I/O psychology publications, we suggested a number of potential barriers which are not intrinsic to the methods themselves, including the role of gatekeepers, the use of inappropriate assessment criteria, presentational constraints, and lack of training. If we wish to encourage the use of qualitative methods within I/O psychology, we may have to address some of these more contextual issues. However, this may be more difficult than immediately apparent.

With our colleagues Phil Johnson, Anna Buehring, and Vicky Bishop we have been exploring the use of qualitative methods in management research in a recent research project sponsored by the UK Economic and Social Research Council (ESRC).[2] Some of the issues arising from this research are pertinent to the use of qualitative methods in I/O psychology. As part of this research, we have interviewed various stakeholders in the management research arena (including journal editors, those from grant-awarding bodies, practitioners, PhD directors, and qualitative researchers themselves). Some of these stakeholders highlight general contextual issues that may constrain the widespread adoption of qualitative research (Cassell, Buehring, Symon, & Johnson, 2005).

In particular, interviewees described the current context of academic research as a whole as not conducive to qualitative research. In the UK (and recently New Zealand) an emphasis on research audit has focused academic attention on the products of research (specifically journal publications) and on the holding of research grants as indicators of academic productivity (Bryson, 2004; Jary & Parker, 1998). Similarly, in North America, the difficulties of achieving tenure may have had something of the same effect. Many of our interviewees argued that this has led to pressures to conduct quantitative research as this is more likely to get published in prestigious journals, more likely to attract research funding, and is less time consuming to conduct.

With respect to publication issues specifically, North American journals are often regarded as most 'prestigious' within our discipline (e.g., *Journal of Applied Psychology* and *Personnel Psychology*), and, as we have seen, such journals do not on the whole publish qualitative research. Thus qualitative research is not being associated with 'prestige'. While some may see journal editors as actively discriminating against qualitative research, we must also see journal editors as operating within a particular context: the need to maintain the current standing of their journals. Such a responsibility may encourage a conservative attitude towards journal content: the familiar is less risky. In addition, in a very pragmatic sense, qualitative research may not 'fit' the presentational parameters of most journals and this may, in itself, discourage its submission for publication.

---

[2] ESRC grant number H333250006, Benchmarking good practice in qualitative management research.

The full reporting of a detailed qualitative study may require the more extended treatment possible in book form. However, as noted above, auditing practices and promotion requirements may focus on journal publications.

From this analysis, the career implications for academics of conducting qualitative research are potentially serious, particularly for new researchers trying to achieve tenure or establish a reputation. Indeed, recent research by Judge, Kammeyer-Mueller, and Bretz (2004) emphasizes that career success in I/O psychology is most closely associated with publication rates. Perceptions that qualitative research will take longer and may be less likely to be published in prestigious outlets may, therefore, be discouraging this line of research. If this is the case, just advocating qualitative research among academics or even providing training in the methods might not be enough. If we are to encourage qualitative research within I/O psychology, we may need to consider how we could tackle some of these contextual issues. One step in this process may be to address current assessment criteria (such as are used in judging journal submissions and grant applications) and we discuss this further below. However, we would, at this stage, also advocate a more specific empirical study to investigate further the claims made above in the field of I/O psychology.

Assessment criteria and the evaluation of qualitative research

Throughout this review we have highlighted that qualitative techniques can be used within a variety of epistemological and ontological traditions. However, in I/O psychology qualitative research has been conducted largely within a positivist framework. Elsewhere, we have emphasized the opportunities that could be provided if I/O psychology as a discipline became more open to alternative epistemological approaches (e.g., Johnson & Cassell, 2001; Symon, 2000c). However, due to the potential epistemological variability of qualitative I/O psychology research, providing criteria for its evaluation is problematic. Whereas there is considerable consensus among I/O psychology researchers about quality criteria for empirical research within a positivist framework, there is far more debate about what makes 'good' research in alternative epistemological approaches (Symon & Cassell, 2004).

Researchers from other disciplines have sought to address this issue by producing quality criteria that are appropriate for qualitative research. For instance, in their early work, Lincoln and Guba (1985) emphasized the need for qualitative researchers within the social sciences to provide audit trails, in a self-critical fashion, that allow audiences to make judgements for themselves as to the rigour of the research process. They suggest the following general principles, which are seen to replace the concerns of positivist evaluation criteria:

• authentic representations (replacing internal validity with credibility);
• extent of applicability (replacing external validity with transferability);

- minimization of researcher idiosyncrasies (replacing reliability with dependability); and
- researcher self-criticism (replacing objectivity with confirmability).

Meanwhile, Morse (1994) focuses upon the inductive analysis of qualitative data through: comprehension (learning about a setting); synthesizing (identifying patterns in the data to produce categories); theorizing (explanations that fit the data); and recontextualizing (abstracting the emerging theory to new settings and relating it to established knowledge). A significant issue here is that the qualitative researcher must provide an account of how an inductive analysis of the organizational settings under investigation was accomplished, by demonstrating how concepts were derived and applied as well as showing how alternative explanations have been considered but rejected.

Hammersley (1990, 1992) adds to the above criteria by suggesting that qualitative researchers ought to be internally reflexive through critically scrutinizing the impact of their field roles upon the research setting and findings, in order to reduce sources of contamination, thereby enhancing 'naturalism' or ecological validity. Therefore, in I/O psychology research, a key aim would be to facilitate access to research participants' 'theories-in-use' (Argyris, Putnam, & Smith, 1985), and the multiple perspectives that abound in organizations (Pettigrew, 1985), while avoiding 'over rapport' with those participants. In this it would be necessary to treat organizational settings as 'anthropologically strange' (Hammersley, 1990, p. 16) while retaining 'social and intellectual distance' and 'analytical space' (Hammersley & Atkinson, 1995, p. 115). As Seale notes (1999, p. 161), through revealing aspects of themselves and the research process as a traceable audit trail, the qualitative researcher persuades readers that they 'can rely on the writer's hard won objectivity' thereby establishing the credibility, dependability, and confirmability of findings.

In assessing these criteria it is worth stating that they may not be appropriate to all types of qualitative research; indeed, some qualitative researchers may argue that criteria like these have a positivist undertone. Therefore, in relation to qualitative research in I/O psychology, the key issue is for the reviewer to be aware of their own criteria in use, and the appropriateness of the criteria they are applying.

Additionally, despite these alternative sets of criteria, there is a debate about the desirability of standardized quality criteria for qualitative research more generally. For example, Seale (1999) argues that it is difficult to regulate an area where the guiding philosophy is one of enhancing creativity and exploration. Additionally, there is a concern that checklists of criteria could potentially lead to the over-formalization of qualitative research and inhibit innovation and the development of new knowledge. This has led to writers such as Schwandt (1996) arguing that:

we must learn to live with uncertainty, with the absence of final vindications, without the hope of solutions in the form of epistemological guarantees.

Contingency, fallibilism, dialogue, and deliberation mark our way of being in the world.

While this suggests there is a need for caution in the development and use of appropriate criteria, there is also the danger that without evaluative guidelines qualitative research within the I/O psychology field will struggle to convince some audiences of its legitimacy—especially those who occupy the quantitative mainstream. Lee et al. (1999), for example, when specifically addressing qualitative research in I/O psychology, argue that in order to address the issue that 'many researchers believe qualitative methods to be inherently inferior to traditional designs' (1999, p. 184), it is imperative that qualitative researchers accept and utilize widely accepted standards for quality which emerge from the positivist paradigm. They propose that:

> ... qualitative researchers adopt the *conventional* and *widely accepted* ideal for methodological descriptions. Simply put, an article's description of its method must be sufficiently detailed to allow a reader (or our peer reviewers) to *replicate* the reported study either in a detailed hypothetical or in an actual manner. Although peer reviewers may not agree with one's interpretations of deductions, how these inferences are drawn must and should be clear. (p. 184, emphasis authors' original)

Although the sentiment behind this recommendation is intended to enhance the quality and profile of qualitative research within the field, and therefore also enhance its perceived credibility, the presentation of specific criteria in this context is quite controversial. The question is the extent to which the criterion outlined can be applied to research from epistemological positions that are alternatives to positivism. Many qualitative researchers would argue, for example, that the strict replication of research techniques is not only impossible, but also not necessarily desirable, as the researchers themselves form a key part of the social world they study (e.g., Hammersley, 1995).

Others within the I/O psychology field have tried to generate sets of criteria that are more appropriate to the epistemological diversity of qualitative research. The *Journal of Occupational and Organizational Psychology*, for example, provides a checklist of criteria for those reviewers who are expected to peer review qualitative articles. Accompanying this set of criteria is the proviso that: 'Given the considerable diversity in research strategies that use qualitative methods, these criteria need to be seen as general guidelines to aid reviewers rather than specific recommendations for all papers' (BPS, 2000).

There are no easy answers to the question of the extent to which specific evaluation criteria are appropriate for the development of qualitative research within the I/O psychology field. The most important challenge in this context is for I/O psychologists and peer reviewers to be aware of the criteria they are using to evaluate qualitative research, and the 'appropriateness' of those criteria for the epistemological position taken by the research in question. What we are advocating here is increased reflexivity in I/O psychology research, a challenge we turn to in the next section.

Reflexivity

One general process that we would argue would enhance the development of qualitative research methods in I/O psychology is a greater orientation to reflexivity in the research process. Reflexivity has had a recent surge of interest in disciplines related to I/O psychology, such as management (e.g., Johnson & Duberley, 2003), but, as yet, has had little explicit recognition in I/O psychology.

By reflexivity, we mean engaging in a critical appraisal of our own practice, whether this be academic research or client work:

> Reflexivity involves reflecting on the way in which research is carried out and understanding how the process of doing research shapes its outcomes.
> (Hardy, Phillips, & Clegg, 2001)

We need to be aware of and acknowledge why we, as I/O psychologists, frame issues in particular ways, investigate them in particular ways, and how these approaches lead us to particular kinds of solutions or theories (rather than others). We might 'develop' theory or 'solve' a particular organizational problem, but whatever the approach adopted, we should also reflect on our role, why we took that approach (e.g., our framing of the problem), whose views we represented, the implications of our theories, and solutions for those involved (e.g., who was advantaged and who was disadvantaged by our conclusions?).

Below, we suggest three different foci for the critical appraisal of our research processes: the methods we use and how we use them; the underlying epistemological assumptions behind our research; and the disciplinary assumptions we make in framing our research.

In the first place, reflexivity with respect to method is centrally concerned with the practices and procedures of research and intervention, and how these are implicated in the conclusions that are reached. By making the research process transparent, it is made public and therefore accountable (Finlay, 2002). Within different research paradigms, I/O psychology might be quite practised at some sorts of methodological reflexivity. With a continuing emphasis on measurement issues, this is probably something that I/O psychologists have thought about most. It is often the aspect of our research that peer reviewers focus on most with questions such as: 'Why these measures?', 'Are there other interpretations of your statistics?', 'Did you use the right statistics?', 'Is your sample skewed?' From more interpretive approaches, the questions may be: 'How were these themes derived from your interviews?', 'How were the interviews conducted?', 'Is the sample size large enough?' One of the issues here, however, is whether appropriate questions are asked of different kinds of data. As suggested above, qualitative research may be subjected to validity critiques based on positivist assessment criteria that it could not be expected to fulfil. I/O psychologists could reflect more on their own (subconscious) judgements of quality (what are they based on? can they be articulated?) and be more aware of possible biases in this area.

In addition, Anderson et al. (2001) suggest that a concern with methodology may have gone too far within (academic) work and organizational psychology, such that academics are more concerned with the rigour of methodological procedures than the relevance of the research conducted to organizational problems. They point to an overemphasis in the major academic publications on 're-finements of measurement procedures in relation to peripheral methodological concerns' (p. 399) and an increasing inappropriate focus on laboratory-based studies and student samples. The implication is that we need to reflect more on how our research methods may help us to achieve valued ends (such as understanding organizational problems) rather than a focus on research methods as an end in themselves. We could consider more what methods are most appropriate, rather than simply accepted or most prevalent. Methods textbooks and methodologically oriented journals may help in encouraging innovation in this area by exposing us to new approaches. In addition, Locke and Golden-Biddle (2002) argue that qualitative research specifically may help in 'helping organizational members gain a perspective on their own situations' (p. 114).

In this context, also, perhaps we have to be aware of how highly technical jargon and increasingly complex research designs and analysis may alienate the organizational audience:

> The complexity of research methods has changed the capability of traditional [management] audiences to understand the level of discourse, and it seems that the audience [for our research] now consists of other I/O psychologists. The peril of this approach is the gradual lessening of the relevance of the field to previous audiences.
>
> (Austin et al., 2002, p. 19)

Some researchers have suggested that the design and conduct of research in organizations should more explicitly involve organizational members (e.g., Bennington & Hartley, 2004; Hodgkinson & Herriot, 2002; Hodgkinson, Herriot, & Anderson, 2001) and this is, of course, a central tenet of action research (e.g., Heller, 2004). It is this issue that Tranfield and Starkey (1998) and Starkey and Madan (2001) address in the context of management research when they argue for a Mode 2 form of knowledge production which would involve all relevant stakeholders and consequently be of more relevance to organizational problems (for a wider discussion of these issues see the Special Issue of the *British Journal of Management* entitled 'Facing the future: The nature and purpose of management research re-assessed' (Hodgkinson, 2001)).

Going beyond methods, it is clear from the above that different kinds of research are based on different assumptions about what we can know and how we can claim to know it: 'An important function of reflexive analysis is to expose the underlying assumptions on which arguments and stances are builts' (Holland, 1999, p. 467).

Epistemological reflexivity concerns reflecting on our knowledge practices—our assumptions about, for example, what we can know about the nature of the world and human action. Conducting a survey, then, is not just about using a particular kind of measure but may imply all sorts of assumptions about how people are able to express their own experiences, about how researchers and practitioners can capture that experience, and so on. Similarly, conducting interviews is often suggested to reveal 'depth' or complexity, but this claim also rests on some assumptions about what people are doing in interviews and the relationship between the interviewer and interviewee that requires critical appraisal.

To the extent that I/O psychology is still dominated by positivist assumptions, as argued above, we do not routinely engage in epistemological reflection. Epistemological reflexivity, however, should be regarded as important for I/O psychology because it provides more potential for 'double-loop learning' (Argyris, 1982). This has enabled some researchers to produce new and different insights into phenomenon that are traditionally the key questions within I/O psychology. Taking the area of selection as an example, Herriot and Anderson (1997) suggest that there is a whole range of questions about the selection process that are rendered inaccessible by the positivist paradigm but that some of those questions lay themselves open to investigation from a social constructionist approach.

An innovative example of paradigmatic reflexivity enabled by the juxtaposition of different paradigmatic interpretations comes from the *Journal of Occupational and Organizational Psychology* (December, 2000). An article by Symon (2000c), critical of received wisdom in the area of technological change, was followed by a commentary from Sonnentag (2000) who disagreed with the underlying assumptions of the approach presented. This was followed by a reply from the original author (Symon, 2000a). In this final rejoinder, Symon explicitly refers to the underlying assumptions of the two authors and thus highlights the potential for paradigmatic debate in this specific field of research. This sort of activity within I/O psychology might help to make underlying assumptions more explicit and illuminate different ways of interpreting organizational processes.

Finally, in the area of social science discipline (e.g., psychology, sociology, organization studies), we need to be aware of our own social and political limitations and ideological functions. Being reflexive in this sense would entail reflecting on how the assumptions of our background discipline have prompted us to create a particular version of reality through our research. We may fit people into our (disciplined) way of thinking about the world. By creating some particular account, we deny other meanings and interpretations. When we are not aware of our interpretive frameworks we may experience the research or organizational problem as 'the reality'. When we are aware of our disciplinary framing, we may be able to note what has been prioritized and what ignored and speculate on the reasons why (Schön, 1991). Thus, as I/O psychologists, we need to consider how our psychological framing may shape our understandings. For example, how do our accounts of leadership or performance create particular identities for employees in organizations or how does I/O psychology promulgate a particular psychologized view of the person (Hollway, 1984, 1991).

An additional consideration in this area is the boundaries we explicitly create around our own expertise, framing who we are. Increasingly within I/O psychology we have put quite a lot of effort into distinguishing our discipline by carefully delimiting the areas of our specialty. While this serves the political purpose of protecting our professional identity, in the longer term it may limit what we can learn and the development of our understanding. Increasingly within the world of work with which we engage, boundaries are becoming less clear. The changing nature of careers and organizational structures means that to achieve a thorough understanding of any work situation we are constantly calling on the expertise of those from other disciplines, including economics, sociology, and law. As an applied discipline, we are probably already better at doing this—at being aware of other systems of knowledge—than our disciplinary colleagues in general psychology, but whether we draw on these other ways of knowing to critique or develop our own perspective is less clear. One of the potential constraints on this is our drive to distinguish ourselves as a 'science' that tends to disallow the credibility of any other system of knowledge, literary criticism, for example. In general we argue that we need to reflect on our accountability as a discipline (as well as individual researchers and practitioners) for creating particular versions of reality, which serve some political purpose.

In conclusion, we suggest that finding space for more critical appraisal of our own practices, while guarding against a self-indulgent focus on our research methods (Seale, 1999), may be a key challenge facing the development of qualitative research methods in I/O psychology.

CONCLUSION

Our aims in this chapter have been to explore the extent to which qualitative methods are being used within I/O psychology research, and to examine the insights they may provide. From our review it would seem that qualitative approaches are more generally known within the I/O psychology field, given the increasing resources available to researchers who wish to use them. However, whether they are used or not is less obvious as research using qualitative techniques is still rarely reported in the key journals in the area. Where such research is reported, however, the authors claim that they achieve insights into their subject matter which they could not have achieved using solely quantitative methods.

We have suggested a number of reasons why qualitative research is not more widely published within I/O psychology (particularly in the more 'prestigious' journals). We have highlighted problems in defining qualitative research, and some of the debates in this area. We have signalled that a far more important issue regarding definition is the underlying philosophies or meta-theories within which a particular technique might be utilized, that is, the epistemological and ontological assumptions that may underpin different qualitative studies. We have suggested that in assessing qualitative work, I/O psychologists might unwittingly draw upon criteria that are more relevant to a positivist tradition of research. As a consequence, researchers may lack confidence in pursuing qualitative work (seeing it as having less credibility) and peer reviewers and editors may be unable to distinguish the insights of the work. In assessing research from a traditional, positivist standpoint, reviewers tend to dwell on the 'technical' or methodological aspects and it is easier to see difficulties with qualitative research rather than quantitative research in this respect. As we have seen, if these problems are to be circumvented, the criteria that we use to assess qualitative work need to recognize the different epistemological traditions within which qualitative researchers work (see also Johnson et al., 2005).

Additionally, with reference to epistemological assumptions, we have argued that within traditional I/O psychology research, higher status has been associated with positivist approaches, approximating a natural science model of knowledge production. We have charted the history of the development of I/O psychology as one where the focus on measurement was the key to the status and credibility of the discipline and, therefore, where considerations of the inherent subjectivity of individuals, and the consequent development of qualitative techniques to address that subjectivity, may be seen to threaten this status. From our review of journals it would seem that such positivist approaches based on measurement through quantification underpin nearly all of the I/O psychology research currently published in the key journals in the field.

Rather than assume that this distribution is because this kind of research is 'better' or of higher 'scientific value', we have drawn attention to some of the more contextual issues that influence the kind of work that gets published. We have argued that our research does not take place in a social vacuum, but rather that a whole range of issues regarding career and status are important and that these issues need to be addressed head on if we want to allow more qualitative research more generally to enter the field of I/O psychology.

It is evident that qualitative work has much to offer I/O psychology researchers. We are not alone among I/O psychologists in arguing this (see, e.g., Lee et al., 1999; Locke & Golden-Biddle, 2002). However, in order for there to be an increased interest or increased use of qualitative methods within I/O psychology research, it is clear that the profile of such work needs to be enhanced. Our assumption behind this review is that a progressive I/O psychology, one that is able to respond to the increasingly diverse and complex issues faced by individuals at work, needs to embrace the potential methodological eclecticism that the enhanced use of qualitative methods can provide. We hope that, collectively, our discipline can rise to this challenge.

REFERENCES

Alvesson, M. & Deetz, S. (2000). *Doing critical management research.* London: Sage.

Alvesson, M. & Skoldberg, K. (2000). Reflexive methodology: New vistas for qualitative research. London: Sage.

Anderson, N. (1998). The people make the paradigm. *Journal of Organizational Behaviour,* **19**, 323–328.

Anderson, N., Herriot, P., & Hodgkinson, G.P. (2001). The practitioner–researcher divide in industrial, work and organizational (IWO) psychology: Where are we now and where do we go from here? *Journal of Occupational and Organizational Psychology,* **74**, 391–411.

Argyris, C. (1982). *Reasoning, learning and action: Individual and organizational.* San Francisco: Jossey-Bass.

Argyris, C., Putnam, R., & Smith, D.M. (1985). *Action science: Concepts, methods and skills for research and intervention.* San Francisco: Jossey-Bass.

Arnold, J. (2004). Editorial. *Journal of Occupational and Organizational Psychology,* **77** (1), 1–10.

Austin, J.T., Scherbaum, C.A., & Mahlman, R.A. (2002). History of research methods in industrial and organizational psychology: Measurement, design, analysis. In S.G. Rogelberg (Ed.), *Handbook of research methods in industrial and organizational psychology.* Oxford: Blackwell.

Bartunek, J. & Seo, M. (2002). Qualitative research can add new meanings to quantitative research. *Journal of Organizational Behavior,* **23**, 237–242.

Bateman, T.S., O'Neill, H., & Kenworthy-U'Ren, A. (2002). A hierarchical taxonomy of top managers goals. *Journal of Applied Psychology,* **87** (6), 1134–1148.

Behling, O. (1980). The case for the natural science model for research in organizational behavior and organization theory. *Academy of Management Review,* **5** (4), 483–490.

Bennington, J. & Hartley, J. (2004). Co-research: Insider/outsider teams for organizational research. In C. Cassell & G. Symon (Eds), *Essential guide to qualitative research in organizations.* London: Sage.

Berry, M. (1996). From American standard to cross-cultural dialogues. In B. Punnett & O. Shenkar (Eds), *Handbook for international management research.* Cambridge, MA: Blackwell.

Bligh, M.C., Kohles, J.C., & Meindl, J.R. (2004). Charting the language of leadership: A methodological investigation of President Bush and the crisis of 9/11. *Journal of Applied Psychology,* **89** (3), 562–574.

Bogdan, R. & Taylor, S.J. (1975). *Introduction to qualitative research methods.* New York: John Wiley & Sons.

Boje, D.M. (2001). *Narrative methods for organizational and communication research.* London: Sage.

Boyatzis, R. (1998). *Transforming qualitative information: Thematic anlaysis and code development*. Thousand Oaks, CA: Sage.

BPS (1988). *The future of the psychological sciences report*. Leicester: British Psychological Society.

BPS (2000). *Journal of Occupational and Organizational Psychology guidelines for reviewers for papers using qualitative methods*. Leicester: British Psychological Society.

Brewer, J.D. (2000). *Ethnography*. Buckingham: Open University Press.

Bryman, A. (1988). *Quality and quantity in social research*. London: Unwin Hyman.

Bryman, A. & Burgess, R. (1994). *Analyzing qualitative data*. London: Routledge.

Bryson, C. (2004). What about the workers? The expansion of higher education and the transformation of academic work. *Industrial Relations Journal*, **35** (1), 38–57.

Burgoyne, J. (1994). Stakeholder analysis. In C.M. Cassell & G. Symon (Eds), *Qualitative methods in organizational research: A practical guide*. London: Sage.

Burrell, G. & Morgan, G. (1979). *Sociological paradigms and organizational analysis*. London: Heinemann.

Cassell, C.M., Buehring, A., Symon, G., & Johnson, P. (2005). *Qualitative management research: A thematic analysis of interviews with stakeholders in the field*. Report for the ESRC.

Cassell, C.M., Close, P., Duberley, J., & Johnson, P. (2000). Surfacing embedded assumptions: Using repertory grid methodology to facilitate organizational change. *European Journal of Work and Organizational Psychology*, **9** (4), 561–574.

Cassell, C.M. & Redman, T. (2001). Editorial: Editorial policy for papers using qualitative methods. *Personnel Review*, **31** (1), 6–8.

Cassell, C.M. & Symon, G. (Eds) (1994a). *Qualitative methods in organizational research: A practical guide*. London: Sage.

Cassell, C.M. & Symon, G. (1994b). Qualitative research in work contexts. In C.M. Cassell & G. Symon (Eds), *Qualitative methods in organizational research: A practical guide*. London: Sage.

Cassell, C.M. & Symon, G. (1998). Quiet revolutions and radical transformations: A reply to H. Peter Dachler. *Organization Studies*, **19**, 1039–1043.

Cassell, C.M. & Symon, G. (2002). *Extending the epistemological boundaries of work and organizational psychology*. Paper presented to the International Congress of Applied Psychology, Singapore, July.

Cassell, C.M. & Symon, G. (Eds) (2004). *Essential guide to qualitative methods in organizational research*. London: Sage.

Cassell, C.M. & Walsh, S. (2004). Repertory grids. In C.M. Cassell & G. Symon (Eds), *Essential guide to qualitative methods in organizational research*. London: Sage.

Coffey, A. & Atkinson, P. (1996). *Making sense of qualitative data: Complementary research strategies*. Thousand Oak, CA: Sage.

Cook, T.D. & Campbell, D.T. (1979). *Quasi-experimentation: Design and analysis issues for field settings*. Boston: Houghton Mifflin.

Creswell, J. (1998). *Qualitative inquiry and research design*. Thousand Oak, CA: Sage.

Crompton, R. & Jones, G. (1988). Researching white collar organizations: Why sociologists should not stop doing case studies. In A. Bryman (Ed.), *Doing research in organizations*. London: Routledge.

Czarniaskwa, B. (2004). *Narratives in social science research*. London: Sage.

Dachler, H.P. (1997). Does the distinction between qualitative and quantitative methods make sense? A review of C. Cassell & G. Symon, Qualitative methods in organizational research. *Organization Studies*, **18** (4), 709–724.

Dalton, M. (1959). *Men who manage: Fusions of feeling and theory in administration*. London: John Wiley & Sons.

Denzin, N. & Lincoln, Y. (2000). *Handbook of qualitative research* (2nd edn). Thousand Oak, CA: Sage.

Finlay, L. (2002). Negotiating the swamp: The opportunity and challenge of reflexivity in research practice. *Qualitative Research*, **2**, 209–230.

Flick, U., Von Kardoff, E., & Steinke, I. (2004). *A companion to qualitative research.* London: Sage.

Ford, L. & Locke, K. (2002). Paid time off as a vehicle for self-definition and sensemaking. *Journal of Organizational Behavior*, **23**, 489–509.

Fryer, D.F. (1991). Qualitative methods in occupational psychology: Reflections on why they are so useful but so little used. *The Occupational Psychologist*, **14**, 3–6.

Fryer, D. & Feather, N.T. (1994). Intervention techniques. In C.M. Cassell & G. Symon (Eds), *Qualitative methods in organizational research: A practical guide.* London: Sage.

Gephart, R.P. (1993). The textual approach: Risk and blame in disaster sensemaking. *Academy of Management Journal*, **36**, 1465–1514.

Gephart, R.P. (1997). Hazardous measures: An interpretive textual analysis of quantitative sensemaking during crises. *Journal of Organizational Behavior*, **18**, 583–622.

Gephart, R.P. (1999). Paradigms and research methods. *Research Methods Forum*, **4** (Summer).

Gibb, G. (2002). *Qualitative data analysis: Explorations with NVivo.* Buckingham: Open University Press.

Gilbert, N. & Mulkay, M. (1984). *Opening Pandora's box: A sociological analysis of scientists' discourse.* Cambridge: Cambridge University Press.

Glaser, B.G. & Strauss, A.L. (1967). *The discovery of grounded theory.* Chicago: Aldine.

Golden-Biddle, K. & Locke, K. (1997). *Composing qualitative research.* London: Sage.

Griffin, C. (1995). Feminism, social psychology and qualitative research. *The Psychologist: Bulletin of the British Psychological Society*, **8** (3), 109–110.

Guba, E. & Lincoln, Y. (1994). Competing paradigms in qualitative research. In N. Denzin & Y. Lincoln (Eds), *Handbook of qualitative research.* Newbury Park, CA: Sage.

Hammersley, M. (1990). *Reading ethnographic research: A critical guide.* London: Longman.

Hammersley, M. (1992). *What's wrong with ethnography?* London: Routledge.

Hammersley, M. (1995). *The politics of social research.* London: Sage.

Hammersley, M. & Atkinson, P. (1995). *Ethnography: Principles in practice* (2nd edn). London: Routledge.

Hardy, C., Phillips, N., & Clegg, S. (2001). Reflexivity in organization and management theory: A study of the production of the research 'subject'. *Human Relations*, **54**, 531–560.

Hassard, J. (1991). Multiple paradigms and organizational analysis: A case study. *Organization Studies*, **12** (2), 275–299.

Heller, F. (2004). Action research and research action: A family of methods. In C. Cassell & G. Symon (Eds), *Essential guide to qualitative research in organizations.* London: Sage.

Henriquez, J., Hollway, W., Urwin, C., Venn, C., & Walkerdine, V. (1984). *Changing the subject: Psychology, social relations and subjectivity.* London: Methuen.

Henwood, K.L. & Nicolson, P. (1995). Qualitative research. *The Psychologist*, **8** (3), 109–110.

Herriot, P. & Anderson, N. (1997). Selecting for change: How will personnel and selection psychology survive? In N. Anderson & P. Herriot (Eds), *International handbook of selection and assessment* (pp. 1–34). Chichester: John Wiley & Sons.

Hodgkinson, G.P. (Ed.) (2001). Facing the future: The nature and purpose of management research re-assessed. *British Journal of Management*, 12 (Special Issue), S1–S80.

Hodgkinson, G.P. & Herriot, P. (2002). The role of psychologists in enhancing organizational effectiveness. In I.T. Robertson, M. Callinan, & D. Bartram (Eds), *Organizational effectiveness: The role of psychology* (pp. 45–60). Chichester: John Wiley & Sons.

Hodgkinson, G.P., Herriot, P., & Anderson, N. (2001). Re-aligning the stakeholders in management research: Lessons from industrial, work and organizational psychology. *British Journal of Management*, 12 (Special Issue), S41–S48.

Holland, R. (1999). Reflexivity. *Human Relations*, 52, 463–483.

Holloway, I. & Todres, L. (2003). The status of method: Flexibility, consistency and coherence. *Qualitative Research*, 3 (3), 345–358.

Hollway, W. (1984). Fitting work: Psychological assessment in organisations. In J. Henriques, W. Hollway, C. Urwin, C. Venn, & V. Walkerdine (Eds), *Changing the subject: Psychology, social regulation and subjectivity*. London: Methuen.

Hollway, W. (1991). *Work psychology and organizational behaviour: Managing the individual at work*. London: Sage.

Hornby, P. & Symon, G. (1994). Tracer studies. In C.M. Cassell & G. Symon (Eds), *Qualitative methods in organizational research: A practical guide*. London: Sage.

Hoshmand, L. (1999). Locating the qualitative research genre. In M. Kopala & L. Suzuki (Eds), *Using qualitative methods in psychology* (pp. 15–24). Thousand Oaks, CA: Sage.

Jackson, N. & Carter, P. (1991). In defense of paradigm incommensurability. *Organization studies*, 12 (1), 109–127.

Jary, D. & Parker, M. (Eds) (1998). *The new higher education: Issues and directions for the post-Dearing university*. Staffordshire: Staffordshire University Press.

Johnson, P., Buehring, A., Cassell, C., & Symon, G. (2005). Evaluating qualitative management research: Towards a contingent criteriology. *Working Paper*.

Johnson, P.D. & Cassell, C.M. (2001). Epistemology and work psychology: New agendas. *Journal of Occupational and Organizational Psychology*, 74, 125–144.

Johnson, P.D. & Duberley, J.P. (2003). *Understanding management research: A guide to epistemology*. London: Sage.

Judge, T., Kammeyer-Mueller, J., & Bretz, R. (2004). A longitudinal model of sponsorship and career success: A study of industrial–organizational psychologists. *Personnel Psychology*, 57, 271–303.

King, N. (2000). Commentary: Making ourselves heard: The challenges facing advocates of qualitative research in work and organizational psychology. *European Journal of Work and Organizational Psychology*, 9 (4), 457–616.

King, N. (2004). Using interviews in qualitative research. In C.M. Cassell & G. Symon (Eds), *Essential guide to qualitative methods in organizational research*. London: Sage.

Kirk, J. & Miller, M.L. (1986). *Reliability and validity in qualitative research (Qualitative Research Methods Series, Vol. 1)*. Beverley Hills, CA: Sage.

Kvale, S. (1996). *InterViews: An introduction to qualitative research interviewing*. London: Sage.

Länsisalmi, H., Pieró, J.M., & Kivimäki, M. (2000). Collective stress and coping in the context of organizational culture. *European Journal of Work and Organizational Psychology*, 9 (4), 527–560.

Larsson, R. & Lowendahl, B. (1996, August). *The qualitative side of management research*. Paper presented at the Annual Meeting of the Academy of Management, Cincinnati, OH.

Latour, B. & Woolgar, S. (1979). *Laboratory life: The social construction of scientific facts.* Beverley Hills, CA: Sage.

Lee, T.W. (1999). *Using qualitative methods in organizational research.* Thousand Oaks, CA: Sage.

Lee, T.W., Mitchell, T.R., & Sablynski, C.J. (1999). Qualitative research in organizational and vocational psychology, 1979–1999. *Journal of Vocational Behaviour,* 55, 161–187.

Lincoln, Y.S. & Guba, E. (1985). *Naturalistic inquiry.* Beverley Hills, CA: Sage.

Locke, K. (2003). *Grounded theory in management research.* London: Sage.

Locke, K. & Golden-Biddle, K. (2002). An introduction to qualitative research: Its potential for industrial and organizational psychology. In S.G. Rogelberg (Ed.), *Handbook of research methods in industrial and organizational psychology.* Oxford: Blackwell.

Mackenzie-Davey, K. & Arnold, J. (2000). A multi-method study of accounts of personal change by graduates starting work: Self-ratings, categories and women's discourses. *Journal of Occupational and Organizational psychology,* 33 (4), 461–486.

Marshall, C. & Rossman, G.B. (1989). *Designing qualitative research.* Newbury Park, CA: Sage.

McAuley, M.J. (2004). Hermeneutics. In C.M. Cassell & G. Symon (Eds), *Essential guide to qualitative methods in organizational research.* London: Sage.

McNiff, J. (2000). *Action research in organizations.* London: Routledge.

Miles, M. & Huberman, M. (1994). *Qualitative data analysis: An expanded sourcebook* (2nd edn). London: Sage.

Morgan, G. & Smircich, L. (1980). The case for qualitative research. *Academy of Management Review,* 5/4, 491–500.

Morgan, S.J. & Symon, G. (2004). Electronic interviews. In C.M. Cassell & G. Symon (Eds), *Essential guide to qualitative methods in organizational research.* London: Sage.

Morse, J.M. (1994). Emerging from the data: The cognitive process of analysis in qualitative enquiry. In J.M. Morse (Ed.), *Critical issues in qualitative research methods.* London: Sage.

Parker, I. (1989). *The crisis in modern social psychology—and how to end it.* London: Routledge.

Patterson, F. (2001). Developments in work psychology: Emerging issues and future trends. *Journal of Occupational and Organizational Psychology,* 74, 381–390.

Patton, M.Q. (1980). *Qualitative evaluation methods.* Beverley Hills, CA: Sage.

Peterson, M. (2001). International collaboration in organizational behavior research. *Journal of Organizational Behavior,* 22, 59–81.

Pettigrew, A. (1985). *The awakening giant: Continuty and change in Imperial Chemical Industries.* Oxford: Blackwell.

Phillips, N. & Hardy, C. (2002). *Discourse analysis: Investigating processes of social construction.* Thousand Oaks, CA: Sage.

Prasad, A. & Prasad, P. (2002). The coming age of interpretive organizational research. *Organizational Research Methods,* 5, 4–11.

Reason, P. & Rowan, J. (1981). *Human inquiry: A sourcebook of new paradigm research*: Chichester: John Wiley & Sons.

Reed, M. (1992). Introduction. In M. Reed & M. Hughes (Eds), *Re-thinking organization: New directions in organization theory and analysis.* London: Sage.

Sackett, P.R. & Larson, J.R. (1990). Research strategies and tactics in industrial and organizational psychology. In M.D. Dunnette & L.M. Hough (Eds), *Handbook of industrial and organizational psychology, Volume 1.* Palo Alto, CA: Consulting Psychologists Press.

Schaubroeck, J. & Kuehn, K. (1992). Research design in industrial and organizational psychology. In C.L. Cooper & I.T. Robertson (Eds), *International review of industrial and organizational psychology* (Vol. 7, pp. 99–121). Chichester: John Wiley & Sons.

Schön, D.A. (1991). *The reflective practitioner.* Aldershot: Ashgate.

Schwandt, T.A. (1996). Farewell to criteriology. *Qualitative Inquiry,* 2 (1), 58–72.

Seale, C. (1999). *The quality of qualitative research.* London: Sage.

Seale, C., Gobo, G., Gubrium, & Silverman, D. (2004). *Qualitative research in practice.* London: Sage.

Shotter, J. (1975). *Images of man in psychological research.* London: Methuen.

Silverman, D. (2000). *Doing qualitative research: A practical handbook.* Thousand Oaks, CA: Sage.

Silverman, D. (2001). *Interpreting qualitative data.* London: Sage.

Smith, J., Harré, R., & Van Langenhove, L. (1995). *Re-thinking methods in psychology.* London: Sage.

Sonnentag, S. (2000). Working in a network context—What are we talking about? Comment on Symon. *Journal of Occupational and Organizational Psychology,* 73 (4), 415–418.

Sparrow, P. (1999). Editorial. *Journal of Occupational and Organizational Psychology,* 72, 261–264.

Spector, P.E. (2001). Research methods in industrial and organizational psychology: Data collection and data analysis with special consideration to international issues. In N. Anderson, D.S. Ones, H.D. Sinangil, & C. Viswesvaran (Eds), *Handbook of industrial, work and organizational psychology, Volume 1.* London: Sage.

Starkey, K. & Madan, P. (2001). Bridging the relevance gap: Aligning stakeholders in the future of management research. *British Journal of Management,* 12 (Special Issue), S3–S26.

Symon, G. (2000a). Talking about working in a network context: A reply to Sonnentag. *Journal of Occupational and Organizational Psychology,* 73, 419–422.

Symon, G. (2000b). Everyday rhetoric: Argument and persuasion in everyday life. *European Journal of Work and Organizational Psychology,* 9 (4), 477–488.

Symon, G. (2000c). Information and communication technologies and the network organization: A critical analysis. *Journal of Occupational and Organizational Psychology,* 73, 389–414.

Symon, G. & Cassell, C.M. (1998). *Qualitative methods and analysis in organizational research: A practical guide.* London: Sage.

Symon, G. & Cassell, C.M. (1999). Barriers to innovation in research practice. In M. Cunha & C. Maques (Eds), *Readings in organization science—Organizational change in a changing context.* Lisbon: ISPA.

Symon, G. & Cassell, C.M. (2004). Promoting new research practices in organizational research. In C.M. Cassell & G. Symon (Eds), *Essential guide to qualitative methods in organizational research.* London: Sage.

Symon, G., Cassell, C.M., & Dickson, R. (2000). Expanding our research and practice through innovative research methods. *European Journal of Work and Organizational Psychology,* 9 (4), 457–462.

Tranfield, D. & Starkey, K. (1998). The nature, social organization and promotion of management research: Towards policy. *British Journal of Management,* 9, 341–353.

Van Maanen, J. (1979). Reclaiming qualitative methods for organizational research: A preface. *Administrative Science Quarterly,* 24, 520–526.

West, M., Arnold, J., Corbett, M., & Fletcher, B. (1992). Editorial: Advancing understanding about behaviour at work. *Journal of Occupational and Organizational Psychology,* 65, 1–3.

Yin, R. (2003). *Case study research: Design and methods.* Thousand Oaks, CA: Sage.

Zjilstra, F. (2000). Editorial. *European Journal of Work and Organizational Psychology*, **9**, 305–306.

Zweig, D. & Webster, J. (2002). Where is the line between benign and invasive? An examination of psychological barriers to the acceptance of awareness monitoring systems. *Journal of Organizational Behavior*, **23**, 605–633.

INDEX

Page references in italics refer to figures and tables.

International Review of Industrial and Organizational Psychology

CONTENTS OF PREVIOUS VOLUMES

VOLUME 17—2002

Coping with Job Loss: A Life-facet Perspective, Frances M. McKee-Ryan and Angelo J. Kinicki; The Older Worker in Organizational Context: Beyond the Individual, James L. Farr and Erika L. Ringseis; Employment Relationships from the Employer's Perspective: Current Research and Future Directions, Anne Tsui and Duanxu Wang; Great Minds Don't Think Alike? Person-level Predictors of Innovation at Work, Fiona Patterson; Past, Present and Future of Cross-cultural Studies in Industrial and Organizational Psychology, Sharon Glazer; Executive Health: Building Self-reliance for Challenging Times, Jonathan D. Quick, Cary L. Cooper, Joanne H. Gavin, and James Campbell Quick; The Influence of Values in Organizations: Linking Values and Outcomes at Multiple Levels of Analysis, Naomi I. Maierhofer, Boris Kabanoff, and Mark A. Griffin; New Research Perspectives and Implicit Managerial Competency Modeling in China, Zhong-Ming Wang

VOLUME 16—2001

Age and Work Behaviour: Physical Attributes, Cognitive Abilities, Knowledge, Personality Traits and Motives, Warr; Organizational Attraction and Job Choice, Highouse and Hoffman; The Psychology of Strategic Management: Diversity and Cognition Revisited, Hodgkinson; Vacations and Other Respites: Studying Stress on and off the Job, Eden; Cross-cultural Industrial/Organisational Psychology, Smith, Fischer, and Sale; International Uses of Selection Methods, Newell and Tansley; Domestic and International Relocation for Work, Feldman; Understanding the Assessment Centre Process: Where Are We Now?, Lievens and Klimoski

VOLUME 15—2000

Psychological Contracts: Employee Relations for the Twenty-first Century?, Millward and Brewerton; Impacts of Telework on Individuals, Organizations and

400   CONTENTS OF PREVIOUS VOLUMES

Families—A Critical Review, Kondradt, Schmook, and Mälecke; Psychological Approaches to Entrepreneurial Success: A General Model and an Overview of Findings, Rauch and Frese; Conceptual and Empirical Gaps in Research on Individual Adaptation at Work, Chan; Understanding Acts of Betrayal: Implications for Industrial and Organizational Psychology, Pearce and Henderson; Working Time, Health and Performance, Spurgeon and Cooper; Expertise at Work: Experience and Excellent Performance, Sonnentag; A Rich and Rigorous Examination of Applied Behavior Analysis Research in the World of Work, Komaki, Coombs, Redding, Jr, and Schepman

VOLUME 14—1999

Personnel Selection Methods, Salgado; System Safety—An Emerging Field for I/O Psychology, Fahlbruch and Wilpert; Work Control and Employee Well-being: A Decade Review, Terry and Jimmieson; Multi-source Feedback Systems: A Research Perspective, Fletcher and Baldry; Workplace Bullying, Hoel, Rayner, and Cooper; Work Performance: A Multiple Regulation Perspective, Roe; A New Kind of Performance for Industrial and Organizational Psychology: Recent Contributions to the Study of Organizational Citizenship Behavior, Organ and Paine; Conflict and Performance in Groups and Organizations, de Dreu, Harinck, and van Vianen

VOLUME 13—1998

Team Effectiveness in Organizations, West, Borrill, and Unsworth; Turnover, Maertz and Campion; Learning Strategies and Occupational Training, Warr and Allan; Meta-analysis, Fried and Ager; General Cognitive Ability and Occupational Performance, Ree and Carretta; Consequences of Alternative Work Schedules, Daus, Sanders, and Campbell; Organizational Men: Masculinity and Its Discontents, Burke and Nelson; Women's Careers and Occupational Stress, Langan-Fox; Computer-Aided Technology and Work: Moving the Field Forward, Majchrzak and Borys

VOLUME 12—1997

The Psychology of Careers in Organizations, Arnold; Managerial Career Advancement, Tharenou; Work Adjustment: Extension of the Theoretical Framework, Tziner and Meir; Contemporary Research on Absence from Work: Correlates, Causes and Consequences, Johns; Organizational Commitment, Meyer; The Explanation of Consumer Behaviour: From Social Cognition to Environmental Control, Foxall; Drug and Alcohol Programs in the Workplace: A Review

and Noe; **Job Performance and Appraisal,** Latham; **Job Satisfaction and Organizational Commitment,** Griffin and Bateman; **Quality of Worklife and Employee Involvement,** Mohrman, Ledford, Lawler, and Mohrman; **Women at Work,** Gutek, Larwood, and Stromberg; **Being Unemployed,** Fryer and Payne; **Organization Analysis and Praxis,** Golembiewski; **Research Methods in Industrial and Organizational Psychology,** Stone